CW00520376

1 MONTH OF
FREE
READING

at
www.ForgottenBooks.com

By purchasing this book you are eligible for one month membership to ForgottenBooks.com, giving you unlimited access to our entire collection of over 1,000,000 titles via our web site and mobile apps.

To claim your free month visit:

www.forgottenbooks.com/free923481

* Offer is valid for 45 days from date of purchase. Terms and conditions apply.

ISBN 978-0-260-03147-1
PIBN 10923481

This book is a reproduction of an important historical work. Forgotten Books uses
state-of-the-art technology to digitally reconstruct the work, preserving the original format
whilst repairing imperfections present in the aged copy. In rare cases, an imperfection in
the original, such as a blemish or missing page, may be replicated in our edition. We do,
however, repair the vast majority of imperfections successfully; any imperfections that
remain are intentionally left to preserve the state of such historical works.

Forgotten Books is a registered trademark of FB &c Ltd.
Copyright © 2018 FB &c Ltd.
FB &c Ltd, Dalton House, 60 Windsor Avenue, London, SW19 2RR.
Company number 08720141. Registered in England and Wales.

For support please visit www.forgottenbooks.com

Sept. 1.

REPORTS OF CASES.

IN THE

SUPREME COURT

OF

NEBRASKA.

JANUARY TERM, 1887.

VOLUME XXI.

BY

GUY A. BROWN,

OFFICIAL REPORTER.

LINCOLN, NEB.:

STATE JOURNAL CO., LAW PUBLISHERS.

1887.

Entered according to act of Congress in the office of the Librarian of Congress,
A.D. 1887,

By GUY A. BROWN, REPORTER OF THE SUPREME COURT,
In behalf of the people of Nebraska.

Rec. Sept. 19, 1887

THE SUPREME COURT

OF

NEBRASKA.

1887.

CHIEF JUSTICE,

SAMUEL MAXWELL.

JUDGES,

M. B. REESE,
AMASA COBB.

ATTORNEY GENERAL,

WILLIAM LEESE.

CLERK AND REPORTER,

GUY A. BROWN.

DEPUTY,

HILAND H. WHEELER.

DISTRICT COURTS

OF

NEBRASKA.

JUDGES.

J. H. BROADY,	FIRST DISTRICT.
THOMAS APPELGET,	FIRST DISTRICT.
S. B. POUND,	SECOND DISTRICT.
SAM. M. CHAPMAN,	SECOND DISTRICT.
E. WAKELEY,	THIRD DISTRICT.
JAMES NEVILLE,	THIRD DISTRICT.
LEWIS A. GROFF,	THIRD DISTRICT.
M. R. HOPEWELL,	THIRD DISTRICT.
A. M. POST,	FOURTH DISTRICT.
WILLIAM MARSHALL,	FOURTH DISTRICT.
W. H. MORRIS,	FIFTH DISTRICT.
T. L. NORVAL,	SIXTH DISTRICT.
J. C. CRAWFORD,	SEVENTH DISTRICT.
ISAAC POWERS, Jr.,	SEVENTH DISTRICT.
WILLIAM GASLIN, Jr.,	EIGHTH DISTRICT.
F. B. TIFFANY,	NINTH DISTRICT.
T. O. C. HARRISON,	NINTH DISTRICT.
F. G. HAMER,	TENTH DISTRICT.
J. E. COCHRAN,	ELEVENTH DISTRICT.
M. P. KINKAID,	TWELFTH DISTRICT.

STENOGRAPHIC REPORTERS.

R. H. POLLOCK, . . . FIRST DISTRICT.
P. E. BEARDSLEY, . . . FIRST DISTRICT.
OSCAR A. MULLON, . . SECOND DISTRICT.
MYRON E. WHEELER, · . . SECOND DISTRICT.
B. C. WAKELEY, . . . THIRD DISTRICT.
C. C. VALENTINE, . . . THIRD DISTRICT.
J. B. HAYNES,. . . . THIRD DISTRICT.
THOS. P. WILSON, . . . THIRD DISTRICT.
FRANK G. NORTH, . . . FOURTH DISTRICT.
EDWIN R. MOCKETT, . . FOURTH DISTRICT.
S. A. SEARLE, ... FIFTH DISTRICT.
FRANK TIPTON, ... SIXTH DISTRICT.
EUGENE MOORE, . . . SEVENTH DISTRICT.
GEORGE COUPLAND, . . SEVENTH DISTRICT.
F. M. HALLOWELL, . . . EIGHTH DISTRICT.
E. B. HENDERSON, . . . NINTH DISTRICT.
CHAS. W. PEARSALL, . · NINTH DISTRICT.
M. B. NEEVES, ... TENTH DISTRICT.
O. C. GASTON, . . . ELEVENTH DISTRICT.
CHAS. W. EARL, . . . TWELFTH DISTRICT.

REPORTER'S NOTES.

The volume of laws quoted as the "Revised Statutes," refers to the edition prepared in 1866 by E. Estabrook.

The volume of laws quoted as the "General Statutes," refers to the edition prepared in 1873 by Guy A. Brown.

The volume of laws quoted as the "Compiled Statutes," refers alike to the first edition, 1881, and second edition, 1885, compiled by Guy A. Brown.

Acts of various years are cited by reference to volume of laws and the year in which they were passed.

This volume contains a report of decisions handed down prior to July term, 1887, except those previously reported, and some cases in which rehearings have been granted.

The syllabus in each case in this volume was prepared by the judge writing the opinion, in accordance with rule 23.

Lincoln, Sept. 1, 1887.

PRACTICING ATTORNEYS.

Admitted since the publication of Vol. XX.

John B. Barnes,
John S. Bennett,
William F. Buck,
Thomas D. Cobbey,
Charles E. Davis,
W. M. Cowell,
John N. Dryden,
W. H. Farnsworth,
N. T. Gadd,
Camden J. Garlow,
William L. Greene,
B. F. Greenwood,
Alfred W. Gregory,
Geo. H. Hilton,
Leslie G. Hurd,
Mell C. Jay,

C. S. Johnson,
George A. Magney,
B. F. McLoney,
H. L. Merriman,
Pliny M. Moodie,
J. W. Provins,
A. M. Robbins,
S. F. Rockwell,
Halleck F. Rose,
W. S. Shoemaker,
R. M. Snavely,
John T. Spencer,
Theodore C. Stevens,
Herman Westover,
A. F. Wilgocki,
John W. Willson.

The following rule was adopted at the January term, 1887:

RULE 28.—In all criminal cases brought on error to this court, where it appears that the court below has passed sentence of death upon the plaintiff in error, it is ordered that the sentence and judgment be suspended until the further order of this court, and it shall be the duty of the clerk to endorse such suspension upon the transcript filed in said cause, and immediately transmit a certified copy thereof to the officer charged with the execution of said sentence.

TABLE OF CASES REPORTED.

A.

B.

O.

P.

R.

S.

2

TABLE OF CASES CITED.

C.

·N.

O.

P.

Q.

R.

S.

T.

U.

V.

W.

CASES

ARGUED AND DETERMINED

IN THE

SUPREME COURT OF NEBRASKA.

JANUARY TERM, 1887.

PRESENT:

HON. SAMUEL MAXWELL, CHIEF JUSTICE.
" M. B. REESE, } JUDGES.
" AMASA COBB,

MARCUS HUTCHINSON ET AL., PLAINTIFFS IN ERROR, V. EVA HUBBARD, DEFENDANT IN ERROR.

Liquors: ACTION FOR DAMAGES: VERDICT. Where in an action by a wife against certain saloon keepers and their bondsmen, to recover for loss of means of support caused by intoxicating liquors sold her husband. the jury returned a verdict for $300, *Held,* That the evidence fully sustained the verdict.

ERROR to the district court for Kearney county. Tried below before GASLIN, J.

Dilworth, Smith & Dilworth, for plaintiffs in error.

Stuart & McPheely, for defendant in error.

3

MAXWELL, CH. J.

This action was brought in the district court of Kearney county, by the defendant in error against the plaintiffs, to recover for loss of means of support, caused by the sale of intoxicating liquors by Hutchinson & Bennett to her husband. In her petition she alleges that Hutchinson & Bennett were duly licensed to sell malt, spirituous, and vinous liquors by the trustees of the village of Minden,.and had given bond duly signed by Hutchinson & Bennett as principals and Herman Wagenknecht, Miles Frien, Josiah Mathers, and Patrick Moran as sureties, with the usual conditions required in a bond of said nature.

3d. That the said Eva Hubbard has been the wife of Delos W. Hubbard for sixteen years last past, that she has five minor children, and that she has resided in Kearney county for more than eight years last past.

4th. That the said Delos W. Hubbard was a farmer by occupation, and while not under the influence of liquor, and abstaining from the use of intoxicating liquors, is industrious and energetic. That the said Eva Hubbard and her children are entirely dependent upon said Delos W. Hubbard for their support, upon the earnings of his labor. That on the 4th of July, 1884, and continuously and at divers times before and since that date, defendants, Marcus Hutchinson and Hiram Bennett, sold and furnished to said Delos W. Hubbard intoxicating liquors, thereby causing intoxication at said times and days, whereby the said Hubbard has been greatly injured in health, unfitted for labor, and has failed to support the said Eva Hubbard and her said family, and has caused her great mental suffering and indignity.

5th. And she alleges that said Delos W. Hubbard has been rendered unfit and disqualified to support and maintain her and her family by reason of the intoxicating liquors sold, given, and furnished him by the said Hutchinson & Bennett.

That she has lost her means of support, that she has been damaged in the sum of three thousand dollars, no part of which has been paid, and asks judgment for three thousand dollars and costs of suit.

The defendants answered, admitting the obtaining of the license and the giving of the bond, and denying each and every other allegation.

On the 13th day of January, 1886, there was a trial to a jury, with verdict for the plaintiff for the sum of $300.

The only errors assigned in this court are that the verdict is not sustained by sufficient evidence, and that the court erred in overruling the motion for a new trial.

A very large amount of testimony was introduced on the trial which is now before us. It is unnecessary in this connection to set it out in full or even give a synopsis of it. That the wife suffered great wrongs by the sale of intoxicating liquor to her husband by Hutchinson & Bennett, is duly proved. That he was in the habit of becoming intoxicated and squandering his means of subsistence when in that condition is not denied, the plea being in effect that the liquor was not furnished by Hutchinson & Bennett. There was sufficient testimony before the jury, however, to justify them in finding that the parties named did furnish the liquor, or at least a portion of it, to produce such intoxication, and this is all that the law requires. *Bauer v. Kerkow*, 15 Neb., 150. It is pretty clear that the error of the jury, if any, consisted in finding an insufficient sum— much less than the actual damages proved. But as no error is assigned on that ground it cannot be considered. There is no error in the record of which the plaintiffs can complain, and the judgment is affirmed.

JUDGMENT AFFIRMED.

THE other judges concur.

P. M. VAN EVERY, PLAINTIFF IN ERROR, V. JOHN FITZGERALD, DEFENDANT IN ERROR.

21   36
33   160
21   36
32   237

Evidence: BOOKS OF ACCOUNT are receivable in evidence only when they contain charges by one party against the other, and then only under the circumstances and verified in the manner provided by statute.

ERROR to the district court of Lancaster county. Tried below before MITCHELL, J.

Lamb, Ricketts & Wilson, for plaintiffs in error.

Marquett, Deweese & Hall, for defendant in error.

COBB, J.

On August 19, 1884, plaintiff filed a petition in court below, alleging in substance:

1st. That defendant is indebted to plaintiff for moving 20,000 cubic yards of dirt on section 25 of Kenesaw and Oxford branch of B. & M. R. R., at agreed price of 18 cents per cubic yard, amounting to $3,600.

2d. That on or about February 1, 1884, plaintiff and defendant entered into contract by which plaintiff was to do the clearing, grubbing, and grading of section 25 of said railroad work, to be commenced on or before March 1, 1884, and done by July 1, 1884.

If in judgment of engineer plaintiff was not prosecuting work with such vigor as to insure it being done as contracted, defendant could serve notice to that effect on plaintiff, and if plaintiff fail for three days to put on enough force defendant could either put on extra force and charge same to plaintiff, or could terminate contract. Plaintiff was at all times ready and willing to perform, and did so except when prevented by defendant. (See contract, exhibit A.)

The work consisted of about 55,000 cubic yards of excavation, and after plaintiff had done the hardest and most expensive part of it the defendant, on or about May 14, 1884, without serving notice, without getting judgment of engineer, took possession of plaintiff's tools, assumed control of work, ordered plaintiff off work, and refused to settle. That work left undone was less expensive and more easily done than that already done. That defendant fraudulently, and for the purpose of cheating and oppressing plaintiff, prevented plaintiff from completing work.

3d. Plaintiff prays damages in sum of $9,900.

On October 29 defendant answered, making a general denial except as to those matters expressly admitted.

1st. Admits the contract as alleged.

2d. Alleges that plaintiff at no time prosecuted work so as to complete it in time contracted, and that defendant duly served notice to plaintiff to increase force. Plaintiff failing to increase force, defendant on 14th of May took possession of work, but not till plaintiff had abandoned it, and defendant then relet a small portion of work, and gave plaintiff benefit of profits. Defendant took possession of work May 14th, 1884.

That after notice was served, and plaintiff failed to increase force, defendant put on extra force and completed work, and charged costs of same to plaintiff. Defendant admits that plaintiff removed and filled 20,000 cubic yards, but alleges full payment as work progressed, by virtue of terms of contract. That defendant was compelled to pay out more for completion of job than plaintiff was to have for all the work, and plaintiff owes defendant $1,469.53.

On December 29, 1884, plaintiff replies:

Denying that any complaint was made about the work, or that engineer ever made any complaint or decision that plaintiff was not vigorously prosecuting work, or that any notice thereof was given plaintiff. Alleges that engineer was under influence and control of defendant, and colluded

and confederated with him, and engineer and defendant
directed plaintiff to do hardest work first, with secret and
fraudulent design to drive plaintiff off work when hardest
work was done.   That after plaintiff had done twenty
fifty-fourths of work defendant began to intermeddle, and
sent one James to superintend work, and James drove off
plaintiff's men and teams by violent, abusial, and tyran-
ranical conduct, and rendered it impossible for plaintiff to
get teams and men to complete work. Defendant, to cheat,
defraud and oppress plaintiff, prevented plaintiff from completing work.   Plaintiff denies that any notice was ever
served on him to increase force on work. . Denies that at
any time force of men and teams was insufficient to do
work in time, if defendant had not interfered.   Plaintiff
denies that he abandoned work.   Denies that defendant
paid out anything to complete work.   General denial, except as specially admitted, answered, or denied.

On the 3d day of June, 1885, there was a trial to a jury,
with verdict for plaintiff for $5.00.

The plaintiff's motion for a new trial having been overruled, and a judgment rendered on the verdict, the plaintiff
brings the cause to this court on error.

There are thirty-three errors assigned; but as we were
all of the opinion at the argument that there must be a new
trial for error in the admission of the time books of the defendant in evidence on the trial, none of the other assignments will be considered.   Our examination will accordingly be confined to number 29 of plaintiff's assignments,
which is as follows:

"29. The court erred in admitting, over the plaintiff's objection, the book account and the account book marked on
the back with lead pencil, 'Holdredge,' and given as a
part of the answer 1126 of the witness John Muldoon."

The book referred to as having been offered and received
in evidence in the above assignment of error is the time
book of the defendant, used to keep the time of the work-

men employed by him in completing the job of railroad work, which, as alleged in the answer, the plaintiff had abandoned and left undone of the job subcontracted by the plaintiff from and under the defendant, and which, as defendant claimed, he had the right to complete, and did complete, at the cost of the plaintiff; and it was for the purpose of establishing before the court and jury the amount of the cost of said work and the completing of said job, that the said time book was offered in evidence. The book was proved by the witness John Muldoon, whose examination is given at length in the abstract. It is not my purpose to examine this evidence as to whether the same is sufficiently full as a foundation for the introduction of the said book in evidence, as the difficulty lies at the very threshold, the admissibility of a book of entries of the character of those in question, and for the purpose of proving an independent fact, value, or quantity, such as that sought to be established here.

Section 346 of the civil code provides that "Books of account containing charges by one party against the other, made in the ordinary course of business, are receivable in evidence only under the following circumstances, subject to all just exceptions as to credibility: 1st. The books must show a continuous dealing with persons generally, or several items of charges at different times against the other party, in the same book. 2d. It must be shown by the party's oath, or otherwise, that they are his books of original entries. 3d. It must be shown in like manner that the charges were made at or near the time of the transactions therein entered, unless satisfactory reasons appear for not making such proof. 4th. The charges must also be verified by the party or the clerk who made the entries, to the effect that they believe them just and true, or a sufficient reason must be given why the verification is not made."

I know of no authority outside of the above section of statute for the admission of books of account or time-books in evidence in a law-suit, and certainly the above provisions of law do not cover books such as the one introduced in evidence in the case at bar. The book in this case does not, nor does it purport to contain entries of charges against the plaintiff, or of dealings with him. It only purports to show by certain lines and cross-lines, with dates between the cross-line at the top, and names on the lines at the left hand side, with check-marks at the intersections of the lines, the number of days worked by each man or hand engaged upon the work. The primary object of these entries was obviously to enable the defendant to settle with his hired men, and perhaps for the secondary purpose of keeping an account of the cost of each job of railroad work. If it appeared on the face of this book that the object of keeping the account was to charge the days' works of these men respectively to the plaintiff, I think under the authorities that it would be admissible in evidence.

In the case of *Mathes v. Robinson*, 8 Met., 269, an account for labor performed by the plaintiff and his apprentice for the defendant, was proven by a book kept in the same general manner as the book in the case at bar, except that there the page of the book ruled off the same as in this case is headed "Mr. David Robinson, Dr. to," then follows the names of plaintiff and of his apprentice on separate lines, etc. Here the name of Van Every does not appear anywhere on the book. There the account was evidently kept for the purpose of charging the work of the plaintiff in that case, and of his apprentice, to the defendant therein; here the account was evidently kept for the purpose of crediting each individual laborer with his time of labor and on the face of the book, its proprietor, the employer of the laborers, was charged in favor of each laborer with the number of days' work, as there shown.

While I am quite clear that a book of account, to be admissible in evidence, as such must consist of charges by one party *against* the other as we held in the case of *Martin v. Scott*, 12 Neb., 42, yet I am equally certain that a witness who has kept a time-book such as the one now under consideration, and who knows that it was correctly kept, can by the use of the said book as a memorandum testify to its contents as independent facts, although at the same time, even with the aid of such memoranda, he does not remember the occurrence of the facts. See *Lipscomb v. Lyon*, 19 Id., 511.

For error in the admission of the said book in evidence, the judgment of the district court is reversed and the cause remanded for further proceedings in accordance with law.

REVERSED AND REMANDED.

THE other judges concur.

CHRISTIAN ENGLEHART, PLAINTIFF IN ERROR, V. PEORIA PLOW COMPANY, DEFENDANT IN ERROR.

Negotiable Instruments: INDORSEMENT OF NOTE BY AGENT OF PAYEE. One D. was a local agent for a Harvester Machine Company, for the sale of its machines. He sold a machine to E., taking his notes therefor, payable to the order of the Harvester Company. One of these notes D. indorsed as follows: "St. Paul Harvester Works, per J. H. Dorrance, agent," and by an arrangement with a person represented to be the general agent of said company, took said note for his commissions, and afterwards passed it to the plaintiff; *Held*, That the property of the Harvester Company in said note was not divested by such indorsement, and that the plaintiff could not recover thereon.

ERROR to the district court for Fillmore county. Tried below before MORRIS, J.

J. W. Eller, for plaintiff in error.

A. A. Whitman, for defendant in error.

COBB, J.

This was an action on a promissory note executed by
the defendant to the Saint Paul Harvester Works, an incorporated company. The following is a copy of the note
as set out in the petition.

"FAIRMONT, July 12, 1882.

For value received, on or before the 1st day of November, 1883, I promise to pay to the order of Saint Paul
Harvester Works sixty-five dollars at the office of Fillmore Co. Bank, in Fairmont, Neb., with interest at ten
per cent per annum from date until paid. Agreed that if
paid within fifteen days after maturity, then the interest
shall be seven per cent. And I further agree that the express condition of the sale and purchase of the harvesting
machine, for which this note is given, is such that the title,
ownership, or right of possession does not pass from the
said Saint Paul Harvester Works until this note is paid
in full. That the Saint Paul Harvester Works have full
power to declare this note due, and take possession of said
machine at any time they deem themselves insecure, even
before the maturity of the note, and to sell the said machine at public or private sale, the proceeds thereof to be
applied upon the balance of the price. (Here follows a
property statement).

Signed,   CHRISTIAN ENGLEHART."

The petition alleged that the said note was endorsed as
follows:

"Dated this 15th day of Nov., 1882, St. Paul Harvester
Works per J. H. Dorrance, agent," and also alleges that
"said note was endorsed by the Saint Paul Harvester
Works as aforesaid, and delivered for a valuable consideration to the plaintiff. No part of said note has been paid,

and there is now due thereon from the defendant to the plaintiff the sum of sixty-five dollars," etc.

The defendant made answer admitting that he made the note; denied that the said note was ever delivered to the Saint Paul Harvester Works. Alleged that the Saint Paul Harvester Works never sold, assigned, or transferred said note to the plaintiff. That J. H. Dorrance had no authority from the Saint Paul Harvester Works to make any endorsement upon said note. Denied that the Saint Paul Harvester Works endorsed and delivered said note to plaintiff. Denied that the Saint Paul Harvester Works endorsed and delivered the said note to the plaintiff for any consideration.

2. Defendant says that said note was made as part consideration for a Saint Paul Binder Machine; that the agreed price for said machine was one hundred and thirty dollars; that he made the note in suit and one other note of the same amount and date; that the said other note was delivered to the said Saint Paul Harvester Works. Defendant says that said binder machine was warranted in writing to be a good machine to bind grain, and that said machine was wholly worthless and would not do good work, and was wholly worthless for the purpose for which it was made. That the said other note which was given for said machine was of the same date of the note in suit and for the sum of sixty-five dollars. That said Saint Paul Harvester Works acknowledged that said machine was worthless, and settled with defendant for said machine and delivered up the said other note and received in settlement for said machine the sum of twenty dollars.

The plaintiff replied to said answer:

1. That said J. W. Dorrance had authority from the Saint Paul Harvester Works to endorse and transfer said note.

2. Denies that said machine was worthless and would not do good work, but alleges that it was a good machine,

and alleges that said warranty was not absolute but was conditional, and that defendant has wholly failed to perform any of the conditions precedent on his part.

There was a trial to a jury, with a verdict and judgment for the plaintiff. The defendant brings the cause to this court on error.

Upon the trial, as appears by the bill of exceptions, the plaintiff offered and gave in evidence a stipulation signed by the respective attorneys, of which the following is a copy:

"STIPULATION OF CERTAIN FACTS.

"That the note in suit was given in part consideration for a St. Paul harvesting machine; that J. H. Dorrance was agent for the sale of machines for the St. Paul Harvester Works, and as such agent sold said machine to defendant; that said machine was warranted in writing to be a good machine and do good work; that the said J. H. Dorrance was also the agent for plaintiff for the sale of plows, and was indebted to said plaintiff; that said note was set apart to said J. H. Dorrance as commission as agent for the St. Paul Harvester Works, and said Dorrance delivered said note to plaintiff (without any notice to plaintiff of any equities against said note) on account of his indebtedness to said plaintiff; that said J. H. Dorrance indorsed on the back of said note the words, 'St. Paul Harvester Works, per J. H. Dorrance, Agent,' without the knowledge of the St. Paul Harvester Works."

Defendant admits the incorporation of plaintiff, as alleged in petition.

Plaintiff also gave in evidence the note as herein copied, and introduced J. H. Dorrance as a witness on its behalf, who testified as follows:

Q. Are you the same J. H. Dorrance who made this sale and took this note of Mr. Englehart?

A. Yes, sir.

Q. You took the note and transferred it?

A.   Yes, sir.

Q.   State to the jury how that happened?

A.   We took the note as commission for the sale of Harvesters.

Q.   By the court.   It was given you by the Saint Paul Harvester Works for your commission?

.   A.   Yes, sir.

Q.   What did you do with that note?

A.   I turned it over to the Peoria Plow Company for some rakes.

Upon cross-examination he testified as follows:

Q.   You was the agent of the Saint Paul Harvester Works for the sale of this machine?

A.   Yes, sir.

Q.   That is all you was agent for, was it?

A.   Yes, sir.

Q.   Was this note in suit here in possession of the Saint Paul Harvester Works?

A.   Yes, sir.

Q.   How did it come to be there?

A.   They took them and looked them over.

Q.   Who took them and looked them over?

A.   I forget his name.

Q.   Where did the Saint Paul Harvester Works do business at that time?

A.   In Omaha.

Q.   They had a branch office at Omaha?

A.   Yes, sir.

Q.   Their headquarters were at Saint Paul?

A.   Yes, sir.

Q.   Did it ever go to that office?

A.   No, sir.

Q.   You kept possesion of it all the time except a few minutes, while you were looking them over?

A.   No, sir.   Mr. Parsons had the notes over night and looked them over.

Q.   In the morning this note was handed back to you as your commission?

A.   Yes, sir.

Q.   Who was that from?

A.   Mr. Parsons.

Q.   By the court.   He is the general agent of the company?

A.   Yes, sir.

Q.   How do you know?

A.   Because we took commission from Mr. Parsons for selling machinery.   We never saw the Saint Paul Harvester Company.   We made our contract with him.

Q.   Is that the only way you know that he is the general agent of the company?

A.   Yes, sir.

Q.   When did you deliver this note to the Peoria Plow Company?

A.   Some time in November, 1883, I think it was. Perhaps it was in 1884.   I know what day it was that we got the note.

Q.   You was not the agent of the Saint Paul Harvester Works, and had authority to sign your name as agent for the transfer of their notes?

A.   I don't know whether I did or not.

Q.   Did you ever have any authority from the company to sign their name on notes?

A.   I don't know.   I had letters directed as agent for the Saint Paul Harvester Works.

Q.   That was as agent for the sale of their machinery?

A.   Yes, sir.

Q.   They didn't give you any direction to sign their name on their notes?

A.   No, sir; not that I know of, only I was acting as their agent.

The plaintiff having rested his case, the defendant was sworn as a witness in his own behalf.   Whereupon his counsel put to him the following questions:

Q. You may state if you received the machine for which this note was given?

Whereupon the court excluded all evidence relating to the machine on the warranty or anything connected with it, for the reason that the same is incompetent.

Counsel then put the following:

Q. You may state whether the machine for which this note was given was a good machine and would do good work?

Upon objection by counsel for plaintiff as incompetent and irrelevant, the objection was sustained by the court and the evidence excluded.

And the following:

Q. You may state to the jury whether or not the machine for which this note was given would do good work, or was of any value as a machine?

Objected to and excluded.

Whereupon the counsel for defendant offered to prove by the witness that the machine in question was warranted to do good work and to be a good machine, and that it was wholly worthless and could not be used for the purpose for which it was sold. The offer was refused by the court.

Defendant having rested his case, the court instructed the jury as follows:

"You will find for the plaintiff and assess his damages at the amount of the note and interest thereon to the first day of this term, according to the tenor thereof."

The pleadings in the case are scarcely sufficient to present a case free from doubt as to the admissibility of evidence to prove a warranty and breach thereof of the machine for which the note was given, even if sued by the payee, but I think they are sufficient to raise the question of the ownership of the note by the plaintiff. If it appeared from the evidence that the endorsement and transfer of the note to the plaintiff was made by Dorrance for a consideration moving from the plaintiff to the Harvester Company, the payee named in the note, it would then be simply a question of authority on the part of Dorrance, as agent, to make the endorsement so as to pass the property of his principal in the note to the endorsee, and even then we look in vain for evidence of such authority. When on the stand he testified that he did not know whether he had such authority or not, and the transaction between him and Parsons, another agent, as he testifies, of the Harvester Company, a general agent fails to develop any authority or power in either of them to indorse the notes of the company. But the case involves another and quite a different question. It is not claimed that the endorsement was made by the payee through its agent to the plaintiff upon a consideration moving from one to the other, but that it was made by the payee to Dorrance himself upon a consideration moving from him to the payee, to-wit, his commissions, and a long time afterwards, by an independent and separate transaction, passed to the plaintiff, by Dorrance in his own right, "for some rakes."

In order to uphold this transaction we must hold that an agent for the sale of agricultural machinery may by virtue of his agency indorse a note taken by him for such machinery, payable to the order of his principal, to himself, in payment for his commissions, and thereby divest his principal of property in such note.

Even if the agency of Dorrance had included generally the power and duty of indorsing the notes of his principal, an indorsement thereof to himself would be void. I quote from Story on Agency, § 210. "In this connection, also, it seems proper to state another rule in regard to the duties of agents, which is of general application, and that is, that in matters touching the agency, agents cannot act so as to bind their principals where they have an adverse interest in themselves. This rule is founded upon the plain and obvious consideration that the princi-

pal bargains in the employment for the exercise of the disinterested skill, diligence, and zeal of the agent for his
own exclusive benefit. It is a confidence necessarily reposed in the agent, that he will act with a sole regard to
the interests of his principal as far as he lawfully may;
and even if impartiality could possibly be presumed on the
part of an agent, where his own interests were concerned,
that is not what the principal bargains for; and in many
cases it is the very last thing which would advance his interest. * * * If, then, the seller were permitted as the
agent of another to become the purchaser, his duty to his
principal and his own interest would stand in direct oppo-
sition to each other, and thus a temptation, perhaps in
many cases too strong for resistance by men of flexible
morals, or hackneyed in the common devices of worldly
business, would be held out, which would betray them into
gross misconduct, and even into crime. It is to interpose
a preventive check against such temptations and seductions
that a positive prohibition has been found to be the sound-
est policy, encouraged by the purest precepts of christi-
anity."

The above principles, more generally applied to cases of
the sale of property, are equally applicable to cases of the
transfer of notes or other choses in action, by indorsement
or otherwise.

In answer to the possible suggestion that the indorsement
of the note in the case at bar is voidable rather than void, I
quote from Story the concluding paragraph of the section
above cited:

"Of course it is to be understood as a proper qualification of the doctrine that the principal has an election to
adopt the act of the agent or not; and that if after a full
knowledge of all the circumstances he deliberately and
freely ratifies the act of the agent, or acquiesces in it for a
great length of time, it will become obligatory upon him,
not by its own intrinsic force, but from the consideration

4

that he thereby waives the protection intended by the law for his own interest, and deals with his agent as a person *quoad hoc*, discharged of his agency."

The plaintiff in its petition alleged the indorsement of the note sued on by the payee therein named to the plaintiff, as it must necessarily do, the note being drawn payable to order. This fact is denied by the defendant in his answer. It was not legally proved at the trial. It necessarily follows that the court erred in directing a verdict for the plaintiff.

The judgment of the district court is reversed and the cause remanded for further proceedings in accordance with law.

REVERSED AND REMANDED.

THE other judges concur.

CHRISTIAN G. HEROLD, PLAINTIFF IN ERROR, V. THE STATE OF NEBRASKA, DEFENDANT IN ERROR.

1. **Constitutional Law**: ACT PROHIBITING FRAUDULENT TRANSFER OF PROPERTY. Section 28 of chapter 32 of the Compiled Statutes—being chapter 46 of the Session Laws of 1883—in so far as it prohibits the fraudulent sale, transfer, secretion, encumbrance, or disposal of property, with the intent to defraud creditors, is constitutional and valid.

2. **Instructions** prayed for and refused. Examined, and *Held*, To have been properly refused. [MAXWELL, CH. J., dissenting.]

ERROR to the district court for Lancaster county. Tried below before POUND, J.

M. A. Hartigan, for plaintiff in error.

William Leese, Attorney General, for defendant in error.

REESE, J.

An information, consisting of three counts, was filed in the district court of Lancaster, against plaintiff in error, by the district attorney, charging a violation of section 28 of chapter 32 of the Compiled Statutes of 1885.

The first two counts of the information are substantially the same, the charges varying only in form; the allegations being that plaintiff in error did unlawfully, fraudulently, and feloniously, sell, transfer, secrete, encumber, and dispose of "a stock of goods, with intent to defraud," etc. The trial resulted in a verdict of guilty as charged in the first and second counts of the information, and not guilty as charged in the third count. From the judgment on the verdict plaintiff in error brings error to this court.

The first contention is that the law under which this conviction was had is unconstitutional and void. This is based upon the alleged failure of the act to comply with the provisions of section eleven of article three of the constitution.

The act of the legislature from which the section above referred to is taken was passed in 1883, and may be found on page 230 of the Session Laws of that year.

The provision of the constitution invoked is that "No bill shall contain more than one subject and the same shall be clearly expressed in its title." Constitution, Article III., Section 11. The title to the act in question is as follows: "An act to prohibit the fraudulent transfer of property and to declare the same a crime, and to prescribe the punishment thereof." It is insisted that "there are several separate and distinct offenses grouped and combined together in this act that in no way or manner are related to the title to the act." As we have seen, the title of the act is to prevent the fraudulent transfer of property. The body of the act is as follows:

"If any person or persons in this state, ·with intent to

cheat or defraud his creditors, or any of them, or with the
fraudulent intent to hinder or delay his creditors, or any of
them, in the collection of his or their demands, shall sell,
transfer, secrete, encumber, or in any way fraudulently dispose of any of or all of his goods, wares, merchandise, chattels, bills receivable, choses in action, or property of any
kind, or who, upon any sale of any goods, wares, merchandise, or property of any kind, with a fraudulent intent to
hinder or delay, or to cheat or defraud his creditors or any
of them, shall secrete, assign, transfer, conceal, or in any
way fraudulently dispose of all or any part of the proceeds
of any such sale or any property, he or they shall be deemed
guilty of a fraudulent transfer of property, and upon conviction thereof shall be punished in the same manner and
to the same extent as if he had been convicted of the larceny
of the same property."

It is argued that this act is amendatory of the act of 1877
(session laws, 1877, p. 5; Compiled Statutes 1885, section
9, chapter 12), and that no greater latitude can be given to
the amendatory act than to the original one, and therefore
the holding in *Ex parte Thomason*, 16 Neb., 238, must apply
to this case. We think this argument is clearly met in
Jones v. Davis, 6 Neb., 33. The act in question is clearly
independent and complete in itself, is not amendatory of
any other law, and is not restricted by any part of the act
of 1877. Neither do we think the act under consideration
is in conflict with section eleven of article three of the constitution. The act has but one subject and that subject is
"clearly expressed in its title." The purpose of the law, as
expressed in the title, is to prohibit the fraudulent transfer
of property, etc. It is nowhere sought to make the secretion,
sale, incumbrance, or fraudulent disposition of property an
offense as such, but the legislature has seen proper to declare
all or any of such acts "a fraudulent transfer of property."
This definition is furnished by the act itself, and the defini-
is as much a part of the act as any other portion. The

right of the legislature to prescribe the legal definitions of its own language must be conceded. Neither does the definition prescribed do any violence to the ordinary use of the language, when applied to the use of property in such a way as to hinder, delay, or defraud creditors.

There is a clear distinction between the principle involved in this case and that of *Ex parte Thomason, supra.* In that case no effort was made by the law-making power to give any legal meaning to any of the terms used. The language of that part of the act which was held valid was in substance the same as is contained in that part of the act under consideration, under which the information was filed. In the former act the language is, "sell, transfer, or in any manner dispose of." In the act in question it is, "sell, transfer, secrete, encumber, or in any way fraudulently dispose of." The word "secrete" is the only one to which any objection could be made, and we think it clearly falls within the legal meaning given it by the legislature when applied to the fraudulent use of property. We therefore hold that, in so far at least as it is applicable to the case at bar, the law is constitutional and valid.

This disposes of all the questions presented by the brief of plaintiff in error, and substantially, all presented by the petition in error, except as to the ruling of the trial court in the refusal of instructions asked by plaintiff in error. Of these the first only need be noticed. It is as follows:

"The state prosecutes the defendant in this case under the act of February 21st, 1883, entitled 'An act to prohibit the fraudulent transfer of property, and to declare the same a crime and to prescribe a punishment therefor."

"Before the jury can find the defendant guilty they must be satisfied beyond a reasonable doubt, not only that the defendant transferred the property or some part thereof, but that such transfer was made with the fraudulent intent to hinder or delay his creditors or some of them, if the jury find from the evidence that he had creditors.

"To transfer, means to convey or pass over the right of one person in property to another, as to sell. It is the act by which the owner of property delivers it to another person with the intent of passing the right he had in it to the latter.

"The jury cannot infer a transfer, but the state must prove it beyond a reasonable doubt, and the jury must be satisfied from the evidence and beyond a reasonable doubt, that the defendant did actually make a transfer of his property or some part thereof as defined in this instruction, and that such transfer was made with the fraudulent intent to hinder, or delay, or cheat, or defraud his creditors or some of them; and if the state fails to convince the jury beyond a reasonable doubt that all these things were actually done, then the defendant shall be acquitted."

By this instruction it was attempted to limit the effect of the act which we have been considering to the one act of the fraudulent *sale* of property. This we have already found, to our own satisfaction, is not the law. But it may be contended that the second paragraph of the instruction should have been given, as by it the question of the fraudulent intent of plaintiff in error—a necessary ingredient of the crime charged—would have been submitted to the jury. To this we answer that the question of the fraudulent intent of plaintiff in error was submitted to the jury by the instructions given by the court on its own motion—especially by the second and fourth—and that the paragraph of the instruction is wrong in itself, and was properly refused, had it been asked in a separate prayer. By it, as by the other instructions asked, it was the clear purpose of counsel for plaintiff in error to limit the criminal act to that by which "the owner of property delivers it to another person with the intent of passing the right he had in to the latter." This construction of the language of the act was insisted upon during the trial as well as in this court. As we have seen, it is not the proper construction. But in any event the instruction was presented to the court as a whole. It was no error to refuse it.

Assuming our interpretation of the law to be the correct one, there can be no question as to the guilt of plaintiff in error. The large amount of his indebtedness, the fraudulent disposition of the goods by shipping them from Lincoln to Cortland, from Cortland to Kansas City, and from Kansas City to Lincoln and elsewhere, consigned to fictitious persons, with other conduct not necessary to be here mentioned, leave no doubt as to his guilt and the righteousness of his punishment. The judgment of the district court is affirmed.

JUDGMENT AFFIRMED.

COBB, J., concurs.

MAXWELL, CH. J.

I am unable to give my assent to the opinion of the majority of the court, and will as briefly as possible state the reasons for my dissent. I agree with them that the act does not infringe any provision of the constitution, and is valid; but in my view the main question in the case—the *intent to defraud*—was not submitted to the jury in an intelligible form. The information consisted of three counts, in the first of which Herold is charged with fraudulently selling, transferring, secreting, encumbering, and disposing of goods and merchandise to the amount of $20,000. In the second count it is charged that he "unlawfully, fraudulently, and feloniously did sell, transfer, secrete, encumber, and dispose of" a large portion of said goods, etc., to divers persons, whose names are unknown, and in the third count it is charged that he "fraudulently, unlawfully, and feloniously did secrete, assign, conceal, and dispose of the proceeds of the said sale," etc. The court, on its own motion, instructed the jury as follows:

"4. There is no evidence that the defendant either sold or encumbered his property within the meaning of the law, and therefore you will inquire whether he transferred, or secreted, or fraudulently disposed of with intent to cheat or defraud his creditors, or any of them, as charged in the first count of the information, or with intent to hinder and delay his creditors, or any of them, in the collection of their demands, as charged in the second count in the information, if you find from the evidence that the defendant was indebted and owed creditors.

" To transfer means to transfer or pass over the right of one person in property to another. It is the act by which the owner of property makes over and delivers possession and control of it to another, with intent to vest the real or apparent ownership of it in such other person. To secrete means to deposit in a place of hiding, to hide, to conceal. To dispose of means to exercise finally one's powers of control over; to pass over into the control of another; to part with; to get rid of.

"5. To justify a conviction it is essential that the prosecution prove, among other things, that the defendant was indebted and had creditors, and was possessed of some kind, and that the defendant committed the offense or offenses charged in the county of Lancaster. It is not necessary that the prosecution prove that the offense charged was committed on the day alleged in the information, but it is sufficient in this respect if it be proven that the defendant committed such offense or offenses on the day alleged, or at any time within one or two months prior thereto.

"6. Intent is an important and essential ingredient in the offenses charged; and if you believe from the evidence that the defendant did transfer, or secrete, or fraudulently dispose of his property or any portion thereof, then, in ascertaining and determining his intent, you should consider all the circumstances surrounding him, as well as what he might have said with respect thereto, as shown by the evidence.

"7. In case you find the defendant guilty, you will find from the evidence, and state in your verdict, the value of the property so transferred or secreted or fraudulently disposed of, as the case may be.

"8. The burden of proof is upon the prosecution to prove every material allegation in the information, and to justify a conviction of the defendant the evidence must satisfy you of his guilt beyond a reasonable doubt. The law presumes the defendant to be innocent, and the presumption of innocence continues until the evidence satisfies you of his guilt beyond a reasonable doubt. If the evidence leaves your minds in doubt and uncertainty, and you have a reasonable doubt of the guilt of defendant, you must give him the benefit of the doubt and acquit him.

"9. If, however, the evidence produces in your mind an abiding conviction of the guilt of the defendant, and satisfies you of his guilt beyond a reasonable doubt, it is your duty to convict him."

To each of which instructions, given by the court on its own motion, and numbered four, five, six, seven, eight, and nine, the defendant excepted at the time the same were given.

The attorney for the prisoner asked the court to give the following instruction, which was refused, and to which exceptions were taken.

"Before the jury can find the defendant guilty they must be satisfied beyond a reasonable doubt that not only the defendant transferred his property, or some part thereof, but that the transfer was made with the fraudulent intent to hinder and delay his creditors, or some of them, if the jury find from the evidence that he has creditors."

This instruction was in harmony with the 4th instruction given by the court on its own motion that the jury "will enquire whether he transferred or secreted or fraudulently disposed of" his property, etc. The 6th instruction given by the court on its own motion, that "intent is an important and essential ingredient in the offenses

charged," not only falls far short of stating the law that
such intent must be proved beyond a reasonable doubt, but
was well calculated to mislead by keeping in the back-
ground the fact it was the gist of the offence. The prisoner was entitled to a clear explicit statement of the law
upon the question of intent, and this court should not give
its sanction to a rule which virtually denies the accused a
fair trial—a fair submission of the cause to the jury. In
my view the judgment should be reversed.

HIRAM J. PALMER, PLAINTIFF IN ERROR, V. WILLIAM
BELCHER, DEFENDANT IN ERROR.

Summons: SERVICE: A summons was issued by a justice of the
peace and delivered to the sheriff of the county for service, who
returned the same with the manner of service endorsed thereon,
as follows: "August 23, 1884. Received this writ, and on the
23d day of August, 1884, I served the same on the within
named defendant, H. J. Palmer, by leaving a copy of the within summons with George Palmer, and by him, the said George
Palmer, in my presence at the time of said service delivered,
the same being a true copy of the within summons with all
endorsements thereon certified by me to be a true copy to said
H. J. Palmer," properly signed by the officer; *Held*, To be a
compliance with the requirements of section 911 of the civil
code, and that the service gave jurisdiction.

ERROR to the district court for Valley county. Tried
below before TIFFANY, J.

Thummel & Platt, for plaintiff in error.

A. M. Robbins and *H. Westover*, for defendant in error.

REESE, J.

The original action was instituted before a justice of
the peace in Valley county. Plaintiff in error appeared

specially and objected to the jurisdiction of the court, alleging as the ground of such objection the defect in service of the summons. The objection was overruled by the justice, to which plaintiff in error excepted and removed the cause into the district court by proceedings in error. In that court the judgment of the justice of the peace was affirmed. Plaintiff now alleges error, and assigns therefor the ruling of the district court in affirming the decision of the justice of the peace.

The return of the sheriff, to which objection is made, is as follows:

"August 23d, 1884. Received this writ, and on the 23d day of August, 1884, I served the same on the within named defendant, H. J. Palmer, by leaving a copy of the within summons with George Palmer, and by him, the said George Palmer, in my presence at the time of said service delivered, the same being a true copy of the within summons with all endorsements thereon certified by me to be a true copy to said H. J. Palmer," properly signed by the officer.

The objection to this service is that the sheriff delivered a copy of the summons to George Palmer instead of to plaintiff in error, and that George Palmer, who delivered it to plaintiff in error, not being an officer with authority to serve a summons, had no power to make the service by delivering it to plaintiff. In other words, the sheriff served the summons on the wrong person, and the fact that he gave it to the one intended to be served would not constitute a valid service.

We concede all that is claimed by plaintiff as to the duty of courts to see that proper service of summons is made before asserting jurisdiction and rendering judgments thereon; and that there must be a compliance with the requirements of the statute before jurisdiction can be obtained. If then the service does not come up to these requirements, the decision of the district court was wrong.

Section 911 of the civil code, prescribing the manner of service of summons in so far as it applies to the case at bar, is as follows:

"The summons must * * * be served at least three days before the time of appearance, by delivering a copy of the summons with the endorsement thereon (certified by the constable or person serving the same to be a true copy), to the defendant, or leaving the same at his usual place of residence."

By an examination of the return of the sheriff, it appears that he served the summons on plaintiff in error by leaving a copy, properly certified, with George Palmer, and that George Palmer at that time, in the presence of the sheriff, delivered it to plaintiff in error. That is, by some mistake, perhaps, the sheriff gave the copy to George. George at once handed it to plaintiff in error. At any rate, the return clearly shows that the copy was delivered to plaintiff in error in the presence and by the act of the sheriff, although passing through the hand of another. It was clearly the act of the sheriff, and it would have been perfectly competent for him to have returned that he delivered the copy to plaintiff in error instead of stating the manner of delivery as he did. Had the sheriff requested George Palmer to return to him the summons, and he then have handed it to plaintiff, the service would have been perfect. Why any more so than for George to hand it at once to plaintiff? Suppose plaintiff had been so situated as to be just out of the direct reach of the sheriff, and another person standing between and in reach of both, had taken the copy from the hand of the sheriff and handed it to plaintiff, as was possibly done in this case, why would the service not have been good? We can see no reason for holding it otherwise, even though the return had been made in the language of the one in the case at bar.

The decision of the district court in holding the service to be a compliance with the statute is affirmed.

JUDGMENT AFFIRMED.

THE other judges concur.

CHRISTIANA E. HENDRICKSON, PLAINTIFF IN ERROR, V. BEESON AND SULLIVAN, DEFENDANTS IN ERROR.

1. **Landlord and Tenant**: ATTORNMENT: TERMINATION OF LEASE. A leased of B certain real estate for an indefinite term, rent to be paid monthly in advance. B afterwards leased the same property to C for the term of one year, subject to the lease of A, the rent accruing from A to be paid to C. A refused to recognize C as her landlord, and failed to pay rent to him. In an action by C for the possession of the property, it was *Held* that the grant of the reversion by B to C was effectual without an attornment by A to C, and *held*, also, that C, the assignee of the reversion, was entitled to collect the rent accruing after the execution of the conveyance to him which had not been paid to B prior to notice of the assignment. In such case the failure to pay rent to C would terminate the lease of A.

2. ———: FORCIBLE ENTRY AND DETENTION : NOTICE. In the absence of a stipulation to the contrary, where a tenant fails and refuses to pay rent according to the terms of his lease when due, such refusal terminates the lease. and by section 1021 of the civil code he is "holding over his term," and liable to an action for the forcible detention of the property. In such case no other notice than the three days' notice to quit, provided by Sec. 1022, Id., is necessary.

ERROR to the district court for Cass county. Tried below before MITCHELL, J.

Caldwell & Christie, for plaintiff in error.

Beeson & Sullivan, pro se.

REESE, J.

This was an action of forcible detention of real property. The suit was instituted in the county court of Cass county, on the 21st of October, 1885, by defendants in error, for the possession of a room in what is known as Union Block, in the city of Plattsmouth. From the testimony it appears that plaintiff in error leased the room in question about the second day of June, 1884. The exact terms of the contract are left in doubt, as it was in parol, and the parties to it do not fully agree as to whether it was a contract of lease from month to month, or for an indefinite time. They do agree that the rent was to be paid monthly in advance. This part of the contract was not strictly observed, and the rent was usually paid about the 15th of each current month. The last payment of rent was made on the first day of August, 1885, and a receipt was given acknowledging full payment to the second day of the same month. On the day of this payment—August 1st—the property was leased to defendants in error, by a written lease in the usual form, for the term of one year. The instrument contained the following clause: "And it is further covenanted and agreed between the parties aforesaid, that the said parties of the second part (defendants in error) take all the said rooms, subject to the present renters, of whom they are entitled to collect rents from this date, or require of them the possession of the rooms and to obtain the same at their own expense."

The contention of defendants in error, who were plaintiffs below, was that plaintiff in error had failed, neglected, and refused to pay the rent due them, and was, therefore, holding over her term, under the provisions of section 1021 of the civil code. It seems to be conceded, and is no doubt the law of this country, that a grant of the reversion is effectual without a formal attornment by the lessee. Taylor's Landlord and Tenant, § 442. *Farley v. Thompson,*

15 Mass., 18. *Burden v. Thayer*, 3 Metc., 76. *Baldwin v. Walker*, 21 Conn., 168. *Coker v. Pearsall*, 6 Ala., 542.

In such case the assignee of the reversion will be entitled to the rent accruing after the execution of the conveyance to him and unpaid to the grantor in default of notice to the lessee. *Birch v. Wright*, 1 T. R., 378. *Ruckman v. Astor*, 3 Edw., Ch. 373. *Breeding v. Taylor*, 13 B. Mon., 481.

The principal question in this case, then, is, was plaintiff in error holding over her term by reason of her nonpayment of rent; or, in other words, had her lease been terminated by reason of such non payment?

By the testimony of R. B. Windham, who was the agent of the M. E. Church, the owner of the property, it appears that on the first day of August—the day of the execution of the lease to defendants in error—he informed plaintiff in error of the lease to them, and that after that date the rent would be payable to them. This notice is admitted by plaintiff in error, but she denied the right of the church or its agents to change her landlord without her consent, and therefore refused to pay rent to defendants in error. She also testified that defendants in error had never demanded rent of her, but also says that at one time on a Sunday evening Mr. Sullivan passed her door and said, "Are you making any calculation to pay your rent?" At another time, she testified, he cursed her, called her an improper name, and asked her why she did not pay her rent. These remarks, even if not couched in the most gallant language, taken in connection with her statement to Mr. Windham that she would not pay rent to defendant, must be held a sufficient demand. Plaintiff in error knew to whom the rent was due. The fact that the treatment received by her was unpleasant or even impolite, if such were the case, would not relieve her from the payment of rent according to her contract of lease.

The next inquiry is as to whether or not plaintiff was

entitled to notice of the termination of her tenancy, aside from the three days' notice to quit which was given. This question must be decided in the negative. Section 1020 of the civil code provides that proceedings under the article for the forcible detention of real estate may be had "in all cases against tenants holding over their terms." Section 1021, above cited, provides in effect that the failure to pay rent shall terminate a tenancy, and that "a tenant shall be deemed to be holding over his term whenever he has failed, neglected, or refused to pay the rent or any part thereof, when the same was due," etc. By section 1022 it is provided that, "It shall be the duty of the party desiring to commence an action under this chapter, to notify the adverse party to leave the premises for the possession of which the action is about to be brought, which notice shall be served at least three days before commencing the action," etc. No other notice is required. It seems plain to us that it was the intention of the legislature that the fact of the failure or refusal to pay rent should bring the lessee within the provisions of section 1020, *supra*, and that in such case but one notice was necessary—the notice to quit. If we are correct in this, the remaining question—as to the non-payment of rent—was one of fact, for the determination of the jury. On this they have found, upon sufficient evidence, against plaintiffs in error, and with that we must be content.

Objection is made to the instructions given to the jury by the court, but as they are consistent throughout with the views here expressed, they need not be further noticed.

The judgment of the district court is affirmed.

JUDGMENT AFFIRMED.

THE other judges concur.

PRENTISS D. CHENEY, APPELLANT, V. B. L. HARDING
ET AL., APPELLEES.

Summons: ACKNOWLEDGMENT OF SERVICE. An acknowledgment
of the service of a summons in writing on the back of such
summons, signed by a person to be served, *Held*, to be equivalent to actual legal service of such summons by the sheriff to
whom the same is directed, made within his proper bailiwick.

APPEAL from the district court of Otoe county. Heard
below before POUND, J.

E. F. Warren, for appellant.

John C. Watson and *Frank T. Ransom,* for appellees.

COBB, J.

This was an action brought by the plaintiff, Prentiss D.
Cheney, to redeem certain lands in Otoe county, upon
which he is the holder of a second mortgage, from a sale
pursuant to a judgment of foreclosure rendered in an action
brought by the holder of a first mortgage upon the same
lands, and in which action the plaintiff was a defendant.

The judgment of the district court was for the defendants dismissing the action, and the cause is brought to this
court by the plaintiff by appeal.   He assigns the following
errors:

"*First.* The court below erred in holding that Cheney's
admission of service, made in Illinois, was equivalent to an
acceptance of service made within the jurisdiction of the
court.

"*Second.* The court erred in holding that the decree in
*Mutual Life Insurance Company v. B. L. Harding and
others* was a foreclosure against Cheney's rights.

"*Third.* The court erred in admitting in evidence the
tax deed from the treasurer of Otoe county to H. H. Gray.

5

"*Fourth.* The court erred in finding for the defendants.

"*Fifth.* The judgment for the defendants is contrary to law.

"*Sixth.* The court below disregarded and violated the rights guaranteed to appellant by the Constitution of the United States, in this: The privileges and immunities enjoyed by citizens of Nebraska, and enforced by the supreme court of the state, were denied to this appellant, who is a citizen of the state of Illinois."

"The court denied to appellant the equal protection of the laws.

"The court deprived the appellant of his property without due process of law."

The principal question involved in the case is presented by the first assignment of errors. Did the district court of Otoe county, in the case of *Mutual Life Insurance Company v. B. L. Harding and others,* acquire and have jurisdiction to render the judgment which it did in fact render in said cause, in so far as said judgment affected the rights of the present plaintiff, one of the defendants in said cause?

Our statute, section 72 of the code of civil procedure, provides that "an acknowledgement on the back of the summons, or the voluntary appearance of a defendant, is equivalent to a service."

It appears from the abstract that upon the trial of the cause, after the introduction in evidence of other parts of the record in the case of *Mutual Life Insurance Company against B. L. Harding and others,* plaintiff introduced a summons (part of said record). I quote from the abstract: "In this summons the sheriff is commanded to summon P. D. Cheney, impleaded with B. L. Harding and others; and it is returned and filed September 3, 1877, and shows the following: 'I admit service of within summons this 29th day of August, 1877, at my residence in Jerseyville, Illinois. P. D. Cheney.'"

It is not shown, either by the abstract or the transcript

itself, whether the above admission is written on "the back of the summons," so as to bring it strictly within the language of 'the statute, or upon some other part of the paper. But as the language of the admission refers to the summons as the *within* summons, I assume that it is on the back of the summons. The *service* to which the statute makes such service the equivalent, is undoubtedly actual legal service, and embraces within its meaning everything necessary to make such actual service legal, as well the place where made, as the officer who makes it. It cannot be conceived that it was the intention of the legislature to make such acknowledgment on the back of the summons the equivalent of substituted or constructive service only, because in cases of constructive service, where the defendant so served does not answer or appear, he may at any time within five years after the date of judgment have the same opened and be let in to defend upon showing by affidavit that during the pendency of the action he had no actual notice thereof in time to appear in court and make his defense. See section 82 of the civil code. I conclude, therefore, that it is the true construction of the statute that the acknowledgment there specified is the equivalent in all respects of a legal service of the summons upon the back of which it is written, by the sheriff to whom it is addressed, made in his proper bailiwick.

The acknowledgment over the signature of the plaintiff, having been introduced in evidence by his own attorney, it will be treated as genuine in all respects. Were authorities necessary to so self-evident a proposition, they are found in the cases cited to that point by counsel for defendants— *Maclin v. The New England Mut. Life Ins. Co.*, 33 La. An., 801, and *Hewitt v. Buck*, 17 Me., 147.

To the general proposition, that a defendant will be bound by an acknowledgment or acceptance of service of a summons outside of the territorial jurisdiction of the court to which it is returnable, counsel for the defendants cites *Ex parte Schollenberger*, 96 U. S., 369. *Vermont Farm Machine Co., v. Marble*, 20 Fed. R., 117, and *Johnson v. Monell*, 13 Ia., 300. The federal cases are, I think, fairly in point to the principle contended for, and the Iowa case holds squarely with it; and the decision being upon a statute almost identical with our own, I regard it as applicable to and as conclusive of the case at bar.

The third error assigned is for the admission of improper evidence. It has been often held in this court, upon what was considered sufficient authority, that error would not lie for the admission of improper or irrelevant evidence in a case tried to a court without a jury.

The second, fourth, fifth and sixth assignments of error are neither of them insisted on in the brief upon which plaintiff submitted the case. They will, therefore, not be considered.

The judgment of the district court is affirmed.

JUDGMENT AFFIRMED.

THE other judges concur.

SAME v. SAME.

1. **Jurisdiction:** ACKNOWLEDGMENT OF SERVICE OF SUMMONS BY NON-RESIDENT. Where in an action to foreclose a mortgage on real estate, a summons was duly issued by the clerk and sent to the sheriff of J. county, Illinois, and endorsed by the defendant, "I admit service of the within summons this 29th day of August, 1877, at my residence in Jerseyville, Illinois," to which he appended his signature, *Held*, Sufficient to give the court jurisdiction.

2. ———: AFFIDAVIT FOR SERVICE. In such case, as it clearly appeared from the record that the defendant resided in another state, the failure to file an affidavit as required by section 78 of the code did not affect the jurisdiction.

REHEARING of foregoing case.

MAXWELL, CH. J.

The plaintiff moves for a rehearing in this case upon the following grounds:

"*First.* No foundation was laid to authorize service out of state, as required in *Blair v. West Point*, 7 Neb., 152.

"*Second.* The writ was directed to the sheriff of Otoe county, but was served by a person in Illinois, not thereunto authorized as required by § 68, code.

"*Third.* Service was made by reading, which is contrary to the requirements of § 69.

"*Fourth.* The officer to whom the writ was directed did not return it as required by § 71.

"*Fifth.* There is not 'an acknowledgment on the back of the summons' as required by § 72.

"*Sixth.* An admission is not an acknowledgment.

"*Seventh.* Service out of the state was not authorized, because *all* the defendants were not non-residents, as required by § 81.

"*Eighth.* Service out of the state is not actual service, but is constructive service only.

"*Ninth.* The judgment is contrary to law and should be reversed."

The service of summons and acknowledgment of service thereof are as follows:

"STATE OF ILLINOIS, COUNTY OF JERSEY, ss.

JERSEYVILLE, IILLINOIS, August 29th, 1877.

I have duly served this writ by reading the same to the within named P. D. Cheney, this 29th day of August, A.D. 1877.

J. M. YOUNG,
Sheriff of Jersey county, Illinois."

Then appears the following:

"I admit service of the within summons, this 29th day of August, 1877, at my residence in Jerseyville, Illinois.

P. D. CHENEY."

Sec. 77 of the code provides that "Service may be made by publication in either of the following cases: *First,* in actions brought under the fifty-first, fifty-second, and fifty-third sections of this code (to recover possession of real estate, partition, foreclosure of mortgages of real estate, specific performance), where any or all of the defendants reside out of the state. *Second,* in actions brought to establish or set aside a will where any or all of the defendants reside out of the state. *Third,* in actions brought against a non-resident of this state, or a foreign corporation having in this state property or debts owing to them, sought to be taken by any of the provisional remedies or to be appropriated in any way. *Fourth,* in actions which relate to, or the subject of which is real or personal property in this state, where any defendant has or claims a lien or interest, actual or contingent therein, or the relief demanded consists wholly or partially in excluding him from any interest therein, and such defendant is a non-resident of the state or a foreign corporation. *Fifth,* in all actions where the defendant, being a resident of the state, has departed therefrom, or from the county of his residence, with intent to delay or defraud his creditors, or to avoid the service of summons, or keeps himself concealed therein with like intent."

Sec. 78 provides that "Before service can be made by publication, an affidavit must be filed that service of a summons cannot be made within this state on the defendant or defendants to be served by publication, and that the case is one of those mentioned in the preceding section, etc."

Sec. 81 provides for personal service of the summons out of the state, by the sheriff or some person appointed by him for that purpose.

In *Blair v. West Point Manufg. Co.,* 7 Neb., 146—an action to cancel a mechanic's lien and quiet the title to the property in the plaintiff—and the defendant being a non-resident, it was held essential that an affidavit be filed setting forth that service of summons could not be made in the state on the defendant to be served. In that case the defendant made a special appearance and moved to quash the service of the summons.

The object of filing the affidavit is to show to the court that the subject matter is within its jurisdiction, but that some or all of the defendants are without the state and cannot be served with process therein. If, however, these facts appear on the record, it will be sufficient. In the admission of service in this case Mr. Cheney says it was "at my residence in Jerseyville, Illinois." This certainly was sufficient to show that he was a non-resident of the state and that service of summons could not be made on him therein. He thus had actual notice of the pendency of the action and could not open the decree under section 82 of the code, unless there was not sufficient time after the service of notice to appear and make his defense, of which there is no claim. He waits nearly eight years and then attempts to treat the entire proceedings as void, not because the action was not brought in the proper county, or that he had no notice of its pendency, nor because he did not admit service of the summons at Jerseyville, Illinois, but solely upon the ground that no affidavit that he was a non-resident was filed. This we think was unnecessary where the fact of non-residence otherwise appears. Every person is entitled to notice, either actual or constructive, before his rights can be barred, but the law favors diligence and requires a party having such notice to appear and assert his rights. The notice in this case therefore was sufficient, and the defendant is barred from maintaining the action. This disposes of all the objections named. A rehearing must be denied.

JUDGMENT ACCORDINGLY.

THE other judges concur.

AULTMAN, MILLER & CO., PLAINTIFF IN ERROR, V.
LEONARD STICHLER, DEFENDANT IN ERROR.

1. **Replevin**: ANSWER. GENERAL DENIAL. In replevin, the
plaintiff's cause of action depending essentially upon his right
to the immediate possession of the property in controversy, a
general denial by the defendant puts in issue not only such right
of possession, but every collateral fact necessary to the establishing of the same. In such case, *Held*, That an answer containing a general denial will not be required to be made more
definite and certain.

2. ———: DAMAGES. In replevin damages, other than legal interest on the value of the property as found, for the detention of
the property. are recoverable only in case of a return. If the
property is not returned the measure of damages is the value of
the property as proved, together with lawful interest thereon
from the date of the unlawful taking. See *Romberg v. Hughes*,
18 Neb., 579.

3. **Warranty**. Plaintiff's contract of warranty construed.

ERROR to the district court for Greeley county. Tried
below before TIFFANY, J.

Henry Nunn and *Paul & Bell*, for plaintiff in error.

Thomas L. Redlon and *H. G. Bell*, for defendant in.
error.

COBB, J.

I. On the 24th day of March, 1885, plaintiff filed petition in the district court of Greeley county, stating its
cause of action to be, that it was the owner of and had a
special property in one span of dark brown horse mules
of the value of $250, by virtue of a chattel mortgage dated
June 9, 1882, and executed by defendant to the plaintiff
on said mules, and one Aultman, Miller & Co. self binder,
to secure the payment of three certain promissory notes of

the said defendant for $95 each, and interest at ten per cent, from July 19, 1881, the date of said notes. Defendant made default in the payment of said notes, and by reason of said default plaintiff claimed right to immediate possession of said mules. That said defendant wrongfully and and unlawfully detained said mules from the plaintiff.

II. On the 3d day of September, 1885, said defendant filed an answer, denying each and every allegation, matter, fact, and thing in plaintiff's petition contained, except as hereinafter stated :

1. That in the month of July, 1881, he bought a Buckeye harvester and self-binder, giving the notes therefor.

2. That at the time of purchase plaintiff made a warranty of said machine.

3. That plaintiff made a printed warranty of said machine.

4. That when defendant bought said machine and gave his notes therefor he relied on said warranty.

5. That said machine did not fill said warranty, and that said machine was useless and worthless as a self-binder..

6. That defendant notified L. A. Devine and John Wacek, the plaintiffs' agents, that said machine would not do its work, and requested them, by letter and otherwise, to put said machine in order.

7. That defendant received no consideration for said notes, because said machine was worthless.

8. That in the month of July, 1882, the plaintiff, by its agent, L. A. Devine, in order to induce the defendant to pay or secure said notes and keep said machine, then and there promised, agreed, and contracted with the defendant in writing to put said machine in order and make the same do as good work as any other machine.

9. That defendant relied on said warranty and gave the plaintiff the chattel mortgage set out in his petition.

10. That plaintiff did not put said machine in order.

11. That defendant tried to run said machine in the har-

vest of 1882. Notified plaintiffs and their agents, L. A. Devine and John Wacek, by letter and otherwise, and requested plaintiff to send a man to put same in order, which plaintiff failed to do.

12. That said machine was worthless and useless and imperfect, and never would do its work in a workmanlike manner.

13. That the value of said mules was $375.

14. That said mules were defendant's only team.

15. That defendant at that time was engaged in farming, and that he was poor and had no means of purchasing another team.

16. That the defendant was damaged in the sum of $2.50 per day, while said team was kept from him, to-wit, from March 14, 1884.

17. That said defendant asked for the return of said mules or $375, their value, and for the sum of $1,337, his damages.

III. The defendant, in his amended answer in the county court under which said case was tried, asked judgment against the plaintiff for return of said mules, or the sum of $375, the value thereof, and $300, his damages, by reason of the unlawful detention of said mules.

IV. On the 4th day of September, 1885, the plaintiff filed a motion as follows: And now comes the plaintiff and moves the court to require the defendant to make his answer more definite and certain, by showing whether said defendant affirmed or rescinded the contract and warranty set forth as made in 1882, and whether the warranty of 1881 was in writing or not. Which motion on the 7th day of September, 1885, the court overruled, to which ruling the plaintiffs duly excepted at the time.

V. On the 7th day of September, 1885, the plaintiff filed a reply to defendant's answer in said court, denying each and every allegation of new matter in said answer contained.

There was a trial to a jury, with a verdict and judgment for the defendant. I copy the verdict and judgment:

"We, the jury duly impaneled and sworn in the above case, find the right of property and right of possession of said property at the commencement of this action, was in the defendant, and we assess the value of said property at $300, and we also assess the damages sustained by him by reason of the detention of said property, at $499. We assess the whole amount of his recovery at $799."

On the 8th day of September, 1885, judgment was given for the defendant for a return of the property taken on said writ of replevin, and that he have and recover of the plaintiff the sum of $499, his damages for withholding the same, or in case a return of said property cannot be had, the defendant have and receive from the plaintiff the sum of $300, the value of said property, and his damages for withholding the same, assessed at $499, and costs of suit, taxed at $213.60.

Defendant then offered to remit $35, being the interest on the value of the property wrongfully held by the plaintiff in replevin.

The cause was brought to this court on error by the plaintiff, who assigns the following errors:

"1st. The court erred in overruling the motion of the plaintiff to require the defendant to make his answer more definite, by showing whether the defendant affirmed or rescinded the contract and warranty of 1882 set forth in his answer.

"2d. The court erred in allowing the defendant to give evidence of a warranty for the year 1881.

"3d. The court erred in refusing to give the second instruction asked by the plaintiff.

"4th. The court erred in refusing to give the third instruction asked by the plaintiff.

"5th. The damages assessed by the jury are excessive and contrary to the law of the case.

"6th. The court erred in overruling a motion of the plaintiff for a new trial."

The first assignment of error cannot be sustained. Had the plaintiff's motion, instead of being to require the defendant to make his answer more definite and certain, been to strike out all of the answer, except the general denial, as redundant matter, it would, as I understand the law, have been sustained. The essential allegation of the plaintiff's petition is his " right to the immediate possession of said mules." Under the general denial contained in the first paragraph of the defendant's answer, he could prove any fact which tended to controvert the said right of possession, and it was not necessary to set up the warranty or breach thereof in order to the admission of evidence of such warranty and breach for the purpose of disproving the plaintiff's claim of the right of possession of the property replevied. See *School Dist. v. Shoemaker*, 5 Neb., 36. *Creighton v. Newton*, Id., 100. *Hedman v. Anderson*, 8 Id., 180. *Ferrell v. Humphrey*, 12 Ohio R., 113. And *Oaks v. Wyatt*, 10 Id., 344.

The above remarks will also apply to the second assignment of error. As we have seen, without an answer in the nature of a special plea, the defendant could give in evidence any warranty of said machine which had been made by the plaintiff. If such warranty had been received in evidence, and had been rescinded by virtue of a subsequent contract between the parties, that was a matter of rebuttal to be proved by the plaintiff.

The third and fourth assignments are based upon the refusal of the court to give the second and third instructions prayed by the plaintiff.

I copy the instructions as prayed.

"II. The court instructs you that if you find from the testimony that the consideration of the chattel mortgage under which the plaintiff claims a special ownership in the property therein described was an extension of time of payment on the three promisory notes introduced in evidence, or if you find that the said extension of time was a part of said contract for said chattel mortgage, then you will find for the plaintiff.

"III. The defense in this case is, that in the year 1882 the plaintiff gave to the defendant a contract and warranty by the terms of which the plaintiff agreed to satisfactorily make work, for the harvest of 1882, the harvester and self-binder sold to said Stichler in the harvest of 1881, on condition that if the binder does not perform its work as well as any binder manufactured, or any other trouble that might arise from its working, notice must be given and time allowed to send a man to put it in order. If it fails to work after this, and with due diligence and care shown, the machine is to be returned to our agency at St. Paul, Nebraska, and notes given for it shall be returned.

"The contract and warranty of plaintiff was upon condition, and these conditions must have been performed by the defendant in order to charge the plaintiff. That is, if the machine failed to work satisfactorily, the defendant must have notified the plaintiff of that fact, and then if the plaintiff failed to send a man to put it in order, or, having sent a man, failed to make it work satisfactorily, then it was the duty of the defendant to return said machine to the agency of Aultman, Miller & Co., at St. Paul, Nebraska; and if you find from the evidence that the defendant failed to do this during the harvest of 1882, then, and in that case, the defendant cannot recover on said contract and warranty set forth in his answer."

There was evidence tending to prove that the defendant purchased the machine of plaintiff for which the notes were given in 1881; that the plaintiff warranted the machine by a printed warranty; that in the harvest of said year the machine failed to comply with the warranty, or to do good work; that defendant notified the local agents of the plaintiff of the failure of the machine to comply with the terms of the warranty, or to do good work, to which no attention was paid. It also appears from the evidence that on or about the 7th day of June, 1882, the agent of the plaintiff went to the house of the defendant for the purpose of collecting the notes given for the said machine. Thereupon the defendant again called the attention of said agent to the failure of said machine to comply with the terms of said warranty or to do good work, which deficiency in the machine was admitted by the said agent, whereupon, in consideration of the giving of the chattel mortgage referred to in the petition by the defendant to secure the said notes, the said agent on the part of the plaintiff agreed to repair the said machine and put it in good working worder for the then approaching harvest, and thereupon executed and delivered to the defendant the warranty called the second or 1882 warranty, of which the following is a copy:

"ST. PAUL, Neb., June 7, 1882.

"We herein agree with L. I. Stichler to satisfactorily make work for the harvest of 1882, the harvester and self-binder sold to said Stichler in harvest of 1881, on consideration that if binder does not perform its work as well as any binder manufactured, or any other trouble that might arise from its working, notice must be given us and time allowed a man to put in order. If it fails to work after this, and due diligence and care shown in its management, the machine is to be returned to our agency at St. Paul, and notes given for it shall be returned." Signed by the plaintiff per agent.

The defendant at the same time, in consideration that plaintiff would put the said machine in good working order according to the terms of the said warranty, that the machine would do good work when so put in order, executed and delivered the chattel mortgage, to foreclose which this suit was brought. It further appeared that the plaintiff failed to put said machine in order, or to do anything with it whatever.

That defendant wrote to the agents of the plaintiff to put said machine in order, but they failed to respond or to again come to the defendant's place until they came to replevy the mortgaged property.

At the argument and consultation we were all of the opinion that it was the true construction of the above warranty that the plaintiff was, in the first place, and without further notice or request, to put the machine in working order for the harvest of 1882, and that the condition of notice giving time for a man to remedy further defects, etc., only applied to defects which might thereafter be developed. After further and careful consideration of the terms of the warranty, and the evidence applicable thereto, I adhere to that construction. With these views of the evidence we must hold that the instructions were properly refused.

The fifth assignment must be in part allowed to the extent of modifying the judgment.

In the case of *Romberg v. Hughes*, 18 Neb., 579, we held that "In replevin, damages for the detention of the property are recoverable only in case of a return. If the property is not returned the measure of damages is the value of the property as proved together with lawful interest thereon from the date of the unlawful taking." Following that case, as we must, believing it to express the law, we must hold that the damages awarded by the verdict are excessive, unless the property can be returned to the defendant. And even if it can be returned we were all of the opinion at the argument that three hundred dollars damages was as large a verdict, in addition to the value of the property as found, as could be sustained.

In case, therefore, that the defendant shall, within forty days from the filing of this opinion, enter a remittitur in this court, of all damages except seven per cent interest on the amount of the value of the property as found ($300) from the date of the taking to the date of such filing of this

opinion in case the property replevied cannot be returned,
or in case the same can be and is returned, then, of all
damages in excess of three hundred dollars with interest
thereon from the date of the judgment in the court below,
then the judgment to stand affirmed as to the value of the
property as found, and the damages in either event not remitted, otherwise the judgment will stand reversed, and
the cause to be remanded for further proceedings.

JUDGMENT ACCORDINGLY.

THE other judges concur.

F. P. HELPHREY, APPELLEE, v. JOHN I. REDICK, JR.,
ET AL., APPELLANTS.

1. **Judgment:** HOW FAR BINDING. A judgment only binds parties and privies. A tax purchaser of real estate not a party to
an action to enjoin the treasurer from issuing a deed, nor appearing in the action, is not bound by the decree.

2. **Taxes:** FORECLOSURE OF TAX LIEN. An action to foreclose a
tax lien on real estate may be brought on the tax certificate
where it is alleged in the petition that a deed would be invalid
if issued, and such action may be brought within the same time
as if brought on a tax deed, the title under which had failed.

3. ———: REDEMPTION: NOTICE. A notice to redeem is not indis-
pensible before bringing an action to foreclose a tax lien, although the failure to give such notice in certain cases may affect
the question of costs. *Lammers v. Comstock*, 20 Neb., 341.

APPEAL from the district court of Douglas county.
Heard below before WAKELEY, J.

John I. Redick and *Redick & Redick*, for appellant.

Groff, Montgomery, & Jeffery, for appellee.

MAXWELL, CH. J.

In December, 1881, the appellee filed a petition in the district court of Douglas county in which he alleged that in September, 1876, he purchased at public tax sale the north half of the north-east quarter of the north-east quarter of section 9, T. 15, R. 13 in said county for $68.18, being the taxes due on said land for the year 1875; that he afterwards paid the taxes due on said land for the year 1876, being $131.70, and for 1877, being $117.35; that before a tax deed was issued to the appellee, the appellant, Redick, obtained an injunction restraining the county treasurer from issuing said deed. The appellee waives all claim to the title to said property, but seeks to enforce his lien for taxes thereon amounting to the sum of $317.23, with interest, etc. In February, 1877, the appellant, Redick, was appointed guardian *ad litem* for the minor defendants, and filed an answer as follows:

"1. That their grantor, John I. Redick, brought suit, and obtained an injunction which was afterwards made perpetual, enjoining the county treasurer from issuing a tax deed for said property to the purchaser, on the ground that all the taxes for which it was sold were illegal and void; and the decree entered therein has never been reversed, and pleading said decree in bar of this action.

"2. That the defendants are all minors, and became the owners of the property March 13th, 1878.

"3. That at the time of sale John I. Redick had plenty of personal property to pay the taxes.

"4. That the cause of action did not accrue within five years next before the commencement of the suit, and is barred.

"5. That the taxes are illegal and void for the want of a valid assessment.

"6. That no notice was served upon them as required by section 123 of revenue law."

And on March 18th, 1885, plaintiff filed his reply as follows:

"That he was not served and did not voluntarily appear in said injunction suit, and denying specifically all the allegations of the answer, except that defendants are minors."

Afterwards there was a trial to the court, and the following proceedings were had:

The plaintiff introduced the petition in the case of John I. Redick vs. W. F. Heins, treasurer of Douglas county, and F. P. Helphrey, alleging that plaintiff was the owner of the N. $\frac{1}{2}$ of N. E. $\frac{1}{4}$ of sec. 9, T. 15, R. 13, in said county; that a portion of it had been sold to said Helphrey for the taxes of 1875; that said taxes were illegal and void for reasons set forth in said petition; that said Helphrey is about to take out a deed, and asking an injunction, etc., etc.

Also the temporary order of injunction enjoining the treasurer from issuing a deed.

Also return on summons showing personal service on said Heins, and that the defendant Helphrey could not be found in Douglas county.

Also entry of default against Heins, and the decree in said cause finding all the allegations of the petition to be true; that the sale and certificate were unauthorized and void; that the assessment was illegal, and did not become a lien on said property, and decreeing that the injunction be made perpetual.

After argument the cause was taken under advisement, and on October 15, 1885, a decree was entered finding in favor of the plaintiff; that the plaintiff's title had failed, and that he had a lien for $628.55; that defendants pay said amount within 30 days or the property be sold, etc. to all of which findings defendants excepted.

Two questions are presented by the record. *First,* Is the appellee estopped from maintaining the action by the decree against the treasurer of Douglas county? *Second,* Is the action barred by the statute of limitations?

First. At the time the proceedings against the treasurer of Douglas county were instituted, the treasurer had sold the land to the appellee for the taxes due thereon. The county, so far as this record shows, had no interest in the controversy, all taxes against the land having been paid. The appellee was not made a party to the proceeding and did not appear therein. It will not be contended that Douglas county, with the money of the tax purchaser in its treasury, which money it had received on a sale of the real estate in controversy for taxes, could bind such tax purchaser without giving him his day in court. Only parties and privies are bound by a decree. To make a matter *res adjudicata*, there must be a concurrence, 1st of identity of the subject matter; 2d, that the former suit was between the same parties in the same right or capacity or their privies claiming under them. *Bigelow v. Winsor*, 1 Gray, 299. The appellee—the real party in interest, not being a party to the action, nor before the court, the decree as to him is no bar to this action.

Second. That the action is barred, not having been brought in five years from the time the cause of action accrued. It will be observed that the tax sale took place in September, 1876, and the action was brought in December, 1881, no tax deed having been issued. The failure of the appellee to obtain a tax deed is explained by the injunction against the treasurer by which he was prohibited from issuing such deed. In a number of cases decided by this court it has been held that the statute did not run against the right to foreclose the lien until the title acquired by the tax deed had failed. *Holmes v. Andrews*, 16 Neb., 296. *Schoenheit v. Nelson*, Id., 235. *Bryant v. Estabrook*, Id., 217. *Zaradnicek v. Selby*, 15 Neb., 579. *Towle v. Holt*, 14 Neb., 222. *Miller v. Hurford*, 13 Neb., 14. *Wilhelm v. Russell*, 8 Neb., 120. *Petit v. Black*, 8 Id., 52. *Peet v. O'Brien*, 5 Neb., 360.

Under our present statute it is unnecessary to take out a

tax deed, but the tax purchaser may in lieu thereof file his petition to foreclose the lien and allege therein that a tax deed would be invalid. He may then, if the taxes are a lien upon the real estate, have a decree of foreclosure and sale. Such action may be brought within the same time that it could have been brought had a deed been issued. The law does not require a needless act. If no title could be acquired by a tax deed it need not be issued as a matter of form before an action of foreclosure is brought. The action could not be brought until the time given to redeem had expired, as the right to a deed in no case would become absolute until after the expiration of the time to redeem, and this would bring the action within the provisions of the statute.

Objection is made that no notice was served upon the appellants, but this is not fatal to an action to foreclose the lien. *Lammers v. Comstock*, 20 Neb., 341. At most it can only affect the costs. No complaint is made as to the amount of the decree, and it is apparent that justice has been done. The judgment is therefore affirmed.

JUDGMENT AFFIRMED.

THE other judges concur.

DEMMITT COLE ET AL., APPELLEES, V. LORENZO COLE ET AL., APPELLANTS.

Deed: CONVEYANCE BY ONE OF FEEBLE MIND: UNDUE INFLU-
ENCE. C., a man past 70 years of age, afflicted with senile cerebral atrophy to such an extent that his mind and memory were
so impaired that he often did not know his own sons with whom
he had resided all their lives, would often become lost in his
own house, door-yard, and orchard. Being possessed of a farm
of the value of nearly twenty thousand dollars, and being the

father of thirteen sons and daughters, all mature men and wo-
men, the fruits of three several marriages, his third wife being
dead, and the youngest son ·being married and occupying the
old homestead with C., the father, a claim was presented to C. by
an attorney on behalf of one Mrs. S., a daughter of the last
wife of C. by a former husband, for her share of $1,500, alleged
to have been received by C. of money inherited by his said last wife
from a deceased uncle's estate in the year 1844, and some of the
sons of C., by the said last wife, including the said youngest
of said sons, co-operated with the attorney to effect a settlement
of the claim of Mrs. S., their half sister, as well as the claim
of the six sons and daughters of C. by his said last wife to the
balance of said $1,500. Whereupon, C. executed and delivered
to the said six sons and daughters by his said last wife, a deed
of general warranty of and to his said farm (the same being
his entire possessions), reserving to himself a life estate therein
and excepting from the covenant of warranty the claim of Mrs.
S. for no other consideration than the said claims. In an action commenced in the name of C., and which at his death was
revived in the name of his seven sons and daughters by the two
former marriages; *Held*, That the judgment and decree of the
district court, whereby the said deed was vacated, annulled, and
declared of no force or effect, be affirmed.

APPEAL from the district court of Cass county.   Heard
below before POUND, J.

Allen Beeson and *Chapman & Polk*, for appellees.

M. A. Hartigan, for appellants.

COBB, J.

This action was brought in the district court of Cass
county by Demmitt Cole, plaintiff, against the defendants.
Pending the action in that court, the death of the plaintiff
was suggested and the action revived in the name of Calvin
H. Parmele as administrator, and Lewis F. Cole, William
Cole, John W. Cole, George D. Cole, Frank Cole, Maud
Cole, and Susanah Drake as devisees under the will of the
deceased, whereupon the cause proceeded to trial and judgment.

I copy from the abstract the entire pleadings in the case, together with the statement of the case by defendants' and appellants' counsel, from which the nature and object of he action, as well as the grounds of the defense will appear.

"Demmitt Cole, plaintiff,   ⎫
           vs.   ⎪
Lorenzo Cole, James M.   ⎪
  Cole, Alfonzo M. Cole,   ⎬ Petition in Equity.
  Joseph F. Cole, Celes-   ⎪
  tine Russel and Dianah   ⎪
  Chalfant, Defendants.   ⎭

"The plaintiff states that he is, and for more than a year last past has been, the owner in fee simple of the following described real estate, situated in Cass county, state of Nebraska, to-wit: The south-west quarter of section No. twenty-four. The west half of the north-east quarter of section No. twenty-four, and the east half of the south-west quarter of section No. twenty-four, which lies east of a small creek which runs northerly through said section, except three acres heretofore deeded to David Brinson; and the north-west quarter and the west half of the north-east quarter of section No. twenty-five, all in township No. eleven, north of range No. 13, east of the 6th P. M. Also about thirty-two and one-half acres of land, described as follows, to-wit:

"Commencing at a point two and $\frac{20}{100}$ chains south of the witness corner, between sections thirteen and twenty-four, of township eleven north, of range thirteen east of the sixth P. M. (said witness corner being twenty-five links west of the true quarter section corner, thence north 61 degrees 35 minutes, east 11 and $\frac{10}{100}$ chains, to a walnut tree on the south bank of Rock creek, thence following the meanders of said creek westward about ten chains, to a point north 8 degrees 50 minutes, east one chain from a large elm tree, thence south 8 degrees, 50 minutes, west by said elm tree 22 and $\frac{60}{100}$ chains to a stake, then south 62 degrees

15 minutes, east 12 and $\frac{60}{100}$ chains, to an old elm stump on the east bank of a small creek, thence following the meanders of said creek north-easterly to the point of beginning, containing twenty-seven and one-half acres, the same more or less being in said sections 13 and 24. Also the following land, viz: Commencing at the quarter section between section 13 and 24, in township 11 north, of range 13 east of the 6th P. M., thence south twenty chains to the south-east corner of the north-east quarter of the north-west quarter of said section 24, thence west about 4 and $\frac{75}{100}$ chains to the center of a small creek, thence down said creek to the place of beginning, containing five acres more or less, said last two descriptions of land being situated in township 11 north, range 13 east of the 6th principal meridian, in Cass county, Nebraska.

"2. That he is seventy-eight years old, a widower, and the defendants, and Lewis F. Cole, John W. Cole, William T. Cole, and Susanah Drake are his children, and only children now living.

"3. That on the 8th day of October, 1881, the defendants, James M. Cole and Alfonzo M. Cole, together with one Michael A. Hartigan, an attorney at law and notary public, came to the home of plaintiff on said land and procured him, by fraud and deception, to sign an instrument of writing, purporting to be a warranty deed of the whole of said lands to these defendants, as grantees, reserving a life estate therein to plaintiff.

"4. That at said time plaintiff was sick and unable to sit up, and in consequence of his age and sickness, his mind was so affected that he did not know what he was doing, and was utterly incapable of transacting any business.

"5. That said defendants, James M. Cole and Alfonzo M. Cole, and the said Michael A. Hartigan, well knew the physical and mental condition of plaintiff at said time, and that he was utterly incapable of transacting business, and purposely took advantage of his helpless condition to obtain said deed, and thus to secure to themselves and their co-defendants the whole of plaintiff's property, leaving nothing for his other children.

"6. That said James M. Cole, and Alfonzo M. Cole, and Michael A. Hartigan procured plaintiff to sign said pretended deed without any knowledge of the character of the instrument whatever, and when his mind was in such a condition that he did not know what he was doing, and said parties refused to tell him what it was or to give him any information in regard to it, but on the other hand carefully concealed from him the nature of the instrument he was signing, and the said Michael A. Hartigan, for the purpose and with the design and intent of assisting, aiding, and abetting the said James M. Cole and Alfonzo M. Cole in perpetrating said fraud upon plaintiff and his other children, falsely and fraudulently certified in his official capacity as a notary public, over his official signature and seal of office on said instrument or pretended deed, that plaintiff personally appeared before him and acknowledged the execution thereof to be his voluntary act, when said Hartigan well knew that plaintiff did not know what he had done.

"7. That plaintiff never designed, intended, or desired to make such disposition of his land, and does not now wish to make such disposition of it.

"8. That the said land comprises all the land owned by plaintiff and constitutes his homestead where he has resided for about fourteen years, and that said defendant procured the execution of said pretended deed for the purpose of securing the whole of said land to themselves, and preventing plaintiff's other children from getting any part thereof.

"9. That there was no consideration ever paid to or received by plaintiff for said pretended deed. Wherefore plaintiff prays that said pretended deed so executed as aforesaid be canceled, set aside, and held for naught, and the defendants and each of them be barred and estopped from having or claiming any interest in said lands by virtue of said pretended deed, and that plaintiff's title thereto be declared absolute as against the defendants, and that he have judgment for costs, and that he have such other and further relief as may be adjudged equitable."

Signed by plaintiff's attorneys and verified.

After filing the petition, but before answer, the plaintiff, Demmitt Cole, appeared in court (in vacation) and filed his motion or paper writing dismissing the suit as follows:

" And now comes the plaintiff in this action and moves the court to dismiss this action for the reason :

" 1. That he now believes said case can be settled without litigation.

" 2. That after further and careful consideration he does not wish said cause to be prosecuted longer, and that the allegations in the petition are not true.

" (Signed)   DEMMITT COLE, by his mark.

" Witness, W. C. SHOWALTER."

Defendants afterwards filed their amended answer as follows:

" Come now the defendants, by leave of court first had and obtained, and file this their amended answer, and therein answering say :

" 1. They deny each and every allegation in said petition contained and not therein expressly admitted.

" 3. They expressly and specifically deny the power of the court to appoint and the power of the pretended administrator to receive the appointment of such trust at the time when the claim of such appointment is made, that there was an attempted will then in existence, with executors named therein, and that said executors had not renounced or surrendered their trust, as by law required, which was then apparent from the records of the probate court of Cass county, and that such appointment was in law and in fact null and void and without force or effect.

"4.   That at the time when the order of revivor was attempted to be made in this court the plaintiff, Susannah Drake, was incapable of commencing or maintaining an action, being legally incompetent from so doing, and confined then and still so confined in a lunatic asylum in the city of Columbus, Ohio.

"5.   They specifically deny all charges of confederation and combination to defraud, charged and alleged against James M. Cole and Alfonzo Cole, with one M. A. Hartigan, as charged in said petition, and allege the truth and facts to be that when said deed was made that said Hartigan then was, and still is, the attorney for one Josephine Scothorne, the half sist : of these defendants, who then and now claims a legal right to the property and estate of their mother, late deceased, and a child's interest therein. And that said Hartigan was called by the defendant's father to make the deed in controversy, and their said father paid for the expense of such deed.

"6.   Defendants further answering say that their father, Demmitt Cole, when said deed was made was competent, mentally and physically, to make the same.   That the making of said deed was in the presence of and in pursuance of an agreement made by their father some months before said deed was made.   That there was time taken by their father to consider and think over the making of said deed.   And that such deed was only made after such consideration and thought, the same being in all things his voluntary, willful act.

"7.   Further answering say that long prior to the making of said deed that their father had often expressed a desire and willingness to convey land to the defendants herein, to requite the claim, 'and if necessary and needful, his then remaining estate' of their mother upon their father, and due and payable to defendants in such right.

"Defendants say that some thirty-five or forty years ago, and at or about the time of their mother's intermarriage

with their father,'she received in her own right, through
and from her uncle's estate, a legacy amounting to fifteen
hundred (1,500) dollars. That when the same was received
their father was in straitened financial circumstances, and
that he made and agreed with their mother that if she
would bring the money received home and pay off the indebtedness then existing on their home farm she could for-
ever hold and own the property; that she did do so and
that said legacy was paid out upon said lands—in pursuance of such agreement and understanding, which would
not have been done otherwise. That their father, as defendants believe and charge the truth to be, made a paper
writing of and concerning this agreement, and that the
same was in the possession of their mother at her death,
but as to its present whereabouts these defendants cannot
say.

"Defendants say the home in Ohio was sold (being the
one purchased by the mother's legacy) and the money invested in the land in suit. And that their father was not
able to purchase when he done so without the mother's
money. Defendants say their father at various times, years
before the deed in controversy was made, and in the lifetime of their mother, had offered to convey portions of the
land in suit to defendants' mother and to these defendants,
and that the reason the same was not done was owing to a
dispute as to the amount to reserve to the father for his life
estate and support.

"Defendants show unto the court that they are the children of their father by a third marriage; that the first and
second wives each had an estate in their own right, and
that upon their death the same was promptly paid, taken
and received by their children—the plaintiffs herein—and
that in addition thereto their father made gifts, advancements and otherwise aided and assisted plaintiffs during his
lifetime.

"Defendants say that the growth of said lands in value

and not their original cost that has made their present value. And that their original cost was not equal to the consideration mentioned in the deed made by their father to these defendants.

"The making, execution, and acknowledgment of said deed being herein admitted, and the same being based upon the condition (with the love and affection borne by the father) hereinbefore named and stated in this answer.

"That in consideration of the obligation resting on their father to their late mother said deed was made to these defendants, and creating and acknowledging the rights of their half-sister, Josephine Scothorne, who claims with and through their late mother, deceased, and who is a needful and necessary party to this action, without whom this cause cannot be fully and fairly heard and the rights of defendants determined. That in making said deed their father secured to himself a life estate in said lands, claiming at the time that was all the interest he sought or needed therein. That these defendants have in no way sought any interference with the care, custody, and management of said lands during his lifetime.

"Defendants deny all purpose or intention to in any manner commit any fraud against the other or older children of their father by prior marriage, and charge the truth to be said children at all times when they came of age took the property of their mothers with other aid and advancements made them by their father. That they received large sums of money and other advances made to them from time to time, much of which was made from the property and earnings of their (defendant's) mother.

"That said older children, particularly Lewis and William, with a fraudulent and dishonest purpose to obtain the property of these defendants through and under their mother, took their father and attempted to have him make a will, and therein and thereby exclude and disinherit these defendants. That said will was not made by their father, but a will was made for their father in which he wholly forgot and overlooked the defendant, Lorenzo Cole.

"Defendants further show unto this court that this suit was commenced without the knowledge, consent, or direction of their said father in his lifetime; that when he learned of the pendency of said action he promptly and of his own will and accord appeared in the district court of Cass county, and therein dismissed the same, as the same appears in the records of this honorable court, and therein and thereby ratified and confirmed his deed and the making of the same.

"In consideration of the premises, defendants ask that this action as to Calvin H. Parmele and Susannah Drake abate, and as to Josephine Scothorne that said action abate she being a needful and necessary party to the determination of said cause. That as to all the several and other plaintiffs, this action be dismissed, and defendants be allowed their costs and disbursements, with such other relief as equity may direct."

Signed by defendant's solicitor and verified.

Reply to amended answer:

"Comes now the plaintiff in the above cause, and for reply to the amended answer of the defendants:

"1. Deny each and every allegation therein contained that is inconsistent with the allegations in plaintiffs' petition.

"2. Plaintiffs further say that on the 20th day of January, 1882, when the motion to dismiss the action was filed, as stated in the amended answer of defendants, the said Demmitt Cole, owing to his great age, and to disease of mind and body, from which he was then and had been for a long time suffering, did not know, and was not capable of knowing, what he was doing. That he did not understand, and was not capable of understanding, the nature and effect of said motion. That what he did at that time was done by the direction and advisal of the defendants, or some of them, and not of his own will. That prior to that time an application had been filed in this court to have a suitable person appointed to conduct this suit on behalf of the plaintiff, on the ground that plaintiff's mind was so affected that he was not capable of attending to business. That said motion to dismiss was afterwards considered by this court and overruled, and the cause ordered to proceed in the name of the guardian of the plaintiff."

Signed by plaintiff's attorneys and verified.

Statement attached to the abstract by defendant's solicitor:

"The plaintiff, Demmitt Cole, in whose name the suit was first commenced, was three times married. There was children born in each marriage—Lewis and Shadrack by the first. Lewis is still alive, and one of the plaintiffs as the suit stands revived. William T. Cole, John Cole, and Susannah Drake are children of the second marriage, and Lorenzo, James, Alphonzo, and Joseph Cole, with Celestine Russell, and Dianah Chalfant, are children of the third marriage, all living, and defendants in the case. Josephine Scothorne was a child of the last wife by a former marriage, before her marriage with Demmitt Cole, so that the record shows the two older sets of children arrayed against the younger ones and their half sister (Mrs. Scothorne), although Mrs. Scothorne is not made a party to the suit.

"The contest grows out of the effort to obtain by the younger children the money the mother brought into the family as her own exclusive property. It appears from the record that there is no dispute as to the receipt and application of this money ($1,500), by Demmitt Cole, in the state of Ohio, to the discharge of the purchase indebtedness of the Ohio farm, which was afterwards sold and the money invested in Nebraska. That to pay off his claim to the younger children and their half-sister the deed in question was made, and to set aside and cancel that deed this suit is brought."

There was a trial to the court, with a finding and judgment for the plaintiffs. And the defendants bring the cause to this court by appeal, and assign the following errors:

"1st. The court erred in retaining said cause in court after the motion of plaintiff Demmitt Cole dismissing the same.

"2d. The court erred in permitting the suit to be maintained and judgment recovered in favor of the present plaintiffs without proof of their succession to the subject of the suit.

"3d. That the court erred in setting the deed wholly aside, but should have permitted it to stand to the extent of defendants' interest therein, or the money actually due the mother of defendants.

"4th. That the court erred in not declaring a trust in said deed for defendants in the right of their mother, to the extent of his estate and interest therein.

"5th. The court erred in not making the claimant, Mrs. Scothorne, a party defendant.

"6th. That the finding (which was general) is not sustained by the evidence; nor is said cause, from the evidence, brought within the limits of equitable relief.

"7th. That the court should not have set aside said deed, but should have made the plaintiffs and defendants distributees under the deed, if plaintiffs were entitled to any relief.

"8th. That said decree should have been for defendants."

I find it impossible, as the case is presented, to understand upon what the first of the above assignments of errors is based. The abstract contains a copy of a motion filed in the district court in vacation by the plaintiff Demmitt Cole to dismiss the action; but I am unable to find, either in the abstract or the record itself, that the attention of the court was called to it or any ruling had thereon. Under the provisions of the statutes, the plaintiff, Demmitt Cole,

estate, to six of his sons and daughters, reserving in himself a life-estate in and to the whole of said farm. The consideration named in said deed is set out therein in the following words: "In consideration of the sum of four thousand dollars, and in consideration of the money due the grantees from their mother's estate in hand paid." The deed also contains a covenant of warranty of seizin against incumbrances, and also to warrant and defend the title to said premises against the lawful claims of all persons whomsoever, "except the claim of Josephine Scothorne through her mother, my late wife, deceased, which they shall pay and discharge, the same being considered a lien on the lands herein described." There was no consideration paid or passed for the land or the conveyance thereof at the time of the execution and delivery of the deed. It may also be said that they are undisputed facts, that the grantees named in said deed are the issue of said Demmitt Cole and his third and last wife, that the plaintiffs are issue of him and his first and second wives respectively, and that the said Josephine Scothorne, named in the said deed, is the daughter of the last wife of said Demmitt Cole by a former husband. There was evidence which tended to prove and is uncontradicted, that said Josephine Scothorne resided in the state of Kansas, and is the only surviving child of her mother, other than the defendants Coles. That after the intermarriage of Demmitt Cole with his said last wife, and about the year 1844, she succeeded to an estate of $1,500, which Demmitt Cole used in paying for a farm which he purchased and occupied with his family in the state of Ohio, and which farm he sold for cash previous to his emigrating to Nebraska Territory some ten or eleven years later. Defendants claim, and it may probably be conceded, that the said $1,500, or a part of it, the estate of the late Mrs. Cole, is traceable and traced into the purchase by Demmitt Cole of the section of land in Cass county which forms the basis of this controversy. There was also evidence that

Mrs. Josephine Scothorne claimed from Demmitt Cole the payment of her share of the said $1,500, as one of the heirs of her deceased mother, and that by correspondence, through an attorney of Paola, Kansas, she placed the said claim in the hands of the defendant M. A. Hartigan, an attorney-at-law, for collection. That shortly after receiving said claim, Mr. Hartigan, through two of the sons, one a plaintiff and one a defendant in this action, procured an interview with Demmitt Cole at the office of the attorney in Plattsmouth. That in said interview Demmitt Cole admitted the facts, or a part of them, upon which the said claim was founded, at least to some extent recognized the claim of the said Mrs. Scothorne, and expressed a regret that the same had not been settled during the lifetime of his deceased wife. He, however, said that he would let the matter rest and fix upon some manner or course of settlement. In this conversation he probably referred to the claim of the defendants, to their distributive shares of the said money, as well as the claim of Mrs. Scothorne, although it does not appear that the said attorney represented any of them. It appears that D. C. afterwards visited the office of said attorney and had further conversation with him, in which he said that he had sent for his son Lorenzo, one of the defendants, who reside in another county. The amount of the claim of Mrs. S., together with those of the defendants, was then figured up by said attorney at the request of D. C., and it was understood between them that upon the arrival of Lorenzo, the whole matter would be fixed up and settled. It further appears that afterward, and during the absence of the said attorney from his office and the state, the said Demmitt Cole, together with the said Lorenzo, and probably all of the male defendants, visited the office of said attorney, presumably for the purpose of carrying out his expressed intention of settling the said business, but the attorney being absent nothing was done, and they went away.

Some time afterwards, and after the return of said attorney, he was requested by James Cole, one of the defendants, to come out to the farm where the said D. C. was residing, and informed that they had agreed upon a settlement. This was a few days prior to the 8th day of October, 1881, and on that day Mr. Hartigan went to the house of Joseph Cole on the said farm, and that then and there, in the apparent consummation of the purpose theretofore talked about between the said Demmett Cole and the said attorney, the deed hereinbefore referred to was drawn up by the attorney and signed and acknowledged; also delivered to the attorney for the parties interested.

As tending to show what occurred at the time and place of the execution and delivery of said deed, I copy from the abstract the testimony of James M. Cole, one of the defendants, given on his examination in chief on the part of the defendants.

Q. What relation, if any, did you bear to Demmitt Cole in his lifetime?

A. Son.

Q. By what marriage?

A. The last marriage.

Q. I will ask you if you were present and heard the conversation, and if so, state what was said between your father and Lorenzo Cole when he came down here in 1881?

. Beeson: You are one of the defendants and one of the parties named in the deed?

A. Yes.

Beeson: I object that this witness is incompetent under the statutes to testify; he has a direct legal interest in the result of the suit, and the adverse party is an administrator. ·

Overruled and exception.

A. I was present and heard the conversation.

Q. What was said that morning?

A. Father had summoned my brother Lorenzo from

Butler county to come down, and he told him in the evening that he wanted him to come over in the morning, that he wanted all us boys there. I went over, and as I went over, my brother Lorenzo was standing on the porch. Father was standing out in front. We all spoke and talked a little about the weather and how he felt. Well, my brother Lorenzo says to him that he was in a hurry to get back home, and what we are going to do about this affair let us be doing. We walked around to the east side of the porch and sat down. And father spoke up. "Now," he says, "boys, you know as well as I do, that I have not got the money to pay off this claim," and he said, "I will deed the land to satisfy that claim if that is satisfactory to you. I want to hear from you all." Lorenzo spoke first: "Father, you can have mine," says he. Says he, "If I do this it will put me on the mercy of the world," and the tears came in his eyes. Lors says, "You can have the use of mine as long as you live, and if it takes it to your support you can have, you will have it." He turned to me and asked me how that was, and I told him I was satisfied. He turned to everyone: "And now, says he, "we will go down."

Q. What did you do after that?

A. We got into the wagon and came down and went to Hartigan's office; found him not there. We asked Mr. Donohue where Mr. Hartigan was, and he said gone to Clarinda, Iowa. Then Lorenzo said he could not stay longer and he must go back. He pressed him about it and he said, "Lors, I would rather you would be here." Lors said, "You can settle it; whatever is satisfactory to you do. You agree to do whatever is satisfactory to him, and whatever you agree it is satisfactory." And with that understanding with us my brother Lorenzo went home. Well, we all went home, and it was about, I expect, two weeks I met Mr. Hartigan at the post-office door. That was the first I had seen of him since. Well, I went home, and as I went home father was standing out at the bars that cuts through the yard over to where I live, and he asked me if I had heard from Lorenzo since he went home, and I said "No." And then he said, "Have you seen Mr. Hartigan?" and I said I had, and he said he was willing to settle it at any time he wanted to come up. That was all that was said at that time, and it was over a week, and possibly two weeks, that I mentioned it to my father. And as he was old and could not stand it to ride in the wagon, he said, "Tell Hartigan," inasmuch as I went there, "you tell him to come down and fix the deed here." He said, "It worries me to ride in the wagon; am getting stiff in the joints and cannot get in and out." I said, "All right, I will tell him any time you want him to come." He said, "Now." I went and saw Hartigan again and told him to come. That was the first of the week, I think, and he did not come until the last of the week. When I went home father asked me if I saw him. Said he, "Said he would be down some time this week, Friday or Saturday; did not think he could be down before that, as he had some cases in the county court, I think." Nothing was said until Hartigan came, which was Saturday, I think; he came out to where I was mowing a little piece of grass. "Now," he said, "I want you to come along with me." I said, "All right," and unhitched the team and went with him. When we started to go over to father's house I don't know whether we met Alphonzo over there at his house or on the road, but anyway he turned and went with us. When we got to the house father was standing at the door, and he spoke to us and said, "Take chairs." We sat down and talked a few words. And the subject was raised then, but who raised it I don't remember, or just the words it was raised on. "Well," he says, "I would rather that Lorenzo was here." We told him, Phonz and I, "Didn't Lorenzo say whatever we would do would be satisfactory?" "Yes," says he, but he would rather he would be here. "Well," he says, "I want it fixed, and I want it done according to law." "Well," says Mr. Hartigan, "that is the way we propose to do it." Agreed to settle it; and then Mr. Hartigan asked about feeding the horse, and we went out to feed and tie the horse, and Joe Cole's wife came to the door and called to him and said that grandpa wanted him to put the horse in the barn and feed it and come in for dinner, and after dinner he would see him. We did that. I went home and took my team and fed it. When I came back Mr. Hartigan was sitting at the table and my father at his left hand. My father had the deed in his hand in this position, and they were talking over about Josephine Scothorne, and father says, "She may come in to-morrow and call for a division of the land, and I don't want to have it divided," and I told him no, she would not. I said, "If that is satisfactory to you here, you have got the deed, and I will take Josephine Scothorne off your shoulders, if that is agreeable to Hartigan." We had a few words in regard to it and he agreed to it. Before it was signed, he said, "Mr. Cole, you understand the facts." He said, "I do." He said, "I am going to read it very carefully, and want you to notice; if there is any change I want you to make it." He says, "There is no change." "Then," says he, "you are ready to sign it." He said, "I am." Hartigan got off the chair and father took the pen and signed it. I sat by and saw him write the deed. Then he pulled out his pocket-book and wanted to pay Hartigan, and just what the consideration was I don't know. Don't know just what was said, whether it was three dollars, two dollars, or two dollars and a half, or a dollar and a half. Father says, "I want you to fix that deed," and handed it to him. "I want you to take that and put it on record." "Very good," says Hartigan, "I will see to it." I went home and saw nothing more of it, knew nothing more of it, until I got the summons in January, I think.

Q. I will ask you if you stayed to dinner at Joseph's house?

A. I did not.

Q. I will ask you to state to the court whether this conversation was brought up that was had between your father and Lorenzo and you boys there before the making of that deed?

A. Yes, it was between four and six weeks.

Q. Before it was made, if you remember whether this conversation was brought up about the making of the deed, conversation between your father and Lorenzo, agreement as to the deed?

Court: At the time the deed was made, if there was any mention made of the prior conversation when Lorenzo was there?

A. Not that I remember of.

Q. I will ask you if the question of the claim of your mother against your father and what—

Witness: When the deed was made?

Q. Yes.

A. Yes.

Q. I will ask you to state at that time if conversation was not brought about in regard to settlement had between you boys and your father at the time Lorenzo was here?

A. Yes.

Q. I will ask you to state to the court what your father said, if anything, there in regard to what this money was applied to?

A. He said it was applied to the old home-place in Ohio, and he regretted that we had not settled it in mother's lifetime. That is my recollection.

Q. You were acquainted with your father's habits of mind and everything of that kind?

A. I have almost all the days of my life.

Q. How did that mind compare at the time Lorenzo was here and had that conversation, and also at the time the deed was made in comparison with his mental condition before that time?

A. Could not see any difference at all.

There was much additional evidence tending to prove that the apparent object and purpose of these negotiations on the part of the defendants—the Coles—was to assist the defendant, Hartigan, in his efforts to secure the claim of Mrs. Scothorne, yet that their real and principal object was to secure for themselves the payment of their claim for their share of the money, which, as was claimed, their father had received belonging to their mother, as hereinbefore stated. And that the sole object and purpose of the defendant, Hartigan, was to secure and collect the share and claim of his client, Mrs. Scothorne.

The consideration then for the execution of the said deed was the money received by Demmitt Cole in 1844 or '5, the property of the mother of the grantees. This money, calling the amount fifteen hundred dollars, the largest fixed by any one, with interest at the rate of seven per cent per annum, would then have amounted to somewhat less than five thousand five hundred dollars. The land at the date of the conveyance was worth, according to the testimony of Lewis Cole, and which I believe was uncontradicted, from sixteen thousand one hundred to nineteen thousand three hundred and twenty dollars. Mere inadequacy of consideration would not be sufficient to avoid the deed, yet it may and should be considered in connection with other facts.

A portion of the brief of appellants is devoted to the argument of, and the citation of authorities to, the proposition that the fifteen hundred dollars received as hereinbefore stated by Demmitt Cole, the property of his wife, was held in trust by him; that when he paid it out in part payment for a farm purchased by him in Ohio, he held the farm partly in trust for his wife; that when he sold that farm and emigrating to Nebraska Territory, accumulated

Cole v. Cole.

the farm in question, the said trust passed into it, and that the execution of the deed under consideration was the execution or discharge of the said trust. The only fault which I care to find with this proposition is, that the essential facts necessary to its establishment are not proved in the case. There are facts alleged in the answer which if proved would go far to establish such trust, but I fail to find any proof of them in the abstract.

I now come to the consideration of the question, whether at the time of the execution of the deed in question, Demmitt Cole, named as the grantor therein, was possessed of the mental capacity and will power necessary to constitute it *his deed*. The most part of the voluminous record is directed to this point. I here copy the substantial part of the testimony in chief of the two medical witnesses introduced on the part of the plaintiffs.

Deposition of Dr. H. Meade:

"Reside at Ogden, Utah. I practice medicine and surgery; been so engaged somewhere about nine years. I am a graduate of Dartmouth and Hahnneman, of Chicago. I practiced medicine in Plattsmounth. I would not be positive about the time that I came here, whether in the spring of 1880 or 1881, and left in January, 1884. I was acquainted with Demmitt Cole; treated him as a physician in October, 1881. Saw him on the evening of the 8th of October. He was lying on the lounge in, I believe, what they call the sitting room. Kind of a lounge bed, or something that he had seemed to favor as a bed. I don't remember exactly what his condition was. Know his bowels were irregular, and he felt in a general malarious condition. Made record of it—at that time when I questioned him I placed no reliance on his answers at all—I depended upon observations and what Mrs. Joseph Cole told me as to his condition. From his condition and appearance, I considered that it was unsafe; that I would not get at the truth if I did. I considered that he was suffering from what we call 'senile cerebral atrophy.' A cerebral atrophy is a disease of the brain itself. It causes diminished power, both physical and mental—loss of memory. I guess that is about the the condition of it. But I was not treating him for the cerebral atrophy at that time—that we do not treat for—I treated him for the minor complaint which arose in the meantime. I did not test his reasoning powers at all, only as far as the questions that I asked him, that he did not answer correctly always. I did not feel like relying upon them, and should not. I do not know his age. He was an old man. The question would indicate mental aberration which would be consistent to which we would expect in senile cerebral atrophy. A person so afflicted would not be competent to transact business, on account of the changed condition of the brain, that they are unable to reason properly. The disease may come gradually, that is the senile cerebral atrophy may arise at any time, and may arise suddenly. The word senile means old, and it is atrophy of old people, old age. I did not see him up, and I don't remember how long he had been in bed; but in the afternoon I might. Just about noon, just after dinner, I met Joe Cole, on my way to the fair 'ground, or from the fair ground, I am not positive which, and he asked me to go and see his father. I asked him if there was any great hurry. He said no. Then I told him I would be down that afternoon or evening. I think I was there between seven and eight. If I am not mistaken I left here about six—possibly I may have left here at five. I had seen him before. I would not be positive whether I had prescribed for him before or not—saw indications of this disease before that time, I cannot say just when. I was there to see Mrs. Cole several times, and while there I saw him, and came to the conclusion that he was suffering from this senile cerebral atrophy, from his actions, general appearance—felt quite certain, quite positive—saw him more than once before; could not say, but three or four times at least. It

had been within a year. The first time I saw him I paid
but little attention to it; as I saw him oftener I took more
notice of it. I saw him at the homestead where Joseph
Cole lived. He lived with Joseph. Joseph was his son.
I think I saw him on the 8th of October at Joseph's. If
I was there I saw him, and noticed the same thing. I
don't remember just what I noticed each time, except the
first time. I might have noticed it, but every time after
this I have seen him at Joseph Cole's place, I am positive.
The last time I noticed more than ever. It was some time
after October 8th, the last time was in the spring of 1883,
at Joseph's house. The last I remember of seeing him was
then; it was very marked then. It had progressed sufficiently. I cannot say to what extent, but that it impaired
it sufficiently that day to unfit him for the transaction of
business, at least I should not want him to transact any for
me in his condition.

"I should say that on the 8th of October he could not
understand the relation of things to each other—most de-
cidedly no. When there on that day he could not give intelligible answers to the questions that I asked him regarding his condition. I asked him but a few questions, and
those I merely put to pacify his mind, and every question
I asked him I turned to Mrs. Joseph Cole for her answer,
and the question as to his bowels I remember most distinctly
that she gave different answers to what he gave. That he
had given a wrong statement of his bowels as to the action.
It is one of those progressive diseases in which we expect
no lucid intervals. The brain is diseased. Part of the
brain has become absorbed, as it were, consequently there
can be no time at which they are entirely free from the
disease, and could be perfectly rational. Could not say
how long the disease was coming on him. It had been
some little time—oh, yes, in October, some months.

"I remember the date, because Miss Barker, that afterwards became my wife, came to town. I learned of it

after I had come to town from the fair. It was the last day of the fair. It was Saturday night, and she came from the country that afternoon. I learned of it, and called to see her on the way out. After my return I made arrangements with Captain Marshall, rented some rooms of him, and the Tuesday following we married—from this, I remember it."

Dr. Scheldnecht sworn and examined:

" Am a practicing physician; about 26 years in Nebraska and Indiana—in Nebraska ever since 1861; was acquainted with Demmitt Cole in his lifetime; was his physician at times; think I was in fall of 1881; prescribed for him occasionally; have not got it down; and when I was not calling there, and called in my office for medicine; cannot remember whether I was called down in the year 1881 or not; yes, sir, he was an old gentleman; quite feeble, sir; quite feeble during the fall and summer of 1881; don't think I could tell exactly; I saw him during that time; I very frequently would see him when I called to see some of the family at Mr. Joe Cole's; well, I don't think he was hardly capable of doing business; he seemed to have an affection of the brain—nervous atrophy, senile atrophy; I think from what I could learn it came on very gradually; quite a little while he was in that way in 1881, and from that on ever since I have known him; he very frequently would commence talking; then he would get through and forget what we were talking about, or quit and talk about something else; very frequently when I saw him at his place he did not seem to know me; I would tell him who I was and then he seemed to know, but not before; had known him ever since he has been in the state; when I first knew him he was a man of sound mind, I should judge; I presume so; he was one of our county commissioners."

I also copy the testimony of Joseph Cole, one of the defendants, called as a witness on the part of the plaintiffs. It was with him that Demmitt Cole resided at the time of the execution of the deed.

"Am a son of Demmitt Cole; age 29 years; am the youngest child in the family; mother has been dead nine years next April; father is dead a little over a year; father lived with me after mother's death; his health—he was not well on the eighth of October, 1881; he was in bed part of the time and up part of the time; he was taking medicines; went to Dr. Scheldnecht and got medicines for him, and took him; I sent Dr. Meade myself; met Mr. Hartigan when I was coming up; he was going down then to see father—to see what he could [do] for the folks in Missouri; did not know he was going for a deed; it was dark when I got home; met Dr. Meade as he was coming away; Hartigan had left; father's age was somewhere in seventy—was over seventy when he died; died year ago this month; he would get up and start away from home— said he wanted to go home, every day or two; he would do that—get lost around the place; he would start off in the house and go in directions, sometimes he would go across the fields, and at other times in the woods north of house; don't think he would be able to get home alone; have seen him when he did not know me, and I have seen him when he would not know other parties; he said he knew their faces, but did not know who they were; could not place their names; I don't [know] how often; several times; a great many times; don't know who this would happen to; some times one and some times the other; don't know hardly; every few days; now and then he would be bad whenever any one of them would come home; I don't know as I ever saw him fail to recognize my wife; he might have done; can't say how he was on the Saturday; I left him in the morning and fetched a load of corn up town and sent a doctor down there; he was not out of bed after I got home [that evening]; asked him how he felt; he was bad off, and gave him some medicine; he talked to me about making the deed; did not seem to understand it alto- gether; did not see how it would benefit him was about all he ever said to me. [About this suit] I don't hardly know; he said he did not want it, and wanted to stop it some way if he could. Yes, he said he did not want to sue any of his children; wanted to stop it if he could; I think Mrs. Cathey was there the day before; on the next Sunday Will and his folks came down; and Mrs. Chalfant and her husband; don't remember that Lew was there; part of the time during Sunday he was in bed, and part of the time he was not; I don't know that there was anything more peculiar that day than he had been before; I was right there with him all the time; I did not notice anything particular."

There was a vast amount of other evidence tending to prove that at the date of the deed Demmitt Cole was beyond seventy years of age, sickly and feeble in body and in mind, far away on the retreat into second childhood. I think it is sufficiently proven that his mind and memory were so far impaired as to render him incapable of giving that mental and intelligent assent to the execution of the deed under consideration, which the law regards as the essence of all contracts. I choose to place this opinion chiefly on the ground of the absence of a mind on the part of the grantor capable of an intelligent assent to the deed, rather than on the ground of fraud or undue influence on the part of the defendants. Indeed, of actual fraud or fraudulent intent on the part of the defendants, or any of them, there is no evidence. And yet the concerted action on the part of the defendants, apparently for the purpose, on the part of the defendants, other than Mr. Hartigan, and really on his part, to secure and collect the alleged claim of Mrs. Scothorne, but really on the part of the defendants, the Coles, to obtain the title to the entire farm for the doubtful and stale claim of their deceased mother; a claim, even if never so well founded and established, amounting to less than one-third of the value of the farm, would probably, upon equitable principles, and in the light of

Cole v. Cole.

many reported cases, be held to be constructively fraudulent, and that the deed thus obtained was obtained through undue influence.

Counsel for defendants takes the position, as I understand him, that by the execution of the said deed, as well as by the admissions made by the said Demmitt Cole, as to the receipt by him of funds belonging to his last wife, etc., he not only admitted the moral and legal obligation resting upon him to account for the same to her children, but waived all defenses, especially that of the lapse of time, which he might otherwise have made. And that the moral and legal obligation thus resting upon him to pay the defendants the amount so admitted to be then due, and having placed in their hands the only fund which he possessed for the purpose of such payment, a court of equity will not scrutinize or weigh the mental power which he possessed at the time of making such disposition, but will regard the act as justified by the motive, however weak the mental power which dictated it. This position is worthy of a respectful consideration, and has the support of many well-considered cases, or would have if the facts in evidence were in all respects as claimed. But neither were the admissions of Cole of the justice of the claim of the defendants sufficiently explicit, nor his mental condition at the time of making them such as to justify the application of the equitable principle contended for. While the evidence is not as satisfactory as could be wished as to the point of time at which the mental faculties of Cole became totally impaired, yet the evidence tends to locate it at a time anterior to that of his conversations with and admissions to Mr. Hartigan as testified to by him. And so the district court was justified in holding him incapable of binding himself by such admissions, or of laying the legal foundation for the deed by such admissions, on the same principles upon which it held him incapable of binding himself or his property by the execution of the deed. With both of which holdings, after mature consideration, I find myself compelled to agree.

The judgment of the district court is therefore affirmed.

JUDGMENT AFFIRMED.

THE other judges concur.

21	113
49	63
53	344

HUBERT M. G. BROWN, PLAINTIFF IN ERROR, V. A. HERR ET AL., DEFENDANTS IN ERROR.

1. **Conspiracy to perpetrate fraud:** DECLARATION ADMISSIBLE IN EVIDENCE. In an action where the cause of action, or ground of defense, is based upon a conspiracy by two or more persons to perpetuate a fraud upon the party asserting such cause of action or ground of defense, the acts and declarations of one of such company of conspirators in regard to the common design as affecting his fellows—a foundation having been laid by proof sufficient in the opinion of the court to establish *prima facie* the fact of conspiracy between the parties, or proper to be laid before the jury, as tending to establish such fact—in pursuance of the original concerted plan, and with reference to the common object, may be given in evidence.

2. The evidence examined and *held* to sustain the verdict.

3. The instructions prayed and refused, and those given by the court on its own motion, as copied at length in the opinion, *Held*, To have been properly refused and given.

ERROR to the district court for Fillmore county, Tried below before MORRIS, J.

W. V. Fifield and *J. W. Eller*, for plaintiff in error.

J. D. Hamilton and *Ryan Brothers*, for defendants in error.

COBB, J.

This action was brought by the plaintiff Brown, against the defendants Amos Herr and eleven others, on a prom-

8

issory note payable to H. M. G. Brown, one year after
date, for the sum of eight hundred and six dollars, with
interest at ten per cent per annum from date. The petition, after setting out the execution and delivery of the
note, with a copy thereof, contains the allegation, "that no
part of the said note has been paid, and there is due thereon
from the defendants to the plaintiff, $806, with interest
thereon at the rate of 10 per cent per annum from February 9, 1882, for which plaintiff demands judgment.

For answer defendants filed a general denial.

On the 21st day of May, 1884, the cause came to a hearing on the motion of the defendants to require the plaintiff
to give security for costs, whereupon it was ordered that
the plaintiff give security for costs, to be approved by
the clerk of the district court within thirty days, and in
case of his failure so to do, the cause to stand dismissed.

On the 28th day of October, 1884, a stipulation was
entered for the setting aside of the order of dismissal, re-
instating the cause, and allowing the defendants time in
which to file an amended answer, and thereupon defendants
filed the following amended answer:

"1. Deny each allegation of plaintiff's petition not
hereinafter specifically admitted.

"2. That the note was obtained, so far as these defendants are concerned, by the fraud and connivance of the
plaintiff and defendant A. Herr.

"That there was no consideration for said note.

"That A. Herr was the principal maker of said note
and these defendants accommodation sureties.

"That said note was drawn up by plaintiff and defendant Herr, or by their procurement, and was signed by
Herr to evidence an indebtedness which in fact had no real
existence, but was falsely pretended by said plaintiff and
defendant Herr to have an existence, and in furtherance of
the scheme between plaintiff and said Herr to collect the
same of other parties who might be induced by them to
sign the same and divide the proceeds.

"The said note so prepared and signed by Herr as aforesaid was presented to each of these defendants, and each was solicited by defendant Herr and plaintiff to sign the same as sureties.

"That by causing some of these defendants to become helplessly intoxicated, and by falsely pretending that the said Herr would pay said note in a very short time, which they said he would be able to do, and that the note was for a *bona fide* indebtedness, these defendants were induced as sureties to sign said note.

"That said defendant Herr was then insolvent and so known to be to plaintiff; that plaintiff knowing that these defendants believed Herr to be solvent, encouraged these defendants to sign said note, and solicited them to so sign as sureties.

3.   That at the date of the note sued on, the plaintiff and Herr were engaged in the saloon business in Geneva—the said business being run in the name of A. Herr, the said Herr being in fact the proprietor.

"That plaintiff was bar tender in said saloon at the date of said note, and so remained until about two months after said date.

"When the said Herr, being unable to obtain a license in his own name, took out a license to run the saloon business as aforesaid, in the name of the plaintiff, and thereafter the said business was run in that manner, until about two months and a half after the note became due.   The said plaintiff during this latter period being nominally the proprietor, but in reality but a bar tender under the same salary and terms as at the date of the note.

"At the date of the note it was represented to these defendants by both Herr and plaintiff that the note was to be taken only to be held for a very short time, in which sufficient money should come into the hands of plaintiff in the course of his employment to pay the amount of said note in full, and the said plaintiff and said Herr then and there, to induce these defendants to sign said note, agreed that the proceeds and receipts in the saloon business aforesaid should be wholly applied to extinguishing said note in full.

"These defendants relying on said representations that payment would be so made and decreased.

" By the fraudulent practices aforesaid of said Herr, and the said plaintiff (having no interest in the note sued on or its proceeds, and simply as accommodation sureties, signed said note, relying on the protection by plaintiff of the rights of these defendants).

"That the income of the said saloon business for the whole time the saloon was running aforesaid, that is, from February 9, 1882, till fourteen and one-half months thereafter, was upwards of $30 net per day, and the application of the same, as agreed when these defendants signed the same as sureties as aforesaid, would have fully paid said note and discharged each of these defendants from any liability on said note."

On the 19th day of May, 1885, plaintiff filed a general denial for reply to the amended answer. There was a trial to a jury, with a verdict and judgment for the plaintiff against the defendant Amos Herr, and for the other defendants against the plaintiff. The cause is brought to this court on error by the plaintiff, who assigns the following errors :

"The plaintiff in error says there is error on the face of the record in this :

"1st. In admitting the testimony of E. Sheppard, as to the solvency of A. Herr at the time the note was signed.

"2d. In admitting the testimony of Josiah Sheppard relating the conversation between himself and defendants Shultz and Herr.

"3d. In admitting the testimony of Josiah Sheppard, stating the conversation with plaintiff after the note became due, relating to the reason why he didn't retain the money out of the proceeds of the saloon.

"4th.   In admitting the testimony of defendant Arnold relating to the income or net proceeds of the saloon.

"5th.   In admitting the testimony of defendant Wintersteen, relating his conversation with Herr and not in the presence of plaintiff.

"6th.   In overruling plaintiff's motion to strike out the testimony of defendant McDougal.

"7th.   In admitting the testimony of Dworak relating to the security for costs.

"8th.   Admitting the bond for costs in evidence.

"9th.   In admitting the testimony of Burt as to signing the bond for security for costs.

"10th.   In the charge of the court, in giving paragraphs numbered *First, Second, Fourth, Fifth, Sixth, Seventh, Eighth, Ninth,* and in giving the charge as a whole.

"11th.   In refusing to give the instructions asked for by plaintiff, number *First, Second, Third, Fourth, Fifth, Sixth, Seventh, Eighth, Ninth, Tenth.*

"12th.   In overruling the plaintiff's motion for a new trial."

Upon the trial there was evidence tending to prove, and it is nowhere denied, that at the time of the execution of the note sued on the plaintiff and the defendant Herr were engaged in keeping a liquor saloon at Geneva; that they came to that place together and had been living and operating together in same business before coming there.   At first the saloon at Geneva was "run" in Herr's name and Brown was ostensibly engaged by him as barkeeper.   But upon the expiration of Herr's license he was unable to procure another license in his own name, and license was procured in Brown's name.   Yet the evidence tends to prove that their relations to the business and to each other remained unchanged in point of fact, although the license being in Brown's name he was necessarily the ostensible proprietor.   It was while this state of things existed that some, at least, of the defendants were induced to sign the note as security for Herr. I quote the evidence in chief of E. Sheppard, one of the defendants:

"Am one of the signers of the note; acquainted with Mr. Herr and Mr. Brown.

Q. You may state the circumstances under which you signed this note.

A. I saw Mr. Herr on the sidewalk; he wanted me to come in and said he wanted to talk with me; previous to this time I had signed a note with Mr. Herr for $600; he wanted I should sign a note with him; this conversation was in the saloon; Brown was in the same room and in hearing distance; (Mr. Herr) said he wanted I should sign a note with him, and he said he wanted to give the note to Mr. Brown, and he had a note drawn up; I told him I was good for nothing, and he said that others said they would sign the note if I would; I signed it; he told me what the proceeds of the bar was and said that Mr. Brown was handling the bar and proceeds of the saloon, and he said the income of the bar should pay the note; he said the income of the bar was from $30 to $50, except on extra days they took in $100 per day; Herr was principal on the note; there were other names on the note besides Herr when I signed it; I think Wintersteen, Josiah Shepard, Eli Shultz, and others.

Q. State whether or not Mr. Herr was solvent at that time or not.

Plaintiff objects. Grounds of objection immaterial, irrelevant, and incompetent. Court overruled objection.

A. He said he was all right for it himself; that was in the presence of Mr. Brown; the saloon was run in Brown's name at the time I signed the note; Brown told me he had to run it in his name because Herr could not get a license; Mr. Herr furnished the money; did not have any conversation with Mr. Brown as to why it was not paid out of the proceeds of the saloon."

There was evidence tending to prove that Herr, in order

to induce the defendants, or some of them, to sign the note, represented that the money which would be taken in over the bar of the saloon, would be applied by Brown to the payment of the note. This in some instances was said by Herr in Brown's presence in the course of conversations in which Brown took part. To some he said that it was their intention to start another saloon in Fairmont, which he would attend to, thus leaving Brown in the sole charge of the saloon at Geneva, and that Brown would apply the proceeds of that business to the payment of the note, and that he "and Brown would make a good thing of it." These conversations in some instances were had with certain of the defendants while they were being bountifully plied with liquor in the saloon by both Herr and Brown. I quote the evidence in chief of Eli Schultz, one of the defendants:

"I think I signed it (the note) some time in February, 1882; that is what I understood afterwards.

"Came up to Geneva with Josiah Sheppard; Sheppard came to court house; I went into Herr's saloon; went to the stove; Herr says, 'Have something to drink,' and I did, and Brown says, 'Take another drink.'

"Herr came to the stove and says, 'Schultz, I have a note here and I want a good signer on it; I have some and I want some more; I want some money at the bank; Brown is going to run this saloon here and I will run another at Fairmont.' He says, 'I want to get you and Sheppard to sign it.'

"I says, I don't want to sign any note. He says, 'I have got Wintersteen and Johnson on the note; Brown and me will make a good thing out of it.'

"Brown spoke up and says, 'I am going to stay in this saloon and Herr will run the one in Fairmont,' and I told him I wouldn't sign the note unless Sheppard would sign it, and Brown says, 'You see if Sheppard will sign it.' I asked him and he said 'No;' we were standing by the window;

and when Herr came where I was Brown was behind the counter.

"Herr called us up to drink and we all drank together; Sheppard told him he wouldn't have anything to do with that; I stayed in the saloon about all day; Brown treated and Herr treated.

"Sheppard came in the saloon after lodge; I was playing pool with Brown; I don't know whether I treated or who treated, but they all kept treating; after awhile this note business was brought up again.

"And there were Brown and Herr and Josiah Sheppard and Carrier and I went back to playing pool, and that was the last I knew about it until Carrier awakened Sheppard and I up in the stable.

"Don't know just where the note was signed.

"In the afternoon Brown told me to sign the note; it was perfectly good, as they would take the money as it came in and pay it off; he said they were clearing any way $25 a day right along and sometimes $30 to $50; that was in the presence of Mr. Herr.

"Don't know what reply Herr made; he told me time and again that he was going to run both saloons; he said they would pay it right back as fast as they could get it; that they would pay it at the bank to Fifield & Fisher.

"Was not asked to sign a note to Mr. Brown.

"The saloon was run by Herr & Brown about fifteen months after the note was given.

Q. At the time you signed that note state whether or not you had any knowledge of the solvency or insolvency of Mr. Herr.

A. I didn't know anything about it. Mr. Brown told me the reason he didn't take the money (out of the proceeds) was because Amos always kicked up a fuss and raised hell with him when he said anything about it, and he kept saying that he would pay him just as soon as he got the money."

I have reluctantly copied the whole of this witness's evidence in chief, as it not only shows some of the nefarious means used to induce the defendants to sign the note, but clearly shows the active participation of Brown, the plaintiff, therein.

The "Sheppard" spoken of by the last witness, is not E. Sheppard, whose testimony I first quoted, but another man of that name, who is also a defendant.

George P. Wintersteen, defendant, testified as follows:

"I signed the note. Recollect the circumstances.

Q. State the circumstances and statements to induce it.

A. Mr. Herr came into the clerk's office; I was county clerk at the time."

(The plaintiff objects to the testimony for the reason that it is irrelevant and incompetent to state any conversation with defendant Herr, not in the presence of plaintiff. Objections overruled. Plaintiff excepts.)

"He says, 'Wintersteen, I am in close quarters. I am owing Mr. Brown some money and I want to raise a little more; Brown wants his money and I can get it with this note.' He says, 'I am doing a good business and I can raise it in a short time, if you will sign this note Brown would accept it.' He said if I did sign it I wouldn't be compelled, in all probabilty, to meet it. He insisted and said there was no question but what he could meet it, and that Brown wanted his money.

"I told him I would like to talk to Mr. Brown, and he said 'Brown is going to run this business here, and I am going to run the business in Fairmont.

"I met Brown. We had a talk about it to the effect that while I was not worth anything, that if I signed that note it would be simply accommodation, and that he must see that the note was paid by Amos before it was due. He said he didn't see any reason why it should not be paid before it was due, that he should stay right with him. He said that the business was certainly paying, and that if he stayed there he would make it his business to look after it till it was paid ; that he wanted his money that would come out of that.

. " It was my idea to charge Mr. Brown's mind to see that Herr did pay it. I knew of no demands being made up to that time that he didn't meet, but the business was very uncertain, and I thought if Mr. Brown looked after it, as he might do, it would be paid within a reasonable time.

Q. What was said about handling the proceeds of the sales from the saloons?

A. He said that he should be there and handling the proceeds of this business here, and that Herr would be at Fairmont.

Q. What did he say?

A. He said that it would be his aim to apply the proceeds to the payment of that note as fast as possible."

Several other of the defendants testified on the trial, but their evidence is chiefly corroborative of the foregoing, and lack of time and space forbid my copying further, except that of the clerk of district court, and the person going security for costs in reference thereto.

V. Dworak testified as follows :

" I am clerk of this court.

Q. Do you recollect the filing and approving the securities for costs in your office in this case?

A. Yes, sir.

Q. By whom was it signed?

(The plaintiff objects to the question for the reason that it is immaterial, irrelevant, and incompetent, and not the best evidence. Objection overruled. Plaintiff excepts.)

A. It was signed by Mr. Burt. Mr. Herr brought him there.

Q. Had he any objections to signing in your presence?

(Plaintiff objects. Ground that it is immaterial, irrelevant, and incompetent, and not in the presence of plaintiff. Objections overruled. Plaintiff excepts.)

A. Mr. Herr and Mr. Burt met me on the street and wanted me to come in the office. Mr. Herr told me that Mr. Burt was going to sign as security for costs, and Burt asked me how much it would be, and I told him it might be fifteen or twenty dollars, and he signed it and I approved the bond. This is the bond."

The defendants offer in evidence the bond which is marked exhibit "B." To the introduction of which bond the plaintiff objects for the reason that it is irrelevant, immaterial, and incompetent. Objections overruled by court, Plaintiff excepts.

J. W. Burt testified:

"I signed the security for costs.

Q. At whose request?

(Plaintiff objects. Immaterial, irrelevant and incompetent. Objections overruled. Plaintiff excepts.)

Mr. Brown first asked me if I would sign it, that was at Alexandria. I told him I would see when I got to Geneva. Next Amos Herr asked me.

Q. What inducement did he offer you if you would sign?

(Plaintiff objects. Irrelevant, immaterial, and incompetent, and no foundation laid. Plaintiff excepts.)

A. He offered me ten dollars if I would sign the bond for security for costs in this case.

Q. Upon that you signed it?

A. I don't know that I did wholly upon that.

Q. Did he pay you anything?

A. He paid me five dollars. I had been asked by Brown at Alexandria to sign it. Herr was up here a day or two after that. Brown was working for Herr at Alexandria.

Q. What other consideration was there that made you sign the bond?

A. Dworak said he didn't think the amount would be over fifteen or twenty dollars, and that also that the time had expired. I didn't believe it would be good, because the time had run out. I knew it was not good so far as I was concerned.

Q. You thought that you would get five or ten dollars for sticking your name where it wouldn't do any good?

A. Yes, sir; and Mr. Herr was owing me money that was repaying me.

Q. You considered that if he paid you anything it was coming in on your debt?

A. I didn't apply it that way."

The first assignment of error is based upon the overruling by the court by the objection of plaintiff to a question put by defendant to the witness, E. Sheppard, as follows:

"Q. State whether or not Mr. Herr was solvent at the time?" To which, after objection overruled, "He said he was all right for it himself, that was in the presence of Mr. Brown." I confess that I do not see the object of the question, but as the answer was entirely unprejudicial to the plaintiff, and amounted simply to a conversation between Herr and one of the other defendants in presence of the plaintiff, and was doubtless but a part of the measures taken by Herr and the plaintiff for the purpose of obtaining signatures to the note, I do not think that error will lie to this point.

Assignments 2, 3, 4, 5, and 6, relate to the evidence of the several parties who were sworn as witnesses on the part of the defense, and the principal objection is, that in some instances they were allowed over the plaintiff's objection to testify to the statements of Herr not made in the presence of Brown, as to the manner in which, and the means out of which, the said note was to be paid, etc. The answering defendants claim, in and by their answer, that the plaintiff and Herr conspired together to defraud the said defendants, by means of procuring them, by false representations and pretenses, to sign the said note with the said Herr, etc. There was some evidence before the jury tending to prove this charge of the answer. That being the case it was competent to prove what was done or said by either of the alleged conspirators in furtherance of the common design, though not in the presence of the other. I quote from Greenleaf on Evidence a part of the section cited by counsel for defendants :

"Section 111. The same principles apply to the acts and declarations of one of a company of *conspirators* in regard to the common design as affecting his fellows. Here a foundation must be laid by proof sufficient in the opinion of the judge to establish *prima facie* the fact of conspiracy between the parties or proper to be laid before the jury as tending to establish such fact. The connection of the individuals in the unlawful enterprise being thus shown, every act and declaration of each member of the confederacy, in pursuance of the original concerted plan, and with reference to the common object, is, in contemplation of law, the act and declaration of them all ; and is therefore original evidence against each of them."

These principles, though most often applied to criminal cases, technically speaking, are equally applicable to cases of conspiracy to perpetuate a fraud, and I deem them applicable to the case at bar; and that "the opinion of the judge" that the proof was sufficient to establish *prima facie* the fact of conspiracy was not erroneous.

The 7, 8, and 9 assignments refer to the admission of evidence to prove that the plaintiff having been required by the court to give security for costs in the action, he being a non-resident of the county, and an order *nisi* dismissing the cause for the want of such security, the defendant Herr aided the said plaintiff to procure such security, even to the extent of hiring a party to become such security and paying him therefor. In an ordinary case and under the usual issue in a civil action, this or similar evidence would probably be inadmissible; but under the issue in this case, and following the other evidence tending to prove a conspiracy and common design between Brown and Herr, to obtain the names of these defendants, and collect the money which it called for off of them, I think that this evidence was properly permitted to go to the jury.

The remaining assignments are of alleged errors for the giving of instructions by the court on its own motion and the refusal of the court to give those prayed for by the plaintiff. I copy the instructions at large.

The plaintiff asked the court to instruct the jury as follows:

"1st. The jury is instructed that the evidence is not sufficient on the part of said defendants to support a verdict in their favor, and you will find for the plaintiff and assess his damages at the face of the note in suit and interest thereon to the first day of the present term of the court, according to the tenor thereof.

"2d. The evidence is not sufficient to establish the claims of defendants, that the note was given without consideration.

"3d. The evidence is not sufficient to support the claim of defendants, that plaintiff was responsible for the drunkenness of any of the defendants when they signed the note.

"4th. The evidence is not sufficient to support the claim of defendants, that plaintiff and defendant Herr concocted or arranged any scheme to obtain to signatures to this note, and then divide the proceeds of the note.

"5th. Although there is evidence that Herr has aided plaintiff to procure security for costs in this case, yet that fact is not material, standing alone. Herr had a perfect right to befriend the plaintiff in that respect.

"6th. The defendant Shultz, who claims he was drunk when he signed the note, cannot take any advantage of that fact, even if you find such to be the fact, for the reason that afterwards when he knew he had signed the note, at a time when Herr told him he had got about all to sign it, he did not ask Herr to take his name off or direct Herr not to deliver it to Brown; he had then by his conduct when sober ratified his act of signing the note.

"7th. Any conversation had by any of the parties with defendant Herr, when not in the presence and hearing of the plaintiff, is not binding upon the plaintiff and should not be considered by the jury in making up their verdict.

"8th. The fact that defendants J. Sheppard and Shultz, after this note had become due, went so far as to sign a new note in renewal of this note, is a circumstance which the jury should properly take into consideration in making up their verdict.

"9th. Unless you are satisfied by a fair preponderance in favor of the defendants, that the plaintiff fraudulently entered into a scheme to defraud the defendants, and that Herr was to have a part of the money, and that plaintiff assisted to get the note in suit for that purpose and not for the purpose of securing his debt, then you shall find for the plaintiff.

"10th. The fact that plaintiff took this note in renewal of a note which was secured by a chattel mortgage, and that plaintiff released his mortgage after this note was given, is of no advantage to these defendants. It was proper for plaintiff to release his mortgage upon the delivery of the note sued upon."

Each of which the court refused to give, to which rulings plaintiff excepted.

The court then charged the jury as follows:

"Gentlemen of the Jury—This action is brought by the plaintiff upon a promissory note signed by Herr and the other defendants herein, signed, made, executed and delivered to the plaintiff, and that the same remains unpaid, and that there is due to him upon that the face of the note and the interest. To this petition of the plaintiff the defendants first admit the making of the note, hence it would follow that the plaintiff would be entitled to recover unless the allegation of the defendants' answer, sustained by the proof, would be sufficient to overcome the claim of the plaintiff.   For defense the defendants allege:

"*First.* That they are sureties only upon this note; that they signed the same without consideration, and that the signatures were obtained by the plaintiff and Herr with the common joint intention of swindling the sureties, by collecting from them the amount of the note.

"*Second.* The answer sets forth that the sureties signed the note upon the representations of Herr and the plaintiff that the plaintiff would have charge of the saloon in Geneva, and would receive the profits and moneys arising from the saloon here, and apply the profits upon the payment of this note as received by him.

"*Third.* To this, for reply, the plaintiff enters a general denial.

"*Fourth.* Either of these defenses, if established by the testimony, would operate as a discharge of the sureties to this note.

"*Fifth.* Fraud is never presumed, but must be proved by the party asserting it by a fair preponderance of the proof, and it may be established as any other fact, by circumstances and circumstantial evidence.   To establish the defense in this case, it is incumbent upon the defendants to establish their allegations by a fair preponderance of the proof.   If they have failed to do this it will be your duty to find for the plaintiff.

"*Sixth.* The liability of surety is only secondary to that of principal, and if you find from evidence that the defendant Herr is principal, and that the other defendants are sureties only, and that no real debt is due from Herr to the plaintiff, and that the note sued upon was obtained for the purpose of defrauding the sureties of Herr, and not for a *bona fide* debt, the verdict should be for the defendants. If you shall find from the proof in this case that there was a common purpose existing between Herr and the plaintiff to obtain the signatures of these defendants to this note, with the intention of defrauding all or any one of them, and that they did so obtain their signatures by furtherance of that common purpose, or by means of misrepresentations in furtherance of the common purpose, then you shall find for the defendants, except the defendant Herr.

"*Seventh.* If you find from the evidence that the plaintiff obtained these signatures or assisted the defendant Herr to obtain the signatures of these alleged sureties, or any of them, upon the representation that he would receive the money and apply the proceeds of the money so received in the business of running this saloon to the payment of this note, and you shall further find from the testimony that he did manage the business and receive the money, and that they were sufficient in amount to have cancelled or have paid this note, then the court charges you that the plaintiff's turning the money over to Herr was a constructive fraud as against the sureties.

"*Eighth.* You are judges of the credibility of each and every witness, and you shall give to the testimony of each and every witness such weight as in consideration of all the facts and circumstances you shall deem the same entitled to, and you have the right to take into consideration the bearing of the witness upon the stand, their relations or their apparent relations, and their relations to each other and their interest in this action; you have also the right to take into consideration, as you shall find from the evidence, the means used to obtain the signatures of the alleged sureties and the representations made to them, and all the facts that have been proven before you, and also the conduct, action, and doings of the defendants themselves.

"*Ninth.* You should be governed, in coming to a conclusion in this case, by the evidence, and that alone, given before you, and not allow yourselves to be governed by remarks or statements of counsel not warranted by the evidence, but by the evidence alone. If you find for the plaintiff upon the evidence, you should find the amount of the

9

note and interest thereon as expressed therein from its date to the day of the first day of this term of the court. If you find for the defendants you will simply find for the defendants, except the defendant Herr."

The first seven of the instructions prayed by the plaintiff were properly [refused, for the reason that to give them would take from the jury the consideration of the evidence of fact, which it is their peculiar province to weigh and decide.

The eighth and ninth instructions prayed for are not specially objectionable, except that the ninth goes too far. It would tell the jury that it was necessary to the defense that they should believe from the evidence that it was a part of the scheme and common design of Brown and Herr, that Herr was to have a part of the money called for by said note, and that Brown assisted to get said note for the purpose of Herr's getting a part of said money. The fraudulent conspiracy is equally available to the defendants as a defense, although it might appear that it was the design of the conspiracy that either Brown or Herr should enjoy the whole of the proceeds of the note; and also with the exception that neither the eighth or tenth instruction prayed is within the pleadings in the case.

Upon a careful consideration of the rather lengthy charge as given, I think that it quite fairly and fully presented the case to the jury, and that as well in detail as in whole it expresses the law of the case.

The judgment of the district court is affirmed.

JUDGMENT AFFIRMED.

THE other judges concur.

EVERETT J. BALLOU ET AL., APPELLEES, V. JOHN
BLACK ET AL., APPELLANTS.

1. **Mechanics' Lien**: PROCEEDINGS TO PERFECT LIEN. Under
sec. 2 of mechanics' lien law of 1881, any person who shall furnish any material to a contractor for the construction of any
building shall be entitled to a lien thereon for the amount due
him from such contractor for the same, upon filing a sworn
statement of such amount with the proper county clerk within
sixty days from the time of furnishing such material.

2. ———: ———: MATERIAL MAN. All payments within the
sixty days by the owner of the building to the original contractor will be at his own risk; and as against one furnishing
material for the construction of the building, the fact that the
original contractor is indebted to the owner will not prevent the
material man from enforcing his lien for such material against
such building and the lot on which it stands.

3, ———: CONTRACT as construed in *Ballou v. Black*, 17 Neb., 389,
adhered to.

APPEAL from the district court of Cass county. Heard
below before MITCHELL, J.

Allen Beeson and *R. B. Windham*, for appellants.

Thurston & Hall and *A. C. Wakeley*, for appellees.

MAXWELL, CH. J.

On the 17th day of March, 1882, the plaintiffs filed petition in court below stating their cause of action to be—
"That during the several times mentioned in the bill of
items hereto attached, one William Winscit was engaged in
the business of a contractor and builder. That on the 2d
day of September, 1881, said Winscit entered into a joint
agreement with one John Black, and the First Methodist
Episcopal Church, of Plattsmouth, who are the owners of
the building and lots upon which the building was erected,
hereinafter described, whereby in consideration of twelve
thousand one hundred dollars, to be paid said Winscit by

said Black and said church, he, the said Winscit, agreed to
erect for said Black and said church certain buildings, to-
wit: A block of buildings upon the following-described
property, to-wit: Lots one (1) and two (2) in block thirty-
six (36), in said city of Plattsmouth, county and state aforesaid, the legal title to a portion of which lots, viz: the
south ninety-two (92) feet of said lots one (1) and two (2),
in said block thirty-six (36), in the name of the trustees of
said Methodist Episcopal Church, the said John Black
owning the remaining portion of said lots, viz: the north
48 feet of said lots. That for the purpose of carrying out
this agreement, and at the request of the said above owners,
the said Winscit purchased of one Otis H. Ballou, a lumber dealer in the city of Omaha, certain building materials
at certain times and prices, to-wit: The several items of
lumber set forth in the itemized accounts hereto attached at
the dates therein mentioned, for which he agreed to pay the
several amounts of money charged opposite the several
items, amounting in the aggregate to fourteen hundred and
eighty-four and $\frac{11}{100}$ dollars, and of the value of fourteen
hundred and eighty-four and $\frac{11}{100}$ dollars.

"That said Otis H. Ballou furnished to said Winscit said
material at the dates therein mentioned, to be used in the
construction of said buildings, and the same were so used
in the construction thereof.

"That the bill of items hereto attached is a true and correct bill of the material furnished to said Winscit; that the
several items of lumber therein mentioned were worth the
amounts severally charged on them, and that no part of
said bill has ever been paid. That the said Winscit ab-
sconded from the city of Omaha, and that according to the
best of plaintiff's knowledge he is financially worthless and
insolvent. That on or about the 25th day of November,
1881, the said Otis H. Ballou did, according to the statute
for such cases made and provided, and before sixty days
had elapsed from the furnishing of said material to said

Winscit, prepare a sworn statement of the items of material furnished said Winscit for said buildings, with the amount due him from said Winscit, together with a description of the land upon which the same were used, which said statement, verified by the affidavit of Otis H. Ballou thereto attached, was filed in the office of the county clerk of Cass county, in which said materials were furnished, and was recorded in a separate book provided by the clerk for that purpose, to-wit: Book A of Mechanics' Liens Record, and he secured a lien on the lots and buildings herein described for the full amount of his said claim, to-wit: The sum of fourteen hundred and eighty-four and $\frac{11}{100}$ dollars ($1,484.11), with interest thereon at the rate of seven per cent per annum from the 28th day of September, 1881.

"That on or about the 10th day of December, 1881, the said Otis H. Ballou did, for value received, assign, set over, and transfer his said claim and lien arising therefrom to one Moses Ballou. That on or about the 16th day of February, A. D. 1882, the said Moses Ballou did depart this life, being at his death a resident of Douglas county. That the said Moses Ballou left a last will and testament. That said last will and testament was duly proved and allowed; that said plaintiffs were severally named therein as executors thereof; that the county court of Douglas county issued letters testamentary thereon to the persons named executors therein, and that said executors accepted the trust and gave the bond required by law; that said defendants, although requested, have hitherto refused and do now refuse to pay the amount of said bill or any part thereof. The plaintiffs pray this court that an account be taken of the amount due and owing them from said defendants, at some early period to be fixed by this court, and that if said defendants do not pay the said plaintiffs the amount so ascertained to be due them, then that the said premises be sold or leased by order of the court as justice and equity may require, and so much of the proceeds thereof as may be necessary be applied to the liquidation of said plaintiff's claim.   That plaintiffs have judgment against the said defendants for the sum of fourteen hundred and eighty-four and $\frac{11}{100}$ dollars ($1,484.11), with interest thereon at the rate of seven per cent per annum from the 28th day of September, A.D. 1881, and for their costs.   That plaintiffs have such other and further relief in the premises as they may be entitled to."

Attached to said petition as an exhibit was the account for lumber, as follows:

"William Winscit, Plattsmouth.   Bought of O. H. Ballou (for John Black and M. L. White for First Methodist Episcopal Church, of Plattsmouth) lumber dealer.   Office North Fifteenth street, near O. & St. Paul Depot:

Sept.	12th	91	2-14	24	5914					
		17	2-14	22	869					
		70	2-12	24	3360					
		57	2-12	22	2508	12649	354	17		
		2216 Lineal	2-2			30	66	48	420	65
	14th	9	2-14	22	462					
		1	2-14	24	56					
		25	2-12	22	1100					
		15	2-12	24	720					
		15	2-8	22	440	28				
		18	2-8	24	576	3354	93	91	93	91
	17th	1	2-14	24	56					
		9	2-14	22	459					
		15	2-12	24	120					
		25	2-12	22	1100					
		218	2-8	24	6976	28				
		15	2-8	22	435	9746			272	88
	20th	49	2-14	24	2744					
		22	2-14	24	1130					
		80	2-12	24	3840					
		16	2-12	22	704					
		2	2-8	24	64	8482	237	50		
		2 m. ft. wa 2 finish				50	100		337	50
	28th	744	1-8 2d clear			50	37	20		
		110	2-8	24	3520	28	98	56		
		34	2-12	22	1496	28	41	89		
		33	2-14	22	1684	28	47	15		
		44	2-14	20	2068	25	50	70		
		4	2-14	24	128	28	3	58		
		24	2-12	24	1152	28	32	25		
		3	2-12	22	132	28	3	69		
		1472 ft. 2-2				30	44	16	359	17
									1484	11

On the 21st day of November the defendant Church filed answer as follows:

"Admits that the said William Winscit entered into a written agreement with the said John Black and the First M. E. Church, of Plattsmouth, defendant, whereby in consideration of the sum of $12,100 to be paid. to the said Winscit by the said defendants, he, the said Winscit, was to erect for the said defendants certain buildings known as the Union Block, and situated in the city of Plattsmouth,. Cass county.

"Defendant further alleges that under the said agreement there was no joint liability created between the defendants; but the said agreement provided that estimates should be made by the architect, as the work on the buildings progressed, as to how much was due from each defendant for work and material, and neither defendant was to be responsible for the other defendant's proportion of the said estimate.

"Defendant, further answering, says that the land upon which said block of buildings are built is not owned jointly by the said defendants, but alleges that Dr. John Black holding the legal title to the north 46 feet of lots 1 and 2, in block 36, upon which his part of the said building is constructed, and this defendant having the legal title to the 44 feet of said lots immediately adjoining the said blocks on the south, upon which their part of the said Union Block is erected.

"Defendants allege that they have no interest in the buildings or that part of said Union Block constructed on the land belonging to Dr. Black, and the said Black has no interest in the building constructed on the land described as belonging to this defendant.

"Defendants further allege that they have paid the said William Winscit in full for all of the material furnished and work done by him upon said building under said contract, and that such payment was made prior to the notice of plaintiff's claim herein, and before this defendant had knowledge of its existence.

"Defendant denies any indebtedness to the said plaintiffs in the said sum of $1484.11, as they allege, or in any part of said sum, or any sum whatever.

"Defendant denies that the said Winscit bought said bill of lumber or any part thereof of the said Otis H. Ballou, with the understanding that it was to be used in the construction of the said Union Block.   Defendant denies that the said Otis H. Ballou sold said bill of lumber to the said Winscit to be used in these particular buildings, and denies that the same was used for that purpose.

"For a further answer to plaintiff's petition, defendant alleges that the said William Winscit never contracted the said account with the said Otis H. Ballou in manner and form as set forth by plaintiffs; but avers that if the said Winscit purchased material of the said Otis H. Ballou to be used in the construction of said block and did not pay for the same, it was then charged to him in one general account without regard as to what building the lumber was to be used in or where it was to be taken.

"Defendant denies that the said Otis H. Ballou had any separate account against the said Wm. Winscit for lumber sold to be used in these particular buildings; but avers that the said Winscit was an extensive building contractor, having at the date said items purport to have been charged a large number of buildings under his control as contractor, and in process of construction, for the building of which he purchased the lumber of the said Otis H. Ballou.   The material he did not pay for at the time was charged to him in one general account, without regard as to what building it was to be used in.   When the said Winscit made a payment to the said Otis. H. Ballou, he was given credit without regard as to who paid it to him (Winscit), or upon what purchases of lumber it should apply.

"Defendant alleges that during the months of Septem-

ber and October, 1881, that these defendants paid the said
Winscit in full the amounts due him under the said contract; and defendant alleges further that on or about the
1st day of October, 1881, and since the last item is purported to have been charged in the said account, the
said Winscit paid to the said Otis H. Ballou the sum of
$400, and that on or about the 8th day of October, 1881,
he paid the said Ballou $845, and that on or about the 16th
day of October, 1881, he paid the said Otis H. Ballou
$140, all of which sums should appear accredited on the
the said account attached to the plaintiffs' petition, a part
of all said sums having been paid to the said Winscit by
these defendants on the contract price of said buildings.
Defendant denies that the said Otis H. Ballou secured a
mechanic's lien upon this defendant's building, or that the
plaintiffs herein hold a lien thereon as alleged in their petition."

On the 21st day of November, 1882, the defendant
Black filed answer as follows:

"1. Denies each and every material allegation in said
petition contained so far as they relate to him, except such
as are hereinafter expressly admitted to be true.

"He admits that William Winscit was a contractor and
builder, and that he and the said M. E. Church are owners
of lots one (1) and two (2), in block thirty-six in the city
of Plattsmouth, and that he and said church entered into a
written contract with said Winscit to erect a block of buildings on said lots for the sum of twelve thousand one hundred dollars ($12,100); but this defendant alleges that he
is the owner in severalty of the north half of said lots only,
and has no interest whatever in the south half thereof, and
said church has no interest, right, claim, or title whatever
to the said north half of said lots. That said block of
buildings covers the whole front of said north half of said
lots, and a part of the south half thereof. That the part
on the north half belongs exclusively to this defendant,

and he has not and never had any interest whatever in the part on the south half. That the right, title, and interest of this defendant and said church to their said parts of said lots and buildings are, and always have been, entirely separate and distinct. That by the terms of said contract with said Winscit it was stipulated that said Winscit should erect a two-story brick building on said lots, as above stated, and furnish all the materials therefor; that this defendant by the terms of said contract was to pay him, the said Winscit, therefor the sum of seven thousand dollars ($7,000) for his part of said building, and he had no interest whatever in the contract between said church and said Winscit, and is not and never was in any way liable for the fulfillment or performance thereof; and said church has not and never had any interest whatever in this defendant's contract with said Winscit. That this defendant's part of said building is separated from that of said church by a partition wall. Wherefore defendant says that there is a misjoinder of causes of action and of parties; and he therefore prays that plaintiffs' bill be dismissed and that he have judgment for cost."

On the 4th day of December, 1882, plaintiffs filed reply to the answer of defendant church as follows:

"They deny that under the said agreement between William Winscit and John Black and this defendant there was no joint liability created between the defendants, Black and said church.

"They admit that the said agreement provided that estimates should be made by the architect, as the work on the building progressed, as to how much was due from each defendant for work done; but deny that the said agreement provided that the said estimates were to show how much was due from each defendant for material, and that neither defendant was to be responsible for the other defendant's proportion of said estimates, as this defendant alleges. That as to whether or not this defendant has no interest in the building in that part of said Union Block constructed on the land belonging to John Black, and as to whether or not the said Black has no interest in the building constructed on the land described as belonging to the said church, these plaintiffs have no knowledge save from the allegation in said answer contained, and they therefore deny the same and leave the defendant to its proof in that behalf.

"That as to whether or not the said defendant has paid the said William Winscit in full for all the material furnished and work done by him upon said building under the said contract, and such payment was made prior to the notice of plaintiff's claim herein and before this defendant had knowledge of its existence, the plaintiffs are not informed save from the allegations in said answer, and they therefore deny the same and leave the defendant to its proof in that behalf.

"That they deny that the said lumber and building material mentioned in the petition herein as purchased of the said Otis H. Ballou by said Winscit was charged to the said Winscit in one general account, without regard as to what building the lumber was to be used in or where it was to be taken, but allege the truth and fact to be that the said lumber was sold to the said Winscit with the understanding that it was to be used in the construction of the said block at Plattsmouth, and was so consigned and was charged to said Winscit separately, and that separate and distinct items thereof were made. But they admit that said Winscit was an extensive contractor and purchased from the said Ballou lumber for the construction of his buildings. But they deny that the lumber he did not pay for at the time was charged to him in one general account, without regard as to what building it was to be used in.

"That they deny that when the said Winscit made a payment to the said Otis H. Ballou he was given credit for the same without regard as to who paid it to him (Winscit), or upon what purchase of lumber it should apply, and allege that upon the receipt of money from the said Winscit there was an understanding in every instance as to where the said payment should apply, and who paid the same, and the payment was credited to that person by whom the payment was made. The plaintiffs admit that the said Winscit paid to the said Otis H. Ballou on or about the 1st day of October, 1881, the sum of four hundred (400) dollars, and on or about the 8th day of October, 1881, the sum of eight hundred and forty-five (845) dollars, and on or about the 15th day of October, 1881, the sum of one hundred and forty (140) dollars, but deny that all or any part of said sums should be credited upon the defendant's account, and deny that all or any part of said sums was paid to the said Winscit by these defendants; but allege the truth and fact to be that all of said sums were paid to the said Winscit by parties in the city of Omaha, for whose houses the said Otis H. Ballou had furnished lumber and material, and was then furnishing lumber and building material; that the said Winscit paid the several sums immediately or soon after receiving them to said Ballou, and directed the said Ballou to credit the several parties with the said several sums, and that said Ballou so did. Save as herein admitted to be true, the plaintiffs deny each and every allegation in said answer contained."

The reply to the answer of Black was substantially the same as that above given.

On the trial of the cause the defendants requested fifteen special findings of facts, as follows:

"1st. What were the terms of contracts between Winscit and the owners?

"2d. Whether O. H. Ballou, plaintiff's assignor, knew at the time he sold the lumber to Winscit, that he, Winscit, had a contract with defendants to build said 'Union Block' in Plattsmouth, and did he sell the lumber described to Winscit with the knowledge that it was to be used in said building and for that particular purpose.

"3d. To whom was the lumber charged on the 'day book,' and to whose account was it posted on the 'ledger?' When posted did Winscit have more than one ledger account, and did that account contain other charges for lumber than those mentioned as having gone into defendants' buildings? On what date does Winscit's general ledger account terminate, and does any credit appear thereon; the amount and date of their entry, the date of the charges for the lumber alleged to have gone to defendants? The date of the letter to Dr. Black demanding payment of $2,600, and if on that date O. H. Ballou, plaintiff's assignor, had any other 'ledger account' against Winscit than the general account found on pages.

"4th. Was the lumber sold on Winscit's credit and charged to him individually?

"5th. Did O. H. Ballou separate 'Winscit's general ledger account' after October 20, 1881?

"6th. . Were the entries 'Gish, Driscol, Wilkins, Coggsell, Plattsmouth, etc.,' made on the 'day book' in connection with charges for the purpose of designating simply to what place the lumber should be delivered, or for the purpose of basing a liability against the owners of the respective buildings?

"7th. How much, if any, lumber sold by plaintiff's assignor to Wm. Winscit was used in the construction of defendant's building? Ans. $1,316.43, at the contract price.

"8th. How much money did Winscit pay Ballou on account between September 12, 1881, and October 20, 1881?

"9th. How much money did Winscit pay Ballou between September 12, 1881, and November 25, 1881?

"10th. How much did the buildings cost defendants independent of any payments they made direct to Winscit?

"11th. How much money did the M. E. Church pay direct to Winscit?

"12th. At the time O. H. Ballou filed the lien did he have knowledge of the overcharges in the account?

"13th. Did Winscit complete the contract according to its terms; if not, did he abandon it wrongfully, and at what stage of completion did he abandon it? Did defendants suffer any damages by reason of Winscit quitting the work?

"14th. At what time was the building completed, and what was the rental value of the M. E. Church part of the block for the months of January, February, and March, 1882?

"15th. Does the contract between Winscit and defendants specifically provide against any liabilities for material until the work was completed and accepted?"

The court made special findings and rendered a decree as follows:

"1st. That the amount of lumber and building material furnished by Otis H. Ballou to William Winscit and used in defendants' block of buildings is $1,316.43.

"2d. That the first item of said lumber was furnished on September 12, 1881.

"3d. That said sum of $1,316.43 is due and unpaid said plaintiffs.

"4th. That William Winscit made no payments to O. H. Ballou upon general account, and that the application of each payment made by said Winscit was directed by Winscit and applied by Ballou as directed, and that said Winscit directed nothing to be applied on the account herein, and that nothing was paid on said account.

"5th. That within sixty days from the delivery of said lumber for said buildings the defendants paid out on account of said building an amount greater than that found due the plaintiffs herein, and that no part of said amount so paid was paid on account of plaintiffs' claim.

"6th. Wherefore it is considered adjudged and decreed that said plaintiffs have a mechanics' lien upon the property in their petition described, to-wit: Lot one (1) and two (2) in block thirty-six (36) in the city of Plattsmouth, Cass county, for said sum of $1,316.43, with interest thereon at 7 per cent per annum from September 28, 1881, and that unless said sum and interest and costs of this suit be paid within twenty days from the entry hereof then that an order be issued to the sheriff of Cass county command-ing him to sell said premises as upon execution and apply the proceeds thereof in payment of the amount so above found due upon the confirmation of said sale.

"7th.   That said lien be satisfied and said premises be sold in the following order, to-wit: That the land of the several defendants be appraised separately, and that the north forty-eight (48) feet of said lots one (1) and two (2) block thirty-six (36), the property of defendant John Black, be sold, and seven-twelfths (7-12) of said amount due be paid out of the proceeds thereof.   That the south ninety-two feet of said lots one (1) and two (2), block thirty-six (36), the property of said Methodist Episcopal Church, de-fendant, be sold and five-twelfths (5-12) of the amount be paid from the proceeds thereof.   And in case the proceeds arising from the sale of either of said parcels of land be insufficient to pay its said proportion of said amount so severally charged upon it, then that the other of said par-cels pay such deficiency in addition to the sum severally charged upon it."

There are twelve assignments of error, as follows:

"1.   The court erred in refusing to make the special findings of facts as requested by the defendants.

"2.   The court erred in its first special finding of fact, 'that the amount of lumber and building material furnished by O. H. Ballou to Wm. Winscit and used in defendants' block of buildings amounted to $1,316.43.'

"3.   The court erred in its third finding of fact, 'that said sum of $1,316.43 is due and unpaid said plaintiffs.'

"4th.   The court erred in its fourth finding of facts,

'that Winscit made no payments to O. H. Ballou upon general account, and that the application of each payment was directed by Winscit and applied as directed, and that Winscit directed nothing to be applied on the account herein.'

"5th.   The court erred in its fifth finding of fact, 'that no part of plaintiffs' claim had been paid.'

"6th.   The court erred in finding and decreeing that plaintiff's were entitled to a mechanics' lien on lots one and two in block thirty-six, in Plattsmouth, for the sum of $1,316.43, and in ordering a sale of said property for the payment of said sum.

"7th.   The court erred in ordering the sale of the whole of said lots.

"8.   The court erred in ordering 'that in case the proceeds arising from the sale of either of said parcels of land be insufficient to pay its said proportion of said amount so severally charged upon it, then that the other of said parcels pay such deficiency in addition to the sum severally charged upon it.'

"8 a.   The findings of facts by the court are vague and uncertain.

"8 b.   The court erred in not rendering judgment against William Winscit.

"9.   The court erred in not finding the issues in favor of the defendants, and dismissing the action.

"10.   The court erred in permitting plaintiffs to introduce evidence tending to prove that the payments made by Winscit were applied as directed by him, and in refusing to give the defendants any benefit or credit for said payments.

"11.   The court erred in permitting the witness Cooper to testify as to the $500 order alleged to have been given by Driscoll, and especially as to the contents of said order, without accounting for its non-production.

"12.   The court erred in refusing to permit the defendants to show by the day books of O. H. Ballou that there were charges for lumber during September and October, 1881, against A. W. Phelps, A. Rosenberry, and R. Stevens, and no designation of the houses in which the lumber was to be used."

It will be observed that no special objections are made to the failure of the judge to make special findings upon some of the requests made, nor does it appear that the defendants were injured by such failure, and that question need not be further considered.

A very large amount of testimony was taken in the case which cannot be set out in this opinion. It tends to show that Mr. Ballou shipped the lumber in question to Mr. Winscit, at Plattsmouth, for use in the construction of said building, and that such lumber was received and applied to that purpose.

Mr. Latham testifies:

"I reside in Plattsmouth. Am agent for the B. & M. R. R. Co. My business is to collect for and receive freight. I kept books. I was not an agent in 1881. I was cashier and kept the cashier's books. My duties as cashier was to collect freight. This is the cash book. By refreshing my memory from the book, I have a perfect recollection of car loads of lumber being shipped from Mr. Ballou to Mr. Winscit. Four cars of lumber were received from Omaha consigned by Ballou and directed to Winscit. They were received some time in September, 1881; do not know whether the dates are correct or not; books show two cars received September 21; one September 27, and one September 30. Those are the dates I collected the freight. The lumber was turned over to Dr. Black. I think he paid the freight on it. Do not know whether he paid it all or not. Mr. Marsland was agent at that time. Dr. Black told me whatever lumber came for him to deliver it to teamster, to Winscit; he would vouch for the freight. I mean by delivery to Black that he vouched for the freight."

This is not denied. The testimony also shows that no

10

payments whatever had been made upon this lumber.   The whole amount of the debt, therefore, was due and unpaid from Winscit.   The testimony also shows that Ballou filed a mechanics' lien within the time required by law, and is entitled to enforce such lien, if valid, as against the defendants, Black and M. E. Church.

Section 2, Chap. 54, Comp. Stat., provides that "Any person or sub-contractor who shall perform any labor for, or furnish any material or machinery or fixtures for any of the purposes mentioned in the first section of this act, to the contractor or any sub-contractor who shall desire to secure a lien upon any of the structures mentioned in said section, may file a sworn statement of the amount due him or them from such contractor or sub-contractor for such labor or material, machinery or fixtures, together with a description of the land upon which the same were done or used, within sixty days from the performing of such labor or furnishing such material, machinery, or fixtures, with the county clerk of the county wherein said land is situated, and if the contractor does not pay such person or sub-contractor for the same, such sub-contractor or person shall have a lien for the amount due for such labor or material, machinery or fixtures, on such lot or lots, and the improvements thereon, from the same time and in the same manner as such original contractor, and the risk of all payments made to the original contractor shall be upon the owner until the expiration of the sixty days hereintofore specified," etc.

It will be seen that under this section any person or sub-contractor who shall perform any labor for, or furnish any material to the contractor or any sub-contractor in the erection or reparation of any building, shall be entitled to a mechanics' lien thereon for the amount due him from such contractor or subcontractor for such labor, material, etc.   The lien to be claimed by filing a sworn statement of the amount due for such labor or material, etc., with the county clerk within sixty days from the performing of such labor or the furnishing such material, and the risk of all payments made to the contractor before the expiration of the sixty days is upon the owner.

Under the Revised Statutes of 1866, pages 257 and 258, the owner was liable to sub-contractors and material men, where there was no contract between them, express or implied, only to the extent of the amount due from the owner to the contractor; in other words, he could be garnisheed for the amount owing by him to the contractor. The present statute, however, makes the owner liable for the labor and material used in the erection of the building without regard to the state of the account between himself and the contractor. ‘ One of the objects of the statute, no doubt, was to prevent collusion between the contractor and the owner, and thus protect those from being defrauded who have performed labor or furnished material in the erection of a building. Therefore payments made to the contractor by the owner within sixty days from the time of furnishing the material for the erection of the building will not absolve such owner from liability therefor to the material man. *Foster v. Dohle*, 17 Neb., 631. *Marrener v. Paxton*, 17 Neb., 634. This disposes of the principal defense relied upon by the defendants. The proper construction of the contract set out in the petition was before this court in *Ballou v. Black*, 17 Neb., 389, and it was held that the building contracted for being a unit, and the contract for its erection containing a convenient method of apportioning its cost between the two owners, the same will be adopted by the court as a proper method of apportioning the lien against the lots upon which the building is situated. This construction was adopted by the court in rendering the decree. This disposes of all questions relating to the state of the account between the defendants and Winscit and the proper construction of the contract between them.

It is unnecessary to notice the other assignments of error as they were not prejudicial to the defendants. The decree is the only one that should have been rendered under the testimony, and there is no material error in the record. The judgment is therefore affirmed.

JUDGMENT AFFIRMED.

THE other judges concur.

N. F. HITCHCOCK ET AL., PLAINTIFFS IN ERROR, v. J. T. McKINSTER, DEFENDANT IN ERROR.

1. **Change of Venue:** PRACTICE WHERE JUSTICE IS BIASED. Where on a change of venue a cause is transferred to a justice of the peace, who, by reason of bias and prejudice, is unable to try the case, a motion to dismiss, filed by the defendant, *Held,* Properly overruled. The proper motion in such case is to remand.

2. ———: MOTION TO CHANGE: PARTY MOVING CANNOT COMPLAIN IF MOTION GRANTED. Where a cause was transferred to a justice of the peace upon a change of venue, and he being unable, by reason of bias and prejudice, to try the case, whereupon the defendant filed a motion to dismiss for said cause, which motion being overruled, he filed a motion supported by affidavit for a second change of venue, which motion was sustained, *Held,* That he could not predicate error upon the sustaining of his own motion.

3. ———: PRACTICE. Where a justice of the peace, on application for a change of venue, made an order transferring the cause to one R., supposed to be the nearest justice to whom no objections would apply; but on the next day ascertained that said justice had resigned, whereupon he changed the order, transferring said cause to one B , the nearest justice exercising the duties of his office, all parties being notified of said change, and a trial was thereafter had before B. and a jury, at which the parties appeared, *Held,* No error.

4. **Forcible Entry and Detention:** COMPLAINT: NOTICE. Where, in a complaint for forcible entry and detention, it is alleged that "plaintiffs served notice on the defendant describ-

ing said premises to defendant," *Held*, A sufficient allegation that the notice was in writing.

5. ———: ———. There being no bill of exceptions, objections to the form of notice cannot be considered.

ERROR to the district court for Otoe county. Tried below before POUND, J.

S. P. Davidson, for plaintiffs in error.

S. J. and *T. B. Stevenson,* for defendant in error.

MAXWELL, CH. J.

This is an action of forcible entry and detainer for the recovery of the possession of certain real estate described in the complaint. On the trial of the cause before a justice of the peace and a jury, a verdict was returned in favor of the plaintiffs, on which judgment was rendered. The case was then taken on error to the district court, where the judgment of the justice was reversed, and from such judgment of reversal the plaintiffs bring the cause into this court on error. There is no bill of exceptions, and the only evidence as to the procedure in the justice's court is contained in the several transcripts set forth in the record, which will be noticed presently.

The action was commenced before one T. J. Smith, a justice of the peace. The complaint is as follows:

"N. F. Hitchcock and J. F. Townsend,
        Plaintiffs,
            vs.
J. M. McKinster,
            Defendant.

"Said plaintiffs allege that they are entitled to the possession of the south-west quarter of section thirty, town seven, range ten, in Otoe county, state of Nebraska; that plaintiffs have been entitled to the possession of said prem-

ises for more than three weeks now past; that said defendant unlawfully and forcibly detains said premises from
said plaintiffs and has so unlawfully and forcibly detained
the same for more than three weeks last past; and on the
6th day of May, 1885, plaintiffs served a notice on defendant, describing said premises, to quit within three days after that time; that said time has elapsed and defendant still
wrongfully detains said premises. Wherefore plaintiffs
pray judgment against defendant for restitution of said
premises and costs of suit."

The defendant filed a motion for a change of venue and
the change was granted to one Charles Turnbull. From
some cause, which does not clearly appear in the transcript,
but which was stated on the argument of the case to be the
bias of Mr. Turnbull, he was unable to act. He thereupon
entered an order transferring the cause to one M. G. Reed;
on the next day ascertaining that Mr. Reed had resigned
the office of justice of the peace, Mr. Turnbull entered a
further order transferring the cause to one C. Bassett, a
justice of the peace, and the papers were transmitted to him.
The defendant thereupon moved to dismiss for the following reasons, viz:

"Because this action is not properly brought before this
justice on change of venue, because the justice from whence
this case was sent could confer no jurisdiction on this justice, to-wit: 'Because there was no authority of law for
said Bassett to entertain and try this action because it is not
properly before him.' Therefore defendant asks that this
action be dismissed."

The motion was overruled, to which defendant excepted.

It was admitted on the argument that Mr. Turnbull
having privately stated to the attorney of plaintiffs and
also of the defendant, that he was unable to try the case by
reason of his bias, the defendant thereupon filed a motion
for a change of venue, which was granted as heretofore
stated. The transcript from Mr. Turnbull's docket is as
follows:

"HENDRICK, OTOE COUNTY, NEB.,

                    May, 19, 1885.

"In justice court, before Charles Turnbull, justice of the peace in and for Otoe county, Nebraska.   N. F. Hitchcock and J. F. Townsend, plaintiffs, vs. J. T. McKinster, defendant.

"May 19, 1885.   A certified transcript from the docket of T. J. Smith, J. P. in the above case, was filed on change of venue being taken from said Smith as such J. P. on application of defendant; May 19, 1885, motion to dismiss filed by defendant and was argued by parties.   May 19, 1885, motion overruled, defendant excepts.   May 19, 1885, defendant files motion for change of venue supported by affidavit.   May 19, 1885, change of venue granted upon defendant paying costs of transfer.   Change of venue granted to Matthew Reed, J. P., South Branch precinct.

"Costs up to date: Docket, 25 cents; transcript and transfer, 75 cents.   Paid by defendant.

                    CHARLES TURNBULL,
                        Justice of the Peace."

Also the following order:

"May 20, 1885.   On taking papers of above cause to Matthew Reed, found that gentleman had resigned the justiceship.   Transferred the cause to C. Bassett and changed time one hour later; wrote and notified all parties concerned of the change.   CHARLES TURNBULL."

Sec. 958*a*, code of civil procedure, provides as follows: "That in all civil and criminal proceedings before justices of the peace, any defendant in such proceedings may apply for and obtain a change of venue by filing an affidavit in the case made by the defendant, his agent, or attorney, stating that the defendant cannot, as the affiant verily believes, have a fair and impartial hearing in the case on account of the interest, bias, or prejudice of the justice, and by paying the costs now required to be paid by defendant on change of venue, for the causes and in the cases mentioned in chapter four of title thirty, part two of the re-

vised statutes, and thereupon the proceedings shall be transferred to the nearest justice of the peace, to whom the said
objections do not apply, of the said county, to be proceeded
with in the manner pointed out for the transfer and procedure in cases of change of venue for cause mentioned in
said chapter four."

Sec. 958 *b*, code of civil procedure, provides that "The
application shall be made before entering upon the merits
of the case by the introduction and reception of evidence;
and no second change of venue shall be allowed for the
same cause in the same proceeding."

1.   The motion to dismiss was properly overruled. The
fact that a cause on a change of venue was transferred to a
justice of the peace who is biased or prejudiced against one
or both of the parties, is no cause for dismissing the action.
The object of granting a change of venue is to secure a fair
tribunal for the hearing of the cause, so that if possible a
correct judgment shall be rendered.   If objections are found
to exist against the justice to whom the cause was transferred
so that a fair trial cannot be had before him, a defendant
no doubt may move to remand the cause to the justice
granting the change, and if he fails to do so, the justice to
whom the cause was transferred may proceed with the trial.

2.   The second change of venue was granted on the
motion of the defendant, and he cannot predicate error upon
the ground that his own motion was sustained.   The statute, while it provides for only one change, does not declare
the proceedings of a second change to be void.   At the
most such second change is erroneous, but only the party
injured thereby can complain.   The defendant, therefore, is
estopped by his own motion from complaining of the ruling
of the court in sustaining it.

3.   Turnbull, in sustaining the motion granting a change
of venue, made an order transferring the case to one Mr.
Reed, whom he supposed to be the nearest justice of the
peace to whom no objection could be made.   On the next
day, ascertaining that Reed had resigned the office of jus-

tice, he changed the entry by ordering the change to be made to one C. Bassett, a justice of the peace.   In this we think there was no error.   Mr. Bassett appears to be the nearest justice to whom no objection could be made, and the entry of the preceding day was made under a misapprehension of the facts and failed to transfer the cause to another justice for trial.   The theory of the code is, that an action having been properly commenced shall not be dismissed upon slight, trivial, or merely technical grounds where the court has jurisdiction of the subject matter and parties, until a trial has been had upon the merits; and this rule applies to proceedings before justices of the peace. There is no complaint that Mr. Bassett was biased or prejudiced, or that a fair trial was not had before him.   We therefore hold that there was no error in his entertaining jurisdiction.

4.   The defendant alleges that there was no allegation in the complaint that written notice to leave was served upon him three days before bringing the action, the language being: " Plaintiffs served a notice on defendant, describing said premises to defendant."

It is unnecessary to allege in the complaint that the notice was in writing, although on the trial it must be proved to be so.   *Meyers vs. Morse*, 15 Johnson, 425.   Moak's Van Santvoords Pleadings, 3d edition, pages 205 and 255. The complaint upon that point, therefore, is sufficient.

5.   Objections are made to the form of the notice and the service of the same; but as there was no bill of exceptions before the district court, hence none before this court, it is impossible to say upon what evidence the judgment of the justice of the peace was predicated; we cannot, therefore, review the facts.   The judgment of the district court is reversed, and that of the justice reinstated.

JUDGMENT ACCORDINGLY.

THE other judges concur.

G. C. UNDERHILL, PLAINTIFF IN ERROR, V. MICHAEL
SHEA AND JOHN DELANEY, DEFENDANTS IN ER-
ROR.

1. **Justice of Peace**: OFFER TO CONFESS JUDGMENT: COSTS.
   Where, in an action for money before a justice of the peace, it is
   shown by the docket of the justice that prior to the day of trial
   the defendant offered to confess judgment in favor of the plaintiff for a certain sum, which the plaintiff refused to accept, there
   is no presumption that the offer was not in writing, and in such
   case the decision of the district court on a motion to tax costs to
   plaintiff for the reason that the judgment did not exceed the
   offer, will not be molested.

2. **Judgment**: OFFER TO CONFESS. An offer to confess judgment
   duly made in the court where the action is brought, under section 1,004 of the code of civil procedure, need not be renewed in
   the appellate court in order to make it available to the party
   making it on final judgment. *Kleffel v. Bullock*, 8 Neb., 336.

ERROR to the district court for Otoe county.   Tried below before HAYWARD, J.

D. T. Hayden and *E. F. Warren*, for plaintiff in error.

F. E. Brown, for defendants in error.

REESE, J.

This action was originally instituted before a justice of
the peace.   It was founded upon a promissory note, dated
November 3, 1883, due seven months after date, for the
sum of $122.50, with interest from date at the rate of ten
per cent.   The docket of the justice contains, among others,
the following entry: "January 20, 1885, 10 o'clock A.M.,
summons returned.   Parties appeared.   Defendants offered
to confess judgment to the sum of $84.25 and costs to date.
Plaintiff refused to accept."

The cause was adjourned to a later date, when a

jury trial was had, resulting in a verdict in favor of plaintiff for $138.35, and upon which judgment was rendered. The cause was taken to the district court by defendant by petition in error, and upon a hearing there the petition in error was sustained, the judgment reversed, costs taxed to plaintiff, and the cause retained for trial. Issues were formed and upon a trial to the court judgment was rendered in favor of plaintiff for the sum of $93.10, with costs taxed at $113.88. Defendant then moved to tax the costs to plaintiff and assigned as their reason therefor the offer to confess judgment in the justices' court before trial. Upon a hearing of this motion the district court taxed to plaintiff the costs of his own witnesses, which amounted to $52.50, but overruled the motion as to the other costs. Both parties complain of the ruling on this motion, but as defendant has filed neither a petition in error nor assignments of errors in this court, he must be taken to have waived his right to complain, and no further attention need be given to that part of the case.

The sole question, then, before us is, whether or not the court erred in sustaining defendant's motion to the extent of charging plaintiff with the costs of his own witnesses. We think not. The real basis of the contention of plaintiff in error is the alleged fact that the offer to confess judgment was not in writing as required by section 1,004 of the civil code. From the record before us we cannot say with certainty whether the offer was made in writing or not. It is only shown that the offer was made and refused by plaintiff. There is nothing in the record which gives any light upon the subject, unless the fact that a fee was charged by the justice for filing the offer might be taken as a suggestion that it was in writing. But as it is a well established rule that error must affirmatively appear before a judgment will be reversed, we need only say that as the record stands we must presume the ruling of the district court to be correct and sustained by the record before it.

As the question whether or not the making of such an offer in open court and its entry on the docket by the justice would be a sufficient compliance with the section referred to is not before us, we have not examined it and express no opinion thereon.

It is next suggested that the offer, if made, was insufficient in amount, not being equal to the judgment finally recovered. The action was upon a promissory note drawing ten per cent interest. Defendant admitted an indebtedness of $75.00 and interest, but claimed that by mistake the note was written for $46.50 more than he actually owed. The amount of his offer was a little more than the $75.00 and interest thereon to the date the offer was made. The trial court found that the true amount of the debt was $75.00 and interest, which was a few cents less than the amount of defendant's offer and interest. The offer, if properly made, became a part of the record of the case, and was as available on final judgment in the appellate court as in the court where made. *Kleffel v. Bullock*, 8 Neb., 341. No objection can be urged to the offer as being too small.

As no error appears upon the record the judgment of the district court is affirmed.

JUDGMENT AFFIRMED.

THE other judges concur.

JOHN DANIELS, PLAINTIFF IN ERROR, V. ELIZABETH COLE, DEFENDANT IN ERROR.

1. **Replevin:** PETITION. A petition in replevin is sufficient if it contain proper allegations that the plaintiff is the owner of the property in dispute and entitled to its immediate possession, and that it is unlawfully detained by the defendant. It is not necessary that it should contain averments that the property was not taken in execution on any order or judgment against

the plaintiff or for the payment of any fine, tax, or amercement
assessed against him, or by virtue of an order of delivery in
replevin or in other mesne or final process against him. These
allegations are required only in the affidavit to be filed at the
commencement of the action.

2. **Evidence examined, and** *Held*, Sufficient to sustain the verdict.

ERROR to the district court for Lancaster county. Tried
below before POUND, J.

Foxworthy & Son, for plaintiff in error.

W. B. Baird, for defendant in error.

REESE, J.

This was an action in replevin instituted by defendant
in error, for the possession of certain property levied on
by virtue of an execution in the hands of an officer, and
which had been issued upon a judgment in favor of plaintiff in error and against the husband of defendant in error.
The trial resulted in a verdict and judgment in favor of
defendant in error.   Plaintiff in error, who was defendant
below, seeks a review by proceedings in error.

Upon the trial plaintiff in error objected to the introduction of any evidence by defendant in error, for the reason
that her petition did not state facts sufficient to constitute a cause of action.   This objection was overruled, and
the ruling thereon is now assigned for error.   The contention is, that as the petition does not allege that the property was not taken in execution, or on any order or judgment, etc., against the plaintiff filing the petition, as is
required in an affidavit for replevin under the provisions
of section 182 of the civil code, it does not state a cause of
action.   In short it is contended that a petition in replevin
should contain the averments mentioned, and failing to do
so, the petition is demurrable.   We know of no rule of
pleading which requires a petition in replevin to contain

these allegations. In fact, the uniform holding of this court upon kindred questions seems to me to lead to a different conclusion. *Haggard v. Wallen*, 6 Neb., 271. *School District v. McIntie*, 14 Id., 48. See also Maxwell's Pl. and Pr., 1885 ed., 293. There was no error in the ruling of the court on the objection to the introduction of evidence.

The remaining contention may be said to be that the verdict of the jury was not sustained by the evidence, although the motion for a new trial consists in alleged errors of the jury in "not giving credence" to certain evidence introduced by plaintiff in error.

It is claimed by defendant in error that the property in dispute, and which was levied on as the property of her husband, was and is her sole and separate property, and that the means with which it was procured were secured from her father's estate, and not from her husband. She in effect so testified, as also did her husband.

On the part of plaintiff in error it was contended that defendant was not the owner, and that the property was the property of the husband; and to sustain this view of the case he introduced, among other testimony, proof that the property in dispute, as well as that through which it was obtained, was listed for taxation for the years 1881, 1882, and 1883, as the property of the husband; that the husband purchased it from Mr. Gillam without disclosing or claiming that he was purchasing for the wife, and that a few days before the levy he executed to defendant in error a bill of sale transferring to her not only the property in dispute, but apparently all the personal property he had, and that defendant in error, at the time of the levy, exhibited the bill of sale and claimed to own the property by virtue thereof. It was also claimed by defendant in error that the property in question was exempt from such levy under the exemption laws of the state.

These questions were properly submitted to the trial

jury, and we think their finding thereon must stand. It
would seem quite probable that the purpose of the husband
of defendant in error in making the bill of sale was a
fraudulent one; yet if the property was exempt from execution such purpose would not make it liable to seizure;
and if the property was the separate property of defendant in error the making of the bill of sale could not
change that ownership.

It appears that the bill of sale was made at the suggestion, and upon the advice, of a third party, and without
consultation between the husband and wife; that it included
a large amount of other property beside the mare in dispute, so that the mere fact of the mare being included in
the bill would not be conclusive that she was not exempt,
nor that she was not the property of defendant in error.
These were the questions presented by her, and the jury
found in her favor, perhaps, on both. She testified that
she received $200 and a span of horses from her father's
estate eleven years ago. That she gave one of the horses
and a part of the money to her husband; that the other
horse was sold and a part of the money applied to the
purchase of a colt; that the colt was traded for a span
of mules, the mules sold and the property in question
purchased with the proceeds, and that her ownership of
the property was maintained throughout. If the jury
believed her, which they perhaps did, the verdict should
be upheld. They were the judges of the weight of her
testimony, as well as that of her husband and the other
witnesses.

It is claimed that plaintiff in error purchased the note
upon which the judgment was rendered, relying upon a
property statement made thereon to the effect that the maker
—the husband—owned in his own name personal property
of the value of $2,000 clear of all incumbrance, and it is
insisted that he is estopped from denying its truth, and
should be bound by it. Were this an action between the

maker of the note and plaintiff in error, this question might arise, but we fail to see that it can in this action. It is not claimed that defendant in error signed either the note or property statement, nor that either were made with her knowledge or consent.

We fail to find any error which requires a reversal of the judgment of the district court, and it is therefore affirmed.

JUDGMENT AFFIRMED.

MAXWELL, CH. J., concurs.

COBB, J., dissents.

160
711

DANIEL FREEMAN, PLAINTIFF IN ERROR, V. HIRAM P. WEBB ET AL., DEFENDANT IN ERROR.

1. **Petition:** AMENDMENT: ADDITIONAL CAUSE OF ACTION. An additional cause of action, which under the provisions of section 87 of the civil code could have been united with the original cause of action, may be added to, and included in, a petition by amendment.

2. ———. The amended petition, as copied at large in the opinion, *Held,* To state a cause of action.

ERROR to the district court for Gage county. Tried before BROADY, J.

A. Hardy, for plaintiff in error.

Pemberton & Bush and *Griggs & Rinaker,* for defendants in error.

COBB, J.

In the district court the plaintiff filed his petition against the defendant Hiram P. Webb, as a former county treasurer of Gage county, and the other defendants as sureties on his official bond. The cause of action, consisted of a breach of the said official bond by the said county treasurer, in entering upon a certain block of real estate in said county, claimed and occupied by the plaintiff, and selling the house and other improvements thereon, as personal property, for the purpose of collecting certain taxes claimed to be due from the plaintiff, etc., to the plaintiff's damage, etc. The principal defendant, having long since left the state, was not served with summons in the case, and made no appearance. The defendants, who were served, demurred to the petition, and their demurrer was sustained. The sustaining of said demurrer is not assigned for error, but the necessity of thus referring to the original petition will be apparent as we proceed. The plaintiff having obtained leave of the court to plead over, filed an amended petition as follows :

"The plaintiff, in this his amended petition, filed by leave of the court, complains of the above named defendants, and for cause of action alleges,

"First.—That at the general election held in and for Gage county, Nebraska, on, to-wit, the second Tuesday of October, 1873, the said defendant, Hiram P. Webb was elected to the office of county treasurer for the period of two years from January 1st, 1874.

"Second.—That on the 25th day of October, 1873, said Hiram P. Webb as principal, and said William Lamb, George Place, James Boyd, Oliver Townsend, H. F. Cook, Phillip Gascoign, Jacob Drum, David Read, Joseph Graff, J. L. Webb, J. F. King, Joseph Saunders, and E. M. Hill, as sureties, made and delivered to said county of Gage, and state of Nebraska, at the said county of Gage, their certain obligation in writing of that date, acknowledging themselves to be held and firmly bound unto the county of Gage and state of Nebraska in the penal sum of eighty thousand ($80,000) dollars, and which said obligation in

11

writing had a condition thereunder written, and which condition is in the following words, viz.: 'Now, if the said Hiram P. Webb shall render a true account of his office and the doings therein to the proper authorities when required thereby or by law, and shall promptly pay over to the person or officers entitled thereto all money which may come into his hands by virtue of his said office, and shall fully account for all balance of money remaining in his hands at the termination of his office, and shall hereafter exercise reasonable diligence and care in the preservation and lawful disposal of all moneys, books, papers, and sureties or other property appertaining to his said office, and deliver them to his successor or to any person authorized to receive the same; and if he will faithfully and impartially, without fear, favor, fraud, or oppression, discharge all duties now or hereafter required of his office by law, then this bond to be void, otherwise in full force.' A copy of said obligation in writing, and the conditions above recited, duly certified, is hereto annexed, marked exhibit 'A,' and made a part of this amended petition.

"And the said plaintiff further alleges that the said Hiram P. Webb did on the 25th day of October, 1873, take and subscribe to the oath of office as such treasurer as aforesaid, a copy of which said oath is also hereto annexed, marked Exhibit 'B,' and made a part of this amended petition. And that said bond or obligation in writing, with the conditions annexed, was on the 25th day of October, 1873, filed in the office of the county clerk of Gage county, and on the first day of November, 1873, the same was duly approved according to law, and said Hiram P. Webb thereafter duly entered upon the duties of said office and at the time of committing the wrong hereinafter complained of was exercising said duties. And for a first cause of action plaintiff alleges that the said Hiram P. Webb, treasurer as aforesaid, on, to-wit, the 16th day of August, 1874, broke the conditions of said bond and committed a breach of the conditions thereof, while acting under and by virtue of his said office, in committing the several acts and wrongs hereinafter complained of and fully set forth and described.

"That the said Hiram P. Webb as such treasurer did not faithfully and impartially, without fear, favor, fraud, and oppression, discharge the duties required of his office by law, but that on the contrary said Hiram P. Webb, acting under and by virtue of his office, committed the several acts of fear, favor, fraud, and oppression hereinafter complained of and fully set forth at the time last aforesaid, and while said bond was in full force. And the plaintiff further alleges that for four years prior to the month of August, 1874, and then, this plaintiff was in quiet and peaceable possession and occupation and claimed to be the owner of a certain block or tract of land in the city (formerly town) of Beatrice, situated and bounded as follows: On the north by Ella street, on the east by Fourth street, on the south by Court street, and on the west by Eighth street, containing about two and one-half acres of land known as Freeman's block, and that said county of Gage also claimed the right of possession of said block of land, but had never had possession of the same adverse to this plaintiff. That during the year 1870, the plaintiff erected upon said premises a dwelling-house, at the cost and of the value of seven hundred dollars, and a privy at the cost and of the value of twenty dollars, and built upon and around said block of land a fence at the cost and of the value of one hundred and fifty dollars, and this plaintiff from that time until the commission of the wrongs hereinafter complained of continued to live and reside in said dwelling-house, upon said premises, with his family, and to occupy the same as a house for himself and family. That on, to-wit, said 16th day of August, 1874, and while the plaintiff and his family were temporarily absent from their said house, the said defendant, Hiram P. Webb, as treasurer of Gage county

aforesaid, acting in his official capacity and under and by
virtue of his office, for the purpose and with the intent of
fraudulently depriving plaintiff of his rights held under
and by virtue of his possession of said block of land, and
to oppress and injure the plaintiff and deprive him of his
property and home and to get in and obtain possession
thereof for the county of Gage, did with his deputy and
others acting under his direction, go upon said block of
land and there detached said house, privy, and fence from
the freehold and carry the same off said block, and under
the pretext of collecting delinquent taxes to an amount not
exceeding $200, levied upon said house, privy, and fence,
and sold the same for the insignificant sum of $102, and
delivered the same to the purchaser thereof, who removed
the same and thereafter wholly deprived plaintiff thereof;
that at the time of said transactions this plaintiff's house-
hold goods were in said house, and that the plaintiff had
in Gage county aforesaid a large amount of personal property, enough to many times pay all the delinquent taxes
claimed by said treasurer from this plaintiff, and that the
delinquent taxes in said county then against this plaintiff
were assessed largely upon lands that this plaintiff had
never owned nor possessed, yet the said defendant, Webb,
acting under and by virtue of his office, practiced the fraud
and oppression aforesaid upon this plaintiff, which he could
not have done but for his office, all contrary to the conditions of said bond, and done with full knowledge of all the
facts aforesaid. That by reason of the premises plaintiff
was damaged in the sum of eight hundred and seventy
($870) dollars.

"Second. And for a second cause of action the plaintiff alleges that said Hiram P. Webb, treasurer as aforesaid, on, to-wit, the said 16th day of August, 1874, further
broke the conditions of said bond and committed a breach
of the conditions thereof while acting under and by virtue
of his said office, in committing the other several acts and

wrongs hereinafter complained of and fully set forth and described. That the said Hiram P. Webb as such treasurer did not faithfully and impartially, without fear, fraud, favor, and oppression, discharge the duties required of his said office by law, but that on the contrary said Hiram P. Webb, after his election to the office of treasurer of Gage county aforesaid, as aforesaid and after he gave the bond (plaintiff's exhibit 'A,' hereto attached and made a part hereof) as aforesaid, and after the same had been duly approved, and while the same was in full force and effect, and after subscribing to and taking the proper oath of office as aforesaid, and while said Webb was acting as the duly elected and qualified treasurer of said county, and while acting under and by virtue of his office, committed the other several acts of fear, favor, fraud, and oppression hereinafter complained of and fully set forth on, to-wit, said 16th day of 'August, 1874, viz., said 16th day of August, 1874, and while the plaintiff and his family were temporarily absent from said Gage county, and after the commission of the several acts above complained of, the said defendant, Hiram P. Webb, as treasurer of said county, acting in his official capacity, and under and by virtue of his office, by his deputy under his directions, for the fraudulent purpose and with the intent of conveying to his said deputy's friend and chum the wheat and barley hereinafter mentioned and described, for little or no consideration, and to deprive the plaintiff of the same, did seize, levy upon, and sell to said chum, one George Dorsey, seven hundred bushels of wheat of the value of one dollar per bushel, and three hundred bushels of barley of the value of one dollar per bushel, all the property of this plaintiff, and then being in said county, and that to oppress and defraud the plaintiff, said Webb, by his deputy acting, took said Dorsey to plaintiff's premises, whereon was said wheat and barley, for the sole purpose of having him, said Dorsey, bid off the same and obtain the same for a slight consideration, and at the sale said treasurer, by his deputy acting, threatened and intimidated the only other person (excepting said Dorsey) then there, and in this way oppressed and defrauded the plaintiff by preventing any competition in bidding and by selling the whole of said wheat and barley to said Dorsey for the insignificant sum of $118.44. That to accomplish the aforesaid purpose said treasurer used the power of his office as such treasurer and claimed to be collecting the balance of the delinquent taxes then claimed against this plaintiff that was left unpaid after selling the house, privy, and fence as aforesaid, and plaintiff alleges that the primary cause of his action was to convey said grain to said Dorsey for as little consideration as possible, and that said pretended delinquent taxes were largely assessed upon lands that this plaintiff never owned or possessed, and had been running since the year 1872, and notwithstanding plaintiff at all times between the years 1872 and 1874 had ample personal property in said county, out of which said taxes could have been collected, no attempt was made to collect the same until after this plaintiff had, with his family, temporarily gone out of said county, yet the said defendant Webb, as such treasurer, well knowing all the facts aforesaid, acting under and by virtue of his office, practiced the fraud and oppression aforesaid upon the plaintiff which he could not have done but for his office, all contrary to the express conditions of said bond, under and by which several acts of oppression and fraud, this plaintiff was wholly deprived of all of said wheat and barley and was damaged in the further sum of one thousand dollars.

" And plaintiff further alleges in addition to both of the foregoing causes of action that on, to-wit, the 11th day of May, 1874, he left and deposited with the defendant, Hiram P. Webb, the promissory notes of several parties living in Gage county, to an amount of over $300, and more than enough to pay all taxes in said county against this plaintiff, all of which and said promissory notes were due and payable between the time they were so deposited with said Webb and the said 16th day of August, 1874, and all of which said notes were worth their face and would have been paid by notifying the makers thereof, yet, notwithstanding, said Webb never notified the makers that he held said notes, nor never attempted to make said taxes out of the same, but held the same and returned the same to plaintiff after his return to this county, upon his order, and thereafter plaintiff, by notifying the makers thereof where said notes were, received full payment of each and every one of said notes.

"Wherefore, and for all of these reasons aforesaid, the plaintiff asks judgment against said defendants for and in the sum of one thousand eight hundred and seventy ($1,-870) dollars, with interest thereon from the 16th day of August, 1874, and for costs of this action."

The plaintiff also set out a copy of the official bond of the said Webb as treasurer of Gage county; but as no question is made on the form of the bond, it is omitted here.

"On the 12th day of June, 1886, the defendants filed a motion in the court below to strike out of the amended petition the second cause of action set out therein, alleging the reason therefor that said cause of action was not included in the original petition, and has since been introduced by amendment of the petition and not otherwise, and that said cause of action is not an amendment to or of plaintff's petition, but is a new, separate, and distinct cause of action attempted to be set up against defendants in favor of plaintiff in addition to the original cause of action set up in the plaintiff's original petition.

"And on the 12th day of June, 1886, the court sustained said motion and struck out of amended petition said second cause of action therein stated.

"On the 12th day of June, 1886, the defendants, except

H. P. Webb, filed a demurrer to the plaintiff's amended petition, in the court below, and stated therein as reason therefor that the facts stated in said amended petition do not constitute a cause of action against said defendents.

"On the 28th day of September, 1886, the court below sustained said demurrer. After which the court below dismissed said action with costs against the plaintiff."

Thereupon the cause was brought to this court on error ·by the plaintiff, who makes the following assignments of error:

"1. The court below erred in sustaining defendants' motion to strike out of the amended petition the second cause of action therein stated.

"2. The court below erred in sustaining the demurrer of the defendants to the plaintiff's amended petition.

"3. The court below erred in dimissing said cause and rendering judgment against the plaintiff of dismissal with costs."

These errors are so closely connected that I deem it most convenient to examine and discuss them together. In the first place it will be observed that the original petition was confined to the alleged injury committed by the principal defendant against the plaintiff, in entering upon the premises of the plaintiff and selling the house and other improvements of the plaintiff for the purpose of collecting certain taxes claimed to be due and delinquent, etc. By sustaining the demurrer to this petitition, the district court held that no cause of action was stated therein. The correctness of this holding is not controverted; but the first question presented is whether, in reconstructing his petition by amendment, the plaintiff was restricted to the identical injury which he had vainly attempted to set out in his original pleading, it will not be denied that in his original petition he could, within certain limits, have set out two or more causes of action. Has he forfeited that right by his futile attempt? Without attempting to reconcile the many conflicting decisions to be found in the reported cases, but endeavoring to follow the dictates of reason and the spirit of the code, I come to the conclusion that upon being permitted to amend, he could bring in any additional cause or causes of action which he could originally have joined with the one which he attempted, unsuccessfully, to plead. Whether he could abandon that one and set up another, or others, without reference to their compatibility with it, is a question which does not arise in this case, and I express no opinion upon it.

By reference to the amended petition, it will be seen that the plaintiff therein set out the original cause of action, supposably in somewhat different language from that of the original petition, and added thereto a second cause of action for the seizing and selling by the said principal defendant Webb, by and through his deputy county treasurer, of a quantity of wheat and barley, the property of the plaintiff, for the purpose of collecting certain taxes then claimed to be owing by the plaintiff, and the unlawful, tortious, and fraudulent manner in which the said Webb, by his said deputy county treasurer, sold the said wheat and barley, to the damage of the plaintiff, etc.

On motion of the defendants the said second cause of action was stricken out by the court on the ground "that the said second cause of action was not included in the original petition filed herein, and has since been introduced by amendment of the petition," etc.

Section 87 of the code of civil procedure is as follows: "The plaintiff may unite several causes of action in the same petition, whether they be such as have heretofore been denominated legal or equitable, or both when they are included in either of the following classes: *First.* The same transaction or transactions connected with the same subject. *Second.* Contracts express or implied. *Third.* Injuries with or without force to person and property, or either. *Fourth.* Injuries to character. *Fifth.* Claims to recover the possession of personal property, with or without damages for the withholding thereof. *Sixth.* Claims to recover real property, with or without damages for the withholding thereof, and the rents and profits of the same. *Seventh.* Claims against a trustee by virtue of a contract, or by operation of law."

While it will not be claimed that the pleader was altogether clear or happy in the use of language in constructing the amended petition, yet when read with that liberality and favor due to all pleadings under the code, it will be seen, I think, that the case falls within the meaning of the first subdivision of the section above quoted. The subject matter of the lawsuit was the seizing and selling by the principal defendant Webb of the property of the plaintiff, by virtue of his office of county treasurer, on a warrant or warrants, legal or illegal, for the collection of taxes, real or pretended; and the two transactions—that which is alleged to have been done by the treasurer himself, in respect to the house and other improvements on the block of land, and that which is alleged to have been done by and through the deputy in reference to the wheat and barley, are certainly "transactions connected with the same subject of action." I am equally clear, in my own mind, that the case also falls within the meaning of the third subdivision. This is an action for injuries to property of the plaintiff. Under the third subdivision all such injuries may be united in the same action, whether with or without force, and may also be united not only with each other, but with injuries to the person.

I come to the conclusion, therefore, that the district court erred in striking out the third paragraph or second cause of action, as it is called, from the amended petition.

As to the demurrer, as above intimated, I think, that by a liberal construction of the language of the petition, it may be held to charge, both in the first and second counts, the doing of the acts complained of on the part of the county treasurer, *virtute officii.* Such was the conclusion to which we all came at the hearing. Such being the case, the petition, even with the second cause of action stricken out, does state a cause of action. It follows, therefore, that the demurrer was erroneously sustained.

The judgment of the district court is reversed, the second cause of action restored to the petition, the demurrer overruled, and the cause remanded for further proceedings in accordance with law.

JUDGMENT ACCORDINGLY.

THE other judges concur.

JOHN YEOMAN, PLAINTIFF IN ERROR, V. THE STATE OF NEBRASKA, DEFENDANT IN ERROR.

1. **Incest**: INDICTMENT. Plaintiff in error was indicted alone for the crime of incest, under the provisions of section 203 of the criminal code. *Held,* That he was properly so indicted, and that it was not necessary that the indictment should be against both parties to the incestuous intercourse.

2. ———: EVIDENCE: CORPUS DELICTI. Where in a prosecution for incest it was proven that the person with whom the incestuous intercourse was alleged to have been had was of the age of sixteen years; that she resided at home with her parents; that the accused also resided with the family; that they were often together alone; that she had no suitor and kept company with no other person; that the relation of uncle and niece existed between them; that she became pregnant, and when her pregnancy was discovered the accused confessed the paternity of the child which was afterwards born, admitted the intercourse, and settled the claims of the mother in satisfaction of proceedings in bastardy, and tried to induce a physician to procure an abortion, it was *Held,* That the *corpus delicti* had been sufficiently proved to require the submission of the case to the trial jury.

3. ——: TIME OF COMMISSION OF OFFENSE. On the trial of the case the court charged the jury that it was not necessary that the offense be proven to have been committed on the date alleged in the indictment, but that it would be sufficient if proven to have been committed within three years prior to the finding of the indictment. The instruction was *Held*, To be correct.

4. ——: EVIDENCE OF CO-FORNICATOR. On a trial of a defendant charged with incest with his neice, the woman was not examined as a witness by the state, but the defendant examined her as a witness in his behalf. On being asked if defendant had ever had sexual intercourse with her, she answered he had not. On the cross-examination counsel for the prosecution presented her with the affidavit which she had made, by which proceedings in bastardy had been instituted; and in answer to his question she stated that she had signed the affidavit. On re-examination she was asked if the signing of the affidavit was voluntary on her part. The question was objected to, and the objection sustained. *Held*, Error.

5. A large discretion is given the district court as to the order in which testimony may be introduced.

ERROR to the district court for Hamilton county. Tried below before NORVAL, J.

J. H. Smith, for plaintiff in error.

William Leese, Attorney General, and *A. J. Rittenhouse*, for defendant in error.

REESE, J.

Plaintiff in error was indicted for a violation of section 203 of the criminal code. The charging part of the indictment was as follows:

"That the said John Yeoman, on the first day of July, 1883, in the county of Hamilton and state of Nebraska, being then and there an unmarried man, did then and there unlawfully, knowingly, and feloniously commit fornication with one Amanda Yeoman, by then and there having sexual intercourse with the said Amanda Yeoman, the said

Amanda Yeoman being then and there a niece of the said John Yeoman, as the said John Yeoman and the said Amanda Yeoman well knew."

The section of the criminal code above referred to is as follows:

" Persons within the degrees of consanguinity within which marriages are declared by the preceding section to be incestuous and void, who shall intermarry with each other, or who shall commit adultery or fornication with each other, or who shall lewdly and lasciviously cohabit with each other, shall be liable to indictment, and, upon conviction, be punished by imprisonment in the penitentiary not exceeding ten years."

The trial resulted in a conviction. Plaintiff brings error to this court.

The first question presented is, does this indictment charge an offence within the section above quoted? Stated otherwise, Is it competent for the state to charge and prosecute but one of the parties to the incestuous commerce? It is urged by plaintiff in error that the act must be the concurrent act and by the consent and agreement of both parties to it, and that both parties must be equally guilty, and therefore both must be indicted together.

It is true that both must be guilty. That the inter-marriage, cohabitation, adultery, or fornication must be by a union of minds as well as of actions. Yet we do not think it necessarily follows that both should be prosecuted jointly. In short, it seems that the rule is the other way. *Hintz v. The State*, 58 Wis., 496.

Upon the trial of the cause the father and mother of Amanda Yoeman were called as witnesses, who testified as to the relationship between the parties (plaintiff in error and Amanda), and that plaintiff in error resided at their house, practically as a member of the family; that Amanda was of the age of sixteen years, and unmarried; that plaintiff in error and Amanda were often together alone; that she had no other escort, and no suitor; that she kept company with no other person, and that she had become a mother, giving birth to an illegitimate child. The father also further testified that when he discovered the pregnant condition of his daughter he went to the stable where plaintiff in error was and said to him, "That girl is in a family way, and he says, 'Yes, Doc. Davis says so.' Then he said he 'did not see how it could be,' and then he showed me a scabbard and said 'That is what they had to use,' and then directly he says 'shoot me.'" He also testified that the bastardy proceeding was settled by the transfer of certain property by plaintiff in error. Another witness, N. W. Titinan, testified that in June or July, 1883, plaintiff in error admitted to him that he had had sexual intercourse with Amanda Yoeman; that she was the third one for him, and that "if he only had to pay for one out of three he was getting along pretty well."

Dr. Davis testified that in the fall of 1883 plaintiff in error and Amanda Yoeman came to his office, and that plaintiff requested him to procure an abortion, which he refused to do. This is substantially all the testimony introduced on the part of the state as to the body of the crime. It is now insisted that the *corpus delicta* was not proven. We think there was sufficient on that point to warrant the submission of the case to the jury. According to the course of nature there must have been sexual intercourse to produce the pregnancy which was clearly established. It was then competent to prove the defendant's guilt by his own voluntary admissions. But it is contended that the admissions were not competent to prove the crime of incest. The relationship—which gave the character of incest to the intercourse—was clearly shown by positive proof without reference to his confessions.

The court gave the jury the following instruction: "It is not necessary that the offense be proven to have been committed on the first day of July, 1883. It is sufficient if it be proven to have been committed within three years prior to May 8, 1885." This instruction was excepted to and is now assigned for error. The first date named refers to the time alleged in the indictment as the date of the commission of the offense, the second to the day after the presentation of the indictment. In the giving of this instruction there was no error. The indictment alleges a single offense. There was but one sought to be proved, hence there could be no election as to which act of fornication was the one upon which the district attorney must rely, as is claimed by plaintiff in error. It is true there was no specific act proven by the positive and direct testimony of a witness to the transaction, but very strong circumstances were shown which tended to prove the one act of intercourse. Whether any others occurred is merely conjecture.

The state did not introduce Amanda Yoeman as a witness. After its evidence had been produced plaintiff in error called her as a witness in his own behalf. We copy, from the abstract, her testimony, with the rulings of the court, in full:

Question (by attorney for plaintiff in error). I will ask you if you are acquainted with the defendant?

Answer. Yes, sir.

Q. I will ask you if you are the oldest daughter of Gilbert Yoeman?

A. I am.

Q. I will ask you to state whether or not you ever had sexual intercourse with the defendant?

A. No, sir.

There is nothing to show whether the right to cross-examine the witness was waived or suspended. At any rate there was none at that time. After the introduction of other witnesses the defense rested. The district attorney then recalled Amanda Yoeman "for the purpose of cross-examination." To this plaintiff in error at the time objected, but the objection was overruled, to which he ex-

cepted, and now assigns the ruling for error. We are not
informed whether there was any showing made upon the
part of the state or not, but for the purposes of this case we
will assume there was not; and yet we do not think there
was such an abuse of discretion, if any, on the part of the
trial court as to call for a reversal of the judgment on that
ground. A certain reasonable discretion is allowed to the
trial court in the conduct of the trial before it, and so long
as it is not clear that that discretion has been abused to
the prejudice of the party complaining, the action of the
trial court will be upheld. In the matter now under consideration we can detect neither abuse of discretion nor
prejudice to plaintiff in error.

The district attorney then proceeded with the cross-examination of the witness, as follows:

Question. You may state whether or not this is your
signature?

Answer. That is my name.

Q. Did you write it?

A. I think I did.

The state then offered in evidence an affidavit, sworn to
by the witness, in which she deposed that she was pregnant
with a bastard child and that plaintiff in error was its
father. The affidavit was sworn to the 17th day of August, 1883; the complaint in the bastardy proceedings. To
the introduction of the affidavit plaintiff objected, but the
objection was, properly, we think, overruled. Plaintiff in
error then re-examined the witness, as follows:

Question. Here is an affidavit in which it is charged
that John Yoeman is the father of a certain child born to
you. I will ask you if the signature and making of that
affidavit was your voluntary act?

The prosecution objects as not cross-examination, incompetent, and immaterial. Sustained, and defendant excepts.

We are unable to say that 'in this ruling of the court
there was no error. It is true the matter was somewhat

awkwardly presented—the re-examination following, instead of preceding the introduction of the affidavit—but, even in that case an answer to the question ought to have been permitted. The witness had testified that plaintiff in error had not committed the offense with which he was charged. She was then confronted with the affidavit which she had made, and which was directly contradictory of her testimony. The presumption was, that it was voluntarily and deliberately made. If so, the effect would be to impair, if not to destroy, the force of her testimony while on the witness stand. But if made under duress, and against her will, it might not have that effect. It was the right of plaintiff in error to have that question submitted to the jury. Again, as the matter was left, it placed the witness under the direct imputation of perjury, for both statements could not be true. It was therefore due to the witness that she be allowed to explain as to the circumstances under which the affidavit was made. But of this plaintiff in error cannot complain, perhaps, except so far as it affected his defense. But it is claimed that the interrogatory did not refer to the affidavit, the effect of which is given above, for the reason that the attorney in putting it refers to an affidavit which charges plaintiff in error with being the father of a bastard child "born to" her. This does not avoid the force of the exception. The affidavit was the same one which she had verified, and which was then before her. The question was, did she voluntarily make *that* affidavit? It is further contended that the question was improper, for the reason that it called for a conclusion instead of calling for the facts and circumstances surrounding the making of the instrument. It evidently would have been better, and more in accordance with the rules of evidence, to have asked the witness to state the fact without putting to her the question in the direct and leading form. But no objection was made on that ground. The

12

subject of the inquiry was "proper cross-examination." It was "competent" and "material."

For this error plaintiff in error is entitled to a new trial.

The judgment of the district court is reversed and the cause remanded for further proceedings in accordance with law.

REVERSED AND REMANDED.

THE other judges concur.

———

A. W. CRITCHFIELD, PLAINTIFF IN ERROR, v. SYL-VESTER REMALEY, DEFENDANT IN ERROR.

1. **Landlord and Tenant.** Where lands are leased to a tenant for one year for a stipulated rent reserved, and after the expiration of the lease the tenant, without further contract, remains in possession, and is recognized as a tenant by the landlord, in the receipt of rent for another year, this will create a tenancy from year to year.

2. ———: TERMINATION OF TERM. In such case the tenancy can only be terminated by the agreement of the parties, express or implied, or by notice given, six calendar months ending with the period of the year at which the tenancy commenced.

ERROR to the district court for Sarpy county. Tried below before WAKELEY, J.

J. P. Grove, for plaintiff in error.

A. N. Ferguson, for defendant in error.

REESE, J.

This action was one of forcible detainer instituted in the county court of Sarpy county. The cause was tried to a jury which returned a verdict in favor of plaintiff. Judgment for restitution was rendered. Defendant then removed the cause into the district court by proceedings in error. Upon a hearing in that court the judgment of the county court was reversed and the cause retained for trial. From the judgment and order of the district court, plaintiff prosecutes error to this court.

The evidence introduced before the county court was preserved in the form of a bill of exceptions, and upon this the decision of the district court was based. From this it appears that one Schaffer had owned the land on which defendant resided, until about the first day of November, 1885, when he sold it to plaintiff. On the first day of March, 1886, plaintiff served upon defendant the usual notice to quit the premises, and on the 5th day oɩ the same month the action was commenced.

The principal question presented is whether defendant was holding over his term, or whether he was a tenant from year to year. If the former, then the notice served was sufficient. If the latter, it was insufficient, as a notice would have to be served at least six months prior to the end of the year in order to terminate the tenancy at that time. Maxwell's Pl. and Pr., 1885 ed., 615. 2 Greenleaf's Ev., sec. 323. Taylor on Landlord and Tenant, sec. 55, et seq. Id., Sec. 475. *Brown v. Kayser*, 18 N. W. Rep., 523 (Wis). *Doe v. Porter*, 3 T. R., 13.

It is the opinion of a majority of the court that the testimony before the county court shows a tenancy from year to year, and that therefore the action was prematurely brought. This conclusion is based principally upon the testimony of Schaffer, the grantor of plaintiff in error· The witnesses all agree that the lease was by the year. Schaffer testified that he leased the land in question to defendant in the spring of 1884, for one year, and that he never made any later contracts with him. That defendant remained on the land during the year 1885, and paid the same rent as during the year 1884. In November, 1885, Schaffer sold the land to plaintiff in error, who seems to have taken no steps to terminate the tenancy until the service of the notice to quit on the first day of March, 1886.

In Maxwell's Practice in Justice's Courts (1884 ed.) 550, it is said: "When a tenant for a year or any other definite period holds over, no notice, except that required in proceedings for forcible entry and detainer, is necessary, because without a new agreement the tenancy is at an end. But when the owner, after the expiration of that period, does any act recognizing the contiuance of the relation of landlord and tenant, it will create a tenancy from year to year, or for a shorter period, depending somewhat on the nature of the original lease."

In a note to the above it is said: "A tenancy from year to year requires a formal notice by either landlord or tenant to terminate the lease, because where after the expiration of a term for years the tenant remains in possession by consent of the landlord, the law will imply, in the absence of express agreement, that the lease is continued for at least another year; therefore the necessity that notice of a purpose to terminate the lease should be given."

The above quotations are made at length for the reason that it is believed by the writer that they correctly state the law applicable to this case and in apt language. It appears by the testimony that the contract of lease was for one year. That after the expiration of that period Schaffer "recognized the continuance of the relation of landlord and tenant" by the receipt of rent for the second year, and no effort to terminate the lease until the first of March of the third year, without any further agreement. The law will therefore imply, "in the absence of express agreement, that the lease is continued for at least another year," and therefore notice of an intention to terminate the lease was necessary.

It was the opinion of the writer that as the ground of

error upon which the judgment of the county court was
reversed was the 6th assignment of the petition in error,
"That the verdict and judgment ought to have been for the
plaintiff in error, and against the defendant in error,"
which was in substance, that the verdict was not sustained
by the evidence, that the question of the character of the
tenancy was one of fact upon which the verdict of the trial
jury should be final.   But it is quite probable that the testimony relied on by defendant in error could not in any
view sustain the verdict.   At any rate, since the cause stands
for trial in the district court, I consent to the affirmance
of the order complained of.

The order of the district court is affirmed.

JUDGMENT ACCORDINGLY.

THE other judges concur.

$\begin{array}{c|c} \text{21} & \text{181} \\ \text{53} & \text{570} \end{array}$

WARREN O. McCLURE, APPELLEE, V. LUKE LAVENDER
AND E. MARY GREGORY, APPELLANTS.

1. **Error**: PRESUMPTION. Before a judgment or decree will be
    rendered for alleged errors occurring on the trial of the cause
    such errors must be made to appear affirmatively of record'
    Error is never presumed.

2. **Limitation on Tax Lien.** The statute of limitations com-
    mences to run on the right to enforce a lien for taxes when the
    title under the tax deed fails. *Bryant v. Estabrook*, 16 Neb. 217.

3. **Taxes**: FORECLOSURE OF LIEN: NOTICE. Under the provis.
    ions of section 3, article 9, of the Constitution, it is not neces-
    sary to serve a notice on the defendant before bringing a suit
    to enforce a tax lien. *Id.*

APPEAL from the district court for Lancaster county.
Tried below before POUND, J.

J. S. Gregory, for appellant.

W. H. Snelling, for appellee.

REESE, J.

This is an action to foreclose tax liens upon the property described in the petition. The petition consists of a number of counts or paragraphs referring to the different parcels of ground purchased and the amount due on each. It is alleged that tax deeds were executed to plaintiff on the various sales, but that the title has failed and a foreclosure of the tax liens is prayed. So far as the record before us discloses, defendant, Lavender, is not seeking a review of the decree of the district court. The abstract of the answer of defendant, Gregory, shows the following defenses to have been presented: *First.* That the petition contained several causes of action improperly joined. *Second.* Plaintiff's claim is barred by the statute of limitations. *Third.* That defendant has continuously occupied the premises since Sept. 1st, 1874, and no notice of tax lien has been served upon her. *Fourth.* That the levy of taxes was largely made for city purposes as upon city lots within the city of Lincoln, while the land was not a part of the city, and was also assessed as "acre" property. *Fifth.* A general denial of the allegations of the petition not admitted.

The decree of the district court being in favor of plaintiff, defendant Gregory appeals and assigns the following errors: "*First.* The amount of the judgment is grossly in excess of all claims of lien shown by the evidence and pleadings. *Second.* The court erred in refusing to require plaintiff to separately state and number his several causes of action. *Third.* The court erred in refusing to find that the clause of lien was barred by the statute of limitations. *Fourth.* The court erred in admitting in evidence the tax certificates and receipts which were not countersigned by the county clerk.

Fifth. The court erred in refusing to find that the plaintiff is estopped from maintaining this action by the provisions of sections 123 and 129 of chapter 77 of the statutes of Nebraska. *Sixth.* The court erred in giving judgment for lien of city tax for the years prior to the lots becoming a part of the city. *Seventh.* The court should have dismissed the plaintiff's action and given defendants judgment for their costs."

As to the second, fourth, sixth, and seventh assignments of error, it must be sufficient to say that the abstract does not furnish sufficient *data* to enable us to say that there was error. There is nothing shown as to the ruling of the court upon any motion for an order to require plaintiff to separately state and number his causes of action, nor are the tax certificates set out so as to show whether they were signed by the county clerk or not. It is quite probable that such signature is not necessary, as sections 103 and 104 of the revenue law make no such requirement. Neither is there anything before us to show whether or not the property was or was not within the city of Lincoln when taxed, nor whether it was taxed as "acre" property or not. It is well settled, by the adjudications of this court that a judgment will not be reversed unless error affirmatively appears of record, and that presumptions are in favor of the regularity of the proceedings of the trial court.

As to the third assignment of error, we are content to refer to *Bryant v. Estabrook*, 16 Neb., 217, wherein it is held that the statute of limitations commences to run on the right to enforce a lien for taxes when the title under the tax deed fails. See also *County of Otoe v. Mathews*, 18 Neb, 466.

The sixth assignment of error evidently refers to the probable fact that no notice was given to the owner of the property of the expiration of the time for redemption. This was not necessary. *Bryant v. Estabrook, supra.*

As to the first, and only remaining assignment of error,

I have not the time at my disposal to make the necessary computation for the purpose of ascertaining whether the amount found due is too large or not.   There are a great number of payments upon which the interest would have to be computed, and no computation is furnished by appellant.   If she so requests within twenty days, the cause will be referred to an accountant for the purpose of making the computation, and upon his report being filed the decree will be modified to correspond thereto.   In case no such request should be made the decree of the district court will be affirmed as it now is.

JUDGMENT ACCORDINGLY.

THE other judges concur.

JOHN P. A. BENDEXEN, PLAINTIFF IN ERROR, v. DAVID W. FENTON, DEFENDANT IN ERROR.

1. **Taxes** : TAX DEED. A tax deed to be valid must have the official seal of the county treasurer attached. *Sullivan v. Merriam,* 16 Neb., 157.

2. ———: ———: LIMITATION. A tax deed must be valid on its face to entitle the party claiming under it to the benefit of the special limitation of the revenue law. *Housel v. Boggs,* 17 Neb., 94.

ERROR to the district court for Douglas county.   Tried below before WAKELEY, J.

C. A. Baldwin, for plaintiff in error.

Warren Switzler, for defendant in error.

REESE, J.

This was an action in ejectment.   Plaintiff in error, who was defendant below, bases his title on a treasurer's tax deed, dated February 6, 1878, for the taxes of 1874. On the trial he offered his deed in evidence, to which objection was made, principally for the reason that it was not under the seal of the county treasurer. The objection was sustained, the deed excluded, and plaintiff in error assigns this ruling of the district court for error.

In deciding as it did the district court followed the cases of *Sullivan v. Merriam* 16 Neb., 157. *Shelley v. Towle,* Id., 194, and *Baldwin v. Merriam,* Id., 199. But plaintiff in error contends that the rule announced in those cases is wrong and should not be followed; that they are technical and do not give expression to the legislative intent as contained in section 67 of the revenue law of 1869, General Statutes, page 923.

We must admit that the rule applied is somewhat technical, but yet we believe it to be correct, and in accord with the holding of courts generally in this country. We do not care to enter into an elaborate discussion of the question, as we are satisfied with the reasons given in the cases cited, but we are reminded that those decisions voice an express provision of the statute which the legislature, for reasons of its own, saw fit to embody therein. As said in *Sullivan v. Merriam,* "a tax deed is executed under a naked power which must be strictly complied with." It is an exercise of the sovereign power of the government by which it appropriates the property of the citizens to the support of the commonwealth. Taxes are assessed and levied upon all property alike, and in this the burden is uniform; but if the taxes are not paid by the owner, then the property is sold for the taxes due without any reference to the relation the price may bear to the value. A few dollars is the price paid for property which is often worth as many thousands. It is the exercise of corporate power whereby it is sought to divest the owner of valuable property for a mere pittance. This was fully understood by the legislature, and was no doubt the reason why a strict compliance with apparent technical requirements was made necessary. But it is urged that by the law then in force the treasurer had no seal, and hence the requirement referred to could not be complied with. To this we can only say, that if the law made no provision for a compliance with its own mandatory provisions, it was an oversight with which the courts have nothing to do. It is enough to know that the requirements exist.

The right to sell property for taxes is one which must exist in order that the public revenues may be collected, but it seems to the writer that the many advantages given to the purchaser of property at tax sale by our statutes clearly indicate that it has not been the intent of the legislature that the property owner should be divested of his title thereto without ample opportunity being given for redemption, and yet that absolute security and a good interest should be given to the purchaser. By law taxes are made a perpetual lien on real estate. A liberal interest is allowed on the money invested in the purchase, and the right of foreclosure is given to the holder of the certificate of sale. All this, too, untrammeled by any advantage which might be sought by reason of any irregularity in the assessment or levy. The principal inquiries are, Was the property subject to taxation? Had the taxes been paid by the owner? Was the taxation substantially uniform, and was no more than a proper proportion levied against the property taxed? If so, the holder of the tax certificate, or deed, has absolute security for his investment and a higher rate of interest than can be obtained in any other real estate loan. I do not hesitate to say that no fairer nor better system for the collection of revenues can be had than has been built up in this state by the legislature, and the construction placed upon our laws by the courts.

These reflections are perhaps not strictly germain to the question in hand, except in so far as they logically lead to the conclusion to which we have arrived, to-wit, that a

strict compliance with the letter as well as of the spirit of the
law is necessary to divest the owner of his title, but that
the payment of the taxes, interest, and costs without reference to any irregularity in the exercise of the taxing power
must be made. We do not hesitate to say that, considering
the revenue laws of the state, and the advantages very properly given to purchasers at tax sale, it is the imperative
duty of the courts to require a most strict and technical
compliance with the law before title can be acquired for
taxes alone. We adhere to the decisions referred to.

The plaintiff in error by his brief insists that his possession is protected by the statute of limitations as prescribed in section 134 of the present revenue law. Comp.
Stats., Ch. 77. It is quite probable that if the three years'
limitation had been applicable to this case, it would have
been. Section 105, page 933, Gen. Stats., 1873. But as no
title passed by the deed the statute does not apply, and
plaintiff could acquire no title until the expiration of ten
years. *Housel v. Boggs*, 17 Neb., 94. *Towle v. Holt*, 14
Neb., 221.

The judgment of the district court is affirmed.

JUDGMENT AFFIRMED.

THE other judges concur.

THE STATE OF NEBRASKA, EX REL. OMAHA & REPUBLI-
CAN VALLEY RAILROAD COMPANY, v. H. A. BAB-
COCK, AUDITOR OF PUBLIC ACCOUNTS.

Internal Improvements: BONDS: PRECINCT BONDS: ELEC-
TION. Under the provisions of section 14, chapter 45, of the
Compiled Statutes of 1885, to authorize the county commissioners to call a special precinct election for the purpose of
voting bonds in a precinct in aid of works of internal improve-

ments, etc., a petition signed by not less than fifty freeholders of such precinct must be presented to such county commissioners, setting forth the nature of the work contemplated, the amount of bonds sought to be voted, the rate of interest, and the date when the principal and interest shall become due. An election called and held without such petition is of no validity.

ORIGINAL application for mandamus.

Williams, Jencks, and Redlon, for relator.

William Leese, Attorney General, for respondent.

MAXWELL, CH. J.

This is an application for a peremptory writ of mandamus to compel the defendant, as auditor of public accounts, to certify certain bonds issued by Dannebrog precinct to the relator. The case is submitted upon the following stipulation of facts:

"1.   That the plaintiff is a railway corporation, organized and existing under the laws of the state of Nebraska, and the corporate successor to the Omaha & Republican Valley Railroad Company, and to all its rights, franchises, properties, and lines of railway, and appurtenances thereunto belonging.

"That the defendant, H. A. Babcock, is the duly elected and qualified auditor of public accounts of the state of Nebraska, and has been performing the duties of such office since the first Thursday after the first Tuesday in the month of January, 1884.

"3.   That Dannebrog precinct was duly erected and denominated as a precinct of Howard county, Nebraska, prior to the 27th day of April, 1885, and that Howard county is duly organized as such county under the laws of the state of Nebraska.

"4.   That on the 27th day of April, 1885, twenty-seven taxpayers and citizens of said Dannebrog precinct petitioned the county commissioners of said Howard county to call a special election in said precinct for the purpose of voting on a proposition to issue bonds of said precinct in the sum of $13,000, to aid the Omaha and Republican Valley Railroad Company in the construction and equipment of its line of railroad through said precinct upon the line specified in the copy of said proposition. * * *

"5. That no bond was executed or filed conditioned to save the said Howard county harmless against the payment of the expenses of such election in case the said proposition should fail to receive the required number of votes to secure its adoption.

"6. That on the 27th day of April, 1885, the Omaha and Republican Valley Railroad Company, by its duly authorized agent, filed in the office of the county commissioners of said Howard county, a proposition to the qualified electors of said Dannebrog precinct, to vote the bonds of such precinct in the sum of thirteen thousand dollars, to aid the company in the construction of its line of railroad through said precinct on the line of route specified in the copy of the proposition. * * * * * *

"7. That on the 14th day of May, 1885, the said county commissioners, in lawful session, called a special election to be holden in said precinct on the 23d day of June, 1885, for the purpose of submitting said proposition to the qualified electors of said precinct.

"8. That due and legal notice of such election, together with said proposition, was published for the time and in the manner and form required by law, and a copy of said proposition was duly posted up at the polls during said day of election.

"9. That said election was held at the time and place designated in said call and notice.

"10. That the result of said election was duly returned and canvassed as required by law, and that the result thereof was duly certified to the said county commissioners, and that the whole number of votes cast at said election in favor of said proposition was two hundred and thirty-three, and that the whole number of votes cast thereat against said proposition was thirty-nine.

"11. That thereupon the said county commissioners declared said proposition adopted, and ordered the same, together with the result of said election, to be spread at large upon the commissioner's record of said county, and ordered notice thereof to be published for the time and manner required by law, all of which was done accordingly.

"12. That the plaintiff and its said corporate predecessor have done and performed all things on their part required by law with reference to the submission of said proposition, and to the construction, equipment, completion, and operation of plaintiff's said line of railroad to insure the issuance to it of valid and subsisting bonds under said proposition; and that prior to the 27th day of November, 1885, the plaintiff had fully complied on its part with all the terms and conditions of such proposition, and that from a time prior to the last-named date, until the present time, the inhabitants of said Dannebrog precinct have been in the enjoyment of the benefits derived from the daily operation of plaintiff's said line of railroad.

"13. That on the 27th day of November, 1885, the county commissioners of said Howard county executed and issued the bonds of said Dannebrog precinct in the aggregate sum of thirteen thousand dollars, under the terms and conditions of said proposition, and delivered the same to the plaintiff, and that the aggregate sum of such bonds is within the limit of the per cent of the valuation of the property of such precinct that may be legally voted by and issued against the same for such purpose.

"14. That at the time the said citizens and taxpayers of said precinct presented their said petition to the county commissioners of said county, and at the time said election was ordered as aforesaid, the act of the legislature of the state of Nebraska entitled 'An act to authorize precincts, townships, and villages to vote bonds to aid works of internal improvements—highways, railroads, bridges, courthouses, jails, and the drainage of swamp lands, and to repeal section 7 of chapter 45 of the Compiled Statutes of Nebraska, entitled, 'Internal Improvements,' approved March 6th, 1885, had not been published according to law, nor otherwise promulgated, and the qualified voters voting at said election had no notice of any defect in the record of the proceedings in relation to the issuance of said bonds.

"15. That the failure on the part of the freeholders of said precinct to present to the commissioners of said county a petition signed by fifty of their number, asking that said election be called, and their failure to execute and deliver to said commissioners a bond signed by them, conditional to save the said county harmless against the payment of the expenses of said election if the proposition should fail of adoption, cannot be said to have changed or affected the result of said election in any way whatever.

"16. That on the ...... day of ......, 188..., prior to the commencement of this action, the plaintiff, by its authorized agent, presented said bonds, together with a duly certified statement of all the proceedings had with reference to the execution and issuance of said bonds, to the defendant, H. A. Babcock, in his official capacity as such auditor, with the request that he register and certify the same in manner required by law, which request was refused by him, and said bonds are still unregistered and uncertified, and that the plaintiff is otherwise remediless.

"17. That the sole ground of objection on the part of the said defendant, H. A. Babcock, to the registration and the certification of said bonds is that the petition and bond mentioned in paragraph 15 of this stipulation were not presented and filed in accordance with the provisions of section 14 of chapter 45 of the Compiled Statutes of Nebraska of 1885, he claiming that the certified statement filed in his office should show that said petition and bond were duly presented and filed—the plaintiff claiming that said bonds ought to be registered and certified, notwithstanding the failure to present such petition and bond, and that the provisions of said section 14 requiring said petition and bond to be presented are unconstitutional and void.

"18. The court is requested to consider and determine all questions of law, whether constitutional, statutory, or otherwise, that may be presented with reference to the foregoing statement of facts, to the end that the matters of contention between the parties may be fully adjusted, and a rule of action be established for the defendant, H. A. Babcock, in the further discharge of his official duties; and it is agreed that if the court should find that the provisions of section 14 of chapter 45 of the Compiled Statutes of Nebraska of 1885 requiring a petition signed by fifty freeholders, and a bond to be executed by them conditioned as aforesaid, are unconstitutional and void, or if the court should find that the said precinct bonds ought to be registered and certified, notwithstanding such petition and bond were not presented, then, in either event, a peremptory writ of mandamus shall issue directed to the defendant, H. A. Babcock, requiring him to register and certify said precinct bonds as required by law, otherwise this action shall be dismissed at plaintiff's cost."

It will be observed that the principal question for determination is the right of the county commissioners to call a special election for the purpose of voting bonds, without a petition duly signed by the requisite number of freeholders presented to them for that purpose.

Section 14 of chapter 45 of the Compiled Statutes of 1885 provides that, "Any precinct, township, or village (less than a city of the second class), organized according to law, is hereby authorized to issue bonds in aid of works of internal improvement, highways, bridges, railroads, courthouses, jails in any part of the county, and the drainage of swamps and wet lands, to an extent not exceeding ten per cent of the assessed value of the taxable property at the last assessment, within such township, precinct, or village, in the manner hereinafter directed, viz.: 1st. A petition signed by not less than fifty freeholders of the precinct, township, or village shall be presented to the county commissioners, or board authorized by law to attend to the business of the county within which such precinct, township, or village is situated. Said petition shall set forth the nature of the work contemplated, the amount of the bonds sought to be voted, the rate of interest, which shall in no event exceed eight per cent per annum, and the date when the principal and interest shall become due; and the said petitioners shall give bond, to be approved by the county commissioners, for the payment of the expenses of the election in the event that the proposition shall fail to receive a two-thirds majority of the votes cast at the election. 2d. Upon the reception of such petition the county commissioners shall give notice and call an election in the precinct, township, or village, as the case may be. Said notice, call, and election shall be governed by the law regulating the election for voting bonds by the county."

Under this section the authority of the county commissioner to call a special election for the purpose of voting precinct bonds, is based upon the fact that a petition, signed by not less than fifty freeholders of the precinct, has been presented to the county commissioners, which petition shall set forth the nature of the work contemplated, the amount of bonds sought to be voted, the rate of interest, and the time when the principal and interest shall become due. It is only upon the reception of such a petition that the commissioners have authority to call an election for the purpose of voting bonds in the precinct. It is claimed on behalf of the relator, that the section above quoted, so far as it requires a petition signed by fifty freeholders, to authorize the county commissioners to call an election, is in conflict

13

with the constitution, because it restricts the right of suffrage, and therefore it is void.

A county or any of its subdivisions has no inherent right to vote bonds. *Hamlin v. Meadville*, 6 Neb., 227. *Hallenbeck v. Hahn*, 2 Neb., 397. The right, therefore, is derived entirely from the statute, the terms of which must be substantially complied with. The effect of voting and issuing bonds by a precinct, is to create a lien upon all the realty of such precinct for the payment of such bonds and interest. It is eminently proper, therefore, that at least fifty freeholders of such precinct should certify to the county commissioners their desire to have such incumbrance placed upon their property. At the election duly called, in pursuance of a petition filed as above, all legal voters of the precinct have the right to vote, whether freeholders or not. It would be possible, therefore, if the petition was dispensed with, for transient persons, temporarily stopping in the precinct, but having no permanent interest in its prosperity, to vote bonds on such precinct to the extent of its legal liability, to the payment of which they would contribute nothing. It is a condition precedent, therefore, to the right of the commissioners to call a precinct election for the purpose of voting bonds of such precinct, that a petition signed by fifty freeholders thereof, stating the facts required by the statute, be presented to such commissioners for that purpose. Whether the failure to give bonds for the payment of the expenses of the election, in the event that the proposition fail to receive a two-thirds majority of the votes cast at such election, would affect the validity of such bonds if voted, we need not now determine. The proper course, however, is for the commissioners to require such bonds in all cases. These provisions of the statute are not in conflict with the consititution, and are valid. As no lawful petition was presented to the county commissioners they had no authority to call the election in question, and the proceedings were void. *People v. Hamilton Co.*, 3 Neb., 244. The writ must therefore be denied.

WRIT DENIED.

THE other judges concur.

THOMAS PRICE ET AL., PLAINTIFF IN ERROR, V. RUFUS F. McCOMAS, DEFENDANT IN ERROR.

1. **Chattel Mortgage**: DESCRIPTION OF PROPERTY. On January 9th, 1885, one A. executed a chattel mortgage to one P. on certain cattle, described as follows: "Ten head of two-year-old past steers, valued at thirty-five dollars per head. * * * * The above described chattels are now in my possession, are owned by me, and are free from all incumbrances in all respects." And on the next day said A. executed a chattel mortgage to one M. on nine head of cattle, described as follows: "Nine head of two and three-year-old steers situate on farm, south of Bennet, Nebraska, 1¼ miles. The above described chattels are now in my possession, are owned by me, and are free from all incumbrances in all respects." A., at the time of executing said mortgages, possessed ninety-eight head of steers of the description named on his farm south of Bennet, and the steers mortgaged were not separated from the others, but the description applied equally to the ninety-eight steers owned by A. *Held*, First, that the mortgages created no liens upon any specific steers, and, as against an attaching creditor, were a nullity.

2. ———: ATTACHMENT: RIGHTS OF CREDITOR. The fact that before the levy of the attachment, certain steers had been separated from the whole number and claimed under the second mortgage, would be unavailing as against such creditor, unless it was also shown that at the time the mortgage was executed there was an agreement that it should apply to such steers.

ERROR to the district court for Lancaster county. Tried below before HAYWARD, J.

. *N. C. Abbott* and *O. P. Mason*, for plaintiff in error.

Edwin F. Warren, for defendant in error.

MAXWELL, CH. J.

In July, 1885, the defendant in error filed a petition in
the district court of Lancaster county, claiming a special
ownership in nine head of two and three-year-old steers by
virtue of a chattel mortgage made by one Robert Arundale, dated Jan. 15, 1885, and filed for record Jan. 13,
1885, in which the plaintiffs in error are charged with the
conversion of said steers, and judgment is prayed for their
value.

The defendants below (plaintiffs in error), in their answer, claim said property by virtue of a chattel mortgage
executed by said Arundale to Thomas Price, January
9, 1885, and filed for record January 12, 1885.   They
also claim by virtue of an attachment levied on said
cattle April 9, 1885.   On the trial of the cause it was admitted in open court that on and prior to the 9th day of
January, 1885, one Robert Arundale was the owner of the
cattle in controversy, and that on said day he executed and
delivered to plaintiff Price a chattel mortgage on certain
property in said mortgage described as "ten head of two-
year-old-past steers, valued at thirty-five dollars per head.
    *   *   *   The above described chattels are now in my
possession, are owned by me, and free from all incumbrances in all respects." Said mortgage was given to secure
the payment of a certain promissory note for the sum of
six hundred ninety-one and fifteen-hundredths dollars, due
and payable.   Said mortgage was on the 10th day of January, 1885, duly filed for record.   Said note and mortgage
was, before due, transferred to one R. C. Outcalt, who was
the owner thereof at the time of the alleged conversion.
That on or about the 9th day of April, 1885, said Outcalt

put said mortgage into the hands of plaintiff Melick for collection and foreclosure, and under said mortgage said Melick took possession of the property described in petition for the purpose of foreclosing the same.

That on or about the 9th day of April, 1885, plaintiff Price, then being a creditor of said Arundale, sued out of the district court of Lancaster county, Nebraska, a writ of attachment against said Arundale for the sum of twelve hundred dollars, which writ was put into the hands of plaintiff Melick, and by him levied upon the property in question, together with other property, as the property of Robert Arundale, and then and there took possession of said property, and held the same by virtue of said chattel mortgage and writ of attachment. The court rendered judgment in the sum of four hundred thirty-nine and fifty-hundredths dollars, in favor of the defendant in error.

The principal error relied upon for the reversal of the judgment is that it is not sustained by the evidence. The testimony tends to show that at the time the mortgage from Arundale to Price was executed, on January 9th, 1885, and and at the time the mortgage from Arundale to McComas was executed, January 10th, 1885, Arundale had on his farm "ninety-eight head of two-year-old steers, coming three," and that the mortgage from Arundale to Price and from Arundale to McComas did not designate any particular steers, the description in the mortgage from Arundale to McComas being "nine head of two and three-year-old steers, situate on farm south of Bennet, Neb., eleven miles. The above described chattels are now in my possession, are owned by me, and free from all incumbrance in all respects."

The description of the property intended to be mortgaged should be such as to distinguish it from other chattels, or should contain some hint to direct such parties as may examine the mortgage to any source of information beyond the words of the same. The description should be such as to enable third parties to identify the property, aided by inquiries which the mortgage itself indicates and directs. *Elder v. Miller*, 60 Me., 118. *Skowhegan Bank v. Farrar*, 46 Id., 293. *Chapin v. Cram*, 40 Id., 561. Herman on Chat. Mort., 574. The general rule is that the description is sufficient if it will enable a third person, aided by inquiries which the instrument itself suggests, to identify the property. Jones, Chattel Mortgages, sec. 54. *Tolbert v. Horton*, 31 Minn., 518. *Tolbert v. Horton*, 33 Minn., 104. *Smith v. McLean*, 24 Iowa, 322. *Yant v. Harvey*, 55 Iowa, 421.

There is no suggestion in the mortgage that the steers mortgaged were all the steers of that age owned by the mortgagor, and in his possession on his farm south of Bennet, nor that they were separated from the whole number of steers and confined in an enclosure by themselves. The description in each mortgage would apply to all the steers owned by the mortgagor on his farm. No case has been cited showing that such a description is valid as against creditors, and we think no such case can be found.

It is claimed, however, that the defendant in error having separated the cattle alleged by him to be mortgaged, from the others, therefore the description was rendered sufficient, and that a chattel mortgage may be created by parol. It is enough to say that he was not claiming under a parol chattel mortgage, but under the one executed Jan. 10, 1885, and then on file in the county clerk's office, and the testimony fails to show that these identical steers, claimed by him under the mortgage, were the ones actually mortgaged. There is a failure of proof, therefore, to sustain the judgment in favor of the defendant in error, and the description in both mortgages is wholly insufficient. The lien acquired by Price, therefore, by the levy of his attachment is superior to the right of the defendant in error. The judgment of the district court is reversed, and the cause remanded for further proceedings.

REVERSED AND REMANDED.

THE other judges concur.

21 199
23 359
21 199
31 456
21 199
35 366
21 199
37 811
21 199
47 118
48 689
21 199
49 190
21 199
57 290

DAVID L. SNOWDEN AND CHARLES SNOWDEN, APPELLEES, v. ELLA M. TYLER, ET ALS., IMP., ETC., APPELLANTS.

1. **Real Estate:** TITLE: EJECTMENT. The remedy for the recovery of real estate by one claiming the legal title thereto against one in possession claiming an estate therein, is an action of ejectment in which the facts may be submitted to a jury; and an action to quiet title, if properly objected to, will not lie.

2. ———: ACTION QUIA TIMET: JURISDICTION. Where a party out of possession of real estate brings an action to quiet title, and the defendant answers, alleging a cloud upon his title, caused by the plaintiff's deed, and prays for a decree cancelling the same, the court will have jurisdiction to determine the title of the respective parties. A defect which appears on the face of the petition should be taken advantage of by demurrer.

3. ———: QUIT-CLAIM DEED: RIGHTS OF BONA FIDE PURCHASER. A quit-claim deed of real estate, while affording cause of suspicion may, where it appears in a chain of title on the proper records of the county, be sufficient to justify a *bona fide* purchaser for a valuable consideration in relying upon it as a valid conveyance. It is a *bona fide* purchaser for valuable consideration, and not a donee, who is protected.

4. ———: ———: CASE STATED. One Shirk, in 1862, conveyed certain real estate to one Snowden, who failed to record his deed. In 1866, Snowden died, and in 1870 one Poe sought to purchase the land of Shirk, but was informed that it had been sold and conveyed to Snowden. Poe then applied to the adult heirs and administrator of the estate of Snowden, and the guardian of the minor heirs, and was informed that the deed in question had been lost or destroyed. Poe thereupon purchased the land,

taking deeds from the adult heirs, and with their consent, a
quit-claim deed from Shirk, which last deed he placed on record;
Held, That a *bona fide* purchaser for a valuable consideration
from a grantee of Poe took the title as against an heir, who was
a minor at the time the deed from Shirk was obtained; but that
a mere donee from Poe was not so entitled.

5. ———: ADVERSE OCCUPANCY: REDEMPTION BY HEIRS. Where
heirs come into a court of equity to claim an interest in lands,
which has not been conveyed, but which lands have been held
adversely by other parties for a long period, they must do equity
by paying a just proportion of the taxes and the interest due
thereon.

6. ———: PURCHASER PENDENTE LITE. A purchaser *pendente
lite* from a purchaser who bought without notice, and for a valuable consideration, may protect himself under the first purchaser.

APPEAL from the district court of Otoe county. Heard
below before MITCHELL, J.

Edwin F. Warren, for appellant.

1. A quit-claim deed acts as an estoppel. *Franklin v. Kelley,* 2 Neb., 111. The holder of title under a quit-claim is
protected by statute. *Morris v. Daniels,* 35 O. St., 406,
420. A quit-claim deed in a chain of title does not deprive him who claims under it of the character of a *bona
fida* purchaser.. *Chapman v. Sims,* 53 Miss., 154. *Brown
v. Banner Coal Co.,* 97 Ill., 215. *McConnel v. Reed,* 4
Scam., 117. *Morgan v. Clayton,* 61 Ill., 40. *Bradbury
v. Davis,* 5 Col., 265. *Fox v. Hall,* 74 Mo., 315. *Wil-
lingham v. Hardin,* 75 Mo., 429; Id., 383. *Springer v.
Bartle,* 54 Ia., 476.

2. A purchaser *pendente lite,* from one who was himself
a purchaser *bona fide,* or even a fraudulent grantee from
such a holder, is protected. A purchaser with knowledge of
equities who buys from one who was an innocent purchaser
for value holds the estate free as his grantor did. *West-
brook v. Gleason,* 79 N. Y., 31. *Varrick v. Briggs,* 6

Paige, 323. *Foot v. Burch*, 5 Denio, 187. *Wood v. Chapin*, 13 N. Y., 509. *Collins v. Heath*, 34 Ga., 443. *Choutcau v. Jones*, 11 Ill., 300. *Erskine v. Decker*, 39 Me., 467. *Fasset v. Smith*, 23 N. Y., 252. *Dexter v. Harris*, 2 Mass., 531. *Crocker v. Bellange*, 6 Wis., 645. *Lowther v. Carleton*, 2 Atk., 242.

3. Innocent purchasers from fraudulent grantees will be protected. *Colquit v. Thomas*, 8 Ga., 258. *Grimstone v. Carter*, 3 Paige, 421. *Scarlett v. Graham*, 28 Ill., 319. *Snyder v. Roberts*, 13 Tex., 598. *Erskine v. Decker*, 39 Me., 467. *Miller v. Fraley*, 23 Ark., 735. *Lea v. Polk Co.*, 21 How. (U. S.), 493. *Brown v. Budd*, 2 Ind., 442. *Godfrey v. Disbrow*, Walker (Mich.), 270. *Holmes v. Stout*, 4 N. J. Eq., 492. *Bumpus v. Platner*, 1 John. Ch., 213. *Garavyn v. Bryant*, 83 Ill., 376; 84 Id., 451; 85 Id., 597. *Corbin v. Sulliran*, 47 Ind., 356. *Stout v. Hyatt*, 13 Kan., 232.

4. Title resting on priority of record of a second deed will prevail against title through a prior unrecorded deed from the same original grantor if any one of the mesne purchasers through whom the former title comes purchased in good faith and for a valuable consideration, without notice of said prior unrecorded deed. *Shotwell v. Harrison*, 22 Mich., 410. *Godfrey v. Disbrow*, 2 Walker Ch., 260. *Pringle v. Dunn*, 37 Wis., 443. *Coffin v. Ray*, 1 Met., 212. *Glidden v. Hurst*, 24 Pick., 221. *Boynton v. Rees*, 8 Pick., 329. And the subsequent recording of a prior deed will not affect purchasers under the prior title. *Somes v. Brewer*, 2 Pick., 184. *Trull v. Bigelow*, 16 Mass., 406. *Hardin v. Harrington*, 11 Bush. (Ky.), 367, and authorities *supra*.

5. For further authorities upon the subject of notice, see: *Low v. Blinco*, 10 Bush (Ky.), 331. *Losey v. Simpson*, 11 N. J. Eq., 246. *Long v. Dollarhide*, 24 Cal., 218. *Chicago v. Witt*, 75 Ill., 211; Id., 354. *Ritzer v. Rankin*, 77 Ill., 289. *Houston v. Stombumer*, 92 Ill., 75; 32 Id.,

529. *Mayhem v. Crombs*, 14 O. St., 428.   *Ogle v. Tur-pin*, 102 Ill., 152.

S. H. Calhoun, for appellees.

MAXWELL, CH. J.

The plaintiffs brought an action against the defendants in the district court of Otoe county, and alleged in their petition—

"That in January, 1867, one Elijah Snowden—the father of the said plaintiffs—died at his residence in Indiana, a widower, and seized of the following described real estate situate in Otoe county, Nebraska, to-wit: Section twenty-three (23) township seven (7) range eleven (11) E., containing 640 acres.

"That said Elijah Snowden, at his death, left the following children: Adaline, now the wife of Samuel J. Leedy; Catharine, now the wife of Sylvester Snodgrass; Margaret, now the wife of James S. Ford; Sally, now the wife of Joseph Leedy; William T. Snowden, and the plaintiffs. That the above-named were all his children surviving him, and were and are his heirs at law. That the said Elijah Snowden derived his title to said real estate from one Elbert H. Shirk, by warranty deed, dated July 25, 1862. That said Shirk derived his title from one Barrett Blue, by warranty deed, dated December 11, 1860; that said Blue derived his title thereto from the United States under an entry made June 21, 1860, and a patent dated October 9, 1860.

"That said Elijah Snowden left no other estate in Nebraska; that all the balance was exhausted in the payment of his debts and expenses of settling his estate; that it was long doubtful whether or not said described lands in Nebraska would also have to be sold in order to pay his debts, but the same were finally settled out of his other property.

This estate was fully settled in the proper tribunals in the state of Indiana, in March, 1882.

"That the above-named children of said Elijah inherited said land as his sole surviving heirs at law, became joint tenants thereof; that since said joint tenancy begun said Sallie Leedy has conveyed all her interest therein to her brother David L. Snowden, who now holds and owns two-sevenths thereof; that Adaline Leedy, Catharine Snodgrass, Margaret Ford, and their respective husbands, and William T. Snowden, have each declined to become plaintiffs, and are therefore made defendants.

"That Ella M. Tyler, formerly Ella M. Poe, and C. L. Tyler, her husband, and E. E. Lyle, and Joseph Mastalka and Herman Floerke, and Connoy Hanks, have set up a claim or claims to said tract of land, and pretended to be owners thereof; that said pretended claim or claims are based upon a pretended quit-claim deed from said Elbert H. Shirk to one Adam Poe; that said quit-claim deed conveyed no right in and to said tract of land, nor to any one claiming by, through or under him, as do the defendants; that said pretended quit-claim deed was of a date long subsequent to the warranty deed from said Shirk to said Elijah Snowden, and that the same was and is a gross fraud upon the rights of said heirs at law in and to said land, and is a cloud upon the title of said heirs in and to the same; that the said defendants pretend to have made some division among themselves of their grantors of said tract of land, and to hold separate and distinct tracts based upon said pretended quit-claim deed from Shirk to Poe, and that by reason thereof the real owners of said land are and will be unable to obtain for said land, or for any portion or portions thereof, the full market value therefor, and will be inconvenienced and hindered in the exercise of their legal rights thereto.

"Wherefore said plaintiffs pray that the said pretended quit-claim deed from Shirk to Adam Poe, and all subsequent deeds from said Poe or any of his grantees, either remote or immediate, may be declared to be a cloud or clouds upon the title of the heirs of said Elijah Snowden deceased; that the same may be set aside and held for naught, and the said defendants Tyler, Lyle, Mastalka, Floerke, and Hanks, may be declared to have held said property as the trustees of, and for the said heirs of Elijah Snowden, deceased; that an accounting may be had, and that the proper parties may be put into the undisturbed and uninterrupted possession and sole control of the same, and for general relief in equity."

ANSWER OF CONNOY HANKS.

" Answer filed in said court October 11, 1884.

" 1.   Denies each and every allegation not expressly admitted hereinafter.

" 2.   Alleges that he is the owner in fee simple, and in the open, notorious, and undisturbed possession of the north-east quarter of section 23, town 7, range 11 east, in said county, being a portion of the same premises described in amended petition; that his said title thereto is derived through and from one Elbert H. Shirk mentioned in the petition, and is adverse, hostile, and independent of and paramount to the pretended title of the said plaintiffs and those under whom they claim, as set out in the petition; that this defendant, and those under whom he claims, have been in the quiet and peaceable possession of said above-described quarter section of land since September 19, 1870, claiming to own the same adversely to all the world by paramount title; that under their said title defendant and those under whom he claims have owned, occupied, and enjoyed the same and every part thereof for more than ten years next preceding the commencement of this action, wherefore the defendant pleads the bar of the statute of limitation.

" 3.   Alleges further that one Lefford H. Purcell was his

grantor, by deed dated December 23, 1882, said deed filed for record in said Otoe county, January 6th, 1883; that defendant paid said Purcell therefor $700 cash, and entered into possession; that at the date of said purchase defendant was entirely ignorant of any claims or demands of said plaintiffs in or to said quarter section; that said Purcell purchased the same October 25, 1881, of one Charles F. Weibke for the sum of $1,500; that said Weibke purchased the same of one George L. Bittinger, June 21, 1875, for $1,600; that said Bittinger purchased the same, including other lands, of one G. Z. Rayhouser, July 14, 187.., for the sum of $2,600; that said Rayhouser purchased the same including other lands, August 4, 1873, of L. F. D'Gette and E. F. Warren, for $2,800; that said D'Gette and said Warren purchased the same from Adam W. Poe, December 1, 1870, for $500; that each of the several deeds aforementioned were recorded in the office of clerk of Otoe county immediately after the execution and delivery. That said several owners, to-wit, Purcell, Weibke, Bittinger, and Rayhouser, were each an innocent purchaser of said premises for value without any knowledge or information of any claim or interest therein on the part of said plaintiffs or anybody else adverse to them. Wherefore defendant pleads and insists that he and his grantors were and are *bona fide* purchasers for value without knowledge or information of the alleged claims of the said plaintiffs, and he is entitled to protection therein as innocent purchaser; that said Poe, claimed to be, and was a purchaser of said lands for value from said Shirk, by deed dated Sept. 19, 1870, recorded in Otoe county clerk's office Sept. 23, 1870. That the alleged deed from said Shirk to said Elijah Snowden, mentioned in the petition as executed July 25, 1862, was not filed for record in said clerk's office before July 14, 1879; that neither defendant nor either of his grantors since said Poe had any knowledge, information or suspicion of said alleged deed from Shirk to Snowden, until a time after it had been recorded as aforesaid in 1879; that defendant was advised by counsel learned in the law that the legal title to said land was vested in his grantor, the said Purcell, and that he could safely purchase the same notwithstanding said deed from Shirk to Snowden, wherefore said last mentioned deed is wholly void and of no effect as against this defendant's title therein.

"4. Alleges on information and belief, that in 1870, one Adam W. Poe, one of the grantors in the chain of title, desired to purchase the whole of section 23, township 7, range 11, aforesaid—which includes defendant's land—of one Elbert H. Shirk, the then apparent owner thereof as shown by records of Otoe county; that said Shirk informed Poe that he had previously sold same to Elijah Snowden then deceased; that thereupon the said Poe and the heirs of said Snowden, including the plaintiffs, agreed upon the purchase price of said section of land, to-wit, $2,000, and the delinquent taxes thereon, which said sum of $2,000 Poe then and there paid to said heirs, including plaintiffs, or to their agent by their direction, said sum being full market value of said land at that time. That thereupon it was agreed between said Poe and said heirs, including the plaintiffs, that in consideration of said sum said Shirk should execute and deliver to said Poe a quitclaim deed to said lands for the expressed consideration of one dollar, the supposed or alleged deed from said Shirk to said Snowden having been, as was said, lost or destroyed, and never recorded. That the same was accordingly done; that thereupon the said heirs of said Snowden, including the said plaintiffs, executed and delivered to said Poe a deed or deeds for their supposed interest in said lands, which said deed also was never recorded. That said $2,000 was paid and deeds executed about September 19, 1870. That said Poe, for value received, conveyed certain portions of said section to said D'Gette and said Warren as aforesaid. That none of the facts stated in this paragraph

were known to this defendant or to either of his grantors
subsequent to said D'Gette and said Warren, but that he
and they and each of them were purchasers in good faith
for value without knowledge of any facts or statements
that the said plaintiffs or any of the heirs of said Snowden,
or any one else, had or claimed any interest in said lands.

" 5.   Alleges that at the date of the purchase of said
lands by said Poe, they were incumbered by taxes delinquent and unpaid, and had been sold therefor on Sept. 7,
1868; that said Poe, the said D'Gette and Warren, and
other successive owners as herein before mentioned, have
paid to redeem said described quarter section—the N. E. ¼
Sec. 23, 7, 11, and for subsequent taxes assessed thereon,
the sums at the dates following, to-wit:

Oct.	8, 1870	paid to redeem		$101 62
Oct.	8, 1870	"	tax of 1868	17 19
June	30, 1870	"	" 1869	22 69
April	19, 1871	"	" 1870	34 80
April	26, 1872	"	" 1871	36 12
Aug.	5, 1873	"	" 1872	33 59
Oct.	23, 1874	"	" 1873	31 06
March	27, 1875	"	" 1874	22 40
June	19, 1876	"	" 1875 ·	25 22
Oct.	22, 1877	"	" 1876	29 13
Nov.	1, 1878	"	" 1877	22 07
Feb.	14, 1880	"	" 1878	21 16
Oct.	29, 1880	"	" 1879	22 53
April	29, 1882	"	" 1880	26 31
April	29, 1882	"	" 1881	20 14
July	21, 1883	"	" 1882	23 59
May	20, 1884	"	" 1883	21 43
	Tax of 1884, due and unpaid			31 37

Aggregating the sum of $542 42

besides interest on the several sums from the dates of their
respective payments.

" 6.   Alleges that by reason of the premises the alleged deed from Shirk to Snowden, dated July 25, 1862, and recorded July 14, 1879, on book 6 of deeds, page 617 in the records of Otoe county, is a cloud on the title of defendant in and to said quarter section, impairs its market value and the sale thereof, and ought not to be allowed to remain thereon.

" 7.   This defendant protests against the jurisdiction of the court to try the question of his title to said lands or his right to the possession thereof in this form of action ; protests against being compelled to defend his said title in common with others and other lands in which he has not the least interest, claim, or demand, and no privity either in law or equity.

"Wherefore the defendant, Hanks, demands judgment that said action be dismissed ; that a decree may be entered quieting his title in and to said described quarter section against the claims and demands of the plaintiffs, and against the claims of the defendants, Adaline Leedy and husband, Catharine Snodgrass and husband, Margaret Ford and husband, and William T. Snowden, and all persons claiming under them by virtue of said deed from Shirk to Snowden, and for general relief."

The separate answer of said Lyle is the same as that of the said Hanks, except as follows:

"Defendant Lyle claims to be the owner in fee simple and in possession of the south-east quarter of said section 23, T. 7, R. 113 E., and derives his title as follows:

"From John J. Burke by special warranty deed dated June 18, 1883, filed for record July 2, 1883, paying therefor $677.50 cash, and took possession.   That said Burke purchased the same of L. F. D'Gette and E. F. Warren for $960 cash, September 24, 1880; that said Burke received a warranty deed from his grantors, which was filed for record October 10, 1870; that Burke was an innocent purchaser without any knowledge of plaintiff's claims;

that D'Gette and Warren claimed to be the owners by deed dated Dec. 1, 1870, from Poe; that Poe derived title from Shirk by deed dated Sept. 19, 1870, which deeds were filed for record immediately."

Also an itemized statement of taxes paid to the year 1884, amounting in the aggregate to $489.79 and interest on the several amounts from the dates of their respective payments.

ANSWER OF JOSEPH MASTALKA,

Filed October 24, 1884.

Same answer as Hanks and Lyle except in chain of title and amount paid for taxes upon forty acres claimed to belong to him, to-wit: The north-west quarter of the south-west quarter of said section 23, Tp. 7, R. 11 E.

His chain of title is as follows:

" 1.   Quit-claim deed from Elbert H. Shirk to Adam W. Poe, dated Sept. 19, 1870, recorded Sept. 23, 1870.

" 2.   Adam W. Poe and wife to L. F. D'Gette and E. F. Warren, Sept. 6, 1870, deed of bargain and sale, recorded Sept. 23, 1870.

" 3.   Another deed from Poe to same grantors, dated Dec. 1, 1870, recorded Jan. 26, 1871.

" 4.   Warranty deed from D'Gette and wife and Warren and wife to Ella M. Poe, dated May 23, 1873, recorded same day.

" 5.   Ella M. Poe (single) by warranty deed to defendant Mastalka, dated May 25, 1876, recorded Aug. 9, 1876."

With itemized statement of taxes paid to the year 1884, amounting in the aggregate to $149.44 and interest on the several amounts from the dates of their respective payments,

ANSWER OF ELLA M. TYLER AND HUSBAND,

Filed Oct. 24, 1883.

Same answer as those of Hanks, Lyle, and Mastalka, except in chain of title and amount paid for taxes upon land claimed to belong to her, to-wit: The east half and

14

the south-west quarter of the south-west quarter; and the south-west quarter of the north-west quarter of said section 23, T. 7, R. 11 E., being 160 acres.

Chain of title:

"1.   Elbert H. Shirk and wife to Adam Poe, quit-claim deed, dated Sept. 19, 1870.

"2.   Adam W. Poe and wife to L. F. D'Gette and E. F. Warren, deed, bargain and sale, Sept. 6, 1870.

"3·   Adam W. Poe and wife to L. F. D'Gette and E. F. Warren, quit-claim deed, Dec. 1, 1870.

"4·   L. F. D'Gette and E. F. Warren and wives to Ella M. Poe (now Ella M. Tyler), May 23, 1883."

And itemized statement of taxes paid to the year 1884, amounting in the aggregate to $507.52, with interest on the several amounts from the dates of their respective payments.

ANSWER OF HERMAN FLOERKE,

Filed in said cause Nov. 18, 1884.

Same answer as those of Hanks, Lyle, Mastalka, and Tyler, except in chain of title and amount paid for taxes on land claimed to belong to him, to-wit: The north half and the south-east quarter of the north-east quarter of said section 23, T. 7, R. 11 E., being 120 acres.

"1.   Elbert H. Shirk and wife to Adam W. Poe, Sept. 19, 1870, quit-claim deed.

"2.   Adam W. Poe and wife to L. F. D'Gette and .E. F. Warren, deed, bargain and sale, Sept. 6, 1870.

"3·   Adam W. Poe and wife to L. F. D'Gette and E. F. Warren, quit-claim deed, Dec. 1, 1870.

"4·   L. F. D'Gette and E. F. Warren and wives, warranty deed to G. J. Z. Rayhouser.

"5·   G. J. Z. Rayhouser and wife to G. L. Bittinger, warranty deed, July 14, 1875.

"6·   Geo. L. Bittinger and wife to Harriet J. Hall warranty deed, July 14, 1875.

"7. Harriet J. Hall and husband, warranty deed, March 11, 1880, to Herman Floerke."

Also alleges that he and his grantors paid for taxes the sum of $500, besides interest from date of payment respectively.

On the trial of the cause the court rendered a decree as follows:

"In this cause * * * the court finds that the prayer of the petition should be granted as to the defendants Ella M. Tyler and C. L. Tyler, her husband, and Epaminondas E. Lyle, and that the same should be denied as to the defendants Joseph Mastalka, Herman Floerke, and Connoy Hanks; that as against the defendants Ella M. and C. L. Tyler, that the said plaintiff David L. Snowden is entitled to two-sevenths; and the plaintiff Charles Snowden is entitled to one-seventh of the SW. $\frac{1}{4}$ of the NW. $\frac{1}{4}$; also the E. $\frac{1}{2}$ of the SW. $\frac{1}{4}$, and the SW. $\frac{1}{4}$ of the SW. $\frac{1}{4}$ in section 23, T. 7, R. 11 E., in Otoe county, Nebraska. The court further finds as against the defendant E. E. Lyle that the said plaintiff David L. Snowden is entitled to two-sevenths, and the said plaintiff Charles Snowden to one-seventh of the SE. $\frac{1}{4}$ of said section (23) twenty-three.

"Further finds as against the said plaintiffs that the defendant Connoy Hanks is entitled to the NE. $\frac{1}{4}$ of said section twenty-three (23).

"Further finds as against the said plaintiffs, that the defendant Herman Floerke is entitled to the E. $\frac{1}{2}$ of the NW. $\frac{1}{4}$, and the NW. $\frac{1}{4}$ of the NW. $\frac{1}{4}$ of said section twenty-three (23).

"Further finds as against the said plaintiffs, the defendant Joseph Mastalka is entitled to the NW. $\frac{1}{4}$ of the SW. $\frac{1}{4}$ of said section twenty-three.

"Further finds that Sarah Leedy has assigned her interest in the said section to the said David L. Snowden; that the defendants Adaline and Samuel J. Leedy, Catharine and Sylvester Snodgrass, Margaret and James S. Ford,

and William T. Snowden, have declined to join as plaintiffs
herein, and have made default as defendants.

"It is therefore ordered, adjudged, and decreed, that the
title of the said David L. Snowden in and to two-sevenths,
and the title of the said Charles Snowden in and to one-
seventh of the SE. ¼, the SW. ¼ of the NW. ¼, the E. ½
and SW. ¼ of the SW. ¼, of section 23, T. 7, R. 11 E, in
Otoe county, Nebraska, be and the same is hereby in all
respects quieted and confirmed; that the quit-claim deed
from Elbert H. Shirk and wife to Adam W. Poe of date
September 19th, 1870, recorded in Book U of Deeds, on
pages 236, 237, and all subsequent and former deeds from
said Poe or any of his grantees either immediate or remote
in and to several tracts of land, are hereby set aside as
clouds upon the title of the said plaintiffs, and are declared
to be null and void; and that the said defendants, Ella M.
Tyler, C. L. Tyler, and E. E. Lyle, hold the same in trust
for the use and benefit of said plaintiffs to the extent of
their several interests as hereinbefore found.

"It is therefore ordered and decreed that the title in and
to the NE. ¼ of said section twenty-three, be and the same
is hereby confirmed in the said defendant Connoy Hanks;
that the title to the E. ½ and the NW. ¼ of the NW. ¼ of
said section 23 be and the same is hereby confirmed in the
said defendant, Herman Floerke; that the title in and to
the NW. ¼ of the SW. ¼ of said section 23 be and the
same is hereby confirmed in the said defendant Joseph
Mastalka.

"The said plaintiffs except to the findings and decree in
favor of the defendants Hanks, Floerke, and Mastalka;
and said defendants Tyler, Tyler, and Lyle, except to the
findings and decree against them respectively.

   *   *   *   *   *   *

"It is further ordered that plaintiffs pay one-half the
costs in this case, and the defendants Tyler pay one-fourth
of the costs, taxed at $75.42."

The plaintiffs appeal, and defendants Ella M. Tyler and husband and E. E. Lyle enter a cross appeal.

The testimony tends to show that in the summer of 1870 one Adam W. Poe, of Ohio, learned that one Elbert H. Shirk, of Indiana, was the owner, as appeared by the records of Otoe county, Nebraska, of all of section 23, township 7, range 11 east, in said county. On his way home he found Mr. Shirk, and on inquiring about the land learned that it had been sold some years before to one Elijah Snowden, then deceased. Mr. Poe found the heirs of said Snowden, consisting of Adaline Leedy, Catherine Snodgrass, Margaret Ford, and William T. Snowden, adults, and Sallie Snowden (now Sallie Leedy), David L. Snowden, and Charles F. Snowden, minors. He also interviewed Jacob Wintrote, administrator of the estate of Elijah Snowden, deceased, and E. J. Anderson, the guardian of the minors. It was ascertained that the adult heirs, the administrator, and the guardian all concurred that the land should be sold to pay the debts owing by the estate of Snowden, deceased. But the deed which Shirk was said to have made to Elijah Snowden had been lost or destroyed, as Mr. Poe was informed, and had never been recorded in Otoe county or elsewhere.

To save the expense and delay of procuring an order from the proper court to sell the minors' interest, it was agreed that Mr. Shirk should make another deed or quitclaim to Mr. Poe for the purpose of making the record title complete, and that the adult heirs and the guardian should join in a deed of the interest of the heirs. Mr. Poe therefore paid to the administrator $1,315.50 for the deed of all the heirs except Mrs. Ford, received also the deed from Mr. Shirk, as agreed, which latter deed was immediately, on September 23, 1870, filed for record in Otoe county. The agreed consideration for the land was $1,500 plus the unpaid taxes thereon—about $500 more.

In this transaction Mr. Poe had two partners, L. F.

D'Gette and E. F. Warren, who lived in Nebraska and man-
aged the land and attended to its sale. Later on they divided the land or its proceeds among themselves.

Inasmuch as the records of Otoe county showed a
straight and perfect chain of title from the United States
to Adam W. Poe and to said D'Gette and Warren, it was
deemed wisest not to record the deed from the Snowden heirs
to D'Gette, as it would only create confusion in the chain of
title, and would injure the sale of the land. In 1870 Mr.
Poe conveyed the whole section to Mr. D'Gette and Mr.
Warren by warranty deed. Shortly afterward D'Gette and
Warren sold the southeast quarter to one J. J. Burke for
$960 cash, by warranty deed, and subsequently the other
portions, to different grantees, always by warranty deed,
except the 200 acres to Ella M. Tyler (then Poe) which
was by special warranty.

In July, 1879, the old deed from Mr. Shirk to Elijah
Snowden, deceased, dated July 25, 1862, was found and
recorded in Otoe county.

That was the first intimation that any one, except Messrs.
Poe, D'Gette, and Warren, had that any of the Snowdens
claimed an interest in said lands.

At the date of the commencement of this action, the
said lands were owned and occupied severally, as follows:

Connoy Hanks owned the NE. $\frac{1}{4}$, 160 acres; J. J.
Burke owned the SE. $\frac{1}{4}$, 160 acres; Ella M. Taylor owned
the E. $\frac{1}{2}$ and SW. $\frac{1}{4}$ of the SW. $\frac{1}{4}$, and the SW. $\frac{1}{4}$ of the
NW. $\frac{1}{4}$, 160 acres.

Joseph Mastalka owned the NW. $\frac{1}{4}$ of the SW. $\frac{1}{4}$, 40
acres.

Herman Floerke owned the E. $\frac{1}{2}$ and the NW. $\frac{1}{4}$ of the
NW. $\frac{1}{4}$, 120 acres.

The plaintiff Daniel L. Snowden claims to own the undivided two-sevenths of said lands—one-seventh in his own
right and the one-seventh as grantee of his sister, Sallie

Leedy, and Charles Snowden claims one-seventh part. These claims are based upon the fact that they never alienated their interest "according to law," by joining in any deed.

The first objection made by the defendants is, that the proper remedy of the plaintiffs was by an action of eject- ment, and that a court of equity has no jurisdiction in the first instance to determine purely legal titles to land, where the plaintiff is out of possession. In other words, when the real estate is in the possession of another the proper remedy of one claiming the legal title is an action of ejectment. *Gregory v. Lancaster Co. Bank*, 16 Neb., 411. This is true, and had the defendants, either by de- murrer or answer, raised an objection to the jurisdiction of the court, the decree would be reversed. In the trial of purely legal titles to land by a plaintiff out of possession against a defendant in possession, either party is entitled to submit questions of fact to a jury and to have the first ver- dict set aside. These provisions, however, may be waived. In the case at bar the defendants do not plead want of jur- isdiction, they merely protest against the jurisdiction of the court, while they ask affirmative relief at its hands. In effect they file cross bills to the petition and ask to have their titles confirmed, thus invoking the equitable powers of the court and giving it jurisdiction. The first objection therefore, is untenable.

(2.) It is objected that the petition is multifarious be- cause the tenants in common are joined in the petition. This defect, if it is one, appeared on the face of the petition and should have been raised by demurrer, and as it was not, it is waived.

(3.) It is claimed that the quit-claim deed from Shirk to Poe conveyed no title, and that *bona fide* purchasers from Poe were not protected. The rule, no doubt, is, that a per- son who purchases of another, real estate, and receives a quit-claim deed only therefor, is bound to enquire and ascertain at his peril what outstanding equities exist, if any, against the title. The reason is, his grantor will not warrant the title even as against himself, therefore, it is a cause of suspicion. We are not prepared to hold, however, that a quit-claim deed, where the grantor has already conveyed, will not in any case convey title. It is not unreasonable to suppose that a quit-claim deed occurs in many titles where there is no outstanding equity. In this case the quit-claim deed in question was made by Shirk to Poe to supply a deed which was supposed to have been lost. It was made to the grantee of such of the heirs of Snowden as were of lawful age. Shirk, upon the records of Otoe county, apparently possessed the legal title to the land in controversy, and a conveyance from him to Poe, although in the form of a quit-claim deed, in form at least, transferred the legal title to Poe. No one seems to have been in possession of the land nor had charge of the same, and from the fact that more than eight years had elapsed from the time of the execution of the deed from Shirk to Snowden without the same having been recorded, certainly was a strong circumstance tending to show that the title still remained in Shirk. It is the policy of the law that titles to real estate shall become matters of certainty as far as possible, and that one who acts in good faith in purchasing, and pays the value of the property, shall be protected in his purchase. Any other rule would operate to prevent settlement and improvements upon lands. A party, therefore, who finds a complete chain of conveyances from the original grantee to his grantor upon the proper records of the county, may rely thereon provided he has no notice, either actual or constructive, of equities affecting the title, and is a purchaser for a sufficient consideration. All those persons, therefore, who purchased from D'Gette and Warren, without notice, for valuable consideration, and their grantees, will be protected. This rule, however, will not apply to those who are mere donees or who purchased with notice. As against such persons, the plaintiff is entitled to relief. The plaintiffs, however, come into a court of equity, and as a condition of obtaining relief, must do equity. The defendants Tyler and Tyler and their grantors have paid the taxes on the land in question for more than twenty years. It is but justice that three-sevenths of these taxes should be refunded to them with interest thereon. The case will therefore be referred to ascertain the amount due for such taxes, and upon the payment thereof the decree of the court below will be affirmed except as to Lyle. We are unable to determine from the evidence the value of the land at the time Poe purchased the same, or the amount of money applied by Snowden's administrator to the settlement of the estate. The question as to the liability of the plaintiffs therefor does not arise in the case. Burke, from whom Lyle purchased, was a *bona fide* purchaser and was entitled to protection, and the fact that he conveyed to Lyle since the action was commenced does not render Lyle's title invalid. A *bona fide* purchaser for valuable consideration without notice, may convey to one with notice. *Alexander v. Pendleton*, 8 Cranch, 462. *Jackson v. Given*, 8 Johns., 141. *Bumpus v. Platner*, 1 Johns. Ch. R., 219. *Demarest v. Wynkoop*, 3 Id., 147. The reason is to prevent stagnation of property, and because the first person being entitled to hold and enjoy, must be equally entitled to sell. The decree as to Lyle will therefore be reversed.

DECREE ACCORDINGLY.

THE other judges concur.

THE STATE, EX REL. FRED. FRANCL, V. ALBERTUS N. DODSON.

1. **Clerk District Court**: ELECTION : MANDAMUS. In an action by mandamus, where it appears that the office of clerk of the district court of S. county became vacant by the removal of M. more than thirty days before the general election of 1886, that upon the canvass of the votes cast at said election, F., the relator, was declared duly elected to said office, which said canvass and declaration is duly evidenced by a certificate of election, issued and delivered to F. under the hand and official seal of the county clerk; that said F. has taken the oath of office, and filed the bond as required by law, which bond was duly approved, and has thereafter demanded the said office and the books and papers belonging thereto of D , who had been appointed to said office by the board of county commissioners, which was refused, *Held*, That a writ of mandamus would issue without inquiry as to the form of the notice of said election or of the ballots cast thereat.

ORIGINAL application for mandamus.

Abbott & Abbott, for relator.

Griggs & Rinaker, for respondent.

COBB, J.

This case arises upon an application for a mandamus by the relator to the respondent, commanding him to forthwith deliver up to him, the said relator, " the office of the clerk of the district court for Saline county, with all things thereunto appertaining," etc.

The respondent filed his answer to the said relation presenting the several defenses and questions hereinafter referred to. It appears from the pleadings that at the general election of 1883 the county of Saline, having a population exceeding eight thousand, and therefore, under the provisions of the statute [Comp. Stat. Ch. 26, sec. 7] entitled to a separate clerk of the district court, one Charles W. Meeker, was elected to said office, qualified, and entered upon the duties thereof. That on the 6th day of March, 1886, the said Meeker was, by the board of county commissioners of said county, legally removed from said office for cause, and that on the same day the respondent was duly appointed to said office by the said board to fill the vacancy caused by the removal of the said Meeker, and that said respondent duly qualified, entered upon the duties of said office and has continued to fill the same hitherto. It also appears that at the general election held in and for said county on the 2d day of November, 1886, the county clerk of said county, by printed notices duly posted throughout said county, gave notice that a clerk of the district court to fill vacancy would, together with other officers to be elected at said election, be voted for thereat. That both the relator and respondent were candidates for said office at said election. It also appears that on the 8th day of November, 1886, the county clerk of said county duly executed under his hand and official seal and delivered to the relator a certificate in due form of his election to said office at the said election, and that on the 24th day of December, 1886, the relator took and subscribed the oath of office and presented to the board of county commissioners his official bond with sureties, which was approved and filed by the said board. It also appears that on the 6th day of January, 1887, the relator demanded of the respondent the possession of the said office and all of the appurtenances thereto, which the said respondent then and there refused to surrender or deliver up.

The points presented and urged by the respondent may be stated as follows:

1. That no election of clerk of the district court in and for said county could be legally held at the general election of 1886.

2. That if such vacancy could in any event have been

legally filled at that election, then, that in the notices of
such election, upon the ballots cast, the canvass made, and
the certificate of election issued, the office must be designated
as "clerk of the district court to fill vacancy."

3.   That at the said election a majority of the votes cast
having the words "for clerk of the district court to fill vacancy" thereon were cast for the respondent and not for
the relator.

The first point, if well taken, will certainly defeat the
case of the relator.   The respondent was appointed to fill
the vacancy caused by the removal of Meeker.   The term
for which Meeker was elected will not expire until January, 1888, so that if the general provisions of law on the
subject of vacancies do not apply to the office of clerk of
the district court he would continue to hold until that time.

Section 7 of chapter 26 Compiled Statutes provides, *inter
alia*, that "In each county having a population of eight
thousand inhabitants or more, there shall be elected in the
year 1879, and every four years thereafter, a clerk of the
district court in and for such county."

Section 101 of the same chapter provides that "Every
civil office shall be vacant upon the happening of either of
the following events at any time before the expiration of
the term of such officer as follows: 1. The resignation of
the incumbent; 2. His death; 3. His removal from office,"
etc.   Section 103 provides that "vacancies shall be filled
in the following manner.   *   *   *   In county and precinct offices by the county board," etc.   Section 105 provides that "Appointments under the provisions of this
chapter shall be in writing and continue until the next
election at which the vacancy can be filled and until a successor is elected and qualified," etc.

The respondent contends that under the above provisions
no successor in the office of clerk of the district court can
be elected until the recurrence of four years from the date
of Meeker's election.   This contention is based upon the

language of the 7th section, that the said officer "shall be elected in the year 1879 and every four years thereafter," and that of the 105th section that the appointments to fill vacancies in such office shall "continue until the next election at which the vacancy can be filled." The language of that seventh section is by no means peculiar to the office of clerk of the district court, but precisely the same language is used in respect to the election of every officer therein named except as to the length of their terms of office, and if the position is correct, that no clerk of the district court could be elected except in the year 1879 and in the quadrennial years thereafter, it then follows that no person can be elected to the office of county judge, sheriff, treasurer, or any other county office, except in the odd-numbered years—the year 1879, and each second year thereafter. But it is sufficient to say that the language of section 7 refers to the regular elections of the officers therein named and not to the filling of vacancies.

It is true that section 105 assumes the fact that there are elections at which certain vacancies cannot be filled and that these elections may occur after the happening of the event causing such vacancy. But we need not resort to a strained construction of any provision of the act in order to give a meaning to the language of this section.

Section 107 provides that "vacancies occurring in any state, judicial district, county, precinct, township, or any public elective office, thirty days prior to any general election, shall be filled thereat," etc. To apply this provision to the case at bar, had Meeker been removed less than thirty days before the general election of 1886, that election would have been one at which the vacancy caused by his removal could not have been filled, not because of any peculiarity in the term of the office, but because of the language of the section last above quoted. But as the office became vacant thirty days before said election it was an election at which said office could be filled. I thus reach the conclusion, and from it I see no escape, that a clerk of district court in and for Saline county could be legally elected at the general election of 1886 whose term of office would expire in the month of January, 1888, and from the certificate of election issued to the relator under the hand and official seal of the county clerk, it appears that the relator was elected to said office. And for the purposes of this action the said certificate is conclusive evidence of the right of the relator to the present possession of the office.

The second and third points are ably presented by counsel for the respondent, and were this a case of *quo warranto*, or one arising on a contest under the statute, they would be entitled to a careful examination and thorough consideration. But these questions do not arise in an action by mandamus. In that form of action the court cannot go behind the canvass evidenced by the certificate of election and inquire as to the notice of election or the form of the ballots cast thereat, but will only inquire as to whether the office is one which could be lawfully filled at said election, and whether the relator by virtue of the canvass thereof has received a certificate of election thereat and has duly qualified for such office by taking the prescribed oath and giving the bond required by law. See *State v. Jaynes*, 19 Neb., 161, and authority there cited. These questions, as we have seen, must be decided in favor of the relator.

A writ of mandamus will issue as prayed.

JUDGMENT ACCORDINGLY.

THE other judges concur.

THE STATE OF NEBRASKA, EX REL. GEORGE P. DA-
VIS, v. GEORGE H. FORNEY, COUNTY CLERK OF
DODGE COUNTY.

1. **Township organization:** VACANCIES IN TOWN OFFICES.
When, in a new town, erected by the county board, in the division of the county into towns or townsh'ps, at the first meeting of said board, the offices of the town board, as well as of
the town clerk, are all vacant, it is the duty of the county clerk
to fill such vacancies as well as all other vacancies in the offices
of such town by appointment.

2. ———— : MANDAMUS. In a proper case, such duty will be enforced by mandamus.

ORIGINAL application for mandamus.

George L. Loomis, for relator.

William Marshall, for respondent.

COBB, J.

This action arises upon the application of George P.
Davis, a citizen of Dodge county, and a resident tax payer
of the town of Cottrell, in said county, for a mandamus to
George H. Forney, county clerk of said county, commanding him to forthwith fill, by appointment, the several vacancies existing in the said town of Cottrell, to-wit, the
several offices of supervisor, town clerk, town treasurer, as-
sessor, two justices of the peace, three judges, and two
clerks of election, of said town.

It appears from the record presented that upon a proper
application by the requisite number of electors of said
county, the question of the adoption of township organization was duly submitted to and adopted by the electors of
said county at the general election for the year 1886.

It also appears that at said election the electors of a ma-

jority of the precincts in said county elected supervisors;
that there was held, commencing on the fifteenth day after
such election, at the county seat of said county, a special
meeting of the newly-elected county board; that at said
special meeting the said board proceeded to divide said
county into towns in accordance with the provisions of the
statute in such case made and provided [Comp. Stat., Ch.
18, Art. IV, Sec. 5]; and that among the other towns into
which the said county was divided as aforesaid, is the town
of Cottrell. It further appears that in the said division of
said county into towns the lines of such towns were so
adjusted in respect to the lines of the precincts theretofore
existing in said county as to leave a full quota of town
officers as elected at said election in and by said several precincts still residing in each of said towns respectively, except the said town of Cottrell; but leaving no town officer,
of any name or grade whatever, residing within the limits
of said town, but leaving each and all of the offices of said
town vacant.

It also appears that before the presentation of the relation in this case, to-wit, on the 11th day of January, 1887,
the relator, together with divers other resident tax-payers
of said towns, personally requested and demanded of the
respondent that he, as county clerk of said county, appoint
proper and suitable persons to fill said several offices of the
said town, which he, the said respondent, then and there
refused to do.

By stipulation the cause is presented to this court to be
considered and disposed of the same as though the matters
of fact stated in the relation were denied by the respondent
and sufficiently proved by the relator; so that the only
question for our consideration is the question of law arising upon the facts pleaded, to-wit, whether upon the above
state of facts the county clerk possesses the power, and is it
his duty, to fill by appointment the vacant offices created by
the creation of the said town of Cottrell?

Section 5, of Article IV, of Chapter 18, of the Compiled
Statutes of 1885, provides that "In case a majority of the
legal votes cast at said election" (referring to an election at
which the question of the adoption of township organization shall be submitted under the provisions of said chapter) "shall be for township organization, and the electors
have chosen supervisors in a majority of precincts of the
county, as provided in the preceding sections, there shall
be held a special meeting of the newly-elected county board,
commencing on the fifteenth day after such election, at the
county seat.   *   *   *   At such special meeting the county
board may transact such county business as may be required
to be transacted before the next regular meeting of the
board, and shall proceed to divide such county into towns,
or townships, making them conform as near as practicable
to townships according to the government surveys," etc.

Section 14 provides that "In case any town in any
county wherein township organization has been, or may be,
adopted, shall refuse or neglect to organize and elect town
officers at the time fixed by law, it shall be the duty of the
board of supervisors of the county, upon the affidavit of
any freeholder, resident of said town, filed in the office of
the county clerk, setting forth the facts, to proceed at any
regular or special meeting of the board, and appoint the
necessary town officers for such town, and the persons so
appointed shall hold their respective offices until others are
chosen or appointed in their respective places, and shall
have the same power and be subject to the same duties and
penalties as if they had been duly chosen by the electors of
the town."

Section 15 provides that "Whenever it shall be made
to appear to the board of supervisors that the town officers
appointed by them or by any preceding board, as provided
in the foregoing section, have failed to qualify, as required
by law, so that such town cannot become organized, the
board of supervisors may annex such town to any adjoin-

15

ing town, and the said town so annexed shall thereafter form and constitute a part of such adjoining town."

By observing the language of section fourteen, as above quoted, it will be seen that the provisions of that section cannot be held to apply to the town of Cottrell, as at present situated, as it has neither neglected nor refused to organize and elect town officers at the time fixed by law—no such opportunity having been offered it. If the provisions of said section be held to apply to the case at bar, then it is the duty of the county board, and not of the county clerk, to appoint officers for said town.

But it is contended by counsel for the respondent, that although it was made the imperative duty of the county board to create the said town (they deeming the same to be necessary) at their meeting held fifteen days after the election at which township government was adopted in said county, yet that the said new town would nevertheless remain a part of the precinct or precincts from which its territory was taken, converted into towns by virtue of said election, until the next annual election, and not until that time be possessed of a separate autonomy. This contention is based upon section 4 of the same article, which, as printed in the Compiled Statutes, and contained in the enrolled bill in the office of the secretary of state, reads as follows: "Sec. 4. For the purpose of temporary organization each voting precinct shall be a township until otherwise ordered by the county board, and at the general election at which the question of adoption of township organization is submitted as aforesaid; *Provided further,* That in wards of cities of the first and second class whose limits are co-extensive with precincts, the electors thereof shall only choose supervisors, assessors, and judges, and clerks of election."

A bare inspection of the above section, or that part of it which comes before the proviso, will not fail to satisfy any one that the legislature never intended to pass it in that form; and an examination of section five as printed, will show that section four as originally drafted contained the words of section five as printed, occurring after the brackets in the twenty-fifth line, and such was the form of the bill as introduced, and as it stood until it came from the hands of the printer, in the form in which it finally passed and stands in the statute book. That part of section four as printed, coming before the proviso, means-nothing at all, and no rule of construction will give any meaning to it. But read in connection with that part of section five above referred to, it will show that the sole object of the section was to provide that the voting precincts should be regarded as towns for the purposes of the first election of town officers, which should take place at the same election, and simultaneously with the voting on the question of the adoption of township organization, and to provide the name and number of several town officers to be elected therein. It also provides, in fact, that the boundaries of the several towns where township organization shall be adopted shall remain the same as those of the former precincts respectively "until otherwise ordered by the county board." In the case at bar it appears from the record that the new county board met as required by the terms of the fifth section of the act on the fifteenth day after the election; and as further required by the terms of the said section, proceeded "to divide such county into towns or townships." Now the said towns held their boundaries the same as those of the old precincts, by virtue of the provisions of the fourth section above quoted, until this act of division by the county board. Then the county board "otherwise ordered." Thenceforward the number and boundaries of the several towns exist by virtue of the division of the county into towns or townships by the county board.

In the case at bar, so far as is shown by the record, the county board in the said division of said county into towns or townships adopted the old division into precincts except in so far as the said town of Cottrell was concerned, which said town was erected out of territory not theretofore constituting a precinct or town, and containing within its boundaries no person elected as a town officer at the said election. As we have seen, none of the provisions of the act which we are considering for the filling of vacancies in town offices apply to vacancies in such offices created by the erection of new towns.   Notwithstanding the omission by the legislature to provide in the act for the filling of such vacancies, I cannot conceive that it was their intention that such vacancies should remain unfilled and the town unorganized for an entire year. If so, why was it made the imperative duty of the county board as it was by the provisions of section five, above quoted, to divide the county into towns or townships at its meeting, held almost immediately after the adoption of that system of government?   It was certainly contemplated that in such division new towns would, or might be, erected, situated, in respect to the offices, precisely as we find the town of Cottrell in the case before us.   To deny the power anywhere to fill these vacancies is to withhold the benefits of local self-government to the people of said town for an entire year, an important fraction of the ordinary life of a town as well as of a natural person.   But while the act now under consideration furnishes no authority for filling vacancies in the offices of a new town created by its erection, we find sufficient reason for the omission of such provision in the fact that the legislature had but four days before the passage of the said law passed a general act on the subject of the filling of vacancies in office, which I believe, and no doubt the legislature believed, fully covered the case.   The provisions of this act applicable to the question before us now constitute section 103 of chapter 26 of the Compiled Statutes of 1885, and are as follows:

"Sec. 103.   Vacancies shall be filled in the following manner. * * * In township offices by the town board,

Graham v. Flynn.

but where the offices of the town board are all vacant the clerk shall appoint, and if there be no town clerk the county clerk shall appoint." In the case at bar the town offices are all vacant. The offices of the town board as well as that of the town clerk being vacant, it is clearly the duty of the county clerk to fill the said vacancies by appointment.

A peremptory mandamus will issue as prayed.

JUDGMENT ACCORDINGLY.

THE other judges concur.

DANIEL L. GRAHAM, APELLEE, V. JOHN FLYNN ET AL., APPELLANTS.

21 299
31 810

1. **Roads**: OPENING: NOTICE: PETITION. Where the testimony tends to show that notices for the location of a public road not signed were duly posted and a petition thereafter presented to the county commissioners, signed by more than ten landholders praying for the location of such road as was described in the notices, and a public road was thereupon located, opened, and traveled for more than ten years, *Held*, A valid public road.

2. ———: PETITION BY OWNER OF LAND. A petitioner for the location of a public road over his own land is not entitled to notice of the pendency of such petition. He is, in fact, a plaintiff in the proceeding, and where a petition signed by the requisite number of landholders has been acted upon by the proper authorities and a road located, a grantee of such petitioner cannot enjoin the use of the road upon the ground of want of notice to his grantor.

APPEAL from the district court of Lancaster county. Heard below before POUND, J.

Lamb, Ricketts & Wilson, for appellants.

Edson Rich and *Harwood, Ames & Kelly*, for appellee.

MAXWELL, CH. J.

Petition of Graham, in Lancaster county district court, filed May 21, 1885, for an injunction to prevent the taking of 33 feet from the west line of N½ of N.W.¼, 2–9–6 E., in Lancaster county, for a public road, the destruction of a crop of rye, and of a hedge growing on said strip, on the grounds that there had been no petition lawfully acted on by the county commissioners for the opening there of a public road; that neither plaintiff nor his grantors had had any notice of the opening of the road; that they had had no opportunity to apply for compensation, and that no compensation for the taking of the land had been offered or tendered them. The answer admits that about May 14, 1885, Flynn, overseer of highways, district No. 1, Yankee Hill precinct, Lancaster county, Nebraska, notified plaintiff to remove hedge aforesaid as an obstruction to the highway there laid out, denying all other allegations. For a second defense the answer alleges petition on July 5, 1871, of C. M. Wittstruck and seventy-five others to the county commissioners of Lancaster county praying for the location of a county road over the land in controversy, due and legal notice of the filing of the same having been given at least twenty days prior thereto, the hearing of said petition on aforesaid day, appointment of a commissioner whose report recommended the granting of the petition and location of road accordingly about August 1, 1871, all the requirements of law to that end having been complied with. For a third defense answer alleges opening of said road, and continued and uninterrupted user for a period of more than ten years.

The petition clearly shows that in the year 1871, E. Veitz, the grantor of Graham, was the owner of the land in controversy and signed a petition with seventy-five others for the location of said road. This is proved beyond controversy by the introduction in evidence of the original

petition containing the name of Veitz which was shown to
be genuine by a witness familiar with his signature. This
petition was presented to the county commissioners of Lancaster county, and by them acted upon by the appointment
of a commissioner who was instructed to proceed to view
the proposed road, and if, in his opinion, the public good
required the road, he was authorized to lay out, mark,
and plat the same. The commissioner did view the road
in question, and being of the opinion that public good
required the location of said road, he laid out, marked and
platted the same and made his report to the county clerk.
The road extended from the city of Lincoln to the southern
portion of the county, and was opened and traveled through
the land in controversy. There is some disagreement among
the witnesses as to the amount of travel, but that is not
material in the case.

It is claimed on behalf of the defendant that no notices
were posted as required by law, and that, therefore, the
commissioners had no jurisdiction. *Robinson v. Mathwick*,
5 Neb., 252. *The State, ex. rel. Sims, v. Otoe county*, 6 Neb.,
129.

In *Robinson v. Mathwick* the plaintiff brought an action against the defendant to recover for trespass; the defendant stated that the alleged trespass was committed on
a public highway duly laid out and established along which
he was traveling as he lawfully might do. In the opinion
in that case it is said, "There was no testimony whatever
offered tending to show that a notice of an application to
the board of county commissioners for the location of the
road was ever given, nor that any petition for such purpose
was ever presented. There was nothing offered tending in
the slightest degree to show that said board ever had the
subject of this road under consideration, nor that any commissioner was appointed to view and lay out the proposed
road. Had such testimony been given even after the irregular admission of said record, that would have obviated

the objections interposed by the plaintiff. But the total failure to produce at any time any evidence whatever to show
that the preliminary steps, which the statute requires, to
authorize the commissioners to take action in the matter,
were taken, leaves the objection to operate with full force,
and renders the error a fatal one."

In *State v. Otoe County*, 6 Neb., 129, 130, the question was
as to the right of the relator to a warrant for $812.36 for
damages alleged to be due him by reason of the location
and opening of a public road through his land. The commissioners denied the opening of the road, and the court
held, no notice having been given in the manner required
by law, the commissioners had no authority in the premises. Where, however, the required number of notices
have been posted prior to the presentation of the petition
to the county commissioners, and proof has been duly
made before them of the posting of such notices, and they
have acted thereon and appointed a commissioner who has
located a public road which has been opened and traveled
for many years, and all parties have acquiesced in the
locating and opening of such road, the rules as stated in
Robinson v. Mathwick, and *State v. Otoe County*, do not
apply.

The rule applied in *Gatling v. Lane*, 17 Neb., 80, *Haywood v. Thomas*, 17 Neb., 237, *Herdman v. Marshall*, 17
Neb., 259; that where a party has been in the actual, open,
notorious, and exclusive possession for ten years, he thereby acquires the absolute right to such exclusive possession
of the same, is applicable to public roads in favor of the
public so far as it relates to a mere easement.

2. The testimony tends to show that Veitz conveyed
to one Leland in 1878, and Leland conveyed to Graham
about the year 1880. The petitioners for a public road may
be regarded as plaintiffs in the proceeding. They were
asking for the location of a public way over their own
lands and those of others, presumably because they and

the general public would derive benefit therefrom. We know of no rule that would require a petitioner to serve a notice upon himself. The very object of the petition is to secure the location of the road, and the fact that a party signs such petition for the purpose indicated is sufficient notice to him of the pendency of the proceedings; as to him it is not an adverse proceeding, but is done not with his assent only but at his instance and request. The road, therefore, having been located on the petition of Veitz while he was the owner of the land in controversy, the plaintiff Graham is estopped by the action of Veitz, and cannot maintain this action.

The judgment of the district court is reversed and the action dismissed.

.   JUDGMENT ACCORDINGLY.

THE other judges concur.

LILLIAN M. JACOBS, ADMINISTRATRIX, PLAINTIFF IN ERROR, v. JOHN C. MORROW, DEFENDANT IN ERROR.

1. **Appeal in Probate Matters**: BOND. On an appeal from a judgment of a probate court in matters relating to an estate, where the judge approves the bond for such appeal, it will be presumed the bond conforms to the orders of such court, although they do not appear in the record.

2. **Appeal not Dismissed though Bond be Defective.** Where a bond for an appeal filed, within the time required by law, has been duly approved by the proper officer, such appeal will not be dismissed although some of the formal requirements of the statute have not been complied with, if the defects can be cured by amendment or the filing of a new bond.

3. **Appeal in Probate Matters**: JURISDICTION OF DISTRICT COURT. On an appeal from the judgment of a county court

overruling an exception to the account of an administrator, the district court may hear evidence and determine the validity of such claim.

4. **Administration of Estates**: LIABILITY OF ADMINISTRATOR. Where the administrator of an estate who had given bond in the sum of $10,000, and had collected and held in his hands more than $12,000, was removed, and the sole surety on his bond appointed administrator *de bonis non; Held,* That it was the duty of such administrator *de bonis non* to charge himself with the penalty of said bond as assets in his hands belonging to said estate. In such case the chose in action is converted into a chose in possession, and is transmitted by the mere operation of law, which is equivalent to a judgment and execution.

ERROR to the district court for Douglas county. Tried below before NEVILLE, J.

George W. Doane, for plaintiff in error.

Congdon, Clarkson & Hunt, for defendant in error.

MAXWELL, CH. J.

In 1875, Henry Gray died intestate, and on the 27th day of February, 1875, one Jonas Gise was appointed administrator of his estate, and was ordered to give bond in the sum of $10,000, which he did, with John G. Jacobs as sole surety.

On the 31st day of August, 1876, Gise was removed as administrator, and John G. Jacobs was appointed administrator *de bonis non,* and qualified as such.

On the 20th day of January, 1881, final settlement was made of the account of Jonas Gise as administrator of Gray, and a balance of $12,730.39 was found still remaining in his hands, and for which he was accountable as such administrator.

On the first day of June, 1880, John G. Jacobs, as administrator *de bonis non* of the estate of Gray, filed his account with said estate for settlement in the county court, to which defendant, on the 15th day of March, 1882, filed exceptions, which were heard, and on April 28, 1882, were determined by the court, and a decree entered thereon on that day.

On the 6th day of May, 1882, a notice of appeal was filed by defendant in the county court, and on the same day an undertaking in appeal was filed and approved.

On the 15th day of May, 1882, the transcript was filed in the district court.

On the 6th day of March, 1883, a motion to dismiss the appeal was filed on behalf of plaintiff in error, which was subsequently overruled, to which an exception was taken.

On the 10th day of December, 1883, the death of John G. Jacobs, appellee, was suggested by appellant, and on his motion the cause was subsequently revived against plaintiff in error as administratrix.

At the October term, 1884, the case was heard on the appeal, and a decree was entered reversing the ruling of the county judge as to one of the exceptions, and sustaining such exception, and affirming his ruling as to the others, and adjudging all the costs of the appeal against plaintiff in error, to which order sustaining such exception and also awarding all the costs against plaintiff in error, exceptions were duly noted.

1. The first question presented is the ruling of the district court on the motion to dismiss the appeal.

Section 3 of the act of 1881 provides that "Every party so appealing shall give bond in such sum as the court shall direct, with two or more good and sufficient sureties, to be approved by the court, conditioned that the appellant will prosecute such appeal to effect without unnecessary delay, and pay all debts, damages, and costs that may be adjudged against him. The bond shall be filed within thirty days from the rendition of such decision; but an executor, administrator, guardian, or guardian *ad litem* shall not be

required to enter into bond in order to enable him to
appeal. If it shall appear to the court that such appeal
was taken vexatiously or for delay, the court shall adjudge
that the appellant shall pay the costs thereof, including an
attorney's fee to the adverse party, the court to fix the
amount thereof; and said bond shall be liable therefor in
cases where it is required." Comp Stat., Ch. 20, sec. 44.

We find no order in the record fixing the amount in
which the appellant was required to give bond; but the
appellant did give bond in the sum of fifty dollars, with
two sureties, that he would secure the appellee for "all
debts, damages, and costs that might be adjudged against
him." This bond was duly approved. Where a bond has
been duly approved by the officer whose duty it was to
approve the same, it will be presumed that it conformed
in all respects to the requirements of such officer, and it
will not be void, even though some of the formalities of
the law have not been complied with, provided the bond
is filed within the time fixed by statute. The appellate
court may permit or require a new bond to be filed, and
will not dismiss an appeal where it is possible by an amendment to correct or replace an erroneous bond. *O'Dea v.
Washington Co.*, 3 Neb., 123. *Casey v. Peebles*, 13 Neb.,
9. The first objection, therefore, is not well taken.

2. The second error assigned is that the court found and
decreed that exception number 1 to the account of John G.
Jacobs as administrator *de bonis non*, was well taken, and
sustained such exception and reversed the order of the
county court thereon.

This exception was as follows:

"That said administrator does not charge himself in his
account as with assets received, with the amount of funds
remaining in the hands of Jonas Gise upon his being removed from his trust as administrator of said estate, on
whose bond said Jacobs was surety, and to whom said
Jacobs is successor."

If the proceeding in the district court had been on error from the county court the objection would be well founded; but sec. 46 of chapter 20 of the Comp. Statutes provides that "When such appeal is taken the county court shall, on payment of his fees therefor, transmit to the clerk of the district court, within ten days after perfecting such appeal, a certified transcript of the record and proceedings relative to the matter appealed from." And sec. 47 of same chapter provides that "Upon the filing of such transcript in the district court that court shall be possessed of the action, and shall proceed to hear, try, and determine the same in like manner as upon appeals brought upon the judgment of the same court in civil actions."

The appeal being taken upon the account mentioned in the above exception, all matters relating to that account were transferred to the district court for its adjudication. In effect the questions relating to this account were to be tried anew in the appellate court. The district court, therefore, possessed the same power as that of the probate court in ruling on the exception named, and it was its duty to hear evidence and determine the validity of such claim and the amount thereof. *In re Raab's Estate*, 16 Ohio St., 274. The second objection, therefore, is overruled.

3. The principal objection of the plaintiff in error is to a judgment charging the administrator *de bonis non* with the amount of the penalty of the bond which he signed as surety for Gise. It is claimed there is no authority to try in this summary manner all the intricate questions which may arise upon the bond; that the proceeding is one to settle the account of Jacobs as administrator *de bonis non*, and not to inquire into his liability as a surety on a bond.

Section 318 of chapter 23 of the Compiled Statutes provides that "When an executor or administrator shall, for any of the causes mentioned in this chapter, be removed from his trust, or shall die, or his authority shall otherwise be extinguished, and a new administrator shall be appointed, such new administrator shall be the party enti-

tled to bring an action upon the bond of the former executor or administrator for any damages sustained by reason
of his neglect or refusal, or the neglect or refusal of his
representatives, to turn over to such new administrator,
pursuant to the order or decree of the probate court, or
according to law, any estate remaining unadministered."

The rule is well settled that the granting administration
of an estate to one indebted to the intestate is an extin-
guishment of the debt. The chose in action becomes converted into a chose in possession, and is transmitted by the
mere operation of law, which is equivalent to judgment
and execution. The debt is thus satisfied and extinguished.
The instant administration is granted, the administrator
being the person to receive and to pay, is considered to
have paid the debt, and as holding the amount in his hands
as assets ; and the debts having once become assets no act
of the parties can return them back to an obligation. *Hall
v. Pratt*, 5 Ohio, 82. *Bigelow v. Bigelow*, 4 Ohio, 147.
Wankford v. Wankford, 1 Salk., 302. *Winship v. Bass*,
12 Mass., 199. *Hays v. Jackson*, 6 Id., 149. *Stevens
v. Gaylord*, 11 Id., 259.

In the last case it is said, "As soon as the debtor was appointed administrator (if he acknowledged the debt) he has
actually received so much money, and is answerable for it.
This is the result with respect to an executor, and the same
reason applies to an administrator, as the same hand is to
receive and pay and there is no ceremony to be performed
in paying the debt, and no mode of doing it but by considering the money to be now in the hands of the party in
his character as administrator." And the sureties on the
administrator's bond were held liable for the amount as
though it had been actually received; and in *Winship v.
Bass* it was held that the sureties of an executor, who was
a debtor to the testator at the time of his appointment, were
responsible for the debt, upon the principle that it must be
considered as having been actually received by the executor.
See also *Marvin v. Stone*, 2 Cowin, 781. *In re Piper's Es-*

tate, 15 Pa. St., 533. *Freakley v. Edward Fox*, 9 Barne-wall and Cress., 130. *Hazelton v. Valentine*, 113 Mass., 472. *Choate v. Arrington*, 116 Mass., 552. *Leland v. Felton*, 1 Allen, 531. *Mattoon v. Cowing*, 13 Gray, 387–390. *Commonwealth v. Gould*, 118 Mass., 300. *Ipswich Mfg. Co. v. Story*, 5 Metcalf, 310. *Benchley v. Chapin*, 10 Cush., 173. *Eichelberger v. Morris*, 6 Watts (Pa.), 42. *Griffith v. Chew's Ex'r.*, 8 Serg & R., 32. *Kinney v. Ensign*, 18 Pick., 232.

Gise, the first administrator, had in his hands more than twelve thousand dollars belonging to creditors of Gray's estate. Gise's bond was in the penal sum of $10,000, Jacobs being the sole surety thereon. As he could not sue himself, the law treats the amount owing by him on the bond as assets in his hands for the payment of creditors of the estate. Any other rule would permit the surety on the bond of a defaulting administrator, upon being appointed to supersede such defaulter in the administration of the estate, to defraud the creditors or heirs of the amount due upon such bond. It was the duty, therefore, of Jacobs to charge himself with the amount of the penalty of Gise's bond and hold the same as assets in his hands for the payment of the debts of the estate. There is no error, therefore, in the ruling of the district court.

4. It is assigned for error that the court ordered all the costs of the appeal against the appellee, and that the same should be taxed against him individually and not as a charge against the estate. We are unable to determine from the abstract upon what the ruling of the court was based, and are therefore unable to review the same. If costs have been improperly taxed, the ruling on a motion to retax may be reviewed in this court. We find no error in the record and the judgment of the district court is affirmed.

JUDGMENT AFFIRMED.

THE other judges concur.

EDWIN F. SEYMOUR ET AL., APPELLANTS, V. JOHN C.
RICKETTS, APPELLEE.

1. **Partition:** NOT MAINTAINABLE BY ONE OUT OF POSSESSION.
   A party out of possession of real estate, whose title is denied,
   cannot maintain an action of partition against one in possession
   claiming the title to said land.   He must first establish his estate in the land.

2. **Administration of Estates:** SALE BY EXECUTOR: TITLE
   ACQUIRED.   Where an executor files a petition in the proper
   court for license to sell real property belonging to the estate of
   the testator, and the heirs and devisees sign a waiver of notice and
   enter an appearance in the case, or are duly served with notice,
   such notice will continue until the debts mentioned in the petition are paid by the sale of the real property described therein,
   and a purchaser under a license issued on such petition, who
   has paid the purchase price, the same being applied to the payment of the debts against the estate of the testator, and the sale
   having been confirmed and a deed made to such purchaser, may
   . rely upon the title so acquired as against collateral attack from
   the heirs and devisees of such testator.

3. **Partition:** EQUITY JURISDICTION.   While in a proper case a
   court of equity will retain a petition for the partition of real
   estate, where the title of the plaintiff is denied or is not clear,
   until he can try his title at law, yet, where it is apparent from
   the whole record that the plaintiff has no interest in the premises, the right will be denied.

APPEAL from the district court of Lancaster county.
Heard below before POUND, J.

John S. Gregory, for appellants.

Lamb, Ricketts & Wilson, for appellee.

MAXWELL, CH. J.

"On the 28th day of February, 1885, the plaintiffs filed
a petition in the court below, stating their cause of action
to be: That they are the sole heirs and legatees of their

father, John W. Seymour, who died July 12, 1872, leaving the real estate in controversy, with all other property, by will to his widow, Sarah J. Seymour, to be held by her during her life, in trust for plaintiffs, and at her death the said property to be equally divided share and share alike between these plaintiffs; that on Aug. 14th, 1884, the said Sarah J. Seymour died, and that plaintiffs were thereupon entitled to a partition of the said lands according to the terms of the will.

"That at the time of the death of the said John W. Seymour, he was the owner of the S. ½ of the S. W. ¼ Sec. 27, and S. E. ¼ of S. E. ¼ of Sec. 28, Tp. 10, Range 6, in Lancaster county, Neb.

"On Nov. 29, 1879, Charles W. Seymour, claiming to act as executor, and under the order of the district court of Otoe county, dated Nov. 15, 1879, sold these lands unto Sarah J. Seymour for $1,120, which sale was by the court duly confirmed, and the said Charles W. was ordered and directed to make deed for same to her, and that said sale and confirmation have never been vacated or set aside.

"On Nov. 29th, 1879, said Charles W. Seymour caused an order to be entered by said district court granting him license to sell so much of said lands as should be necessary to pay the debt, taxes and costs of said estate, and on the 28th day of Dec. 1880, he sold the same unto defendants' grantee for the sum of $945. Said sale was on the same day confirmed by the judge of Otoe Co. district court, at Lincoln, Lancaster county, Neb.

"By virtue of said sale and confirmation, Chas. W. Seymour executed to said defendant a deed to said premises, and by virtue of said deed, plaintiffs claim that defendant became seized in fee of one-ninth interest, being the title of said C. W. Seymour in said land, and that defendant is the tenant in common therein.

"That no notice was ever served upon any of the plaintiffs that application would be made for said sale. No

16

order was made by the court citing them to appear and
show cause why such license should not be granted, and no
appearance was by them made in court, and plaintiffs, who
all resided in Ohio, never knew or had any intimation of
any of the said proceedings until shortly before the commencement of this action ; that at the time said last order
was obtained, all debts of the estate had long prior thereto
been paid, and no taxes were ever by said Chas. W.
paid, and no part of the purchase money was paid or
tendered to these plaintiffs ; that said Chas. W. gave no
bond, and did not take the oath required by law ; and said
sale was fraudulent and void.

"Plaintiffs offer to pay their proportion of taxes and improvements, and pray a partition."

The defendant demurred to the petition upon the ground
that it failed to state a cause of action. The demurrer was
overruled, to which the defendant excepted. He then filed
answer as follows:

"For first defense, that he admits the death of John
W. Seymour, his will, his title in fee at the time of his
death, the sale of Dec. 28, 1880, of the property in controversy, the confirmation and deed of Chas. W. Seymour, as
alleged in the petition ; he denies each and every other
allegation, and claims to be sole owner in fee.

"Second and third defenses, that defendant is seized in
fee of said premises by virtue of certain tax deeds to Chas.
L. Flint, and to E. Howard, and by mesne conveyance
from said Flint and Howard ; and under virtue of said
title defendant has been in possession of said premises since
Dec. 18, 1880, and has paid the taxes thereon.

"Fourth defense, that Charles W. Seymour was duly
appointed administrator and executor under the will of
John W. Seymour, by the probate court of Otoe county,
Nebraska; that he duly qualified ; that by the terms of
the will large legacies were directed to be paid out of the
estate; that the estate was subject to large indebtedness

which had been proved up and allowed by the probate court
of said Otoe county; that the personal estate was inadequate to pay the same; that on May 3d, 1875, said executor filed his petition in Otoe county district court praying
assignment of dower, license to sell these lands with other
lands; that these plaintiffs were duly notified and filed their
voluntary appearance and assented to the sale in accordance
to the prayer of petition; and said court only licensed
said Chas. W. to sell said lands; that said cause was
continued from time to time until June 8th, 1878, when
all the lands were sold (except 40 acres) to the widow,
Sarah J. Seymour, or some of the plaintiffs, and defendant is not advised whether any money was paid for
such of said property as was sold to the widow or not, but
alleges that no money was paid.

"That December 9th, 1880, the district court renewed
and enlarged the former license and thereunder the said
administrator did, on Dec. 28th, 1880, at the west front
door of the U. S. building, in Lincoln, sell said lands to
A. C. Ricketts for $980, and on the same day S. B. Pound,
judge of said Otoe county district court, duly confirmed
said sale, and a deed was duly executed to said Ricketts;
that prior to said sale, Shambaugh & Richardson held
judgment against the estate of J. W. Seymour of about
$1,000, and had caused execution to be levied on the
Seymour house property, and that all the proceeds of said
sale were used in paying said judgment and saving said
Seymour house property.

"That defendant has occupied said lands and improved
them to the value of about $5,000 and paid all taxes
thereon, and that the plaintiffs were fully advised of all
C. W. Seymour's proceedings as before mentioned.

"Fifth defense, that in January, 1880, said C. W. Seymour was the duly constituted agent of the several heirs,
including plaintiff, and in behalf of all said heirs he entered into an agreement with defendant to sell him said

lands, subject only to tax liens, and advised defendant to
purchase the outstanding tax title, under which advice he
did purchase the same, and by reason of the premises
plaintiffs are now estopped to claim any interest therein.

"That the administrator's prior sale to Sarah J. Seymour
was void, and that she refused to pay the purchase money
bid therefor and the administrator refused to make her a
deed. .

"That this suit is being conducted by the plaintiff's attorneys under a champertous agreement for fees, and defendant prays that the action be dismissed."

The reply is a general denial.

In April, 1886, there was a trial to the court and judgment dismissing plaintiff's petition at their costs. The
plaintiffs appeal.

The petition shows on its face that the title of the plaintiffs is not clear. They claim to be the owners of eight-
ninths of the legal title of the property in question, and
that the defendant is the owner of one-ninth part thereof;
but they do not state that they are in possession of the
premises. Where the complainants' legal title is disputed, courts of equity decline the jurisdiction to try
this question, but in a proper case will retain the petition
for a reasonable time until the question of title can be determined at law. *Slade v. Barlow*, L. R., 7 Eq., 296.
Giffard v. Williams, Id., 5 Ch., 546. *Bolton v. Bolton*,
Id., 7 Eq., 298 n. *Potter v. Waller*, 2 De G. & Sm.,
410. *Simpson v. Wallace*, 83 N. C., 477. *Mattair v.
Payne*, 15 Fla., 682. *Hardy v. Mills*, 35 Wis., 141.
Hoffman v. Beard, 22 Mich., 59. *Wilkin v. Wilkin*, 1
Johns. Ch., 111, 118. *Manners v. Manners*, 1 Green Ch.,
384. *Currin v. Spraule*, 10 Gratt., 145. But all persons,
whether in possession or expectancy, are proper parties to
the action. *Evans v. Bagshaw*, L. R., 5 Ch., 340. *Agar
v. Fairfax*, 2 L. Cas. in Eq., 468; 3 Pom. Eq., § 1388.
As the plaintiffs claim under a purely legal title against

the defendant in possession, claiming a legal estate in the land, the demurrer to the petition should have been sustained.

2. The testimony tends to show that in the year 1875 C. W. Seymour, as executor of the last will and testament of John W. Seymour, filed a petition in the district court of Otoe county, setting forth that certain debts were due from the estate of said Seymour, and that it was necessary to sell a sufficient quantity of land belonging to such estate to pay such debts. The petition included lands belonging to the estate situated in Otoe, Cass, and Lancaster counties, and included the land in controversy. Eight of the heirs signed a waiver of service of notice and entered a general appearance in the case, and service by publication was had upon the ninth. A license was thereupon duly issued to said executor to sell certain lands in Otoe county. The executor at that time took the oath required by statute before Judge GANTT, but was unable to effect a sale of the real estate. A number of renewals of the license took place, and in 1879 the license issued included the lands in controversy, and they were sold to the widow of the testator. This sale took place in Otoe county and seems to have been confirmed in that county. But she paid no portion of the price bid, nor was a deed ever executed to her. In 1880 a renewal of the license was granted by the district court of Otoe county to sell the land in controversy, and under such license the executor advertised the land for sale, and sold the same to the defendant for the sum of $980 in cash, which money was applied to the payment of debts of the estate of said John W. Seymour. The sale was confirmed and a deed made to the purchaser—the defendant—who thereupon took possession of the land and has made valuable improvements thereon.

The principal objections made by the plaintiffs against this sale relate to irregularities in the proceeding. Where, however, the court has jurisdiction of the subject-matter and the parties, its judgment is not open to collateral attack.   This question was very fully considered in *Trumble v. Williams*, 18 Neb., 144, and it was held that a petition for a license to sell real property for the payment of debts of an estate, filed in the court having exclusive original jurisdiction, and which was acted upon by that tribunal and treated as sufficient, was not, in the absence of fraud or collusion, subject to attack in a collateral proceeding, and that the authority to grant a license to sell real estate carries with it the implied power to determine the necessity for such sale and the sufficiency of the pleadings presented to the court for that purpose.   In that case it was also held that where license to sell real estate had been unavailing by reason of the want of bidders, and the necessity for a sale continued to pay debts due from the estate, that the court might grant a second or other license upon the original petition.   There would seem to be no necessity for filing a new petition, unless new facts had arisen which it was necessary to bring to the attention of the court, of which there is no evidence in this case.   The original petition, therefore, was sufficient, and the waiver of service, and service of notice continued until the debts were paid. The court, therefore, had jurisdiction, and its judgment must be held valid and sufficient.   It is unnecessary to notice the matter relating to the defendants' tax deed.

The plaintiffs claim that even if the court will not sustain an action for partition where the title is denied, or is not clearly established, yet the petition will be retained to give the plaintiffs an opportunity to establish that title at law.   This is the general rule, and where questions on the title of the plaintiff are strictly of a legal character, the court will give the plaintiff a reasonable opportunity to try his title at law, and in the meantime retain the petition. *Wilkin v. Wilkin*, 1 Johns. Ch., 111.   *Blynman v. Brown*, 2 Vern, 232.   *Parker v. Gerard*, 1 Amb., 236.   If it clearly appeared that the court below had dismissed the action because plaintiffs were not in possession of the premisess we would order a stay of proceedings until the plaintiff, could try their title in an action at law. It is apparent, however, that the court decided the case upon the merits, and held that the plaintiffs had no interest in the lands in controversy, and in this there is no error. The judgment of the district court is therefore affirmed.

JUDGMENT AFFIRMED.

THE other judges concur.

CITY OF BLAIR, APPELLEE, v. VICTOR G. LANTRY ET AL., APPELLANTS.

1. **Municipal Corporations:** CONTRACTS OF OFFICERS. The city council of a city of the second class, or any committee or member thereof, officer or department of the corporation, cannot incur any expense or enter into any contract, whether the object of the expenditure shall have been ordered by the city council or not, unless an appropriation shall have been previously made concerning such expense; except in cases where the proposition has been sanctioned by a majority of the legal voters of the city, etc.

2. ——: ——: LIABILITY OF OFFICERS. Where the mayor and council of a city of the second class drew an order upon the cemetery fund of such city for $716.66, there being at the time $1,000 in such fund in the treasury of such city, and applied the proceeds to the payment of lands purchased as an addition to the cemetery of such city, but no appropriation had been previously made concerning such expense; *Held*, No act of ratification being proved, that the mayor and clerk were liable for the amount drawn on such order.

APPEAL from the district court of Washington county. Heard below before NEVILLE, J.

W. H. Eller, Congdon, Clarkson & Hunt, and *Jesse T. Davis,* for appellants.

George B. Lake and *W. H. Farnsworth,* for appellee.

MAXWELL, CH. J.

In March, 1886, the plaintiff filed its petition in the district court of Washington county, stating its cause of action, as follows:

"1.   That it is a legally organized city of the second class.

"2.   That in May, 1884, the defendant Lantry was the mayor of the city of Blair, and the defendant Farr was the city clerk thereof.

"3.   That during the month of May, 1884, the plaintiff opened negotiations with the defendants Weimers for the purchase of a tract of land adjoining said town, and containing ten acres, which it desired for cemetery purposes.   That in the month of September, 1884, and before such negotiations had been consummated, the defendants Lantry and Farr, conspiring with each other, and with the defendants Wiemers, to cheat and defraud the plaintiff, without any authority of law, in fraud of the rights of the plaintiff, drew a warrant on the treasurer of the city of Blair in favor of the defendant Lantry, for the sum of $716.66 for the pretended purchase of said land, and without the consent or authority of plaintiff, placed upon the records of Washington county a deed from the defendants Weimers, pretending to convey said land to the plaintiff.

"4.   Alleges that the plaintiff never purchased said lands, and that the deed from Weimers was a nominal conveyance only.

"5.   That at the time of such conveyance, said real estate was largely encumbered by mortgage in an amount unknown to plaintiff. That the title to said land was imperfect, and not complete in defendants Wiemers, and that it was worth far less than the amount of the order above referred to and the encumbrance thereon.

"6. That on the 8th of September, 1884, the defendant Lantry wrongfully presented said order to the treasurer aforesaid and received therefrom the sum of $716.66 of the funds of plaintiff, of which said amount plaintiff was thereby defrauded.

"7. . That it has never taken possession of said land, or exercised control or ownership thereof, nor ratified said purchase, but has at all times disclaimed the same.

"8. That before the commencement of this suit, plaintiff offered to reconvey said lands to defendant Weimers, and demanded of each of the defendants the said sum of $716.66, which was refused, and further offers now to make a delivery of such conveyance."

The following is a copy of the order:

"$716.66.   BLAIR CITY ORDER.

BLAIR, Neb., Sept. 6th, 1884.

Cem. Fund.

The Treasurer of the Incorporated City of Blair, pay to Victor G. Lantry, or order, Seven Hundred and Sixteen and 66-100 Dollars.

By order of City Council.

Edward J. Farr, Clerk.   Victor G. Lantry, Mayor.

[WEIMER LAND BUSINESS.]

"Endorsements thereon as follows, to-wit: [Victor G. Lantry.]

"Prays that the above order may be adjudged unauthorized and illegal; that the deed from defendants Weimers to the plaintiff be adjudged unauthorized, null and void; that the title in the lands be quieted in the defendants Weimers and that the defendants, or such of them as the court shall think proper, may be adjudged to refund to the plaintiff the amount found due, with costs of suit, and for general relief.

* * * *

"Thereafter and on April 5th, 1886, the defendants, Weimers, demurred to the petition for the reason that it did not state facts sufficient to constitute a cause of action against them. This demurrer was subsequently overruled.

* * * *

"The defendant Farr answered, admitting that defendant Lantry was mayor of said city ; that he was the clerk thereof, and alleging that John W. Boggs, Neil McMillan, Allen C. Jones, and Pat Quinlan were councilmen of said city, and Edward C. Jackson was treasurer thereof. That on the 10th day of July, 1884, a committee was appointed by the said city to confer with defendant Weimers with reference to buying the land in question for cemetery purposes; that said committee was composed of said McMillan, Jones, and Quinlan; that afterwards, on the 5th day of August, 1884, on motion, it was resolved that the city of Blair do purchase said ten acres of ground for cemetery purposes at the agreed price of $1,250, and that said D. D. Weimer present an abstract of title and necessary papers to close the purchase at the next regular meeting of the city council. That said minutes were approved by the council on the 18th of August following; that on the 1st day of September following, at a meeting of said council at which all members were present, on motion, the chairman of the Finance Committee, to-wit, John W. Boggs, above named, was instructed to close the contract with D. D. Weimer for ten acres of land for cemetery purposes when he was satisfied the title was good; and on motion, the clerk was instructed to draw a warrant for the sum of $761.66, when the said chairman of the finance committee reported to him the title good for the land bought of Weimer. That the minutes of said meeting above were approved September 5th, 1884. Further alleges that in pursuance of the above resolutions and ordinances and relying upon said instructions, and in good faith, after the said purchase by said city had been completed fully by the said city and its agents, and after the said Boggs as chairman of said committee had reported to him that the title to said land was good, he drew the order complained of in the presence of said Boggs, with his knowledge and consent and under his directions, and payable to said V. G. Lantry, as ordered by him, for the reason as he [Boggs] said, that Lantry understood the business and would pay over the money to said Wiemers when the deed was made by them conveying said land to said city, which he believes said Lantry did so pay over to said Wiemers when said deed was delivered; that said order was drawn on the cemetery fund of said city in the amount named, and that the money belonging to said fund was in the treasury of said city at the time, and that the treasurer of said city honored said order and duly paid the same from the said cemetery fund in the sum of said $716.66, and that the balance due on said land, to-wit, the sum of $533.34, was secured by mortgage referred to in plaintiff's petition in favor of A. E. Wells, of Burt county; and that said mortgage includes all the encumbrance upon said title; and that said city is seized in fee simple in and to said premises whenever it pays said mortgage to said Wells with interest thereon as it agreed to do.   Further alleges that he relied upon the acts of said plaintiff so openly done, published and announced as aforesaid; that he acted within the scope of his authority without connivance, collusion, conspiracy, or fraud.   And further alleges that said lands were valuable and the only available that can be had as an addition to the cemetery of said plaintiff; that the present cemetery is already inadequate to its wants, and prays that the above proceedings be ratified and confirmed, and that he be dismissed with his costs."

The defendant Lantry answered as follows:

" 1.   Denies each and every allegation in the petition contained, except such as are expressly admitted.

" 2.   Admits the organization of the city; that he was legally elected and·qualified mayor.

" 3.   Admits the negotiations by said city with said Weimers for the land described.

" 4.   Admits the order mentioned was drawn in his favor, but avers that the same was drawn at the instance and request of said city ; that the money was paid out for the use and benefit of Annie Weimer.

" 5.   Denies any conspiracy, collusion, or fraud.

" 6.   Denies that he had any part in the negotiations with said Weimer, or any one for her ; that he never received and retained a cent of said money ; was not profited by said purchase, either directly or indirectly.

" 7.   Denies any tender of title, and prays to be dismissed."

The reply consists of denials.

On the trial the following decree was rendered : " This cause coming on for trial at a former day of the present term, the plaintiff and defendants being present, it was submitted to the court upon the pleadings and testimony and was argued by counsel and taken under advisement, and now, on this day, the court being fully advised in the premises, finds, as to the said defendants Victor G. Lantry, Annie Weimer, and D. D. Weimer, that there was no fraud or conspiracy,·and no intention to defraud, and finds that the warrant described in said petition was drawn and appropriated without authority of law, and the proceeds thereof should be refunded.

" It is therefore considered, adjudged, and decreed that the plaintiff, by its proper officers, within forty days, formally execute and deliver to the said Annie Weimer a quitclaim deed of the premises described in the plaintiff's petition and deposit the same with the clerk of this court for her use, namely :   [Description.]

"And it is further ordered and adjudged that upon the delivery of said deed the said Victor G. Lantry, Annie Weimer, and D. D. Weimer pay to this court for the use of the plaintiff the sum of $812.14, together with the costs of the plaintiff in this behalf expended, taxed at $ ————, and in default of such payment an execution issue therefor.

"It is further considered that the said defendant Farr go hence without day and recover from the plaintiff his costs herein."

The testimony shows the appropriation ordinance for the city of Blair for the fiscal year commencing on the first Tuesday of May, 1884, and ending on the first Tuesday of May, 1885, to be as follows:

"There is hereby appropriated out of the levy of taxes for the fiscal year commencing as above, the sums of money for the purposes and objects, to-wit:

For street purposes	$500
For fire purposes	500
For printing and stationery	150
For criminal prosecution and jail fees	350
For officers' salaries	1,500
Aggregating	$3,000

"W. H. Farnsworth, sworn for the plaintiff, testified that he was city attorney; that he had examined the ordinances passed by the city during the year in controversy and in reference to the purchase of the land in question; that he found none in reference thereto; that he further examined them in reference to the appropriation ordinances and found none other than the ones offered in evidence."

The city clerk produced the records of the proceedings of the council in 1884, from which it appeared that on August 5th and 18th respectively the following orders were made:

"On motion it was ordered that the city of Blair, Ne-

braska, do purchase ten acres of ground for cemetery purposes at the agreed price of $1,250, said ten acres being
north of the county road and adjoining Catholic and City
Cemetery on the east, and including all buildings and appurtenances thereon; and said D. D. Weimer to present
an abstract of title and necessary papers to close purchase
at next regular meeting.

" On motion the charman on finance committee was instructed to close up the contract with D. D. Weimer for
ten acres of his land for cemetery purposes, when he was
confident the title was good.

" On motion the clerk was instructed to draw a warrant
for $716.66 when the chairman of finance committee re-
ported to him the title good for land bought of Weimer."

At the meeting of the council September 15, 1884, the
minutes of the preceding meeting were read and approved.

" J. W.Boggs made a verbal report that he did not think
the title to the Weimer land complete.

" On motion, the motion made September 1st, instructing
the finance committee to close up the bargain for the Weimer land, was reconsidered.   Original motion coming up
was lost."

The clerk further testified that he found from the record
that Mr. Boggs was then chairman of the finance committee.

V. G. Lantry testified as follows:

" I am one of the defendants in this case and, commencing in May, 1884, was mayor of the city of Blair; that
after the city decided to purchase that land and authorized
the chairman of the finance committee to complete the
transaction, he called me into his office and told me that he
knew but little about abstracts and wished me to complete
it.   He authorized Mr. Farr to draw a check and have it
ready whenever I called for it, and I examined the abstract and took the deed and took the money and paid for
it.   I put the deed on record.   I did that as a favor to

Mr. Boggs. I paid a mortgage of $525.80 to George B. Lane, and there was an existing mortgage in favor of A. E. Wells for $533.34. Deducting these items from $1,250, the agreed price, it left $190.86, which I paid to Mrs. Weimer, less $1.80 for mortgage discharge. I think I charged them but one dollar for drawing the discharge, and eighty cents for recording it. That was the disposition that I made of the money. This was done from the 6th to the 8th of September, 1884, and on the 15th of September, during my absence, Mr. Boggs reported the title was bad, and on the strength of that the city council ordered that transaction off. I think there is a minute to that effect on the record. That was the only transaction I had in the premises. There had been no tender of the title of this land by the city. The city attorney came to me and said he was directed by the city council to fix up that Weimer matter, and I think the language I used to the city attorney was, I told the city council to go to the place not polite to mention."

Edmond J. Farr testified as follows:

"I was city clerk in the year 1884. I was instructed by the city council, I think somewhere about September, that whenever the chairman of the finance committee reported to me that the title to the Wiemer land that they were trying to buy for cemetery purposes was good, to draw an order for $716.66. I think it was September 6th. Mr. Boggs came to my office with Mr. Lantry and told me that the title to the land was good, and told me to draw the order in favor of Mr. Lantry. I asked him if I should not draw it in his favor, and Mr. Lantry said it would be better to draw it in that way, and Mr. Boggs said, 'No, draw it in your name, Vic, because you understand the business. You go ahead and close up the deal'; and they went over to a desk near by and were talking there, and one of them told me the amount to draw. I did not know the exact amount at the time, and asked them, and they told me, and I drew it in their presence. They started out, Mr. Boggs first and Mr. Lantry next, and as he got to the door I asked if he was going to take the order, and he said, ' No, I will call for it in a day or two; just leave it there. You need not tear it out of the book.' I think about September 8th I was away from town; Mr. Lantry came to my office and got the order. September 15th Mr. Lantry was absent from the meeting, and Mr. Boggs reported that he did not think that the title was good, and ordered the previous order rescinded, although it had been issued at his instance. I never got any of that money. Do not know personally what was done with it. I never saw the order after I issued it."

It was agreed that there was $1,000 in the cemetery fund in the city treasury at the time the order was drawn.

There is other testimony in the record to which it is unnecessary to refer.

Section 86 of chapter 14 of the Compiled Statutes provides that "The city council of cities, and board of trustees in villages, shall, within the first quarter of each fiscal year, pass an ordinance to be termed the annual appropriation bill, in which such corporate authorities may appropriate such sum or sums of money as may be deemed necessary to defray all necessary expenses and liabilities of such corporation, not exceeding in the aggregate the amount of tax authorized to be levied during that year; and in such ordinance shall specify the objects and purposes for which such appropriations are made, and the amount appropriated for each object or purpose. No further appropriations shall be made at any other time within such fiscal year, unless the propositon to make such appropriation has been first sanctioned by a majority of the legal voters of such city or village, either by a petition signed by them or at a general or special election duly called therefor; and all appropriations shall end with the fiscal year for which they were made."

Sec. 87 of same chapter provides that "Before such annual appropriation bill shall be passed the council or trustees shall prepare an estimate of the probable amount of money necessary for all purposes to be raised in said city or village during the fiscal year for which the appropriation is to be made, including interest and principal due on the bonded debt and sinking fund, itemizing and classifying the different objects and branches of expenditures as near as may be, with a statement of the entire revenue of the city or village for the previous fiscal year, and shall enter the same at large upon its minutes, and cause the same to be published four weeks in some newspaper published or of general circulation in the city or village."

Section 88 of same chapter provides that "The mayor and council, or board of trustees, shall have no power to appropriate, issue, or draw any order or warrant on the treasurer for money unless the same has been appropriated or ordered by ordinance, or the claim, for the payment of which such order or warrant is issued, has been allowed according to the provisions of this chapter, and the appropriations for the class or object out of which such claim is payable has been made as provided in section 88. Neither the city council or board of trustees, nor any department or officer of the corporation, shall add to the corporation expenditures in any one year anything over and above the amount provided for in the annual appropriation bill for that year, except as herein otherwise specially provided; and no expenditure for any improvement, to be paid out of the general fund of the corporation, shall exceed in any one year the amount provided for such improvement in the annual appropriation bill; *Provided, however,* That nothing herein contained shall prevent the city council or board of trustees from ordering, by a two-thirds vote, the repair or restoration of any improvement, the necessity of which is caused by any casualty or accident happening after such annual appropriation is made. The city council or board

17

of trustees may, by a like vote, order the mayor or chairman of the board of trustees and finance committee to borrow a sufficient sum to provide for the expense necessary to be incurred in making any repairs or restoration of improvements, the necessity of which has arisen, as is last above mentioned, for a space of time not exceeding the close of the next fiscal year, which sum, and interest, shall be added to the amount authorized to be raised in the next general tax levy, and embraced therein. Should any judgment be obtained against the corporation, the mayor, or board of trustees, and finance committee, under the sanction of the city council or board of trustees, may borrow a sufficient amount to pay the same for a space of time not exceeding the close of the next fiscal year, which sum, and interest, shall in like manner be added to the amount authorized to be raised in the general tax levy of the next year, and embraced therein "; and section 89 of same chapter provides that " No contract shall hereafter be made by the city council or board of trustees, or any committee or member thereof, and no expense shall be incurred by any of the officers or departments of the corporation, whether the object of the expenditure shall have been ordered by the city council or board of trustees or not, unless an appropriation shall have been previously made concerning such expense, except as herein otherwise expressly provided."

It will be seen that no contract can be made by the city council or any committee or member thereof, or any expense incurred by any of the officers or departments of the corporation, whether such expense shall have been ordered by the city council or not, unless an appropriation shall have been previously made concerning such expense, except in certain cases where a further expenditure is sanctioned by a majority vote of the legal voters of the city, etc.

The testimony clearly shows that the appropriation ordinance in the year 1884 did not include the amount required for the purchase of the lands in question, and the case is not within any of the exceptions named in the statute. Hence the contract was directly prohibited. The city council, no doubt, in entering into negotiations for the purchase of the land in controversy, as also the defendants in this case, acted in the utmost good faith, and there is not a particle of proof tending to show fraud or collusion, or an intention to disregard the law. Their action, however, was entirely unauthorized, and for that reason the city is entitled to recover the money drawn upon the order.

Upon what theory the court below found against Lantry, and dismissed the action against Farr, we are unable to discover. The statute makes it the duty of the city clerk to countersign all warrants drawn upon the city treasurer, and provides that each warrant shall state the particular fund or appropriation to which the same is chargeable, and the person to whom payable, and for what particular object; and that no money shall be otherwise paid than upon such warrants so drawn, and each warrant shall specify the amount levied and appropriated to the fund upon which it is drawn, and the amount already expended upon such fund. Comp. Statutes, Ch. 14, Art. 1, Sec. 66. The money could not have been drawn from the treasury, therefore, without the joint act of the mayor and clerk of the city. The conduct of Mr. Boggs, as shown by testimony in the record, is inexcusable. As chairman of the finance committee he was entrusted with the examination of the title to this land, and was authorized so far as the city council could authorize him, to purchase the land if he found the title perfect. He made verbal report to the defendants Farr and Lantry, that the title was good, and induced them to issue the order in question, and afterwards reported to the city council that the title was defective, whereupon the council repudiated the purchase. Had the city in any manner ratified this contract after

full notice of its terms and conditions, it would be estopped
from alleging its illegality; but no act of ratification has
been shown.

The petition as to the Weimers wholly fails to state a
cause of action. So far as it appears they acted in the utmost good faith. The order was not drawn in their favor,
nor did they draw any money from the treasury of the
city of Blair; and if the defendants purchased without
authority, the contract would seem to be sufficient to bind
them personally. Mr. Lantry was not acting in an official
capacity. Suppose he had purchased chattels in place of
real estate, and the city had disclaimed authority, it will
not be contended that he could compel the seller to take
the property again and refund the money? The same rule
would seem to apply in this case. The court erred, therefore, in overruling the demurrer as to Weimers.

In view of the fact that this order was drawn under a
mistake as to the law, and there is no proof that the funds
in question were drawing interest, therefore no interest will
be allowed. The judgment of the district court as to
Weimers will be reversed, and the action as to them dismissed. The judgment dismissing the action as to Farr is
reversed, and judgment will be entered in this court against
Farr and Lantry for the sum of $716.66, to be paid within
ninety days, provided the city within that time shall execute and deliver to them a good and sufficient deed conveying to them the title of the city to the land in question.

JUDGMENT ACCORDINGLY.

THE other judges concur.

THE VILLAGE OF WEEPING WATER, PLAINTIFF IN
ERROR, V. EUGENE L. REED AND THE WEEPING
WATER ACADEMY, DEFENDANTS IN ERROR.

21
40

1. **Notary Public:** SEAL. The seal of a notary public which
contains the words "Notarial Seal," the name of the county for
which he was appointed, and the word "Nebraska," is sufficient
for the authentication of his official acts. Section 5 of chapter
sixty-one of the Compiled Statutes does not require the name
or initial of the notary to be engraved in the seal. The provision of the section concerning the name or initials of the name of
the notary is permissive only.

2. **Town Sites:** EXECUTION AND ACKNOWLEDGMENT OF PLAT.
In the year 1868 the owners of real estate caused the land upon
which the village of W. now stands to be surveyed as a town
site, and in 1870 the plat thereof to be recorded. All the owners
signed and acknowledged the plat except one, whose name
was signed by another one of the platters as "attorney." The
person whose name was thus signed, but who did not acknowledge the plat, afterwards conveyed to a third party his interest
in the town site, excepting certain lots and blocks, as designated by the plat. His grantee and all others have at all times
recognized the validity of the plat. *Held*, That under the provisions of section 115 of chapter 14 of the Compiled Statutes,
the execution and recording of the plat sufficiently complied
with the provisions of section 42 of chapter 53 of the revised
statutes of 1866—as amended by the act of February 8, 1869—
and that by the provisions of section 43 of the same chapter,
the recorded plat was equivalent to a deed in fee simple from
the proprietors to the public of all portions of the platted land
dedicated to public use.

3. ——— : ——— : DEDICATION : EJECTMENT. Where in such
plat a square is marked and designated therein as "College
Square," the lots in adjoining blocks, abutting thereon, being
only one-half the size of other lots in that part of the plat, and
so laid out as to front to the square, and held at a higher valuation by reason thereof in order to secure compensation for the
land included in such square, it was *Held*, That there was a
dedication of College Square to the public, with a right to the
use thereof for the purpose of an institution of learning so long
as the user continued ; the title remaining in the public, as

represented by the municipal corporation (after being incorporated) for that use, and ejectment will lie to remove any person
unlawfully in possession.

4. **Ejectment**: LIMITATION: BURDEN OF PROOF. Where, in
an action of ejectment, the defendant in possession of the real
estate, the subject of the action, relies upon the statute of limitations as a defence, the burden of proof is on him to show that
his possession has been continuous, adverse, hostile and exclu
sive during the ten years last preceding the commencement of
the action.

ERROR to the district court for Cass county.   Tried below before HAYWARD, J.

H. D. Travis, for plaintiff in error.

J. H. Bellows and *E. H. Wooley*, for plaintiff in error.

REESE, J.

This was an action in ejectment instituted by the village of Weeping Water for the possession of a parcel of
land designated on the village plat as "College Square."
The action was instituted for the purpose of ejecting the
defendant Reed, but before the cause was tried the Weeping Water Academy appeared and made claim to the property, and asked to be made a defendant, which was done.
Each defendant then filed separate answers denying the
plaintiff's title or right of possession.   Upon trial judgment was rendered in favor of the defendants, and plaintiff
prosecutes error to this court.

From the testimony it appears that on the 19th day of
December, 1870, the owners of the land upon which
Weeping Water now stands filed in the office of the county
clerk the plat and field notes of the town.   The survey
had been made in March, 1868, and the acknowledgment
taken on the 29th day of June of the same year.   In a
part of the plat rather remote from what seems to have
been intended as the business portion of the town, a block

was left undivided and designated as "College Square." The lots surrounding this block and fronting towards it were of one-half the size of other lots in that part of the plat as is shown by the following diagram :

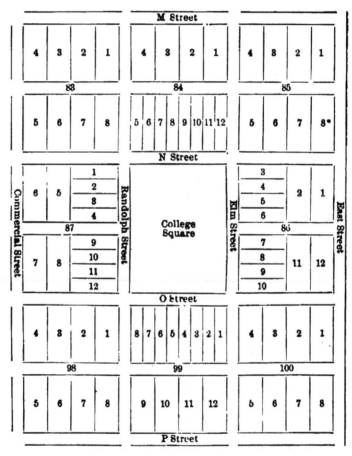

For some years after the platting of the ground, there appears to have been no demand for the lots in that part of the town where College Square was located, and a part of the square and a considerable portion of the other blocks, streets, and alleys were enclosed with a fence, and the grounds used for pasturage and other purposes, but as the demand grew up for the property the fence was removed.

On the 20th day of June, 1885, and about ten days before the commencement of this action, the Weeping Water Town Company, by E. L. Reed, president, and F. Bellows, secretary, deeded the property to the defendant academy, and its claim of ownership is based upon this deed.

A great many questions are presented by plaintiff in error, growing out of alleged errors of the trial court in its rulings in admitting in evidence deeds and other documents presented by defendant on the trial. As the trial was to the court without a jury we shall disregard these exceptions and take it for granted that the court was as able to pass upon the admissibility of the evidence in considering the whole case as during the trial. We will, however, notice one which seems to require some attention because of its general importance. It appears that one of the deeds introduced and objected to was acknowledged by the grantor before a notary public having a seal, the impression of which appeared on the paper. This impression did not contain the name nor the initials of the name of the notary before whom the acknowledgment was taken. The objection to the introduction of the deed was that the acknowledgment was not authenticated and proved as required by law.

Section 5 of chapter 61 of the Compiled Statutes, Laws 1869, p. 22, sec. 5, provides that "Each notary public, before performing any of the duties of his office, shall provide himself with an official seal, on which shall be engraved the words 'Notarial Seal;' the name of the county for which he was appointed and commissioned, and the word 'Nebraska,' and in addition, at his option, his name, or the initial letters of his name, with which seal, by impression, all his official acts as notary public shall be authenticated."

It is contended that the requirement of this section is, that the seal must contain either the name of the notary or the initials of his name, as he may prefer, and to this extent he may exercise his choice—his option—but no further. On the part of defendant in error it is insisted that the proper construction of the section is, that the seal must contain the words provided for, and if the notary so desire, he may add his name or the initials thereof; that he may exercise his option as to either, and that the seal is as good without either as with. This, we think, is the correct view. The proper construction of the section, as we think, is, that the seal shall contain the words, "Notarial Seal," the name of the county for which the notary was appointed, and "Nebraska"; and that, if the notary so desire—at his option—he may add his name or the initials thereof. This has been the construction placed upon this section by the bar of the state, and, so far as we know, by the officers of the state and of the counties throughout the state, and it would require a strong case indeed to justify a court at this late day in adopting the construction contended for and thus destroying the evidence of the title to real estate throughout the state upon which reliance has been placed since the date of the enactment of the law. We therefore hold that the court did not err in admitting in evidence the deed referred to.

There are two principal questions involved in this case, which are: Was the filing and recording of the town plat in connection with the conduct and representations of the parties in interest a dedication of College Square to the public? and if such was the effect, can plaintiff maintain ejectment for its possession? These questions arise upon the allegations of the motion for a new trial and the petition in error, that the findings and judgment of the district are not supported by the evidence, and are contrary to law.

First, Was there a dedication of College Square?

The affirmative of this question is insisted upon by plaintiff in error with much earnestness and apparent confidence, while the negative is as strongly contended for by defendant in error. This contention arises out of a defective acknowledgment attached to the town plat. The "explanation" and plat are executed by F. M. Wolcott, Hattie B. Wolcott, E. L. Reed, Annie B. Reed, Garry Treat, Kate Treat, Levina Hunter, and S. Clinton and Mary Clinton, by their attorney, E. L. Reed. The justice before whom the acknowledgment was taken certified therein that all the parties named in the certificate appeared and acknowledged the plat, but no mention is made of the Clintons, and there is no proof of their having signed or acknowledged the plat. Their names appear thereto, but it is signed "by their attorney, E. L. Reed," the defendant, and there is no proof of the existence of any authority on the part of Reed to sign their names. But it appears that the Clintons have never questioned the legality of the platting of the town, and on the 4th day of August, 1875, they executed a deed to L. F. Reed, by which they conveyed to him all their interest in the town site, excepting certain lots and blocks, thereby recognizing the existence and legality of the plat. Again, the defendant, E. L. Reed, did sign and acknowledge the plat, and since Clinton has recognized the validity of the act of Reed for him, we do not see that Reed can at this day very well question the validity of his own act.

The plat was filed for record on the 19th day of December, 1870, and therefore must be governed, so far as the effect of the platting and recording is concerned, by sections 42 et seq. of chapter 53 of the Revised Statutes of 1866, as amended by the act of February 8, 1869. Laws 1869, p. 26. Sections 42 and 43, as amended, are as follows:

"Section 42. The proprietor of any land may lay out a town or addition to any town, and shall cause an accurate map or plat thereof to be made out under the name of .... (naming it), designating explicitly the land so laid

out, and particularly describing the lots, streets, avenue ·
lanes, alleys, or other grounds belonging to such town or
addition; the lots must be designated by their numbers,
and the streets, avenues, lanes, and other grounds by names
or numbers; and such plat shall be acknowledged before
some officer authorized to take the acknowledgment of
deeds or conveyances of real estate, and shall be filed and
recorded in the office of the county clerk of the county;
and in case the land so platted, acknowledged and recorded,
be an addition to any town incorporated under the general
laws of this state, said lands shall be a part of such incorporated town for all purposes whatsoever, and the inhabitants thereof shall be entitled to all the rights and privileges
and be subject to all the ordinances, by-laws, rules and
regulations of the town to which such land is an addition.

"Section 43.   Such plat and acknowledgment, being so
recorded, shall be equivalent to a deed in fee simple from
the proprietor, of all streets, alleys, avenues, squares, parks,
and commons, and such portion of the land as is therein
set apart for public, county, village, town, or city use, or
is dedicated to charitable, religious, or educational purposes."

As we have said, Clinton has never questioned the legality and regularity of the platting of the town, but, upon
the contrary, has expressly ratified it by his deed to L. F.
Reed.   So, also, has E. L. Reed, by his deed to L. F.
Reed, dated June 12th, 1875, ratified it (if, indeed, any
ratification was necessary on his part), and in which he
conveyed his interest in the town site, excepting certain
lots and blocks reserved.   On the 13th day of August,
1875, L. F. Reed and wife conveyed all of the unsold portion of the town site by particular descriptions of lots and
blocks, according to the plat, to the Weeping Water Town
Company. Under this conveyance defendant academy claims
by deed of June 20, 1885, in which the property is deeded
to it by the Town Company, and designated as "all that

portion of said village of Weeping Water known and platted as College Square, and reference is hereby made to the recorded plat of said town," etc. All parties to this action, therefore, are claiming under the plat referred to, and no one is disputing its validity for the purposes of a town plat. Under these circumstances it seems to us that section 115 of chapter 14 of the Compiled Statutes (enacted in 1879) must be held as curing any defects which may have existed in the acknowledgment of the plat. This section is as follows: "None of the provisions of this chapter shall be construed to require re-platting in any case where plats have been made and recorded in pursuance of any law heretofore in force; and all plats heretofore filed for record, and not subsequently vacated, are hereby declared valid, nothwithstanding irregularities and omissions in manner or form of acknowledgment or certificate; but the provisions of this section shall not affect any action or proceeding now pending."

It is claimed by defendant in error that such a construction of the section above quoted as would hold it to cure the defect in the plat would be a violation of both the constitution of the United States and of this state, because it would have the effect of depriving the owner of his property without due process of law, and of taking private property for public use without compensation. To this we cannot give our assent. It cannot deprive Clinton of his property, for he claims no interest in the land in dispute. Neither can it affect his grantees, for they hold under him with direct reference to a lawful and valid plat. We therefore hold that, at least so far as the present action is concerned, the plat must be treated as having been lawfully made, and that it was equivalent to a deed in fee simple, under the provisions of section 43 above quoted.

It is insisted by defendants in error that even under the construction here given, there is no proof that the plattors intended to dedicate College Square to public use or to the village of Weeping Water, and that it remained their property. Aside from the plat itself, the testimony upon this point is somewhat meager, yet we think it is sufficient. It will be observed that the lots in the adjacent blocks were laid out with direct reference to the square in question. The lots were only one-half the size of other lots in that part of the plats. The designation "College Square" was evidently intended to mean that it was set apart for a use or purpose not private in its character, and in which the public would have an interest. That its use would make the adjacent property more valuable, and that the square was a donation or dedication. Mr. Barnes purchased two of the adjoining lots of Mr. Reed, and in his testimony, referring to the transaction, says: "I asked him the price of them and Mr. Reed spoke of the numbers as being one and two, and it looked like a small piece of ground to contain two lots. I asked him why he called it two lots, and he said the lots opposite College Square were divided into two rods wide instead of four as elsewhere in the town. I asked him why the lots were divided in that way, and he said it was in order to get compensation for College Square." In this transaction Reed was acting for the town company. In the testimony of Mr. Reed, in his cross-examination, the following question was propounded to him: "Will you explain why these lots fronting on College Square were less than the other lots?" His answer was, "The lots fronted on the public square and would be more valuable." It is also admitted of record that this square has not been taxed since 1875. These facts are sufficient to establish a dedication to the uses indicated. *Hannibal v. Draper*, 15 Mo., 634. *Doe v. Attica*, 7 Ind., 641. *Winona v. Huff*, 11 Minn., 75. *Church v. Hoboken*, 33 N. J. L., 13. *Baker v. Johnson*, 21 Mich., 319. *Cincinnati v. White*, 6 Peters, 431. *Trustees v. Havens*, 11 Ill., 554. *Gregory v. Lincoln*, 13 Neb., 353.

The effect of the plat being a deed in fee, and the facts

and circumstances connected with the platting and conduct
of the original owners showing a dedication, the question
arises as to whom the fee was conveyed and for what purpose. Evidently the fee was conveyed to the public as
represented by the citizens and property holders of the
town, and, when incorporated, in their corporate capacity
for the purpose, only, for which the dedication was made,
and no conveyance would be necessary to entitle the proper
occupant to the possession. Therefore the village holds
the title for that use. Such being the case, ejectment will
lie to remove any person from the possession who might
be using the square for a purpose not contemplated by the
dedication. Dillon on Mun. Corp., sec. 648. *Church v.
Scholte*, 2 Iowa, 27. *San Francisco v. Sullivan*, 50 Cal.,
603. Sedgwick & Waite on Trial to Title to Land, sec.
267, *et seq.*

It is contended that Reed, by himself and grantors, has
held adverse possession of the square in question for more
than ten years before the commencement of this suit, and
that plaintiff's action is barred by the statute of limitations.
The testimony shows that prior to the year 1875 a part of
the square, with other blocks, streets, and alleys, was enclosed with a fence and used for pasture, etc., but that about
that time a market for the lots arose, and that they might
be sold, the fence was removed. No actual possession was
afterwards had until in the year 1882, during which time
the property was unenclosed and subject to the use of the
public. In 1882 it was again fenced for the purpose of a
base ball ground and used as such, but upon objection being made by the citizens the fence was removed. Afterwards the ground was again enclosed with a wire fence, and
trees were set out on the square and surrounding streets.
The enclosure was also used for a pasture lot for cows. At
this time there were a number of residences of considerable
value as well as other valuable improvements upon the lots
fronting the square. It is pretty clear that the possession

has not been such as to protect defendant under the statute. In order to do so it must have been continuous, adverse, hostile, and exclusive during the ten years next preceding the commencement of the suit. Instead of such a possession there was an apparent abandonment of the property for a number of years—1875 to 1882—and at no time since the first named year has defendant caused the property to be taxed or in any way treated by the public as private property. It has sustained none of the burdens of the government, either municipal or otherwise. It is quite clear that the action was not barred.

The possession of Reed being in contravention of the purpose of the grant or dedication, it follows that the judgment of the court should have been in favor of plaintiff instead of defendant, and this without any reference to any title the defendant academy may have. For neither it nor its grantees or tenants have any right to occupy or use the premises in any other manner than in accordance with the dedication.

The answer of the academy is the same as that of Reed. No affirmative defense is presented. No relief, equitable or otherwise, is sought. It bottoms its defense alone on the weakness of plaintiff's case. Therefore the conclusion as to the rights of plaintiff as against Reed virtually disposes of the whole case. But the question might arise as to what rights, if any, has the academy in the square. We answer, as to the deed from the Weeping Water Town Company, of June 20, 1885, it has none. The town company having no title could convey none. But under the dedication, the rights of no educational institution having intervened, it will have all the rights of possession and use so long as it may see proper to occupy it as a site for an institution of learning. It may hold the possession as the beneficiary so long as it holds within the provisions of the dedication. In short it may use it for a "college square," but for no other purpose. So long as its occu-

pancy is in accordance with the grant, so long will its right
of possession be unimpaired.   But upon its failure to so
use the property its rights cease and are terminated. Anything short of this would be to sanction a violation of the
contract of dedication and an act of injustice to those of
the residents of the village who have bought and improved
property on the faith of the dedication and the expected
future use of the square.

The judgment of the district court is reversed and the
cause remanded for further proceedings.

REVERSED AND REMANDED.

THE other judges concur.

BERTHA DOGGE, PLAINTIFF IN ERROR, V. THE STATE
OF NEBRASKA AND S. M. MELICK, SHERIFF, DE-
FENDANTS IN ERROR.

1. **Witnesses.**   Under the provisions of the statutes of this state
   the parties to a civil action are competent witnesses, and each
   may be compelled to testify in favor of the adverse party the
   same as any witness.

2. **Notary Public:** DEPOSITION: CONTUMACIOUS WITNESS.   A
   notary public has power to commit for contempt a witness who
   refuses to give his deposition in a proper case.

ERROR to the district court for Lancaster county. Tried
below before POUND, J.

Billingsley & Woodward and *H. J. Whitmore,* for plaintiff in error.

Field & Harrison and *W. J. Houston,* for defendant in
error.

REESE, J.

On the 23d day of July, 1886, plaintiff filed her petition for a writ of habeas corpus before the Honorable S. B. Pound, judge of the District Court of the Second Judicial District, as follows, to-wit:

"Your petitioner, Bertha Dogge, respectfully represents to S. B. Pound, judge of the district court for the county of Lancaster, that she is unlawfully deprived of her liberty by one S. M. Melick, sheriff of Lancaster county, in this state.

"Your petitioner alleges the facts in regard to said detention to be as follows, to-wit: This petitioner is one of the defendants in an action pending in the district court of said county, wherein Hart Bros. et al. are plaintiffs and Bertha Dogge et al. are defendants; that one of the plaintiffs in said action on the 16th day of July, 1886, served upon the attorneys of your petitioner a notice that they would on the 21st day of July, 1886, at the office of James L. Caldwell, in the city of Lincoln, Nebraska, take the deposition of your petitioner; that on the 19th day of July, 1886, an alleged subpœna commanding your petitioner to appear before W. J. Houston, a notary public, at the office of J. L. Caldwell, in the city of Lincoln, in said county, on the 21st day of July, 1886, at nine o'clock in the forenoon, and give evidence in a suit between Hart Bros., plaintiffs, and Bertha Dogge and Otto H. Dogge, defendants, on the part of said Hart Brothers, plaintiffs.

"That your petitioner failed and refused to comply with the order of said pretended subpœna, and thereupon the said notary public, W. J. Houston, issued a writ of attachment, directed to the sheriff of said county, and caused your petitioner to be arrested and brought before him to give said deposition; that your petitioner refused to be sworn in said case and refused to answer the questions put to her by the said notary public and by the attorneys for

18

the said Hart Brothers; that thereupon the said notary public, W. J. Houston, made out a writ of commitment, directed to the sheriff of Lancaster county, the said S. M. Melick, commanding him to take your petitioner into his custody and to imprison her in the county jail of said county until such time as she would be willing to give her said deposition, or was otherwise released by law.   That this petitioner is set out in the notice to take depositions served herein in the pretended subpœna served upon her, and in all the papers filed herewith, as one of the parties defendant to the action; that there is no provision of the statute of the state of Nebraska whereby a defendant to an action can be compelled to testify in a cause before the time of trial thereof; that your petitioner is a resident of Lancaster county, Nebraska, is in good health, and capable of being present at the trial of the cause set out in said pretended subpœna, and has no intention of being absent from the county when said cause comes up for trial, of all of which the said attorneys for plaintiffs and the said notary public, W. J. Houston, had due notice in writing before the issuing of said writ of attachment, and before the issuing of said commitment; that the action of said notary public, W. J. Houston, in committing your petitioner to jail was illegal and unwarranted by law, and that the detention of your petitioner by said S. M. Melick is therefore illegal and wrong.   A copy of the warrant of commitment is hereto attached marked Exhibit 'A.'

"Your petitioner therefore prays that a writ of habeas corpus may be issued, and that she may be discharged from said unlawful imprisonment."

A writ was issued, but upon a hearing plaintiff in error was remanded to the custody of the sheriff, and she brings error to this court.

We have set out the petition in full in order that it may appear just what the legal propositions involved in the case are.

From the record before us it appears that a notice to take the deposition of plaintiff and Otto H. Dogge was given their attorneys, and a subpœna was served upon them.   These papers were in the usual form and need not be further noticed.   Prior to the time fixed for taking the deposition, plaintiff and Otto H. Dogge served upon the notary public a notice which we also copy in full.   It is as follows:

"July 21st, 1866.

"To William J. Houston,
        Notary Public, Lincoln, Nebraska.

"We have been notified and summoned to appear at your office this day for the purpose of giving our testimony on behalf of the plaintiffs in the above entitled action; the above-named plaintiffs are all non-residents of this state; we are citizens and residents of the city of Lincoln, Lancaster county, Nebraska; are in good health, and have no intention of changing our residence.

"Under and by virtue of the laws of this state, there is no legal or sufficient reason for the taking of our deposition at this time, or our evidence had in this cause, before the trial of the same.

"We respectfully decline to appear at your office as requested in said summons, and decline to give our evidence in said cause at this time.

"You are hereby notified that we will hold you responsible in damages as such officer, for any and all acts, official or otherwise, in which it may be attempted to coerce us into giving our testimony in this case prior to the hearing of said cause in our district court.

"We give you this notice prior to the hour set for our appearance before you, that you may act advisedly in the premises.   .   .

BERTHA DOGGE,
OTTO H. DOGGE."

Upon plaintiff's failure to appear at the time fixed for taking her deposition, an attachment was issued by the notary and she was arrested and taken before him and required to be sworn and give her testimony, which she refused to do. She was then found guilty of contempt by the notary, and ordered to be committed to prison until she should consent to testify. The record made and entered by the notary is as follows:

"The said Bertha Dogge being brought before me on said attachment and by me being requested to be sworn and testify in the above cause of Hart Brothers, plaintiffs, and Bertha Dogge and Otto H. Dogge, defendants, refused to be sworn and refused to testify as a witness in the above action.

"Whereupon, I found Bertha Dogge guilty of contempt, and entered the following judgment:

"It is therefore ordered and adjudged by me, that the said Bertha Dogge be imprisoned in the county jail of Lancaster county, Nebraska, there to remain until she shall submit to be sworn to testify and to give her deposition in the above entitled cause.

(Seal.)   W. J. HOUSTON,
                                  Notary Public."

The warrant of commitment is in the usual form.

In the brief and argument of plaintiff in error, she says: "Two important questions are brought before this court for decision in this case.

"1. Whether the adverse party to a suit can, in this state, be compelled to testify?

"2. Has a notary public in this state power to commit for contempt, a witness who refuses to give his deposition?"

These questions alone are presented, and they alone were argued at the bar of the court, and they alone will be considered.

We are thus specific for the reason that, in the consultation room, the suggestion was made that the action in which the deposition was sought was perhaps against husband and wife, that relation existing between plaintiff and Otto H. Dogge, and that, therefore, plaintiff might be protected by the provisions of section 331 of the civil code, which provides in substance that the wife can in no case be a witness against the husband except in a criminal proceeding for a crime committed by him against her. But upon a careful examination of the petition, abstract, and briefs, we find that this question is not presented in any form. There is no mention of any such relation existing between the parties named, and therefore that question cannot enter into the case, and is not decided.

First, then, can the adverse party to a suit be compelled to testify?

Section 328 of the civil code provides that all persons with sufficient capacity to understand the obligation of an oath, are competent witnesses in all cases, civil or criminal, except as is otherwise declared. Neither in this section nor in any other part of the law of evidence, as regulated by the statutes of this state, do we find any exception which would render a party to an action an incompetent witness. There is no express provision of law rendering parties to an action competent witnesses, excepting as contained in the section above referred to. It is conceded that such a person is a competent witness when called by the adverse party if he willingly testifies, but it is insisted that the law nowhere gives one party to an action the right to call and examine an opposite party without his consent. From an examination of the statute we are convinced that it was the intention of the legislature, in the enactment of the chapter on evidence, to remove every barrier to the discovery of truth, where the parties to the action have equal opportunity to testify. And where necessary, either party may call the other to testify as to facts exclusively within his knowledge, provided the questions are not privileged. This intention is clearly shown by section 398, which is as follows: "In addition to the above remedies, if a party to a suit in his own right, on being duly subpœnaed, fail to appear and give testimony, the other party may, at his option, have a continuance of the cause as in case of other witnesses, and at the cost of the delinquent." This section would be without effect and the "remedy" given by it would be no remedy at all, if when the party appeared in answer to a subpœna he could refuse to be sworn and thus deprive a party of the benefits of the rights given by the provision.

The next question, as to the power of a notary public to commit for contempt, a witness who refuses to give his deposition, involves the whole judicial power of that officer; for, if he has any power of the kind mentioned, the right to commit for contempt is clearly given by sections 356 *et seq.*, civil code. The contention that a notary public cannot exercise judicial functions is based upon section 1 of article 6, of the constitution of the state, which is as follows:

"The judicial power of this state shall be vested in a supreme court, district courts, county courts, justices of the peace, police magistrates, and such other courts inferior to the district court as may be created by law for cities and incorporated towns."

It is said that the commitment of a person to jail for a contempt presupposes a judicial inquiry, judgment and sentence, and that the officer who exercises these functions must of necessity do so in the exercise of judicial power. This is true; and if the constitution must be treated as limiting the exercise of all judicial functions to the courts named in the section above quoted, then the position of plaintiff in error is unassailable, unless another provision of the constitution hereafter noticed, continues in force the laws conferring judicial powers which were in existence at the time of its adoption. But the question might arise as to whether or not such is the purpose of this section, or whether it does not have reference to the creation and organization of courts for trial of causes, civil and criminal, and the administration of justice in accordance with the forms of law in the protection of rights and the enforcement of remedies? If it was the intention of the framers of the constitution to prevent the exercise of *all* judicial functions except by the courts referred to, and to prohibit their exercise by *all* persons except such courts, then indeed would the administration of the law be exceedingly difficult. As illustrative of the idea here suggested, we might refer to the matter of the appraisement of property.

In *Sessions v. Irwin*, 8 Neb., 5, it is held that appraisers selected by a sheriff to appraise real estate levied upon by him, act judicially in making the appraisement. If this is true they must in some degree exercise judicial power, and if true why do not other appraisers act judicially; such as in the appraisement of lands taken for drains, for school house sites, for the establishment of roads, for the right of way for railroads, changing the grade of streets, of property for county buildings, or of university and school lands, or on the foreclosure of tax liens, or of property taken in attachment or replevin, or of homesteads, estrays, effects of decedents, estates assigned for the benefit of creditors, or of animals killed by live stock sanitary commission?

Again, county boards in the discharge of their duties are continually called upon to exercise judicial functions. The same may be said of many other officers, and persons, whom we need not mention. Are their acts of the character named all void by reason of this section of the constitution? We think not.

But it may be insisted that the judicial functions of a notary public or board of county commissioners, in imprisoning for contempt, are the functions of a *court*, and therefore are not governed by the same principles as those to which we have referred. While not adopting such a suggestion, we need only say that if this is true, yet we think the judicial functions of a notary public are continued by section 4 of article 16, of the constitution. This section provides that "all existing courts which are not in this constitution specifically enumerated, and concerning which no other provision is herein made, shall continue in existence, and exercise their present jurisdiction until otherwise provided by law."

The law authorizing the imprisonment of witnesses for refusing to testify or give deposition, and also the law creating the office of notary public, with the powers and duties thereof, were in force at the time of the adoption of the present constitution. Now, if a notary public in the exercise of the judicial functions or power given by law, is a *court* as claimed by plaintiff in error, then we must hold that the authority and power of that court is " continued in existence," and will be authorized to "exercise their present jurisdiction until otherwise provided by law," by virtue of the section of the constitution last above quoted.

The judgment of the district court is affirmed.

JUDGMENT AFFIRMED.

THE other judges concur.

FIRST NATIONAL BANK OF CENTRAL CITY, PLAINTIFF IN ERROR, V. JONAS E. LUCAS, DEFENDANT IN ERROR.

1. **Landlord and Tenant**: IMPROVEMENTS. Where a landlord leases real estate, to be occupied by a tenant at a future time, and before such occupancy, without request from the tenant, makes certain improvements which are necessary to prepare the property for such occupancy, there is no legal liability against the tenant to pay for such improvements unless created by contract or agreement to pay the same.

2. Corporations: BANK: LIABILITY OF PRESIDENT SELLING
    PROPERTY WITHOUT AUTHORITY. As between the corporation
    and himself, a president of a bank ordinarily has no authority
    to sell the property of the corporation of which he is such offi-
    cer.   Before he can legally do so he must have authority by the
    charter, the direction of the board of directors, managing com-
    mittee, or by usage.   And where the property of a bank is sold
    by a president without authority and the bank suffers loss
    thereby, he may be held to respond in damages to the extent of
    such loss.

3. ———: ———: PAYMENT OF LOSS: ESTOPPEL.   Where the
    president of a bank without authority disposes of the property
    of the bank, and the bank is damaged thereby, and for the pur-
    pose of making good the loss, either temporarily or perma-
    nently, transfers to the bank promissory notes held by him in
    an amount equal to the loss sustained ; and where afterwards
    he disposes of his interest in the bank and induces others to pur-
    chase a controlling interest in the stock upon the representation
    that he has no demand against the bank, he cannot afterwards
    recover of the bank the amount of the notes transferred to it
    for the purpose of making up the deficiency caused by the loss
    resulting from the sale of the bank's property.

ERROR to the district court for Merrick county.   Tried
below before POST, J.

Webster & White and *John Patterson,* for plaintiff in error.

A. L. Reinoehl and *A. Ewing,* for defendant in error.

REESE, J.

This action was instituted by defendant in error for the
recovery of the sum of $890.50, alleged to be due him
from plaintiff in error.

The allegations of the petition are as follows: "That
plaintiff from on or about August 1st, 1882, to April 1st,
1885, was a stockholder and the duly elected and qualified
president of defendant bank, and on the last date named
resigned his position as president, and disposed of his stock
and all interest and withdrew from the corporation.

"That during said time defendant in error expended out of his individual funds, for the use and benefit of defendant bank, the following items:

Court and sheriff's costs in the cause of the First National Bank of Central City, Neb., vs. Jos. N. Osterlind	$ 63	85
Attorney fee in said cause	100	00
Attridge & Keeney, labor in bank	30	10
Lunquist	2	15
Judgment in Hall Co., Neb., in favor of Whitney & Whitney	106	40
Costs in said cause	18	00
Attorney fee in said cause	25	00
Clerk of Nance Co. for abstract of Patrick lands..	20	00
Railroad fare and expenses incurred in negotiating and discounting $6,000 in notes belonging to bank	25	00

"That said amount is due and not paid. Further, said plaintiff alleges that on April 30th, 1885, he was the owner of certain promissory notes of the value of $500; that said notes were placed in the bank as his individual notes; that title had not passed from him, and that on the 30th day of April, 1885, he was entitled to the possession thereof; and that on the last mentioned date the defendant unlawfully and wrongfully converted said notes to its own use and to plaintiff's damage in the sum of $500.

"Plaintiff prays for judgment for the sum of $890.50 and costs."

The answer filed by plaintiff in error consisted of a general denial.

The trial court instructed the jury that the only items which they need consider were the charges for labor done upon the bank building, money paid for abstract of title to lands in Nance county, money paid as expenses in traveling to Fullerton, Omaha, and Lincoln in the negotiating of the notes of the bank, and the charges of conversion of the $500 in notes, thus withdrawing from the consideration of the jury the other items of the account.

The verdict of the jury was in favor of defendant in error for the sum of $453.30, upon which judgment was rendered. One of the grounds alleged in the motion for a new trial and the petition in error is that the verdict is not sustained by sufficient evidence.

Referring to the item of $30.10 paid Attridge & Keeney for labor in bank, we find the testimony of defendant in error as shown by the abstract to be as follows: "I was the owner of the building, and rented it to the bank. I made improvements. This bill was for work on counter and around the vault. The work was done before the bank moved in. I brought this up before the directors, and they did nothing with it." This is all the evidence we find on this item of account. If 'this were all, and by the record we must presume it was, there was nothing to support a verdict for the value of labor mentioned. It is true that if the labor was done by the procurement of the bank, or if it agreed to pay for the improvements made prior to its occupancy of the building, it would be bound by its contract. But there is nothing disclosed which would show any such procurement or contract on its part. It follows therefore that this item also should have been withdrawn from the consideration of the jury. The instruction withdrawing a part of the account substantially informed the jury that they might consider the remaining portion. There was no evidence to support a verdict for the item named.

The principal contention is as to the second alleged cause of action contained in the petition of defendant in error. The allegation is that on the 30th day of April, 1885, he was the owner of certain promissory notes of the value of $500; that said notes were placed in the bank as his individual notes; that he was entitled to them, and plaintiff in error had converted them to its own use to his damage, etc.

From the abstract of the testimony it appears that about the time of the organization of the bank an exchange committee, was formed, consisting of defendant in error, who was president of the bank, J. J. Chadwick, who was cashier, C. S. Lucas, about whose eligibility there was some question, and one other person, whose name is not given. This committee was formed under the by-laws of the corporation, and it was their duty to formulate rules and regulations by which the president and cashier were to be governed in making discounts, and in buying notes and in making rediscounts. In the latter part of 1884 the bank was the owner of promissory notes to the amount of $6,000, drawing interest at nine per cent per annum, which were secured by mortgage on real estate. Defendant in error sold these notes for the sum of $5,500 in money. In his testimony defendant in error testified that the notes were well secured "and were worth dollar for dollar on the market." This sale was made without any direction or authority from the exchange committee, and was never ratified by them or by the board of directors or the stockholders. The only evidence of any authority to make the sale was to the effect that defendant in error and J. J. Chadwick had a conversation upon the subject, and agreed that $5,500 in money was worth more than $6,000 in notes. C. S. Lucas objected to the sale. After the sale, whether upon the demand of the directors of the bank or not is not shown, defendant in error placed the notes referred to in the bank to make up the deficiency occasioned by the loss on the notes sold. The amount represented by the notes transferred to the bank is not given, but it is to be inferred that it was more than $500, as a certificate of deposit for the amount in excess of that sum was given him to be paid when collections were made. It seems to be quite clear that at the time the transfer of the notes was made it was understood to be for the purpose of repaying the loss to the bank occasioned by the improvident sale of the $6,000 of notes. It is also equally clear that defendant in error so understood it, and that he had no expectation of receiving either the notes or their value from the bank.

The sale of the $6,000 notes was without authority. At least none is shown. No rules or regulations had ever been made by the exchange committee which would authorize it, and it was not authorized by the board of directors. There is nothing in the act concerning the organization of national banks which would authorize it, and it is not shown to have been the custom of the bank to permit the president to make such sales to be subsequently ratified. Ordinarily the authority of a president of a bank, as such, is very much limited. He may bring an action at law and employ counsel for the purpose of protecting the rights of the bank, but he is not its executive officer nor has he charge of its moneyed operations. He has no more power of management, or disposal of the property of the corporation, than any other member of the board of directors. Morse on Banks and Banking, 146 *et seq.* It is true that extensive powers may be, and are, quite often, given to presidents of banking organizations by the charter of the bank or by the action of the managing board, and where so conferred, the right to proceed thereunder will exist; but there is no proof in this case, shown by the abstract, of any such power.

The fifth instruction given to the jury by the court is as follows: "The plaintiff, as president of the defendant bank, had the authority to sell and dispose of the notes belonging to said defendant when necessary or proper for the interest, or in order to protect the credit, of said bank, and money honestly and necessarily expended for railroad fare in negotiating said securities, or for abstract of title to lands mortgaged would be a just and legal demand against the defendant."

As we have seen, in the light of the testimony before us,

that part of the instruction which informs the jury that, as matter of law, the president had authority to dispose of the notes of the bank, was erroneous.

There is an additional reason why we think the verdict was not sustained by the evidence. This is shown by the uncontradicted testimony of N. R. Persinger, which we here copy in full:

"N. R. Persinger called and testified: Am a resident of Central City; am president of the First National Bank and was so engaged on 1st of April last. At or about that time I purchased some $38,000 and agreed to make purchase of stock up to $42,000 in bank. About the middle of February, 1885, Lucas came to me and proposed to sell me a controlling interest in bank. After some conversation J. J. Chadwick and Mr. J. E. Lucas at that time entered into a contract to sell me for $26,000 a controlling interest. I asked for a statement of liabilities and resources, which was furnished, and upon strength of which we entered into an agreement. The statement was furnished me about February 14th. The same was never claimed to be untrue until some five or six months after I purchased a controlling interest in the bank. He made no demand, merely handed me a list which he said the bank owed him. I knew of no claims until after my purchase. The statement furnished me purported to be a tabular statment of all liabilities and resources. Cross-examination: The statement is a transcript of the balance sheet. Contract I first made was to take possession of the bank on the 30th of April, and they sold stock to Lazear, and I took possession April 20th. I looked over the books. I made my bargain upon the strength of statements that I supposed correct, and disputed items should have appeared. I purchased the bank from the stockholders through Lazear, their agent. Lucas and Chadwick had sold their interest. Lucas said if I became purchaser he had no claims. Lucas and Chadwick sold to Lazear, and after the sale both came to me and urged me to buy, and said that whatever I made out of the books they would stand by. Re-direct: Notes deposited—Fagerstrom paid his. Wallenstein, maker of other two notes, came in and said they were obtained by fraud. I finally got him to execute a new note for the one then due. Both notes are unpaid. There was some kind of a statement attached to these notes showing their discount to the bank. There was also a certificate of deposit attached and stamped paid. The statement said portions of notes when collected should be paid to Lucas. The amount to be paid was the amount of the certificate."

The only testimony introduced which tended in any degree to contradict the foregoing was that of Mr. Chadwick on rebuttal, which we here give in full from the abstract:

"Chadwick recalled: Statement is in my hand-writing. I handed same to Persinger in presence of Lucas, and said it contained a copy of the balance sheet for that day, and said it was not exactly correct. I said loans and discounts did not agree with statement. Cross-examination: Am a practical book-keeper. I said bills receivable did not correspond with that statement. I said the books were in the same condition. I don't remember now what was the difference. We thought bills receivable overrun that day, but we were mistaken; they were short that amount."

It will be seen that this falls far short of contradicting the testimony of Mr. Persinger, that he knew of no claims of defendant in error until after his purchase of the stock, and that defendant had told him that if he became the purchaser he (defendant in error) had no claims. Defendant in error testified in the cause during the trial. He was, no doubt, present in court at the time Persinger gave his testimony, yet he failed to go upon the stand and rebut it. We can call to mind no rule of law which would permit him, by the representations described, to induce another to expend his money in purchasing the stock, and after the purchase is made upon the faith and credit of his statements, to turn about and recover for demands which he had declared did not exist.   Upon the contrary we think the rule of law to be well settled, that where one, by his words or conduct, wilfully causes another to believe the existence of a certain state of things, and induces him to act on that belief so as to alter his previous position, the former is concluded from averring against the latter a different state of things as existing at the same time.   Bigelow on Estoppel, 4th ed., 547, and cases there cited.   *Newman v. Mueller*, 16 Neb., 527.

It may be truthfully said that this action was not against Persinger and that he was not a party to the suit as shown by the record.   This is true; but the fact still remains that the effect would be the same, since by the representations of defendant in error Persinger was induced to expend his money in purchasing a controlling interest in the bank.

For the foregoing reasons a new trial should be awarded.

The judgment of the district court is reversed and the cause remanded for further proceedings.

REVERSED AND REMANDED.

THE other judges concur.

JOSEPH P. MANNING ET AL., PLAINTIFFS IN ERROR, V. DENNIS CUNNINGHAM, DEFENDANT IN ERROR.

1. **Errors must be assigned in Motion for New Trial.** In an action at law, to obtain a review of errors which have occurred during the progress of a trial, they must be assigned in the motion for a new trial.

2. **Chattel Mortgage:** PRIORITY OF LIENS.   A chattel mortgage, executed by the mortgagor in possession of the property as owner, although the legal title was not to pass to him until the chattels were paid for, where such contract of conditional sale was not filed for record, will take precedence over the secret lien of the party claiming to hold the legal title.

3. **Assignment of Error:** VERDICT. Where the only assignment of error in the motion for a new trial is that the "verdict is contrary to the facts," the verdict will not be set aside unless clearly wrong.

ERROR to the district court for Douglas county. Tried below before WAKELEY, J.

David Van Etten, for plaintiff in error.

Constantine J. Smyth, for defendant in error.

MAXWELL, CH. J.

This is an action of replevin brought by Cunningham against Black to recover the possession of a span of mules. Manning claimed a special ownership in the mules, by virtue of a chattel mortgage executed by Black to him, and on his motion he was permitted to intervene. The property was taken on the order of replevin and delivered to Cunningham. On the trial of the cause the jury returned a verdict finding the right of possession of the property at the commencement of the action to be in Cunningham, and awarding him five cents damages. Manning thereupon filed a motion for a new trial, "because said verdict is contrary to the facts, and upon the ground of newly discovered evidence." The motion was overruled, to which he excepted, and now assigns errors in this court as follows:

1st. The judgment of the court, that defendants pay the cost of action, when the evidence shows that they were in the rightful possession of said property, and when the action was commenced without demand made upon them, or either of them, to yield possession to the plaintiff, is contrary to law.

2d. The court erred in overruling a motion for a new trial.

19

3d. That the verdict of the jury is not sustained by sufficient evidence in finding the plaintiff entitled to the possession of the mules in controversy at the time of the commencement of the action.

4th. That the verdict of the jury is contrary to law, in finding the plaintiff entitled to the possession of said mules under the issue joined, without also finding him the owner of the same, which it did not find.

5th. That the instructions of the court given to the jury on its own motion were insufficient, vague, misleading, and contrary to law.

6th. That said judgment is not sustained by the verdict rendered.

7th. That the verdict is contrary to law.

8th. That said verdict is not sustained by sufficient evidence.

The plaintiff therefore prays:

1st. That said judgment be reversed.

2d. That judgment be rendered in favor of said Manning and against said Cunningham for the sum of $250, with interest from the 21st day of November, 1883, as the proof shows they were wor.h that sum on that day, with costs of suit; or

3d. In lieu thereof, that said action be remanded for a new trial, and for such other relief as justice may require.

The rule is well settled in this court that errors which are alleged to have occurred during the trial must be assigned in the motion for a new trial, or they will be waived. *Horbach v. Miller*, 4 Neb., 43. *Singleton v. Boyle*, 4 Id., 415. *Horacek v. Keebler*, 5 Neb., 356. *Hosford v. Stone*, 6 Neb., 381. *Walrath v. State*, 8 Neb., 88. *Stanton County v. Canfield*, 10 Neb., 390. *Russell v. State*, 13 Neb., 68. *Dodge v. People*, 4 Neb., 228. *Light v. Kennard*, 11 Neb., 130.

There is no evidence set out in the abstract as newly

discovered. The only ground of error, therefore, is that the "verdict is contrary to the facts."

The testimony tends to show that in the year 1881 Cunningham purchased the mules in question for Black, and delivered possession of the same to him. Cunningham claims that the mules were not sold to Black, but merely delivered to him, and not to be his until paid for, while there is other testimony in the record from which it appears that Black was the owner of the mules. In December, 1882, Black executed a chattel mortgage upon the mules in question to Manning to secure the payment of the sum of $800. At the time of the execution of the mortgage Cunningham had no actual notice of any claim or lien on file in the office of the county clerk. There is no doubt that a mortgage executed by Black upon said property to a mortgagee, who took the same in good faith, would take precedence of a secret lien in favor of Cunningham, and if the decision rested upon this question alone the judgment would be reversed. The testimony shows, however, that after the execution and delivery of the chattel mortgage Black transferred certain real estate to Manning, the value of which was $4,000 to $5,000, in which transaction it is claimed by Black the debt secured by the mortgage on the mules was included and satisfied. There is some testimony tending to corroborate his evidence. Manning, while admitting the transfer of the real estate, denies that the entire debt secured by the chattel mortgage has been paid. There is thus a direct conflict of evidence on that point, and the case was one proper to submit to a jury; and as the verdict is not against the weight of evidence, it will not be disturbed. The judgment of the district court is therefore affirmed.

JUDGMENT AFFIRMED.

THE other judges concur.

KENDAL S. JOHNSON, PLAINTIFF IN ERROR, V. HORACE
E. POWERS, DEFENDANT IN ERROR.

1. **Receiver.** An order appointing a receiver in a case brought
for the foreclosure of a mortgage without notice served on the
defendant, or his solicitor, as required by section 267 of the
code of civil procedure, *Held*, to be void.

2. ————: LIABILITY FOR MONEY COLLECTED. Money collected
by a receiver acting under a void appointment, as such, may be
recovered from him by the party entitled to it in an action for
money had and received to the use of the plaintiff.

ERROR to the district court for Washington county.
Tried below before NEVILLE, J.

John Lothrop, for plaintiff in error.

W. C. Walton, for defendant in error.

COBB, J.

This action was brought in the district court of Washington county by the plaintiff in error against the defendant
in error for certain moneys alleged to have been collected
and received by said defendant for the rent of property
belonging to the plaintiff by virtue of his appointment as
receiver by the said court in a certain action then pending therein, such appointment being claimed to be void.
As the cause was disposed of in the district court upon demurrer I copy the petition at length:

"1st. Plaintiff for cause of action says that he is
owner of lots three, four, and five in block No. 30 in the
city of Blair, Washington county, Nebraska, and has been
such owner continuously for the last past three years, and
that all of said time he has been in peaceable, undisputed
possession of the same, either in person or by tenant, up to
the 27th day of June, 1885.

"That there has been for more than two years immediately before filing this petition, and there is now on said
lots costly and valuable improvements consisting of a good
brick two-story dwelling house in good repair and condition, and a good two-story frame barn, wells, cisterns,
fruit trees, and shrubbery and all other necessary buildings and improvements for to make said premises very
valuable as a family residence; that the rental value of said
premises is and has been for the last year two hundred
dollars a year, payable in advance.

"That on or about the 3d day of April, 1885, the
Omaha Savings Bank commenced an action in this court
to foreclose a mortgage on said premises and made this
plaintiff defendant as mortgagor, and A. Castetter, E. H.
Monroe, and Palmer & Ryan defendants as subsequent
purchasers or incumbrancers; that on the 27th day of June,
1885, at an adjourned term of this court, the defendant, A.
Castetter, made application to said court for the appointment of a receiver to collect the rents and profits of said
premises. Such application was supported by affidavit
filed on said 27th day of June, 1885. That on said day
the court appointed this defendant receiver of said rents
and profits.

"This plaintiff further alleges that he had no knowledge
or notice of said application and proceedings until several
days after the receiver was appointed; that his attorney
had no notice until said proceeding came up for hearing;
that plaintiff was a resident of this county, and that no notice
by publication was made in any manner; that he did not
appear in said proceedings either in person or by attorney,
and alleges that no notice was issued or served as is required by law, and that no notice whatever was issued or
served on any of the parties or their solicitors; that for
the want of notice as is required by law this court had
no power to appoint this defendant receiver or to make any
appointment, and that said pretended appointment is void

and of no effect; that this plaintiff had a good and valid defense to said proceedings, as he believes and has been advised by counsel; that he would have made said defense had he been served with notice as is required by law.

"2d.   That on the said 27th day of June, 1885, and all the time since, this defendant has been in possession and exercised control over said premises under said proceedings. This plaintiff alleges that this pretended receiver has not filed in the office of the clerk of this court the bond required by law, and that no bond whatever has at any time been filed in said proceedings; that on the 27th day of June, 1885, this defendant, without authority, urged and persuaded the tenant then on said premises to pay the rent for the future use of said premises to this supposed receiver, which has been done, and by such payment this defendant has received of such rent the sum of two hundred and twenty dollars; that on the 6th day of March, 1886, this plaintiff demanded of defendant the said rent, and defendant refused to pay the same or any part thereof.

"Therefore plaintiff asks judgment against said defendant for the said sum of two hundred and twenty dollars, and cost of this action, and that defendant cease to act as such receiver, and for such other and further relief as this case may require."

Defendant filed a demurrer to the petition for the reason it does not state facts sufficient to constitute a cause of action.

On April 13th, 1885, the cause came on for hearing on demurrer, and the court sustains the demurrer and dismisses the case.

Assignments of error are: 1st. The court erred in sustaining demurrer.   2d. The court erred in dismissing the case.

Before the adoption of the code and the abolition of the difference in the systems of practice in courts of law and of equity, it was the practice of the latter courts to appoint receivers in proper cases on motion at any time after the service of subpœna and the appearance of the defendant, without notice to the opposite party other than such as might be given in open court. Then, there was usually no statute regulating the practice, which was left to the discretion of the judge or chancellor. Now, the whole matter of the appointment of receivers is regulated by statute, and the principal question involved in the case at bar is whether the method prescribed is to be deemed as exclusive of all others.

Section 266 of the civil code points out the several cases in which receivers may be appointed, among others: "In an action for the foreclosure of a mortgage, when the mortgaged property is in danger of being lost, removed, or materially injured, or is probably insufficient to discharge the mortgage debt."

Section 267 provides as follows: "No receiver shall be appointed except in a suit actually commenced and pending, and after notice to all parties to be affected thereby, of the time and place of the application, the names of the proposed receiver and of his proposed securities, and of the proposed securities of the applicant. Such notice shall state upon what papers the application is based, and be served upon the adverse party or his solicitor, at least five days before the proposed hearing, and one additional day for every thirty miles of travel from the place of serving the notice to the place where the application is to be made, by the usually traveled route; or shall be published in the same manner as notice of the pendency of suit to non-residents."

Section 274 provides that "Every order appointing a receiver without the notice provided for herein, shall be void," etc.

Considering these two sections together, there can be no

doubt, even if there could have been upon the language of
sec. 267 alone, that it was the intention of the framers of
the statute that the form and method there prescribed for
the appointment of receivers by a court should be exclusive of all others, and that all orders for the appointment
of receivers made by any court, without the notice therein
prescribed, should be not merely voidable but void.

The allegations of the petition being for the purposes of ·
this opinion assumed to be true, and the defendant having
had no authority to act as receiver, his appointment as
such being absolutely void, he must be held to have possessed himself of the rent money of the plaintiff by his
own voluntary and unauthorized act, and to be liable
therefor as for money had and received.

Defendant in error contends, that even if it be held that
his appointment as receiver was null and void, that nevertheless the judgment of the district court in sustaining the
demurrer was right; that in that case the tenant is not discharged of his obligation to pay the plaintiff by reason of
his having already paid the rent to the defendant in his
assumed character of receiver, so that the plaintiff's remedy is still against the tenant.

While it is possible that the plaintiff might maintain an
action against the tenant for the rent of the premises, and
that the latter would be unable to maintain the defense,
that he had already paid the same to the defendant as
receiver, yet the defendant is entitled to avail himself of
no such consideration. Should the plaintiff collect the
rents from the tenant the latter would certainly have a
cause of action against the defendant for the money paid
him, so that this would lead but to a multiplicity of actions
which the law as well as equity abhors. ·The action of assumpsit was sometimes called "the equitable action of the
common law," because it can generally be maintained by
the party entitled to a fund against one who has no right
to retain it.

The judgment of the district court is reversed and the cause remanded for further proceedings in accordance with law.

REVERSED AND REMANDED.

THE other judges concur.

GOTLIEB KILLINGER ET AL., PLAINTIFFS AND APPEL-LANTS, V. JOHN GEORGE HARTMAN, DEFENDANT AND APPELLEE.

Trusts: PETITION FOR ACCOUNTING: SUPPLEMENTAL PETITION. The grantee in a deed from a grantor who had received a conveyance from a trustee, filed a bill to require the trustee to account, and to have him removed; and subsequently, having purchased in certain general interests in the trust, asked leave to set up the same by supplemental petition; *Held*, 1. That having shown no interest in the trust in the original petition, he could not aid the same by a supplemental petition; and, 2. That having no interest in the trust at the commencement of the suit, he could not maintain the action.

APPEAL from the district court of Douglas county. Tried below before WAKELEY, J.

E. W. Simeral and *George W. Doane*, for appellants.

Congdon, Clarkson & Hunt, and for appellee.

COBB, J.

This case comes to this court on appeal from the district court of Douglas county. As it is an important, as well as a peculiar case, I copy the pleadings at length.

The plaintiffs in and by their petition allege:

"That on May 10, 1857, a society was organized and incorporated in the city of Dubuque, Iowa, known as the 'Homestead Society of Dubuque, Iowa,' and which was formed for the purpose of buying real estate to be divided among the members for homes; that the plaintiffs are members and shareholders of said society, and that they or those from whom they derived their rights were each original members of said society; that in pursuance of the purpose of said organization, purchases were made of two tracts of land near Omaha, described in the petition, which were conveyed by the grantor to John George Hartman, 'in trust for the use and benefit of the shareholders in the Homestead Society of Dubuque, and by the said Hartman to be conveyed in lots or parcels in severalty to each member of said society, his heirs, or assigns, who were entitled thereto, according to his several interest in said premises; that said deeds were duly recorded; that Hartman took possession for and in behalf of said shareholders, and undertook to administer said trust; that in order to do so the more conveniently, he laid out said land into an addition to Omaha known as 'Hartman's Addition,' a plat of which was duly signed and acknowledged by him and recorded in the records of deeds of Douglas county, and a copy of which plat is attached to the petition as 'Exhibit A'; that said addition was so laid out into 84 lots; that that the larger number of said lots were allotted and deeded by defendant to the members of said society, or their assigns, but that a number of them have never been allotted to any of the members, but still remain in the possession of said defendant as trustee; a list of twelve of which lots so remaining unallotted is given in the petition by numbers; that in addition to the lots, a portion of the land, containing about seven acres, was left undivided, and was laid out on said plat and designated as 'Hartman's Reserve,' and which still remains in defendant's possession; that said seven acres have been used and occupied by defendant, upon which he has had a house erected and a fence placed around it, and has cultivated and used it as a garden for a number of years for his own use and benefit, which was of the rental value of at least $10 per acre for each year; that during a portion of the time the defendant leased the land, and derived large profits therefrom; that a large number of the lots in said addition have been deeded by defendant to persons who were not members of said 'Homestead Society,' in fraud of his trust, and for the purpose and with the intention of cheating and defrauding the society, and the shareholders thereof, out of their just rights; that by fraud and misrepresentation he induced a number of the shareholders to deed to him their interest in that portion of said addition designated as 'Hartman's Reserve,' which was done without consideration and through fraud of said defendant as such trustee, and that said tract of land is now held by him in fraud of the rights of the members of said society; that large sums of money have at various times come into the hands of said defendant as such trustee, arising out of said trust property, the amount of which, and the times when received, plaintiffs are unable to state; that defendant has not faithfully discharged his trust, in that he has not accounted for or paid over to the shareholders of said society, or to plaintiffs, any of the money received by him as such trustee; that he has conveyed a number of said lots to persons of his own family and others not entitled thereto, said persons not being members of said society; that he has used and occupied said seven acres called 'Hartman's Reserve' for several years, and now claims to own the same, and to exclude plaintiffs and all other shareholders in said society from participation therein, and has refused and still refuses to make deeds to shareholders entitled thereto, and has abused his trust by obtaining from shareholders conveyances of their interest in said reserve of seven acres.

" Prays that defendant be required to render an account

of his trust, showing amount received by him in money or property as trustee, and the manner the same has been disposed of, and the income derived therefrom and payments made on account of his trust, with dates, etc., and also of all other matters arising out of said trusteeship; that he be adjudged to pay to the shareholders all monies which of right belongs to them or any of them, and that he be removed from said trust, and that some fit and suitable person be appointed in his stead, to whom defendant shall turn over all monies and other property in his hands belonging to said society, and make deeds to all lands still remaining in his hands as trustee, and that in the meantime, and until final hearing, he be enjoined from conveying, disposing of or in way intermeddling with said property, and for general relief."

And on the 14th day of February, 1881, the defendant filed his answer, setting up his defenses as follows:

"1st.   General denial except as to admissions subsequently made.

"2d.   While 'denying right of plaintiffs to bring and maintain this action for the reason that they have not the rights or interests claimed by them in the trust, the defendant having performed towards all of them the duties resting upon him as such trustee, and all of said parties or their assignors or grantors having selected and had allotted and deeded to them lots in said Hartman's Addition and all having quit-claimed their interest in the seven acres reserve mentioned in said petition, nevertheless for the purpose of fully answering said petition, and to terminate said trust if the court has jurisdiction and power in this action so as to say,' as follows:

"Admits incorporation of 'Homestead Society,' of which a copy of articles is attached to answer marked ' Exhibit A'; that 83 shares of stock were issued and that corporation dissolved on the 28th day of May, 1860, by the terms of its articles of incorporation; that certain conveyances had

been made to the Homestead Society of real estate near
Omaha, the title to which had failed, and thereupon the
defendant was given the power of attorney by the proper
officers of the society, on September 8, 1858, authorizing
him to act for said society, and to take such legal steps as
might be necessary to secure the rights of the society, which
power of attorney was duly recorded; that acting thereunder he expended much time and labor in endeavoring to
adjust the matters in controversy between said society and
the grantors in said deeds, etc.; that failing in that he began suit against them in the district court of Douglas county,
and after many years of vexatious trouble and litigation,
the same was in January, 1867, finally settled, the said defendant as trustee for shareholders in said society taking
conveyances for certain lands in lieu of those the title to
which had failed, and which lands so received constitute
what is now 'Hartman's Addition to the City of Omaha,'
all of which was ratified by the holders of shares in said
Homestead Society. That the defendant expended of his
own moneys in the prosecution and maintenance of said
action prior to January 1, 1860, certain sums, to-wit:

For court costs, $28.00, which, with interest
        from Jan. 1st, 1860, to Jan. 1st, 1881,
        makes due thereon .... $ 71.30
Attorneys' fees to five different attorneys, $617.70,
        which, with interest at 10 per cent from
        Jan. 1, 1860, to Jan. 1, 1881, makes
        due on that item 1914.80

"That the words of the trust expressed in the deeds to
defendant are as follows: 'In trust for the use and benefit
of and by the said J. George Hartman, to be conveyed to
the members of the Homestead Society at Dubuque, in
the state of Iowa, in the proportions and according to the
several interests in and to said premises to which said members are severally entitled.'

"That defendant took possession of the lands as alleged in petition, and entered upon the trust. The trust existed in favor of parties whose interests were measured by eighty-three shares of stock, which constituted all the shares issued. That by reason of defendant's services rendered from 1858 until 1867, the holders of shares awarded to him a parcel of land in said addition 410 feet east and west by 680 feet north and south, being the seven acres reserve mentioned in the petition. That defendant reserved the seven acres accordingly and divided the remainder into 84 lots, which constituted Hartman's Addition. That to equalize values, the lots were made of different sizes according to location. That he awarded and deeded said lots to the shareholders, one lot for each share, as the same were selected by them, and in the order of their demands for deeds. That he has up to date awarded and deeded such lots at such times, etc., as shown by 'Memorandum of lots,' etc., attached to and made part of answer as 'Exhibit B.' That all of these acts of his were done under the instruction and with the acquies-cence of the shareholders. That prior to January 1, 1868, he expended of his own moneys for the benefit of the share-holders for drawing and printing deeds, $62.00, which with interest at 10 per cent to January 1, 1881, makes due deft. thereon $114.00. That prior to January 1, 1871, he pub-lished notices in newspapers in different states notifying shareholders of their interests, etc., for which he expended $18.00, which with interest at 10 per cent, makes due thereon January 1, 1881, $36.00. That prior to January 1, 1866, he expended for surveying and cutting brush, $55.00, which with interest at 10 per cent makes due January 1, 1881, $137.50. That he expended for laying out addition $420.00' and that he has received from share holders thereon $320.00, leaving balance due him thereon $100.00, which with in-terest at 10 per cent makes due thereon January 1, 1881, $200.00. That he expended prior to May 1, 1871, for fence posts, fencing, and material used on lots still held by him, $84.50, which with interest to January 1, 1881, is $165.00. Also prior to January 1, 1875, for cutting brush, digging stumps, and grubbing on same lots, $175.00, which with interest at 10 per cent makes due January 1, 1881, $280.00. That he has paid for taxes the amounts and at the times shown in schedules attached to answer marked 'B,' 'C,' 'D,' and 'E,' upon which there is due January 1, 1881, to defendant $1,236.29. That for 14 years' services as trustee he has received no compensation, and that they are reasonably worth $300 per year, making due him for services as trustee January 1, 1881, $4,200. That each of the shareholders to whom a deed of a lot has been made has quit-claimed to the defendant all his interest in the seven acres reserve, and that he, the defendant, is trustee for the plaintiffs only to the extent that the plaintiffs together with all other *cestui que trusts* are entrusted or have rights in one uncertain lot in said Hartman's addition, which results from the fact that said addition was laid out into 84 lots represented by 83 shares, and which said lot remains in the hands of said trustee.

"Admits that the said defendant has sold lots to parties other than those holding shares in said Homestead Society, a list of which, with parties to whom sold, prices, etc., is given in 'schedule A' attached to answer and made part of same. That the sums realized from said sales with interest at 10 per cent, make in hands of defendant January 1, 1881, the sum of $3,988.06, but insists that he is under no obligation to account to plaintiffs for said sum for the reason that they have no interest therein, although willing to do so, if court adjudges that plaintiffs are entitled to an account.

"Admits that defendant has leased parts of lots 60, 61, 66, 67, 72, 73, and 78, and has received therefrom, including interest up to January 1, 1881, not to exceed $60. That all such acts above enumerated have been done in his capacity as trustee and for the benefit of and with the con-

sent and acquiescence of the *cestuis que trust*. That there is
due him for disbursements, etc., as above set forth, including
interest to January 1, 1881, the sum of $8,354.59. That he
has received from all sources as above set forth, including
interest to January 1, 1881, the sum of $4,048.06, which
leaves due him the sum of $4,306.53.

"Wherefore defendant, desiring a full and final settlement with said plaintiffs of the matters set forth, and
wishing to be relieved of the burdens resting upon him as
said trustee, joins said plaintiffs in their prayer in regard
to terminating said trust, and prays the court that if in the
judgment of the court the power exists, said trust be
brought to an end, and that all *cestuis qui trust* having interests in said Hartman's Addition have their rights and
interests by the order of this court herein particularized
and ascertained, and that the sum of $4,200 claimed for
services as said trustee be allowed to defendant. That an
account be taken of the moneys expended and received
under said trusteeship, and that there be adjudged and decreed as due to defendant the sum of $4,306.53. That
said sum be declared a lien upon all lots and lands remaining unsold in hands of defendant, and that unless the same
is paid by a day to be fixed by the court the said lots, etc.,
be sold to satisfy said sum. Also that it be adjudged that
plaintiffs have no rights or interests whatever in said seven
acres reserve. That the only rights and interests of said
plaintiffs exist in said one undetermined lot. That the interests of plaintiffs in said lot be determined. That said
lot be ascertained and named, and if in the judgment of
the court the power exists the same be sold subject to defendant's heir and out of proceeds said *cestuis que trust* be '
paid according to their several interests therein, and for
general relief."

On the 7th day of May, 1883, an amended reply was
filed denying all allegations of the answer not expressly admitted:

"Admits incorporation of the Homestead Society and that articles were duly filed and recorded in Dubuque county. Admits failure of first title taken by society, and the giving of power of attorney to defendant. Denies that defendant acting under said power expended much time and labor, etc., in relation to said lands, etc. Admits the making of deeds by Redick to the defendant as trustee of said society of the lands was known as Hartman's Addition. Denies the expenditure by defendant of his own moneys in prosecution of suit, etc., but alleges that when any moneys were paid out the defendant received the same from funds of the society. Denies that defendant is entitled to intrust. Denies that the words of trust expressed in the deeds from Redick are as alleged in answer, but aver that they are as follows: 'In trust for the use and benefit of and by the said John George Hartman to be conveyed to each member of the Homestead Society of Dubuque in the state of Iowa, his heirs or assigns who are entitled thereto according to his several interests in said premises, and not otherwise.' Denies that defendant expended much time and labor in adjusting the business of the society or that the same was done through the personal efforts of defendant, or that the *cestuis que trust* in consideration of his services awarded to defendant seven acres of land mentioned in answer. Denies that the holders of eighty-three shares conveyed to defendant all their right, title, and interest in and to said seven acres or any portion thereof, or that they acquiesced in any way in allowing defendent to reserve to himself said seven acres. Denies that the eighty-four lots were laid out in different sizes for the purpose stated in answer. Denies each and every allegation in answer wherein defendant claims to have expended money of his own for the benefit of his *cestuis que trust*. Denies that defendant is entitled to charge $300 per annum or any sum whatever for his services, or that $4,200, or any other sum was due him January 1, 1881, for his services. De-

20

nies that defendant, under the instruction and with the acquiescence of the *cestuis que trust*, deeded to them such lots as they might select or in the order of the demand for lots, or that he deeded to said *cestuis que trust* all the lots set forth in 'Exhibit B,' attached to answer, but avers the fact to be that many of the lots set forth in 'Exhibit B' were deeded by defendant to persons other than those entitled thereto under the terms of said trust, and were in fraud of his trust. Denies that all of the *cestuis que trust* to whom defendant has deeded a lot have quit-claimed to defendant their interest in the seven acres.

"Avers that defendant has disposed of lots to a much larger amount in value than $3,988.06 as set forth in answer. That he has leased and enjoyed rents and profits and use of much more of the land than is set forth in answer, and has received a much larger sum therefor than $60 as in answer stated, and that the same amounts to and is reasonably worth $1,000. That defendant was not authorized to expend money in fencing, grubbing, or clearing said lots, and whatever was done by him in that regard was for his own individual gain and profit. That he received large sums of money from sale of wood cut off from said lots for the occupation and cultivation of them. Also that in disposing of lots to persons other than shareholders, defendant violated the express terms of his trust. That in addition to the sums admitted to have been received by defendant, he received of Kountz & Ruth about the time of the settlement of the controversy in regard to the land purchased from them, the sum of about $1,200 as trustee.

"Denies that defendant advertised in newspapers in different states for claimants of lots, and denies that there is due defendant from said society the sum of $4,306.53 or any other amount. Alleges that the persons to whom defendant deeded lots in said addition who were not shareholders, were mostly his own sons or other members of his family. That the sums expressed as the consideration therefor, were much less than the real value of the lots, to-wit: That lot 55 deeded to Mary Arnold, the mother-in-law of Christian Hartman, for the consideration of $100 was worth then $300; that lots 60, 79, and 84, deeded to sons of defendant for the nominal sum of $350 were at that time worth $1,000.

"Prays that the sale of lots made by defendant to other, than shareholders be set aside and declared null and voids and for other relief as prayed for in petition."

By consent of parties the cause was referred to a member of the bar, as referee, to try the issues of law and fact, and report his findings to the court. After taking a large amount of testimony, the substance of which is contained in the abstract, the referee reported his findings to the court as follows:

"1st. That the 'Homestead Society' was organized May 14th, 1857, at Dubuque, Iowa. That there were eighty-three certificates of capital stock issued to subscribers therefor. The object being to purchase with the money paid in, a tract of land to be sub-divided among the members so as to give each one a home.

"2d. That in pursuance of such purpose a piece of land was bought of Kountz & Ruth in Omaha, and a bond for a deed taken October 13, 1857, which was paid for by the moneys received for subscription to the capital stock.

"3d. That the corporation expired in three years from the time of its organization according to the articles of incorporation.

"4th. That after the corporation expired in May, 1860, the individual stockholders, each of whom had contributed equally to the capital stock, continued to act together as an association of persons for the purpose of carrying out the original design of the society, as their several interests might appear.

"5th. That the title of said piece of real estate having

failed, the association sent defendant, one of the members, to Omaha for the purpose of taking such steps as might be necessary to secure a legal title to said land, or to secure other lands in lieu thereof.

"6th. That defendant, acting for himself and associates, commenced and conducted a series of litigations concerning the title to said real estate, and that finally, in full settlement of all such suits, he secured conveyances, one June 30th, 1865, and one December 26th, 1867, to himself in trust for the original shareholders in said Homestead Society, of the tract now known as 'Hartman's Addition,' which said tract of land when so secured became in equity the joint property of the several parties who had contributed to the capital stock, and each of said members who had paid for one share of stock became entitled to the 1-83rd undivided interest in and to said real estate now known as Hartman's Addition.

"7th. That said defendant, still acting for himself and associates at some time prior to January 1, 1868, laid off and platted said real estate as 'Hartman's Addition,' and caused a map to be made showing the several lots and tracts into which the same had been divided.

"8th. That said real estate was so subdivided as to consist of 84 lots, and also of a tract containing about 7 acres, designated upon the plat and map as 'Hartman's Reserve.'

"9th. That said defendant from time to time conveyed information by letter and word of mouth to the members of said society of the action taken by him; that he sent a copy of the plat to the members residing in Dubuque, Iowa, for their inspection and approval, and also called a meeting of such members as resided in Omaha or were represented here, for the purpose of considering the matter of the subdivision as shown by the plat.

"10th. That said meeting was held at Turner Hall, in Omaha, January 2d, 1868; that a large number, and probably a majority, of the stockholders were represented at said meeting; that it was explained at said meeting that defendant had reserved to himself the tract known as 'Hartman's Reserve,' to reimburse him for moneys expended and expenses incurred in and about the litigation, etc., and also to pay him for services performed by him in relation thereto, said reserve being of but small value at that time, and defendant having given much time and attention to the conducting of the litigations and settlement, and having expended more or less money.

"11th. That the members present and represented at said meeting, as well as most or all of the members living at Dubuque, acquiesced in the proposed subdivision of said land as platted, and consented that defendant should receive said "reserve" in full payment for all such expenditures, expenses, and services; that it was also acquiesced in by himself and all the members at said meeting, and by the other members of said society, that one of said lots should be given to Wm. Baumer, secretary of said society, in payment for services performed by him, and that of the remaining eighty-three lots each member or representative of a member of the society who had been or was entitled to one share of the capital stock of the original corporation, should be entitled to receive one lot in full satisfaction and settlement of his interest in said entire tract, and that defendant should convey to each of the members, or his representative, upon demand, one of said lots, and that the person applying for conveyance should be entitled to select each his own lot in the order of application.

"12th. That the entire arrangement was acquiesced in by all the members of said society for more than ten years without objection or question.

"13th. That defendant conveyed a large number of said lots to various of said members and their representatives upon demand made of him, and so conveyed to all such members who made demand therefor.

"14th. That many of said lots have never been conveyed

by defendant to any ot the other stockholders or their representatives, and are still held in trust by him for them.

"15th. That defendant at various times sold several of said lots to members of his own family and other persons, and executed to them what purported to be full and complete deeds of conveyance of the same, and said persons have now been in possession of several of said lots for many years, and there are several of the lots still unclaimed, and held in trust by defendant.

"16th. That plaintiffs, named as such, had all received lots in said addition by conveyance from defendant for all shares or interest held and owned by them up to the time of the commencement of this action.

"17th. That Streitz, one of the plaintiffs, has secured assignments and conveyances to himself, since the commencent of this action, of one or more shares or interests in said association, and is entitled to receive from defendant the conveyance of one lot for each of said shares, to be selected by him from the lots not yet conveyed to any shareholder."

Referee finds in addition to the above as matter of law :

"1st. That the arrangement by which defendant was to have 'Hartman's Reserve,' and Wm. Baumer was to have one lot for services, and by which each shareholder was to receive one of the other of said lots, there being eighty-three shareholders, was agreed to and acquiesced in so as to be binding upon all the members of said society, their heirs and assignees.

"2d. Finds that such action amounted to a complete partition and apportioning of said real estate among the members or individuals entitled to an interest therein. That in order to determine which particular lot each member was entitled to, there was nothing to be done except by way of selection according to the arrangement recited above.

"3d.   That by said subdivision said society and association ceased to exist as such, and the members and share-holders ceased to be joint owners or tenants in common in said real estate, and ceased to have any common interest therein, and each one became entitled to and owned a separate interest in a determined portion of the same.

"4th.   Finds that each member of said association or his representative became entitled to demand and receive from defendant one certain unconveyed lot, according to his own selection, and that this was the extent of his interest in said property or of his claim against said defendant.

"5th.   Finds that there is no joint interest in the plaintiffs in this suit. That each one of them, at the commencement of this action, had received in full his entire interest and share in said real estate, and was not entitled to demand any further conveyance from defendant, and had no right of action against him.

"6th.   Finds that the conveyance by defendant of certain of said lots to relatives and persons not members of said association, and not entitled to said lots as such, was a legal fraud upon the members who had not prior to that time received a conveyance of their respective lots from defendant.

"7th.   Finds that such conveyances by defendant to third parties were and are in law null and void.

"8th.   Finds that any person being the owner or assignee of an original interest in said Homestead Society, for which no lot has been deeded, is entitled to a conveyance from defendant of any lot he may select in said addition, not conveyed to a member or shareholder in said association, whether said lot has been conveyed to third parties or not.

"9th.   Finds that if any right of action exists in favor of any shareholder as against defendant for the rents or profits of any lot in said addition, such right can only exist in favor of each individual shareholder for the account of rents and profits of the particular lot selected by such shareholder as his own.

"10th.   Finds that none of the plaintiffs had a cause of action against defendant at the time of the commencement of this action.   That the interest of Streitz acquired subsequent to the commencement of this action, does not entitle him to relief in this case.

"Finds therefore that there is no cause of action in favor of plaintiffs, or any of them, against defendant, and that this cause should be dismissed."

On the 25th day of November, 1884, a motion to confirm the report of the referee was filed by attorneys for defendant.

On the 17th day of December, 1884, exceptions to the report were filed by attorneys for plaintiffs on the following grounds :

"1st.   That the findings of fact made and reported by the referee, numbered 10th, 11th, 12th, 13th, and 16th, are not supported by the testimony.

"2nd.   That so much of No. 1 as refers to the object of the organization is not supported by the testimony.

"3d.   That so much of the 4th finding of fact as relates to the "understanding" as to disposition that was to be made of the land purchased for the benefit of the society was not sustained either by the law or the testimony.

"4th.   To so much of the 6th finding of fact as states the interest to which each shareholder became entitled in Hartman's addition.

"5th.   To the conclusions of law made and reported numbered 1, 2, 3, 4, 5, 9, and 10, and to the concluding finding that no cause of action existed in favor of plaintiffs, or any of them, as against defendant, and that case should be dismissed."

On the 16th day of July, 1885, a decree was entered as follows :

" This cause being heard at the last term of court upon

report of the referee filed herein, motion of defendant to confirm same and exceptions thereto by plaintiffs, and having been argued by counsel and submitted, the court being fully advised in the premises, does on consideration overrule said exceptions except as to the 12th, 14th, 15th, and 17th findings of fact, and the 1st, 2d, 3d, 4th, 6th, 7th, 8th, and 9th conclusions of law, and as to the said enumerated findings and conclusions, the exceptions thereto are sustained for the reason that the same relate to matters not material to the issues in this action, and save as aforesaid the report of the said referee is approved and confirmed.

" It is therefore considered and adjudged that this action be dismissed, and that the said defendant go hence without day and recover from the said plaintiffs their costs, etc. To which findings and decision plaintiffs except, etc."

The first point presented by plaintiffs and appellants, in this court, arises upon the overruling, by the district court, of the motion made by them after the coming in of the report of the referee, and before the final judgment, for leave " to file an amended and supplemental petition—to amend so as to conform to the facts as they appear in the evidence; and supplemental so as to set up the after-acquired rights of Streitz, one of the original plaintiffs."

I understand it to be an inflexible rule of practice, that in order to predicate error upon the refusal of a trial court to permit a supplemental pleading to be filed, the paper proposed, or at least the substance of it, must be made a part of the record.

Section 149 of the civil code provides that "Either party may be allowed, on notice, and on such terms as to costs as the court may prescribe, to file a supplemental petition, answer, or reply, alleging facts material to the case, occurring after the former petition, answer, or reply."

Under this provision the better practice, doubtless, is that the notice be accompanied by a copy of the pleading in the form in which it is proposed to file it; but it would probably be sufficient if it contain the substance of the pleading. Here there does not appear to have been any notice, nor does the motion even contain the substance of the amendatory or supplemental matter of the proposed pleading.

We are informed by the brief of counsel, as we were at the bar, that the supplemental fact sought to be set up by way of a supplemental petition was that one of the plaintiffs, Streitz, had, since the commencement of the action, by purchase and assignment of other parties, become the owner of certain shares or rights in the property involved in the litigation, in addition to the interest which he had or claimed therein, at the date of the commencement of the action. It is contended by counsel for defendant that the above facts are not such as would be allowed to be set out in a supplemental petition, or in other words, that they do not constitute a cause of action which could be availed of in an action commenced before their occurrence.

The case of *Evans v. Bagshaw*, 5 Chancery Appeal Cases, 340, seems to be in point; so I will cite it in the absence of any case cited by counsel on either side. In that case the suit was brought by a married woman and her husband, together with their mortgagee, for a partition of certain real estate, of which the married woman was tenant in common in fee in one-sixth. The defendants, by their answer, stated, as was the fact, that the husband had been bankrupt before the mortgage was executed, and that all of his interest in right of his wife was therefore vested in his assignee; and the defendants submitted whether such a suit, being in fact a suit by the wife as reversioner, could be maintained. The mortgagee thereupon bought the life estate from the assignees of the husband, and the bill was amended by stating that fact.

The master of the rolls was of the opinion that the original bill, being by a reversioner for a partition, could not be maintained, and that the plaintiffs could not carry on the suit upon a title different from that which they originally stated, and he dismissed the bill with costs. This decision of the master of the rolls was affirmed by the court of appeals. I quote the syllabus: "If a plaintiff has no title to maintain his suit at the time when the bill is filed, he cannot carry on the suit by subsequently acquiring a title and amending the bill accordingly." See also Daniel's Chancery, *page 1515 *et seq.*, and notes.

From the testimony of Mr. Streitz, who was sworn as a witness on the part of the plaintiffs, it appears that he had never demanded deeds from the defendant on the shares which he had purchased since the commencement of the suit, to use his own language, "Because I was not ready yet—could attend to but one thing at a time." Had he been allowed then to file a supplemental bill it would only have contained the allegation of his purchase of said three shares since the commencement of the action, his present ownership of them, and that he had made no demand of the defendant in respect thereto.

As I understand the theory of the case, as well from the reading of the bill as from the brief and argument at the hearing, the action was brought as well in behalf of the shareholders in the original homestead society who never had appeared at Omaha and claimed their lots or shares as of those who had; so that the case of the owners of the shares afterwards purchased by Streitz was already before the court by general allegations, which would apply to him or any other person who might become the owner and holder of them. I therefore cannot see that anything would have been accomplished by setting out such subsequent purchase of these shares by Streitz by a supplemental petition.

The second point arises upon the overruling by the district court of the exceptions of the plaintiffs to the first. fourth, sixth, tenth, eleventh, thirteenth, and sixteenth findings of fact, and the fifth and tenth conclusions of law, as contained in the report of the referee, as well as the finding and conclusion of no cause of action, and that the case should be dismissed, as contained in said report. This point also covers the final judgment of the district court, and under it the entire case will be considered.

It appears from the pleadings, evidence, and findings that in the month of May, 1857, there was organized at Dubuque, Iowa, under the general incorporation laws of that state, a company known as the Homestead Society, though it is not shown to have adopted any name. This society was composed of eighty-three members or shareholders, who seem to have, each and all of them, contributed equally to the funds of the society. The object of said society was found by the referee, and claimed by counsel at the hearing to have been, to purchase with the money paid in, a tract of land to be subdivided among the members so as to give each one a home. But such purpose cannot be gathered from the articles of association, a copy of which is contained in the abstract, but rather that the object was to engage in town site speculations. But, be that as it may, the fact is undisputed that in the month of October of said year the society purchased a tract of land adjoining the city of Omaha, taking a title bond for conveyance thereof. That said tract of land was divided into lots so as to give each member of the society three lots in severalty, and this division of the property among the members, or shareholders, seems to have been consummated by the society executing to each member a deed of the corporation to the three lots assigned to such members respectively, and by the said members accepting the same, presumably in full satisfaction of their claims upon the society.

But it seems that as early as the year 1858 the title to the said land failed, and the defendant, a member of said society, and who had become its president, was sent out to Omaha to look after the interests of the society, or of the shareholders and holders of the said lots in severalty, which, it does not appear. It is admitted that he had a power of attorney, but as that paper is not before the court, it does not appear whether he was the attorney in fact of the society, or of the individual holders of the corporation deeds of the lots.

The defendant, after instituting a lawsuit and prosecuting it in the district court of Douglas county for some seven or eight years, for the purpose of securing a title to said land, finally in the year 1865 affected a compromise and received from the defendants in said litigation, or a party acting for them, the tract of land, also adjoining the city of Omaha, the subject of this suit, in full of the claim of said society, or of the said lot holders, or both, as his authority to act in the premises was measured by the said power. The title to said last-mentioned tract of land was conveyed to the defendant in trust, the language of the deed being as follows: "In trust for the use and benefit of and by the said John George Hartman to be conveyed to each member of the Homestead Society of Dubuque, in the state of Iowa, his heirs or assigns, who are entitled thereto, according to his several interests in said premises, and not otherwise."

This tract of land was surveyed off into lots and streets, leaving an oblong piece of land in the south-west corner 410 by 680 feet, said to contain seven acres, which was called Hartman's Reserve, though not so marked on the plat before us. There were 84 lots, not all of the same size. There is some confusion in the testimony as to why there were 84 lots when there were but 83 shareholders. Yet the conclusion seems to be that Colonel William Baumer, one of the original shareholders, who in the meantime had removed to Omaha, had acted as secretary of the society and superintended the surveying and platting of the said tract, had been by some of the parties interested, promised an additional lot or share in the land for his services, and

so made the survey and plat that there would be one extra
lot for that purpose.   In the meantime a few of the original shareholders, in addition to the defendant and the said
Colonel Baumer, had removed from Dubuque to Omaha,
besides a few shares had been transferred to parties residing at Omaha.   After the said land had been surveyed
and platted as above stated there was in the month of January, 1868, a meeting held in the Turner Hall at Omaha,
for the purpose, so far as can be gathered from the evidence,
of ratifying the acts of the defendant in making the said
division, survey, and plat of the said land, and especially
in reserving to himself the seven acre piece called Hartman's Reserve, as his compensation for his time, services,
and expenditures in and about the said litigation, taking
care of said property, etc.   It appears to a reasonable degree of certainty that this meeting was attended by all the
shareholders then residing in Omaha, and the proceedings
of that meeting, together with the approval thereof by the
shareholders at Dubuque, upon the same being reported to
them as testified to by the defendant, may upon due consideration of the peculiar and anomalous facts of the case,
together with the lapse of time since their occurrence, be
deemed and taken as a ratification of such acts, in so far as
the same were susceptible of ratification by the members
of the society or shareholders, as such.

When we come to measure and define the rights and
duties of the parties by the language of the deed, recognizing rather than creating the trust, and consider the
same in connection with all the antecedent facts, I think
it indisputable, that upon the delivery of the deed to the
trustee, the shareholders or their assigns, if living, and
the heirs of such as were deceased, become the equitable
owners of the land as tenants in common.   It necessarily
follows that they divide the land among themselves.   A
part only of them being present near the property, and the
others being widely scattered and residing at a great dis-

tance, it was competent for those present to agree upon a plan of division which would be binding upon them, but not upon the absentees until ratified by them ; and this plan being that the shareholders present should each select his lot and receive a deed therefor from the trustee in severalty, and the same right and privilege be extended to the absentees as fast as they should come forward and demand it ; those of them who have availed themselves of this right are equally bound by the arrangement, division, and partition with those who were present at the meeting and were original parties to the plan of partition. Such plan of partition, including the partition and assignment to the defendant of the reserve of seven acres, as a compensation for his time, services, and money laid out in procuring the estate, laying out and caring for the same, being just, reasonable, and equitable, and the parties thereto having acted in the utmost good faith, so far as is shown by evidence in the case, it will be upheld.

It appears that each of the plaintiffs have ratified the plan of partition and division by availing themselves of its rights, privileges, and benefits, and by selecting and receiving conveyances for their respective shares in severalty. They have therefore ceased to have any interest in the balance of the estate, that being held by the defendant in part at least in trust for those of the shareholders, their heirs or assigns, who have not ratified the said plan of partition, or received conveyances for their several lots, and for them alone, free from and disconnected with any claim or equity on the part of any of the shareholders who have ratified as aforesaid.

I have purposely avoided incumbering what I have had to say by any reference to the quit-claim deeds executed to the defendant by the plaintiffs and other shareholders receiving conveyances of lots from him, as I do not deem any consideration of them necessary to the conclusion to which I have come, and there being no evidence of any circumstance of duress accompanying the giving of any of them.

It appears from the complaint, and there is some evidence in support of the allegation, that one of the plaintiffs made selection of, and demanded a deed for a certain lot upon a corporation deed of which he was the owner, which the defendant, for some reason, refused to convey to him; but it appears that he thereafter selected another lot upon the same right, which was conveyed to him, and thereby waived whatever right he may have had to his original selection.

I do not express any opinion as to the right of the holders of shares in the society, or of corporation deeds, who have not received deeds thereon from the defendant, or in any manner ratified the plan of partition as agreed upon at the Turner Hall meeting, to call in question the title of the defendant to the seven acre reserve, so far as their rights are concerned, or the title to lots conveyed by defendant to parties not members of the society, or holders of corporation deeds, not deeming those questions to be before the court. But so far as the questions before the court are concerned, the equities are with the defendant.

The judgment of the district court is affirmed.

JUDGMENT AFFIRMED.

THE other judges concur.

THE STATE, EX REL. LEGRAND B. THORN, V. JAMES H. FLEMING.

1. **Execution:** STAY: WRIT TO ISSUE AGAINST DEBTOR AND SURETIES. Where, upon a judgment rendered in a county court, in a sum exceeding two hundred dollars, exclusive of costs, a stay has been taken by filing a bond with sureties in accordance with the provisions of the statute, and such judgment is not paid within the time limited by law and the terms of such stay bond, it is the duty of the county judge, upon demand, to issue a joint execution against the property of all of the judgment debtors and sureties in such stay bond, describing them as debtors and sureties therein.

——————: ——: MANDAMUS. In a proper case such duty will be enforced by mandamus.

ORIGINAL application for mandamus.

Dilworth, Smith & Dilworth, for the relator.

James H. Fleming, pro se.

COBB, J.

This is an original application for a mandamus to the county judge of Adams county, commanding him to issue an execution out of the county court of said county against Spencer W. Clark, John S. Chandler, and B. F. Kellogg, for the sum set out in the relation.

The answer of the respondent is equivalent to a demurrer. It expressly admits all the facts stated in the relation, but denies the lawful power of the county court to issue the execution demanded by the relator.

The only question involved in the case is, whether, where a judgment is rendered in a county court in what is usually called a term case, in an amount exceeding the jurisdiction of a justice of the peace, a stay is taken under the provisions of the statute, and the judgment is not paid

21

according to the statute and the terms of the stay bond, an execution may be issued out of the county court against the sureties on such stay bond without further proceedings ?

Section 17 of chapter 20, Compiled Statutes, which chapter is entitled "Courts—Probate, County," provides as follows: "Any person against whom a judgment is rendered, on all sums exceeding two hundred dollars, may have stay of execution in like manner as upon judgments rendered in the district court, and upon the same conditions; and upon sums of two hundred dollars and under, the same as provided for in actions before justices of the peace."

Section 477c of the code of civil procedure (which is chiefly devoted to procedure in the district courts) provides as follows:

"Sec. 477c. On all judgments for the recovery of money only, except those rendered in any court on an appeal or writ of error thereto, or against any officer or person or corporation, or the sureties of any of them, for money received in a fiduciary capacity, or for the breach of any official duty, there may be a stay of execution if the defendant therein shall, within twenty days from the rendition of judgment, procure two or more sufficient freehold sureties to enter into a bond acknowledging themselves surety for the defendant for the payment of the judgment, interest, and costs from the time of rendering judgment until paid, as follows: 1st. If the sum for which judgment was rendered, exclusive of costs, does not exceed fifty dollars, three months. 2d. If the sum for which judgment was rendered, exclusive of costs, exceeds fifty dollars and does not exceed one hundred dollars, six months. 3d. If the sum for which judgment was rendered, exclusive of costs, exceeds one hundred dollars, nine months."

Section 477i provides that "At the expiration of the stay the clerk shall issue a joint execution against the property of all the judgment debtors and sureties, describing them as debtors or sureties therein."

Construing the above provisions of law together, it seems to me that there can be no doubt that it was the intention of the legislature in framing them to place the rights of parties in the several cases provided for upon the same basis, regardless of the court in which they are being administered. No other meaning can be given to the words of the seventeenth section of chapter twenty, "and upon the same conditions." It is certainly one of the conditions upon which a party obtains a stay of execution upon a judgment rendered in the district court, that upon his failure to pay the same within the time limited, an execution will issue against his sureties as well as against himself.

So, as the statute gives the party against whom a judgment is rendered exceeding two hundred dollars, in the county court, the right to a stay of execution, "in like manner as upon judgments rendered in the district court, and upon the same conditions," it necessarily follows that in such case, upon a like default, execution may issue against both principal and sureties.

The framers of the statute, no doubt, had also in view the consideration that to authorize the issuing of executions against the sureties on the stay bond, as well as against the principal, without further proceedings, would tend to save costs and prevent a circuity of actions.

The writ will issue as prayed.

WRIT AWARDED.

THE other judges concur.

EX PARTE D. A. HOLMES.

1. **Criminal Law**: MOTION FOR NEW TRIAL. The time within which a motion for a new trial may be filed in a criminal case is fixed by statute, which is during the term of court at which the verdict is rendered, and, except for newly-discovered evidence, within three days after the verdict was returned, unless unavoidably prevented.

2. ——: ——: FILED OUT OF TIME. The filing of a motion for a new trial at a term of the district court subsequent to the term at which a defendant was tried and convicted, and six months after he had been imprisoned in the penitentiary for the purpose of serving out his sentence, would confer no authority upon such district court to set aside the verdict and judgment and grant a new trial. And in such case, where the motion was sustained and a new trial granted, the order being void, the warden of the penitentiary would have no authority to surrender the prisoner to the sheriff of the county in which such conviction was had.

Application for *habeas corpus.*

D. A. Holmes, pro se.

William Leese, Attorney-General, contra.

REESE, J.

This is an application to this court, in the exercise of its original jurisdiction, for a writ of *habeas corpus* for the purpose of releasing one Henry Paulson from the custody of the warden of the penitentiary, and causing him to be delivered into the custody of the sheriff of Cherry county.

From the petition and papers in the case, the following facts with reference to the imprisonment of Henry Paulson appear:

At the March (1886) term of the district court of Cherry county he was tried upon a charge of murder and found guilty of the crime of murder in the second degree. No motion for a new trial was made, and he was sentenced to hard labor in the penitentiary for the term of fifteen years. Court adjourned *sine die* soon after pronouncing sentence, and within two or three days thereafter Paulson was conveyed to the penitentiary and placed in the custody of the warden, as a convict, in execution of the sentence. On the 11th day of October, 1886, at the next succeeding term of court, a motion for a new trial was filed, and on the second day of December, of the same year, the motion was sustained, the verdict and judgment set aside, a new trial ordered, and the warden of the penitentiary directed to deliver the prisoner to the proper authorities of Cherry county, in order that he might be there held for a second trial. The warden not feeling satisfied of the authority of the district court to grant a new trial, upon a motion filed so long after judgment and sentence, upon the advice of the attorney-general declined to surrender the custody of the prisoner, and this action being brought, seeks the direction of this court as to his duty.

The only question presented is as to the jurisdiction or authority of the district court to set aside the verdict and judgment and grant a new trial upon motion filed after the adjournment of the court. In the case at bar the time which elapsed between judgment and sentence and the filing of the motion was about six months, and until action on the motion about nine months. The motion appears to have been filed at the next succeeding term of court after judgment, by leave of court, and by the consent of the district attorney. If there was jurisdiction to hear the motion and make a legal order granting a new trial, it is the duty of the warden to surrender the prisoner. If there was no such authority or jurisdiction, the order was simply void, and the prisoner must remain in the penitentiary as a convict, so far as this proceeding may be concerned, no matter how just the order may have been, nor how much the present appearances of the case may indicate an unjust conviction.

District courts have no inherent or common law power to grant new trials in criminal cases. Their power originates and exists alone in the statutes.

Looking then to the statute as the sole authority for the granting of new trials, we find the following provisions:

"A new trial after a verdict of conviction may be granted on the application of the defendant, for any of the following reasons affecting materially his substantial rights: *First.* Irregularity in the proceedings of the court or the prosecuting attorney, or the witnesses for the state, or any order of the court, or abuse of discretion by which the defendant was prevented from having a fair trial. *Second.* Misconduct of the jury or the prosecuting attorney, or of the witnesses for the state. *Third.* Accident or surprise which ordinary prudence could not have guarded against. *Fourth.* That the verdict is not sustained by sufficient evidence, or is contrary to law. *Fifth.* Newly discovered evidence, material for the defendant, which he could not with reasonable diligence have discovered and produced on the trial. *Sixth.* Error of law occurring on the trial." Sec. 490, Cr. Code.

"The application for a new trial shall be by motion, upon written grounds, filed at the term the verdict is rendered, and shall, except for the cause of newly discovered evidence, material for the party applying, which he could not with reasonable diligence have discovered and produced at the trial, be 'within three days after the verdict was rendered, unless unavoidably prevented. In assigning the grounds of such motion it shall be sufficient to assign the same in the language of the statute, and without further or other particularity." Sec. 491, Id.

"The causes enumerated in subdivisions two, three, and five of section 490, must be sustained by affidavits showing their truth, and may be controverted by affidavits." Sec. 492, Id.

It has been the holding of this court, in construing

section 491, that the motion for a new trial must be made during the term at which the verdict was rendered, and, except for newly discovered evidence, within three days after the verdict was rendered, unless unavoidably prevented. *Bradshaw v. The State*, 19 Neb., 644. Our attention has again been called to section 491, with the request that we re-examine it. It is contended that a proper construction would be that a motion for a new trial may be filed not only after the expiration of the three days, but that it may be filed after the term where " unavoidably prevented." As we read the section, it is that the application for a new trial, if made at all, *must* be made during the term at which the verdict was rendered, and must, except for the one cause of newly discovered evidence, be made within three days. In the latter case, " if unavoidably prevented," it may be made after the expiration of the three days, but not beyond the term. This, to the mind of the writer, is clearly the meaning of the section. If we are correct in this, it must follow that upon the final adjournment of the term the right to make applications for new trial ceases and the court can have no jurisdiction to entertain them. And in the case at bar the jurisdiction of the district court to make orders affecting the judgment having ceased, the order granting a new trial after execution of the sentence has been commenced must be held to be void.. *State v. Hughes*, 35 Kan., 632. *Com. v. Weymouth*, 2 Allen (Mass.), 144. *State v. Daugherty*, 30 N. W. Rep. (Iowa), 685.

Another reason why this writ must be denied is found in the fact that no provision is made by law for the surrender of a convict for a new trial upon any order of a district court. Section 510 of the criminal code provides for the suspension of sentence by the court allowing the writ of error.

Section 512 provides that " When the defendant has been committed to the penitentiary of this state, and the

judgment by virtue of which the commitment is made
shall be reversed on a writ of error, by which reversal the
defendant shall be entitled to his discharge or to a new
trial, the clerk of the court reversing said judgment shall,
under the seal of the court, forthwith certify the same to
the warden of the penitentiary."

Section 514 is as follows: "In case a new trial be ordered, the warden of the penitentiary shall forthwith cause
said defendant to be taken and conducted to the county
jail and committed to the custody of the keeper thereof in
the county in which said defendant was convicted."

Our attention has been called to no other sections providing for the removal of a defendant from the penitentiary, when serving out a sentence, to the county jail for
the purpose of a new trial. The warden was, therefore,
justified in declining to surrender Paulson to the sheriff of
Cherry county, or to any other person for that purpose,
except upon the certificate of the clerk of the appellate
court.

It may be that injustice has been done to the prisoner
and that the order of the district court seemed to be demanded by the highest considerations of justice and right,
yet in the absence of any authority to make such an order
one could not be made. As said in *Bradshaw v. The State*,
supra, the rule permitting a motion for a new trial to be
filed at any time within one year from the rendition of the
judgment should be extended to criminal cases where serious doubts are thrown upon the correctness of the verdict.
But such is not the law and the courts are without authority to act, except as provided by law.

The writ is therefore denied.

WRIT DENIED.

THE other judges concur.

21 399
24 706
21
25
21
439
21
45

THE STATE OF NEBRASKA, EX REL. JASON G. MILLER,
v. ROBERT B. GRAHAM, COUNTY TREASURER.

1. **School Lands:** DEFAULT IN PAYMENT OF INTEREST. On
the facts proved, *Held*, That a preponderance of the testimony
showed that the relator had been duly notified of the default
in the payment of the interest on his school lands before the same
were declared forfeited to the state and resold.

2. ——: ——: NOTICE: FORFEITURE: RE-SALE. The statute, while it requires notice to be given to the purchaser of
school lands of his default in paying the interest thereon before
said lands are declared forfeited, yet it is the duty of such purchaser to pay the interest due thereon annually, and when he
has failed for many years to perform his duty in that regard
and the lands in the meantime have been declared forfeited
and resold, it will be presumed that proper notice was given
before forfeiture was declared, upon the principle that official
acts of public officers, which presuppose the existence of other
acts to make them legally operative, are presumptive proof of
the latter.

3. **Estoppel:** ACTS IN PAIS. If a party knowingly, though it be
done passively by looking on, suffers another to purchase and
expend money on land under an erroneous opinion of title
without making known his own claim, he will not afterwards
be permitted to exercise his legal rights against such person.

ORIGINAL application for mandamus.

Marquett, Deweese & Hall, for relator.

Harwood, Ames & Kelly, for respondent.

MAXWELL, CH. J.

This is an application for a writ of mandamus to issue
out of this court, commanding Robert B. Graham, county
treasurer of Lancaster county, Nebraska, or his successor
in office, to receive from the relator the several sums of
money that may be due from the relator to the respondent

on four certain contracts of purchase entered into by the relator with the state of Nebraska, and commanding the said county treasurer to give a receipt therefor showing that final payment of the balance of the principal and interest has been paid on the contracts of purchase. It is alleged in the plaintiff's petition that on the 15th day of June, 1868, the relator purchased from the state of Nebraska lot 14, being a part of the north-west quarter of section 36, town 10, range 6, for one hundred dollars per acre, and that he paid one-tenth cash payment as required by law, and gave his note as required by law of Nebraska for the residue of purchase money, to-wit, $450.

"The contract of purchase entered into by the state of Nebraska with your relator is as follows:

"Whereas, in pursuance and by virtue of an act of the legislative assembly in such case provided, and after due public notice, the state of Nebraska, on the day of the date hereof, has struck off at public sale to J. G. Miller, as purchaser thereof, the following described tract of land, situated in the north-west quarter of section 36, town 10, range 6 east, in Lancaster county, Nebraska, described as lot number 28, according to the survey and recorded plat of said section 36, containing five acres more or less, at and for the aggregate price of $420; and whereas the said J. G. Miller has this day paid to the treasurer of Lancaster county, for the state of Nebraska, the sum of $42, being the one-tenth part of said purchase money aforesaid, and to secure the payment of the other part of said purchase money has executed and delivered his certain promissory note, indorsed by P. Peck and M. M. Culver, by which he has promised to pay to the order of the state of Nebraska, on the first day of January, A.D. 1880, the sum of $378, with interest thereon at the rate of ten per cent per annum from date hereof, said interest to be promptly paid annually in advance on the first day of January in each year until said note shall be fully paid.

"Now, therefore, I, J. G. Miller, the said purchaser aforesaid, of Cass county and state of Nebraska, in consideration of the premises aforesaid, and of the extension of time of payment of the aforementioned purchase money, do hereby for myself, my heirs, executors and administrators, covenant, promise, and agree to and with the state of Nebraska that so long as said purchase money, or any part thereof, secured by the above-mentioned promissory note remains unpaid, I shall not, nor will not commit or permit to be committed, in or upon the above-mentioned and described premises, tracts, or parcels of lands, any waste or spoils whatever, in timber or otherwise; and I do hereby, for myself, my heirs, executors, and administrators, further covenant, promise, and agree to and with said state of Nebraska, that upon the non-payment in advance by me, my heirs, executors, and administrators, of the annual interest, or any part thereof aforesaid, at the time when the same shall become due and payable, or upon the non-payment of said principal sum of $378 in said note mentioned, on the first of January, A.D. 1880, according to the tenor and effect of said promissory note above mentioned, or upon the commission of any waste or spoil whatever, by me, my heirs, executors, or administrators, in or upon said premises so struck off to him as purchaser as aforesaid, then and in that case all the said tract or parcel of land above mentioned and described, and all improvements thereon, shall be surrendered and absolutely revert to the state of Nebraska.

"In witness whereof I have hereunto set my hand this eleventh day of June, A.D. 1868.

J. G. MILLER.

In presence of
    S. B. LINDERMAN.

"That the relator paid the interest on the balance of the said purchase money, for which he gave his note for the years 1869, 1870, 1871, 1872, 1873, 1874, up to the first of January, 1875; that on the 16th day of June, 1876, the

said lot number 14 was again sold, and the county treasurer pretended to cancel the contract of purchase which
had formerly been made by the state of Nebraska with this
relator; that the relator had no notice of any kind of the
• attempted or pretended cancellation, and that your relator
did not know until after the cancellation had taken place
that his contract had been or was to be cancelled; that he
was never notified by any one in any manner that his interest in the purchase money of the above-described tract
of land was due and unpaid.

"It is further alleged that the county treasurer and
county commissioner, without any authority of law, pretended to cancel said contract of purchase, and proceeded to
and did re-sell the said land to other and different parties,
which sale was made on the 16th of June, 1876, for the
sum of $350; that the said lots were sold at public sale
without having given notice by publication, as required by
law, and said sale was null and void and made without any
authority of law, and in contravention of the statutes.

"The relator further alleges in his petition that ever
since the said pretended sale and cancellation of this contract the county treasurer failed and refused to accept from
the relator the said payment due on the balance of purchase
money which fell due annually. The relator has always
been ready and willing to make said payment under his
contract.

"It is further alleged that on the 5th day of May, 1885,
relator tendered to Robert Graham, county treasurer of
Lancaster county, Nebraska, the sum of $991.08, being the
balance of purchase money due the state of Nebraska, together with interest, interest on interest then due from
relator to the state of Nebraska, as the balance of the purchase money on said lot number 14; that said Robert
Graham's acknowledgment of the said tender, and the refusal of the same, is in words and figures as follows, to-wit:

"'I hereby acknowledge the tender of the above sums of

money as the correct amounts, and being the balance due the state of Nebraska as the purchase money due on said several tracts of land purchased by J. G. Miller from the state of Nebraska, and refuse to receive the same and give Miller final receipt for the same. This refusal on my part is made under the instructions of the board of public lands and buildings of the state of Nebraska.

Signed, R. B. GRAHAM,
County Treasurer.'

"It is further alleged by the relator that he is ready and willing, and at all times has been ready and willing, to pay to the state of Nebraska the balance of money due on the contract, together with interest thereon, and has been ready and willing to perform all things necessary to carry out and fulfil the said contract made with the state of Nebraska, and now brings the said sums of moneys into court, to-wit, the sum of $991.08, and offers the same in payment of the balance of purchase money due on said note and contract from him to the state of Nebraska.

"It is further alleged that unless Robert Graham, the county treasurer, is commanded and required to receive the said money, to-wit, the sum of $991.08 from your relator, and give him a final receipt therefor, showing that this is the balance of the purchase money, your petitioner will be remediless in the premises, and that your petitioner is wholly remediless in the premises except by the interposition of this court by the writ of mandamus to compel the said county treasurer to receive said sum of money on said contract of purchase in payment of the balance of the purchase money due on said land contract.

"These are the allegations constituting relator's first cause of action. In regard to lot number fourteen the petition for mandamus contains four causes of action. The second cause of action is the same as the first heretofore set out, which involves the title to lot 28, being part of the north-west quarter of section 36, town 10, range 6.

This lot was purchased from the state of Nebraska at the same time, and on the same terms as lot fourteen, for $84 per acre. The interest payment for the same years was made on this lot as on the former lot, and a tender of the balance of purchase money was made to Robert Graham at the same time the tender was made for lot fourteen, and was refused in the same terms by the county treasurer.

"The third cause of action is the same as the first and second, with the changes in the amount of purchase price, and change in the amount of money tendered as the balance of purchase money due on said lot.

"The fourth cause of action is the same, with these changes :

"Notice was served on the respondent at the time of the filing of the petition, which notice stated that on the 11th day of August, 1885, or as soon thereafter as the relator could be heard, he would apply to the supreme court for a peremptory writ of mandamus to issue against defendant herein, to require him to receive and accept from the relator $4,083.79, or whatever sum may be due the state of Nebraska on said contract of purchase referred to in this application for a writ of mandamus, and require you to give receipt therefor, showing that final payment has been made on said contract of purchase.

"The prayer is as follows :

"' Wherefore your petitioner respectfully prays this honorable court that a writ of mandamus may issue commanding the said R. B. Graham, county treasurer of Lancaster county, Nebraska, to receive from your relator the said sum of $991.07, as the balance of the purchase money due the state of Nebraska on the contract of purchase entered into by your relator with the state of Nebraska, and to issue to your petitioner receipt therefor, showing that final payment of the balance of the purchase money and interest has been made on said contract of purchase on said lot No. 14, and commanding the said R. B. Graham to also receive from your relator the further sum of $832.47, as the balance of the purchase money due the state of Nebraska on lot number 28, being a part of the north-west quarter of section 36, town 10, range 6, Lancaster county, Nebraska, and to issue a receipt therefor showing that your petitioner has paid the balance of the purchase money due the state of Nebraska on his said contract of purchase heretofore referred to, and command the said R. B. Graham, the county treasurer, to receive the further sum from your petitioner of $1,076.97, as the balance of the purchase money due the state of Nebraska from your petitioner on his contract of purchase for lot 30, being a part of the north-west quarter of section 36, town 10, range 6 east, Lancaster county, Nebraska, and to give a receipt for the same showing that final payment has been made of the purchase money due the state of Nebraska from your petitioner on said contract of purchase; and that the said R. B. Graham be commanded to receive from your relator the further sum of $1,181.17, as the balance of purchase money due the state of Nebraska from your petitioner on the contract of purchase for lot number 6, being a part of the north-west quarter of section 36, town 10, range 6 east, Lancaster county, Nebraska, and to issue to your petitioner a receipt therefor showing that the balance of the purchase money due the state of Nebraska on the said contract has been paid, and as in duty bound your petitioner will ever pray.'

" The respondent filed an answer to the said petition August 25th, 1885, in which he admits that the title to the property described in relator's petition was, on the 15th day of June, 1868, in the state of Nebraska, and a part of the common school lands of said state; admits that the said land was appraised and advertised for sale in the manner provided by law, and that relator bid off said land described in said petition at public sale at the price alleged in the petition; but respondent avers that the only pay-

ments ever made by said Miller on account of said sale or
pretended sale were one-tenth of said principal sum and
annual interest on the residue thereof for the years 1869,
1870, 1871, 1872, and 1874; that after the first day of
January, 1876, and more than thirty days prior to the 9th
day of May in said year, one C. C. White, then treasurer
of said Lancaster county, duly served on the relator a
written or printed, or partly written and partly printed,
notice, stating, in substance, that said relator was delinquent for installment of interest then accrued on account
of his said purchase of said lot, and that unless such delinquency should be removed within thirty days after the
date of said notice, said lot would be forfeited to the state,
and said purchase cease to be of force by reason thereof,
and that said lot would then again be offered for sale and
sold in the manner as provided by law.

"Respondent further avers that thereafter one W. A.
Sharrar, then clerk of said county, pursuant to said notice
and in accordance with the statute in such case made and
provided, published in the Nebraska *State Journal*, a newspaper printed, published, and of general circulation in said
county, a notice to the effect that said lot, together with
other tracts of land therein particularly described, belonging to the common school lands in said county, had been
theretofore sold, but had reverted and become forfeited to
the state by reason of non-payment of interest installments
thereon, and would be again offered for sale; that said notice
was published first on the 9th day of May, 1876, and
therein continuously until the day of the sale, which was on
the 15th day of June, 1876; pursuant to said last-named
notice, and in accordance with the statute in such case made
and provided, a sale of said lands was duly had and held
at the time and place in the manner provided by law, at
which sale a large number of lots and tracts of land which
had reverted and become forfeited to the state in all respects in like manner as the said lot 14, and descriptions

of which were inserted in said notice so published in said newspaper, were offered for sale and sold, and among others of said lots the said lot 14 was in manner and form as aforesaid, offered for sale and duly sold at said sale to one William Miles, for the price of three hundred and fifty dollars, he being the highest and best bidder therefor, and that thereupon the said county, on account of said sale, received such sum of money, and executed and delivered such notes and contracts on account thereof as were by law required. And respondent avers that said relator was present at said sale and had full and personal notice and knowledge of all and singular the matters in this answer alleged, and that the relator, so far from making any objection or protest on account of said sale, or asserting any rights to said lot, or to any lot mentioned in his application herein, or intimating that he had or claimed any interest therein, actively participated in said sale as bidder and purchaser thereat, and did in fact purchase several lots so described in said published notice as having reverted and become forfeited to the state. And respondent further avers that thereafter the said Miles duly sold and assigned his right as such purchaser to one Celia Wallingford and one Jerome Schamp, and that on the first day of January, 1880, said assignees being still the holders and owners of said right and of said contract of purchase, and the same not being delinquent or in any way invalid, paid to the treasurer of said county the full amount of principal and interest then unpaid on said contract, and received his receipt therefor in duplicate as provided by law, and afterwards obtained deed to the said property from the state of Nebraska."

The second cause of defense is an answer to plaintiff's second cause of action, and is substantially the same as the first cause of defense heretofore set out in respondent's answer, which said defense refers to lot 28.

It is not alleged in this defense that the holder of the
22

contract of purchase of said lot has ever received any deed from the state of Nebraska. Defendant's answer to the relator's third cause of action is substantially the same as the second cause heretofore set out and refers to lot 38, and as to the title to this lot defendant's answer shows that the holder of the contract of purchase has not yet received a deed to the said lot from the state of Nebraska.

The fourth defense, which is in answer to the relator's fourth cause of action, is the same as the cause of defense preceding this, with the exception that it alleges that the holder of the contract of purchase received a deed from the state of Nebraska in 1879.

The parties entered into a stipulation of facts as follows:

"That on and prior to the 15th day of June, 1868, the state of Nebraska was the owner in fee of lot six in the north-east quarter of section number 36, in township 10 north, of range 6 east of the 6th P. M. in Lancaster county, in said state, also of lots 14, 28, and 30 in the north-west quarter of said section, and that each of said lots was a part of the lands set apart for the permanent support of the common schools of said state, and was prairie land.

"That prior to said 15th day of June, 1868, said lands had been duly appraised and advertised for sale by the officers of said county, and on said day were duly advertised for sale in the manner provided by law ; and that at such sale the relator was the highest and best bidder for each of said lots, and that each of them was struck off to him thereat at the following prices, viz.: Lot 6 at $59.50 per acre, lot 30 at $101 per acre, lot 14 at $100 per acre, lot 28 at $84 per acre. That thereupon the relator paid to the treasurer of said county one-tenth of the sum for which each of said lots was so struck off to him, and that thereafter the relator paid to the treasurer of said county interest on the residue of the purchase price of said lots 6, 14, and 28, at the rate required by law, as the same accrued, on

the first days of January from the year 1869 to and including the year 1874 to January, 1875, and on the said
lot 30 from the year 1869 to the first of January, 1875.
That the sums for which said lots were struck off to the
relator were not less than $7 per acre, nor less than the
appraised value thereof.

"That on the 5th day of May, 1885, the relator tendered to the treasurer of said county, on account of said
lot 14, the sum of $991.08, and on said lot 28 the sum of
$832.47, and on said lot 30 the sum of $1,076.97, and on
said lot 6 the sum of $1,181.17, and that said treasurer
refused to receive each and every of said sums.

"That on the 9th day of May, 1876, one William A.
Sharrar, who was then clerk of said county, published in
the Nebraska *State Journal*, a newspaper then and thereafter printed and published daily and weekly and of general circulation in said county, a notice, of which a true
copy is hereto annexed, marked 'Exhibit A,' and made
a part thereof; and that said notice was published in said
newspaper three weeks consecutively, and that the first
publication thereof therein was on said 9th day of May,
1876.

"That at the time and place specified in said notice, to-
wit, at the clerk's office in said county, on the 16th day of
June, 1876, each and all of said several lots and tracts of
of land were duly offered for sale, and at said sale and at
private sale thereafter, pursuant to said notice, sold by the
clerk and treasurer of said county, said county clerk acting
as crier at said sale, and the county treasurer attending receiving the money and issuing receipts therefor. That prior
to said sale, on June 16, 1876, the treasurer of said county
entered opposite the description of said lots on the school
land register of said county the word 'reverted' and afterwards the words 'and resold.'

"That at said sale, on June 16, 1876, said lot 14 was
sold to one William Miles, he being the highest and best

bidder therefor, at the price of $350, and the lot 28 was sold to one J. H. McMurtry at the price of $200; and the said lot 30 was sold to one N. S. Harwood for the price of $200; and the said lot 6 was sold to one William Miles for the sum of $350. Said several sums being not less than $7 per acre for said lots, not less than the appraised value thereof.

"That at the date of said sale, on the 16th day of June, 1876, each of said purchasers paid to the treasurer of said county, in cash, one-tenth of the said purchase price of the lot by him respectively so purchased as aforesaid, and received the county treasurer's receipt therefor, and executed and delivered to said treasurer his promissory note, stipulating in manner and form as provided by law for the payment to the state of Nebraska the residue of said purchase price ten years after said date, with interest at the rate of ten per cent per annum, payable annually in advance, the first payment of interest being computed to the first day of January after the said date of said note, and being paid accordingly.

"That on the 9th day of May, 1885, said N. S. Harwood, being still the owner of said contract of purchase of said lot number 30, paid to the treasurer of said county, in cash, all the rest and residue of the said purchase price of said lot then remaining unpaid, together with interest thereon at ten per cent per annum until January 1st, 1886, and received said treasurer's receipt in duplicate.

"That on the 11th day of June, 1885, one George P. Tucker was the owner, by purchase and assignment, of the said contract of purchase by said J. H. McMurtry of said lot 28, and on said day paid to the treasurer of said county, in cash, all the rest and residue of the said purchase price of said lot then remaining unpaid, with interest thereon at ten per cent per annum until January 1st, 1886, and received said treasurer's receipt therefor in duplicate.

"That on the 11th day of September, 1879, one J. M.

Knox was the owner, by purchase and assignment, of the said contract of purchase by the said William Miles, of said lot number 6, and on said day paid to the treasurer of said county, in cash, all the rest and residue of the said purchase price of said lot then remaining unpaid, together with interest thereon at the rate of ten per cent per annum until January 1st, 1880, and received said treasurer's receipt therefor in duplicate. And that thereupon said Knox surrendered said receipt to the commissioner of public lands and buildings of said state, whereupon, by order of the board of public lands and buildings, the said commissioner and the governor and secretary of said state executed and delivered to said Knox, under their several hands officially, and the great seal of the said state, a deed or patent purporting to convey said lot to said Knox in fee simple absolute, which deed or patent was duly filed for record and recorded in the clerk's office of said county on the 13th day of September, 1879. And that thereafter the said Knox, in consideration of $1,000 to him paid, conveyed said lot by deed of general warranty to one Daniel S. Owen and one Solon Hazelton in joint tenancy, which deed has also been filed for record in said clerk's office.

"That on the 1st day of January, 1880, one Celia Walingford, and one Jerome Schamp were jointly the owners, by purchase and assignment, of the contract of purchase by the said William Miles of said lot number 14, and on said day paid to the treasurer of said county, in cash, all the rest and residue of the said price of said lot remaining unpaid, together with interest thereon at the rate of ten per cent per annum until said date, and received said treasurer's receipt therefor in duplicate. And that thereupon said Wallingford and Schamp surrendered said receipt to the commissioner of public land and buildings of said state, whereupon, by order of the board of public lands and buildings of said state, the said commissioner, and governor, and secretary of said state executed and delivered to said Wallingford and Schamp, under their hands officially, and the great seal of the state, a deed or patent purporting to convey said lot to said Wallingford and Schamp jointly, in fee simple absolute. That said deed or patent was thereupon duly filed for record in the clerk's office of said county, and duly recorded therein, and that since the date of the said instrument aforesaid, the said Wallingford and Schamp have occupied and now occupy said lot as their several homesteads for themselves respectively and their families, both of said persons being married.

"This stipulation is conclusive as to the facts herein agreed upon, but shall not be construed as precluding either party from proving, or offering to prove, any other fact or facts material to the controversy, or from introducing or offering any testimony tending to prove any additional fact.

"It is further stipulated that the school land record for Lancaster county, in the year of 1876, shows that the relator purchased on the 14th day of July, 1876, lot 2 in the south-west quarter of section 36, township 10, range 6, and that on the 20th day of July, 1876, he also purchased lot 20 in the north-west quarter of said section.

"That the contract of sale of the said last-named tract was, on the 16th day of October, 1878, assigned by said Miller to one F. W. Ware, and was thereafter assigned through mesne assignments to one Isaac Oppenheimer, and was treated as being in force, and payments were made thereon by the holders thereof, from time to time, until May 11th, 1885, when final payment was made by said Oppenheimer, and the deed executed and delivered to him by the governor, land commissioner, and secretary of state.

"The records in the office of said land commissioner show that, as to lots 14, 38, and 30 in the north-west quarter of section 36, township 10, range 6, and lot 6 in the north-east quarter of said section, annual payments accruing under the contract of sale of June 16, 1876, have all been made up to and including full and final payment.

"The published notice, a copy of which is annexed to the stipulation heretofore made in this action, appears upon the book in which appears the record of the appraisement of school lands in Lancaster county for the years 1875 and 1877.

"That there is no record in the land commissioner's office, state of Nebraska, of any notice of the relator being in arrears for payments on the lots set forth in the relator's bill, neither is there any record showing any notice was ever given the relator that his contracts of purchase to said property would be forfeited and cancelled unless his delinquent payments were made."

The testimony of the relator was taken by interrogatories, as follows:

Int. 1st. "Where did you reside in the month of May and June, 1876?"

Answer to Int. 1st. "At the corner of P and 18th streets in the city of Lincoln, state of Nebraska."

Int. 2. "Were you a subscriber to the Daily Nebraska *State Journal*, then published at Lincoln, Nebraska?"

Answer to Int. 2. "I think not; am not positive."

Int. 3. "Did you know, or were you informed in any manner prior to the 16th day of June, 1876, that the lots in controversy in this suit were to be offered for sale by the clerk and treasurer of said county on said day?"

Ans. to Int. 3. "I did not know of any cancellation of my contracts for these lots prior to said date, or of any intended cancellation, or of any contemplated sale of said lots; had never received any notice of delinquency or of cancellation, or of any sale to take place; never had any notice served on me, either printed, written, or verbal, that I was delinquent or of any danger of an effort to cancel

my contracts, or that my contracts had been cancelled, or
that there was to be a sale of these lots on the 16th day of
June, 1876, or at any other time.   Never saw any notice
in any newspaper or posted in any place on this subject,
nor had I any information of any kind, or intimation that
said sale was to take place on said day.   I was not present
at the sale; was not in Lincoln at the time.   I feel the
more certain and positive that I had no information of this
proposed sale, as I was interested in the lots to be sold to
the amount of several thousand dollars, perhaps more interested in the sale of lots in section 36, T. 10, R. 6, than any
other man, having purchased near one hundred acres, I
think, at the sale of June 15th, 1868, and still held a large
proportion of these lots by contract from the state of Nebraska, upon which I paid ten per cent of the purchase
at the time; also ten per cent interest in advance annually
for six years, so that I was largely interested in said sale,
and could not have forgotten if I had received any information of said sale.   Another reason I feel sure I had
no information of said sale is, that I had been annually
annoyed and out of humor on account of the course pursued by the county and state in levying, assessing and collecting taxes on these lots in open violation of the express
conditions of the sale that these lots were to be free from
taxation, which statement was made publicly on the day of
sale by the county clerk and the state officers.   This statement was made repeatedly during the sale as an inducement to purchase said lots and to advance the prices.   The
same statement was also published in the Lincoln papers,
over the signature of the the county clerk, prior to the
sale.   I had paid these taxes under protest all these years
with the investment in these lots in controversy of nearly
one hundred dollars per acre on an average, counting the
first payment of one-tenth of the purchase money with ten per
cent interest in advance, and ten per cent interest in advance
on the deferred payment for six years, counting the inter-

est at ten per cent per annum on these separate payments, together with the annual taxes, together with the interest on these several sums at ten per cent per annum, which constituted the amount of my vested interests and rights in these lots. I cannot conceive that I could have been informed that there was an effort being made to cut off my right and interest in these lots and set me out in the cold after six years and one-half of constructive possession, without due process of law, and I made no protest against it, especially when the state held my obligations with approved endorsers for the residue of the purchase money as required by the state officers at the time of the purchase. I feel certain as . I know myself, that I should have enjoined that sale if I had been informed concerning it; another reason that confirmed me that I knew nothing of the sale prior to said day, by the utter surprise which I experienced and well remember, when informed by J. V. Hoagland—I think it was him, on O street, in Lincoln, in front of the First National Bank, that all my lots above referred to in section 36 were sold; this was the first intimation I had of the sale or intended sale of these lots. This was in the afternoon of June 16th, 1876, on my way home from the B. & M. train. I hastened at once up to the county treasurer's office, and learned from C. C. White, county treasurer, that the sale was closed and all my lots in section 16 were sold."

Int. 4. "If you had any such knowledge or information as is mentioned in the last preceding interrogatory, state what it was and how it was obtained."

Ans. to Int. 4. "I had no such knowledge or information."

Int. 5. "Did you purchase from any person or persons any contract or contracts of sale executed by the treasurer of said county, or by any purchaser or purchasers, pursuant to any sale or sales of land that were made on the said · 16th day of June, 1876?"

Ans. to Int. 5. "On the afternoon of June 16th, 1876, after being officially informed by the county treasurer that all my lots were sold, I asked and received from him a list of the names of the purchasers of my lots, with the number of the lots that each had purchased. As I remember them now, the purchasers were C. C. Burr, R. R. Tingley, J. H. McMurtry, N. S. Harwood, and one Miles, first name forgotten. I was acquainted with all the purchasers except the last one named. I immediately went to C. C. Burr and made a statement of the facts in connection with my former purchase, of the payments made thereon on my contracts, of interest and taxes from June 15th, 1868, and told him that I considered I had vested rights in the lots, and that I considered my claim equitable to the lots, and he took the same view and offered to release his claim to me. I done the same thing with Dr. Tingley with the same results. I think Mr. Burr purchased three of the lots and Dr. Tingley one. The others refused to relinquish their claims. I had a long corespondence with Miles, lasting for months, in which I presented my claims to the lots, with all the facts connected with my purchase and payment, but he refused to do anything about it. I paid neither C. C. Burr nor R. R. Tingley for their supposed rights under their bids for the lots, and they asked me nothing. My recollection is that neither of them had paid any money on the lots, and do not think they made any assignment of contracts. I think they had no contracts made out. I do not think they made any written assignment of their bids or purchase to me, but think they went in and made a verbal release to the county treasurer. I think that was all that was done about it at the time. I think I paid no money to either of them; do not think I paid any money on the lots to the county treasurer at the time, nor till some time after; I think not till after my return from a trip to Chicago a month or so later. But when I did go into the treasurer's office to fix up the mat- ·

ter I was presented by the county treasurer with a written
release of these lots to the state from my former purchase
of the same lots on June 15, 1868, giving as the reason that
most of the counties had not re-sold their delinquent school
lands, and that there were conflicting opinions and doubts
as to the legality of the sales, which release I signed.

"I paid the one-tenth of the purchase money, with the
interest, ten per cent in advance, and received my contracts
for the lots. Whether this was a legal purchase from C.
C. Burr and R. R. Tingley or from the state of Nebraska
I cannot answer. I call it a kind of swap, in which the
state got all I had previously paid on these lots, being more
than double what they were now appraised at and sold for,
besides paying the amount for the new contracts, said lots
having been greatly depreciated in value by the state's illegal taxation on them. I have found myself unable to give
a categorical answer to Interrogatory 5, but have tried to
give an exact account of the whole transaction as it occurred,
to the best of my knowledge and belief."

Int. sixth. "If you purchased any such contracts as are
mentioned in the last named interrogatory, state from whom
you got the same, what tract or tracts of land were named
in the contract or contracts so purchased, whether the same
were assigned to you, and what, if anything, you afterwards did with reference to compliance with the terms of
said contracts, and whether you disposed of the same or
any of them, and if so, what disposition you made of
them?"

Answer to Int. sixth. "I did obtain several such contracts in the way and under the circumstances as related in
my answer to the last preceding interrogatory, but whether
I obtained them legally from C. C. Burr and R. R. Tingley or from the state of Nebraska, or whether the release
required by the county treasurer of my former purchase of
these lots made a new transaction, I am unable to decide,
but I got contracts for the lots that were struck off at that

time to C. C. Burr and R. R. Tingley, but which lots were
sold to Burr and which to Tingley I do not now recollect.
I think the two lots named in the first paragraph of the
second stipulation were some of them. I cannot now give
the number of the lots I got contracts for; I think there
were four of them; do not think there was any written
assignment of either of them to me from Burr or Tingley
after the release of the old contracts. I complied with all
the conditions of the new contracts while I held them, I
think. I sold them all; do not now recollect to whom.

J. G. MILLER."

Theo. F. Hardenberg, being examined as a witness, testified as follows:

Question (4). What was your occupation March, '76?
Clerk in the county treasurer's office.

(5). Do you recollect the sales of land in 36–10–6, in
June of that year? I do.

(6). State whether you had anything to do with making
out notices of delinquency of the payment of interest on
the lands in that section? I did; I made up the notices
preparatory to the sale of school lands.

(7). What steps did you take to notify delinquents of
their delinquency in payment of interest, if any? Answer.
I made up a list of all delinquent school lands that were
delinquent for over two years for the county of Lancaster.
I prepared notices showing the amount of delinquency.
To all persons whose address I knew, the notices were
mailed to them through the post-office.

(8). Do you recollect whether or not you sent a notice to
the relator, Jason G. Miller? Ans. I know that his notice
was prepared, and I have every reason to believe it was
mailed to him with the others.

(9). If I understand you correctly, then is this what you
mean to say, that all the persons whose addresses were
known you sent written notices to? Ans. Yes, sir, written notices through the post-office.

(10). And such as were not known, what was done? They were advertised through the papers.

(11). Have you a copy of the notice such as mailed? I have not ; I think all those things were destroyed when the county treasurer's office was removed from the old building to the new.

(12). Have you made a search for them? I have. I think those papers were in a bundle by themselves and were all destroyed.

(13). Can you state from memory what that notice contained, in substance? I can tell the substance of it. It contained the amount of each year's delinquency, with the interest added to it, showing the total amount of delinquency up to that time, and, as near as I remember, a statement that if this delinquency was not paid at once the lands would be forfeited.

CROSS-EXAMINATION.

Question (1). Who was treasurer at this time? Mr. Chas. White.

(2). When did you say these notices were sent out? In the spring of '76·

(3). What time in the spring? I don't remember.

(4). Who prepared them? I prepared them all.

(5). Who signed them? I think I signed them.

(6). As deputy treasurer? No, sir, I was not deputy.

(7). How does it come, then, that they were signed by you? I think I just signed his name, White.

(8). Did you ever show them to Mr. White? Yes, sir.

(9). You say you sent out the notices to all persons who were delinquent two years or over? Yes, sir.

(10). Then if it should turn out that Miller was not delinquent two years, was a notice sent to him? Probably not.

(11). When did you see one of these notices you prepared last? I don't remember.

(12). Have you seen one in five or six years? I can't say.

(13). You swear that you sent a notice to Jason G. Miller? Yes, sir.

(14). You swear positively that you sent him a notice, do you? Yes, sir.

(15). You are just as positive about that as that he was delinquent two years, are you? Just as positive.

(16). Have you ever seen that notice since? No, sir.

(17). Were any of them ever returned? I think not.

(18). What time were these notices sent out? In the spring of '76·

(19). Don't you know what time in the spring it was? No, sir ; it was in the spring of the year.

(20). What makes you think it was in the spring of the year? Because it was some time before Mr. White went away. I think he went away some time along in June.

(21). How long do you think it was? I don't know— two or three months.

(22). And he went away in June? Yes, sir.

(23). What lots did you notify Mr. Miller that he was delinquent on? I can't state now.

(24). Do you know how many or what lots? No, sir.

(25). Now if it should turn out in evidence that J. G. Miller was not delinquent, you didn't send the notices, did you? It would seem so.

(27). When did you have your attention called to the fact of your having sent out these notices? I don't remember now. I have always known that there has been more or less controversy about it ever since they were sent out.

(28). What was the usual mode of sending them? By mail.

(29). Did you put the notice in the post-office to J. G. Miller? I have every reason to believe that I did if his lands were delinquent at the time I made out the list.

(30). You didn't skip any one? I know I couldn't skip anybody; I know I didn't skip Miller.

(31). How do you know? Because it wasn't possible to skip anybody, and I have a distinct recollection of this one.

(32). Do you remember any others? I mailed one to F. B. Cheney. I don't remember any others.

(33). How is it that you remember only these two? I was acquainted with the parties.

(34). Weren't yon acquainted with any others? I don't remember.

(35). You think these notices stated that if they didn't pay up immediately these tracts would be forfeited? Exactly.

RE-DIRECT.

Question (1). Do you remember who prepared the form for these notices? I think Mr. White, the county treasurer, prepared them.

(2). You signed these notices under the direction of Mr. White? Yes, sir.

(3). Were these notices sent out before or after the publication to the non-residents? I suppose about the same time; I have no distinct recollection. I suppose it was about the same time.

C. C. White being called as a witness, testified as follows:

Question (2). What official position, if any, did you hold in Lancaster county in 1876? That of county treasurer.

(3). Do you remember the forfeiture sale of school lands in section 35, 10, 6, adjoining the city of Lincoln? Yes sir. I remember taking steps looking to the forfeiture and sale of lands in which lessees and purchasers were delinquent in payments to the state.

(4). State what steps you took. I may not be able to state all the steps that were taken, but my mind is refreshed

in regard to certain of them, such as serving notices upon
parties whom the books showed to be delinquent, and furnishing a list of said delinquents to the district attorney,
and proceeding according to his directions in the case.
Just what those directions were specifically I am not able
now to recollect.

(5). Do you recollect what kind of notice was used,
whether printed or written? I am unable to recollect the
exact form of the notices; they were probably printed, as
there were a good many of them. In substance they were
notified formally of their delinquency, and that unless
within a short time these delinquencies were paid up, the
premises would be forfeited to the state.

(6). In what manner were these notices served? I am
unable to recollect. I may be able to refresh my memory
by this letter.

(7). You think you can remember distinctly if you
refresh your memory by the letter, do you? Yes, sir.
This letter was written to the district attorney, in which I
state that notices were served on non-residents by publication and upon residents by personal notice. I rely largely
upon this letter, and it only refreshes and corroborates the
indistinct recollection I had. When I knew the residence
of the delinquent I served the notice personally.

(8). Can you state at about what time these notices
were served? I don't know that I am able to recollect the
date. I might say that this letter was dated March 27th,
1876. The notices were served prior to that time.

(9). Were you at that time acquainted with the relator,
Jason G. Miller? Yes, sir. I was very well acquainted
with him.

(10). Did you know at that time that he was delinquent on some of his contracts? I must have known it.

(11). Did you know where he resided at that time? I
undoubtedly did.

(12). Will you consent that the letter to which you

refer may be attached as an exhibit to your deposition? Yes, sir.

(13). This letter was written in your official capacity as treasurer of Lancaster county to the district attorney in his official capacity, was it not? Yes, sir; as a report of what I had done, and asking for advice.

"The exhibit hereto annexed is a true copy of the letter to the district attorney above referred to.

CHAS. C. WHITE."

EXHIBIT "A."

"LINCOLN, NEB., March 27, 1876.

"*Hon. J. H. Broady, Dist. Atty., Judl. Dist., Brownville, Neb.:*

"DEAR SIR—Enclosed find list of the school lands of this county, the lessees and purchasers of which are delinquent in their payments of interest and lease money to the state. I have endeavored to comply with the law (chap. 70, sec. 18) in notifying them of such delinquency, and herein find copies of the notices served by me. The *published* notice is for those whose places of residence are to me unknown, the other, a copy of the one served personally or by mail upon resident owners.

"Will you, as attorney for county treasurers in such matters in your district, please advise me whether my action in the case is strictly legal, and what other steps, if any, are necessary for me to take. Also please return the enclosed list, if not needed by you.

Yours respectfully,
C. C. WHITE."

"TREASURER'S OFFICE, LANCASTER COUNTY,
NEB., March 23, 1876.

"Whereas, the following named persons, whose places of residence are to the subscribers unknown, have severally violated the covenants of their respective bonds and

23

contracts with the state of Nebraska, relating to the purchase by them of the tracts or parcels of school land hereinafter described, and which appear opposite their respective names. Said violation consisting in the failure of said parties to pay interest money to the state of Nebraska, when by the terms of said bonds and contracts became due. Now, therefore, in pursuance of the statute in such case made and provided, notice is hereby given that unless said delinquency is removed within thirty days from the date hereof, by the fulfillment of the covenants of said bonds and contracts, then said lands shall revert to, and the title thereof be revested in the state of Nebraska."

Then follows names of purchasers with the tracts purchased and the amount due from each thereon.

There is a large amount of other testimony to which it is unnecessary to refer. It will be observed that in March, 1876, the relator was in default in paying interest on the amount due the state on the lands in question for two years, viz., 1875 and 1876. Hardenburg swears positively that he notified all persons who were in default two years in the payment of interest, and in this he is corroborated by the treasurer, White. A clear preponderance of the testimony, therefore, tends to establish the fact that the relator had notice. The law requires good faith on the part of purchasers of school lands and a reasonable compliance with the terms of the contract. The interest is to be applied annually to the support of the common schools. If one purchaser may neglect for years the payment of interest owing by him, and still maintain his contract, all other purchasers may do likewise, and thus the purpose of the grant be entirely defeated; and where a forfeiture has been declared of which the party had notice, and no steps were taken at once to set it aside, a presumption, after a great lapse of time is, that the necessary notice was given. In other words, the law will presume official acts of public officers to have been rightly done unless the circumstances of the case overturn this presumption; and acts done which presuppose the existence of other acts to make them legally operative, are presumptive proof of the latter. *Bank of the United States v. Dandridge*, 12 Wheat., 70. *Coombs v. Lane*, 4 Ohio State, 112. *Ward v. Barrows*, 2 Id., 241.

The notice therefore was sufficient, and the relator's rights are barred.

(2). But suppose the relator was not served with notice, still he is not entitled to the writ. The testimony is undisputed that he was informed in the afternoon of the day on which the sale took place that the lands in controversy had been sold by the state under an alleged forfeiture, and that the purchasers had paid one-tenth of the purchase price. These purchasers and their assignees have held undisputed possession of said real estate from the time of purchase until this date, and have paid the interest on such purchases, and some of them have paid in full and have made valuable improvements on the land, and during all this time the relator has taken no steps to assert his alleged rights to said premises. In effect he has stood by, and by his silence said to said purchasers and their assignees that he had no claim upon the property. This question was before this court in *Gillespie v. Sawyer*, 15 Neb., 536, in which the law of estoppel was applied. REESE, J., in quoting from *Kirk v. Hamilton*, 102 U. S., 68, said, "There is no principle better established in this court, nor one founded on more solid considerations of equity and public utility, than that which declares that if one man knowingly, though he does it passively by looking on, suffers another to purchase and expend money on land under an erroneous opinion of title, without making known his own claim, shall not afterwards be permitted to exercise his legal right against such person. It would be an act of fraud and injustice, and his conscience is bound by this equitable estoppel." It may be contended that his action is not against the purchasers of the land, hence that the

rule above stated would not apply.   All the facts, however,
upon which the relator bases his claims to the lands, and
also in regard to the alleged · forfeiture of said lands, the
sale to other parties, the payment by them of interest from
the time of purchase until this date, and the erection of
valuable improvements thereon, are before the court, from
which it appears that said purchasers and their assignees
have been in possession for more than ten years, claiming
the land as their own, and it is apparent that the relator is
estopped to assert any title in said lands.

(3). The supreme court of Minnesota, in *McKinney v.
Bode*, 23 N. W. Rep., 852, where one M., at a sale of school
lands in 1872, purchased a tract of such land, paid part of
the purchase price and the interest on the remainder to the
succeeding June, received the usual certificate, went into possession, built a house, paid the interest due June, 1873, and
remained in possession till December, 1873, when he executed an assignment of the certificate to his wife, and abandoned the land and his wife and family, and never afterwards
resumed possession, nor gave any further attention to the
matter.   The wife and family remained in possession, and
from December, 1873, a son who remained with his mother
paid the taxes and the interest on the unpaid purchase
money, for and on account of his mother, until her death
in 1880, and after her death, for and on account of her estate, until November, 1880, when the administrator of her
estate, under license from the probate court, sold and assigned the certificate to A.   The latter thereupon paid to
the land commissioners all arrears of principal and interest
on the certificate, and a patent for the land was issued to
him; it was held that, although the assignment of the certificate to the wife was void, M. had at the time of issuing
the patent no equity to the land as against A.

That a party may abandon his contract with the state
there is no doubt; but as the question of abandonment is
not discussed in the brief of either counsel, we will not con-

sider it here. It is clear that the relator has no interest in the lands in controversy, and the writ must be denied and the action dismissed.

JUDGMENT ACCORDINGLY.

THE other judges concur.

MARY J. SELLS, PLAINTIFF IN ERROR, V. D. D. HAGGARD & CO., DEFENDANTS IN ERROR.

1. **Appeal**: PLEADING CAUSE OF ACTION : EVIDENCE. While a plaintiff in an appellate court must prosecute the same cause of action as in the court of original jurisdiction, yet so long as the identity of the cause of action is maintained he may plead and prove any fact to show its validity.

2. **Evidence.** A letter held to be incompetent and properly excluded.

3. ——— : DEPOSITIONS : NON-RESIDENT WITNESS. Where from the deposition of certain witnesses it appears that they are non-residents of the state, it is unnecessary for the party offering the depositions in evidence to prove they are not present in court.

4. ——— : ——— : NON-RESIDENT PLAINTIFF. A party plaintiff who is a non-resident of the county where the trial is held need not appear personally to testify in the case, but his deposition may be taken as in the case of other non-resident witnesses.

5. **Evidence**: FOREIGN LAWS. Where the statute of another state is pleaded, and offered, and allowed in evidence, but not introduced, it will be unavailing to the party offering the same.

6. ——— : ——— : The statutes of another state must be pleaded as facts and the proof submitted to the jury.

ERROR to the district court for Platte county. Tried below before POST, J.

McAllister Bros., for plaintiff in error.

Sullivan & Reeder, for defendant in error.

MAXWELL, CH. J.

This action was brought on a promissory note, of which the following is a copy:

"$100.00.   ANCHOR, ILLINOIS, October 17th, 1882.

"On or before the first day of December, 1883, for value received, I or we, the undersigned, of Anchor Township, county of McLean, state of Illinois, promise to pay to the order of D. D. Haggard & Co., one hundred dollars, at C. A. Schurman & Co.'s bank at Saybrook, Ill., with exchange and expense of collection and interest at eight per cent per annum, payable annually from date until maturity, and eight per cent per annum from maturity until paid. If this note is not paid at maturity and is placed in the hands of an attorney for collection, in consideration of the credit herein given, we agree to pay its holder ten per cent additional upon the amount due as liquidated damages for non-payment at maturity, and also other expenses incurred in its collection. Demand, protest, and notice of non-payment waived by drawers and indorsers.

her
MARY J. ⋈ SELLS.
mark
J. A. SELLS."

Witness: O. PATTER.

The answer is as follows:

"Now comes the said defendant, Mary J. Sells, and for answer to the plaintiffs' petition states:

"*First.* She admits that she signed the note mentioned and referred to in plaintiffs' petition, but alleges that it is null and void for the following reasons.

"*Second.* Said defendant alleges that at the time she signed said note she was a married woman and living with her husband, that said note was not given for any debt or obligation owing by this defendant to said plaintiff, or for any claim or obligation against the separate property of this defendant.

"*Third.* Said defendant alleges that said note was obtained by said plaintiff by force and duress, and was not her voluntary act, in this, to-wit, defendant alleges that W. H. Haggard, of the firm of D. D. Haggard & Co., plaintiffs, on the day that said note was executed, told this answering defendant that if she did not give and sign this note then he would have her husband, Basil Sells, arrested and prosecuted and sent to the penitentiary of Illinois, that this defendant then and there believed that if she did not give and sign the note in suit that said W. H. Haggard would immediately arrest and imprison her said husband."

The reply was as follows:

"Comes now the said plaintiffs, D. D. Haggard & Co., and for a reply to defendant's answer filed herein admits:

"(1) That defendant was a married woman at the time she executed the note in question.

"(2) And plaintiffs aver that said note was signed and said contract entered into in the state of Illinois, and that at the time said note was so signed and said contract entered into that section number six of chapter number sixty-eight of the statutes of the state of Illinois was as follows: 'Contracts may be made and liabilities incurred by a wife and the same enforced against her to the same extent and in the same manner as if she were unmarried, but except with the consent of her husband she may not enter into or carry on any partnership business unless her husband has abandoned or deserted her, or is idiotic or insane, or is confined in the penitentiary;' said statute was then and now is in force in said state.

"(3) Plaintiffs deny each and every other allegation in said answer contained."

To this reply the defendant filed a motion supported by an affidavit as follows:

"Now comes the said defendant, Mary J. Sells, and moves the court to strike out the second paragraph or count of plaintiffs' reply, for the reason that said count raises a new and different issue from any issue that was raised or pre-

sented in the trial of this case in the court from which it
was appealed."

In support of this motion defendant refers to the files
in this case in the county court of Platte county, and also
the affidavit of Stephen S. McAllister herewith filed and
made a part hereof as follows:

"Stephen S. McAllister, being first duly sworn according to law, deposes and says that he was one of the attorneys for said defendant in the trial of this case in the
county court of Platte county, and was present during the
entire trial of said cause, acting as the attorney for said
defendant, and that on said trial no reference was made to
the statute of Illinois, mentioned and set forth in the 2d
count of plaintiffs' reply, nor was the said statute of Illinois offered in evidence by said plaintiffs, nor was any isssue
raised on or concerning said statute of Illinois in said
county court.

(Signed)   STEPHEN S. McALLISTER."

The motion was overruled, to which the defendant below
(plaintiff in error) excepted, and now assigns the overruling
of said motion for error.

In *O'Leary v. Iskey*, 12 Neb., 137, it was held that a
case is to be tried in an appellate court upon the same
issues which were presented in the court from which the
appeal was taken. This rule was approved and adhered
to in *U. P. R. R. v. Ogilvy*, 18 Neb., 638. That is, the
action is to be brought on the same claim and substantially
the same defenses to be made against it in the appellate
court as in the court of original jurisdiction. In this case
the defendant below admits the making of the note, but
pleads coverture as a defense against it and that it was not
made in reference to her separate estate. That portion of
the reply objected to simply states in effect that she had
authority under the statutes of Illinois, and therefore the
note is valid. The reply does not change the nature of the
cause of action. So long as the identity of the cause of

action is maintained a party may prove any fact in the appellate court proper to be received in evidence which tends to sustain sustain the cause of action.

The rule that causes are to be tried in the appellate courts upon substantially the same issues as in the court of original jurisdiction, is intended to require the respective parties to settle the controversy in the first trial if possible. If, however, either party is dissatisfied with the judgment, the statute gives the right of appeal. In the appellate court the plaintiff's claim is to be set forth substantially the same as in the court below, and substantially the same defenses made, otherwise it would not be be an appeal. But neither party, in the first instance, is required to produce all the evidence in support of his claim or defense. He may not deem it necessary to do so, or may be unable to produce the same. Therefore in the trial in the appellate court the plaintiff may produce any testimony tending to establish his claim, and the same rule applies to the defendant. Otherwise the ends of justice would frequently be defeated. The court did not err, therefore, in overruling the motion of the defendant.

Second. Error in refusing to receive the following letter:

"D. D. HAGGARD.   W. H. HAGGARD.
Office of .
D. D. HAGGARD & Co.,
Hardware, Stoves, and Farm Machinery,
210, 216, and 218 West Washington Street,
BLOOMINGTON, Ill., Sept. 19th, 1882.

BASIL SELLS, Saybrook, Ill., Dear Sir: We have sent your note for $81.55 and interest to the bank at Saybrook, Ill., for collection. We find that the property statement you made on that note is false, and would advise you, if you wish to avoid serious trouble, that you pay the note at once.   Respectfully,
D. D. HAGGARD & Co."

This was objected to by plaintiffs as immaterial, irrelevant, and incompetent.   Objection sustained.

There was no error in sustaining the objection; the letter, if admitted, would not tend to prove any issue made by the answer, while it would distract the attention of the jury from the real questions at issue.

Third, That the court erred in receiving the depositions of W. H. Haggard and O. Potter, it being alleged that there was no foundation laid for the admission of the depositions, as it was not shown that they could not be present at the trial, and W. H. Haggard being one of the plaintiffs.

Section 372 of the code of civil procedure provides that " The depositions of any witness may be used only in the following causes: *First.*   When the witness does not reside in the county where the action or proceeding is pending, or is sent for trial by change of venue, or is absent therefrom. *Second.*   When from age, infirmity, or imprisonment, the witness is unable to attend the court, or is dead. *Third.*   When the testimony is required upon a motion, or in any other case where the oral examination of a witness is not required."

Section 386 provides that "When a deposition is offered to be read in evidence, it must appear to the satisfaction of the court, that for any cause specified in section three hundred and seventy-two, the attendance of the witness can not be procured."

The depositions in this case appear to have been taken in another state, of witnesses whose places of residence were in another state.   It being thus clearly shown that they were non-residents, their absence from the county at the time of trial would be presumed, and such depositions are admissible without further proof of the absence of the witnesses. A plaintiff who is a non-resident of the county where the action is tried cannot be required to appear in person at the trial, but his deposition may be taken the same as other non-resident witnesses.   This objection therefore is untenable.

Fourth. The court erred in refusing to set the verdict aside as against the evidence. This is predicated principally upon the alleged duress set up in the answer. There is a large amount of testimony on this point which we will not discuss, as for reasons hereinafter stated there must be a new trial. If, however, the decision of the case rested upon the question of duress alone, the verdict would not be disturbed. The plaintiff below sought to introduce the statute of Illinois to prove the authority of Mrs. Sells to make the note in question. Objection was made to the introduction of the statute but was overruled; the statute, however, was not introduced. The plaintiffs then offered to introduce the decision of the supreme court of Illinois in *Taylor v. Boardman*, 92 Ill., 566, and offered to read the same to the jury. The defendant below objected, and the objection was sustained. It will thus be seen that the statutes of Illinois authorizing a married woman to execute a note like the one sued on were not submitted to the jury. By stipulation of the attorneys in the supreme court the case above referred to, cited in 92 Illinois, was to be considered by the court in connection with a bill of exceptions; but as the statutes of another state are to be pleaded and proved as facts, the testimony must be submitted to a jury. There is a failure of proof therefore as to the authority of the wife to execute the note in question, and for that reason the judgment of the court below must be reversed and a new trial granted.

REVERSED AND REMANDED.

THE other judges concur.

364|
646|

LEVI CARKINS, PLAINTIFF IN ERROR, V. JOSEPH AN-
DERSON AND HANNAH M. ANDERSON, DEFENDANTS
IN ERROR.

1. **Public Lands of the United States**: SALE BY TIMBER
   CULTURE CLAIMANT: SPECIFIC PERFORMANCE. In 1874, one
   C. was possessed of a timber claim of 160 acres on public lands,
   upon which he had broken up about forty acres in 1875 ; he set
   out about twenty acres of this to timber in 1876; the claim with
   the improvements was worth about one thousand dollars; he
   sold the same to one A. upon consideration that he was to enter
   the same as a homestead under the laws of the United States,
   and after final proof to convey eighty acres of said land to C.;
   Held, That A. having obtained title to the land as the result
   of the transaction, would not be permitted to set up the illegality
   of the contract to permit him to retain the entire property.

2. ———: SALE OF IMPROVEMENTS. Under the statute of Nebraska all contracts, promises, undertakings, either written or
   verbal, made in good faith, and without fraud, collusion, or
   circumvention, for the sale, purchase, or payment of improvements made on the lands owned by the government of the
   United States, are valid in law and equity, and an action may
   be brought thereon and a recovery had as on other contracts.

ERROR to the district court for Adams county.   Tried
below before MORRIS, J.

A. H. Bowen, for plaintiff in error..

Batty & Castro and *J. M. Woolworth*, for defendants in
error.

MAXWELL, CH. J.

In October, 1885, the plaintiff filed a petition in the
court below stating, that on December 16, 1876, defendants owning and being in possession of the south half of
the south-east quarter of section 10, town 8, range 10, did

on said day sell the same to plaintiff, and entered into an agreement in writing of that date, whereby in consideration of one hundred dollars paid by plaintiff to defendants, said defendants sold said tract of land to plaintiff, and therein agreed to execute and deliver to plaintiff on or before May 1, 1881, a good and sufficient warranty deed to said premises, clear of all incumbrances, binding themselves, their heirs, executors, administrators, and assigns.

That plaintiff had performed all conditions on his part; that he has frequently demanded of defendants the fulfillment of said contract and the execution of said deed of conveyance, which they have ever and still refuse to make. Plaintiff prays for a decree requiring specific performance, and for such other relief as he may be entitled to.

The following is the contract upon which the action was brought:

"This agreement, made and entered into this 16th day of December, A. D. 1876, by and between Joseph Anderson and Hannah Anderson, his wife, of the county of Adams, and state of Nebraska, parties of the first part, and Levi Carkins, of Adams county, Nebraska, party of the second part, witnesseth: That the said parties of the first part have this day sold for and in consideration of the sum of one hundred dollars, to them in hand paid by the said Levi Carkins, the receipt whereof is hereby acknowledged, the following real estate, to-wit: The south one-half of southeast quarter of section ten (10), in town eight (8), range ten (10) west in Adams county, Nebraska.

"And the parties of the first part further agree with the party of the second part, that they will make and execute to him, on or before the first day of May, 1881, a good and sufficient warranty deed of said premises, clear of all incumbrance, and for the faithful performance of this contract they hereby bind themselves, their heirs, executors, administrators and assigns.

" In witness whereof, they have hereunto set their hands and seals this 16th day of December, 1876.

Signed,   JOSEPH ANDERSON,
                                 HANNAH M. ANDERSON.
                                         Parties of the first part.

                                     LEVI CARKINS,
In presence of   Party of the second part.
L. P. HAWLEY."

The defendants filed an answer as follows: Denying that when the contract was made that they were owners, or in possession of said tract of land, and alleging that when the contract was made the land belonged to the general government; that contract was made to homestead tract under acts of congress.   In March, 1877, Joseph Anderson, defendant, entered the tract with other land, as a homestead, and resided on and cultivated the land until March 31, 1884, when he made final proof at land office, and subsequently received patent for tract.   That when he made contract he was ignorant and unacquainted with the law governing homestead; that plaintiff seeking to cheat and defraud defendants out of their rights, pretended that he had a claim on the land, and represented that if defendants would make contract he would convey his right to them.   Defendant was thereby induced to make contract.   That as soon as defendants learned contract was contrary to law they repudiated the same, and have ever since treated the same as null and void.   That no consideration was paid for sale of land. That contract is void as against public policy.

Plaintiff filed his reply, denying that said contract was without consideration, and alleging that the consideration was valuable, to-wit: the transfer by plaintiff of property to defendants, which was received by defendants, and is still retained by them; that such property was worth more than $100.

There a trial to the court and judgment was rendered against the plaintiff, dismissing the action.

The testimony shows that in 1874 the plaintiff was possessed of a timber claim of 160 acres on the government land, and had broken up 40 acres of said land; that in 1875 he set out about 20 acres thereof with forest trees; that in 1876 the plaintiff sold the claim in controversy to the defendant Anderson, who was to enter the same as a homestead under the laws of the United States, and who, after making final proof, was to convey one-half of said land to the plaintiff.

Chapter 38 of the Comp. Statutes of Nebraska, provides that "All contracts, promises, assumpsits, or undertakings, either written or verbal, which shall be made hereafter in good faith, and without fraud, collusion, or circumvention, for sale, purchase or payment of improvements made on the lands owned by the goverment of the United States, shall be deemed valid in law or equity, and may be sued for and recovered as in other contracts."

Sec. 2. "All deeds of quit-claim or other conveyance, of all improvements upon public lands, shall be as binding and as effectual in law and equity between the parties, for conveying of the title of the grantor in and to the same, as in cases where the grantor has the fee simple to the premises."

This statute was in force when this contract was made and authorized a recovery for improvements on the public lands.

The defendants now refuse to execute the contract upon the ground that it is against public policy, and therefore void. This question was before this court in *Simmons v. Yurann*, 11 Neb., 518. *Bateman v. Robinson*, 12 Neb., 511. In the last case there was a re-argument ordered and the authorities were fully examined and cited, and it was held in substance that where acts are merely prohibited by statute and the parties are not *in pari delicto*, the party upon whom no penalty is imposed, may upon non-performance enforce his contract against his co-contractor. *Jaques v. Golightly*, 2 Wm. Blacks., 1073.   *Browning v. Morris*, 2 Cowp., 790. *Williams v. Hedley*, 8 East., 378. *Inhabitants of Worcester v. Eaton*, 11 Mass:, 368. *White v. Franklin Bank*, 22 Pick., 181. *Lowell v. Boston & Lowell R. R. Co.*, 23 Pick., 24. *Schermerhorn v. Talman*, 14 N. Y., 93. *Blanchard v. Jamison*, 14 Neb., 246. This principle is recognized by the supreme court of the United States, and it has been held in a number of cases that when an illegal contract is completed, and money or property has been received by a joint owner by force of the illegal contract, he will not be permitted to retain the whole by setting up the illegality of the transaction by which he procured it; but must account to his associates. *McBlair v. Gibbes*, 17 Howard, 237. *Brooks v. Martin*, 2 Wall., 70, and cases cited. *Wann v. Kelley*, 2 McCrary, 628. *Planters Bank v. Union Bank*, 16 Wall., 483.

In this case the timber claim and improvements are shown, by the testimony, to have been worth about one thousand dollars this the defendant obtained under his promise to convey one-half the land to plaintiff. The defendant's title to the land is the result of the entire transaction, and he cannot be permitted to retain the entire results upon the sole grounds that the means by which he obtained the same were unlawful. The case of *Dawson v. Merrille*, 2 Neb., 119, is the only case cited by the defendant in support of his claim, and that case was practically overruled in *Simmons v. Yurann*, 11 Neb., 518; *Bateman v. Robinson*, 12 Neb., 511; and *Blanchard v. Jamison*, 14 Neb., 244. We hold therefore that the plaintiff is entitled to the performance of the contract. The judgment of the district court is reversed and a decree of specific performance will be entered in this court.

DECREE ACCORDINGLY.

THE other judges concur.

HENRY COOK, PLAINTIFF IN ERROR, V. MELVILLE C.
HESTER, DEFENDANT IN ERROR.

1. **Justice of Peace**: PRACTICE. Bill of particulars examined
   and *Held*, Sufficient when attacked after judgment in a cause
   where the parties had appeared and a trial was had upon the
   merits of the case.

2. ——— : PROCEDURE. Where jurisdiction appears, all matters
   relating to the form of procedure in justice courts will be construed with great liberality.

ERROR to the district court for Adams county. Tried
below before MORRIS, J.

John M. Ragan and *J. B. Cessna*, for plaintiff in error.

Hester & McCreary, for defendant in error.

REESE, J.

This action was instituted before a justice of the peace
in Adams county. On the day fixed for trial the parties
appeared, defendant in error in person, plaintiff in error
in person, and by his attorney. A trial was had to the
court which found in favor of defendant in error and rendered judgment thereon.

The recital of the justice's docket is that "a trial was
had to the court, a jury being waived by both parties."
Plaintiff and defendant, with their several witnesses, were
sworn and the cause submitted upon its merits without any
objection being made to the form or substance of the bill
of particulars. After judgment the cause was removed to
the district court on error by plaintiff in error—who was
defendant below—and upon an affirmance of the judgment
of the justice the cause is brought to this court by like proceedings.

24

The only contention of plaintiff in error is that the bill of particulars filed before the justice of the peace did not state facts sufficient to constitute a cause of action.

The following is a copy of it:

"STATE OF NEBRASKA, ⎱ ss.
  Adams County, ⎰

Bill of particulars before John F. Battenger, a justice of the peace of Denver Township, Adams county.

MELVILLE C. HESTER, plaintiff, ⎱
              vs.   ⎰
  HENRY COOK, defendant.

The plaintiff in the above-entitled action says the said defendant was and is indebted to the plaintiff in the sum of eighty-nine dollars and sixty cents for seventeen stock hogs weighing 2,240 pounds gross on the 20th day of December, 1884, with interest thereon at seven per centum from said day, for which sum and interest, with his costs herein, plaintiff asks judgment.

MELVILLE C. HESTER."

Section 952 of the civil code provides that "The bill of particulars must state in a plain and direct manner the facts constituting the cause of action," etc.

In *Freeman v. Burks*, 16 Neb., 328, and *Wells v. Turner*, 14 Id., 445, it was held that the filing of a promissory note with the justice before whom an action was commenced was a sufficient compliance with the foregoing section, and in *Crossley v. Steele*, 13 Id., 219, it was held that a bill in the form of an account, with a statement that the plaintiff charged the defendant with damage to crops as stated in the account was sufficient.

As stated in the latter case, all matters relating to the form of proceeding in justice courts will be construed with great liberality.

In the case at bar the cause was tried upon its merits. There is no doubt but that the bill of particulars fully apprised plaintiff in error of the nature of the claim against him. No objection was made until after judgment. In such case there would have to be a clear and palpable failure to comply with the law, resulting in prejudice to the party complaining, before a reviewing court would interfere. In this case there is a substantial compliance with the section above quoted, and there is no prejudice resulting from the defect of form.

The judgment of the district court is affirmed.

JUDGMENT AFFIRMED.

THE other judges concur.

CHARLES J. HULL, PLAINTIFF IN ERROR, V. THE CHICAGO BURLINGTON AND QUINCY RAILROAD COMPANY, HUMPHREY BROTHERS HARDWARE COMPANY, SPENCER A. BROWN, FRANK E. PARISH, AND AUSTIN W. WIER, DEFENDANTS IN ERROR.

1. **Railroads**: POWER OF EMINENT DOMAIN: EJECTMENT: TRESPASS. The remedy given by statute to land-owners for injuries sustained by taking land for railways is exclusive of all other remedies. But this rule does not preclude the land-owner from bringing ejectment for the possession of real estate illegally occupied by a railroad. Where a railroad company without consent of the owner takes and occupies real estate as a part of its right of way without pursuing the statutory method of appraisement and condemnation, and thus making its possession rightful, it is, as all others under like circumstances would be, a trespasser and cannot justify its possession. In such case the usual common law remedies are available to the owner.

2. ———: ———: DEFECTIVE PROCEEDINGS. Where proceedings to condemn real estate, instituted and carried through by a railroad company, are so defective as to be void for want of jurisdiction, such proceeding will afford no defense to an action

of ejectment instituted by the land-owners to recover the possion of the land taken and occupied by the railroad for right of way purposes.

3. ——: ——: CONSTITUTIONAL LAW. The constitutional guaranty that "the property of no person shall be taken or damaged for public use without just compensation therefor" makes it incumbent upon a railroad company, or other governmental agency, exercising the right of eminent domain, to render such compensation before the right to appropriate the property will exist, and in case of failure to agree upon the damages accruing from the taking, the railroad company must proceed to condemn under the forms of law (unless such proceedings are instituted by the land-owner); and in case of failure so to do the possession of the real estate by the company for railroad or other purpose will be illegal, and ejectment may be maintained by the land-owner.

4. ——: ——: WITHDRAWAL OF DEPOSITED CONDEMNATION MONEY. Where a railroad company condemns private property to public use and deposits the condemnation money with the county judge of the proper county, in accordance with law, and takes possession of the condemned land, the subsequent withdrawal of the deposit from the county judge, for the reason that the proceedings were illegal, will be an abandonment of all right to claim the possession of the real estate under such proceedings. COBB, J., dissents.

5. ——: ——: SERVICE BY PUBLICATION. Where, in a proceeding to condemn the right of way through or over the real estate of a non-resident, notice is given by publication in a newspaper, that if the owner fails to apply for an assessment of damages by a date named, then the railroad company will apply therefor, and that the appraisement will be made at the premises on a day and hour named in the notice, such publication will give no authority for the assessment of damages nine months after the day fixed therefor in the notice.

6. ——: ——: ——. Where it is sought to exercise the right of eminent domain in the condemnation of the real estate of a non-resident and notice of such intention is given by publication, the publication must be made in one newspaper four successive weeks. The publication of such notice in a daily newspaper a part of the time and the remainder of the time in a weekly, (the papers being sent to different sets of subscribers in different localities,) will not confer jurisdiction and all proceedings thereunder will be void.

7. **Limitation of Actions**: REAL ESTATE: POSSESSION. A party in order to acquire title to land by the statute of limitations must not only have a possession adverse to the true owner, but must occupy the same as the owner during the entire statutory period.

8. ——: ——: EJECTMENT: PROPERTY CONDEMNED BY RAILROAD. In an action in ejectment against a railroad company for real estate occupied by it as a part of its right of way, the company claimed title to the property by reason of the statute of limitations. Within the ten years last preceding the commencement of the action the railroad company sought to condemn the property to its use under the provisions of the statute for the condemnation of real estate. These proceedings were instituted against the real owner by name, and the condemnation money deposited with the county judge for him. It was *Held* that these proceedings amounted to a recognition of the ownership of the person against whom they were instituted, and would arrest the running of the statute, even though the proceedings were void for want of jurisdiction by reason of a failure to comply with the law in the publication of the notice.

ERROR to the district court for Lancaster county. Tried below before HAYWARD, J.

Lamb, Ricketts & Wilson, for plaintiffs in error.

O. P. Mason and *Marquett & Deweese*, for defendant in error.

REESE, J.

This was an action in ejectment instituted in the district court of Lancaster county for the possession of lots 14, 15, 16, and 17 of block No. 70 of the city of Lincoln. Upon a trial in that court judgment was rendered in favor of plaintiff for the possession of lots 14 and 17 and in favor of defendant for lots 15 and 16. Plaintiff in error, being dissatisfied with the finding of the trial court as to the latter described lots, seeks a review thereon by proceedings in error. The defendant has filed a cross-petition in error,

and seeks a reversal of the judgment in so far as its right
to the possession of the former is affected.

It is insisted by defendant in error that ejectment is not
the proper remedy, that the remedy given by statute to
land owners, for injuries sustained by taking land for railways, is exclusive of all other remedies and not cumulative.
This rule seems to be well settled by adjudications.   Mills
on Eminent Domain, sec. 87, and cases there cited.   See
also *R. R. Co. v. Fink,* 18 Neb., 88.   But if the theory of
plaintiff in error is the correct one, that all the proceedings
to condemn the real estate in question were void, and defendant acquired no rights thereunder, then it seems to us
that the rule as to the statutory remedy being exclusive
would not be applicable here, for the action is not one for
injuries sustained by taking the land, but for the land
itself. Stated differently, the contention on the part of
plaintiff in error is that the whole proceeding to condemn
the property is a nullity, and that defendant in error is a
trespasser from the beginning.   If this is true the action
in ejectment is the proper remedy.

In *R. R. Co. v. Fink, supra,* the present Chief Justice,
MAXWELL, in writing the opinion of the court, says: "The
law does not require the citizen to institute proceedings to
protect his rights, but merely permits him to do so.   Constitutional guarantees of the rights of property would be
of little value if the corporation could seize the property of
an individual, and say to the owner, 'If you want compensation for this property institute proceedings to condemn it,
and after we think the proper amount is awarded we will
pay you.'"   While the manner of ascertaining the damages
is exclusive, yet if a railroad company takes and occupies
real estate without taking the necessary legal steps to condemn the land and thus making its possession rightful, it
is, as all others under like circumstances, a trespasser, and
cannot justify its possession.   Therefore the usual common
law remedies are available to the owner. *R. R. Co. v.*

Menk, 4 Neb., 24. *Blaisdell v. Winthrop*, 118 Mass., 138. *Ewing v. St. Louis*, 5 Wall., 413. The owner may enjoin the entry. *R. R. v. Menk, supra. Ray v. R. R.*, Id., 439. *Cameron v. Supervisors*, 47 Miss., 264. *Paris v. Mason*, 37 Texas, 447. *Floyd v. Turner*, 23 Id., 292. *Pierpoint v. Harrisville*, 9 W. Va., 215. Or he may bring ejectment. *R. R. Co. v. Smith*, 78 Ill., 96. *Smith v. R. R.*, 67 Id., 191. *R. R. v. President of Knox College*, 34 Id., 195.

Where ejectment is brought, the pendency of proceedings to condemn will be no defense to the action. *Coburn v. Lumber Co.*, 46 Cal., 31. And for stronger reasons it would follow that if the proceeding to condemn had been completed, and was so defective as to be void for want of jurisdiction or for other cause, the same rule would apply, and such void proceeding would furnish no defense.

This question being presented by the record and being as we think, of vital importance to the case, we will consider it as next in order.

The answer of defendant in error consists of four separate defenses, which may be stated as follows:

First. A general denial.

Second. That on the 12th day of December, 1879, and long prior thereto, the Burlington and Missouri River Railroad Company in Nebraska was a corporation under the laws of the state, and had built and operated a railroad in said name from Plattsmouth through the counties of Cass, Saunders, and Lancaster, through the city of Lincoln, and thence westward to Kearney. That at said date the business of said company required said lots 14, 15, 16, and 17, in block 70, for the use and operation of its railroad. That said company, in pursuance of the statutes, made application on the 12th day of December, 1879, by filing an application and petition for the condemnation of said lots to the use of said company. A transcript of all the proceedings of condemnation, showing the deposit of the con-

demnation money with the county judge, is attached to the
answer.   It is alleged that the money, amounting to one
thousand dollars, being deposited, the said railroad company being in possession of the property, the same was occupied by it, and its successor, the Chicago, Burlington
and Quincy Railroad Company, to the present time.   That
no appeal or writ of error to reverse or modify the proceedings, had ever been had, and they were wholly unre-
versed, unmodified, and in full force, and by which defendant had the right to use and occupy the lots, and could
not be ejected therefrom.

Third.   That plaintiff's cause of action did not accrue
within ten years next immediately preceding the commencement of this action and is barred by the statute of limitations.

Fourth.   That in July, 1874, the Nebraska Railway
Company, a corporation under the laws of Nebraska, and
operating a road from Nebraska City through the city of
Lincoln to Seward, took possession of said lots, and in the
fall of 1874 took open, notorious, and public possession of
said lots, laid side tracks across and over them, and said
company from that time to the present, together with its
legal successors, has continued in open, public, notorious,
and exclusive use and occupancy of said lots for more than
ten years next prior to the commencement of this suit;
that the Nebraska Railway Company was legally leased to
the Burlington and Missouri River Railroad Company,
and said lots were used and occupied with station-house,
coal-house, side tracks, and in the open, public, notorious
and exclusive possession of said Burlington and Missouri
River Railroad Company by virtue of said lease.   That
afterward said last-named company consolidated all its
lines of road in Nebraska with the company known as
the Chicago, Burlington, and Quincy Railroad Company,
and said company has continued in the constant, continuous, notorious, public, and exclusive possession of said lots,

and has by its predecessor aforesaid and by itself, occupied
the said lots, and been in the public, open, notorious and
exclusive use of all of said lots and duly using and occupying the same, with its station-house, coal-house, side
tracks, and turnouts for more than ten years next prior to
the commencement of this suit, and during all of said time
said defendant and its legal predecessors have occupied the
same and claimed title thereto, which claim was never questioned until the bringing of this suit.

The answers of the defendants, Humphrey Bros., and
of S. A. Brown and Company, each consisted of general
denials.

Plaintiff filed his reply to the answer of the defendant
railroad company, which consisted of a general denial except as to matters expressly admitted and a specific denial
that on the 12th day of December, 1879, or at any other
time the Burlington and Missouri River Railroad Company filed any application for the condemnation of the
property in question. Alleges that the condemnation proceedings described and set out in defendant's answer are
void because the county judge had no jurisdiction over the
property and never had jurisdiction to appoint appraisers.
That the appraisers had no power to assess damages for
taking the property. That no notice was given or served
upon the plaintiff as required by law to give said court
jurisdiction.

It is alleged that the notice was never published four
weeks in any newspaper, but that the same was published
in the daily *State Journal* January 24, 1880, and in the
weekly *State Journal* January 30, February 6 and 13, and
at no other times; that the daily *State Journal* and weekly
State Journal at said time were wholly different newspapers,
with different subscribers, and circulated in different com-
munities.

It is denied that the Chicago, Burlington, and Quincy
Railroad Company and the Burlington and Missouri River

Railroad Company ever needed said property, or that they have used or occupied it for railroad purposes, but have leased it to private individuals who use the same for wholly private purposes in no way connected with the business of said companies as common carriers.

It is alleged that whatever possession the said Nebraska Railway Company ever had of the property in question was under and by virtue of certain pretended condemnation proceedings which expressly recognized the title and ownership of plaintiff. That in 1879, or prior thereto, the Nebraska Railway Company surrendered whatever possession it had theretofore had of said property and abandoned the use and occupation thereof. That the B. & M. R. R. Co., the successor of said Nebraska Railway Company, withdrew from the county judge the money deposited by the said Nebraska Railway Company as damages assessed under said pretended condemnation proceedings taken by said Nebraska Railway Company and abandoned all right, title, and interest in said property derived through and under said pretended condemnation. Denies that said Nebraska Railway Company ever occupied said lots under claim of title thereto. Denies that the B. & M. R. R. Co. received possession of said lots from the Nebraska Railway Company, but alleges that the B. & M. R. R. Company expressly recognized the title and ownership of the plaintiff by its proceedings to condemn, set forth in answer that the B. & M. R. R., in 1880, by their lessees took possession of said lots and have ever since held the same by virtue of the pretended condemnation proceeding in said amended answer set forth.

Plaintiff also filed his motion for an order to compel defendant to elect whether it would stand upon the second or fourth defense contained in its answer for the reason that these defenses were inconsistent and could not be joined. This motion was overruled and plaintiff now assigns this ruling for error. As we view this case the question here presented is not material to its determination. But we deem it proper to say that upon consultation we were unanimously of the opinion that the defenses were not inconsistent, and that in the ruling on plaintiffs' motion there was no error. The cause was tried to the court without the intervention of the jury, with the result above stated.

The following facts were found by the court specially:

"1st. That the title of the premises described in plaintiff's petition, to-wit: Lots 14, 15, 16, and 17, in block 70, passed by patent and mesne conveyances from the United States to the state of Nebraska, and then by deeds dated the 10th day of Nov., 1868, and the 9th day of July, 1868, the title in fee to the same vested in the plaintiff herein.

"2d. That in May and June, 1875, the Nebraska Railway Company entered upon said lots 15 and 16, and laid thereon a road bed and a side track or switch, and at the same time laid their main track along the west side of said lots, as shown by the map introduced in evidence, the same being the tracks next east and west of the building designated as Humphrey's warehouse, and said company or its successors have ever since used such tracks.

"3d. That about December, 1875, the said Nebraska Railway Company moved its depot on to lot number 15 as described in plaintiff's petition.

"4th. That about November 4th, 1875, the Nebraska Railway Company filed a petition in the county court of Lancaster Co., to condemn the property described in plaintiff's petition, and that thereafter appraisers were called and report made, and on May 5th, 1876, $668.55 were deposited with the then county judge as damages awarded to the plaintiff for the taking of the said property. In such proceeding the county court acquired and had jurisdiction of the subject matter.

"5th. That on March 6th, 1880, the Burlington and Missouri River Railroad Company in Nebraska, the successor of the Nebraska Railway Company, withdrew the

money theretofore deposited by the said Nebraska Railway
Company as damages of the alleged ground.

"6th.   That about 1877, the Nebraska Railway Company leased its road and right of way to the said Burlington & Missouri River Railroad Company in Nebraska.

"7th.   That said depot building was, about 1879, by
the Burlington & Missouri River Railroad Company,
leased to the defendants Humphrey Bros., for the period
of five years at the annual rent of $150, and that said les-
sees have ever since held possession thereof under said lease.

"8th.   That on the 12th day of December, 1879, the
Burlington & Missouri River Railroad Company in Nebraska filed with the county judge of Lancaster county, an
application for the appointment of appraisers to condemn
certain property for right of way in and about the city of
Lincoln, and that the plaintiff's property now in controversy was not described, and his name is not mentioned in
said application; that on the third day of April, 1880, appraisers appointed upon said application proceeded to appraise the property in controversy, and their report was
duly filed on the 5th day of April, 1880, and that on the
7th day of April $1,000 was deposited with the then
county judge as plaintiff's damage for the taking of said
property, and on the said 7th day of April, 1880, there
was filed in the county court of said county due and regular proofs by affidavit of the publication of the notice to
the plaintiff Hull, as set out in the answer herein filed.
That such notice, proof of publication, and all such proceedings were regular upon their face.

"9th.   That the said notice was in fact published in the
daily *State Journal* of dates January 24th and 25th, 1880,
and in the weekly *State Journal* of dates January 30th and
February 5th and February 13th, 1880, and that the same
was not published at any other time or date. Such papers
are published at the same office by the same company, but
are different and separate papers.

"10th. That no affidavit, or other proof of non-residence of the plaintiff Hull, was made to the county court in either of said condemnation proceedings.

"11th. That in 1881 the Burlington & Missouri River Railroad Company in Nebraska leased lots 14 and 17 to Doolittle & Gordon, to be used for a private lumber yard for the period of five years at a nominal rental.

"12th. That in 1881 the said Railroad Company at the request of said Doolittle & Gordon laid a side track or switch over said lots 14 and 17 as shown by the map put in evidence in this case.

"13th. That thereafter and before the commencement of this suit the said Doolittle & Gordon sold their business and stock to the defendants S. A. Brown & Company, together with their rights under said lease.

"14th. That since 1881 said Doolittle & Gordon and S. A. Brown & Company have had exclusive and entire possession and control of said lots 14 and 17 for the use of their said lumber business, and have fenced and enclosed the same.

"15th. That the plaintiff has never received or accepted any of the moneys deposited with the county judge of Lancaster county, in pursuance of either of the condemnation proceedings.

"16th. The court in this case finds that lots 15 and 16, in block 70, are necessary for the operation of defendants' said railroad, and are being used so far as they are occupied by the tracks, road beds, and grades.

"17th. The court further finds, as to lots 14 and 17 in block 70, that while they are not at the present time being used for railroad purposes, that in anticipation of the increase of business and consequent necessity for a greater amount of ground, the proof shows that they will be necessary in the near future to facilitate the operation of its said road and leased lines concentrated at Lincoln."

By reference to the fifth finding it will be seen that the

condemnation proceedings of 1875 were abandoned by de_
fendant, and the damages which had been paid ·to the
county judge were withdrawn.   This action by the railroad company was for ·the reason that the proceedings
were illegal and irregular, and it is quite clear that no right
of defendant can be based thereon.   We quote from the
record a receipt executed for the money withdrawn.   It is
as follows:

"LINCOLN, March 6, 1880.

"Received of ex-county judge, A. G. Scott, six hundred
and fifty dollars, being the amount of condemnation as
above set out on lots 14, 15, 16, and 17 of block 70, city
of Lincoln.   The said condemnation having been illegal
and irregular, and this company having become the successor of the Nebraska Railway, and entitled to this money,
the same is withdrawn.

THE B. & M. R. R. Co. IN NEB.,

By J. W. DEWEESE, Agent."

Since no rights can be claimed under or by virtue of the
condemnation proceedings referred to in the receipt here
set out, we deem it scarcely worth while to notice that part
of the case further, yet another reason might be assigned
why they conferred no right to the possession of the property.

It appears that on the 4th day of November, 1875, the
application or petition for the appointment of appraisers
was filed with the county judge.   Plaintiff was a non-resident.   A notice was published "to the owners" of the
property in question in the Nebraska *State Journal*, notifying them that the Nebraska Railway Company had
located its depot thereon, and "if the owner or owners of
said lots aforesaid, and each of them, shall not within
thirty days from the 3d day of January, 1875, apply to
the probate judge of Lancaster county, in the state of Nebraska, to have the damages assessed in the mode prescribed
by law, the said Nebraska Railway Company will apply

to the probate judge of Lancaster county, in the state of
Nebraska, to have the damages assessed in the mode prescribed by law.   The said assessment of damages for the
said lots on behalf of the said Nebraska Railway Company
will take place on the said lots aforesaid at the city of Lincoln, in Lancaster county, Nebraska, on Monday, the 3d
day of February, 1876, at 11 o'clock A.M. of said day."
No action was taken by plaintiff as the owner of the lots,
nor was any taken by defendant until November 4th, 1876,
when proof of the publication of the notice was filed with
the county judge, and on the 6th day of the same month
an order was issued to the sheriff commanding him to summon the appraisers named therein to appraise the damages
to the property.   The appraisement was made on the 13th
day of November of the same year.

Section 100 of chapter 16 of the Compiled Statutes,
which was in force at the time referred to, is as follows:

" If, upon the location of said railroad, it shall be found ·
to run through the lands of any non-resident owner, the
said corporation may give four weeks' notice to such proprietor, if known, and if not known, by a description of
such real estate, by publication four consecutive weeks in
some newspaper published in the county where such lands
may lie, if there be any, and if not, in one nearest thereto
on the line of their said road, that said railroad has been
located through his or her lands; and if such owner shall
not within thirty days thereafter apply to said probate
(county) judge to have the damages assessed in the mode
prescribed in the preceding section, said company may proceed as herein set forth to have the damages assessed, subject to the same right of appeal as in case of resident
owners; and upon payment of the damages assessed, to the
probate (county) judge of the proper county for such owner,
the corporation shall acquire all rights and privileges mentioned in this subdivision."

While it does not seem to be required by the section

above quoted that the notice shall fix the day at which the
railroad company will cause the appraisement to be made,
yet, as we have seen, the time was fixed in the notice as the
third day of February, 1876, at 11 o'clock A.M. We are
unable to see how a notice fixing the third day of February as the time when "the assessment will take place,"
could confer authority to make the appraisement more than
nine months thereafter. Where a time is fixed for the appraisement, and no action then taken, the land owner
would be justified in supposing that all action had been
abandoned, and that appraisement would not be made. If,
then, the appraisement might be made months after without further notice, it would have the effect of depriving a
non-resident owner of "the same right of appeal as in case
of resident owners," which is given by the section above
copied. We think it clear that jurisdiction to make the
appraisement under the notice given had been lost, and all
proceedings thereunder were void.

We next come to the condemnation proceedings of 1879–
80. By the 8th and 9th findings of the trial court it appears that a new petition was filed with the county judge
seeking the appraisement of property. Plaintiff being a
non-resident, notice was again given by publication. The
essential question as to these proceedings is found in the
fact that the notice was "published in the daily *State Journal*, January 24th and 25th, 1880, and in the weekly *State
Journal* January 30th, February 5th, and February 13th,
1880, and that the same was not published at any other
time nor date. Such papers are published at the same
office by the same company, but are different and separate
papers." See 9th finding of fact.

As we have seen by the section above copied (100), the
corporation may give notice to the land owner "by publication four consecutive weeks in some newspaper published in the county" where the real estate sought to be
appropriated is situated. Did the publication referred to

comply with the requirements of the law? Clearly not·
As well might the publication have been in four "different
and separate" newspapers as in two. The fact that the
papers were published by the same publishing company
could have no bearing upon the question. The testimony
shows that at the time of the publication but few subscribers
took both papers, the daily and weekly. The daily had
the largest circulation in the city, and the weekly the
largest in the country. Each had its separate subscription
list and circulation.

It is well settled that in proceedings of this kind, depending upon a compliance with statutory provisions for
their existence and validity, the statute giving the power
to divest an individual of his property, in order that it may
be appropriated to the use of the public, must be strictly
followed in matters affecting jurisdiction. The right is
given by statute. The statute must be complied with to
secure it. The notice must be given substantially in accordance with the statutory requirement or the proceedings
will be void. *Curran v. Shattuck,* 24 Cal., 427. *State ex
rel. v. Otoe County,* 6 Neb., 129. *Doody v. Vaughn,* 7 Id.,
28. *Robinson v. Mathwick,* 5 Id., 252. *Case v. Thompson,* 6 Wend., 634. *Case v. Myers,* 6 Dana, 330. *Wood
v. Commissioners,* 62 Ills., 391. *Seifert v. Brooks,* 34 Wis.,
443. *People v. Kniskern,* 54 N. Y., 52. *Skinner v. Avenue Co.,* 57 Ills., 151. *People v. Supervisors,* 36 How.
Pr., 544. *Stone v. Boston,* 2 Metc., 220.

The statute requiring the notice to be published in "*some
newspaper* published in the county" clearly means that the
whole publication shall be made in *one* paper "four consecutive weeks." This was not done and no jurisdiction
was acquired. Virtually no notice was given. The proceedings constitute no justification. *R. R. Co. v. Fink,
supra.*

The next question presented is as to the statute of limitations. This point in the case is referred to but not dis-

25

cussed by defendant in error in its brief. It is true that
defendant in error and its predecessors were in possession
of a part, if not all, of the property in dispute more than
ten years prior to the commencement of this suit. But we
cannot see how it can be held that this possession was, during all of the time alluded to, *adverse* to the title or ownership of plaintiff. In the first instance the title and ownership of plaintiff—or some other person unknown, perhaps
—was recognized by the condemnation proceedings of 1875.
The damages to the owner as found by the appraisers was
placed to his credit with the county judge, where it remained until it was withdrawn in 1880. Had it not been
for the fact that at that time new proceedings had been instituted against plaintiff by name *as the owner*, it might be
that subsequent to that date the possession of defendant
would have been adverse. But by that proceeding his title
and ownership were directly admitted and recognized, and
on the 7th of April, 1880, the condemnation money found
due by the appraisers was deposited with the county judge
as plaintiff's damages. These acts amount to a clear and
definite acknowledgment of plaintiff's ownership of the
property, and would arrest the statute of limitations even
if it had commenced to run. *Erskine v. North*, 14 Gratt.,
60. *Walbrunn v. Ballen*, 68 Mo., 164. Wood on Limitations, 578. *Lovell v. Frost*, 44 Cal., 471. *Dietrick v. Noel*,
42 O. S., 18. *Stump v. Henry*, 6 Md., 201. Tyler on
Ejectment and Adverse Enjoyment, 125 and 921. *Koons
v. Steele*, 19 Penn. St., 203.

We hold, therefore, that neither the condemnation proceedings nor the statute of limitations, as shown by the evidence on the trial, constituted a defense to plaintiff's action.

Other questions are presented by the record, but as their
consideration is not essential to the decision in this case they
will not be noticed.

The judgment of the district court so far as it refers to
lots 14 and 17 in block 70 is affirmed. So far as it refers

to lots 15 and 16 in block 70 it is reversed, and the cause, as to them, is remanded for further proceedings.

REVERSED AND REMANDED.

THE other judges concur.

NETTIE B. SHEDENHELM, PLAINTIFF IN ERROR, V. JAMES W. SHEDENHELM, DEFENDANT IN ERROR.

1. **Divorce:** SUMMONS: SERVICE BY PUBLICATION. An affidavit for service by publication in an action for divorce was as follows:

"In the district court of Saline county, Nebraska,

NETTIE B. SHEDENHELM, plaintiff,
  vs.
JAMES W. SHEDENHELM, defendant.

STATE OF NEBRASKA,
  Saline County.

Nettie B. Shedenhelm, plaintiff in the above action, being first duly sworn, on oath says: She has this day caused a petition to be filed in said court against the said defendant, the object and prayer of which are to obtain a divorce, with alimony, from said defendant; that the defendant is a non-resident of the state of Nebraska, and that service of a summons cannot be had on him in this state. Wherefore plaintiff prays for service upon said defendant by publication.

NETTIE B. SHEDENHELM.

Subscribed in my presence and sworn to before me this 9th day of September, 1886.

[NOTARIAL SEAL.]   L. H. DENNISON,
                                       Notary Public."

Held, Sufficient. It is unnecessary in the affidavit for publication to set forth the particular cause or causes upon which a divorce is sought, and the affiant may state or omit the same at his option.

2. **Default:** FINAL ORDER. The overruling a motion to take a default against the defendant is not a final order, and not reviewable in the supreme court until after final judgment.

ERROR to the district court of Saline county. Heard below before MORRIS, J.

Abbott & Abbott, for plaintiff in error.

No appearance for defendant in error.

BY THE COURT:

This is an action for divorce brought by the plaintiff against the defendant in the district court of Saline county. The defendant being a non-resident of the state, an affidavit to that effect was filed and service had by publication. Proof of publication was duly filed, and after the time to answer had expired, no appearance being made by the defendant, the plaintiff moved for a default against him. The motion was overruled, the order being as follows: "And now on this 8th day of December, A.D. 1886, being one of the days of the adjourned October, 1886, term of this court, this cause came on to be heard upon the motion of the plaintiff for default, against said defendant. The plaintiff appearing by her attorney, and the defendant failing to appear, upon due consideration by the court, the said motion is denied, because the court has acquired no jurisdiction, by reason of the affidavit for publication being insufficient in this, that it fails to set out facts showing a cause wherein publication can by law be made."

The affidavit for publication is as follows:

"In the district court of Saline county, Nebraska. Nettie B. Shedenhelm, plaintiff, v. James Shedenhelm, defendant.

STATE OF NEBRASKA, } ss.
    Saline County.   }

Nettie B. Shedenhelm, plaintiff in the above action, being first duly sworn, on oath, says: She has this day caused a petition to be filed in said court against said defendant, the object and prayer of which are to obtain a divorce, with alimony, from said defendant; that the defendant is a non-resident of the state of Nebraska, and that service of summons cannot be had on him in this state. Wherefore plaintiff prays for service upon said defendant by publication.

NETTIE B. SHEDENHELM.

" Subscribed in my presence and sworn to before me this 9th day of September, 1886.

L. H. DENNISON,

[NOTARIAL SEAL.] *Notary Public.*"

The published notice was as follows:

"IN THE DISTRICT COURT OF SALINE COUNTY, NEBRASKA.

Nettie B. Shedenhelm ⎫
    vs.   ⎬
James W. Shedenhelm. ⎭

PETITION FOR DIVORCE AND ALIMONY.

To James W. Shedenhelm: You will take notice that I have this day caused a petition to be filed in the above court against you, praying a divorce from you, with reasonable alimony, on the ground that you have cruelly neglected and refused to furnish me with reasonable support, you being of sufficient ability so to do.

That unless you answer said petition on or before Monday, October 18th (eighteenth), 1886, you will be in default, and said petition will be taken and confessed, and judgment entered accordingly.

Crete, September 6th, 1886.

NETTIE B. SHEDENHELM.

ABBOTT & ABBOTT, Att'ys for Plaintiff."

The plaintiff now prosecutes a petition in error in this court.

Section 10, chapter 25 of the Compiled Stautes, provides that "A petition or bill of divorce, alimony, and maintenance, may be exhibited by a wife in her own name, as well as a husband, and in all cases the respondent may answer such petition or bill without oath; and in all cases of divorce, alimony, and maintenance, when personal service cannot be had, service by publication may be made as is provided by law in other civil cases under the code of civil procedure, and either party may be a witness as in other civil cases."

Section 77 of the code of civil procedure provides that "Service may be made by publication in either of the following cases: 1st. In actions brought under the fifty-first, fifty-second, and fifty-third sections of this code, where any or all the defendants reside out of the state (for the recovery of real property, partition of same, foreclosure of mortgages, and specific performance of real estate contracts). 2d. In actions brought to establish or set aside a will, where any or all the defendants reside out of the state. 3d. In actions brought against a non-resident of this state, or a foreign corporation, having in this state property or debts owing to them, sought to be taken by any of the provisional remedies, or to be appropriated in any way. 4th. In actions which relate to, or the subject of which is, real or personal property in this state, where any defendant has or claims a lien or interest, actual or contingent therein, or the relief demanded consists wholly or partially in excluding him from any interest therein, and such defendant is a non-resident of the state or a foreign corporation. 5th. In all actions where the defendant, being a resident of the state, has departed therefrom, or from the county of his residence, with intent to delay or defraud his creditors or to avoid the service of a summons, or keep himself concealed therein with like intent."

Section 78 of the code of civil procedure provides that "Before service can be made by publication an affidavit must be filed that service of summons cannot be made within this state on the defendant or defendants to be served by publication, and that the case is one of those mentioned in the preceding section.   When such affidavit is filed the party may proceed to make service by publication."

All that is required by section 78, above quoted, is that the nature of the cause of action shall be stated in the affidavit and that service of a summons cannot be made within this state on the defendant or defendants to be served by publication.   The object of stating the nature of the cause of action is to show that the cause is one in which service may be made by publication.   The nature of this cause is an action for divorce.   The particular grounds upon which a divorce is sought need not be set forth in the affidavit, although a statement to that effect will not impair its validity, and may be stated or omitted at the option of the affiant.   The grounds upon which a divorce is sought, however, should be set forth in the notice of publication, and that was done in this case.

In *Atkins v. Atkins*, 9 Neb., 191, the affidavit for publication failed to state the nature of the cause of action, the allegation being "that this cause is one mentioned in section No. 77 of title V. of the Revised Statutes of Nebraska as amended."   In no case could the section mentioned relate to actions for divorce, and therefore the affidavit was insufficient.

The order complained of is not a final order, and therefore the judgment of the court below cannot be reviewed. *Mills v. Miller*, 2 Neb., 309.   *Smith v. Sahler*, 1 Neb., 311. *Scofield v. State National Bank*, 8 Neb., 17.   *School Dis- v. Brown*, 10 Neb., 441.   *Sprick v. Washington County*, 3 Neb., 255.   *Nichols v. Hail*, 5 Neb., 195.   *Riddle v. Yates*, 10 Neb., 511.   *Green v. State*, 10 Neb., 104. *Preuit v. People*, 5 Neb., 382.   *Miller v. B. & M. R. R.*, 7 Neb., 228.   *Hall v. Vanier*, 7 Neb.; 398.   *Meglemere v. Bell*, 14 Neb. 378.   *Brown v. Edgerton*, 14 Neb., 453. *Wilson v. Shepherd*, 15 Neb., 17.   The court is unable, therefore, to correct the error until final judgment has been rendered.   The action here is dismissed.

JUDGMENT ACCORDINGLY.

LOEB & HIRSCH, PLAINTIFFS IN ERROR, v. SAMUEL
MILNER, DEFENDANT IN ERROR.

1. **Chattel Mortgage**: FORECLOSURE: REMOVAL OF PROPERTY
TO ANOTHER COUNTY. Under the act of 1867, in foreclosing a
chattel mortgage by a sale of the property, such sale is to take
place in the county where the mortgage was first recorded,
or in any county where the property may have been removed by
consent of parties, and in which the mortgage was duly recorded. Under the act of 1879 the proper filing of a chattel
mortgage takes the place of recording. But to authorize a sale
under the statute where the property has been removed by consent of parties, into a county other than that where the mortgage
was first filed, the mortgage must be duly filed in the county
where the sale is to take place.

2. ———: SALE BY MORTGAGEE. A sale by the mortgagee under
the statute in which he fails to comply with any essential requirement of such statute will render him liable to the mortgagor for the damages which the latter may thereby sustain.

3. ———: SALE IN ANOTHER COUNTY. A provision in the mortgage
that the mortgaged property may be sold in a county other than
that in which the mortgagor resides does not waive the statutory
requirement that the mortgage is to be filed in the county where
the sale is to take place.

4. ———: POSSESSION BY MORTGAGEE. A provision in a mortgage
that the mortgagee may take possession of the property at any
time he feels insecure, and advertise and sell the same, does not
authorize him to apply the proceeds to the payment of a note
not then due.

ERROR to the district court for Adams county. Tried
below before MORRIS, J.

Dilworth, Smith & Dilworth, for plaintiffs in error.

J. B. Cessna and *Ragan, McDonald & Shellenbarger,*
for defendant in error.

MAXWELL, CH. J.

In June, 1885, the defendant in error filed petition in
the court below, stating that on the 2d day of May, 1882,

he became indebted to the plaintiffs in error in the sum of $280, and delivered to them two notes; one for $150, due November 10, 1882, and one for $130, due November 1st, 1883, each drawing interest at ten per cent. That to secure the payment of said notes he made a chattel mortgage on one brown horse mule, one bay horse mule, one black mare, one roan mare, one second hand Studebaker wagon, one set of harness, one white cow, one roan cow, one roan heifer, and one white heifer.

At the date of making said note and mortgage he resided in Webster county, Nebraska, and the property was in said Webster county, and he resided there, and said property remained there until the happening of the grievances hereafter mentioned. That the mortgage was filed in the county clerk's office of Webster county, and in no other county.

That on December 19th, 1882, he paid the plaintiffs in error, to be applied on the first note, $110, which left a balance due of $49.37 on the first note, and the second note of $130, due November 1st.

That on the 18th day of December, 1882, they without any justifiable cause took possession of the above property, of the value of $700, and carried the same away from said Webster county into Adams county, and wrongfully without his consent converted it to their own use. That they kept said property and the proceeds thereof to the value of $700 when he was only indebted to them in the sum of $180, and defendants are liable, to-wit, in the sum of $520, for which with costs he prays judgment.

The plaintiffs in error filed an answer to said petition, stating:

1st. That they deny each and every allegation therein contained.

2d. That on or about the 2d day of May, 1882, at the special instance and request of defendant in error, they sold and delivered to him one brown horse mule and one bay

horse mule of the value of $280, which were sold on credit
and evidenced by two promissory notes dated May 2d,
1882, one for $150, due on or before November 10, 1882,
and one for $130, due on or before November 1, 1883,
drawing interest at ten per cent from date until paid, and
to secure the payment of said notes he gave them a chattel
mortgage upon the following described property, to-wit:
one brown horse mule, one bay horse mule, one black mare,
one roan mare, one second-hand Studebaker wagon, one
set double harness, one white cow, one roan cow, one roan
heifer, one white heifer. That said mortgage was filed in
the county clerk's office of Webster county on the 3d day
of May, 1882.

3d. That on the 2d day of May, 1882, the defendant in
error became indebted to one G. H. Pratt in the sum of
$39.45, which was evidenced by note of said defendant in
error due on the 2d day of November, 1882, with interest
at ten per cent, and to secure said note he gave a chattel
mortgage to said Pratt on one red and white cow, one white
cow, one yearling heifer, one white yearling heifer, and said
mortgage was duly filed on the 3d day of May, 1882, in
Webster county, and they allege that the said G. H. Pratt
was about to foreclose said mortgage, and that for a valuable consideration they guaranteed and did assume to pay
the said debt of G. H. Pratt.

4th. They further allege that the defendant in error paid
to their agent the sum of $150, and that the said sum of
money was applied in the payment of said Pratt debt and
the expenses of collecting the same, and that the balance
thereof was applied upon the payment of the notes held by
them against the defendant in error.

5th. They further allege that default was made in the
conditions of the mortgage given by the defendant in error
to them, and that they felt unsafe and insecure, and that
on or about the 20th of January, 1883, they took possession of the property mentioned in the mortgages, and after

having duly advertised the same for sale for at least twenty days they did on the 21st day of February sell said property or so much thereof as they got possession of for the sum of $329.25. That the debt, interest, costs, expenses of taking and feeding the said property amounted at that time to $318.04, excluding the payment of the Pratt note and all payment previously made by him, leaving in their hands the sum of $11.21, which sum they then and there tendered and offered to pay to said defendant in error, but he refused to receive the same. That they have always been ready and willing to pay him and are now ready to pay the same and hereby tender him and pay into this court for his use the said sum of $11.21.

They therefore plead not guilty to the charge in the petition and pray that they may recover their costs in this action.

To which answer there was attached as "Exhibits A and B" the two mortgages set forth in said answer. In Exhibit "A" the following condition was made:

"And I, the said S. L. Milner, do covenant and agree to and with the said Loeb & Hirsch that in case of default made in the payment of the above-mentioned promissory notes or any part thereof, or in case of my attempting to dispose of or remove from said county of Webster the aforesaid goods and chattels or any part thereof, or if at any time the said mortgagee, his heirs or assigns, should feel unsafe or insecure, then and in that case it shall be lawful for the said mortgagee or his assigns by himself or agent to take immediate possession of said goods and chattels wherever found, the possession of these presents being sufficient authority therefor, and to sell the same at public auction, or so much thereof as shall be sufficient to pay the amount due, as the case may be, with all reasonable costs pertaining to the keeping, advertising, and selling said property, together with the sum of $..... as liquidated damages for non-fulfillment of the contract. The money remaining after paying said sums, if any, to be paid on demand and to the party of the first part. Said sale to take place in Hastings in the county of Adams and state of Nebraska after giving at least twenty days' notice of such sale by advertisement published in some newspaper printed in the county in which the sale is to take place, or in case no newspapers are printed therein by posting up notices in at least five public places in said county, two of which shall be in the precinct where the mortgaged property is to be offered for sale.

"Witness my hand and seal this 2d day of May, 1882.

S. L. MILNER."

A trial was had to a jury, with a verdict for defendant in error. At the trial the following proceedings were had:

John Milner, called and sworn on the part of the defendant in error, testified "That he was the son of the defendant in error. That he was acquainted with the property his -father mortgaged to Loeb & Hirsch. That Thomas M. Abbott in December, 1883, took away a big mule, also a brown horse mule, one roan mare and a wagon, a double set of harness, one roan or spotted cow, one white heifer. He was acquainted with and raised with the stock. The brown mule was worth about $135 or $140. The bay horse mule was worth about the same. The wagon was worth about $30 or $40. The harness probably $10 or $15. The roan cow about $50. The white heifer about $15. His father was not there the day he took them."

Samuel Hirsch, one of the plaintiffs in error, testified as follows; "He remembered the mortgage S. L. Milner gave to Loeb & Hirsch. He never filed the mortgage in Adams county."

S. L. Milner, called in his own behalf, testified: "Identifies 'Exhibit A,' which was used in evidence without objection. Also identifies the mortgage that he gave to Pratt. Says he paid it to Jay Cherry. Jay Cherry had it in his possession. Identifies the receipt from Jay Cherry.

Copy of receipt attached marked 'Exhibit B.' $39.45
was to pay the mortgage marked 'Exhibit A.'   Paid
another sum of money to Loeb & Hirsch, to-wit: to Jay
Cherry.   Said he came to see about it, when I could pay
it. He gave me a receipt. That was to go on the note I
owed Loeb & Hirsch. Identifies paper which is attached
as 'Exhibit C.' That was to apply on the first note.
Never paid any other money than that mentioned in the
receipt.   I wasn't at home when Abbott took the property.
He didn't demand it of me. Was acquainted with the
value of the property at that time. The brown horse mule
was worth $150, the bay horse mule about $150, the black
mare $125, the roan mare about the same, the wagon worth
about $45, the harness worth about $15, the roan cow $50,
the white heifer $25."

Mason Fisher, called on behalf of the defendant in error,
testified that he was acquainted with the property mortgaged to Loeb & Hirsch by the defendant in error. The
brown horse mule was worth about $150, the bay horse
mule about $125, the black mare worth $85, the wagon
worth $35, the roan mare $85, the harness worth $5, the
roan cow worth $40, the white cow $25.

Joseph Acre, called by the defendant in error, testified
that he was acquainted with the cows, horses, wagon,
heifers, mules and harness that the defendant in error
owned. The mares were worth at that time $165. He
knew nothing more about it..

EXHIBIT B.
"CENTRAL HOTEL, M. S. McCLELLAN, Proprietor.
BLUE HILL, NEB., Dec. 19, 1882.
$39.45.
Received of S. L. Milner thirty-nine and 45-100 dollars
as the supposed amount of a note held by the First Na-
tional Bank of Hastings, Neb., dated May 2d, 1882.
FIRST NATIONAL BANK,
(Signed.)   By JAY CHERRY."

And thereupon the plaintiffs in error filed a demurrer to the evidence as follows:

"Come now the defendants, plaintiffs herein, by their attorneys, and demur to the evidence of the defendant herein, and say that the same is not sufficient in law under the pleadings to constitute a cause of action against the defendants, plaintiffs herein, and in behalf of the plaintiff, defendant herein."

Does this testimony, taken as true, entitle the plaintiff below to recover? The statute relating to foreclosure of chattel mortgages, so far as it relates to the testimony in this case, is as follows:

Sec. 1 of chapter 12, Comp. Stat., provides that "Every mortgage of personal property, containing or giving to the mortgagee or any other person a power to sell the property described therein, upon default made in any condition of such mortgage, may be foreclosed in the cases and in the manner hereinafter specified."

Sec. 2, same chapter, provides that "To entitle any person to foreclose a chattel mortgage as hereinafter prescribed, it shall be requisite, 1. That some default in a condition of such mortgage shall have occurred, by which the power to sell became operative. 2. That if no suit or proceeding shall have been instituted at law to recover the debt then remaining, secured by such mortgage on any part thereof; or if any suit or proceeding has been instituted that the same has been discontinued, or that an execution upon judgment rendered thereon, has been returned unsatisfied, in whole or in part, and, 3. That such mortgage containing the power of sale has been duly recorded."

Section 3, same chapter: "Notice that such mortgage will be foreclosed by a sale of the mortgaged property, or some part thereof, shall be given as follows: By advertisement published in some newspaper printed in the county in which such sale is to take place, or in case no newspapers are printed therein, by posting up notices in at least five public places in said county, two of which shall be in the precinct where the mortgaged property is to be offered for sale, and such notice shall be given at least twenty days prior to the day of sale."

Section 6, same chapter, provides that " Such sale shall be at public auction in the day time between the hours of 10 A.M., and 4 P.M, in the county where the mortgage was first recorded, or in any county where the property may have been removed by the consent of parties, and in which the mortgage was duly recorded, and in view of said property."

Section 8, same chapter, provides that "When a mortgage shall have been foreclosed, as herein provided, any and all right of equity of redemption, which the mortgagor may or might have had, shall be and become extinguished."

While the rule is well settled that a chattel mortgage transfers to the mortgagee the legal title to the things mortgaged, subject only to be defeated by the peformance of the condition; *Butler v. Miller*, 1 N. Y., 496; *Tallon v. Ellison & Sons*, 3 Neb., 74; *Brown v. Bement*, 8 Johns., 96; *Ackley v. Finch*, 7 Cow., 290; yet the mortgagor has an equity of redemption in the chattels and may redeem the same at any time before the sale. *Tompkins v. Beatie*, 11 Neb., 151. *Charter v. Stevens*, 3 Denio, 33. *Lansing v. Goelet*, 9 Cow., 372. *Hart v. Ten Eyck*, 2 Johns. Ch., 100. To extinguish this equity of redemption the statute provides the mode of foreclosing the mortgage and selling the property ; the sale is to take place " in the county where the mortgage was first recorded, or in any county where the property may have been removed by the consent of parties, and in which the mortgage *was duly recorded,* and in view of said property." The use of the words in section 6, "duly recorded," shows the intention of the legislature to require the filing of the mortgage in the county where the sale is to take place. This intention is clear and explicit, the language being that the sales shall take place in the county where the mortgage was first recorded, or in any county where the property may have been removed by consent of parties and in which the mortgage was duly recorded.

Since the act providing for foreclosure of mortgage was passed in 1867, the law relating to chattel mortgages has been changed by providing that " a mortgage or true copy thereof shall be filed in the office of the county clerk of the county in which the mortgagor executing the same resides, or in case he is a non-resident of the state, then in the office of the clerk of the county where the property mortgaged may be at the time of executing such mortgage." Sec. 14, chapter 32, Compiled Statutes.

The filing of a chattel mortgage in the proper county takes the place of recording the same and is sufficient. But the filing of a chattel mortgage in the county to which mortgaged property may be moved by consent, is a condition precedent to the right to sell the same in such county, and the sale made without complying with such condition is unauthorized. If the mortgagee may disregard the provisions of the statute in one essential requirement and not be liable to the mortgagor for the abuse of power, he could disregard all other provisions, and suit his own convenience and pleasure in the disposition of the property. The statute, while it protects the rights of the mortgagee and enables him to sell the property under certain conditions and thus divest all interest of the mortgagor, also protects the rights of the mortgagor and requires the mortgagee to conduct the sale in the manner prescribed. How far these statutory requirements may be waived by the parties is not now before the court, as there is no waiver in this case. The provision in the mortgage authorizing the sale to take place at Hastings does not waive the requirement that the mortgage be filed in Adams county. The rule is well settled that if a mortgagee in possession of the mortgaged goods sell them before he has complied with all the requirements of the statute, he will be liable to the mortgagor for any damage he may sustain thereby. 6 Wait's Actions and Defenses, 196. Jones' Chattel Mortgages, 730 § 774. *Simpson v. Carleton*, 1 Allen, 109. *Botsford v. Murphy*, 11 N. W. R., 376, Mich. *Denny v. Faulkner*, 22 Kas., 89 ; also 27 Kas., 437. *Kopmeier v. O'Neil*, 3 N. W. R., 365 Wis. *Black v. Howell*, 56 Iowa, 630. *Stromberg v. Lindberg*, 25 Minn., 513. *Brink v. Freoff*, 40 Mich., 610. Cooley's Const. L., 77–8. *French v. Edwards*, 13 Wall., 80 U. S., 506.

It being in effect conceded that the plaintiffs in error failed to comply with the statute, the court would have been justified in directing the jury to find a verdict for the plaintiff below. The instructions therefor need not be considered. There is no complaint that the verdict is excessive or that the mode of assessing damages was incorrect. Those questions, therefore, are not before the court.

It will be observed that the second note was not due until November, 1883. This was the contract of the parties. The right to take possession of the property at any time, reserved in the mortgage, did not authorize the mortgagee to apply the proceeds arising from the sale of same, to the payment of the note before it became due, even if the sale had been authorized. Yet the defendants below, in plain violation of their duty to the mortgagor, sold the property, and without his consent applied the proceeds to the payment of a note that was not due for nearly a year afterwards; this they had no authority to do. There is no material error in the record, and the judgment of the court below is affirmed.

JUDGMENT AFFIRMED.

THE other judges concur.

JAMES H. CLARK, APPELLEE, V. GEORGE A. CLARK ET AL., APPELLANTS.

1. **Trust:** EVIDENCE. In an action to establish a trust and for a decree quieting the title of certain lands in the plaintiff, *Held*, That a preponderance of the testimony established the trust, and that the plaintiff was entitled to the relief prayed for.

2. ———: DEFENSE: EVIDENCE. *Held*, That an allegation in the answer of certain defendants that a deed was obtained by fraud and misrepresentations, was not sustained by the evidence.

3. ———: LIMITATION. Where the statute of limitations has begun to run in favor of a *cestui que trust* it will not be suspended by the death of the trustee.

4. ———: ———. Where a *cestui que trust* is in possession of the trust property as his own, the statute of limitations will not run against him in favor of the trustee so as to bar his right to the property.

5. **Action quia timet:** MINOR HEIRS AS DEFENDANTS NOT LIABLE FOR COSTS. Where an action was brought against certain minor heirs and others to quiet the title of real estate in the plaintiff, the principal object of the action being to divest the title of the minor heirs, *Held*, That as such minor heirs were unable to convey by deed, they should not be taxed with the costs of the action, and that the relief will be granted to the plaintiff upon the payment of all costs.

APPEAL from the district court of Johnson county. Tried below before BROADY, J.

C. M. Easterday and *S. P. Davidson*, with *V. D. Metcalfe*, guardian *ad litem*, for appellants.

C. E. White and *T. Appleget & Son* (*Bingham, Mitchell & Batchellor*, of New Hampshire, with them), for appellee.

MAXWELL, CH. J.

In November, 1884, plaintiff filed his amended petition, stating his cause of action to be:

" That he is, and has been for about twenty years, the

owner and in possession of the north-east quarter of section five, town five, range ten, in Johnson county, Nebraska; that he purchased said land of one James Clark prior to the year 1866, for a valuable consideration; that on or about September 4, 1866, a deed to said land was made by said James Clark to one Albert W. Clark, a brother of plaintiff; that said deed, which is duly recorded in the records of deeds of said county, was made without consideration and with the purpose and intent of him the said James Clark, who at the time was old and infirm, that said land should be conveyed by said Albert W. Clark to the plaintiff, who was absent from the home of said parties in New Hampshire and engaged in business in Massachusetts; soon after the making of said deed, to-wit, March 27, 1867, said Albert W. Clark suddenly died; very soon after his death, Philinda G. Clark, his widow, at the request of James Clark and one Farr, a lawyer and near friend, deeded said land to plaintiff, acting for herself and as guardian of her three minor children, defendants; but said deed was not recorded and has since been lost; that plaintiff has been in continuous and undisputed possession of said land from 1866 to the present time and has paid all the taxes thereon since said date, amounting to about $400; that about March, 1883, defendants herein, the legal heirs of said Albert W. Clark, made a deed to this plaintiff for said land, understanding at the time that said deed was for the purpose of placing the legal title to said land of record in plaintiff; said deed is duly recorded in book "Q" of deeds for said county at page 388; that plaintiff claims title to said land in fee and defendants claim an estate or interest adverse to plaintiff which is without any right whatever, and that they have no interest or estate in said premises or any part thereof. Plaintiff prays that all adverse claims of defendants may be determined by decree of court; that said deed from James Clark to Albert W. Clark may be declared null and void; that by decree it be declared that defendants have no estate or interest whatever in and to said land; that the title of plaintiff be declared good and valid; that defendants be barred from asserting any claim whatever to said lands adverse to plaintiff, and that plaintiff have general relief."

On motion of plaintiff V. D. Metcalfe was appointed guardian *ad litem* for defendants, George A. and Eva M. Clark, minors.

V. D. Metcalfe, guardian *ad litem* for said minor defendants, filed answer to amended petition and cross petition, by which he is joined by Philinda G. Clark, guardian and next friend of said minor defendants, in which they admit "that on or about September 4, 1866, said James Clark, the owner of the lands in controversy, conveyed the same to said Albert W. Clark by deed of that date duly executed and acknowledged and since recorded in Johnson county; that on or about March 27, 1867, said Albert W. Clark died; that all of the defendants are his legal heirs, and these answering defendants are minors of young and tender years, do not clearly know all their rights herein involved, and ask the court to fully protect their rights to the same extent as if they were fully set out and claimed; and they deny each and every other allegation in said amended petition contained.

"That said deed from James Clark to Albert W. Clark was made for and in consideration of full value paid to said James Clark by said Albert W. Clark,·who was the father of the defendants, and at his death said Albert W. Clark was the owner and in possession of the lands in controversy.

"At the death of said Albert W. Clark one Charles H. Clark, his brother, was appointed administrator of his estate, and because defendants reposed confidence in him, he and said plaintiff were permitted to have the management of said lands with other lands in Gage county for the defendants herein ever since the death of said Albert W. Clark, and during that time they have collected for rent of said lands $500; and for valuable timber thereon cut down and sold, $100; and for right of way across said land of the A. & N. railroad in 1872, $50, all of which sums said plaintiff has wrongfully converted to his own use.

"Defendants never saw said lands, and at all times prior to the commencement of this suit were entirely ignorant of the quality, location, surroundings, and value of the same, but plaintiff was well acquainted therewith, as well as the quality and value of said land in Gage county on and before March 8, 1883, when said plaintiff, for the purpose of cheating, defrauding, and circumventing said defendants, did falsely and fraudulently represent to defendants that all of said lands were wild, uncultivated, situated in an uninhabited wilderness, far removed from any settlements or markets, that they were of poor quality not worth to exceed $200, and that defendants held but a small undivided interest in all of said lands; all of which representations were false and untrue, as plaintiff well knew. Defendants, being entirely ignorant as to whether said representations were true or false, but relying thereon and being influenced thereby, were induced by said plaintiff to sign and deliver to him what purported to be a deed to all of said lands, including that of Gage county, for $200, and no more; but as defendants are informed said deed is not legally acknowledged, but plaintiff has caused the same to be spread upon the records of said Johnson county at page 388 of Book Q of Deeds.

"Since signing said papers these defendants have learned and aver the facts to be that they each own one-third interest in said lands in controversy, subject to the dower of defendant, Philinda G. Clark, and one-fourth of the land in Gage county; that plaintiff has no interest therein whatever; that said land in Gage county is adjacent to the city of Beatrice and is very valuable; that the land in controversy lies within two miles of a railroad station, in a thickly settled neighborhood; that a large portion of it has

been under cultivation for twenty-six years, that a portion
of the balance was valuable timber land, and that said land
is of a very superior quality, that a fourth of said land in
Gage county, on March 8, 1883, was worth not less than
$1,000, and the land in controversy was then worth not
less than $3,500, all of which facts plaintiff then well
knew, but defendants were entirely ignorant thereof.

"At the time said deed was signed these answering defendants were minors, and they now disaffirm, renounce,
and repudiate the same and charge that the same was procured from them by fraud and circumvention and by false
and fraudulent representations of said plaintiff. The one-
fourth interest in said lands in Gage county was then worth
a great deal more than said two hundred dollars, the consideration of said deed, and the amounts received by said
plaintiff for rent, for timber and for right of way as above
mentioned largely exceed the amounts paid out by him for
taxes.

" Defendants deny that plaintiff has ever been, or claimed
to be, in possession of said land adverse to any of said defendants until about the time of the commencement of this
suit, and during all the time from March 27, 1867, till the
commencement of this suit he fraudulently concealed from
defendants the character, condition, surroundings, and value
of said lands, the amount he was receiving as rent therefrom, and the interests of defendants therein.

"2d. As a second and further defense defendants aver
that the cause of action sued on did not accrue within ten
years next prior to the commencement of this suit; and the
same had long theretofore been barred by the statute of limitations.   Defendants pray that said deed recorded in book
Q, page 388, be delivered up and cancelled, that the same be
discharged from record, the cloud occasioned thereby upon
defendants' title be removed, that the title of each of these
defendants to the undivided one-third of said land in controversy, subject to Philinda G. Clark's dower, be quieted

and confirmed in each of them, that plaintiff's petition be dismissed, and that defendants have general relief."

On same day defendants Philinda G. Clark and Israel J. Clark filed their answer, making substantially the same averments and denials therein as those contained in the answer of the other defendants above mentioned, and specially denying that plaintiff ever was the owner of the lands in controversy or was ever in possession of the same adverse to defendants, until about the time of the commencement of this suit; and denying that in the year 1867, or at any other time, Philinda G. Clark, acting for herself and as guardian for her minor children, ever deeded said land to plaintiff, and averring that defendant, Israel J. Clark, became of age May 27, 1881, and that defendants, Eva Clark, and George A. Clark are still minors, and making substantially the same prayer as that made by the other defendants, and in addition asking that the right of dower in said lands of defendant, Philinda G. Clark, be declared and confirmed to her.

The reply is substantially a general denial, with the additional averment that defendants' claim is barred by the statute of limitations.

On the trial of the cause in the court below, a decree was rendered in favor of the plaintiff, quieting and confirming the title of the land in question in him, and taxing all the costs, including the fee of the guardian *ad litem*, against the defendants. The defendants appeal.

It appears from the testimony that in the year 1863, one Leroy C. Clark was possessed of the lands in controversy, and also of certain lands in Gage county. He died in that year, leaving a widow, but no children. Under the statutes of this state, such lands, subject to the life estate of the widow, descend to the father of such decedent. An adjustment was made between the widow and the father of the deceased by which she conveyed to him her interest in the lands in controversy, and he seems to have conveyed to her his interest in certain lands in Gage county.

In September, 1866, James Clark, the father of Leroy Clark, conveyed to Albert W. Clark the lands in question by a special warranty deed. The plaintiff claims that this conveyance was made in trust for him, and his right to recover in this action depends upon the establishment of the trust. The testimony shows that the plaintiff and one Charles H. Clark are also sons of James Clark. In 1867, Albert W. Clark died suddenly. At the time of the conveyance from James Clark to Albert W. Clark, the plaintiff was a resident of Lynn, Massachusetts, and was engaged in business there; and one of the witnesses swears that he was "not meeting with very good success."

His father, James Clark, and Albert W. Clark, were at that time residing in New Hampshire, and the plaintiff does not seem to have met Albert W. after the execution of said deed. There is a large amount of testimony tending to show that the plaintiff paid his father the consideration for the land conveyed to Albert W., and that the said land was conveyed to Albert W. in trust for the plaintiff.

There is testimony also tending to show that Albert W. admitted that he held the lands in trust for his brother James H., and that after the death of Albert W., James Clark, the father, the plaintiff, Charles H. Clark, and Philinda G. Clark, the widow of Albert W., went to one Farr, an attorney, who was at that time counsel for said Philinda G. Clark, telling him the circumstances. He advised her to deed the land to the plaintiff for herself, and as guardian for her children. This the plaintiff claims she did. The deed, however, if made, was not recorded, the reason given by the plaintiff for not recording the same being, "I retained this deed and did not record it because I consulted other counsel and found it was not sufficient to pass the title to me." In 1868, James Clark died. In August, 1883, certain depositions were taken at the office

of Bingham, Mitchell & Batchellor, a law firm at Littleton, New Hampshire, before one E. C. Steveans, a notary public, to which depositions the deed, purporting to
have been made by Philanda G. Clark to plaintiff, was
attached.   E. C. Steveans testifies as follows: "I was the
notary who wrote the deposition above mentioned by Mr.
Batchellor.   The deed was given to me to be annexed to
the deposition.   It was in the handwriting of E. W. Farr,
from Philinda G. Clark and her children to James H.
Clark, of lands in Johnson county, Nebraska.   It was so
annexed and mailed by me to the clerk of the district of
Johnson county, Nebraska."   In this he is corroborated
by one A. S. Batchellor, a member of the law firm heretofore referred to, at whose office the deposition was taken.

There is no evidence that this deposition containing the
deed in question was ever received by the clerk of the
district court of Johnson county, his testimony being: "I
do not remember what depositions were received and filed
in the case of Clark v. Clark during that time (in 1883).
I do not find any such depositions now.   My term expired
in January, 1884.   The fee-book does not show the filing
of any such depositions.   As a matter of fact I was not
in the habit of entering depositions in this book or on the
appearance docket at the time of receiving them.   Upon
examination of appearance docket, I cannot say whether
I filed any depositions in this case."

Mary Jane Richardson, a sister of the plaintiff, testifies:
" I reside at Littleton; the plaintiff is my brother.   I had a
brother, Leroy, who owned land in Nebraska and died there;
he had no children.   My father and his wife settled up about
the property.   He said he wanted J. H. Clark to have this
land.   J. H. Clark was away at this time, and he deeded
the land to the Doctor with the intention to deed it to J.
H. Clark.   The Doctor never paid anything for the land.
The family all knew why it was deeded to him.   After
the doctor died, my father, Henry, and Philinda said they

had fixed it all right. She always called it Henry's land. I never heard it mentioned that she had a dollar there for herself or children until within two years.

"There was two pieces of land above mentioned, one piece called the forty-acre parcel in Beatrice, and the larger piece was in Gage county. I cannot tell whether both pieces were in the same county or not."

CROSS-EXAMINATION.

" The only reason I know of why the land was not conveyed directly from father to Henry was, Henry was not here. I could not tell how much Henry paid father for the land. It was not considered very valuable then. I think a part was paid before and a part after the deed to the Doctor. I could not tell how long before the conveyance to the Doctor; the bargain was made and part of the money paid. I don't know that I ever saw a dollar pass, but I have heard my father say he paid him. I have seen him pay my mother. I do not know how I knew the money was intended as part consideration for the land, only I know it."

The only testimony that tends to show that A. W. Clark paid anything for this land is that of his widow, Philinda G. Clark, who testifies that: "My husband sent money out to pay for it. This I know of my own knowledge, though I was not present when he deposited it in the office to send to his brother. It was one or two years previous to the war of the rebellion that my husband raised the money about which I have testified."

In this she is directly contradicted by the widow of Leroy C. Clark, a disinterested witness, who testifies that: "He (Leroy C. Clark) purchased these lands and paid the consideration himself. Albert W. Clark had nothing to do with the purchase of these lands." A clear preponderance of the testimony, therefore, establishes the fact that the plaintiff paid the consideration for this land, and that it was held in trust by A. W. Clark as trustee for him.

In 1883, the defendants executed a conveyance of the lands in controversy to the plaintiff, and their mother was paid the sum of $200 for the same. One of the children, Israel, was more than twenty-one years of age at the time of executing this conveyance. The defendants assert that this conveyance was obtained by means of fraudulent representations by Charles H. Clark. This Charles H. Clark denies. So far as the testimony shows, he was and is a disinterested party. He had been the administrator of the estate of Albert W. Clark, and so far as it appears, had performed his duty to the satisfaction of the defendants.

Considerable time had been spent in 1883 in conducting the negotiations, and the defendants evidently were in possession of the principal facts of the case before executing the deed of that date. During the summer of 1883, George A. Clark, one of the minor defendants, spent several weeks on a visit at the home of his uncle Charles H. Clark, which, if the alleged fraudulent conduct of the uncle was true, he probably would not have done. In our view, therefore, the testimony fully justifies the court below in finding, as it must have done, that the deed given plaintiff by defendants in 1883 was not obtained by fraud.

There is some testimony tending to show that the plaintiff took possession of this land about the year 1864, and has retained possession from that time till the present; that he has paid the taxes on the land and received the rents and profits therefrom. The plaintiff contends that if the statute of limitations had commenced to run in his favor before the death of A. W. Clark, that such statute would continue to run in his favor notwithstanding such death; that is, if the statute has begun in favor of the *cestui que trust* during the life of the trustee, it will not be suspended by his death. *Wooldridge v. Planters' Bank*, 1 Sneed., 297. *Worthy v. Johnson*, 10 Ga., 358. *Williams v. Otey*, 8 Humph., 563. *Long v. Cason*, 4 Rich. Eq., 60. *Pulteney v. Warren*, 6 Ves., 73. *The East Indian Company v. Cam-*

pion, 11 Bligh, 158, 186, 187.   *Williams v. Presbyterian Society,* 1 Ohio Stats., 478.

It is claimed on behalf of the defendants that the statute of limitations has run against the plaintiff in their favor, more than ten years having elapsed since the creation of the alleged trust.   No case has been cited showing that the statute of limitations would run against the *cestui que trust* in possession of the trust property, and bar his right to the same in favor of the naked trustee.   The statute of limitations does not begin to run against a *cestui que trust* in possession in favor of the trustee until after the trustee has disavowed the trust.   *Williams v. Presbyterian Society,* 1 Ohio State, 478.   *Willison v. Watkins,* 3 Peters, 48. "The same principle (that governing landlord and tenant) applies to mortgagor and mortgagee, trustee and *cestui que trust,* and generally to all cases where one man obtains possession of real estate belonging to another, by a recognition of his title."   The statute therefore forms no bar.

The court below taxed all the costs to the defendants, including the fee of the guardian *ad litem,* although he was appointed on the plaintiff's motion.   The principal ground of the action is to obtain a title from the minor heirs, and as they were unable to convey by deed they should not be subjected to costs.   All the costs in the case, therefore, including the fee of the guardian *ad litem,* will be taxed against the plaintiff in the case, and as thus modified the judgment of the court below is affirmed.

JUDGMENT AFFIRMED.

THE other judges concur.

JAMES M. PARKER, APPELLEE, V. NORMAN A. KUHN
ET AL., APPELLANTS.

1. **Statute of Limitations**: FRAUD. An action for relief on
the ground of fraud may be commenced at any time within four
years after a discovery of the facts constituting the fraud, or of
facts sufficient to put a person of ordinary intelligence and prudence on an inquiry, which, if pursued, would lead to such discovery.

2. ———: REDEMPTION. An action by a junior encumbrancer to
redeem land sold at execution or judicial sale, being an action
for relief other than those specifically mentioned, must be brought
within four years after the cause of action shall have accrued.

APPEAL from the district court of Douglas county.
Heard below before NEVILLE, J.

H. D. Estabrook, for appellants.

George W. Doane, for appellee.

COBB, J.

This is an action in the nature of *quia timet,* brought by
the appellee against the appellants in the district court of
Douglas county for the purpose of quieting his title in and
to the real property described in the petition.

The plaintiff alleged that he is the owner in fee of said
lands, that he acquired the title to the same and took actual
possession thereof, and has for about twenty years last past
remained in the actual, undisputed, notorious, and adverse
possession of said lands, claiming title thereto against all
the world.   That he has erected on a portion of said lands
large and valuable improvements ; that he has during a
portion of said time had a considerable part of said lands
under cultivation, and still has; that for many years he
occupied a portion of the said lands as his home and the

same is still occupied by a part of his family.   That plaintiff acquired title to said lands by virtue of certain judicial proceedings instituted against the Florence Land Company, resulting in decrees rendered on the 14th day of February, 1860, in all except one case, and in that on the 21st day of November, 1862, ordering sale of these lands in foreclosure of certain mortgages and deeds of trust given by said Florence Land Company, and that plaintiff was the purchaser at said sales and received deeds in fee simple for said lands.

That the only title under which the said defendants claim any interest in said lands is by virtue of a certain judgment obtained at the October term, 1859, of said court by John M. Kuhn against the Florence Land Company, execution issued thereon and sheriff's sale of the same on the 23d day of February, 1860, at which sale John M. Kuhn was purchaser.   That no steps toward a confirmation of said sale were ever taken until within the year last past, when John M. Kuhn made a quit claim deed of said lands to his son Norman A. Kuhn, one of the defendants. That the defendants Kuhn and Estabrook, conspiring together to cast a cloud upon the title of plaintiff to said lands, made application and obtained an order for confirmation of said lands without notice to any person whatever, and caused deeds to be executed for said lands under said execution sale to John M. Kuhn.   That said judgment and any lien acquired thereunder were subsequent to the liens of the said mortgages and were subject to the decrees of foreclosure entered thereon.   That in the last of said proceeding for foreclosure of one of said mortgages, said John M. Kuhn was made a party defendant and appeared and filed his answer and took testimony therein, and a final decree was entered therein in which, among other things, it was found that whatever interest the said John M. Kuhn had or pretended to have in said mortgaged premises was subject and subsequent to the interest of the said complainants by virtue of said mortgage, which decree remains un-reversed. That after the above narrated proceedings de-fendant Kuhn, on or about the ... day of ......, 1880, made to defendant Estabrook a deed conveying to him a portion of the lands by quit claim. Thereupon they together con-veyed to the defendants Rasmussen, Tiedeman, and Priess a portion of said lands, which said portion of said lands was covered with timber; that the same was so conveyed as the result of a conspiracy to enable the parties last named to cut the timber from said land and thereby deprive it of its value.

That plaintiff is informed and believes that said defend-ants Kuhn and Estabrook are making efforts to dispose of other portions of said lands and thereby cast a cloud upon the title of plaintiff thereto.

With other allegations for the purpose of obtaining an order of injunction against the defendants, and a prayer for judgment cancelling and declaring null and void the said conveyances of the defendants and removing all cloud cre-ated thereby from said lands, declaring the plaintiff's title thereto to be clear and perfect, etc., and for general relief.

The defendant Tiedeman answered said petition, denying each and every allegation thereof, except that Norman A. Kuhn on or about the 9th day of December, 1880, for a valuable consideration conveyed (describing a tract of land the same as in the petition) to J. K. Rasmussen and John Tiedeman, alleging that said grantees purchased said land in good faith and without any knowledge of any claim to the same by the plaintiff; that they thereupon entered upon the land and proceeded to cut timber therefrom and had open and notorious possession thereof until the plaintiff by his agents drove them off with threats and force of arms.

That the deed conveying the said land was recorded, etc. That on the 29th day of January, 1881, Rasmussen conveyed all of his right, title, and interest to said lands to John Tiedeman, with prayer that defendant may be adjudged to be the owner in fee simple of said lands, etc., and for general relief.

The defendant, Norman A. Kuhn, also answered, denying each and every allegation contained in the plaintiff's petition, except as otherwise expressly admitted. He also alleged that he is the owner in fee simple of the property described in the plaintiff's petition, "that these lands are vacant and unoccupied, and have been so for twenty years last past, except a few acres upon which plaintiff has erected certain buildings. That the pretended title of plaintiff is null and void as against this defendant, for that the mortgage under which it was executed was made without authority, of which the plaintiff had notice. For that plaintiff was a judgment purchaser without notice of said mortgage, said mortgage never having been recorded. For that the said mortgage was made to defraud the creditors of the said Florence Land Company, of which plaintiff had notice."

As evidence of fraud, defendant alleges the following facts:

1. That said company was greatly embarrassed at the time of said loan.

2. That it pledged all of its property as security for said loan.

3. That said plaintiff was authorized to borrow at twenty per cent interest, and after his authority expired loaned the money himself at forty per cent.

4. That the money so loaned was not used by said company for the payment of its debts, but was converted by the stockholders.

5. That the president of said company acknowledged the deed of trust as notary.

6. That said mortgage was made as an absolute deed with a bond of defeasance, the deed only being recorded.

7. That said plaintiff was a member of said company, and virtually executed a mortgage to himself.

8. That there were a great many suits pending against said company at the time of the making of said mortgage.

9. That said mortgage was made secretly, and never recorded.

10. That said loan was for payment of warrants to pre-empt the lands by the party, and that said mortgage was void on that account. That said John M. Kuhn was never made a party to any foreclosure proceedings; that he authorized no one to contest said mortgage; that he always believed himself to be the owner of said lands.

That he is, and has been for the twenty years last past, a non-resident of the state of Nebraska, with no means of knowledge of suits pending in the courts of Nebraska.

Wherefore he asked judgment that the title to said lands be decreed in him; and if said mortgage of Cook, Sargent and Parker was valid and binding upon said defendant that he may be permitted to redeem therefrom, and for general relief.

The plaintiff replied to the answer of the defendant, Tiedeman, specifically denying each and every allegation of defense therein stated.

The plaintiff also replied to the answer of the defendant, Norman A. Kuhn, denying each and every allegation contained in the second defense of said answer. Plaintiff also in his said reply says: "That in a certain action begun and prosecuted in the district court of Douglas county, in which Ebenezer Cook, George B. Sargent, and James M. Parker were plaintiffs, and the Florence Land Company and others defendants, John M. Kuhn, from from whom the defendant, Norman A. Kuhn, derived all the interest or title which he has or claims in any of the real estate described in the petition filed herein, appeared as a party defendant, and filed his answer, setting up the same matters substantially which are alleged by the defendant Kuhn in the second defense in his answer.

"That a decree was rendered in said cause in favor of

27

Cook, Sargent, and Parker, finding all of the equities of
said case with said complainants. It ordered, adjudged,
and decreed, among other things, that the mortgaged
premises should be sold, and that the master should make
a deed to the purchaser, who should be let into the possession of the premises on production of said master's deed;
further, that the purchaser at such sale should take and
hold such premises absolutely freed and released of all
claims or interest of the defendant, John M. Kuhn, and
all other persons who may have acquired any interest
therein during the pendency of said cause, and that the
entire right, title, and interest of the Florence Land Company should be by such sale vested in such purchaser.
Plaintiff says further, that he became the purchaser of the
lands at the sale made under this decree, and afterwards
received the master's deed therefor, and was let into possession of the lands, claiming title thereto for more than
twenty years last past as stated in petition.   Plaintiff
therefore says that all the matters alleged by way of defense in the said answer have been already adjudicated between the plaintiff and the grantor of the said defendant,
and that the defendant is barred from again litigating the
same in this action.

" Plaintiff states further that the rights alleged and claimed
by the defendant Kuhn in the second defense of his answer, and by reason whereof he claims affirmative relief
therein, did not accrue to the defendant or his grantor at
any time within ten years before the commencement of this
action, or before the filing of the answer herein; therefore
the defendant is barred by the statute of limitations of this
state from alleging or receiving any advantage from any
of the matters contained in his second defense.

" Plaintiff says further that the facts stated in the second
defense of the answer are not sufficient to constitute any
defense in favor of the defendant to the relief prayed for
by the plaintiff in his petition, or to entitle him, the de-

fendant, to any relief against the plaintiff, and he prays
the same benefit of this reply as if taken advantage of by
way of demurrer, and he therefore prays relief as in his
petition," etc.

At the close of the pleadings there is printed in the abstract the following : "Note. Defendants admit that plaintiff has shown a connected chain of title in himself to all
the lands here in dispute so far as the records are concerned.
Therefore to save encumbering the records, numerous pat-
ents, deeds, and court records in foreclosure cases showing
this chain of title from the U. S. to plaintiff, defendants
admit to be regular upon their face and admit all inferences
to be drawn from such regularity ; all exhibits to this point
will be marked 'admitted.'

"Defendants admit that said court proceedings are in due
form and substance in all the cases of *Cook, Sargent, and
Parker v. The Florence Land Company*, and of *Hays v.
The Florence Land Company*, identical with the proceedings
as shown in exhibit G, the description of the land being
the only difference."

The cause was tried to the court with a finding and decree for the plaintiff, and is brought to this court by the
defendants by appeal.

The testimony is very voluminous, the abstract of which
fills forty-one closely printed pages.   Therefore, even were
it necessary, it would be impossible to set out in this opinion more than the briefest summary of it.   But I do not
think it necessary.   By the note or stipulation above copied
the defendants admit the paper or record title to all the
lands involved in the suit to be in the plaintiff, and to be
regular on its face.   This title as to nearly all of the lands
had its inception in mortgages, or conveyances found and
held by the district court to be mortgages, executed and
dated in 1857, and was perfected by legal proceedings and
a master's deed in 1860; and as to the balance of the lands
it had its inception in a mortgage executed in 1859, and

was consummated by legal proceedings and master's deed in 1863. The plaintiff in and by his reply to the answer of the principal defendant pleads and invokes the protection of the statute of limitations.

The language of the statute of limitations, taken in its literal sense, limits the time in which actions may be commenced after the accruing of the cause of action, or the right to enforce which the action is brought only, but it applies equally to the same facts or rights when they are plead as a defense or counter claim or in the nature of a cross-action. That part of the code of civil procedure from section 5 to section 22, both inclusive, is usually referred to and known as "the statute of limitations." This statute prescribes the time within which actions may be brought for the redress of every class of wrongs and the enforcement of every species of rights provided for in the civil code, and it is worthy of notice that the longest time prescribed within which any action can be commenced "after the cause of action shall have accrued" is ten years.

The sections of the above statute especially applicable to the case in which it is here invoked are sections 6 and 12. Section 6 provides that "An action for the recovery of the title or possession of lands, tenements, or hereditaments can only be brought within ten years after the cause of such action shall have accrued," etc. Section 12 places within the class of cases which by the previous section are required to be brought within four years "after the cause of action shall have accrued," the following: "An action for relief on the ground of fraud, but the cause of action in such case shall not be deemed to have accrued until the discovery of the fraud."

I do not deem it necessary or expedient to follow counsel to the discussion of the question as to whether the above statute applies to equity cases. The language of the clause last above quoted seems to me to be conclusive that it was intended to apply to cases where relief is sought in equity,

even if it can be conceived that its application is not confined to such cases.   The defendant Kuhn, being sued in a
court of equity, seeks relief not only against the case alleged against him by the plaintiff, but also prays both specific and general relief against the plaintiff "on the ground
of fraud."   In this state all courts of general jurisdiction
are courts of equity.   The system of procedure under the
code is patterned after that formerly prevailing in courts of
equity rather than that prevailing in courts of law.   The
statute in its terms applies generally to suits in such courts
"for relief on the ground of fraud;" it must therefore be
held to be applicable to the case at bar.

There is an apparent conflict in the authorities as to when
the statute, in cases like the one which we are now considering, commences to run.   This question has been twice
presented to this court and to some extent considered.

The case of *Blake v. Chambers,* 4 Neb., 90, was an action
for the fraudulent misapplication of trust funds by an executor and to subject certain real property into which such trust
funds had been converted, to the payment of the plaintiff's
claims against the testator.   Among other defenses the defendant invoked the statute of limitations.   In delivering the
opinion of the court, then C. J. LAKE said: "As to the
statute of limitations, on which some reliance seems to have
been placed, it is well settled in courts of equity in cases
like the one under consideration, that the statute will not
commence to run until the discovery of the fraud.   And
in this state such is the statutory rule.   General Statutes,
525, sec. 12.   In this case it is expressly alleged that this
fraudulent misapplication of the assets of the estate was not
discovered until after the first day of January, 1874, so
that in any event the statute did not begin to run until after that time, which was but a few days prior to commencing the action."

The other case was that of *Welton v. Merrick County,* 16
Id., 83.   This action was brought to recover back money

paid to the county for taxes alleged to have been unlawfully demanded and received by the county in the year 1876 on certain unpatented railroad lands.   The plaintiff alleged that he had no knowledge of the illegality of such taxes prior to the 1st day of December, 1881.   The defendants' demurrer invoking the statute of limitations was sustained, which was assigned for error in this court.

The present Chief Justice, in delivering the opinion of the court, said: "It is very clear that there is no error in the ruling of the court below.   Even if a cause of action had existed in favor of the plaintiff upon the payment of the taxes in controversy, it was barred by the statute of limitations.   If a party with ordinary care and attention could have detected even fraud, he will be charged with actual knowledge of it; that is, the mere fact that a party is not aware of the existence of certain matters where there is no concealment, will not prevent the running of the statute of limitations.   Angel on Lim., § 187.   But in this case there is no pretense of fraud."

The point of divergence in these cases is readily seen to be where, in the latter case, the statute is declared to have commenced to run when the party with ordinary care and attention could have detected the fraud, rather than when it was discovered.   None of the English cases can be relied upon as authority upon this point as to the true construction of the meaning of our statute.   Their statutes of limitations, from that of 32 Henry VIII. to 3 and 4 William IV., exclusive of the latter, are silent on the subject of fraud or other matters of equitable jurisdiction, and the clause of the 26th section of the latter statute applicable to the point now being examined, is in the following language: "XXVI. That in every case of a concealed fraud, the right of any person to bring a suit in equity for the recovery of any land or rents of which he, or any person through whom he claims, may have been deprived by such fraud, shall be deemed to have first accrued at and not before the time at which such fraud shall or with reasonable dilligence might have been first known or discovered," etc.   This statute is, I think, still in force.   At all events it was under it that *Vane v. Vane*, L. R., 8 Ch., 383, and *Chatham v. Hoar*, L. R., 9 Eq., 571, cases cited in the note to 2 Story's Eq. Jur., 13 ed., § 1521, as "the more exact rule" were decided. That the more exact rule under that statute is that the statute commences to run at "the time at which such fraud shall or with reasonable diligence might have been first known or discovered," cannot be doubted; but does it follow that it is the rule under a statute, like ours, which lacks the words to which that statute doubtless owes such construction?

Of the states of the Union, so far as my limited time enables me to examine, only Michigan, Wisconsin, Iowa, California, Minnesota, Kansas, and New York have, or had at the date of Mr. Angel's compilation, provisions in their statutes of limitations like our own.   I do not find that such provision has been construed by the supreme courts of either of the three first mentioned states.   The provision of the statute of California corresponding to that of our own which we are now considering, was considered and construed by the supreme court of that state in the case of *Boyd v. Blankman*, 29 Cal., 19.   The case is long and much involved. I quote that part of the syllabus which is in point.

"An action for relief on the ground of fraud may be commenced at any time within three years after a discovery of the facts constituting the fraud, or of facts sufficient to put a person of ordinary intellegence and prudence on enquiry."

In the state of Minnesota, the case of *Commissioners of Mower County v. Smith*, 22 Minn., 97, an action brought by the county commissioners against a defaulting county treasurer, and in which the bar of the statute was pleaded, came before the supreme court by appeal.   In the opinion the court say: "If the defendant, occupying as he did a fiduciary relation to the county, converted the money, it was a fraud within the rule in *Cock v. Van Elten*, 12 Minn., 522, and the time limited for the commencement of the action began to run upon the discovery by the plaintiff of the fraud or notice to it of such facts and circumstances as, if investigated, would lead to such discovery." But strange enough, we find in the syllabus of the case written by the chief justice who wrote the opinion, the following: "Where there has been a fraudulent conversion, the time limited for the commencement of the action is to be counted from the discovery of the fraud."

The corresponding section of the statute of Kansas was in a manner before the supreme court of that state in the case of *Marbourg v. McCormick*, 23 Kas.; 38. The plaintiff in error, an agent of the McCormicks, in settling with them, had passed to them as genuine, and by false representations induced them to receive in payment of a balance due them on such settlement, a certain note of hand which proved to have been signed by him with the name of a fictitious person, and to be worthless. Upon suit by the McCormicks for such fraud, Marbourg plead the statute of limitations. Upon the trial the court gave the following instruction to the jury: "The time when the statute of limitations would commence to run would not be when mere suspicions were aroused, as that would not be in itself regarded as a discovery, but as a circumstance leading to further investigation. So that in this case, if you find from the evidence as adduced any fraud on the part of defendant, the discovery of such fraud would be when the plaintiff had knowledge thereof, and not when they had mere suspicions only." The giving of this instruction was assigned for error in the supreme court. In the opinion of the court, Judge Brewer, after quoting said instruction, said: "The testimony upon which such instruction was founded was that of plaintiff's agent, that when he made settlement with defendant and received the note his suspicions were aroused by noticing that it was all in the handwriting of the defendant, the maker not signing but making his mark; that thereupon he enquired of defendant concerning the maker, and received in reply the statements and representations heretofore noticed; that these suspicions were afterwards strengthened by the return of a letter uncalled for which he had directed to Patrick Flynn at Kennekuk. Now, in view of these facts, we think the instruction correct. 'Discovery of the fraud' is the language of the statute. That implies knowledge, and is not satisfied by mere suspicion of wrong. The suspicion may be such as to call for further investigation, but is not itself a discovery. A party, even though his suspicions have been aroused, may well be lulled into confidence and take no action by such representations as were made. And it would be strange if a party who had disarmed suspicions by his representations could thereafter plead those suspicions as ground for immediate inquiry and action," etc.

Strange as it may seem, the precise point now before us does not appear to have been directly considered by the courts of New York. The statute is cited, however, and to some extent considered by the superior court of New York city in the case of *Mayne v. Griswold*, 9 New York Legal Observer, 25. I quote from the syllabus: "A bill filed for relief on the ground of fraud, which shows on its face that the fraud was committed more than six years before the filing of the bill, should not merely state in anticipation of the defense of the statute of limitations, that the fraud was discovered within six years, but show that it could not with reasonable diligence have been discovered sooner." To the same effect is the case of *Bertine v. Varian*, 1 Edwards' Ch., 343.

From these cases it would seem that none of the courts have been content to leave to the statute the plain import of its words. This may arise from the use of the word "discovery." This word, when used in reference to past transactions or omissions can not have the same literal meaning as when applied to the discovery of a new continent or of a principle in physics. Fraud in a past and consummated transaction cannot be the subject of direct ocular or auricular discovery or knowledge. The discovery, then, of which the statute speaks, is of evidence or of evidential facts leading to a belief in the fraud and by which its existence or perpetration may be established, and not of the fraud itself as an existing entity.

If I am correct in the above, the inference follows that it is impossible to lay down any general rule as to the amount of evidence or number or nature of evidential facts which must be discovered before the statute will commence to run; therefore the rule supplied by the clause of sec. 26, chap. 27, 3 and 4 William IV. above quoted, and which seems to be followed more or less closely by the cases above cited, is after all, "the more exact rule."

To return to the case at bar. The frauds or facts alleged to have been fraudulent on the part of the plaintiff, and relied upon by the defendant Kuhn as a defense to the action, and as the ground of relief to himself, all occurred more than ten years, in point of fact more than twenty years, before the commencement of the action. The defendant is then barred of his defense unless it be true that down to a point of time less than four years before the commencement of the action, the defendant was in ignorance thereof or of any fact or circumstance connected therewith sufficient to put a person of ordinary intelligence and prudence upon inquiry in respect thereto.

Before entering upon an examination of defendant's evidence as to its application to the above proposition, our attention naturally turns to his answer. For if the fraud relied upon as a defense, or the facts and circumstances leading to a knowledge thereof, were first discovered by the defendant within four years next before the commencement of the suit, that was a fact of very great importance, indeed the fact, if the position of defendant as to the fraudulent source of the plaintiff's title be conceded, upon which the case turns.   It should therefore be distinctly alleged in the pleadings.

The case of *Godden v. Kimmell*, 99 U. S., 201, is authority to this point.   In that case Mr. Justice Clifford, in delivering the opinion of the court, said : " Courts of equity, acting on their own inherent doctrine of discouraging for the peace of society antiquated demands, refuse to interfere in attempts to establish a stale trust except where the trust is clearly established, or where the facts have been fraudulently and successfully concealed by the trustee from the *cestui que trust*.   Relief in such cases may be sought, but the rule is that the *cestui que trust* should set forth in the bill specifically what were the impediments to an earlier prosecution of the claim, and how he or she came to be so long ignorant of their alleged rights, and the means used by the respondent to keep him or her in ignorance, and how he or she first came to a knowlege of their rights :" citing *Badger v. Badger*, 2 Wall., 87, and *White v. Parmeter*, 1 Knapp, C. C., 227.

To the same effect is the case of *Bertine v. Varian, sup.* I quote from the syllabus : " Ignorance of rights and concealment will prevent the operation of the statute, but a party must set these up distinctly in his pleading.   An averment that the complainants had not been in a situation to call the guardians or their representatives to an account is too indefinite."

The only allegation of defendant's answer tending to explain the reason of his ignorance of his rights is in the following words : " That he is and has been for the 20 years last past a non-resident of the state of Nebraska, with no means of knowledge of suits pending in the state of Nebraska;" nothing whatever as to the time when or how he first came to a knowledge of his rights or of the facts which led him to such knowledge. The allegations of fraud against the plaintiff as contained in the defendant's answer are copied at length in the fore part of this opinion. As none of them relate to suits pending in the courts of Nebraska, or other-wheres, except the reference therein to suits pending against the Florence Land Company as evidence of its insolvency, it must be obvious that the defendant's want of knowledge of suits pending in the courts of Nebraska furnishes no rea-son for his ignorance of any one of the ten facts or groups of facts which he sets out as "evidences of fraud." And it is not stated, either in the answer or evidence, when he first discovered them, or either of them. I copy at length the abstract of the testimony of John M. Kuhn as given at the trial, with the observation that the defendant Norman A. Kuhn did not testify.

"I was plaintiff in the case of John M. Kuhn against the Florence Land Company; first came to Nebraska in the fall of 1856—the last week of December—and returned in April, 1857, and remained until the following October again. I then went back to Ohio, where I had been, and was never in Nebraska again until August, 1881; I re-mained in Ohio from 1857 to 1881; I suppose the debt was contracted and I obtained judgment against the Flor-ence Land Company through money that I left in the hands of W. Y. Brown to invest for me; I understood from him that he was secretary of the company; there was no specific way pointed out for investing this further than that he was to invest it upon real estate security and personal individual in-dorsers. I got this note in this way. He came to Salem, Ohio, where I was living and have lived ever since, whatever date it was, in March, April, or May, I don't remember, of 1858, and negotiated with me about this note, and I gave it into his hands and never saw it since until I saw it a few days ago; I never saw the note from that day until the com-mencement of this suit; I could not say where I did learn that it was in judgment; it was prior to 1858; I think it was in the winter of 1857 or 1858; I cannot remember the date; to the best of my knowledge I never authorized Mr. Seymour or any one else to appear for me as my agent in any case involving the lands in question between Cook, Sargent & Parker and the Florence Land Company—had I ever done so I think I would be apt to remember it; I was never notified or advised that any one put in an appearance in such a case for me; think I had no knowledge of it until the commencement of this suit, to the best of my recollection; not until the commencement of this suit did I first discover the fact that Mr. Parker held the lands in controversy, or a portion of them, as trustee of certain individuals by virtue of a secret trust; I have had no correspondent out here to instruct me as to the state of this property or its condition since 1859 or 1860, when Dr. Seymour went into the army; Mr. Brown told me that the mortgage given by the Florence Land Company to Sargent and Parker was fraudulent as to its character; I heard that there was fraud in giving the mortgage; I heard that some time prior to that note that I received from Mr. Brown as secretary of the company; I heard in what it consisted; I know nothing of my own knowledge in regard to this being a fraudulent transaction."

CROSS-EXAMINED BY MR. DOANE.

"William Y. Brown became a brother-in-law to me after I went home from here in the fall of 1857, before this note was given; at the time he gave me this note he was my brother-in-law, lately married in my family, and he had been my agent for investing my money; in consideration for that note, in addition to the money directly left with him, I had other claims here that were owing to me when he came there in 1858; it was for the proceeds of the money that he had left in his hands that was coming to me; he gave me to understand that the Florence Land Company owed him, and I suppose it was for the purpose of settling

his indebtedness to me that he gave me the note on the
Florence Land Company. I feel sure that he was indebted
to me in that full amount at the time that note was given
in 1858; I had no accounting with him at that time; that
was the amount that was coming to me as the proceeds of
that money that I left in his hands. I understand that the
Florence Land Company owed him more; he said that
$1,142 was the amount that he was owing me; he gave it
as being the balance that he owed me; we did not come to
any settlement at that time; it was not my understanding
that the note was given by Brown to me so as to enable me
to bring suit against the Florence Land Company to
recover judgment against them rather than that Brown
should bring suit against them on his own account; after
taking the note I returned it to Brown to bring it here and
get the money on it; Brown was managing my finances; I
left this whole matter in regard to this suit and its collection
with Brown; corresponded with Brown concerning it for
some time; Dr. Seymour was my brother-in-law; after the
judgment was obtained I think that William Y. Brown
was not here at the time and he wrote me what was done
and asked me to correspond with Dr. Seymour, and I did
have some correspondence with him afterwards. Dr. Seymour wrote me about my having obtained a judgment
against the Florence Land Company for so much, and that
the lands were sold, and that John Hellman, who was
sheriff of the county, wrote him that there was so much
cost—I think $62.50—in the case, saying that if the costs
were not paid until the June term the lands would be sold
again for the costs. I paid the costs, and before the June
term Seymour wrote me saying that the Florence Land
Company was going to pay the claim. I don't know where
I could find any of these letters; have not seen any of
them since after the lands were sold; I looked over the
letters before I came out here and burned bushels of them;
it is possible I brought the correspondence relating to this

period with me; will look for them; when I wrote to
Brown making inquiry about it he told me that he had employed Redick, and I think I wrote one letter to Redick
about it. I have no idea of its date; it was after the suit
was over. I did not know at that time of the pendency
of the suit to foreclose the lien on the Florence Land Company's lands; I never received any letter from Redick &
Briggs in regard to it. I wrote Redick after the foreclosure, asked him how the matter stood. I knew that he
was the proper person to refer to to get information. I
think James H. Seymour appeared for me voluntarily or
by the advice of W. Y. Brown in the suit brought to enforce my rights. I had some correspondence with him
about the matter after it was over; I could not tell at what
time the first correspondence took place; think it was after
the suit was over—I mean the foreclosure of the mortgage
after I had obtained judgment against them. I could not
say how soon after; I only know of one foreclosure suit;
I don't think I heard anything of the pendency of this suit
until after it was put into effect; never paid any fees for
the services of Redick in this suit; no claim was ever presented. James H. Seymour is now dead; he was in the
army. All that I knew in regard to this matter was before he went into the army. It was my understanding that
he went with the First Nebraska Regiment soon after the
opening of the war. If Mr. Redick had succeeded in
getting the money out of this land I would have supposed
it was coming through W. Y. Brown, and I would have
accepted the money as a matter of course. I would say that
whatever W. Y. Brown did in the matter of enforcing my
claim against the Florence Land Company he did as my
agent. I knew nothing about land, and was supposed to
rely upon him."

RE-DIRECT BY MR. SIMERAL.

"Mr. Brown gave me to understand that he would go
on and collect that note; he signs himself attorney on that

note for the company. I never thought of his employing any other counsel than himself, and supposed there would be no necessity; the substance of what he said is that he would go on and collect that note, and that it was sure to me."

BY MR. ESTABROOK: "He said that there was some mortgages that would have to be contested; he didn't say he would do it; I could not say whether it was at the time I gave him the note, or previous; I could not say concerning the conversation between Brown and myself, except that he would get the money for me and that it was a very sure thing; he tried to impress that upon my mind very strongly—that it was sure."

The only fact or circumstance stated in the testimony to have been discovered by the said John M. Kuhn at any time, is that the plaintiff held the lands in controversy, or a portion of them, as trustee of certain individuals by virtue of a secret trust. This he says, he discovered after the commencement of the suit. This refers to the fact testified to by the plaintiff that he bid off the lands at the mortgage sales in his own name, but in point of fact for the benefit of all the members of the firm of which he was a member, which was the owner of the mortgages, and the members of which were the plaintiffs in the suits in which the mortgages were foreclosed, and the sale of said lands made, and that he afterward bought in the respective shares of his partners and co-plaintiffs in said actions, in said lands. The purchase of these lands in his own name by the plaintiff constituted a trust in favor of his co-partners, which had he denied, equity would enforce, but it constituted no trust in favor of any other creditor of the mortgagor. If there was any fraud in the transaction, it was in the making of the notes and mortgages by the Florence Land Company. If the plaintiff and his co-mortgagees, or any of them, were cognizant of such fraud, then it must be admitted that the foreclosure of the mortgages, including the sale of the lands, was but a continuing fraud; but it had its inception, if at all, in the original transaction. Of this the defendants' grantor had notice, according to his testimony, twenty-three years before the commencement of this action, and, indeed, before the receipt by him of the note of the company upon which the judgment was rendered under which defendant claims.

All of the transactions alleged to have been fraudulent had occurred more than four years before the commencement of the action, and the defendant, or his grantor, having knowledge of such fraud (if any there was), or of such facts in connection therewith as would put a person of ordinary intelligence and prudence upon inquiry that would have led to such knowledge, the defendant is barred by the statute.

The defendant claims, as an alternative relief, that he should be allowed to redeem the lands in question from the mortgage sales.

As to a portion of the lands, it is difficult, if not impossible, to learn from the abstract whether the judgment under which defendant claims was rendered prior to the commencement of the foreclosure proceedings or not. As to the other portion, defendant's grantor was a party defendant, and appeared, answered, and defended by attorney. It is true that the authority of the attorney to appear for John M. Kuhn is denied.

The claim of a party of the right to redeem lands sold on execution or at judicial sale, on the ground of his being the holder of a subsequent lien, and has not had notice of the proceeding under which the land was sold, is doubtless a matter within the jurisdiction of a court of equity. It would be an action for relief, and therefore falls within section 16 of the statute of limitations, and must be brought within four years after the cause of action shall have accrued, so that the bar of the statute invoked by the plaintiff is equally applicable to the defendant's answer viewed as a bill to redeem.

28

In any view of the case, we must hold, as we do, that the decree of the district court be and it is affirmed.

DECREE ACCORDINGLY.

THE other judges concur.

JOHN CURRAN, PLAINTIFF IN ERROR, V. ELDRED PER-
CIVAL ET AL., DEFENDANTS IN ERROR.

1. **Trial**: JURORS: CHALLENGES. Where objections are made to certain jurors, and the record fails to show that the party exhausted his peremptory challenges, the objection will be unavailing in the supreme court.

2. **Witnesses**: CROSS-EXAMINATION. A witness cannot be cross-examined as to an independent collateral matter in no way connected with the subject of the action, in order to show contradictory statements made by him, for the purpose of impeaching his credibility.

3. **Liquors**: SALE: EVIDENCE. The sale of intoxicating liquor in a saloon may be proved by circumstantial evidence, and where the circumstances establish such sale the jury will be justified in disregarding the positive assertion of the bar-tender that the liquor sold by him was not intoxicating.

4. ———: ———: PRESUMPTION. An instruction that "If you shall find from the evidence that the deceased went into the saloon of the defendant, and that the business of the defendant was to sell intoxicating drinks, and that deceased was sober when he went into the saloon, and that he came out of the saloon intoxicated, these facts raise a presumption that such person obtained intoxicating liquor in such saloon, but such presumption may be overcome by the proofs and circumstances; and if you shall find from the evidence that deceased did not procure liquor from the defendant that caused him to be intoxicated, or that contributed thereto, you should find for the defendant," *Held*, Not erroneous.

5. ———: ———: INSTRUCTIONS. Instructions referred to in the opinion *Held*, Properly refused.

6. ——: ——: DAMAGES. *Held*, Excessive, and leave given to
remit $500 from the judgment within thirty days.

ERROR to the district court for Adams county. Tried
below before MORRIS, J.

Ragan, McDonald & Shallenberger (*Marquett, Deweese
& Hall* with them), for plaintiffs in error.

Dilworth, Smith & Dilworth, for defendants in error.

MAXWELL, CH. J.

This action was brought by the defendant in error, in behalf of herself and four minor children, against John
Curran, the plaintiff in error, who was a duly licensed
saloon keeper in the city of Sutton, county of Clay, for
selling her husband intoxicating liquor, which contributed
to cause his death by freezing, February 6th, 1883.

The complaint alleges that the defendant kept a licensed
saloon in the village of Sutton, etc., on February 6, 1883.
That the plaintiffs were the wife and children of one Mark
Percival. That on the 6th day of February, 1883, the
defendant sold and furnished to said Mark Percival intoxicating liquors, and thereby caused said Mark Percival to
become intoxicated so that in attempting to go from the
saloon of said defendant to his home, he became helplessly
drunken and overpowered by the effect of the liquors so
sold to him, and falling in a state of intoxication perished
and died.

That the plaintiffs were all dependent on the said Mark
Percival for support. That it amounted to $300 yearly,
whereupon they ask judgment for $5,000 against the de-
fendant.

The answer was a general denial.

On the trial of the cause the jury returned a verdict in
favor of the plaintiffs below for $2,500, upon which judg-

ment was rendered. The defendant below brings the cause into this court on petition in error. There are fifty-two assignments of error, most of which are unimportant and need not be noticed. Only the errors relied upon in the brief of the plaintiff in error will be considered.

The first objection urged is as to the qualification of certain jurors. From an early period in the history of this state, the practice has been in the district courts to allow each party to challenge peremptorily a certain number of persons called as jurors. The object is to enable either party to exclude from the jury such persons called thereon whom they may regard as unfriendly to them, or unfit from any cause to sit in the case. In this case the jurors objected to were not peremptorily challenged, the plaintiff in error not having exercised any of his peremptory challenges, and therefore the objection to the competency of such jurors was waived. *Palmer v. People*, 4 Neb., 68. *Burnett v. B. & M. R. R. Co.*, 16 Neb., 332. *Kremling v. Lallman*, 16 Neb., 280. There was no error, therefore, in the impaneling of the jury.

Second. Errors in the admission of testimony. The testimony tends to show that on the 6th day of February, 1883, one Mark Percival, the husband of Eldred Percival and father of the minor children, plaintiffs below, defendants in error, went into the saloon of the plaintiff in error, John Curran, in the city of Sutton; that at that time he was sober. There is a contradiction in the testimony as to the time he remained in the saloon, but none of the witnesses fixed it less than half an hour. There is considerable testimony tending to show that when he came out of the saloon he was intoxicated. As testified to by one of the witnesses: " I observed he was so drunk he could hardly walk." The testimony shows that he drank twice at the bar of the saloon. Mr. Clyde, the bar-tender, testifies that the only drink he furnished him was soda pop, and that he was not in the habit of giving him anything strong.

That Percival went into the saloon sober is clearly established, and that after 'remaining there some time he came
out drunk was also proved ; the jury, therefore, were not
compelled to believe Mr. Clyde that the liquor he furnished
to Percival was not intoxicating.

In *McDougall v. Giacomini*, 13 Neb., 435, it is said :
"Suppose it is shown that a place is a licensed saloon, and
that persons go in there sober and come out under the influence of liquor. These facts raise a presumption that such
persons obtained intoxicating liquor in the saloon. *Com.
v. Van Stone*, 97 Mass., 548. *Com. v. Kennedy*, Id., 224.
The business of a saloon-keeper is to sell intoxicating drinks
by the glass. If, therefore, the proof shows that he has
sold or furnished liquor at his place of busness, the presumption would seem to be that such liquor was such as his
business required him to keep and furnish to his customers
—intoxicating liquors. The fact of intoxicating liquor
being furnished by a saloon-keeper may be proved like any
other fact.

Suppose a murder was committed in a saloon and no one
present to witness the deed, could the murderer not therefore be proved guilty because these was no direct evidence
that he committed the crime? In such case, when the fact
of murder was proved, all the facts and circumstances
which tended to show that the person accused committed
the crime would be competent evidence, and if this proof
reached that degree of certainty required by the criminal
law, would justify the conviction and execution of the accused, although no one had seen him commit the offense.
If such testimony is sufficient to authorize a conviction
for offenses where the punishment involves the life or liberty of the accused, and where the proof must establish the
guilt beyond a reasonable doubt, the same kind of proof
certainly is sufficient to establish the sale of intoxicating
liquors, where the punishment is merely pecuniary compensation, and the degree of proof required merely a prepond-

liquor, and that you didn't know whether any one of those
liquors were intoxicating or not?

Defendant objects that it is immaterial, irrelevant, incompetent, and no foundation laid.   The objection was
overruled, and the defendant duly excepted.

A. I can't remember what I did swear to at that time.
I will tell you what I remember I swore to.   I swore that I
did not know whether the drink that that man Stewart
drank was intoxicating or not—the man that he was arrested for treating.

The question was again repeated, the same objection
made, overruled, and exception taken, and the witness answered :

A. I can't remember what I did swear to at that time,
as I could not tell, it was so long ago."

These questions were clearly improper.   The statement
which may be drawn out on cross-examination with a view
to show a contradictory statement by the adverse witness
in respect to it, must not only relate to the issue, but it
must be a matter of fact, and not merely a former opinion
of the witness in relation to the matter in issue.   2 Phil-
lips on Evidence, 903 (4th ed.)   *Lawrence v. Barker*, 5
Wendell, 301.   1 Starkie Ev., 134.   There are many cases
where great latitude of cross-examination may be permitted, to show the bias, prejudice, interest, disposition, and
conduct of the witness; but a distinct collateral fact, un-
connected with the cause on trial, should not be inquired
into, as the effect is to distract the attention of the jury
from the matter on trial before them.   The answers of the
witness, however, were not of such a character as to materially prejudice the plaintiff in error before the jury,
therefore not sufficient to warrant the granting of a new
trial.

Third. Objections are made to the 8th paragraph of the
instructions given by the court to the jury on its own motion.   It is as follows:

"If you shall find from the evidence that the deceased went into the saloon of the defendant, and that the business of the defendant was to sell intoxicating drinks, and that deceased was sober when he went into the saloon, and that he came out of the saloon intoxicated, these facts raise a presumption that such person obtained intoxicating liquor in such saloon, but such presumption may be overcome by the proofs and circumstances; and if you shall find from the evidence that deceased did not procure liquor from the defendant that caused him to be intoxicated, or that contributed thereto, you should find for the defendant."

It is claimed that it was for the jury to say what presumption or conclusion the facts warranted, and that it was error for the court to assume that the proof raised a presumption. This instruction is in exact accordance with the testimony in the case, and is not objectionable.

Exceptions were also taken to the refusal of the court to give the following instruction asked by the defendant below:

"The court instructs the jury, as a matter of law, that while a man is answerable for the natural and probable consequence of his own acts, still if his acts happen to concur with something extraordinary, and not reasonably to have been foreseen, and thus produce an injury, he will not be liable therefor, provided such extraordinary and unforeseen conditions were not produced by or were not the direct result of his own wrongful act."

The rule is well settled that a party is not responsible for all the remote and possible consequences which may result from his act, although he be a wrong-doer, and the damages must be the natural and probable result of the act complained of. *Union Trust Co. v. Cuppy*, 26 Kas., 754. *Fuller v. Chicopee Mfg. Co.*, 16 Gray., 46. *Dickens v. Beal*, 10 Peters, 572. *Beach v. Ranney*, 2 Hill, 314. *Vandenburg v. Traux*, 4 Denio, 464. We are unable to see what application the instruction asked for has to the testimony in this case. The natural and probable result of the intoxication

Curran v. Percival.

of Percival was to cause him to become confused, stupefied, and unable to reach his home, whereby he was exposed to the elements during the night and frozen to death. A person furnishing intoxicating liquor to another is liable to pay all damages which the community or individuals may sustain in consequence thereof. In a recent case in this court, where the person who procured liquor and thereby became intoxicated, and while stupefied and unconscious by such liquor lay out of doors during a cold night, by reason of which his legs were frozen and had to be amputated, and he was thereby unable to follow his occupation and was deprived of his means of livelihood, it was held that he could recover from the saloon-keeper the damages sustained by him from his inability thereafter to support himself. That the freezing and consequent death of Percival were occasioned by his intoxication and inability therefrom to reach his home is fully established by the evidence, and the person furnishing the liquor to him is liable. There was no error, therefore, in refusing to give the instruction.

It is claimed on behalf of the plaintiff in error that the damages are excessive, and that the verdict was rendered under the influence of passion and prejudice. The testimony shows that Percival was fifty-eight years of age at the time of his death; that for several years prior thereto he had contributed, in part, at least, to the support of his family, but to what extent is not clear. It is evident, however, that he did not entirely support his wife and family. As this action is for loss of means of support, the damages are to be graduated by the loss sustained, and the verdict exceeds the amount of damages proved on the trial. The defendants in error have leave within thirty days to remit from the judgment the sum of $500, and upon condition that such remittitur be made, the judgment of the district court will be affirmed.

JUDGMENT AFFIRMED.

THE other judges concur.

J. E. PHELPS, PLAINTIFF IN ERROR, V. GEORGE W. STOCKING, DEFENDANT IN ERROR.

1. **Promissory Note: PROTEST: NOTICE.** Where a promissory note payable at W., was duly presented to the makers on the last day of grace and demand of payment made, which was refused, *Held*, That a notice received on the following day by the endorser, who resided a few miles from W., was within a reasonable time.

2. ——— : ——— : ———. Where the endorser receives his mail at the place where the note is payable, a notice of nonpayment, actually received by him through the mail on the day following the last day of grace, is sufficient to charge him as endorser.

ERROR to the district court for Saunders county. Tried below before POST, J.

E. S. Merritt and *J. R. Gilkeson,* for plaintiff in error.

Bell & Sornborger, for defendants in error.

MAXWELL, CH. J.

This action was brought upon a promissory note executed by Byron Wise and Peter Marsh to George W. Stocking, Jr., and by said Stocking endorsed before maturity to the plaintiff. On the last day of grace demand was duly made of the makers of said note for payment, and upon their failure to pay, said note was duly · protested, and notice thereof given to the endorser.

Wise and Marsh appear to have been residents of Wahoo, while Stocking resided near there and received his mail at that place. The notice was sent through the post office on the day that demand of payment was made and was received by Stocking in the forenoon of the following day.

On a trial of the cause in the court below a jury was

waived and the cause submitted to the court, which rendered judgment in favor of the defendant, Stocking.

Two questions are presented. First, Was the notice received by the defendant, Stocking, on the day after the dishonor of the note, within a reasonable time? Second, Was a notice sent through the post office sufficient to charge the endorser? The rule seems to be well established that the holder is not obliged to give notice immediately on the very day of dishonor. 2 Daniel Neg. Inst., sec. 1037. *Darbishire v. Parker*, 6 East., 8. *Tindal v. Brown*, 1 T. R., 168. *Burridge v. Manners*, 3 Camp., 193. *Russel v. Langstaffe*, Doug., 515. *Muilman v. D'Eguino*, 2 H. Black., 565. Chitty on Bills [*482], 544. 1 Parsons on N. & B., 515, and cases cited. The notice, therefore, was forwarded in time.

In *Forbes v. Omaha National Bank*, 10 Neb., 338, where Forbes resided about one and one-quarter miles outside the corporate limits of the city of Omaha, where the bank was located, and received his mail at the post office in that city, it was held that notice sent through the Omaha post office was insufficient to charge Forbes as endorser. In that case there was nothing to show that Forbes had received the notice in a reasonable time. In this case, however, the testimony is undisputed that Stocking received the notice the next day after the failure to pay the note. It certainly could make no difference to him in what manner he received notice. One of the objects in requiring personal service of notice of protest, is to give the endorser a fair start with others in pursuit of the property of the defaulting principals. If in such case it could be shown that the endorser did not receive the notice until several days after the same had been placed in the post office, such notice would not be sufficient, as there is an implied agreement that the endorser shall be notified within a reasonable time after the dishonor of the note.

Where a person endorses commercial paper payable at a

distant place he by implication agrees to receive notice of dishonor through the post office, as that is the usual channel of communication between distant points.   This rule, however, does not apply to an endorser of paper payable at a place situated within his own post office delivery. *Forbes v. Omaha National Bank, supra.*   But where the endorser receives notice through the post office within a reasonable time, so that he is enabled to take proper steps for his own security, he will be bound thereby, even if such notice was mailed in the post office at which he received it. *Terbell v. Jones*, 15 Wis., 278.   *Bradley v. Davis*, 26 Me., 45. *National Bank v. Wood*, 51 Vt., 473.   *Cabot Bank v. Warner*, 10 Allen, 524.

The judgment of the district court is reversed, and as the facts are undisputed, judgment will be entered in this court in favor of the plaintiff and against the defendant, Stocking, for the amount of the note and interest thereon.

JUDGMENT ACCORDINGLY.

COBB, J., concurs.

REESE, J, having been of counsel, did not sit.

WILLIAM A. DENTON, PLAINTIFF IN ERROR, v. THE STATE OF NEBRASKA.

Medicine: PHYSICIANS: COMPLAINT FOR PRACTICING WITHOUT QUALIFICATIONS.   The complaint under which plaintiff was convicted charged that at a time and place named plaintiff in error did "commit the offense of practicing medicine, claiming to be a physician, in violation of the provisions of chapter 55 of the Compiled Statutes of the state of Nebraska, in this, that having registered under section 2 of said chapter, he was not entitled to make such registration or to practice as a physician, not being possessed of any of the qualifications in section 4 of said chapter," etc.   It was *Held* that the complaint did not state facts sufficient to constitute an offense and that the accused was improperly placed upon his trial thereunder.

ERROR to the district court for Burt county.   Tried below before WAKELEY, J.

Jesse T. Davis and *Horace E. Powers*, for plaintiff in error.

William Leese, Attorney General, for the state.

REESE, J.

This was a criminal prosecution instituted against plaintiff in error before the county judge of Burt county, charging him with a violation of the provisions of the act of March 3, 1881, entitled "An act to regulate the practice of medicine in the state of Nebraska."   Session Laws 1881, page 282; Compiled Statutes 1881, chapter 55. The trial before the county judge resulted in a conviction, and from that judgment he appealed to the district court. A motion to quash the complaint was made in the district court, and was sustained, and the prosecutor ordered to file a new one, which was done, and on which the cause was tried, another conviction being the result.   Plaintiff in error now prosecutes error to this court.   Prior to the trial plaintiff in error filed a motion to quash the new complaint.   This motion was overruled and the ruling thereon is assigned for error.   The grounds of the motion were as follows:

"1st.   The complaint does not charge in what particular defendant has violated the chapter mentioned therein.

"2d.   The complaint does not charge any crime under the laws of this state.

"3d.   The complaint is vague, indefinite, and uncertain as to the crime charged."

The complaint charged that plaintiff in error "on the

first day of March 1883, in the county aforesaid, then and there being, did then and there commit the offense of practicing medicine, claiming to be a physician, in violation of the provisions of chapter fifty-five of the Compiled Statutes of the state of Nebraska, in this, that having registered under section two of said chapter, he was not entitled to make such registration, or to practice as a physician, not being possessed of any of the qualifications in section four of said chapter, contrary to the form of the statute in such case made and provided, and against the peace and dignity of the state of Nebraska."

Does this complaint charge plaintiff in error with the commission of an offense, and if so, what one? It would not do to say that it is sufficient to charge that he committed "the offense of practicing medicine, claiming to be a physician, in violation of the provisions of chapter fifty-five of the Compiled Statutes," for it is no offense to practice medicine or to claim to be a physician unless such conduct would violate some specific prohibition of the criminal statutes of the state. There are two classes of persons who are prohibited from practicing medicine by the act in question. One is, those who are unregistered, and the other, or second class, those who do not possess any of the qualifications required by section four, whether registered or not. There are three qualifications mentioned in said section, any one of which will entitle a person to registration. *First*, a graduate of a legally chartered medical college or institution having authority to grant the degree of "Doctor of Medicine." *Second*, a person who on the first day of June, 1881, had attended one full course of lectures in a chartered medical college or institution having authority to confer the degree of Doctor of Medicine, and had practiced medicine three years, one of which was in this state. *Third*, a person who at the date named had been engaged in the practice of medicine, etc., for a livelihood for ten years, the last two of which was in this state.

The complaint contains the allegation that plaintiff in error was "registered under section two of said chapter," therefore he is not of the first class of persons above alluded to.   It was evidently the purpose of the pleader to charge that he was one of the second class named: that is, that he was not a graduate, nor had he taken the course of lectures and practised medicine three years, one of which was in this state, nor had he practised such profession ten years, two of which was in this state.   But does the complaint so charge?   We think not.   While much of the strictness of the former rules of practice has been dispensed with, yet sufficient must be alleged to indicate clearly the crime charged.   It is also true that where a statute in apt words describes the act declared criminal, it is sufficient to charge the commission of the crime in substantially the words of the act.   But the description of the "qualifications" necessary is not found in the section (9) which provides the punishment and defines the crime, but are contained in section four, which permits the registration. Therefore it was necessary to go to that section for the allegation descriptive of the offense.   It was necessary that the fact that plaintiff in error engaged in the practice of medicine, etc., should be alleged, and that either one or all of the qualifications mentioned in section four, according to the fact, did not exist.   This should be done, substantially, in the language of the statute in which they occur.   This was not done, and the motion to quash the complaint should have been sustained on the ground that it did not charge an offense.

The judgment of the district court is reversed, the motion to quash the complaint sustained, the prosecution dismissed, and defendant discharged.

JUDGMENT ACCORDINGLY.

THE other judges concur.

SCHOOL DISTRICT NUMBER 20, OF STANTON COUNTY, PLAINTIFF IN ERROR, V. THOMAS O'SHEA, DEFEND-ANT IN ERROR.

Practice in Supreme Court: DISMISSAL OF ACTION. Plaintiff filed its petition in error on the 22d day of February, 1886, since which time it has not appeared in the case. No abstract or brief having been filed, and no reason being shown for the delay, defendant is entitled, under rule four, to a dismissal of the petition in error.

MOTION to dismiss.

J. T. Brown and *Allen & Robinson,* for the motion.

BY THE COURT.

Defendant in error files a motion to dismiss petition in error in this cause for want of prosecution.

By reference to the record it appears that the judgment was rendered by the district court on the 24th day of February, 1885, and that the petition in error was filed in this court on the 22d day of February, 1886, and was placed on the docket for the January term of that year. Since that time no action has been taken by plaintiff in error to bring the cause on for hearing; no brief nor abstracts having been filed. The case having now been reached the third time, and no appearance having been made by plaintiff in error since the filing of his petition in error, and no reason being shown for the delay, defendant is entitled to have it dismissed under rule four of this court.

The proceedings in error are therefore dismissed.

JUDGMENT ACCORDINGLY.

29

PAUL BARBOR, PLAINTIFF IN ERROR, V. CATHARINE
BOEHM, DEFENDANT IN ERROR.

1. Trial. Questions of fact and upon conflicting testimony, are to
    be decided by the trial court, or jury, and a finding or verdict
    will not be set aside on the ground of a want of sufficient evi-
    dence to support it unless the want is so great as to show that
    the verdict is manifestly wrong.

2. Insurance: NOTE GIVEN IN PAYMENT OF PREMIUM. A
    promissory note given for the premium on an insurance policy
    issued by an insurance company which had not complied with
    the laws of the state in filing its statement and procuring the
    certificate of the state auditor authorizing it to issue policies, is
    void as between the parties to the contract, and cannot be en-
    forced.

ERROR to the district court for Hall county. Tried below before NORVAL, J.

Thummel & Platt and *T. O. C. Harrison*, for plaintiff in
error.

O. A. Abbott, for defendant in error.

REESE, J.

This action was founded upon a promissory note executed by defendant in error to plaintiff in error. The defense presented by the answer was, that the note, with
another, was given as and for the premium upon two policies of life insurance, one of which was for the sum of $5,000,
issued by the Continental Life Insurance Company, of
Hartford, Connecticut, the other being issued by the United
States Life Insurance Company, of New York city, for the
sum of $10,000, and that there was no other consideration
for said notes. It is further alleged that at the time of the
issuance of said policies the said United States Life Insur-

ance Company was a corporation organized under the law of the state of New York, and that it had not complied with the law of this state in the matter of filing with the auditor of state the statements required by law, and that no certificate had been issued by the auditor authorizing said insurance company to transact business as such within the state. That the application and contract of insurance were made and the notes executed within the state, all of which was contrary to law, and by reason whereof the note was void and of no effect. The premium on the policy issued by the Continental Insurance Company was $163; on that of the United States Insurance Company, $374.80, making a total of $537.80, one half of which—$268.90 —is included in the note upon which this suit was brought.

The real and controlling question is one of fact. It is claimed by plaintiff in error that the note in suit does not represent any part of the premium on the policies of insurance, but that he loaned to defendant in error the $537.80 to pay the premium on the two policies, and took the notes referred to, payable to himself, advancing the money for the policies, and thus becoming the creditor of defendant in error for that amount. Upon the other hand it is contended by defendant in error that the notes were given for no other consideration than for the premium on the policies, and that no contract or agreement ever was made by which the money was to be advanced by plaintiff in error as a loan to defendant in error, or otherwise.

The cause was tried to the court who found in favor of defendant. The testimony was conflicting. Defendant testified that the contract was that she was to give her notes for the premium as she did do, and that the notes were given for no other purpose. Plaintiff testified in the main to the opposite, yet both in his testimony in chief and cross-examination he stated that the notes were given for the premium on the two policies. Each party was supported by corroborative testimony, more or less direct. The question at issue was submitted to the court upon conflicting testimony and the finding thereon must stand.

The court, by its decision having found that the note was given for the premium on the policies of insurance, and the evidence being undisputed that the United States Company was a foreign corporation, and that it had not complied with the law of this state and received the certificate of the auditor authorizing it to transact business in the state, it follows that as between the parties to the contract it is void, and payment of the note cannot be enforced. *Health Association v. Rosenthal*, 55 Ill., 85. *Insurance Co. v. Harvey*, 11 Wis., 412.

The judgment of the district court is affirmed.

JUDGMENT AFFIRMED.

THE other judges concur.

———

HIRAM J. PALMER, PLAINTIFF IN ERROR, V. ABRAHAM ROWAN AND WILLIAM BELCHER, DEFENDANTS IN ERROR.

1. **Party Under Indictment in County other than his Residence, not Liable to Civil Action there.** A party who is charged with a criminal offense in a county other than that in which he resides, and who has given bail for his appearance at the next term of the district court of such county, and who in pursuance of such bail, attends said court at the time and place stated, and who upon the trial is discharged, is not liable to be served in such county with process in a civil action until after a reasonable time has elapsed to enable him to return to his home.

2. ———. The immunity is not confined to witnesses, but extends also to parties.

Error to the district court for Hall county. Tried below before NORVAL, J.

Thummell & Platt, for plaintiff in error.

O. A. Abbott, for defendants in error.

MAXWELL, CH. J.

The plaintiff sued defendants on a promissory note for the sum of $530, executed and delivered by them to plaintiff in the city of Grand Island, county of Hall. The case was filed in the county court on the 7th day of September, 1885, summons issued and delivered to the officer to serve, returnable on the first Monday of October, 1885, or on the first day of the next term of the county court of said county.

The defendants were under indictment to appear and answer at the September, 1885, term of the district court of said county, to-wit: September 8th. They had been indicted a long time previous, and had given bail for their appearance at said term. They appeared, and after several days' trial were acquitted. On the afternoon of the day of acquittal the officer having said summons in his possession served the defendants with a copy of the writ for their appearance at the next term of the said county court in said county to answer to the action on the note. On the answer day, to-wit, October, 5th, 1885, the defendants filed a plea to the jurisdiction of the court over the person of the defendants, for the reason they were served while in attendance on court, without being subpœnaed, they being residents of another county in this state.

To this plea the plaintiff filed a demurrer. The demurrer was overruled and the case was dismissed at the cost of plaintiff. Plaintiff took the case to the district court, where the same ruling was made, the court dismissing and overruling the petition in error.

At common law, parties and witnesses attending in good faith any legal tribunal, were privileged from arrest on civil process during their attendance and for a reasonable time in going and returning. *Thompson's Case*, 122 Mass., 428. And this whether they attend on summons or voluntarily, and whether they have or have not obtained a writ of protection. *Walpole v. Alexander*, 3 Doug., 45. *Meekins v. Smith*, 1 H. Bl., 636. *Arding v. Flower*, 8 T. R., 534. *Spence v. Stuart*, 3 East., 89. *Ex parte Byne*, 1 Ves. & B., 316. *Persse v. Persse*, 5 H. L. Cas., 671. *McNeil's case*, 6 Mass., 245. *Wood v. Neale*, 5 Gray, 538. *May v. Shumway*, 16 Gray, 86. Gray, J., in *Thompson's Case*, *supra*.

In some of the early cases in this country it was held that the privilege of suitors and witnesses extended no further than exemption from arrest, and that service by summons was legal, and where an arrest was made, common bail must be filed or a general appearance entered. *Blight v. Fisher*, Pet. C. C., 41. *Hunter v. Cleveland*, 1 Brev., 167. *Taft v. Hoppin*, Anthon, N. P., 255. *Booraem v. Wheeler*, 12 Vt., 311. The tendency of the courts, however, has been to enlarge the privilege and to afford full protection to suitors and witnesses from all forms of process of a civil nature during their attendance before any judicial tribunal, and for a reasonable time in going and returning.

In *People v. Judge*, 40 Mich, 729, in a well considered opinion by Judge Cooley, it is said, "There is no doubt whatever that the privilege exists in the case of all proceedings in their nature judicial, whether taking place in court or not. *Fletcher v. Baxter*, 2 Aik. (Vt.), 224; *Sanford v. Chase*, 3 Cow., 381; *Clark v. Grant*, 2 Wend., 257; and in *Reinmer v. Green*, 1 M. & S., 638, it was very justly recognized in the case of bail attending for the purpose of justification. In *Commonwealth v. Hawes*, 13 Bush., 699, where the privilege was allowed in the case of one brought within the jurisdiction on process of extradition, it is clearly shown that the reason of the privilege must determine its extent." To the same effect see *Cannon's Case*, 47 Mich., 482. *Baldwin v. Judge,* 48 Mich., 525.

In *Mitchell v. Huron Circuit Judge*, 53 Mich., 541–542, where a resident of Bay county, who was a party to two suits pending in the county of Huron, and went into the latter county to attend the trial thereof. He was examined as a witness in one of the cases, and the other case was continued. While so in attendance he was served with summons in the latter county in another case; he applied to the court on a showing of the facts to set aside the service, but the application was refused; he then applied to the supreme court for a mandamus. The court per COOLEY, J., say: "We think the case is within the principle of *Watson v. Judge of Superior Court*, 40 Mich., 729, and that the writ should issue. Public policy, the due administration of justice, and protection to parties and witnesses alike demand it. There would be no question about it if the suit had been commenced by arrest; but the reasons for exemption are applicable, though with somewhat less force, in other cases also. The following cases may be referred to for the general reasons: *Norris v. Beach*, 2 Johns., 294. *Sanford v. Chase,* 3 Cow., 381. *Dixon v. Ely*, 4 Edw. Ch., 557. *Clark v. Grant*, 2 Wend., 257. *Seaver v. Robinson*, 3 Duer, 622. *Person v. Grier*, 66 N. Y., 124. *Matthews v. Tufts*, 87 N. Y., 568. *Hall's Case*, 1 Tyler, 274. *In re Healey*, 53 Vt., 694. *Miles v. McCullough*, 1 Binn., 77. *Halsey v. Stewart*, 4 N. J. L., 366. *Dungan v. Miller*, 37 N. J. L., 182. *Vincent v. Watson*, 1 Rich. Law, 194. *Sadler v. Ray*, 5 Rich. Law, 523. *Martin v. Ramsey*, 7 Humph., 260. *Dickenson's Case*, 3 Harr. (Del.), 517. *Henegar v. Spangler*, 29 Ga., 217. *May v. Shumway*, 16 Gray, 86. *Thompson's Case*, 122 Mass., 428. *Ballenger v. Elliott,* 72

N. C., 596. *Parker v. Hotchkiss*, Wall. C. C., 269. *Juneau Bank v. McSpedan*, 5 Biss., 64. *Arding v. Flower*, 8 Term, 534. *Newton v. Askew*, 6 Hare, 319. *Persse v. Persse*, 5 H. L. Cas., 671. See also *Matter of Cannon*, 47 Mich., 481."

In *Compton v. Wilder*, 40 O. S., 130, one U., a resident of Pennsylvania, was extradited from that state upon a requisition issued by the governor of Ohio upon application of one C. in a criminal prosecution; it was held that the service of summons and an order of arrest issued in a civil action brought by C. against U. and made upon U. directly after he had entered into a recognizance to appear before the court of common pleas at its next term, and before he had an opportunity to return to his home, was rightly set aside.

In *Person v. Grier*, 66 N. Y., 124, it is said: "It is the policy of the law to protect suitors and witnesses from arrest upon civil process while coming to and attending the court and while returning home. Upon principle as well as upon authority their immunity from the service of process for the commencement of civil action against them is absolute *enudo, morando et redenudo*. This rule is especially applicable in all its force to suitors and witnesses from foreign states attending upon the courts of this state. In some instances witnesses and suitors, residents of the state, have only been discharged from arrest upon filing common bail, but the service of process upon non-resident witnesses and suitors has been absolutely set aside, thus giving color to a distinction between the two classes in respect to their immunity. Whether any distinction should or does in fact exist is at least doubtful. This immunity is one of the necessities of the administration of justice, and courts would often be embarrassed if suitors or witnesses, while attending court, could be molested with process. Witnesses might be deterred and parties prevented from attending, and delays might ensue or injustice be done. In *Norris v. Beach* (2 J. R., 294), the defendant, a resident of the state of Connecticut, attending in this state to prove a will, was held exempt from the service of a *capias* and discharged absolutely from the arrest. The like relief was granted in *Sanford v. Chase*, 3 Cow., 381, and the defendant, a resident of Massachusetts, arrested upon civil process while attending as a witness before arbitrators, was discharged absolutely without filing common bail, the court saying: 'The privilege of a witness should be absolute.' The court in *Hopkins v. Coburn* (1 Wend., 292), expressly affirm the absolute immunity of foreign witnesses attending our courts from the service of civil process for the commencement of an action. The same rule was held in *Seaver v. Robinson* (3 Duer., 622), and *Merrill v. George* (23 How., 331), and the service of a summons upon persons attending from other states was in each case set aside. This case in *Van Lieuw v. Johnson*, (decided in March, 1871, but not reported), substantially adjudged that a summons could not be served upon a defendant, a non-resident of the state, while attending a court in this state, as a party. Four of the judges taking part in that decision were of the opinion that neither a party nor a witness attending court in this state from a foreign state could be served with a summons for the commencement of an action."

In *Matthews v. Tufts*, 87 N. Y., 570, the case of *Van Lieuw v. Johnson*, above referred to, is cited with approval, and the court say: "This immunity does not depend upon statutory provisions, but is deemed necessary for the due administration of justice; it is not confined to witnesses, but extends to parties as well, and is abundantly sustained by authority."

In *Huddeson v. Prizer*, 9 Phila., 65, the court says the immunity "is alike the privilege of the person and the privilege of the court; it renders the administration of justice free and untrammelled and protects from improper interference all who are concerned in it." See also *Larned v. Griffin*, 12 Fed. Rep., 590, where many of the cases are reviewed. *Atchison v. Morris*, 11 Id., 582. *Plimpton v. Winslow*, 9 Id., 365. *Bridges v. Sheldon*, 7 Id., 19. *Brooks v. Farwell*, 4 Id., 166. *Parker v. Hotchkiss*, 1 Wall. Jr., 269.

The defendants in their answer, in addition to showing that they had given bail to appear at the time and place stated, allege that they were necessary witnesses on the trial and therefore could not be served with summons in a county in which they did not reside. We do not wish to place our decision upon the narrow ground that the immunity applies only to witnesses; it applies also to parties and is necessary to the due administration of justice. The defendants therefore would have been entitled to immunity from service of civil process upon them if they had not given bail for their appearance at the time and place stated. They were defendants to an action in which the state was the party prosecuting, and they were entitled to defend the same without fear of molestation from the commencement of civil actions against them. The rule applies with greater force, however, when they had given bail to appear. We hold, therefore, that they could not be served with summons until reasonable time had elapsed after their discharge to enable them to return to their homes.

There is no error in the record and the judgment will be affirmed.

JUDGMENT AFFIRMED.

THE other judges concur.

THE GOODMAN, BOGUE & SHERWOOD COMPANY, PLAIN-
TIFF IN ERROR, v. J. W. PENCE, DEFENDANT IN
ERROR.

1. **Evidence.** *Held,* That a preponderance of the testimony sustained the finding of. the court below as to the amount due from
   the defendant to the plaintiff.

2. **Mechanic's Lien.** A mere inchoate right to a mechanic's lien
   is not assignable; such lien passes with an assignment of the
   debt only where it has been perfected under the statute.

3. **Justice of Peace:** JURISDICTION: COSTS. Where a justice
   of the peace has jurisdiction of the cause of action and it is
   brought in the district court the plaintiff will not be entitled to
   recover costs.

ERROR to the district court for Hall county. Tried below before NORVAL, J.

T. O. C. Harrison and *Thompson Brothers,* for plaintiff
in error.

O. A. Abbott, for defendant in error.

MAXWELL, CH. J.

This is an action to enforce mechanic's liens upon certain
real property in the city of Grand Island. There are
three counts in the petition, in the first of which the plaintiff claims there is due to it from the defendant the sum
of $31.50 with interest from January 10, 1885; on the
second count the sum of $47.50 with interest from the
20th day of December, 1884, and on the third the sum of
$102.50 with interest from the 20th day of December,
1884.

The plaintiff claims as assignee of a verbal contract
made by one Benjamin Berry with the defendant to erect
and repair certain houses on lots owned by the defendant.

The account on which it is claimed the defendant is indebted to Berry was assigned to the plaintiffs before Berry had perfected a mechanic's lien on the premises by filing the same in the office of the county clerk.

On the trial a jury was waived and the cause was submitted to the court, which rendered a degree as follows:

"This cause came on to be heard on the issues joined between the parties, and after hearing the evidence of the witnesses, and the arguments of the counsel, the court finds that the said J. W. Pence, one of the defendants, is justly indebted to the plaintiff in the sum of one hundred one dollars and eighty seven cents, on account of the work, labor and material mentioned in said plaintiff's petition.

"And the court further finds that the liens mentioned and described in said plaintiff's petition as Exibit 'A,' filed against lots one (1), and two (2), in block nine (9), of Clark's Addition to the city of Grand Island, in said Hall county, was not filed within four months next following the date of the completion of the work on the building on said lots. And the court do further find that the plaintiff is entitled to a mechanic's lien on lots one and two, in block six, in Clark's Addition to the city of Grand Island, in said Hall county, in the sum of three dollars and seventy-five cents ($3.75), part of the sum so as aforesaid found due the said plaintiff. And the court do further find that said accounts and claims of lien in plaintiff's petition described, were duly assigned by the said defendant, Benjamin Berry, to the said plaintiff.

" It is therefore considered by the court now here, that the said plaintiff do have and recover of and from the said J. W. Pence the said sum of one hundred and one dollars and eighty-seven cents, so as aforesaid found due. And it is further ordered, adjudged, and decreed that unless the said J. W. Pence, defendant, shall within thirty days from the 23d day of February, A.D. 1886, that being the first day of the February, A.D. 1886, term of this court, pay to said plaintiff the said sum of three dollars and seventy-five cents, found to be a lien as aforesaid, with the costs of this suit taxed at the sum of $61.62, that an order issue to the sheriff of this county, commanding him to cause the lands and tenements herein before described, to-wit: lots one and two, block six, in Clark's Addition to the city of Grand Island, to be appraised, advertised, and sold according to law, and out of the proceeds of said sale, pay the costs of this action, and all increase costs, and pay to the plaintiff the said sum of three dollars and seventy-five cents ($3.75), with interest from the 23d day of February, A.D., 1886, that being the first day of the February, A.D., 1886, term of this court.

"And it is further ordered, adjudged, and decreed, that the plaintiff within thirty days from the 23rd day of February, A.D., 1886, execute and deliver to said J. W. Pence, defendant, a release of the liens now on record against lots one and two, in block nine (9) in Clark's Addition to the city of Grand Island. And in default thereof, that this decree operate as such release."

Two questions are presented for determination. *First*, that the judgment is not supported by the evidence. There is direct conflict in the testimony as to the amount agreed to be paid for certain work, at whose request such work was performed, and as to the materials furnished. We have read the record carefully twice, and find a preponderance of the evidence sustaining the amount found due by the court below.

The judgment of the court below as to the amount found due is, therefore, affirmed.

Second. It appears from the pleadings and evidence that Berry did not acquire a mechanic's lien upon the premises described in the petition, but that an attempt was made by the plaintiff to perfect such lien. The question therefore presented is, does the assignment of the debt carry with it the lien or vest in the the assignee the right by complying with the statute, to a lien? The mere performance of labor or furnishing material to another is not sufficient to entitle a party to a mechanic's lien. His right to the same depends upon compliance with the statute. Until he has so complied he has no lien which he can assign. When, however, he has acquired a lien, he may assign the same with the account to another. In other words, a mere inchoate right to a mechanic's lien is not assignable, although the lien when acquired passes with an assignment of the debt. ·

In Iowa, where by statute " Mechanics' liens are assignable, and shall follow the assignment of the debt" (Miller's Code, sec. 2139), it was held that the mere right which follows the performance of labor, and which for its existence depends upon the volition of the sub-contractor, was not assignable. *Brown v. Smith*, 7 N. W. R., 401. The court says : the language of the statutes is, the lien is assignable, and not the mere right. See also *Merchant v. Ottumwa Water Power Co.*, 6 N. W. R., 709. *First Nat'l Bank v. Day*, 3 N. W. R., 728. The mere assignment of the account therefore did not carry with it the right to a mechanic's lien.

If the mere assignment of the debt gave the assignee the right to assert the lien, then in cases where portions of the debt were assigned to different persons, each must file a lien for the amount due to himself, and thus instead of one lien against the property, there might be fifty or an indefinite number, which would render the proceeding cumbersome and oppressive. Before the assignment of the debt, therefore, will carry the right to a mechanic's lien, it must be perfected by properly filing the same in the office of the county clerk before the assignment is made.

The judgment of the district court, so far as it finds that there is a lawful mechanic's lien upon the real estate of the defendant, is therefore reversed, as also the judgment for costs in favor of the plaintiff in the court below, and as a justice of the peace had jurisdiction in the case the plaintiff below cannot recover his costs.

As thus modified, the judgment of the court below is affirmed.

JUDGMENT ACCORDINGLY.

THE other judges concur.

21
44
21
45

JOHN McCONAHEY, APPELLANT, V. SARAH McCON-
AHEY, APPELLEE.

1. **Appeal to Supreme Court.** In a case brought to the supreme court on appeal, where it is claimed that the finding and decree of the district court is not supported by the evidence, such finding will not be disturbed if the testimony is conflicting unless it appears that the finding is clearly wrong.

2. **Divorce:** TRIAL: EVIDENCE. In an action for divorce, tried to the district court without a jury, the fact that incompetent evidence was admitted over the objection of the party complaining, will not of itself require a reversal of the decree, if upon the whole case there was sufficient competent evidence admitted to sustain it.

3. ————: ————: ALIMONY: DECREE MODIFIED. Where it was shown that the husband was possessed of property of the value of $2,200, and the wife was possessed of $500 worth of property in her own right, it was held that a decree allowing the wife $800 of alimony and $150 attorney's fees, was excessive, and the decree for alimony was modified, and the sum of $500 allowed in addition to the attorney's fees, it not appearing that the wife had contributed to the common fund.

APPEAL from the district court of Dakota county. Heard below before CRAWFORD, J.

Isaac Powers, Jr., and *John T. Spencer,* for appellant.

Mell C. Jay, Joy, Wright & Hudson, and *Barnes Brothers,* for appellee.

REESE, J.

This action was instituted by plaintiff, by which he sought a divorce from defendant on the ground of abandonment. Defendant answered denying 'the charge of abandonment, but alleging that her departure from the home of plaintiff was made necessary by the cruel treatment of plaintiff. She also presented her cross-petition for divorce and alimony, alleging as ground therefor the extreme cruelty of plaintiff.

The cause was tried to the district court, resulting in a finding in favor of defendant and a decree of divorce and $800 alimony in her favor. Plaintiff appeals.

The first contention on his part is, that there was no evidence to support the findings of the trial court. This involves: *First.* The finding against plaintiff on the allegations of his petition; and, *Second.* The finding in favor of defendant on the allegations of her cross-petition.

The testimony is quite voluminous, and in many respects unsatisfactory. We do not see that any good purpose would be subserved by setting it out at length, nor by even giving a synopsis of it. We have read it carefully and find in it, especially on the part of defendant and her witnesses, many apparently contradictory and unreasonable statements, some of which seem to challenge particular attention. But when the whole case is considered together and the testimony is examined in the light of the rule stated in *Callahan v. Callahan*, 7 Neb., 38, and re-affirmed in *Powers v. Powers*, 20 Neb., 529, we must hold that the findings of the trial court cannot be disturbed, even though they may not be entirely satisfactory to the mind of the appellate court. There is enough in the testimony of defendant and her witnesses, if believed, to sustain the decree. The trial court was the judge of its weight as well as of the weight of the testimony given by plaintiff and his witnesses. We cannot molest the decree upon the general proposition that it is not sustained by sufficient evidence, nor that it is against the preponderance of the testimony.

It is next urged that the court erred in the admission in evidence of an alleged copy of a letter written by plaintiff to defendant. There was no proof of the loss of the original and the copy offered was mutilated so that only a part of it could be read. It is fundamental that a copy of an instrument in writing cannot be received in evidence without preliminary proof of the loss or destruction of the original, or some other fact which would make the copy the best evidence attainable. It is also insisted that the court erred in admitting the testimony of defendant wherein she detailed the conversation of third parties in plaintiff's absence. It is not entirely clear that this testimony was inadmissible, as the purport of it seems to have been communicated to plaintiff soon after, and the peculiar circumstances surrounding the alleged conversation, *if true,* might tend to throw light on the conduct of plaintiff. The conversation testified to had reference to a proposition made by the party named to place defendant in a bath immediately after the birth of her child, and from which defendant suspicioned a criminal purpose. She testified that she afterwards communicated the fact of the proposal to plaintiff. Yet it is not material to this decision whether the testimony was properly admitted or not, as the same strictness is not to be applied to the rulings upon the admissibility of evidence where the trial is to the court instead of to a jury. This suggestion must also apply to the ruling upon the copy of the letter above noticed. We know of no rule which would require the reversal of a judgment for the sole reason that the rulings of the court upon the admission of evidence were erroneous, when the cause is tried to a court, if the testimony which was properly admitted is sufficient to sustain the finding, for the court was as competent to exclude the force of the testimony at one stage of the trial as at another. 1 Greenleaf on Evidence,

30

§ 49. If there is sufficient to sustain the finding of the
trial court after the elimination of the testimony improperly received the verdict must still be sustained.

It is next contended that the court erred in rendering its
decree in favor of defendant for divorce and alimony on
her cross petition. This is based upon the alleged fact that
defendant was a non-resident of the state, and therefore
the court had no jurisdiction to render affirmative relief.
We are unable to see that this question can arise in this
case, for the reason that if the finding of the district court
that there had been no abandonment was correct, then the
residence of defendant would still be in this state notwithstanding the fact that she was temporarily in Ohio. If
there was a final separation and an abandonment of plaintiff her domicile or residence might be in Ohio. But if
there was no such abandonment or separation her legal residence would still remain in this state. *Smith v. Smith*, 19
Neb., 706. The finding of the district court being against
plaintiff on the allegations of his petition must be final as
to the question of jurisdiction.

The testimony on the trial, which was uncontradicted,
shows that the value of plaintiff's property is $2,200 over
and above his indebtedness, while defendant is possessed
of property worth about $500. In addition to the $800
alimony allowed defendant, an additional sum of $150 was
allowed for her attorney's fees, making in all $950. By
this it will be seen that the alimony allowed defendant
was excessive. The decree for alimony will be modified
and the sum of $500 will be allowed, to be paid as follows:
$100 in six months, $100 in one year, $150 in two years,
and $150 in three years; with the option to plaintiff to
pay sooner if he so desires, the decree to draw seven per
cent interest until paid. And as modified, the decree of
the district court is affirmed at plaintiff's costs.

DECREE ACCORDINGLY.

THE other judges concur.

GEORGE D. RATHMAN, PLAINTIFF IN ERROR, V. PETER NORENBERG, DEFENDANT IN ERROR.

21
28
—
21
50

1. **Trial:** CONFLICTING EVIDENCE. Where the testimony is conflicting and nearly equally balanced, the verdict will not be set aside as being against the weight of evidence.

2. **Roads:** ESTABLISHMENT BY USER. A public road over wild unenclosed prairie lands cannot be established by mere user, yet where the testimony shows that the land owner assisted in staking out and afterwards dedicated such road to the public, which accepted and worked the same, the jury will be justified in finding the establishment of such public road.

3. ———: DEDICATION. Where there is testimony tending to show a dedication, *Held*, That the following instructions were properly refused : I. That there is no evidence from which the jury would be warranted in finding a dedication by the plaintiff to the public of a right of way across his lands where alleged trespass was committed. II. There has not been shown affirmative act of dedication to the public of right of way across the plaintiff's land by any previous owner thereof when the alleged trespass was committed.

ERROR to the district court for Washington county. Tried below before WAKELEY, J.

Jesse T. Davis, George B. Lake, and *H. E. Powers,* for plaintiff in error.

W. C. Walton and *Osborn & Farnsworth,* for defendant in error.

MAXWELL, CH. J.

This action was brought in the district court of Washington county by the plaintiff against the defendant to recover damages for breaking down the fences and destroying the crops growing on the plaintiff's land. The defendant filed an answer as follows:

"Denies that on the 8th day of July, 1885, or at any

other time, either prior or subsequent thereto, he did unlawfully, willfully, and with force break and enter upon
the lands of plaintiff described in plaintiff's petition, or
upon other lands of plaintiff. Defendant denies each and
every other allegation of fact in plaintiff's petition contained, except such as are admitted, or otherwise explained
or answered.

"Defendant alleges that on the 8th day of July, 1885,
and for a long time prior thereto, defendant was the road
overseer of road district No. 2, of Washington county,
Nebraska, and that the lands described in plaintiff's petition are included in and comprise a part of said road district over which defendant is overseer as aforesaid.

"And this defendant further states that for more than
twenty years last past there has been, and still is, and was
on the 8th day of July, 1885, a public road or highway
over and across the lands described in plaintiff's petition
and through the cultivated farm now occupied by the plaintiff, being the premises described, which has been during
all of said time continuously traveled by the public generally with the knowledge and consent of the owner, and
since the spring of 1869 has been one of the main
thoroughfares leading to the present city of Blair, over
which the travel to and from said city passed, and for more
than fifteen years has been kept, maintained worked, improved, repaired, and accepted by the public and by the
public authorities of Washington county, Nebraska.

"Defendant further states that in the month of June,
1885, written notice was served upon him as such overseer, by citizens who had a right to travel over said road,
notifying him that said road had been obstructed and fences
placed across the same by the plaintiff, and demanding of
him that as such overseer he remove said obstructions and
open up said highway for travel by the public.

"Defendant further states that immediately thereafter
he as such overseer notified said plaintiff to remove said

fence and obstructions from said road, which plaintiff refused to do.

"Defendant further states that on or about the 8th day of July, 1885, after repeated notices to said plaintiff to remove said obstructions, this defendant, in his official capacity as overseer as aforesaid, opened said fences at the point where the same crossed said highway, sufficiently to allow the passage of vehicles, and with his team drove along said highway, and defendant denies that he did any other damage than to open said fences and drive along said highway, and denies that he trespassed upon said lands and that he did any damage whatever, or that he did any act except to remove a portion of the obstructions that plaintiff had unlawfully placed in said public road, and which it was the duty of defendant, by law, to do as such overseer."

The reply denies the facts stated in the answer.

On the trial of the cause the jury returned a verdict in favor of the defendant, upon which judgment was rendered.

The errors assigned are:

1st.   Error of the court to charge the jury as requested by the plaintiff.

2d.   Error of the court in the admission of testimony over the objections of the plaintiff.

3d.   Error of the court in the rejection of the testimony and evidence offered by the plaintiff.

4th.   Error of rule occuring at the trial and excepted to by the plaintiff.

5th.   The verdict is not sustained by sufficient evidence, and is contrary to law.

The testimony tends to show that in 1857 one Zimmerman settled upon the land over which the road in controversy is located and soon afterwards pre-empted the same; it also shows that in order to enter the land he borrowed a land warrant from one George Mallow, and gave Mal-

low a mortgage on the land to secure the amount due for
the land warrant; that in the year 1860, being unable to
pay Mallow the amount due on the land warrant, he conveyed the land to him.   There is also testimony tending
to show that in the year 1857, Mallow and others staked
out the road in question, and that after the land was entered and Mallow became the owner thereof, he recognized
the existence of said road and claimed to one Wild, who
desired to purchase the land, that the land was thereby rendered more valuable. The road passes near the head of two
gulches, and the testimony tends to show that the soil at the
head of each of the gulches has been cut away somewhat by
the action of the water from rains and melting snows, so
that the track at those points has been moved somewhat
away from the original line.   The lands over which the
road runs was unimproved, but a considerable portion of
it was used as hay land, and was mowed yearly.   There is
a direct conflict in the testimony as to the amount of travel
over the line of road originally located, a number of witnesses swearing that the travel diverged a considerable distance from the line as first located, while an equal number
testify that the travel, except during the winter or early
spring, when the road was bad, has followed the original
location.   In this condition of the testimony, it is impossible for a reviewing court to hold that the jury were not
warranted in finding as they have done.

If the testimony is true that Mallow assisted in staking
out this road and gave his consent to its continued use after
he became the owner of the land, the jury were justified
in finding that there had been a dedication.

In *Graham v. Hartnett*, 10 Neb., 518, it was held that
the existence of a public road by mere user did not apply
to wild unenclosed prairie land. We adhere to that decision;
but this rule will not apply where the land owner per-
manently surrenders the tract or tracts as traveled, for
public use. There was no testimony tending to show a

dedication in *Graham v. Hartnett, supra.* The rule as stated in that case, therefore, is not applicable to this.

The testimony shows that Mallow conveyed to the plaintiff, in the year 1884, the land over which the road was located, Mallow having been continuously the owner thereof from the year 1860, and said road during all that time having been travelled substantially on the line as staked out. The plaintiff, therefore, was bound by the acts of his grantor in locating and dedicating the road in question. *Graham v. Flynn, ante,* p. 229; S. C., N. W. R., 742.

The plaintiff asked the following instructions:

" I. That there is no evidence from which the jury would be warranted in finding a dedication by the plaintiff to the public of a right of way across his land where the alleged trespass was committed."

Refused. It is for the jury. E. W. Ex. by plaintiff.

" II. There has not been shown by the testimony affirmative act of dedication to the public of a right of way across the plaintiff's land by any previous owner thereof when the alleged trespass was committed."

Refused. It is for the jury. E. W. Ex. by plaintiff.

" III. A public highway across the land of a private person cannot be established as against him by mere user, but in addition thereto there must be such attendant circumstances as show that the user was under a claim of right to use it to the exclusion of all control or dominion of the owner."

Given. E. W.

" IV. In order to establish a public highway or road over the land of a private person by use, it must not only be used in such manner as to show that the public accommodation requires it, but also that during the time of such use it was the intention of the owner to dedicate the way to the public."

Refused. Given as deemed correct in other instructions. E. W. Ex. by plaintiff.

We think there was no error in the refusal to give the instructions named. The last instruction had already been given by the court on its own motion, while the first and second were not justified by the evidence, as there was testimony before the jury from which they might find a dedication, and also that the public had accepted the same by repairing and improving the road. The court did not err, therefore, in its refusal to give the first, second, and fourth instructions asked. There is no error apparent in the record, and the judgment of the court below is affirmed.

JUDGMENT AFFIRMED.

THE other judges concur.

THOMAS WOLF, PLAINTIFF IN ERROR, V. JOSEPH L. MURPHY, DEFENDANT IN ERROR.

All the parties in a joint judgment are necessary parties to a petition filed by one of their number to reverse it, and may be made so as plaintiffs or defendants, in conformity with the provisions of the code as to parties to civil actions. *Smetters v. Rainey*, 14 O. S., 287.

ERROR to the district court for Seward county. Tried below before NORVAL, J. Heard here on motion to dismiss.

Lamb, Ricketts & Wilson, for plaintiff in error.

Norval Brothers, for defendant in error.

COBB, J.

This action was brought in the district court of Seward county by Joseph L. Murphy, plaintiff, against Thomas Wolf, T. W. Boies, C. W. Barkley, L. G. Johns, Henry

Vanderhoof, and Aeneas Hurlburt, defendants, on several causes of action. The causes of action were all joint in form against all of the defendants. The defendants all appeared and answered. A trial was had to the court, which found the issues and rendered judgment in favor of the plaintiff as against the defendants Wolf and Boies, but against the plaintiff and for the defendants Barkley, Johns, Vanderhoof and Hurlburt. The defendant Thomas Wolf alone brings the cause to this court upon error. No mention is made in the petition in error of either of the other defendants.

In this court the defendant in error moves to dismiss the petition in error upon the following grounds:

1. This court has no jurisdiction of the subject matter.

2. That all the parties interested in the judgment sought to be reversed, as shown by the record, have not been brought before the court.

3. The record shows a judgment against Boies and Wolf for $575.90 and costs, and a judgment of no cause of action as to the defendants Barkley, Johns, Vanderhoof, and Hurlburt, yet neither Boies, Barkley, Johns, Vanderhoof or Hurlburt have been made parties in this court.

4. The petition in error and summons in error do not set out the names of all the parties to the judgment of the court below.

The argument on the motion was directed chiefly to the omission on the part of the plaintiff in error to make the parties in the court below, in whose favor judgment was rendered, parties to the proceedings in error, plaintiffs or defendants. I do not think that the motion can be sustained on that ground. But I think that it must be sustained for his failure to make Boies, against whom the judgment was rendered, jointly with himself, a party, either plaintiff or defendant, in the proceedings in error.

The point was before the supreme court of Ohio in *Smetters v. Rainey*, 13 O. S., 568, and again S. C., 14 Id.,

287.   In that case the judgment was a joint one against all of the defendants, one only of whom sought to prosecute error without mentioning his co-defendants.   I quote from the syllabus of the case as last presented:

"All the defendants to a joint judgment are necessary parties to a petition filed by one of their number to reverse it, and may be made so as plaintiffs or defendants in conformity with the provisions of sections 34, 35, and 36 of the code as parties to civil actions."   Both the reason and authority of this case are confined to a case of a joint judgment against all of the defendants in the lower court.   So also of the case of *Fotterall v. Floyd*, 6 Sergt. & Rawle, 313, cited by counsel for the motion.   The point has been often presented to the supreme court of the United States, in the cases cited by counsel, and others.   In the case of *Simpson v. Greeley*, 20 Wall, 152, cited by counsel for the motion, Mr. Justice Clifford, in delivering the opinion of the court, said: "Cases arise beyond all doubt where only one of several defendants is affected by the judgment or decree, and it is well settled that in such cases the party whose interest only is affected by the alleged error may carry up the case without joining the others in the appeal or writ of error," citing *Forgay v. Conrad*, 6 How., 203. He continues: "Exceptional cases of the kind occasionally arise, but where the interest is joint and the interest of all is affected by the judgment, the rule is universal that all must join in the writ of error, else it is open to the other party to demand that it be dismissed unless a severance of the parties in interest has been effected by summons and severance, or by some equivalent action appearing in the record."

Following the rule laid down in these cases the motion must be sustained, for the omission to make Boies a party or show any reason for not doing so.

JUDGMENT ACCORDINGLY.

THE other judges concur.

THE STATE OF NEBRASKA, EX REL. THOMAS M. FRANSE,
v. WILBUR F. BRYANT.

Judgment: COLLECTION WITHOUT EXECUTION: COMMISSION.
The commission of one per cent authorized by sec. 11, chap. 28,
of the Compiled Statutes, on money collected on judgment without execution by a justice of the peace or a county judge is to
be paid by the judgment debtor.

ORIGINAL application for mandamus.

Thomas M. Franse, pro se.

Wilbur F. Bryant, pro se.

MAXWELL, CH. J.

The defendant is the county judge of Cuming county.
The First National Bank of West Point recovered a judgment before him on a promissory note against one Fer-
dinand A. Mervis as principal and Thomas M. Franse and
William Boldt as sureties.

On the same day upon which judgment was rendered
the sureties paid to the defendant the amount of the judgment and costs and tendered him twenty-five cents to enter
satisfaction of the judgment. He refused to enter such
satisfaction unless he was also paid one per cent on the
judgment as commission. The relator thereupon brought
this action to compel satisfaction of said judgment.

Section 9, chap. 28, of the Compiled Statutes provides
that "For any service performed by the probate judge in
any matter within the jurisdiction of justices of the peace
he shall be allowed the same fees as are allowed by law to
justices of the peace for like services, and no more; in all
civil actions triable in the probate court, of which a justice
of the peace has not jurisdiction, the probate judge shall
be entitled to receive the trial fee as is now allowed to justices of the peace for like service in justice's court."

Section 11, same chapter, provides that for "Docketing each cause twenty-five cents. Taking affidavit, twenty-five cents. Filing petition, bill of particulars, or other paper necessary in a cause, ten cents. Issuing summons, capias, subpœna, order of arrest or venire for jury, fifty cents. Issuing execution, order of sale, order of attachment, order of replevin, and entering return therein, fifty cents. Issuing writ of restitution and entering return therein, one dollar. Administering oath or affirmation to witness, ten cents. Entering judgment in any cause, fifty cents. Taking acknowledgment of deed or other instrument, fifty cents. Swearing jury, twenty-five cents. Copy of appeal, certiorari, or copy of pleadings or other papers for any purpose, for each ten words, one cent. Taking deposition, for each ten words, one cent. Certificate and seal, twenty-five cents. Issuing warrant or mittimus, one dollar. Taking information or complaint, fifty cents. Discharge to jailor, twenty-five cents. Dismissal, discontinuance, or satisfaction, twenty-five cents. Written notice to party or parties, ten cents. Filing notice and opening judgment for rehearing, thirty cents. Each adjournment, fifty cents. Performing marriage ceremony, three dollars. Each day's attendance upon trial of a cause after the first day, one dollar. Taking and approving bail bond, twenty-five cents. Entering voluntary appearance of defendant, twenty-five cents. Issuing attachment, fifty cents. Entering motion or rule, ten cents. Rule of reference to arbitrators, fifty cents. Entering award of arbitrators, twenty-five cents. Commission on money collected on judgment without execution shall be one per cent on the amount."

The question for determination is, is this one per cent commission to be paid by the debtor or by the creditor?

Sec. 828 of the revised statutes of the United States, under the title "Clerk's Fees," provides that "for receiving, keeping, and paying out money in pursuance of any statute or order of court, one per centum on the amount so received, kept, and paid, shall be allowed." There are no decisions, however, under this statute.

In *Pixley v. Butts*, 2 Cow., 421, it was held that to entitle a constable to his fees upon an execution he must sell the property unless prevented by the plaintiff or by operation of law; and in *Hildreth v. Ellice*, 1 Caines, 192, where the sheriff had levied upon the property of the defendant sufficient to satisfy the execution, but before the sale the parties settled, it was held the sheriff was entitled to his fees, and in *Adams v. Hopkins*, 5 John., 252, where the sheriff had arrested a defendant, who was afterwards discharged under the insolvent act, it was held that the sheriff was entitled to his fees, as the defendant was discharged by operation of law; the same point was decided in *Boswell v. Dingley*, 4 Mass., 413.

After an exhaustive examination of the authorities the the writer has been unable to find any case exactly in point. The case turns, therefore, upon the proper construction of our statute.

Where an execution is issued upon a judgment the costs of issuing such execution, together with commission on all money received and disbursed by the sheriff on the sale of property, for each dollar, not exceeding $400, three cents, for every dollar above $400, not exceeding $1,000, two cents; for every dollar above $1,000, one cent. Constables are allowed the same fees as are paid to sheriffs for like services. These fees are chargeable to and are to be paid by the judgment debtor. The creditor is entitled to the full amount of his judgment. It would seem that the same rule would apply where the debtor pays the amount of the judgment to the justice of the peace or the county judge before whom the judgment was rendered. The money is collected by the officer in his official capacity for the benefit of the creditor; it is also for the benefit of the judgment debtor, as the costs of issuing execution, levying upon property, advertisement, and commissions to the sheriff or constable are thereby saved. In some of the states a sheriff is entitled to half commission where levy has been made and debt paid to the plaintiff, or otherwise settled by the parties without a sale. This allowance is made for the trouble, care, and risk of the officer in discovering and levying on the property of the defendant, and its safe keeping for the purpose of a sale, and securing the payment of the amount due. *Sturgis v. Lackawanna, etc., Co.*, 27 N. J. L., 424. Murfree on Sheriffs, sec. 1068. *Gaty v. Vogel*, 40 Mo., 553. In Indiana it was held that the sheriff was entitled to no commissions whatever on money paid by the defendent to the plaintiff, where the payment was made before the execution was served. *Miles v. Ohaver*, 14 Ind., 206. Whether this rule would prevail under our statute is not now before the court. We are of opinion that the commission of one per cent on money collected on judgment without execution is to be paid by the judgment debtor, and not by the creditor. The writ will therefore be denied.

WRIT DENIED.

THE other judges concur.

JAMES E. FULTON ET AL., PLAINTIFFS IN ERROR, V. JOHN H. LEVY, DEFENDANT IN ERROR.

1. **Mortgage Foreclosure**: SERVICE BY PUBLICATION: AFFIDAVIT. In an action to foreclose a mortgage of real estate, when service upon the defendants by publication is desired, an affidavit in the following form, *Held*, Sufficient: " Byron Reed, being first duly sworn, says he is the agent for the plaintiff in the above entitled action, who is now absent from said Douglas County. That on the 29th day of August, 1876, the said plaintiff com-

menced his civil action in said District Court for Douglas County,
Nebraska, by filing therein his petition against the defendants
above named, praying that certain lands situate in Douglas
County, and in said petition particularly described, may be decreed to be sold to satisfy certain mortgages given by the said
Emma Williams to said plaintiff, to secure the payment of a
certain sum of money therein named; and the said Emma
Williams has since conveyed the said premises to the said Eliza
Whalen; and affiant further says that service of a summons
cannot be made upon the said Emma Williams and Eliza
Whalen within said state of Nebraska. That this affidavit is
made for the purpose of obtaining service upon them by publication, this cause being one of those mentioned in section 77 of
the Code of Civil Procedure of the General Statutes of Nebraska, to-wit: Being for the sale of real property under a
mortgage; and further affiant saith not."

2. ———: ———: ———. Where there is a total failure to state
a material fact in the affidavit, the court will acquire no jurisdiction by publication of the notice; but where there is not an
entire omission to state such fact, but it is not fully set forth,
the proceedings are hot void but merely voidable.

3. ———: EJECTMENT. Whether ejectment will lie against the
mortgagee in possession under a proceeding in foreclosure, claimed
to be void, without tendering the amount of the mortgage debt
less the rents and profits, *Quaere.*

Error to the district court for Douglas county. Tried
below before WAKELEY, J.

G. W. Shields, for plaintiff in error.

W. J. Connell, for defendant in error.

MAXWELL, CH. J.

This is an action of ejectment brought by the plaintiff
against the defendant to recover the possession of lots 6
and 7 in block 233 in the city of Omaha. On the trial of
the cause in the court below a verdict was returned in favor
of the defendant, upon which judgment was rendered.
The testimony shows that in October, 1867, one Emma

Williams, who then owned said lots, executed to the defendant a promissory note in the sum of $1,000, and on May 1st, 1868, a second note in the sum of $600, and to secure the payment of said notes executed two mortgages upon the lots in question; that afterwards said Emma Williams conveyed her interest in said lots to one Eliza Whalen; that in 1876 the defendant brought an action against Emma Williams and Eliza Whalen to foreclose said mortgages. Service was had by publication, and a decree of foreclosure and sale rendered, a sale had and confirmed, and a deed made to the purchaser.

The plaintiffs claim that said foreclosure proceedings were void, because the affidavit for publication was insufficient.

The affidavit was as follows :

"STATE OF NEBRASKA,

IN DISTRICT COURT, DOUGLAS COUNTY.

JOHN H. LEVY,
    Plaintiff,
      vs.
EMMA WILLIAMS,
ELIZA WHALEN,
    Defendants.

Affidavit for Publication.

STATE OF NEBRASKA, }
  Douglas County. } ss.

"Byron Reed, being first duly sworn, says he is agent for the plaintiff in the above entitled action, who is now absent from said Douglas County; that on the 29th day of August, A. D. 1876, the said plaintiff commenced his civil action in said District Court for Douglas County, Nebraska, by filing therein his petition against the defendants above named, praying that certain lands situate in Douglas County, and in said petition particularly described, 'may be decreed to be sold to satisfy certain mortgages given by the said Emma Williams to said plaintiff, to secure the payment of a certain sum of money therein named, and the said Emma Williams has since conveyed said premises to the said Eliza Whalen. And affiant further says that service of a summons cannot be made upon said Emma Williams and Eliza Whalen within said state of Nebraska, and that this affidavit is made for the purpose of obtaining service upon them by publication.

"This case being one of those mentioned in section 77 of the Code of Civil Procedure of the General Statutes of Nebraska, to-wit, being for the sale of real property under a mortgage.

"And further affiant saith not.

BYRON REED.

"Subscribed in my presence and sworn to before me this 29th day of August, A. D. 1876.

WM. H. IJAMS, *Clerk*."

Section 78 of the code of civil of procedure provides that "Before service can be made by publication, an affidavit must be filed that service of a summons cannot be made in the state on the defendant or defendants to be served by publication, and that the case is one of those mentioned in the preceding section. When such affidavit is filed the party may proceed to make service by publication."

Section 77 provides that "Service may be made by publication in either of the following cases: *First*. In actions brought under the fifty-first, fifty-second and fifty-third sections of this code (recovery of real property, partition thereof, foreclosure of real estate mortgage and specific performance of real estate contracts), where any or all of the defendants reside out of the state. *Second*. In actions brought to establish or set aside a will, where any or all of the defendants reside out of the state. *Third*, In actions brought against a non-resident of this state, or a foreign corporation, having in this state property or debts owing to them, sought to be taken by any of the provisional remedies, or to be appropriated in any way. *Fourth*. In actions which relate to, or the subject of which

31

is real or personal property in this state, where any defendant has or claims a lien or interest, actual or contingent therein, or the relief demanded consists wholly or
partially in excluding him from any interest therein, and
such defendant is a non-resident of the state or a foreign
corporation. *Fifth.* In all actions where the defendant
being a resident of the state has departed therefrom, or
from the county of his residence, with intent to delay or
defraud his creditors or to avoid the service of summons,
or keeps himself concealed therein with like intent."

It will be seen that the affidavit in question conforms to
the requirements of section 78. It states the nature of the
cause of action, not in apt words, perhaps, but sufficiently,
so that the case appears to be one in which service by
publication was authorized, and that service of summons
could not be made in this state on the defendant or defendants to be served by publication. The rule stated in
Atkins v. Atkins, 9 Neb., 200, that "If there is a total
want of evidence upon a vital point in an affidavit, the
court acquires no jurisdiction by publication of the summons ; but where there is not an entire omission to state
some material fact, but it is insufficiently set forth, the
proceedings are merely voidable," is the true rule. The
proceedings to obtain service by publication should be lib-
erally construed in order that justice may be done.

In *Atkins v. Atkins supra,* there was a total failure to state
a material fact in the affidavit,—the nature of the cause of
action—hence the affidavit was held insufficient. Where,
however, the statement is merely defective, but the essential
facts are stated in the affidavit, although somewhat in-
definitely, the affidavit will not be void. We hold, therefore, that the affidavit in this case was sufficient, and the
judgment of the court below must be affirmed.

Even if the foreclosure proceedings had been void, the
right of the plaintiff to bring ejectment without first tendering the amount due upon the mortgage, less the rents and

profits, is very doubtful. The statute of limitations certainly would not run against the mortgagee in possession so as to bar his right to the amount due upon the mortgage. This branch of the case has not been discussed in the brief of either attorney, and need not be decided here. See *Kortright v. Cady*, 21 N. Y., 343 and 365. *Hubbell v. Moulson*, 53 N. Y., 225. *Pell v. Ulmar*, 18 N. Y., 139, *Watson v. Spence*, 20 Wend. (N. Y.), 260. *Fox v. Lipe.* 24 Id., 164. *Phyfe v. Riley*, 15 Id., 248. *Van Duyne v Thayre*, 14 Id., 233. *Forgal v. Pirro*, 10 Bosw, 100. *Chase v. Peck*, 21 N. Y., 581, 586. *Roberts v. Sutherlin*, 4 Oregon, 219. *Dickason v. Dawson*, 85 Ill., 53. *Nicholson v. Walker*, 4 Bradw. (Ill.), 404. *Martin v. Fridley*, 23 Minn., 13. *Brinkman v. Jones*, 44 Wis., 498.

The judgment of the court below was clearly right and is affirmed.

JUDGMENT AFFIRMED.

THE other judges concur.

I. OBERFELDER & CO., PLAINTIFFS IN ERROR, V. D. C. KAVANAUGH, DEFENDANT IN ERROR.

1. **Conversion:** EVIDENCE● OWNERSHIP OF PROPERTY. In an action against a sheriff for taking and carrying away a stock of millinery goods and notions, the point in dispute being whether the goods were the property of B. F. S., or of his wife, Mrs. B. F. S., it having been proved that both of them had up to a certain point of time, under some authority and in some capacity, exercised control over the said stock of goods and the store in which the same was kept, *Held*, Competent on the part of the defendant, who claimed under Mr. B. F. S., to prove any fact connected with the business of the Stumps, which from its nature must have been known to Mrs. S., inconsistent with her claim of ownership.

2. ——: ——: ——. The fact that goods purchased for
said business at different times, extending over a period of four
or five years, and amounting to several thousand dollars, had
been shipped to B. F. S., and all correspondence in relation to
such goods and purchases had been carried on between the
wholesale merchant selling such goods and B. F. S., and in his
name, *Held*, To afford some evidence, however slight, that B. F.
S. was acting in the capacity of owner rather than that of clerk,
agent, or manager.

3. **Trial**: EXAMINATION OF WITNESS. A trial court will always
allow a witness to explain an error, mistake, or oversight in his
testimony when he requests to do so before leaving the stand.
At what point of time is a matter of discretion with the court.

4. **Evidence**: PROOF OF LEASE. Where a lease purporting to
have been executed by and between strangers and a party to
the suit is offered in evidence, and its execution is not admitted
by the opposite party, such execution must be proved. Where
such lease purports to be signed by a subscribing witness, proof
of such signature being the genuine handwriting of the witness
is sufficient.

5. **Witnesses**: CROSS-EXAMINATION. A witness for defendant
being under cross-examination, plaintiff's counsel asked him
whether he had not at a certain time and place—naming them—
offered certain inducements of a pecuniary nature—specifying
the same—to Mrs. B. F. S., if she would "come up and testify
in the county court" (the said Mrs. S. having afterwards given
her deposition on the part of the plaintiff). Defendant's objection to such question, *Held*, Properly sustained.

6. **Conversion**: EVIDENCE. When an officer attaches property
found in the possession of a stranger claiming title, in an action
for such taking, the officer, in order to justify it, must not only
prove that the attachment defendant was indebted to the attachment plaintiff, but that the attachment was regularly
issued.

ERROR to the district court for Platte county. Tried
below before POST, J.

McAllister Brothers, for plaintiff in error.

John M. McFarland, for defendant in error.

COBB, J.

The defendant in error, who was also defendant in the court below, is the sheriff of Platte county. On or about the 7th day of December, 1884, he had in his hands two certain orders of attachment, issued out of the county court of said county against one B. F. Stump, one in favor of Lederer, Strause & Co. for the sum of $970.86, the other in favor of Roll, Thayer, Williams & Co. for the sum of $247.88. These orders of attachment he levied upon a certain stock of millinery goods, notions, and store fixtures then in a certain storehouse in the city of Columbus, and took and carried the same away.

The plaintiffs were in the possession of the stock of goods at the time of the levy and taking, by virtue of a chattel mortgage thereof, executed to them by Mrs. B. F. Stump, dated and duly recorded on the 8th day of December, 1884.

The action was brought for the value of the property taken, alleged in the petition to be $2,091.87. The defendant admitted the taking, justifying the same under and by virtue of the two orders of attachment above referred to, and alleging said property to be of the value of $1,142.63, and no more.

There was a trial to a jury, which found for the defendant. The plaintiff's motion for a new trial having been overruled a judgment was rendered for the defendant, and plaintiffs bring the cause to this court on error.

The following are the errors assigned:

"1. The court erred in allowing the witness, Charles McDonald, to answer questions 5 and 6 on page 8 of the bill of exceptions.

"2. The court erred in allowing the witness, Charles McDonald, to answer questions on page 9 of the bill of exceptions.

"3. The court erred in admitting exhibit 'D' in evidence.

"4. The court erred in not allowing the witness, D. N. Meyers, to answer the last question put to him on page 24 of the bill of exceptions.

"5. The court erred in overruling plaintiffs' motion for a new trial on the ground that the verdict was against the evidence and contrary to law.

"6. The court erred in overruling the plaintiffs' motion for a new trial generally.

"7. The court erred in entering judgment against the plaintiffs and in favor of the defendant."

The plaintiffs proved their cause of action *prima facie*. Of this there can be no doubt. The plaintiffs' agent testified to the ownership and possession of the goods by Mrs. B. F. Stump at the time of the execution of the note and mortgage to the plaintiffs. The note and mortgage were introduced and received in evidence; that after the execution and delivery of the mortgage, Mrs. Stump delivered the keys and possession of the store to the witness as agent of the plaintiffs, and that the store and goods were in such possession when the goods were levied on by the defendant. The balance of plaintiffs' evidence, up to their first rest, was confined to the question of the value of the goods taken by the defendant.

The defendant then called Charles McDonald, who testified that he was acquainted with B. F. Stump and Mrs. B. F. Stump; had known them for about four years; had been dealing with them during that time; had sold them goods from four to six times per year, amounting in all to several thousand dollars. The following question was then put to witness by counsel for defendant:

Q. I will ask you to whom you always shipped and billed the goods, in dealing with them?
The question was admitted over the objection of plaintiffs as immaterial and incompetent, and answered.

A. To B. F. Stump.
Again the following:

Q. With whom was the correspondence in regard to the business transactions with the firm of B. F. Stump carried on?

Over the same objection admitted, and witness answered, "With B. F. Stump"

I cannot say that these questions, or the answers thereby elicited, were either immaterial or incompetent, although I think they were very near the line. The question at issue before the court and jury was, as to the ownership of the attached property. It was, and is, an undisputed fact, that such property had constituted the stock and fixtures of the store and business in which both Mrs. Stump—under whom plaintiffs claimed—and Mr. B. F. Stump—under whom defendant claimed—had, up to a certain point of time, under some authority, and in some capacity, exercised control. Upon the plaintiffs' theory, Mrs. Stump was the owner of the goods, fixtures, and business, and B. F. Stump was her agent, clerk and manager; while upon the defendants' theory, B. F. Stump was the owner, and Mrs. Stump employed by him as a trimmer. Either of these theories, proved to be the true one, would be conclusive. After the departure of B. F. Stump, if never before, Mrs. Stump had exercised in her own right, real or assumed, exclusive ownership and control of the property, and in her deposition, then on the files of the court, had sworn to such ownership. It was then competent on the part of the defendant to prove any fact connected with the business, and which, from its nature, must have been known to Mrs. Stump, inconsistent with her ownership. The fact that goods purchased for said business at different times, extending over a period of four or five years, and amounting to several thousand dollars, had been shipped to the house in the name of B. F. Stump, and that all correspondence in relation to such goods and purchases had been carried on between him and the wholesale merchant selling them, afforded some evidence—probably slight under the circumstances of this case—that he was the owner rather than acting in the capacity of clerk, agent, or manager; and it was certainly material to the case, that defendant prove such fact if he could. The latter question was objectionable, in that it assumed that there was such a *firm* as B. F. Stump, but it was not objected to on that account.

Upon cross-examination the witness identified two papers as being in his own handwriting; one as part in his and part in the handwriting of Miss McCartney, a clerk in his employ, and one as being wholly in the handwriting of Miss McCartney, and as relating to a matter within the line of her duty.

Upon redirect examination, counsel for the defendant put to the witness the following question:

Q. Do you desire to make an explanation in regard to these letters?

Plaintiff's counsel objected to the question as "incompetent, immaterial, and irrelevant. Upon the overruling of his objection to the above question, the plaintiffs base their second assignment of error. The error, as counsel insist in the brief, consisted in permitting the witness to explain his testimony in regard to the papers identified by him before they were offered in evidence. Had this been deemed important, plaintiff could have prevented it by offering the papers in evidence upon their identification by witness and before turning him over to the defendant for re-examination. But I do not think the point of time important. A court ought always to permit a witness to explain his testimony before leaving the stand—at what point of time before his final dismissal is a matter of discretion with the court.

Henry Hockenburger, a witness on the part of the defendant, testifies as follows:

Q. Do you know what lot and on what part of it the business of the Stump outfit was done on?

A. It was the middle third of lot one, block 119.

Q. Do you know the handwriting of Mr. Stump?

A. No, sir.

Thereupon defendant offered in evidence a certain lease in writing purporting to have been executed between Daniel Condon and B. F. Stump, whereby the former leased to the latter the middle one-third of lot one, block one hundred and nineteen, with the building thereon except the cellar, from September 26, 1884, to September 26, 1885, for the consideration of $240, with stipulations, etc., to which the plaintiffs objected as immaterial and incompetent. The objection was overruled and the lease admitted in evidence and marked exhibit " D."

This paper, in the absence of proof of its execution, was incompetent evidence. It purports to have been witnessed by Gus G. Becher. Upon proof of his signature as the handwriting of the witness it would doubtless have been admissible, and would have been material as tending to show that the building in which the goods were kept and the business carried on was held in the name of B. F. Stump, and not in the name of Mrs. Stump. And in that view it probably had weight with the jury.

It was stated by counsel at the hearing that the family residence of the Stumps was also in the building on the said lot. Had this fact been proved at the trial it would not only have rendered the lease inadmissible as evidence, even if its execution had been proved, but would have destroyed its weight as evidence if admitted, it being the duty of the husband to furnish a residence for his wife; her use of it for other purposes might be merely incidental.

D. N. Meyers was sworn as a witness on the part of the defendant. He testified, among other things, that he was a traveling salesman for the firm of Lederer, Strause & Co. Upon his cross-examination, he having stated that he went to Ulysses in the month of January then last past and had a paper with him which he wanted Mrs. Stump to sign, plaintiffs' counsel put the following question to him:

Q. Did you not at that time when you saw Mrs.
Stump in January last, when you had that paper with you,
offer to put up $500, $400 or $500 in one of the banks at
Ulysses, to guarantee that you and your house would return
all of the goods that had been taken by you and your house
on the attachment here, if she would come up and testify
in the county court.

To this question the counsel for defendant objected as
incompetent, immaterial, and irrelevant, and not proper
cross-examination. Which objection was by the court sustained and the question excluded.

Counsel in the brief says that "The error complained
of here is in not being allowed to show by the cross-examination of D. N. Meyers that he had tried and endeavored
to suborn and corrupt another witness," etc. But, so far
as I can see, no answer which the witness could have made
to the question would have tended to prove that the witness
had tried or endeavored to suborn or corrupt Mrs. Stump.
Had he offered to put up money to induce her to stay away
from court or to testify falsely, or to a particular fact which
may have been false, it might have been different. But
the answer contemplated by the question could only have
shown that he offered her an extravagant inducement to go
to court and testify—presumably, of course—to testify truly.
I fail to see how his answer to the question, either in the
affirmative or negative, would have tended to prove any
attempt on the part of the witness to bribe or corrupt
another witness.

The fifth assignment of error indirectly presents the
question whether the verdict is sustained by the evidence.
This point divides itself into two branches: 1. Does the
evidence sustain the finding as to the ownership of the
goods being in the defendant in the attachment proceedings?
2. Has the defendant sufficiently shown and proven his
right and authority to take the goods from the possession
of the plaintiffs?

Having come to the conclusion, upon consideration of the second branch of the point, that there must be a new trial, I do not deem it expedient to discuss the first branch.

Upon the second branch the papers introduced or offered in evidence by the defendant were the two orders of attachment issued out of the county court. There was evidence of the indebtedness of B. F. Stump, the defendant in the attachment proceedings, to the firm of Lederer, Strause & Co., but no evidence of his indebtedness to Roll, Thayer, Williams & Co., nor any evidence that either of said plaintiffs in such attachment proceedings made or filed the oath required by statute before the issuance of an order of attachment. As before stated, the goods when attached were in the possession of the plaintiffs in this action, who were strangers to the said attachment proceedings.

Drake, in his valuable work on attachment, states the law as follows : " When the officer attaches property found in the possession of the defendant he can always justify the levy by the production of the attachment writ, if the same is issued by a court or officer having lawful authority to issue it, and be in legal form. But when the property is found in the possession of a stranger claiming title, the mere production of the writ will not justify its seizure thereunder; the officer must go further and prove not only that the attachment defendant was indebted to the attachment plaintiff, but that the attachment was regularly issued." Drake on Att., 6 ed., § 185a. The above is adopted by the author almost literally from the opinion of the court in *Thornburgh v. Hand*, 7 Cal., 554, and is sustained by other authorities cited : *Noble v. Holmes*, 5 Hill (N. Y.), 194; *Van Etten v. Hurst*, 6 Id., 311 ; *Mathews v. Densmore*, 43 Mich., 461, as well as by authorities here cited by counsel for plaintiffs.

Some courts have made a distinction between attachments issued by courts of general and those of limited jurisdiction. It may be doubted, however, whether there is any difference under a statute like ours, where the authority to issue an order of attachment by any court is limited to the special cases therein provided for, and in which the plaintiff shall conform to certain conditions precedent, amongst others that of filing an affidavit alleging certain facts therein indicated. It therefore follows that in order to justify the seizure by virtue of an attachment of goods found in the possession of and the title to which is claimed by a stranger against whom no element of estoppel exists, the party so justifying must both allege and prove not only the issuing of the attachment but every material fact and condition necessary to the regularity of its issue. But if there is any difference in the application of the rule to the different classes of courts, there can be no doubt of its strict application to courts of such limited jurisdiction as that of county courts.

The judgment of the district court is reversed and the cause remanded for further proceedings in accordance with law. The costs in the district court to abide the final result.

REVERSED AND REMANDED.

THE other judges concur.

ETHAMER PELTON AND FRANK MOORE, PLAINTIFFS IN ERROR, V. E. E. DRUMMOND ET AL., DEFENDANTS IN ERROR.

1. **Liquors**: APPLICATION FOR LICENSE: NOTICE. In an application for license to sell intoxicating liquors under the provisions of chapter 50 of the Compiled Statutes, it is necessary to give at least two weeks' notice of the same in the manner provided by law, and where the notice is published in a newspaper, the county (city or village) board has no authority to take any action thereon until the expiration of the time during which the notice must be given. Any action taken by them before the expiration of the two weeks will be void.

2. ———: NOTICE: APPLICATION. Notice of application for a
license was published in a newspaper, the first publication being
on Saturday, the 5th day of June. The time for hearing the
application was fixed in the notice at the third Friday in June,
which was the 18th day. On that day, the village board being
in session, the application was considered, and there being objections to the issuance of the license, the 22d day of June was
appointed for the hearing. It was *Held* that the board had no
authority to make the order, the notice being insufficient.

ERROR to the district court for Furnas county. Tried
below before GASLIN, J.

John Dawson, for plaintiffs in error.

W. S. Morlan, for defendants in error.

REESE, J.

Plaintiffs in error filed with the clerk of the village of
Arapahoe their petition for license to sell intoxicating
liquors. Certain citizens appeared and filed their remonstrance and protest against the issuance of the license.
The matter was heard by the village board and a license
granted. The remonstrants appealed to the district court,
and upon a hearing there the order of the village board
was vacated and the license refused. Plaintiffs bring error
to this court.

. As shown by the abstract the decision of the district
conrt was based upon the finding that the bond filed and
notice given by plaintiffs in error were insufficient. But
one of these questions need be noticed here, for the reason
that the decision thereon must result in an affirmance of
the judgment of the district court. This question is as to
the finding that the notice was insufficient.

The petition was filed in the office of the village board
on the 3rd day of June, 1886. A notice of the filing of
the petition was then published in the *Arapahoe Pioneer*.
This notice was as follows:

"APPLICATION FOR LICENSE.

Notice is hereby given that we, Ethamer Pelton and Frank Moore, have filed with the clerk of the board of trustees of the village of Arapahoe, Furnas county, state of Nebraska, a petition for the sale of malt, spirituous and vinous liquors, for the ensuing municipal year, and that we will apply for such license at the regular meeting, on the third Friday in June, of said board of trustees.

ETHAMER PELTON.
FRANK MOORE.

Dated June 3d, 1886."

As shown by the affidavit of the publisher, the notice was published on the following dates, to-wit: June 5th, June 12th, and June 19, 1886. As will be observed, the notice fixed the third Friday in June as the date of hearing. This day came on the 18th day of the month. One day before the last publication. On that day the board met in regular session and "on motion, Tuesday, the 22d day of June, 1886, commencing at seven o'clock P.M., was appointed for the hearing of said case."

Section 2 of chapter 50 of the Compiled Statutes—relating to the license and sale of intoxicating liquors—is as follows:

"No action shall be taken upon said application until at least two weeks' notice of the filing of the same has been given by publication in a newspaper published in said county, having the largest circulation therein, or if no newspaper is published in said county, by posting written or printed notices of said application in five of the most public places in the town, precinct, village, or city in which the business is to be conducted, when, if there be no objections in writing made and filed to the issuance of said license, and the county board is in session, and all other provisions of this chapter have been fully complied with, it may be granted."

Section three provides that "If there be any objection, protest, or remonstrance filed in the office where the application is made against the issuance of said license, the county board shall appoint a day for the hearing of said case, " etc.

By these provisions of the law we understand that when an application for a license is filed in the proper office, it is necessary to give notice of the fact in the manner provided by law. This notice must be given "at least two weeks before" any action can be taken by the board. The language of the law is plain and imperative. "No action shall be taken upon said application until at least two weeks' notice of the filing of the same has been given."

What action could the board take until the expiration of that time? Simply none.

Section 895 of the civil code provides that "The time within which an act is to be done as herein provided shall be computed by excluding the first day and and including the last; if the last day be Sunday it shall be excluded.".

The language of section two of the act, as above quoted, requires the application of this rule to the computation of the time during which the notice is to be given. Saturday the 5th of June—the day of publication—must be excluded. The two weeks, then, would expire with Saturday, the 19th. If Sunday must be excluded—and it must, for the board could not legally be in session on that day to appoint the time for hearing—Monday, the 21st, would have been the first day on which the board could take any action whatever on the application. The "action" was taken by the board on the 18th, three days before they had any authority or jurisdiction to act.

This objection was presented to the board by the remonstrance. It was clearly such an "objection" as should have defeated the license, at least under the order of the 18th of June.

The appeal brought the issue to the district court and its decision thereon was clearly right.

The judgment of the district court is affirmed.

JUDGMENT AFFIRMED.

THE other judges concur.

ABRAM C. WRIGHT, PLAINTIFF IN ERROR, v. THE STATE OF NEBRASKA, DEFENDANT IN ERROR.

Evidence Held Insufficient. The evidence examined and held not sufficient to support a verdict of guilty of the crime of burglary.

ERROR to the district court for Gosper county. Tried below before GASLIN, J.

James M. Hamilton, for plaintiff in error.

William Leese, Attorney General, for state.

REESE, J.

An information was filed by the district attorney of the eighth judicial district in the district court of Gosper county, charging plaintiff in error with the crime of burglary and larceny.

The trial resulted in a verdict of guilty of burglary, whereupon he was sentenced to the penitentiary for the term of one year.

The principal error now alleged is that the verdict of the jury was not sustained by sufficient evidence.

The crimes charged are, that of breaking and entering a dwelling-house, and stealing therefrom a quantity of meat alleged to be of the value of forty dollars. The verdict of the jury fixed the value of the meat taken at six dollars.

The house broken into was a dwelling-house, used in part for a temporary school-house and was not occupied on the night of the alleged breaking. The fact of the burglary was not known until the next day in the forenoon. The evidence was circumstantial. On the part of the state it was shown that the last person at the house on the afternoon before the burglary (January 10, 1884) left the premises about sun-down, and returned the next morning about sun-up, when the evidences of the crime were discovered. On that day tracks of horses were discovered about the stabling on the premises. These tracks were followed about three-fourths of a mile in the direction of the residence of plaintiff in error, which was about two and a half miles from the place where the crime was committed. The tracks showed evidence of having been made on the night of the 10th, having been made when the ground was frozen, and the road being muddy during the day of the 10th. During the afternoon of the 11th horse tracks were followed to the residence of plaintiff in error. But it was not shown that these tracks were followed continuously through the whole distance. One of the state's witnesses, Ellwood Thomas, testified that they followed the tracks to a cross-road running east and west, "and as cattle had been running over there so much we could not follow the tracks from there on for about one hundred rods; there we saw some pony tracks again on the road," and followed them to the residence of plaintiff in error. It seems that no comparison was made between the two sets of tracks by measurement or otherwise for the purpose of determining whether they were made by the same horses or not. While it was entirely competent for the state to present these facts as circumstances tending to prove, in some degree, the guilt of plaintiff in error, yet much of their force is destroyed by the want of proof of their identity. One of the witnesses testified that he measured the tracks, but whether those first followed, or those discovered after the trail had

32

been lost in the cattle tracks, does not appear, and that three or four days thereafter he applied his measuring stick to a track made by one of plaintiff's horses and they were the same size. If this measurement was made first of the tracks at the place of the commission of the crime and applied to the tracks of plaintiff's horses, the conviction produced thereby upon the mind would necessarily be much stronger than if the first measurement had been made of the tracks discovered after passing where the cattle had been. This matter is left unexplained by the proof.

On the evening of the 11th, after or about dark, plaintiff in error was arrested and taken to Homerville, where he gave bail and returned home at night. Some of the witnesses followed him home, and remained about his premises during the night, for the purpose of watching him. He and they arrived at his house about eleven o'clock, but he had no knowledge of their presence. About an hour after that time he came out of the house, went to his stable, and soon after returned with a stick of wood, or timber, on his shoulder, which he cut up for use, and carried it into the house. Afterwards he came out again and went to the well and seemed to be drawing water. This was repeated two or three times in succession, his wife accompanying him the last time. Each time he carried something which appeared about the size of a water-bucket. He then saw the watchers and informed them they could remain there as long as they desired, but that he should go in and go to bed. The next day, in the afternoon, the premises were searched, and about 100 to 150 pounds of meat was found in the well referred to, and taken possession of by the officer, and taken to Homerville. The property was not identified by the person from whom the meat was stolen as his; yet he testified that it resembled his in two or three particulars, which he described.

These facts constituted quite a strong array of circumstances, and if unexplained would perhaps be sufficient to sustain a conviction. But when the testimony on the part of plaintiff in error was presented, it seems to us to have been quite sufficient to so far destroy the force of the circumstances proven as to create very serious doubts in the minds of an impartial tribunal as to plaintiff's guilt. Mr. King, the owner of the stolen property, testified that from 300 to 350 pounds of meat was stolen, but only 100 to 150 pounds was found in the well. It would seem probable that if plaintiff had stolen the 350 pounds, the whole of it could have been found. It was shown on the cross-examination of plaintiff that when his premises were searched a quantity of meat was found in his house; but it was not disturbed, and it seems to have been conceded that it belonged to him. As to the conduct of plaintiff on the night of his arrest, he testified that his horses became untied during the night, and that he caught them at the well by drawing water into the trough and catching them when they came to drink. He also testified that one of the persons engaged in watching the premises assisted in catching the horses, and that occasion was the only time he was at the well. This was not contradicted by the state, although the witnesses were present who knew of the facts. The well in which the meat was found was upon adjoining land, about ninety steps from plaintiff's house, and was used but little by him, except for stock water. Plaintiff and his wife both testified that plaintiff was at home all of the night on which the crime was committed, and that they knew nothing of the meat being in the well until it was found. Plaintiff also, in the most positive terms, denied any knowledge of the commission of the crime. He also testified that but one of his horses was broken to ride, and that he passed over the ground where the tracks near his house were discovered on the evening before the burglary, with some wild ponies, on his way home from town. William Gath testified that he measured the tracks followed by the witnesses Burke and Thomas, and also the feet of

Wright's horses, and. that their feet were one quarter of an
inch larger than the tracks, and that the horse that made
part of the tracks "overreached," while plaintiff's horses
did not; also that one of the hoofs of plaintiff's horse was
badly broken out on one side, while the tracks followed
were made with unbroken hoofs.

It seems to us, upon the whole case, that the verdict of
guilty of burglary was not sustained by the testimony.
Every criminative circumstance was either explained or
denied in such a manner as to render plaintiff's guilt ex-
tremely doubtful, and the motion for a new trial should
have been sustained on that ground.

The judgment of the district court is therefore reversed,
the motion for a new trial sustained, and the cause remanded for further proceedings in accordance with law.

REVERSED AND REMANDED.

THE other judges concur.

IN RE BABCOCK.

Insurance. That portion of section six, chapter 16, Comp.
Stat., requiring a company or association, partnership, firm, or
individual to be possessed of $100,000.00, refers to life insur-
ance companies.

2. ———. Bankable notes cannot be, under the statute, included
as a part of capital stock of life insurance companies.

THIS was a matter coming before the court upon a letter
addressed to it by the auditor of public accounts, which
letter is as follows:

"*The Honorable Supreme Court, State of Nebraska.*

"Gentlemen—In the transaction of business in my office
it has become necessary for me to know the law regarding

the capital, if any, required of a life insurance company organized within the state of Nebraska.

"If it is not inconsistent with your duties, in order that I may fully understand what law is applicable, I respectfully solicit your opinion upon the following questions:

"1st. Does that part of section six, of chapter 16, Comp. Statutes, 1885, pages 182 and 183, which requires a company or association, partnership, firm, or individual, to be possessed of a capital of $100,000, refer to life insurance companies organized within the state of Nebraska?

"2d. If it does, would *bankable notes* be considered capital within the meaning of the law?

"Respectfully submitted,

H. A. BABCOCK,

Auditor Pub. Acc'ts."

To this, the court made the following reply:

BY THE COURT:

Chapter XXV. of the Revised Statutes, revision of 1866, entitled, "Incorporations—Insurance Companies," contained provisions regulating all kinds of insurance companies. That is, its provisions were general, making no distinction between the legal regulations of life, fire, accident, or any other kind of companies or business. That chapter contained section 6, precisely as it is now contained in chapter sixteen of the Compiled Statutes, and it clearly embraced in its provisions every kind and character of insurance known to the business of this state, including life insurance.

Subsequently, on the 25th day of February, 1873, there passed the legislature, and took effect June 1, of that year, the act entitled, "An act regulating insurance companies," which was published in and constitutes chapter 33 of the General Statutes, compiled and published that year. Section 41 of said chapter is in the following words: "Sec. 41.

That portion of chapter twenty-five, of the revision of 1866, which relates to insurance companies, and all acts and parts of acts amendatory and supplementary thereto, are hereby repealed, except so far as the same relates to the business of life insurance companies; and the auditor of state is authorized to return the deposits made under section twelve, chapter twenty-five, of the revision of 1866, when the companies making the same shall have complied with this act; *Provided*, such deposits shall not be needed for the payment of losses due from the company having made the same."

The said chapter twenty is carried forward in the latest compilation as chapter sixteen, and is believed to remain in force for some purpose, manifestly for that of controlling life insurance companies and the business of life insurance; and clearly all of its provisions, including the one requiring a corporation or association, partnership, firm, or individual to be possessed of a capital of $100,000, which are applicable, in the nature of things refer to life insurance companies organized within the state of Nebraska as well as those organized in other states and countries.

2. No mention being made in the section referred to of bankable notes, or securities other than "stocks of some one or more of the states of this union, or of the United States, * * * or bonds of cities of the United States." We have no doubt that the securities must be confined to those thus designated, which does not include bankable notes.

EPHRAIM K. ROBERTS, APPELLANT, V. SARAH E. FLAN-
AGAN AND W. H. MCCLELLAND ET AL., APPEL-
LEES.

1. **Will:** PROBATE. In February, 1873, one S., a resident of Wayne
    county, Michigan, made a will, and soon thereafter died. Said
    will was thereupon duly admitted to probate in the proper
    court of Wayne county, Michigan, and soon afterwards in the
    probate court of Gage county, Nebraska, certain lands belong-
    ing to the estate of S., being situated in said county, which lands
    were afterwards sold by the executors under a power in said
    will. *Held,* The probate court of Gage county, in 1873, having
    jurisdiction, the admission of said will to probate in 1873 was
    valid, and that said court properly refused to again admit said
    will to probate in 1883.

2. **Summons:** SERVICE BY PUBLICATION: PROOF. Where publi-
    cation has actually been made for the time and in the manner
    required by law, the failure to file proof of such publication
    before the hearing will not render the judgment void.

3. **Will:** PROBATE: ENDORSEMENT: EVIDENCE. The certificate to
    be endorsed on a will, required by section 160 of the Dece-
    dents Act, is not essential to the validity of the probate thereof,
    but merely provides that a will so certified, and the record there-
    of, or a transcript of such record, duly certified, may be read in
    evidence in all courts within this state, without further proof.

4. ———: JURISDICTION OF PROBATE COURT: PRESUMPTION. Where
    a probate court has jurisdiction in admitting a will to probate,
    all presumptions are in favor of the regularity of its proceedings,
    and in a collateral attack upon such probate the court will not
    inquire into the degree of proof required by the probate court.

5. ——— : ———. Mere irregularities in the proceedings, where
    the court has jurisdiction, are not subject to collateral attack.

APPEAL from the district court for Gage county. Tried
before BROADY, J.

Hazlett & Bates, for appellant.

Griggs & Rinaker and *T. D. Cobbey,* for appellees.

MAXWELL, CH. J.

In February, 1873, one Jeremiah Scanlon made a will as follows:

" Know all men by these presents, That I, Jeremiah Scanlon, in the city of Detroit, in the county of Wayne, and state of Michigan, being of the age of thirty-eight years, and being of sound mind but in feeble health, do publish and declare this my last will and testament, hereby revoking and cancelling any and all wills by me heretofore made.

" First.   I appoint as the executors of this my last will and testament John Heffron and Edward Reidy, both of Detroit, Michigan.

" Second.   I request my executors to pay all and singular my just and lawful debts and funeral expenses.

" Third.   My property, being chiefly real estate, I desire my executors to sell the same as soon as practicable after my decease for the purpose of paying the following legacies :

" Fourth.   I give and bequeath unto my beloved mother, Winifred Scanlon, of Detroit, the sum of three hundred dollars ($300) per annum for her life, for her sole and separate use, and I authorize and request my executors to take the necessary steps to secure the certain payment of the same.

" Fifth.   I give and bequeath unto my sister, Mary Burkery, of Detroit, Michigan, the sum of sixteen hundred ($1600) dollars.

" Sixth.   I give and bequeath unto my sister, Bridget Scanlon, of Detroit, Michigan, the sum of three thousand five hundred ($3,500) dollars.

" Seventh.   I give and bequeath unto my brother, John Scanlon, of Garranboy, County Clare, Ireland, the sum of one thousand ($1,000) dollars.

"Eighth. I give and bequeath unto my sister, Ann Scanlon, of Garranboy, County Clare, Ireland, the sum of fifteen hundred ($1500) dollars.

"Ninth. I give and bequeath unto my sister, Margaret Scanlon, of Detroit, Michigan, the sum of seven hundred ($700) dollars.

"Tenth. I give and bequeath unto my sister, Sarah Flanagan, of Cleveland, Ohio, the sum of sixteen hundred ($1600) dollars.

"Eleventh. I give and bequeath unto my brother, Michael Scanlon, of Greenfield, Wayne county, Michigan, the sum of eight hundred ($800) dollars.

"Twelfth. I give and bequeath unto my nephew, John Scanlon, of Detroit, the sum of one thousand ($1,000) dollars.

"Thirteenth. I give and bequeath unto my niece, Mary Scanlon, of Detroit, the sum of five hundred ($500) dollars.

"Fourteenth. I give and bequeath unto my nieces, Mary Berkery and Winifred Berkery, the sum of one hundred dollars to each.

"Fifteenth. I give and bequeath unto the St. Anthony Male Orphan Asylum the sum of five hundred ($500) dollars.

"Sixteenth. I give and bequeath unto the St. Vincent's Orphan Asylum the sum of five hundred ($500) dollars.

"Seventeenth. I give and bequeath the House of Providence, situated on Fourteenth street, the sum of five hundred ($500) dollars.

"Eighteenth. I request my executors to set apart the sum of five hundred dollars for the purpose of erecting a monument to my memory over my grave.

"Nineteenth. I give and bequeath to Rev. James Savage, of Detroit, the following sums in trust to be paid in the settlement of the following debts owing to the undermentioned persons:

Chas. H. Coil, Cleveland, Ohio	$300 00
Rasson Gartner, Kalamazoo, Michigan	100 00
Proprietor Adams hotel, Dexter	21 43
Total	$421 43

Making a total as above of four hundred and twenty-one dollars and forty-three cents.

"Twentieth. All the rest, residue, and remainder of my property, if any there be left after the foregoing distribution, I give, bequeath and devise in equal shares to my brothers and sisters, Mary Berkery, Bridget Scanlon, Margaret Scanlon, John Scanlon, Ann Scanlon, Sarah Flanagan and Michael Scanlon, to be divided equally, as aforesaid, after the foregoing legacies have been paid."

Scanlon seems to have died soon after making the will, and on the 25th of the following March the will in question was duly proved before the probate court of Wayne county, Michigan, and letters testamentary issued by said court to John Heffron and Edward Reidy.

In April, 1873, Heffron and Reidy filed their petition in the probate court of Gage county, Nebraska, setting forth that Scanlon departed this life on the 23d day of February of that year, leaving a last will and testament, which had been duly admitted to probate by the probate court of Wayne county, Michigan, and praying that said will might be admitted to probate in the county of Gage, state of Nebraska, and that letters testamentary might be issued to the petitioners.

Thereupon a notice was ordered published for three consecutive weeks in the Beatrice *Express*, which notice is in the words and figures following, to-wit:

"To all persons interested in the estate of Jeremiah Scanlon, late of the county of Wayne, and state of Michigan, deceased: You are hereby notified that application by petition has been made to me, probate judge of the county of Gage and state of Nebraska, by John Heffron and Ed-

ward Reidy, praying that the last will and testament of
said Jeremiah Scanlon be admitted to probate in said county
of Gage; also praying that administration of said estate be
granted to said John Heffron and Edward Reidy, and I
have appointed Thursday, the 5th day of June, A.D. 1873,
at the hour of 10 o'clock A.M., at my office in the city of
Beatrice, in said Gage county, as the time and place for
hearing said application, when you can be present and
show cause, if any there may be, why the prayer of said
petitioners should not be granted.

" J. W. CARTER,

"Dated May 4, 1873.   <i>Probate Judge.</i>

" Now, on this 5th day of June, 1873, this cause came on
further to be heard, and further hearing is postponed until
July 1, 1873.

"And now, on this 1st day of July, 1873, comes S. C. B.
Dean, attorney, and files an affidavit of publication, which
is in words and figures as follows, to-wit:

"AFFIDAVIT OF PUBLICATION.

"STATE OF NEBRASKA, ⎱ ss.
  COUNTY OF GAGE, ⎰

" Theodore Coleman, being duly sworn, says he is one
of the publishers of the Beatrice <i>Express</i>, a weekly newspaper printed in Gage county, Nebraska, and of general
circulation therein, and that a notice, a true copy of which
is hereto annexed, was published in said paper three consecutive weeks, or four times, once in each week, commencing on the 15th day of May, 1873.

"THEODORE COLEMAN.

"Subscribed and sworn to before me this 7th day of
July, 1873.   ALBERT TOWLE,
Notary Public."

Also, on the same day, was filed a copy of letters testamentary granted to the said Heffron and Reidy in the state
of Michigan, county of Wayne, from the probate court
thereof.

The court thereupon made the following order:

"No person appearing to contest the above said last will and testament of Jeremiah Scanlon, deceased, and the same having been duly proved and allowed by the honorable the probate judge of Wayne county, Michigan, it is hereby ordered that said will be approved and allowed, and it is further ordered that John Heffron and Edward Reidy, named in said will, be and are hereby appointed executors, with the will annexed, of the estate of Jeremiah Scanlon, deceased, upon their filing an undertaking in the sum of $5,000.

"And now, on the 15th day of August, 1873, a bond was filed and approved." Then follows copy of bond.

Under the probate of said will, in Gage county, the executors named sold certain real estate in that county belonging to the estate of the testator. In June, 1883, the plaintiff filed his petition in the probate court of Gage county, in this state, together with the exemplifications of the records of the probate court of Wayne county, Michigan, and praying that all persons interested in the estate of Jeremiah Scanlon, deceased, be duly cited to appear, and that the last will and testament of said Scanlon be probated and allowed as provided by law, and that administration of said estate, with the will annexed, be granted to one Alfred F. Wilcox, upon his giving bond, etc. Upon the hearing of this application it was dismissed at the plaintiff's costs. The plaintiff then appealed to the district court of said Gage county, where the judgment of the probate court was affirmed. The plaintiff appeals to this court.

It is claimed on behalf of the plaintiff that the will was not legally probated in Gage county in 1873, because the hearing of the petition was ordered for June 5th of that year, on which day, without proof of publication of notice, the hearing was adjourned until July 1st, 1873, and that the affidavit of publication was not filed until July 7th, 1873.

JANUARY TERM, 1887.		509

All the evidence before the probate court of Gage county,
as to the publication of notice, may not be embodied in the
record. The fact is clearly made to appear that the notice
was published for the length of time required by law, and
the mere failure to file proof of such publication until after
the time set for hearing would not oust the court of jurisdiction nor render its judgment void.

Second. That the will has no certificate of probate endorsed upon it, as required by statute.

Section 160, chapter 23, Compiled Statutes, provides that
"Every will, *when* proved as provided in this subdivision,
shall have a certificate of such proof endorsed thereon or annexed thereto, signed by the judge of probate and attested
by his seal; and every will so certified, and the record thereof, or a transcript of such record, certified by the judge of
probate, and attested by his seal, may be read in evidence
in all courts within this state without further proof."

It will be seen that the endorsement of the certificate on
the will is not a part of the probate of the same, but is
simply evidence that the will has been admitted to probate,
as "every will so certified, and the record thereof, or a
transcript of such record, certified by the judge of probate,
and attested by his seal, may be read in evidence in all
courts within this state, without further proof." That is,
the certificate attached to the will authorizes it to be used
in evidence without further authentication, but the failure
to endorse the certificate on the will does not affect the validity of the probate thereof.

Third. That the will was admitted because no one objected, and that it had been admitted in Michigan, and that
no evidence of the execution of the will, or of the testamentary capacity of the deceased, was produced.

If this was a direct proceeding to set aside the probate of
the will, and all the evidence upon which such probate was
made was before the court, we might hold that the proof
was insufficient; in this collateral proceeding, however, we

cannot so hold. Jurisdiction being established, all presumptions are in favor of the judgment of the probate court.

The fourth, fifth and sixth objections relate to irregularities in the proceedings, which, even if they existed, would not affect the validity of the acts of the executors. The plaintiff in this case claims under the will of Scanlon, which was admitted to probate in Wayne county, Michigan, in 1873.   He claims in his petition to be the owner, by purchase and assignment, of all the legacies in said will provided for, excepting that of Sarah Flanagan, and alleges that she is indebted to said estate, and has assigned her interest therein to said estate, and that there are no debts.

So far as this record discloses, the former executors sold the land belonging to the estate in Gage county, Nebraska, for the purpose of paying the debts and legacies. If, as claimed by the plaintiff, the former executors are largely indebted to the estate, and insolvent, still this will not authorize him to disregard sales made by them, permit them to retain the money obtained from the former sales, and again sell the land under the will. It is very clear that the probate court of Gage county, in 1873, had jurisdiction, and that the probate of the will in question by said court was sufficient and valid, and that it properly refused to permit proceedings to be again instituted in 1883 under the same will.

The judgment of the district court, and also of the probate court, is therefore affirmed.

JUDGMENT AFFIRMED.

THE other judges concur.

WILBURN BILLINGS, PLAINTIFF IN ERROR, V. ELIJAH
FILLEY, DEFENDANT IN ERROR.

1. **Sale of Stock**: INCORRECT WEIGHT: EVIDENCE. One B. sold
   forty-two head of fat steers and one hundred and four fat hogs
   to F. at an agreed price per one hundred pounds. The stock
   was weighed on the scales of F. and delivered, and on the succeeding day it was discovered that the scales were incorrect. In
   an action by B. against F. to recover the difference between the
   weight of the stock given and the actual weight, *Held*, That
   a preponderance of the evidence showed that the scales of F.
   were incorrect, and that B. had thereby sustained damages.

2. ———: ———: RIGHTS OF SELLER: CONSIDERATION. Where
   a party sold stock to be paid for by weight, and said stock was
   weighed on the scales of the buyer, which on the next day were
   found to have been out of order, and to have favored the buyer,
   Held, That the seller was entitled to have the stock weighed
   correctly, and that a promise by him to pay the buyer a bonus
   to weigh the stock correctly was without consideration.

3. ———: ———: RATIFICATION OF CONTRACT. Where one F.
   purchased forty-two fat steers, which were delivered and accepted by him, and on the succeeding day, at the request of the
   seller, reweighed forty-one of said steers, but refused to accept
   the forty-second, but retained possession of said steer, and afterwards disposed of the same, *Held*, A ratification of the original contract, and the purchaser was liable to the seller for the
   purchase price agreed upon.

4. **Instructions**: EXCEPTIONS. Instructions not excepted to cannot be reviewed in the supreme court.

ERROR to the district court for Gage county. Tried below before BROADY, J.

A. Hardy, for plaintiff in error.

Hazlett & Bates, for defendant in error.

MAXWELL, CH. J.

The plaintiff filed his petition in the court below, stating
his cause of auction to be: "That on the 11th day of March,

1884, the parties to this action entered into a written agreement, whereby plaintiff sold defendant forty-two head of steers, at $5.35 per hundred pounds (from the weight there was to be taken three per cent for shrinkage, and no more), and one hundred hogs, at six cents per pound, said stock to be delivered at Filley, Gage county, Nebraska, from May 1st to 15th, and correctly weighed and paid for, on which defendant advanced to plaintiff $1,000 (said contract is attached to petition marked exhibit A). That all of said stock was delivered April 21st, 1884, and received and weighed on Filley's scales; that defendant's scales, on which he weighed said stock, were grossly incorrect and wrong, and did not give the true weights of said stock within at least twenty-five per cent, making the weights that much too low; that said forty-two steers were falsely and fraudulently weighed, so that their combined weights, as given by defendant, only aggregated 48,645 pounds, when, in fact, they weighed twenty-five per cent more, and not less than 60,606 pounds, of which fact plaintiff was wholly ignorant; and that after shrinking the three per cent, defendant only allowed plaintiff for 47,185$\frac{65}{100}$ pounds, and paid plaintiff only $2,424.45 for said steers, whereas he should have been allowed and paid $3,155.52 therefor; that plaintiff was thereby wronged, cheated, and defrauded to the amount of $731.09; that said one hundred hogs were then by defendant falsely and fraudulently weighed upon said scales, so that their combined weight only aggregated 14,-335 pounds; that the hogs honestly weighed at least twenty-five per cent more, and not less than 17,918 pounds, of which fact plaintiff was then ignorant; that said Filley only allowed and paid plaintiff on account of said hogs $860.10, whereas he should have allowed him and paid therefor, $1,075.10, whereby plaintiff was further wronged, cheated and defrauded to the amount of $215.

"4th Paragraph.   And for a further cause of action, plaintiff alleges that during and immediately after the

weighing of said stock plaintiff was satisfied in his own
mind that the scales upon which the stock was weighed
were wrong, and the weights given fraudulent and unjust
to him; that the plaintiff then sold defendant nineteen
more hogs to be weighed at Filley, and one other hog, for
$20, all of which were delivered at Filley, April 22, 1884;
that while weighing said last hogs, plaintiff discovered that
said scales were grossly inaccurate and unjust; that said
hogs weighed several hundred pounds less on the end of
the scales where they stood while being weighed than on
the other end, and not enough by several hundred pounds
on either end, and that he had been grossly cheated and defrauded in weighing said stock the day before; and thereupon plaintiff insisted and demanded that said Filley again
weigh all the said stock he had received of plaintiff under said
contract, which said Filley refused to do, until he had first
extorted from the plaintiff an agreement to pay said Filley
$25 for reweighing the said stock, and to allow Filley to
shrink said steers one more per cent, said Filley then having all of said stock in his possession, to which proposition
the plaintiff, by force of circumstances, was compelled to do,
and did agree to, upon the express condition that said Filley
should correctly weigh all of said stock and make right
the wrong already done plaintiff, which Filley agreed to do;
that then Filley weighed forty-one head of said steers on
another pair of scales of insufficient capacity, and wholly
unfit for that purpose, and that the steers while being
weighed rested much of their weight off said scales and on
the frame surrounding them, and said frame rested wholly
upon the ground, and bore up and supported much of the
weight of said steers, so that their full and true weight
could not be, was not given; yet the forty-one steers weighed
fifteen pounds more than forty-two did the day before on
said cattle scales.   That said Filley then refused to weigh
the other or forty-second steer, that he had weighed and accepted the day before, but has ever since kept, and now

33

has said steer, which Filley claimed weighed 1,050 pounds, and absolutely refused to go on and weigh said one hundred hogs, or any part thereof, and broke and ended the contract by which he was to reweigh all of said stock. Yet, having the said stock, and the whole business in his hands, said Filley wrongfully kept and retained out of purchase price of the last hogs the said sum of $25, so by him exacted for reweighing all of said stock, and kept and retained the further sum of $32.50 as a further shrinkage of said steers, one additional per cent, making in all $57.50, so by said Filley, of Filley, Nebraska, wrongfully kept and retained out of monies justly due and belonging to the plaintiff, whereby plaintiff has been further wrongfully cheated and defrauded by said defendant in the further sum of $57.50.   Plaintiff asks judgment for $1,005.50.

The plaintiffs exhibit "A" is as follows:

"FILLEY, NEB., March 11th, 1884.

"Received of Elijah Filley $1,000, as part pay on forty-two head of fat steers that I am now feeding, and which I am to feed from the first to the fifteenth of May next. Said cattle to be driven from feed lot on day of delivery, and stand one hour, and then weighed at Filley, and shrunk three per cent, for which Filley agrees to pay $5.35 per hundred pounds. Also one hundred head of choice hogs I am now feeding—now with the cattle—which I am to deliver at the town of Filley, for which I am to have six cents per pound, to be delivered from first to fifteenth of May. Should Filley advance any more money, Billings to pay ten per cent for it.

"[Signed.]   WILBURN X BILLINGS.
                                                  His   Mark.
                                  ELIJAH FILLEY."

The defendant in his answer admits the making of the contract, and alleges that in pursuance thereof forty-two head of steers, and one hundred and four hogs, were delivered by the plaintiff to defendant, and that he has paid plaintiff for the same in full.

The reply is a general denial of new matter.

On the trial of the cause a verdict and judgment were rendered in favor of the defendant.

The plaintiff testified: "April 22d, defendant wanted the stock delivered next day. I delivered next day forty-two steers, and one hundred hogs. Filley weighed the stock. I could not read the writing. I was dissatisfied with the weight of the steers. There was a plank off the side, about as high as a steer's head. Alva Lamb stood there. When he punched the steers back to the other end of the scales I saw the beam run up. I said: 'Filley, your scales are not right.' He said, 'Ah! it's the wind.' I said: 'The wind don't make two or three thousand pounds difference in the scales.' Every time the cattle crowded to the south side the beam would go up. I remarked this several times to him. He said he knew they were right because he sold on them. I told him: 'They are not right, and I think you know it.' Weighed a bull after steers. I knew scales were not right from weight of bull, but could not get Filley to examine them. He stuck to it that they were right, and I was not a judge of scales. We then weighed the hogs. That evening I sold Filley twenty other fat hogs, nineteen at five cents per pound, and one for $20, and took them up next day. Alva Lamb, Miller, and Bill Grady were with me. Filley was not there when we got there. His weigher, Boughman, weighed first eleven hogs, then drove on the other eight. He weighed them. I asked him to weigh them on south end of scales. There they weighed two hundred fifty-five pounds more than on north end. This was on same scales the cattle and hogs were weighed the day before. Mr. Filley then came down. I told him there was something wrong with his scales, and was yesterday, and now I am going to convince you. He said something had got between the sill and the frame, and the scales were all right. I said: 'Let us find what it is.' He went to one end of frame and sawed between frame and a piece of studding that had worked against it. Got that off clean. He then weighed the hogs on one end and then on the other end of the scales, and they weighed just the same as when Boughman weighed them. We then took those eight hogs on to his office scales, and they weighed there four hundred eighty pounds more than they did on one end of cattle scales. I then told him I wanted him to weigh the stock all over. He said he could not do it, and wouldn't do it. He said he would not weigh them over but would give me $225 to say no more about it. I told him I wanted the weight of the stock and that was all I did want—agreeable to contract. I told him I wanted him to weigh them over. He said he would not. He was not fixed to—had no other stock scales. I told him I wanted them weighed over. And he would not unless I shrunk the steers one per cent and gave him $25—that would make four per cent shrinkage. He said if I would give $25 and shrink one per cent he would weigh the stock over and weigh them right. I said rather than get in trouble I'd rather shrink one per cent and give $25 and weigh them over. He said he would. He put frame that was around cattle scales around his wagon scales and spiked frame to studding, and here he weighed all the cattle but one steer. There was something the matter with the one. He weighed forty-one steers. Then he did not weigh the hogs over. He was to weigh the stock all over—the hogs and cattle. He took $50 out of the hogs I took up the next day, for weighing over and shrinkage of the steers. He paid me some money on the first lot of stock the first day—that was on basis of first weights. He has never settled in any other way. The last I saw of the forty-second steer he was at Filley's. He accepted him the first day and threw him out the second day.

"CROSS-EXAMINATION.

"I cannot read nor write. I had a man taking the weights. He and Filley figured together. It was Charley

Wininger, Alva Lamb and John Miller. Miller was then working for me. I think they all agreed on their figures the first day. I was paid according to their figures and weights.

Q. 154. Now the agreement was, you say, between you, that you would weigh the stock over again and allow Filley, or pay him, $25?

A. Yes.

Q. 155. And four per cent shrinkage?

A. Yes.

Q. 156. You wanted him to weigh the hogs, did you?

A. I did. I don't think there was anything said about the hogs until we got done weighing the cattle. 'I told him I wanted the hogs weighed, that was my contract.' I wanted him to weigh them. Don't know that I asked him to weigh them, because I saw it was not worth while, seeing he would cheat me out of them. I did not want them weighed the way he weighed the cattle.

Q. 165. Is it not a fact that after you weighed the cattle you went in and settled up the whole business?

A. Never settled a thing; he took $50 out of last hogs I took in, and he was to give me $20 for a black sow, and agreeably they only figured nineteen hogs, and the black sow was never figured in.

Defendant objected and asked to have this answer stricken out.

Overruled. Defendant excepted.

Q. 176. He did not pay for the black sow and took out $25 and one per cent shrinkage?

A. Yes. Second day Filley did not tell me there was something wrong with scales, that they did not balance. I saw him clean them off with the saw and balance them. Cannot tell how many dollars I got the second day; got what the nineteen hogs came to, is my opinion, besides what they took out in one per cent weighing, and $25 for weighing the cattle over. That is what I lacked of getting what the nineteen hogs came to. The steer not weighed the second day was a spotted three-year-old. He got down on scales the first day. Don't think I had any agreement with Filley about the steer, something wrong with him. He drove him into the yard. Think there was something said about my taking the steer back if he did not get well, the second day.

Q. 235. What was done about the settlement? Did you settle up on those new figures, you, and Brown, and Wininger and Miller?

A. Never had any settlement, only he took so much out of the hogs and I took the balance and went home.

Q. 256. The balance he paid?

A. The balance all paid, only the steer. He wanted I should take the steer home.

Q. 257. You agreed to take him?

A. I don't know whether I did or not. I don't know whatever became of the black hog. Charles Wininger helped drive steers up Filley's; aggregated weight first day, forty-two steers, 48,645 pounds. Said hogs weighed first day, aggregate weight, 14,335."

John I. Parker testified: "Am a millwright and carpenter. He removed these cattle scales after this stock was weighed. Found on side the cattle were driven in it was banked up with clay and there was a block under that to support the top of the frame, and that block had pressed against the adjustable frame and caused some friction. That is all I found. The block pressed against the platform. It was under the stationary platform that supports the scales."

Samuel Cowan testified: "I'm a carpenter. Parker called my attention to the block he spoke of. He showed me what was the matter with the scales."

The defendant testified: "The hogs and cattle were delivered April 21, 1884. We balanced the scales in the first place. They were correct. I did the balancing. I weighed in different drafts. After last steer went on scales, balanced them and found fifty-five pounds of mud on the scales. Took one-half of fifty-five pounds for each draft, making twenty-seven and one-half pounds for each draft. We then weighed the hogs. Scales were all right at this time. Billings spoke once or twice to know if the scales were correct. I told him they were. He thought they did not weigh just exactly right each time. I think he was weighed a couple of times; my recollection is that there were about five pounds difference on the two weights. I accounted for it that it was the difference in the wind, or something made the difference, or a break in the scales. We figured the hogs at $6 a hundred; had figured the cattle already. We then settled up, and I finished paying him. No difference in the figures. No dispute as to figures. No objection made by Billings. One steer fell down near Billing's yard before we started. At my place he fell down on the scales. I told Billings, 'We will figure them up, and if he gets better I will pay for him. If he don't, you will take him back.' He said, 'All right.'

Q. 1,043. Was he included in the figures you paid him?

A. Yes, in this settlement. The next day, right after this settlement, I bought twenty hogs of Billings; one for $20—it was spotted—the other nineteen was to be $5.50 per hundred. While at dinner, Boughman, the man who weighs for me, came in and told me there was something wrong with the scales; I would have to go up. I went out, took hold of the beam to weigh the hogs, and I saw at once the scales were out of whack—something the matter with them. I weighed the hogs on one end of the scales; they weighed about 1,850 pounds. On the other end they weighed 2,000 and something. Billings was saying they were out of fix the day before, and I had beat him over $1,000 on the stock the day before. I told them to take the eight hogs on the scales—the office scales are

grain scales—and weigh them on the office scales. Billings
and myself kept them together and went to the office scales
and weighed these eight hogs there, and found they weighed
over 2,300. Billings was in a sweat about it; thought he
had been beaten that much the day before. I was in a
sweat about it. We then weighed the twenty hogs on
office scales; then we weighed the one hog we lumped off,
and deducted its weight. This left 3,852 pounds I was to
pay for, which came to $211.86. This did not include the
black sow. I added to that $20 for her, making $231.86
for the twenty hogs, coming to him. Billings was then
wanting to weigh the stock over I had bought the day before, claiming I beat him $1,000. I claimed all the time
I had not beat him $1,000; there was not stock enough to
beat him $1,000. He then testifies to how he figured
the matter, if the scales were the same the day before, and
made about $225. Billings would not take that, and
wanted to weigh over. I said 'I will weigh over if you
can get at it so as to make a fair shrinkage and run the
cattle around.' He asked what I thought was right. I
told him I would not have a bunch of cattle out of the yard
for less than $25. I said, 'Give me $25 and shrinkage of
cattle four per cent.' He says, 'I will do it.' So we went
at it.

Q. 1,054. What was the reason of giving that shrinkage of one per cent more?

A. That would offset the drive of four miles the day
before.

Q. Anything for feeding?

A. For the reason the cattle were filled up.

Q. 1,061. What was said about whether the hogs—
what was said about them?

A. The talk was about the cattle principally. He
spoke about weighing the hogs over. I said 'I will
weigh the stock over; you pick out the hogs if you
can get into the lot and sort them out, and we will weigh

them over.' I had about three hundred hogs in the yard. He then describes the manner of weighing; took rack off cattle scales and set them around office scales the best we could set them around the scales. They were nailed up, did not rest on scales, but on frame-work around the scales. There was one steer we did not weigh; he had a fit; the same one that tumbled over before. I said he was not right and I would not take him. He said 'All right, I will take him and work him off on the butchers.' Total gross weight of the forty-one steers was 48,660 pounds. After deducting net weight was 46,714 pounds. I figured this amount at $5.35 a hundred, then deducted $25 for reweighing the cattle, leaving a balance they came to of $2,474.19. I said 'Now then we will weigh the hogs over.' He said he was satisfied it was weighed correct. I then took out $10.75 out of $231.86 for twenty hogs, and gave check for $221.11. He was to pay me back the $10.75 and take the crazy steer home. He seemed satisfied, any more than this, his cattle did not weigh as heavy as he expected. He said he was satisfied.

CROSS-EXAMINATION.

Boughman is a fair weigher and pretty accurate at balancing the scales. If he had weighed a draft of hogs on these scales and they were in the condition I described when I came, I think he would have discovered it; think any man would. We call it four miles the stock was driven. The forty-one we weighed the second day weighed forty-one pounds more than the forty-two. We guessed the one we did not weigh at 1,000 pounds.

Q. 1,188. By the way, tell us what became of that steer? Where he is?

A. I don't know.

Q. 1,189. What did you do with him?

A. I kept him there in the lot waiting for Billings to take him away.

Q. 1,190. What became of him and what did you finally do with him? Is he in your lot yet?

A. I think not.

Q. 1,191. What did you do with him, Elijah?

A. I didn't do anything with him.

Q. 1,192. Haven't you sold him or sent him away to market, shipped him to market?

A. I told some parties there was a steer there that was not mine, and I did not care what became of him. I sold the forty-one steers to Wagner, of Chicago. I said to Billings on the 19th of May, 'You were going to take him away?' He said he wouldn't do it; said, 'You have bought the steer, you will keep him.' He went home without him. I says to the Chicago party, 'Go look at that steer, and if he is of any account you take him along;' and he went up and looked at the steer, and I think shipped him with his cattle.

Q. 1,213. You told Billings this would disturb the cattle a good deal to get them up and weigh them again, didn't you?

A. Yes. Here he is asked to explain, and testified : 'I don't think they would lose in weight so much, but it would be a damage to the cattle.'

Q. 1,216. They would lose in flesh?

A. Yes, in one sense of the word, I think they would.

Q. 1,221. Wear off $25 worth of flesh to drive them ten or fifteen rods on the scales and back again?

A. Think ten pounds, eight or ten pounds off from a steer.

Q. 1,222. You told Billings you would weigh them over if he would pay you $25?

A. I told him it would be worth $25 to weigh them over.

Q. 1,223. And then he must shrink them how much?

A. One per cent additional.

Q. 1,225. You were satisfied your scales were wrong?

A.   I was satisfied the scales were wrong at this time.

Q. 1,226.   But you would not weigh them over unless he allowed you $25 and shrunk them four per cent?

A.   As soon as I made the proposition he took me up. I had paid him for the stock the day before, and had the stock in my hands.   I think Wilks Gale bought hogs with me, you might say.

Q. 1,271.   Do you remember about telling him about five years ago, and while engaged in business, that you could not make money in the business and give honest and good weights?

Objected to as immaterial, irrelevant, incompetent and too remote.

Sustained.   Exception noted.

Q.   Did you offer Billings $225 to settle, after you discovered this difficulty?

A.   I think not.   I have heard the witnesses testify to that.   I think they are mistaken."

There is considerable other testimony in corroboration of the plaintiff to which it is unnecessary to refer.   It will be observed that the defendant does not deny the essential facts testified to by the plaintiff, that the scales would not weigh correctly; in fact he corroborates the plaintiff's testimony that the scales were incorrect, that forty-one steers weighed more on the office scales than forty-two had done the day before on the other scales; he also corroborates the plaintiff that he agreed to pay the defendant $25 to reweigh the stock delivered the day previous, and that he refused to reweigh the hogs.   His excuse is that the plaintiff expressed himself as satisfied with the weights the day before, and therefore stated that he did not desire to have the hogs reweighed; this statement is not very probable when we consider that the actual weight of the cattle was considerable more than the weights as given the day previous. A clear preponderance of the testimony tends to show that the scales, on which the forty-two head of cattle and the one hundred and four hogs were weighed, were incorrect, and that the incorrect weights were in favor of the defendant, and that thereby the plaintiff sustained damages. If the scales were so arranged on purpose, it was a gross fraud on the plaintiff, and if accidental, the plaintiff should not be permitted to sustain loss by the mistake.

The defendant was to pay the plaintiff $5.35 per hundred for the steers, and six dollars per hundred for the hogs. These prices were for the actual weight of the stock so delivered, and when it was found that the scales were incorrect the plaintiff was entitled to have the stock weighed ·correctly, and this without payment of any consideration. Until the stock had been weighed correctly it had not, so far as the rights of the seller were concerned, been weighed—that is, the fraudulent or incorrect weighing of the stock was not a weighing within the meaning of the contract. The $25, therefore, which the plaintiff agreed to pay the defendant was a mere gratuitous promise, and for which he received no consideration.

2.   Even had the promise been supported by a sufficient consideration, still unless the plaintiff waived the reweighing of the hogs the defendant failed to perform his· part, and therefore is not entitled to recover.

3.   As to the forty-second steer.the defendant testifies: "I says to the Chicago party, 'Go look at that steer, and if he is of any account take him along,' and he went up and looked at the steer, and I think shipped him with his cattle."

This will make him liable for the value of the steer. This steer he purchased with the others, and received him the day the cattle were delivered, but on the second day, when the cattle were reweighed, he attempted to throw him back on the plaintiff. The steer, however, was left in the defendant's possession, and by him turned over to the parties who purchased the other steers, whether by gift or sale is immaterial to the plaintiff. The assumption of ownership by the defendant ratified the previous contract and made him liable to the plaintiff for the contract price of the steer.

4. A large number of instructions were given in the case to which no exceptions were taken, therefore they cannot be reviewed by this court. The judgment of the district court is reversed, and the cause remanded for further proceedings.

REVERSED AND REMANDED.

THE other judges concur.

BELL BROTHERS, PLAINTIFFS IN ERROR, v. WHITE LAKE LUMBER COMPANY, DEFENDANT IN ERROR.

1. **Justice of Peace**: JUDGMENT: PRESUMPTION. Where in an action tried before a justice of the peace no bill of particulars is set out in the record, but there is a finding of the justice that "there is due and owing from defendant to plaintiff upon the account sued upon the sum of fifty-two dollars and seventy-seven cents, with interest from June 1st, 1885," it will be presumed that the account was before the justice when he rendered judgment.

2. **Jurisdiction**: TECHNICAL OBJECTIONS NOT CONSIDERED. Where a party appears in court and objects by motion to the jurisdiction of the court over his person, he must state specifically the grounds of objection. Technical objections to the jurisdiction of the court, over the person of the defendant, will be unavailing unless they are specific.

3. **Justice of Peace**: MOTION TO DISMISS: JUDGMENT. A party who appears before a justice of the peace and moves to dismiss the action, which motion was afterwards overruled, and the party not desiring to appear further, judgment was rendered against him, cannot afterwards have the judgment set aside upon his offering to confess judgment for costs.

4. ———: APPEAL: UNDERTAKING. Where an undertaking for an appeal is filed with the justice more than ten days after the rendition of the judgment, it is not error for him to refuse to approve the same.

5. **Error Must Affirmatively** appear in the record and will not be presumed.

ERROR to the district court for Franklin county. Tried below before GASLIN, J.

A. E. Fletcher, for plaintiffs in error.

Sheppard & Black, for defendant in error.

MAXWELL, CH. J.

This action was originally commenced before a justice of the peace in Franklin county by the White Lake Lumber Company against Bell Bros., and judgment rendered in favor of said lumber company. Bell Bros. then took the case on error to the district court where the judgment of the justice was affirmed. The cause is now brought into this court on petition in error.

The attorneys for the defendant in error now move to dismiss the proceedings in error in this court for the following reasons:

First. No abstract of the record of this case has been, printed and filed in this court by the plaintiffs in error.

Second. No objections were made or exceptions taken in the court below, of the errors complained of here.

Third. It does not appear by the record in this case that the attention of the court below was directed, by the plaintiff in error, to the rulings of the court objected to here.

The motion is evidently made under a misapprehension of the facts of the case, as there is a printed abstract of the case on file, and certain exceptions were taken to the rulings of the justice, and the alleged errors were specifically assigned in the district court. The motion is therefore overruled.

The cause was originally commenced before one Isaac Black, a justice of the peace of Franklin county, and upon a motion for change of venue, it was transferred to one

John Earson, and by him was set for hearing on the 20th day of June, 1885, at 10 o'clock A.M.

At the time stated the attorney for Bell Bros. appeared and filed a motion as follows:

"Comes now the defendant above named, by its attorney, reserving the privilege of appearing for the purpose of this motion only, and moves the court to dismiss this cause of action for the following reasons, to-wit:

"First. The court has not obtained jurisdiction over the person of the defendant.

"Second. The court has not jurisdiction over the subject matter of said cause of action."

The motion was overruled, and Bell Bros. not desiring to answer, their default was taken, and judgment entered against them for $52.77, and costs of suit.

Five days afterward the attorney for Bell Bros. filed a motion to set aside the default and offered to confess judgment for costs up to that time. This was taken up and overruled on the 13th of July, 1885. On the 6th of July, 1885, Bell Bros. filed their undertaking for an appeal with the justice, which he refused to approve, because not filed within the time required by law.

The errors assigned in the district court were the following:

"The court erred in rendering judgment in said cause for any amount whatever.

"The court erred in overruling plaintiffs' motion to dismiss said cause.

"The court erred in overruling motion to set aside judgment by default rendered in said cause filed by plaintiff in error.

"The court erred in refusing to approve the bond for appeal, filed by plaintiff in error, asking that an appeal be allowed to the district court.

"The court erred in rendering judgment against Joseph Bell and Rob't Bell."

No copy of the bill of particulars is set out in the record or abstract, but that there was such a bill there is no doubt, as the justice finds "That there is due and owing from defendant to plaintiff, upon the account sued upon, the sum of fifty-two dollars and seventy-seven cents, with interest from June 1st, 1885." That there was evidence to support this finding will be presumed, as the evidence is not preserved in the record.

The second objection is untenable. A party who objects by motion to the jurisdiction of the court over his person must state specifically the reasons for the objection. He who raises an objection upon technical grounds must himself be technically correct; that is, the cause of objection must be distinctly pointed out, otherwise the motion should be overruled; so with the objection that the court has not jurisdiction over the subject matter, although usually this will appear from the statement of the cause of action. So far as this record discloses, the justice had jurisdiction both over the person of the defendant and the subject matter of the action. There was no error, therefore, in overruling the motion to dismiss.

3.   There was no error in overruling the motion to set aside the judgment by default. Bell Bros. were present by attorney when the judgment was rendered, and so far as appears had an opportunity to make a defense if they so desired. Having failed to do so, they could not afterwards move to set aside the default.

4.   The justice properly refused to approve the undertaking for an appeal. The statute requires such undertaking to be filed "within ten days from the rendition of judgment." The justice has no discretion in the matter, and it is his duty to refuse to approve such undertaking, unless filed within the ten days.

5.   The subject-matter of the action was upon an account, the nature of which is not set out, and as error

It is apparent that justice has been done. It is not the
policy of the law to encourage parties to file motions and
dilatory pleas in an action, which do not affect the merits
of the case; such pleas are usually intended for delay, and
not as a means of obtaining justice for the parties.

There is no error in the record, and the judgment of the
court below is affirmed.

JUDGMENT AFFIRMED.

THE other judges concur.

JOHN W. KERN, PLAINTIFF IN ERROR, V. AUGUSTUS
KLOKE ET AL., DEFENDANTS IN ERROR.

1. **Statute of Limitations:** DAMAGES FOR BREACH OF WAR-
RANTY. An action for damages, for the breach of the covenants
of warranty contained in a deed conveying land, is an action
upon a specialty, within the meaning of the 10th section of the
Code of Civil Procedure, and may be brought at any time within
five years after the cause of action shall have accrued.

2. ———— : ————. Such action may be maintained by the direct
covenantee irrespective of the question whether the covenant
upon which it is brought would run with the land.

ERROR to the district court for Cuming county. Tried
below before CRAWFORD, J.

T. M. Franse, for plaintiff in error.

M. McLaughlin, for defendants in error.

COBB, J.

The plaintiff commenced his action in the district court,
filing the following petition:

34

must affirmatively appear to justify this court in reversing a judgment, it will not be presumed.

"1.   The plaintiff complains of the defendant for that
on the 28th day of May, A.D. 1879, the defendant in consideration of the sum of $250.00, then paid, delivered to
plaintiff a warranty deed, duly executed, and thereby sold
and conveyed to plaintiff the following described land, viz.:
The north-west quarter of section twenty, township twenty-
three north, of range four east, of the sixth principal
meridian, containing one hundred and sixty acres, in Cuming county, Nebraska.

"2.   By said deed defendants covenanted as follows,
to-wit: 'And we, the said Augusta Kloke and Herman
Kloke, do hereby covenant with the said John W. Kern,
and his heirs and assigns, that we are lawfully seized of
said premises; that they are free from encumbrance; that
we have good right and lawful authority to sell the same,
and we do hereby covenant to warrant and defend the title
to said premises against the lawful claims of all persons
whomsoever.'

"3.   That afterwards, viz., on the 27th day of November, 1880, your plaintiff, by warranty deed, conveyed said
premises to one J. T. Hart, in consideration of the sum of
$250.00, by him in hand paid; that on or about the 21st
day of July, 1883, one Nathaniel Gordon commenced an
action in the district court of Cuming county, Nebraska,
to quiet the title of said premises against the grantee of
your plaintiff, J. T. Hart, and on the 8th day of March,
1884, recovered the judgment canceling the defendant's,
J. T. Hart, claim of title.

"4.   That on or about the 24th day of March, 1884,
the plaintiff satisfied the claims of his grantee, J. T. Hart,
on the warranty contained in his deed to said J. T. Hart
in full, as per the following receipt:

"WEST POINT, NEB., March 24th, 1884.

"Received of John W. Kern the following sums, viz:

Amount of purchase money.............................$250 00
Interest on same from May 28th, 1879.............. 123 00
Taxes paid on same.................................... 30 00
Costs and expenses in defending title to lands...... 150 00
Value of said lands.................................... 500 00

$1053 00

in full of all demands for a breach of warranty in a deed
given by said John W. Kern to me on the north-west
quarter of section twenty-three north, of range four, in
Cuming county, Nebraska, having been evicted by paramount title after due course of law.

"J. T. HART.

"5. At the date of the execution and delivery of said
deed by defendants to plaintiff, said defendants did not
have a good and sufficient title to said premises, but, on the
contrary, the paramount right and title to the same was in
one Nathaniel Gordon, who has ousted and dispossessed
and evicted J. T. Hart, the grantee of plaintiff, therefrom,
by due course of law.

"6. The defendant, J. T. Hart, gave due notice to said
plaintiff of the filing and pendency of the action against
him immediately after the commencement thereof; that
plaintiff has sustained damages by reason of the premises,
the sum of $1,053.00.

"Wherefore plaintiff prays judgment in his favor and
against the defendant in the sum of $1,053.00, and costs
of suit."

To which petition defendants presented the following
demurrer:

" And now comes the defendants and demur to the petition of the plaintiff in the above action, and say : That
the petition does not state facts sufficient to constitute a
cause of action against said defendants, or either of them.

"2. The plaintiff's said petition shows upon its face that the plaintiff's cause of action is barred by the statute of limitations."

The demurrer presents two questions:

1. Do the facts alleged in the petition, if proved, under the law, entitle the plaintiff to a judgment?

2. . Is the plaintiff's right of action barred by the statute of limitations?

The second question comes first in natural order, and will be first considered.

Section 10, of the Code of Civil Procedure, is in the the following words:

"Sec. 10. Within five years, an action upon a specialty, or any agreement, contract, or promise in writing, or a foreign judgment."

This action is brought on a deed. A deed is one of the instruments embraced within the meaning of the word "specialty," as used in the section quoted, and is therefore within the terms of the statute. The deed was delivered according to the allegations of the petition, on the 28th day of May, 1879. The action was commenced in the district court, on the 2d day of April, 1884, somewhat less than five years after the delivery of the deed. It therefore becomes unnecessary to discuss or decide the question argued by counsel for plaintiff, as to whether the statute, in such cases, commences to run at the date of the delivery of the deed, or at the date of the breach of its covenants.

Upon the first point, counsel, in support of the demurrer, in the first place cites an authority to the effect that this being an action for the breach of a covenant of seizin, and the measure of damages being the amount of the consideration paid by the covenantee to the covenantor, and lawful interest thereon, if there was no consideration there could be no damage. He then says, "subsequent facts appearing in the petition lead us strongly to believe that no consideration, in fact, ever passed between the plaintiff and the defendant for this conveyance." By reference to the petition it will be seen that the allegation of the payment of the consideration of two hundred and fifty dollars for the land and the warranty of title thereto is as direct and positive as is required by our liberal system of pleading. Whether the allegation is true as a matter of fact, is a question which does not arise upon the consideration of a demurrer.

In the case of *Real v. Hollister*, 20 Neb., 112, the suit was brought, not by the covenantee of the defendants, but by a subsequent purchaser under covenants from him. It appeared affirmatively by the pleadings that the defendants had no title in the land conveyed, and it did not appear that they had actual possession. We therefore held in that case that "the only covenant contained in the deed of plaintiffs in error (defendants) which can be deemed available to the defendant in error (plaintiff) is that contained in the following words 'they do hereby covenant to warrant and defend the title to said premises against the lawful claims of all persons whomsoever.'", Which words we held to be equivalent to a covenant for quiet enjoyment, and that in order to maintain an action for a breach of that covenant it was necessary to both allege and prove that the covenantee or those claiming under him have "been actually turned out of the premises by legal process based upon a title, or some right existing in another at the date of the covenant, or that such outsta n ling title having been asserted he has yielded to it and surrendered the possession thereto." In that case, as in this, there was a covenant of scizin in the deed, but we held that it was unavailable to the plaintiff, because the defendants having no title, their covenant of seizin did not run with the land into and through his immediate grantor. But in the case at bar, the covenant of seizin, under which the plaintiff claims, is made directly and personally to him, and hence the question as to whether it ran with the land upon his conveying it to

another, does not arise.   So far as I am able to see, or as is
developed by the briefs and the authorities cited, the petition states a case upon which the plaintiff can recover.
What may be the amount of such recovery, or as to the
measure of damages, cannot be here discussed.

The judgment of the district court is reversed, the demurrer overruled, and the cause remanded for further proceedings in accordance with law.

REVERSED AND REMANDED.

THE other judges concur.

E. M. BISBEE, JOHN AUSTIN, WALTER H. CLARK, AND
N. H. VANDERBILT, PLAINTIFFS IN ERROR, V. ISAAC
HENRY GLEASON, DEFENDANT IN ERROR.

1. **Guardian and Ward:** ACTION ON GUARDIAN'S BOND.   A
    right of action on a guardian's bond to recover the amount re-
    maining in the hands of the guardian first accrues to the ward
    when such amount is ascertained by the county court on the
    settlement of the guardian's final account. *Ball v. LaClair*, 17
    Neb., 39.

2. ———: ACCOUNTS OF GUARDIAN: DUTIES OF COUNTY COURT.
    Where a guardian is cited by the county court to appear and
    settle his accounts upon the termination of his trust, and he re-
    fuses to appear in answer to such citation, it is the duty of the
    county court to ascertain and declare the condition of the ac-
    counts in his absence and charge him with the money and prop-
    erty in his hands, after allowing all just credits; and for the
    purpose of such settlement the jurisdiction of the county court
    is exclusive.

ERROR to the district court for Dixon county.   Tried
below before CRAWFORD, J.

W. E. Gantt, for plaintiffs in error.

Barnes Bros., for defendant in error.

REESE, J.

This action was commenced in the district court by defendant in error, in which he sought to recover a judgment for $1,900, and interest, against E. M. Bisbee, as principal, and the other defendants in the action, as sureties, upon a guardian's bond, executed by them in favor of defendant in error, as the ward of said Bisbee. Plaintiffs in error demurred to the petition upon the ground that it did not state facts sufficient to state a cause of action. The demurrer was overruled. Plaintiffs in error refused to answer, and judgment was rendered against them for $2,615.05, the amount found due upon the bond. The error assigned is that the district court erred in overruling the demurrer.

For the purpose of presenting the question involved we copy the petition at length. It is as follows. For cause of action it is alleged:

"1st. That on or about the fifth day of July, 1880, the said E. M. Bisbee, one of the defendants, was duly appointed by the county court of Dixon county, Nebraska, guardian of the estate of this plaintiff, to-wit: Isaac Henry Gleason, who was at that time a minor, of the age of sixteen years, residing in said county and state.

"That on said date, said E. M. Bisbee, together with John Austin, Walter H. Clark, and W. H. Vanderbilt, executed and delivered to the county judge of said county of Dixon, in the state of Nebraska, the following obligation in writing:

"STATE OF NEBRASKA, ⎱ ss.
    Dixon County, ⎰

"Know all men by these presents:

"That we, E. M. Bisbee and John Austin, Walter H.

Clark, and W. H. Vanderbilt, as sureties, all of said county and state, are held and firmly bound unto the state of Nebraska, and its assigns, in the sum of three thousand ($3,-000) dollars, to be paid to the said state of Nebraska, or its assigns; to which payment well and truly to be made we hereby bind ourselves, our and each of our heirs, executors, and administrators, jointly, severally, and firmly by these presents.

"Dated at Ponca, in the said county and state, this 14th day of July, 1880.

"WHEREAS, The above bounden E. M. Bisbee has been appointed by the probate court of said county, guardian of the estate of Isaac Henry Gleason, a minor, of the age of sixteen years, and a resident of Dixon county, Nebraska, till he arrives at the age of majority:

. 'Now, the condition of the above obligation is such that if the said E. M. Bisbee, as such guardian as aforesaid, shall make and return to the probate court aforesaid, within three months, a true and perfect inventory of all the real and personal estate of the said Isaac Henry Gleason that shall come to his possession or knowledge, and shall dispose of and manage all such estate and effects of the said minor that may come into his hands according to law, and for the best interest of the said minor, and faithfully discharge his trust as such guardian, and shall make an account, on oath, of the property in his hands, including the proceeds of all real estate which may be sold by him, and of the management and disposition of such property within one year after his appointment as such guardian, and at such other times as the court shall direct, and shall, at the expiration of his trust, settle all of his accounts with the court, or with the said Isaac Henry Gleason aforesaid, or his legal representatives, and pay over and deliver all the estate and effects remaining in his hands, or due from him on such settlement to the person or persons who shall be lawfully entitled thereto, then the above obligations to be

null and void, otherwise to be and remain in full force and
effect.

E. M. BISBEE.

"Signed and delivered in the   JOHN AUSTIN.
    presence of R. H. Knapp.   WALTER H. CLARK.

W. H. VANDERBILT.

"2d.   That said instrument was duly approved by the
county judge of said county, and said E. M. Bisbee thereupon entered upon the duties of said guardianship, and
collected a large amount of money belonging to said estate,
and to said minor, to-wit, the sum of $1,900.04; that all
of said money came into the hands of said E. M. Bisbee,
guardian as aforesaid, on or before the 28th day of April,
1881, and that all thereof still remains in the hands of said
E. M. Bisbee, guardian as aforesaid.

"3d.   That on or about the first day of January, A.D.
1886, said plaintiff demanded a settlement of the said matters of his said estate, of the said E. M. Bisbee, and the
said E. M. Bisbee has failed, and refused, and neglected to
settle his said business as such guardian of said estate.
That on the 16th day of March, A.D. 1886, the county
court of said county of Dixon duly issued its citation to
said E. M. Bisbee to appear before said court forthwith to
report his doings as such guardian, and to settle said business and pay over the said money to plaintiff, as required
by law and the terms of said bond; which citation was
duly served upon the said defendant Bisbee, and yet the
said defendant has failed, neglected, and refused so to do.
That said E. M. Bisbee has converted said money to his
own use, and refuses, fails, and neglects to settle and account for said money and pay the same to the plaintiff.

"That said E. M. Bisbee, guardian as aforesaid, has not
paid any debts, or incurred or paid any expenses whatever,
for or on account of said estate of said plaintiff.

"4th.   The plaintiff further states that he is of lawful
age and entitled to the full use and control of his said
estate.

"5th.   That there is due the plaintiff from said defendants, on said bond, the sum of $1,900.04, with interest on
the same, at the rate of ten per cent per annum, from the
28th day of April, A.D. 1881.

"The plaintiff therefore prays judgment against said defendants for the sum of $1,900.04, and interest thereon
from the 28th day of April, 1881, and costs of suit."

It will be seen that the petition contains no averment
that any settlement with the guardian had ever been made
by the county court, nor that any sum had ever been found
due plaintiff by that tribunal.

Substantially the same question presented here was before this court in *Ball v. LaClair*, 17 Neb., 39, and it was
there held that a right of action upon a guardian's bond
first accrues to the ward when the amount remaining in the
hands of the guardian is ascertained by the county court
on the final settlement of the guardian's account.

This, we think, correctly states the law.   Section 9, of
chapter 34, of the Compiled Statutes of 1885, provides
that "Every such guardian shall give a bond, with surety
or sureties, to the judge of probate, in such sum as the court
shall order, with condition as follows: *   *   *   *

"Fourth.   At the expiration of his trust, to settle his
accounts with the court, or with the ward, or his legal representatives, and to pay over and deliver all the estate and
effects remaining in his hands, or due from him on such settlement, to the person or persons lawfully entitled thereto."

We need not here copy the provisions of the constitution
and statutes of the state, which confer exclusive jurisdiction upon the county courts in all matters relating to the
settlement of the accounts of guardians, as they are fully
set out in the opinion of the court, in *Ball v. LaClair*,
written by the then chief justice, Cobb; and in so far as
that decision is applicable to the case at bar we shall be
content with it as fully stating the law and meeting all the
requirements of the case.   But it is claimed that since it is

alleged in the petition in this case, that plaintiff in error, Bisbee, was cited to a settlement by the county judge, and refused to obey the citation, this case is brought directly within the language of the opinion in *Ball v. LaClair*, wherein the writer thereof says that the liability of a guardian "to a suit in a court of law for the balance due her wards on her guardianship account, and certainly the liability of her sureties would arise only upon her refusal or failure to obey some order of the county court in that behalf." We do not so understand the meaning of the language referred to. To the mind of the writer the meaning clearly is, that the county court had jurisdiction to cite . the guardian to a settlement, and when such settlement was made to order such guardian "to pay into court, or to . pay over to her late wards such sum as should be found due them upon such settlement." Or, in other words, if either order was made and not complied with, the action could be maintained, and not otherwise.

Neither do we think that the fourth clause above quoted from section nine, of chapter thirty-four, can be so construed as to confer the right to sue without such settlement having first been made. Substantially the same language occurs in the statutes of California, and in *Allen v. Tiffany*, 53 Cal., 16, it was held that no action could be maintained until after the settlement was made. In the opinion it is said: "Within a reasonable time after the ward arrives at full age the statute provides that the guardian may settle his accounts with the ward; but, considering the previous relations of the parties, it is not to be supposed that it was the intention that such settlement should of itself constitute a discharge, or that it should not be subject to the approval or disapproval of the probate judge prior to the discharge by him. The probate judge has the exclusive jurisdiction to determine the state of accounts between the guardian and ward. The ward may agree upon a settlement with his guardian, subject to the approval of the probate judge, or may apply for a citation compelling the guardian to settle his accounts before the probate judge. But to hold that prior to such accounting before the probate judge, or to his order at proving the settlement *in pais*, the ward may bring suit in the district court for a supposed balance, would destroy the symmetry and efficiency of the system furnished by our law for the appointment and conduct of guardians of infants."

To the same effect see also *Newton v. Hammond*, 38 O. S., 430, and cases there cited.

But it is said that the county court cited plaintiff in error, Bisbee, to appear and settle his accounts, and that he ignored the citation, and no settlement could be made, and that for that reason this action should be maintained. We can see no sufficient reason for such conclusion. As we have seen, the county court not only has the authority to require settlements to be made, but it has exclusive jurisdiction in such matters. · It is true that a guardian may ignore the citation to settle, but it is equally true that the county court has full power to examine into his accounts and charge him with a balance, after such citation, in his absence as in his presence.

It also has all the facilities that any court has for bringing evidence before it, and can just as well settle the accounts of a guardian upon default as can the district court. It has the same power to compel the attendance of witnesses as the district court, and its powers in that behalf are just as extensive. But the provision of the statute giving the exclusive jurisdiction to the county court must be decisive of the whole question, without reference to any other considerations.

The judgment of the district court is therefore reversed, the demurrer sustained, and the cause is remanded for further proceedings.

REVERSED AND REMANDED.

THE other judges concur.

JOHN MANN, PLAINTIFF IN ERROR, V. BARNABAS WEL-
TON, DEFENDANT IN ERROR.

1. **Exemption.** The exemption of five hundred dollars in personal property in favor of a judgment debtor, provided by section 521 of the civil code, in lieu of a homestead, must depend
upon the filing of the inventory as provided by section 522
of the civil code, and the selection of property claimed by the
debtor to be exempt.

2. ———: REPLEVIN. Replevin cannot be maintained against an
officer for property levied upon and claimed to be exempt under
said section until after the inventory is filed and the appraisement and selection are made.

3. **New Trial.** A new trial will not be granted where it appears
as matter of law that upon the conceded facts the result must
be the same.

ERROR to the district court for Holt county. Tried below before POST, J.

Uttley & Small, for plaintiff in error.

M. P. Kinkaid, M. F. Harrington, and *H. C. Brome,*
for defendant in error.

REESE, J.

This was an action of replevin instituted by plaintiff in
error against defendant in error for the possession of personal property, consisting of a stock of harness and sad-
dlery goods. It is alleged in the petition that plaintiff is
the head of a family; that he is not the owner of town lots,
lands, nor homestead exempt to him as a homestead; that
the property described in his petition is exempt to him in
lieu thereof, under the provisions of the statute of exemp-
tions, and that defendant has wrongfully levied upon the
property, and without any authority so to do. That the

execution to satisfy which the levy was made was void on its face, and that the pretended judgment upon which the execution was issued was void for want of jurisdiction. A trial was had which resulted in a verdict and judgment in favor of defendant. Plaintiff brings error to this court.

The controlling question in the case is presented by the sixth instruction given to the trial jury by the court, and to which plaintiff excepted. It is as follows: " 6th. To enable plaintiff to claim the benefit of the exemption provided in section 521, it was necessary for him to file an inventory, under oath, of the whole of the personal property owned by him, and inasmuch as the proofs in this case show that no such inventory was filed, you are charged that the plaintiff cannot recover under the provisions of said section 521."

It is not claimed that any of the property. in question was exempt to plaintiff under the provisions of section 530 of the civil code, but it is insisted that as the property taken did not aggregate the value of $500, and constituted substantially all the property owned by plaintiff, which was not exempt from execution under the specific exemptions of that section, and as plaintiff was not the owner of a homestead, the property was exempt and the levy was wrongful.

Section 521 of the civil code, referred to in the instruction, is as follows: "All heads of families, who have neither lands, town lots, or houses subject to exemption as a homestead, under the laws of this state, shall have exempt from forced sale on execution the sum of five hundred dollars in personal property." It will be observed by this that no specific property or kind of property is named, but that the language is general. "Five hundred dollars in personal property" is exempt from forced sale on execution.

Section 522 provides that " Any person desiring to avail himself of the exemption as provided for in the preceding section must file an inventory, under oath, in the court

where the judgment was obtained, or with the officer holding the execution, of the whole of the personal property
owned by him or them at any time before the sale of the
property; and it shall be the duty of the officer to whom
the execution is directed to call to his assistance three disinterested freeholders of the county where the property may
be, who, after being duly sworn by said officer, shall appraise said property at its cash value."

Section 523 provides that, "Upon such inventory and
appraisement being completed, the defendant in execution,
or his authorized agent, may select from such inventory an
amount of such property not exceeding, according to such
appraisal, the amount or value herein exempted, but if
neither such defendant nor his agent shall appear and make
such selection, the officer shall make the same for him."

By these sections it clearly appears that if the execution
debtor desires to avail himself of the benefits which are
placed within his reach by section five hundred and twenty-
one, he must file an inventory under oath, and procure the
appraisement of his property in the manner prescribed.
When the inventory and appraisement are completed, if
the property is found to be of less value than five hundred
dollars it would be sufficient justification for the officer to
return the property and refuse to proceed further under the
execution, but if the value is greater than that amount the
defendant must proceed to the selection of such part of the
property as he may desire to retain, equal to that sum.
When this is done by him or his agent, or in case they fail
to do so, by the officer, then, and not until then, does the
character or quality of exemption attach to the specific property to the extent that replevin may be maintained for its
possession. It has been twice decided by this court that if
the inventory was filed, and the officer refused to cause the
appraisement to be made, mandamus would lie to compel
him to do so. *People v. McClay,* 2 Neb., 8; *State, ex rel.
Metz, v. Cunningham,* 6 Id., 92.

If replevin could be maintained in the first instance, it would follow that an action for conversion would also lie. These two remedies would certainly furnish "a plain and adequate remedy in the ordinary course of the law," and mandamus could not be resorted to under the provisions of section 646 of the civil code.

This reasoning is sustained by a comparison of the language contained in the two sections (521 and 530) referred to. In 521 it is said that the debtor shall have exempt from forced sale the sum of "*five hundred dollars*" in personal property. By section 530 it is provided that "No property hereinafter mentioned shall be liable to attachment, or execution, or sale on any final process issued out of any court in this state against any person being a resident of this state and the head of a family." Then follows a designation of the particular property. By this section there is an absolute prohibition of the seizure. The property shall not "be liable." The officer who violates the section by the seizure of the property protected is a trespasser and wrong-doer, and is liable in replevin or for conversion, and can be made to respond in damages to the extent of the full value of the exempt property taken. But by section 521 the debtor shall have a specific *value* of property exempt upon a compliance with the provision of sections 522 and 523. It is optional with him whether he will have it or not. But it is said that since the enactment of the sections above considered, the legislature has amended the law of replevin—section 182, civil code—so that replevin will lie for exempt property, and that this section must refer as well to property exempt by virtue of section 521 as of section 530. This is, perhaps, true after the quality of exemption is fixed upon property by the appraisement and selection, but as replevin must be for "specific personal property" (sec. 181) it must follow that the property must be susceptible of identification before it can be replevined. In reply to this it is said that the value of plaintiff's property was less than five hundred dollars and therefore the identification is complete. This is not, and could not be true, until the appraisement was made in the manner provided by law, and the fact of the value thus legally ascertained. Furthermore if the officer should, upon demand, refuse to make the levy on the ground that the property was exempt it would be quite doubtful if he could urge such exemption as a justification, if the debtor made no claim thereto. It therefore follows that the instruction was correct.

It is claimed that the verdict is excessive; that the value of defendant's possession, being limited to the amount due on the executions with interest and costs, any valuation in excess of that amount would be excessive. This is true, and if the verdict exceeds that amount defendant will be required to remit the excess, or in default thereof a new trial will be given. The cause will be referred to the clerk of this court to make the necessary computation from the bill of exceptions, and if the verdict is found to be excessive the judgment must be reversed, if the excess is not remitted within thirty days.

Other errors are assigned, but they are not vital to the case and need not be noticed. A new trial will not be given where it appears as matter of law that the verdict upon the conceded facts must be the same upon another trial as at the first.

The judgment of the district court will be affirmed upon the condition above named. If the verdict is found to be excessive the costs in this court will be taxed to defendant in error.

JUDGMENT ACCORDINGLY.

THE other judges concur.

546
434
834

CHURCHILL PARKER, PLAINTIFF IN ERROR, V. ELLA
    MATHESON ET AL., DEFENDANTS IN ERROR.

546
685

1. **Taxes**: FORECLOSURE OF LIEN: LIMITATION. An action to foreclose a tax lien on real estate may be brought on the tax certificate, when it is alleged in the petition that a deed would be
invalid if issued. In such case the cause of action would accrue at the expiration of the time within which the land owner
might redeem, and suit may be brought at any time within five
years thereafter.

2. ——: ——: ——: A. purchased land at tax sale, on the
5th of February, 1878. A deed was refused by the treasurer,
when demanded, for the reason that no notice was given of the
expiration of the time for redemption, and that the sale was
void. On the 21st day of February, 1885, more than five years
after the expiration of the time for redemption, he commenced
this action to foreclose the tax lien. *Held*, That his cause of
action was barred by limitation.

ERROR to the district court for Antelope county. Tried
below before TIFFANY, J.

Groff, Montgomery & Jeffrey, for plaintiff in error.

W. J. Connell and *William A. Redick*, for defendants in
error.

REESE, J.

The only question involved in this case is the statute of
limitations.

Plaintiff filed his petition in the district court seeking to
foreclose a tax lien on the land described therein, and alleged
in substance that on the 5th day of February, 1878, he
purchased the same for the taxes then delinquent, and that
a certificate of purchase was executed to him by the county
treasurer. That the certificate of purchase had been tendered to the county treasurer and he had refused to execute

a deed thereon, "on the ground that a due and legal notice of said sale, and of the time when the right of redemption would expire, had not been served upon the occupant of said real estate, and also on the ground that plaintiff had no right to a tax deed pursuant to said sale." Plaintiff waives title and asks an accounting and foreclosure.

Defendants demurred to the petition upon the ground that it did not state a cause of action. The demurrer was sustained and the cause dismissed. Plaintiff brings error thereon.

As we have seen the sale was on the fifth day of February, 1878. Since the notice was not given, no deed could have legally issued. The action to foreclose could not have been brought until the time given to redeem had expired. *Helprey v. Redick, ante* p. 80; S. C., 31 N. W. Rep., 257. An action could have been maintained at any time after that event. Therefore the statute began to run at that time. There never was any *title* to "fail." The sale was simply void and conferred a lien for the taxes which might be foreclosed after the expiration of the time in which the defendant might redeem. That time was two years from date of sale. February 6th, 1880, the action could have been maintained. The suit was instituted February 21st, 1885, five years and fifteen days after the expiration of the time for redemption. At the time of the sale the law of 1875 (Laws 1875, 107) was in force, but the act of 1879 must apply to the foreclosure wherein the former act has been changed or amended. It is urged that a material difference in the two acts is that, by the act of 1875, the foreclosure might be had notwithstanding the tax deed, and by the act of 1879 he is entitled to foreclose instead of demanding a tax deed. This is true, but he could not demand a tax deed until after the expiration of the two years; therefore the landowner had that time within which he could redeem, without consulting the purchaser, and the right to foreclose did not accrue until the right to redeem by the payment of the money to the treasurer ceased. Under the rule stated in *Helprey v. Redick, supra,* the statute began to run February 6th, 1880. Five years from that time the cause of action would be barred. The action not having been commenced within that time, the demurrer was properly sustained.

The judgment of the district court is affirmed.

JUDGMENT AFFIRMED.

THE other judges concur.

WESTERN HORSE AND CATTLE INSURANCE COMPANY, PLAINTIFF IN ERROR, V. THOMAS O'NEILL, DEFENDANT IN ERROR.

Insurance on Live Stock. One O'N. insured a mare for the sum of $100 in the W. H. & C. Ins. Co., and afterwards violently beat and abused said mare by striking her with an iron rod *Held*, That a preponderance of the testimony clearly established the fact that the death of said mare was the result of such striking and abuse, and that O'N. was not entitled to recover the amount of the insurance for the death of said mare.

ERROR to the district court for Platte county. Tried below before POST, J.

Higgins & Garlow and *Charles Ogden,* for plaintiff in error.

McAllister Bros., for defendant in error.

MAXWELL, CH. J.

This is an action brought upon an insurance policy on one bay gelding, six years old, and one bay mare, eight years old, it being alleged said gelding died from disease

April 18th, 1885, and said mare died from disease May 13th, 1885.

The defendant in its answer admits insuring the property, but alleges "that said bay gelding died by reason of abuse of plaintiff, and for want of proper and reasonable care, and defendant denies that said policy was in force at the time of the death of the said mare, but alleges that said policy contained a condition that the defendant corporation reserved the right to cancel said policy at any time by giving notice to that effect to the policy holder, and returning to him the amount of unearned premium; and that in pursuance of said condition said defendant did, on the 9th day of May, 1885, cancel said policy in accordance with said condition.

"And defendant further alleges that said last named animal died by reason of the abuse of said plaintiff, and for want of proper and reasonable care."

In reply the plaintiff admits that said policy of insurance contains a provison therein as stated in defendant's answer, viz., that said defendant corporation reserves the right to cancel said policy of insurance at any time by giving notice to that effect to the policy holder, and returning to him the unearned premium; but denies that said defendant canceled said policy in manner and form as stated in their answer, also denies all other new matter contained . in said answer as a defense.

On the trial of the cause the jury returned a verdict in favor of O'Neill for $227, and judgment was rendered thereon.

The gelding was insured for the sum of $115, and the mare for the sum of $100.

After a pretty careful examination of the testimony we think the insurance company has failed to establish any defense against the payment of the insurance on the gelding, as there is no proof that such gelding died from the fault of O'Neill.

In regard to the mare, however, we think the company
has established a complete defense against the payment of
the insurance on her.

One W. M. Abbott testifies as follows: " I reside in
Humphrey, Platte county; have lived there for two years;
am acquainted with Thomas O'Neill; was acquainted with
him last spring; I saw Mr. O'Neill in Humphrey in the
early part of the month of April of last year (1885), when
he came to take a calf from my house; had a conversation
with him; Mr. O'Neill stated in my presence that the animal he whipped was one covered by this insurance; it was
after he had commenced this action; it was in Humphrey;
he took an iron rod out of the wagon and whipped her with
it; I thought at the time it was an end-gate rod; he
whipped her very hard, knocked her down several times
with the rod and beat her bad; he struck her pretty near
all over with the rod; he bent the rod several times by
beating her and then would straighten it out again; he beat
her over the head and over the sides and back; she looked
pretty hard when he was through beating her, she had been
badly whipped; there were ridges on her, she was swelled
up in places, and the blood run from her nostrils; cannot
say how long this beating continued, should think something like half an hour; when the animal was down he
kept on pounding; there were several of the citizens came
around and interfered and caused him to desist; it caused
quite a crowd to come around, several tried to stop him;
I think he told one man that it was his horse and he would
whip it as long as he pleased, and if he didn't get away he
would whip him; he had an iron rod in his hand at the
time, a rod about the size of an end-gate rod; I thought it
was the end-gate rod, and think so yet; about every time
he would hit her she would grunt; I think Mr. Bloedorn
came up and caused him to desist beating her; when he
stopped beating I think she was lying down, she did not
lie long; he was beating her over the head when she fell;

I think her method of going down indicated that she was knocked down.

I think it was the mare that he whipped, a bay mare, very thin in flesh; I do not think she fell over the tongue; she would not often rear up when he struck her over the head; a balky horse sometimes throws himself.

Q. State what statements Mr. O'Neill made to you when you say he talked to you in the saloon.

A. He said if they would pay him for the other horse that died he would not sue for the mare that was whipped. Mr. O'Neill spoke of this mare as having died; he told me she was dead, after he commenced this action; I didn't think she would live to get home."

There is a large amount of other testimony corroborating that of Mr. Abbott, and a clear preponderance of the testimony establishes the fact that the mare died as a result of the beating. O'Neill therefore cannot take advantage of his own wrong, and is not entitled to recover for the loss of the mare.

The insurance company attempted to cancel the policy in question on the 9th day of May, 1885, after the death of the horse but before the death of the mare. There is a conflict in the testimony as to the time such cancellation actually took place, but in the view that we take of the case it is immaterial whether it was canceled before the death of the mare or afterwards.

The judgment for the amount of insurance on the mare is reversed, and for the insurance on the horse is affirmed, and judgment will be entered in this court in conformity to this opinion.

JUDGMENT ACCORDINGLY.

THE other judges concur.

CLIFFORD B. SMITH, PLAINTIFF IN ERROR, V. THE
STATE OF NEBRASKA, DEFENDANT IN ERROR.

1. **Practice in Supreme Court:** HABEAS CORPUS: FILING
   BRIEFS. Where a habeas corpus case is brought on error from a
   district court the ordinary rules as to the time of filing briefs
   will not be adhered to, but the case will be heard as soon as
   practicable after the petitioner's brief is filed.

2. **Criminal Law:** COMPLAINT. A complaint must charge explicitly all that is essential to constitute the offense, and it cannot
   be aided by intendments.

3. ———: FUGITIVE FROM JUSTICE: COMPLAINT. Section 330 of
   the Criminal Code contemplates that the charge of the crime
   against the person to be arrested and delivered up must be made
   in the state where the offense was committed. The charge must
   be to some court, magistrate, or officer in the form of an indictment, complaint, or other accusation known to the laws of such
   state or territory, and a complaint made before a magistrate in
   this state which fails to allege that such charge is pending
   against the accused in the state where it is alleged the offense
   was committed will not confer jurisdiction on such magistrate.

ERROR to the district court for Lancaster county. Tried
below before POUND, J.

Sawyer & Snell, for plaintiff in error.

J. E. Philpott, for defendant in error.

MAXWELL, CH. J.

On the 4th day of March, 1887, the plaintiff was arrested by a policeman of the city of Lincoln, on a telegram,
and lodged in the city jail, where he remained until the 9th
of March, when between 10 and 11 o'clock at night he
was removed to the county jail. He was imprisoned in
the city jail from the 4th to the 7th of March without any
warrant for his arrest having been issued. On the 7th of
March the following information was filed:

" THE STATE OF NEBRASKA   } In the police court of the
         vs.   } city of Lincoln, Lancas-
     C. B. SMITH.   } ter county, Nebraska.

" THE STATE OF NEBRASKA, } ss.
   Lancaster County,   }

"The complaint and information of J. K. Post, of the county of Lancaster, made before me, A. F. Parsons, judge of the police court, within and for the city of Lincoln, Lancaster county, Nebraska, on this 7th day of March, A.D. 1887, who, being duly sworn, on his oath says that C. B. Smith is now within said last named county and city, and that said Smith stand charged with the commission of a criminal offense against the laws of the territory of Dakota, which if committed in this state would by the laws thereof have been a crime, and said Smith is now a fugitive from justice, contrary to the form of the statute in that behalf provided and against the peace and dignity of the state of Nebraska.   J. K. POST.

"Subscribed in my presence and sworn to before me this 7th day of March, A.D. 1887.

                 " A. F. PARSONS,
         Police Judge of the City of Lincoln."

Upon this complaint being filed an examination of the plaintiff herein was thereupon had, and he was remanded to prison. A copy of the commitment will be found in the answer and return of A. C. Langdon to the writ of habeas corpus hereafter referred to.

On the 10th day of March the plaintiff presented a petition to a judge of the district court of Lancaster county for a writ of habeas corpus, which writ was duly issued on said day, to which the party having said plaintiff in custody made the following answer and return:

"STATE OF NEBRASKA, } ss.
   Lancaster County,   }

"A. C. Langdon, for answer and return to said writ, states that Clifford B. Smith, on the 9th day of March,

A.D. 1887, was placed in his custody by virtue of a warrant of commitment, by authority of which he now holds said Smith in custody, of which the following is a copy:

"THE STATE OF NEBRASKA }
         vs.
   C. B. SMITH.   }

"In Police Court of the City of Lincoln, Nebraska.

"THE STATE OF NEBRASKA, } ss.
      Lancaster County.   }

"The State of Nebraska to the keeper of the jail of said county, greeting:

"You are hereby commanded to receive into the 'jail of said county C. B. Smith, and him safely keep, unless sooner discharged by due course of law, he having been brought before the undersigned police judge in and for said city, on the 7th day of March, 1887, charged in writing, on the oath of J. K. Post, with the commission of a criminal offense against the laws of the territory of Dakota, which, if committed in the said state of Nebraska, would, by the laws thereof, have been a crime, and that the said Smith is now a fugitive from justice from the said territory of Dakota, and on the day first aforesaid, having been by the court duly advised in the premises, found and adjudged guilty of the offense with which he stands charged, and ordered and adjudged to be committed to the county jail of Lancaster county, until discharged by due process of law, and be delivered to some suitable person to be removed therefrom to said territory of Dakota, the proper place for the further prosecution of this cause. You will make return of this writ and of your proceedings thereunder as required by law.

"Witness my hand this 9th day of March, 1887.

                              "A. F. PARSONS,
                                        Police Judge.

"And said A. C. Langdon further says upon information and belief that the said Clifford B. Smith now stands charged, and that a warrant has been duly issued for his arrest for the crime of grand larceny and malicious mischief, having been committed by him in the county of Fall River, in the territory of Dakota, during the year 1886. That said county of Fall River is five hundred miles northwest from Lincoln, Nebraska, and that Hot Springs, the county seat of said Fall River county, is situate from Bismarck, the capital of Dakota, by the usual mail route, about 900 miles. That H. A. Goddard, sheriff of Fall River county, received on the 9th day of March the first telegram from said J. K. Post, that the said Smith had been examined and held by said police judge as a fugitive from justice from said territory of Dakota; that upon the receipt of said telegram one E. D. Norton, the duly authorized district attorney for said Fall River county, on said 9th day of March, made up and forwarded to the governor of said territory at Bismarck an application for a requisition from the executive of the state of Nebraska for the said Clifford B. Smith, and that on the 9th day of March said H. A. Goddard, sheriff as aforesaid, left said town of Hot Springs for Lincoln, Nebraska, and is now here awaiting for a reasonable time to elapse for the transmission to him by the governor of Dakota of his application and demand of said governor of Nebraska for a requisition and delivery thereunder of the said Smith to him as the agent duly authorized therefor, and that such reasonable time has not yet elapsed.

"A. C. LANGDON,

Keeper of the County Jail of Lancaster County, Nebraska."

On the hearing the district court refused to discharge the plaintiff, and caused him to be remanded to the jail of said county.

He then filed a petition in error in this court in order that the judgment of the district court might be reviewed. The attorney for the defendant in error contends that he

cannot be compelled to submit the cause until more than
fifteen days have elapsed from the time of filing the petition in error. In answer to this objection it is sufficient to
say that the ordinary rules governing civil actions do not
apply. If the plaintiff is unlawfully restrained of his
liberty as he contends, the case should be heard with all
convenient speed, and a determination had as to the nature
of the alleged unlawful restraint. The court therefore will
not delay the hearing of the case.

2. It will be observed that the plaintiff is charged
"with the commission of a criminal offense against the
laws of the territory of Dakota, which, if committed in the
said state of Nebraska, would, by the laws thereof, have
been a crime, and that the said Smith is now a fugitive
from the said territory of Dakota." The nature of the
crime is not set out. This question was before the supreme
court of Ohio, in *Lamberton v. State*, 11 Ohio, 284, where
it is said: "It is a rule of criminal law, based upon sound
principles, that every indictment should contain a complete description of the offense charged. That it should
set forth the facts constituting the crime, so that the act
cused may have notice of what he is to meet; of the ac-
done, which it behooves him to controvert, and so that the
court, applying the law to the facts charged against him,
may see that a crime has been committed.

"A contrary doctrine would deprive the accused of one of
the means humanely provided for the protection of innocence." An indictment must charge explicitly all that is
essential to constitute the offense. It cannot be aided by
intendments, but must positively and explicitly state what
the prisoner is called upon to answer. *State v. Seay*, 3
Stewart, 123; *Com. v. Waters*, 6 Dana, 290. This is specially the case in criminal prosecutions of the grade of
felony. *Kit. v. State*, 11 Humph., 167; *Bulloch v. State*,
10 Ga., 46; *Stephen v. State*, 11 Ga., 225; *State v. Hand*,
1 Engl. (Ark.), 165; *State v. Wilson*, 2 Const. (S. C.), 135;

State v. Henderson, 1 Rich, 179; *State v. Wimberly*, 3 Mc-
Cord, 190; *State v. Philbrick*, 31 Maine, 401; *State v. Fields*,
Mart. & Yerg., 137; *Com. v. Clark*, 6 Gratt., 675; *Markle
v. The State*, 3 Ind., 535; *Lambert v. The People*, 9 Cowen,
579; 1 Archbold's Criminal Practice and Pleading, 265
(8 ed.); *Ex parte Eads*, 17 Neb., 145; Maxwell's Crim.
Pro., 284, 286.

The complaint, therefore, is wholly insufficient.

3. Section 330 of the criminal code provides that
"When an affidavit shall be filed before any judge of a
district court, or any judge of probate or police court, or
any justice of the peace, within this state, setting forth that
any person charged with the commission of any criminal
offense against the laws of any other state, or any of the
territories of the United States, and which, if the act had
been committed in this state, would, by the laws thereof,
have been a crime, is at the time of filing such affidavit
within the county where the same may be filed, it shall be
lawful, and it is hereby made the duty of such judge or
justice of the peace to issue his warrant, directed to the
sheriff or any constable of the county, commanding him
forthwith to arrest and bring before the officer issuing such
writ the person so charged."

The word "charged" in the statute contemplates that the
person arrested and delivered up committed the offense in
another state, and is in such state charged either by indictment, information, or accusation known to the law of
such state before some court, magistrate, or officer thereof.

In *State v. Hufford*, 28 Iowa, 391, the information charged
substantially that the defendant, James Hufford, was guilty
of murder in the second degree, committed in Knox county,
Illinois, by producing an abortion upon one L. L. Strayer,
a pregnant woman, which caused her death.   It contained
no averment that the accused was charged with the crime
in the county where it was committed, and contained nothing further than the allegations of the commission of the

crime by the accused, and the place, time, and manner of its commission.   The court, by Beck, J., after citing the provisions of the Constitution of the United States, and the act of congress, February 12th, 1793, says: "It is quite clear that our statute, being enacted in aid of the foregoing constitutional and statutory requirements of the United States, contemplates that a charge of the crime against the person to be arrested and delivered up must be made in the state where the offense was committed.   This charge must be made to some court, magistrate, or officer, in the form of an indictment, information, or other accusation known to the laws of the state in which the offense was committed.   We conclude, therefore, that unless the accused in this case was so charged, the magistrate had no jurisdiction.   *Ex parte Smith*, 3 McLean, 121 ; *Ex parte Clark*, 9 Wend., 212; *Matter of Heyward*, 1 Sandf., 701."

The same ruling was made by the supreme court of California in *Ex parte White*, 29 Cal., 433, and by the supreme court of Nevada in *Ex parte Lorraine*, 16 Nev., 63, and by the supreme court of Missouri in *State v. Swope*, 72 Mo., 399.   These cases, in our view, state the law correctly. The charge referred to in the statute means a prosecution lawfully instituted against the defendant, and then pending, and the complaint must set forth the essential facts to show that such charge is pending, otherwise a magistrate in this state will acquire no jurisdiction by the filing of the complaint.

A form of complaint will be found in Practice in Justices' Court (4th ed.), p. 586.

While it was not necessary to the decision of this case, the plaintiff filed a certificate from the private secretary of the governor stating that up to the 30th day of March no application for extradition of the plaintiff had been made by the governor of Dakota, thus giving strength to the presumption that no prosecution is pending against the plaintiff in such territory.

The judgment of the district court is reversed and the prisoner discharged.

JUDGMENT ACCORDINGLY.

THE other judges concur.

GUSTAV UECKER, APPELLANT, V. GUSTAV KOEHN AND EMIL KOEHN, APPELLEES.

1. **Evidence Conflicting.** When the evidence is conflicting and it is apparent that some of the witnesses—the defendants—were mistaken, and that their testimony was disregarded by the court, the judgment will not be set aside as being against the weight of evidence.

2. **Infancy:** MORTGAGE BY INFANT. Where an infant purchases real estate, and receives a conveyance thereof, and at the same time executes a mortgage upon the land to secure notes given for the purchase money, such mortgage is voidable only, not void; and when, on reaching his majority, he sells and conveys such real estate, he thereby confirms the mortgage.

APPEAL from the district court for Pierce county. Tried below before TIFFANY, J.

Wigton & Whitham, for appellant.

H. C. Brome and *N. A. Rainbolt,* for appellees.

MAXWELL, CH. J.

December 1, 1885, the plaintiff filed in the district court of Pierce county his petition, stating his cause of action to be: "That on the 19th day of January, 1884, the defendant, Gustav Koehn, was the owner and in possession of the south half of the north-east quarter of section thirty-three, and the south half of the north-west quarter of section thirty-four, of township twenty-five north, of range one west of the sixth principal meridian, in Pierce county, Nebraska; that on the said 19th day of January, 1884, said defendant, Gustav Koehn, sold and conveyed said premises by his deed of general warranty to defendant, Emil Koehn; that in consideration of and for said sale of said premises, defendant Emil Koehn assumed the payment of certain mortgage liens then resting thereon, to-wit: one lien in favor of ——— for $——, and one lien in favor of ———, for $——; and in addition thereto and as a further consideration for said premises, said defendant, Emil Koehn, executed and delivered to said defendant, Gustav Koehn, on the same day, twelve promissory notes in writing of that date, each of said promissory notes being for the sum of $208.33, and falling due respectively one, two, three, four, five, six, seven, eight, nine, ten, eleven, and twelve years from said date, and all of said notes bearing interest at the rate of ten per cent per annum from the date thereof, payable annually; and the said defendant, Emil Koehn, did on said date and to secure the payment of said notes execute and deliver to said defendant, Gustav Koehn, a mortgage deed upon said premises, witnessed and acknowledged in the manner provided by law, said mortgage being given for the express purpose of securing the payment of the portion of the purchase price of said premises represented by said notes, to-wit: the sum of $2,500.00, together with such interest and costs as might legally become due thereon, said notes being particularly referred to and described in said mortgage deed; that by the terms of said mortgage deed it was provided that 'If the said Emil Koehn shall well and truly pay or cause to be paid the said sums of money in said notes mentioned, with the interest thereon, according to the tenor and effect of said notes, then these presents shall be null and void, but if said sum of money or any part thereof or any interest thereon is not paid when the same is due, then in

that case the whole of said sum and interest shall become
due by the terms of this indenture; or if the taxes and assessments of every nature which are or may be assessed or
levied against said premises, and not paid at the time when
the same are by law made due and payable, then in like
manner the whole of said sum shall immediately become
due and payable, and upon forfeiture of this mortgage, or
in case of default in any of the payments herein provided,
the said Gustav Koehn shall be entitled to the immediate
possession of said premises;' that afterwards, and on the
9th day of August, 1884, the defendant, Gustav Koehn,
did for a valuable consideration sell and transfer, by endorsement to this plaintiff, seven of the above described
promissory notes, to-wit: the notes falling due respectively
one, two, three, four, five, six, and seven years after the
19th day of January, 1884; that at the time plaintiff purchased said notes, said defendant, Gustav Koehn, fraudulently and falsely represented and stated to plaintiff that
the mortgage hereinbefore referred to, and by which the
payment of said notes was secured, was duly recorded in
the office of the county clerk of Pierce county, Nebraska;
that plaintiff, relying upon said statements with reference
to the recording of said mortgage deed, and believing the
same to be true, was induced to and did purchase said notes;
that said mortgage deed was not recorded in the office of
said county clerk, nor has the same ever been recorded in
the office of said county clerk, all of which Gustav Koehn
well knew when he made said statements, and at the time
he sold and delivered said notes to plaintiff.

"After the transfer and sale of said notes said defendant,
Gustav Koehn, did, without the knowledge or consent of
this plaintiff, deliver said mortgage deed to said defendant,
Emil Koehn, and said mortgage was thereupon, and without knowledge or consent of this plaintiff, wholly destroyed; that plaintiff has no remedy in the premises except
such as may be afforded by the interposition of this court.

36

"Wherefore plaintiff prays that. plaintiff be adjudged
and decreed to have a first mortgage lien upon said premises for the amount then due or to become due on said promissory notes, and that it be further decreed that if said
defendants or either of them shall fail to pay the amount
of said notes, with interest thereon, according to the tenor
thereof, or any part thereof when the same shall become
due and payable, then and in that event plaintiff may and
shall be entitled to foreclose said mortgage as in other cases
by law provided for the foreclosure of mortgages, and for
such other relief as may be just and equitable."

Gustav Koehn, in his answer, "admits that on the 19th
day of January, 1884, he was the owner of the land described in plaintiff's petition; that on said day he conveyed
said premises by his deed of general warranty to defendant, Emil Koehn; that as a part of the consideration for
said conveyance said Emil Koehn executed and delivered
to this defendant on said day the promissory notes described in plaintiff's petition, and to secure their payment
executed and delivered to this defendant the mortgage deed
described in plaintiff's petition; that said mortgage deed
was never recorded or filed for record in the office of the
county clerk of Pierce county, Nebraska, or anywhere.

"Denies each and every allegation in plaintiff's amended
petition not herein admitted to be true.

"Alleges that on or about the 8th day of April, 1884,
and before plaintiff obtained possession of any of said
notes, and while all the notes described in plaintiff's
amended petition were owned by and in possession of this
defendant, this defendant, for good, sufficient, and valuable
consideration, endorsed in blank all of said notes and returned and redelivered to defendant Emil Koehn all of
said notes and said mortgage deed, with the intent thereby
to release, cancel, and annul all of said promissory notes
and said mortgage deed, and the lien, if any there was,
created by said mortgage deed, and defendant Emil Koehn

accepted the redelivery of said notes and mortgage deed with the same intent. This defendant has not, since the said redelivery of said notes and since the month of April, 1884, been the owner of said notes or any of them, nor has this defendant since April, 1884, had any right or any authority to sell or transfer said notes, or any of them, to any one.

"On the 22d day of April, 1884, defendant Emil Koehn delivered said promissory notes, endorsed in blank as above alleged, to this defendant for safe keeping only, subject at all times to the order of said Emil Koehn.

"On or about the 9th day of August, 1884, plaintiff obtained possession of said seven promissory notes especially mentioned in plaintiff's petition, but gave no consideration whatever for said seven notes or for the possession of said seven notes. Plaintiff knew when he obtained possession of said notes that the said notes belonged to defendant Emil Koehn, and had been canceled, and that this defendant had no authority to give or transfer to plaintiff any right, title, or interest in said notes."

Emil Koehn, in his answer, admits the purchase of the land in question, and the execution and delivery of the notes and mortgage; but alleges that "in April, 1884, said notes and mortgage were canceled by Gustav Koehn and redelivered to him, but that they were left in the possession of said Gustav Koehn; that on the 9th day of August, 1884, and while the said notes were in the possession of said Gustav Koehn for safe keeping only, plaintiff obtained from said Gustav Koehn, wrongfully and without any consideration therefor, the possession of said seven promissory notes, and still retains possession of the same. This defendant never authorized said Gustav Koehn or any person to deliver said seven notes or any of them to plaintiff or to allow plaintiff to obtain possession of said notes. Plaintiff knew when he got possession of said notes that this defendant was the owner of said notes and that said notes had been canceled and said Gustav Koehn had no right or authority to deliver said notes or any of them to plaintiff.

"On or about the 15th day of August, 1884, this defendant demanded of plaintiff the possession of said seven notes, but plaintiff then refused and still refuses to deliver said notes or any of them to this defendant.

"The plaintiff is wholly insolvent."

The plaintiff in his reply denies the new matter stated in the answers of the defendants, and alleges that after Emil Koehn became of age he ratified and confirmed said notes and mortgage by selling the land in question for which they were given.

On the trial of the cause the court below rendered the following decree:

"That on the 19th day of January, 1884, the defendant, Gustav Koehn, was the owner and in possession of the south half of the north-east quarter of section thirty-three, and the south half of the north-west quarter of section thirty-four, in township twenty-five north, of range one west of the sixth principal meridian, in Pierce county, Nebraska. That on the said 19th day of January, 1884, said defendant, Gustav Koehn, sold and conveyed said premises by his deed of general warranty to said defendant, Emil Koehn. That in consideration of and for said sale of said premises, said defendant, Emil Koehn, executed and delivered to said defendant, Gustav Koehn, on said 19th day of January, 1884, twelve promissory notes, each of said promissory notes being for the sum of $208.33, and falling due respectively one, two, three, four, five, six, seven, eight, nine, ten, eleven, and twelve years from date, all of said notes bearing interest at the rate of ten per cent per annum from the date thereof, payable annually; and the said defendant, Emil Koehn, did, on said date and to secure the payment of said notes, execute and deliver to said defendant, Gustav Koehn, a mortgage deed upon said premises

signed, witnessed, and acknowledged in the manner provided by law, said mortgage being given for the express
purpose of securing the payment of the purchase price of
said premises, represented by said notes, to-wit: the sum
of $2,500, together with such interests and costs as might
legally become due thereon. That by the terms of said mortgage deed it was provided 'that if the said Emil Koehn shall
well and truly pay or cause to be paid the said sums of
money in said notes mentioned, with the interests thereon,
according to the tenor and effect of said notes, then these
presents shall be null and void ; but if said sums of money
or any part thereof or any interest thereon is not paid
when the same is due, then in that case the whole of said
sum and interest shall become due by the terms of this indenture, or if the taxes and assessments of every nature
which are or may be assessed or levied against said premises are not paid at the time when the same are by law made
due and payable, then in like manner the whole of said sum
shall immediately become due and payable, and upon forfeiture of this mortgage or in case of default in any of the
payments herein provided, the said Gustav Koehn shall be
entitled to the immediate possession of said premises.'

"That afterwards and on the 9th day of August, 1884,
the defendant, Gustav Koehn, did for a valuable consideration sell and transfer by endorsements six of the above described promissory notes, to-wit: the notes falling due
respectively one, two, three, four, five, and six years after
the 19th day of January, 1884. That at the time plaintiff purchased said notes, the defendant, Gustav Koehn, represented and stated to him that said mortgage deed was duly
recorded in the office of the county clerk of said Pierce
county. That plaintiff relied upon said statements with
reference to the recording of said mortgage deed, and believed that said mortgage was so recorded at the time
of said purchase. Said mortgage deed was not recorded in
the office of said county clerk nor has the same ever been
recorded in the office of said Pierce county.

"That said mortgage deed was at the time of the commencement of this action, and now is, a valid subsisting lien
upon the above described premises for the amount due or
to become due on said several promissory notes with the
interests and costs accruing thereon, and that plaintiff is
entitled to enforce said lien and foreclose said mortgage in
the same manner as he might do were said mortgage deed
duly recorded.   The court further finds generally upon the
issues joined herein for plaintiff, to all of which findings
the defendants at the time excepted.

"It is therefore considered, adjudged, and decreed by the
court that the plaintiff, Gustav Uecker, have a first mortgage lien upon the above described real estate, to-wit:

"The south half of the north-east quarter of section
thirty-three, and the south half of the north-west quarter
of section thirty-four, in township twenty-five north, of
range one west, for the amount now due or that may hereafter become due upon said several promissory notes, and
in default of payment thereof, said plaintiff be and is hereby authorized to foreclose said mortgage lien in the manner
provided by law for the foreclosure of mortgages."

The defendants appeal.

Two questions are presented by the record. *First*, were
the notes and mortgage above described actually canceled
and redelivered to Emil Koehn in April, 1884? *Second*,
if not so canceled, does the proof show sufficient ratification after Emil Koehn became of age to justify the court
in enforcing the contract against him?

The testimony shows that in July and August, 1884,
Gustav Koehn was in the employ of Gustav Uecker; that
during that time he purchased from Uecker a half interest
in certain real estate, shown by the following contract:

"NORFOLK, Nebraska, August 9th, 1884.

This agreement made this day witnesseth that for and in
consideration of twelve hundred and fifty dollars in hand
paid by Gustav Koehn to said Gustav Uecker, the said

Gustav Uecker has agreed and does agree to convey to said Gustav Koehn by warranty deed one undivided half interest in and to the saloon property on Main street, including the bowling alley, stables, and all buildings, said property being free from taxes and all incumbrances excepting two mortgages of $500 each on which interest is paid up, said property being parts of lots 4 and 5, of block 1, of Mathewson's addition to the town of Norfolk.

In presence of   GUS. UECKER.
AUGUSTUS SATTLER."

This contract was drawn by one August Sattler, a notary public, who, in the previous January, had drawn the notes and mortgage in question. He testifies in substance that the parties came to his office and stated that they had made a trade of some property and desired to have the contract put in writing, and also that Mr. Koehn turned over $1,250 in notes. Sattler inquired of Koehn if these were the same notes that were secured by mortgage, and he answered that they were. Mr. Sattler then desired the mortgage to make the assignment on the back of the mortgage. Koehn stated that the mortgage was at his brother's place. He appears to have conveyed the impression that the mortgage was recorded. The testimony also shows that Uecker wanted a formal assignment of the mortgage, but Sattler seems to have advised him to wait until Koehn brought the mortgage in order that the assignment might be made on that. But as Koehn failed to procure the mortgage to make the assignment thereon, he executed the following assignment:

"Know all men by these presents that I, Gustav Koehn, in consideration of fifteen hundred dollars to me paid by Gustav Uecker, have granted, bargained, and sold, and by these presents do grant, bargain, and sell to Gustav Uecker, his heirs and assigns, a certain deed of mortgage from Emil Koehn to Gustav Kochn, of the south half of the north-east quarter of section thirty-three (33), and the south half of the north-west quarter of section thirty-four (34), township twenty-five (25) north, of range one west, in Pierce county, Nebraska—said mortgage deed is recorded in book —, page —, one of the land records of Pierce county to be found at the county clerk's office— together with seven notes of two hundred and eight and $\frac{33}{100}$ dollars each, due respectively in 1, 2, 3, 4, 5, 6, and 7 years from date, being part of the original purchase price debt of said premises for the securing of which said mortgage deed was given.

In presence of   GUSTAV KOEHN.
    AUGUSTUS SATTLER.

"STATE OF NEBRASKA, ⎫
    MADISON COUNTY.   ⎬

                        Before me, Augustus Sattler, a notary public in and for said county, personally appeared above named Gustav Koehn, who is known to me personally to be the identical person whose name is affixed to within, grantor, and acknowledged the same to be his free act and deed.

    Witness my hand and seal this 29th day of August, 1884.

⎧ Madison County ⎫   AUGUSTUS SATTLER,
⎨ NOTARIAL SEAL. ⎬   Notary Public."
⎩   Nebraska.   ⎭

The testimony on the part of the defendants tends to show the following facts: That during the month of April, 1884, a new arrangement was entered into between Gustav Koehn and Emil Koehn, whereby the price of the land was to be reduced to $2,000, and new non-negotiable notes, unsecured by mortgage, taken in place of the twelve heretofore referred to. Both of the defendants swear positively that that agreement was consummated; they fail, however, to explain satisfactorily why the old notes and mortgage were preserved if they were canceled, or why the new notes, which they allege were to be given, were not executed. This arrangement is said to have taken place in

April, and the transfer by Gustav Koehn of the notes and
mortgage in question was made in the following August,
and the defendant, Emil Koehn, when spoken to about the
first of September, 1884, says, "I simply told him (the
plaintiff) I was a minor and wouldn't pay, and the notes
and mortgage belonged to me. I never did ask him to
give them back to me." It also appears that some time
during the fall of 1884 the plaintiff procured a pony for
Emil Koehn to ride from Norfolk to the residence of his
brother, August Koehn, in Pierce county, and procure the
mortgage in question, and that he rode to his brother's but
did not bring the mortgage, his excuse being that "August
had it and wouldn't give it up." When we compare the
contradictory statements of the brothers we find that there
is a want of directness and. consistency which casts suspicion upon it. The testimony of Gustav Koehn is directly
impeached upon important points by the assignment of the
mortgage made by him on August 29th, 1884. There are
other points in which there is a direct contradiction and a
want of consistency in the defendant's testimony, to which
it is unnecessary to refer. In our view the court below was
fully justified in disregarding such testimony and finding
for the plaintiff.

2. Does the proof show sufficient ratification, after
Emil Koehn became of age, to justify the court in enforcing the contract against him? The decisions upon an infant's liability after he reaches his majority, on a contract
made by him during infancy, are directly in conflict.

In *Proctor v. Sears*, 4 Allen, 95, it was held by the supreme court of Massachusetts that when an infant had made
a promissory note, and after majority he admitted the debt
and promised to pay the same, it was not sufficient, as a mere
acknowledgment, would not have the effect to make the
obligation valid.

In 2 Kent's Com., 237, it is said : "The books appear
to leave the question in some obscurity, when and to what

extent a positive act on the part of the infant is requisite."

In *Henry v. Root*, 33 N. Y., 545, it is said : "I think that the course of decision in this state authorizes us to assume that the narrow and stringent rule, formerly enunciated, that to establish the contract, when made in infancy, there must be a precise and positive promise to pay the particular debt after attaining majority, is not sustained by the more modern decisions."

In *Zouch v. Parsons*, 3 Burrows, 1794, it was held that a conveyance by a lease and release executed by an infant without livery of seizin was voidable only; Lord Mansfield cites Bro. Abr. to prove that the delivery of a deed cannot be void but only voidable; and he adds: "There is no difference in this respect between feoffments and deeds which convey an interest."

In *Conroe v. Birdsall*, 1 John. Cas., 127, it was held that the bond of an infant, which takes effect by delivery the same as other deeds, was only voidable, and this rule was affirmed in *Jackson v. Todd*, 6 John., 257 ; *Jackson v. Carpenter*, 11 John., 539; *Roof v. Stafford*, 7 Cow., 179.

The question was before this court in *Kleffel v. Bullock*, 8 Neb., 336. That was an action for goods furnished and labor performed, the balance claimed to be due being $66.90. Kleffel offered to confess judgment for $40 with costs then accrued; this was not accepted. A trial was had and judgment rendered for a less sum than $40, and the costs, which amounted to a very large sum (more than $400), were taxed to Bullock. Upon his coming of age he refused to avail himself of the judgment, and the court held that as no guardian had been chosen for him he was not liable for the costs. It is said, page 344 : " From analogy to the cases of the ratification of the voidable acts of infants after becoming of full age, we think it clear that if, after reaching his majority, he had either assented to judgment on the verdict or taken a single step in the further prosecution of the action,

all the privileges of infancy would thereby have been fully
waived, and he would have been bound by the action of
the court. But the record shows that at the very first opportunity after he reached the age of twenty-one years, he
disclaimed all benefit from what had been done in the case,
and in the most unequivocal manner denied the jurisdiction of the court to proceed further."

In *Philpot v. Sandwich M'fg Co.*, 18 Neb., 54, it was
held that contracts of an infant other than for necessaries
were voidable only, and upon coming of age he had the
right to affirm or avoid in his discretion; and in *Ward v.
Laverty*, 19 Neb., 431, and *O'Brien v. Gaslin*, 20 Neb.,
352, it was held that an infant becoming of age must disaffirm a deed within a reasonable time or be barred of
the right.

These cases seem to be based upon sound principles. The
contract is merely conditional that the infant shall not disaffirm after becoming of age. The law, however, is to be used
as a shield—as a means by which he may be protected
against inequitable bargains; it is not designed as a means
of enabling him to rob others by procuring and retaining
their property without paying for it. The principles of
justice apply to an infant as well as an adult; therefore if
he purchases real estate and receives a deed therefor, and to
secure the consideration he executes a mortgage upon such
land, and after coming of age sells the real estate as his own,
his plea of the invalidity of the mortgage will be unavailing. That is, he cannot confirm that part of the transaction
which is beneficial to him and repudiate that which im-
poses an obligation.

This rule was very carefully considered in *Philpot
v. Sandwich Mf'g Co., supra*; and it was held in that
case that if an infant purchased personal property and
gave his promissory note therefor, he cannot, upon ar-
riving at the age of twenty-one years, retain the property
and plead infancy as a defense to the note. This, we think,

is the correct rule.   See also *Delano v. Blake*, 11 Wend., 85; *Jones v. Phœnix Bank*, 4 Seld., 228 ; *Kitchen v. Lee*, 11 Paige, 107; *Lynde v. Budd*, 2 Id., 191; *Deason v. Boyd*, 1 Dana, 45; *Cheshire v. Barrett*, 4 McCord, 241 ; *Ottman v. Moak*, 3 Sandf. Ch., 431.

The plaintiff is entitled therefore to have the mortgage duly established and recorded in the proper records of Pierce county.   The value of the property does not appear in this record, and the question of the personal liability of Emil Koehn does not arise in the case.

3.   An attempt was made by the proof to show a partial rescission of the contract between Gustav Koehn and the plaintiff; no issue of that kind is made in the pleadings, and we cannot consider it in this collateral proceeding. There is no error in the record and the judgment of the court below is affirmed.

JUDGMENT AFFIRMED.

THE other judges concur.

THE STATE OF NEBRASKA, EX REL. JAMES P. HYMER, V. TYRA NELSON ET AL.

1. **County Seat**: RELOCATION: PETITION: JURISDICTION. Where a petition was presented to the county commissioners of F. county purporting to contain the names of 644 resident electors of said county, asking said board to call a special election for the relocation of the county seat, the whole number of votes cast in said county at the preceding general election being 729; a remonstrance, signed by 1,164 persons purporting to be electors of said county, against the calling of said election, was thereupon presented to said board alleging that said petition was signed by persons who were non-residents of said county, and by minors and others not authorized to sign such petition; *Held*, That a general finding of said board that a large number of persons so disqualified had signed said petition, and that the

whole number of lawful petitioners was less than three-fifths' of all the votes cast in said county at the preceding general election, was not subject to collateral attack; but if erroneous must be reviewed on error. *State v. Nemaha County*, 10 Neb., 32.

2. **Jurisdiction.** The decision of a special tribunal, where it has jurisdiction of the subject-matter and parties, is conclusive, unless reversed or modified in the mode provided by law.

3. **Mandamus.** A writ of mandamus will not be granted unless the right of the relator thereto is clear.

ORIGINAL application for a mandamus.

Marquett, Deweese, & Hall, for relator.

George H. Stewart, O. P. Mason, and *H. L. Merriman,* for respondents.

MAXWELL, CH. J.

The relator alleges that he is a resident of the county of Frontier, and that he is a taxpayer in said county; that on the 21st day of February, 1887, said defendants being in lawful session at the county seat of said county, the following petition was presented to them:

"To the Honorable Board of County Commissioners of Frontier county, Nebraska: We, the undersigned, resident electors of Frontier county, Nebraska, do most respectfully petition your honorable body to forthwith call a special election in said county, for the purpose of submitting to the qualified electors thereof a question of relocation of the county seat." This petition was signed by E. K. Bowman, W. G. Phelps, and six hundred and forty-two other citizens and resident electors of said county, and following each name of the petitioners on said petition there was designated the age of the petitioner, and the section, township, and range or lot on which, or the town or city in which, the petitioner resided, and also the time that said petitioners had resided in said county, in days and years.

That at the last general election, held prior to the presentation of this petition, of said county in the fall of 1886, there were seven hundred and twenty-nine votes cast in said county, and no more.

That the petitioners making said application to the said board constituted more than three-fifths of all the resident voters and electors in said county.

It is also alleged that defendants refused to call such election.

An alternative writ was allowed, to which the defendants made return as follows :

"That during the session duly appointed and held of the board of commissioners of the county of Frontier, state aforesaid, and on the 21st day of February, 1887, a petition, the one referred to in the petition in this cause filed, purporting to contain the names of 644 resident electors of said county was filed in the office of said board praying for the submission to the electors of said county the question of the relocation of the county seat of said county.

"That thereafter, and during the said session, remonstrance, protest, and answer to said petition for submission were filed in the office of said board.

"That thereafter and during said session the board proceeded to and did hear said petition, remonstrance, protest, and answer, and the allegations, proofs, and arguments of the respective parties, and did try the same.

"That all the allegations above set forth and in this answer contained more fully and at large appear by reference to the proceedings had before said board on the hearing and trial aforesaid, a certified transcript of which is hereto attached.

"That all the facts and things stated in said proceedings, certified as aforesaid, are true and correct, and it did appear to said board on said hearing that the inhabitants of said county were not desirous of changing their county-seat; that said petition for submission was not supported

by any proof that it contained the names of resident electors of said county equal in number to three-fifths of
the votes cast at the last general election held in said
county; that persons who had signed said petition for submission had subsequently thereto signed the remonstrances
against the same, as alleged in said protest and answer;
that others who had signed said petition for relocation had
personally appeared before the board and withdrew their
names from said petition for submission; and that a number of the signers on said petition for submission were
minors and others non-residents of said county of Frontier,
and others not electors of said county, as alleged in said
protest and answer; and that no proof was introduced
showing that any of those signing said petition for submission were electors of said county; and that the tax levy
of said county had been exhausted, and there were no
funds out of which the expenses of such election, if called,
could be paid, and such election, if ordered, would create
an indebtedness in excess of the amount levied for the
county general fund.

"That the proceedings in said record, certified as aforesaid, were in fact had, and the acts and things therein stated
were done at the times therein named, and the said board,
being duly and fully advised in the premises, and having
the facts and proofs referred to before it, did find and enter of record the motion or order set forth in said proceedings as shown by 'Exhibit A' aforesaid, refusing to grant
said petition for submission or the prayer thereof.

"That on February 21st, 1887, a petition was presented
to these respondents while sitting and acting as the board
of commissioners of Frontier county, Nebraska, signed
by 644 names, giving age, section, town, and range upon
which said petitioners claimed to reside, and time of residence in said county, the prayer of which petition was to
call a special election to submit to the electors of said
county the question of the relocation of the county seat

of said county; that said petition was not supported by any
proof to the effect that it contained the names of *bona fide*
electors of said county equal in number to three-fifths of all
the votes cast in said county at the last general election held
therein, voluntarily signed to said petition, and the prayer
of said petition was denied and the said petition was dismissed; and said respondents submit, under the advice of
counsel, that they had power and jurisdiction to pass upon
the question of whether the names signed to said petition
were electors or minors, or fictiticus and apparent and
not real and *bona fide* electors of said county as required by
Section 1, Art. III., Relocation of County Seats, Compiled
Statutes of Nebraska, p. 232, which said original petition
is herewith submitted to the court, together with the original remonstrances signed by 1,164 electors of said Frontier county, and residents therein, all of which is respectfully submitted to this Honorable Court."

The proceedings of said board on the 21st of February,
1887, are as follows:

"And the matter of the petition coming on for hearing
upon the petition, protest, and answer, and the board, having heard the allegations, proofs, and arguments of the respective parties, adopted and entered of record the following order in the premises:

"It is ordered that the petition asking for a special election for the relocation of the county seat be dismissed and
the prayer therein be not granted, for the following reasons,
to-wit:

"1st. Because it appears of record that the inhabitants of
Frontier county do not want the county-seat relocated.

"2d. Because it appears that a number of the signers on
said petition are minors, non-residents and not electors of
said Frontier county, and state of Nebraska.

"3d. Because there is no proof that the signers upon said
petition are electors of said county and state.

"4th. Because the levy of said county has been exhausted,

and there are no funds out of which the expenses of such
election can be paid.

" 5th. Because by ordering such election an indebtedness
will be created in excess of the amount levied for a county
general fund."

These proceedings were signed by all the defendants.
The pleadings filed before the defendants by the attorneys
for the persons who presented their remonstrance to said
board need not be referred to here. The cause was submitted to this court upon the writ and return thereto. It
will be observed that the defendants concede that the petition presented to them contained 644 names, praying them
to call a special election to vote upon the question of relocation of the county seat of Frontier county, and that that
number was more than three-fifths of all the votes cast
at the last general election in said county; but they find
that minors, non-residents, and others not electors had
signed said petition, and that the number of persons thus
disqualified when deducted from the whole number of 644
reduced the number of qualified signers to less than three-
fifths of all the votes cast in said county, at said election.
The findings of the board are general, vague, and somewhat
indefinite; but they are sufficient, if true, to justify them in
refusing to call the election.

Section 1, Art. III., Chap. 17, Compiled Statutes, provides that, " Whenever the inhabitants of any county are
desirous of changing their county seat, and upon petitions
therefor being presented to the county commissioners, signed
by resident electors of said county equal in number to
three-fifths of all the votes cast in said county at the last
general election held therein, said petition shall contain in
addition to the names of the petitioners the section, town,
and range on which, or town or city in which, the petitioners reside, their ages, and time of residence in the county,
it shall be the duty of such board of commissioners to forthwith call a special election in said county for the purpose
37

of submitting to the qualified electors thereof the question of the relocation of the county seat."

It will thus be seen that the defendants were the proper persons to determine, in the first instance at least, whether the petition presented to them was signed by resident electors of said county equal in number to three-fifths of all the votes cast therein at the last general election.

In *Smiley v. Samson*, 1 Neb., 56, it was held that the power to hear and determine the matter in controversy was jurisdiction, and that it is *coram judice* whenever a case is presented which brings the power into action. This case was cited with approval in *Franklin v. Kelley*, 2 Neb., 96, and by Judge REESE in *Van Sant v. Butler*, 19 Neb., 354, and in *Parker v. Kuhn*, Id., 396. If the decision of said board was unsatisfactory to the petitioners it was subject to review by the district court, and the error, if any, could thereby be corrected. No fraud is charged, and such decision cannot be treated as void, nor can the errors of the board be corrected in this proceeding.

To entitle the relator to the writ it must appear that he has a clear legal right to the performance of the duty, and that the law affords no other adequate remedy. *State v. School District*, 8 Neb., 94.

In *State v. Ramsey*, 8 Neb., 286, this court refused to compel the county commissioners of Cass county to call a second election for the relocation of the county seat, for the reason that the right of the relator was not clear, there being an allegation that certain illegal votes were cast at the previous election; and in *State v. Nemaha County*, 10 Neb., 32, where the commissioners rejected certain petitioners, thereby reducing the number of petitioners to less than three-fifths of all the votes cast in said county at the preceding general election, it was held that the error, if any, in rejecting said names could not be reviewed by proceedings in mandamus. The case last cited would seem to be decisive of this. The action of the board if unwarranted by the evidence before it may be corrected by proceedings in error, but in a matter in which they have original jurisdiction cannot be treated as void.

A peremptory writ is denied and the action dismissed.

JUDGMENT ACCORDINGLY.

THE other judges concur.

ARTHUR PERRY AND HENRY JOHNSON, PLAINTIFFS IN ERROR, V. JOHN GRANGER, DEFENDANT IN ERROR.

1. **Tenant in Common:** CHATTELS. Where a joint owner of personal property assumes without authority to sell the interest of his co-tenant, the latter may repudiate the sale and sue for the conversion of the property, or he may ratify it and sue for his share of the money received.

2. ——: ——. If one tenant in common of a chattel, without authority sell it, an action for conversion by his co-tenant will lie against him.

ERROR to the district court for Saunders county. Tried below before TIFFANY, J., sitting for POST, J.

Bell & Sornborger, for plaintiffs in error.

J. R. & H. Gilkeson, for defendant in error.

MAXWELL, CH. J.

This action was brought by the defendant in error against the plaintiffs, for the conversion of certain personal property. The cause of action is stated in the petition as follows:

"That on and prior to the 25th day of October, 1884, this plaintiff and S. Scott Case were the owners of, and in the possession of, the following described personal property,

to-wit: Two jacks and seven jennets; that said plaintiff
and said Case each owned an undivided half interest in
said property; that on or about the 15th day of November,
1885, the interest of said S. Scott Case was sold on an execution, and said Case since said sale had no interest therein; that said defendants took possession of said property
on or about the first day of March, 1885, and claim to be
the owners of the whole of said property, and have taken
the same from the possession of the plaintiff; that said
plaintiff has demanded possession of said property and
demanded his interest therein; but defendants refused to
deliver said property to the said plaintiff, or to recognize
his right in and to the possession, and claim and exercise
ownership over the whole of said property, and deny that
the said plaintiff has any right or interest to the same."
The value of the property was alleged to be $1,400.

The defendants below (plaintiffs in error) in their answer
allege that they purchased said property for a valuable
consideration without notice of plaintiff's claim.

On the trial of the cause the jury returned a verdict of
$400 in favor of Granger, and a motion for a new trial hav-
ing been overruled judgment was entered on the verdict.

A large number of errors are assigned, which in view of
the nature of the evidence need not be considered in detail.

The undisputed testimony shows that in January, 1883,
John Granger purchased of one S. S. Case a half interest
in the property in question for the sum of $600, and that
he has never sold his interest in such property.   It also
shows that Granger was absent from Saunders county, where
the property was kept, from October, 1884, until March,
1885.   About the 15th day of November, 1884, one-half
interest of the property in question was sold under legal
process against S. S. Case to one Smith.   Smith took entire
possession of the property, and about the first of March,
1885, sold, or attempted to sell, the entire interest in said
property to the plaintiffs in error for "$700 in trade."   To

this point there is no conflict in the testimony. Granger swears positively that he demanded his interest in the property from the plaintiffs in error, which they deny. Mr. Perry, however, does not make an unequivocal denial. His testimony is: "I heard Mr. Granger's testimony and the testimony of the other witnesses about a conversation with me at our barn. He made no such demand, and no such conversation took place. He was never there but once; the three Grangers and Mr. Gilkeson were there at that time * * * as we started out of the gate, this gentleman with gray whiskers remarked that there would be trouble about them (the property in question), and that was all there was said. I made no reply to that." From his own testimony it is apparent that he knew that Granger claimed a half interest in the property; but notwithstanding this knowledge, on the 9th day of April, 1885, he sold the entire property and the same was transferred to another county.

The rule is, that where a joint owner of personal property assumes without authority to sell the interest of the other owner, such owner may repudiate the sale and sue for the conversion of the property, or he may ratify it and sue for his share of the money received. *Small v. Robinson*, 9 Hun, 419.

Tenants in common are not like partners; the latter may dispose of chattels by virtue of an implied authority to sell without being liable for a tort, whilst the former can not dispose of them without violating the right of his co-tenant. For an unauthorized sale, therefore, of a chattel, an action of trover will lie by one tenant in common against another. *Wilson v. Reed*, 3 Johns., 175. *Hyde v. Stone*, 9 Cow., 230. *Gilbert v. Dickerson*, 7 Wend., 449. *Mumford v. McKay*, 8 Wend., 442. *Dyckman v. Valiente*, 42 N. Y., 549. *Weld v. Oliver*, 21 Pick., 559. *White v. Brooks*, 43 N. H., 402. *Neilson v. Slade*, 49 Ala., 253. *Courts v. Happle*, 49 Ala., 254. *Green v. Edick*, 66 Barb., 564. *Wheeler v. Wheeler*, 33 Me., 347.

Under the testimony the verdict is the only one that should have been rendered, and the judgment of the court below is affirmed.

JUDGMENT AFFIRMED.

THE other judges concur.

MARTHA I. COURTNAY, PLAINTIFF IN ERROR, V. C. B. PARKER ET AL., DEFENDANTS IN ERROR.

1. **Judgment:** LIEN. Where judgment is recovered in a district court against a vendor who has sold certain real estate in the same county but has not made a deed therefor, nor received the whole of the purchase money, such judgment is a lien on the vendor's interest in the land.

2. ———: ———. A party purchasing real estate subject to a judgment lien has notice of the extent to which such property may be subjected in satisfying the judgment, and where a vendor had retained the legal title in his own name and afterwards became security for the purchaser for money to enable such purchaser to build a house on such land and received a lien on such house which he failed to record; *Held*, That a purchaser under said judgment acquired all the interest of the vendor, including the lien on said house, the aggregate not to exceed the amount of the judgment lien. That is, he acquires the interest of the judgment debtor in the real estate.

ERROR to the district court for Lancaster county. Tried below before MITCHELL, J.

O. P. Mason and *D. G. Courtnay*, for plaintiff in error.

Lamb, Ricketts & Wilson, for defendants in error.

MAXWELL, CH. J.

This case was before this court in 1884, and is reported in 16 Neb., 311, the judgment of the district court being reversed and the cause remanded. The plaintiff claims a legal estate in lot 3, block 10, Lavender's addition to Lincoln, and that the defendants unlawfully hold possession of said premises.

The defendants in their answer set up certain equitable defenses which will be noticed hereafter.

On the trial of the cause a jury was waived and the cause submitted to the court, which found there was due the plaintiff upon the lot in question the sum of $76.85, the balance of the unpaid purchase money from one Parmenter to Luke Lavender.

The plaintiff appeals.

On the 19th of July, 1871, Luke Lavender sold to B. O. Kenable and C. O. Parmenter lots 1, 2, 3, and 4 in block 10 of Lavender's addition to the city of Lincoln for the sum of $1,600, $100 being paid at the time the contract was entered into, $500 to be paid on or before August 19th, 1871, $500 on or before February 19th, 1872, and $500 on or before August 19th, 1872, with interest at ten per cent on deferred payments. Upon the failure to make payments as above, the contract to be void at the option of Lavender, the amount paid to be held as stipulated damages for non-performance.

There is a contradiction in the testimony as to whether the $500 due August 19th, 1871, was paid. Lavender testifies that he never received but $100 upon the contract, while there is other testimony tending to show that he received $600 thereon.

The testimony shows that in October, 1872, Parmenter, being unable to pay for the lots in question, requested one Joseph W. Hartley to purchase lots 1, 2, and 4, which he did, and received deeds from Lavender therefor. The reason assigned by Parmenter for desiring Hartley to purchase was that "he (Parmenter) could not pay the balance of the purchase money."

From the testimony of Joseph W. Hartley it appears

that Lavender sold him said lots 1, 2, and 4. Whether Lavender had exercised his option to declare the contract at an end prior to the sale, does not appear. In October, 1871, Parmenter, desiring to borrow some money from one John C. Johnson, sought to obtain a release of lot 3 so that he could mortgage the same to obtain money to erect a house thereon. He stated to Lavender that he had paid $600 on the four lots and it would be safe therefore for him to release lot 3 and hold the other lots for the residue of the purchase money. This Lavender refused to do, but stated that he would sign Parmenter's note as surety for the money. Parmenter thereupon procured a loan from Johnson of $500, for which he gave a note with Lavender as surety. Parmenter then gave Lavender a lien upon the house on said lot 3. This lien was not recorded, and the court below refused to receive it in evidence. The above note Lavender was afterwards compelled to pay.

On the 30th day of January, 1874, Parmenter and wife conveyed to Joseph W. Hartley lot 3 in block 10, Lavender's addition to Lincoln, and on the 30th day of March of that year Hartley and wife conveyed said premises to the the defendants.

On the 4th day of November, 1873, one Henry Atkins recovered a judgment in the district court of Lancaster county against Luke Lavender. Various executions were issued on said judgment, and on the 3d day of November, 1879, said premises were sold to the plaintiff on an execution issued thereon. The sale was thereafter confirmed and a deed made to the plaintiff. It will thus be seen that the plaintiff is entitled to whatever interest in the premises Lavender had at the time the judgment in question became a lien. At the time that Hartley purchased said lot 3, and also at the time that defendants purchased the same, the judgment appears to have been entirely unsatisfied on the records of the district court of Lancaster county. They thus purchased with notice of the possible liability to which said property might be subjected under said judgment.

Lavender swears positively that he was paid but $100 on the purchase price of lot 3, but that Parmenter paid him $500 for one Kellogg who had bought lots 11 and 12 in the same block. We find no direct denial of this in the testimony.

It is also clearly proved that Lavender paid the note for $500, upon which he was surety, given by Parmenter to Johnson. To what extent, if any, Lavender was authorized to apply the money arising from the sale of lots 1, 2, and 4 upon the original contract does not appear from the testimony; it does appear, however, that Parmenter gave him a lien upon lot 3. This lien was not recorded, and as against a *bona fide* purchaser would be unavailing, but as against one purchasing with notice of a judgment against Lavender, the lienholder is entitled to show all of Lavender's interest in said premises. It is upon this equitable principle that one having contract of sale for certain real estate, where the legal title is in the name of the judgment debtor, is protected, and the land held liable upon the judgment only for the unpaid purchase money. The court erred, therefore, in excluding the lien given by Parmenter to Lavender on lot 3 in block 10, Lavender's addition.

If this lien was one proper to have been enforced by Lavender against Parmenter, and which upon a proper decree and a sale thereunder would have divested his title, it is proper for a court of equity to consider, in marshaling the several amounts to which the plaintiff would be entitled in purchasing the interest of Lavender in said premises. In other words, the lien is an interest, and as Lavender held the legal title, the judgment creditor is subrogated to all his rights in the land.

Whether Lavender had declared the contract for lots 1, 2, and 4 terminated, and the amount paid thereon as forfeited, before he sold said lots to Hartley, does not appear from the testimony.   The judgment of the district court is reversed and the cause remanded for further proceedings.

REVERSED AND REMANDED.

THE other judges concur.

M. W. BUTTS, PLAINTIFF IN ERROR, V. CAPITAL NATIONAL BANK, DEFENDANT IN ERROR.

1. **Negotiable Instruments:** EVIDENCE OF PAYMENT IN PART: BURDEN OF PROOF. Where an action was brought upon a promissory note for the sum of $250, and it appeared that originally the loan had been made for $500, that a number of renewals had been had, and it was claimed by the payee that the note sued on was for the balance of the original loan; *Held*, That a letter written by the payee to the maker, as follows: " LINCOLN, NEB., June 1, 1883. *Mrs. M. W. Butts*—Your letter received, and we credit $300 on note," imposed on the payee the burden of showing that the note referred to in such letter was not that held by the payee against the defendant.

ERROR to the district court for Lancaster county. Tried below before POUND and HAYWARD, J.J.

Harwood, Ames & Kelly and *Edson Rich*, for plaintiff in error.

Chas. O. Whedon, for defendant in error.

MAXWELL, CH. J.

This action was brought in the court below upon a promissory note, of which the following is a copy :
" $250.00.   LINCOLN, NEB., Nov. 25, 1884, No. 7183, A.

Ninety days after date I promise to pay to the order of Capital National Bank two hundred and fifty dollars, for value received and payable without defalcation or discount, at their bank in Lincoln, Nebraska, with interest at the rate of ten per cent per annum, from maturity until paid.

"P. O. BUTTS.

"Due Feb'ry 23–25, '85·   M. W. BUTTS."

M. W. Butts makes answer for herself as follows:

"She admits the plaintiff is a corporation under the laws of the United States, and that on the 25th day of November, 1884, she signed a note with P. O. Butts for $250 and ten per cent interest from February 26th, 1885, to said bank; but denies each and every other allegation in said plaintiff's petition contained.   And this defendant further answering says she is the wife of said P. O. Butts, having been married to him October 12th, 1882, and that about two weeks after such marriage defendant P. O. Butts informed this defendant that he was owing the plaintiff about the sum of $450, and wanted her to sign a note with him for that amount, stating that it was a mere matter of form as the banks require two signatures to a note, but that she would never have it to pay.   Relying on these statements this defendant went with P. O. Butts.   That afterwards the same was renewed at various times, until some time in January, 1884, said P. O. Butts paid a part of said note, and induced this defendant, by the same representations as at first, to sign a renewal note for the balance of said note unpaid in the sum of $250;   that said note of $250 was afterwards renewed from time to time until the note herein sued on was signed as such renewal by P. O. Butts; and this defendant further says that the debt so contracted with said plaintiff bank was the sole and individual debt of said P. O. Butts, and the same was contracted prior to the marriage of said P. O. Butts with this defendant; that this defendant never had a particle of benefit from the proceeds of said note or notes, and that said P. O. Butts has never contributed anything to the support of this defendant or her children since said marriage; and this defendant fur-

ther avers that said note has been fully paid to said bank
by said P. O. Butts, and that this suit is brought in the name
of said bank solely for the use and benefit of said P. O.
Butts, who thereby seeks to collect said note from the property of this defendant. Wherefore this defendant prays the
court that she be discharged from any indebtedness on said
note and may be hence dismissed with her reasonable
costs."

The reply admits the marriage of the defendant, but denies each and every other allegation in the answer.

On the trial of the cause a jury was waived and the
cause tried to the court, which rendered judgment in favor
of the bank for the sum of $287.50

The bank contends that but one note was given which
was for $500 loaned the plaintiff in error on the 31st
of October, 1882. On the amount thus loaned the plaintiff below admits there was paid on the 21st day of February, 1883, $100; on the 21st of May; 1884, a second
$100; and on the 29th of November, 1884, $50, new
notes being given at each of the times stated and the interest up to those dates being paid. It is contended on
behalf of the bank that the note in controversy was given
for the unpaid balance of the $500 loaned October 31st,
1882.

On behalf of the plaintiff in error the following letter
was introduced in evidence, signed by the proper officers of
the bank :

"LINCOLN, NEB., June 1, 1883.

Mrs. M. W. Butts—Your letter received, and we credit
$300 on note."

The letter also contains a reference to her business, to
which it is unnecessary to refer. The letter to which this
was an answer was not produced by the bank, nor was
any attempt made to explain it, except that the amount of
$300 was not entered on the books of the bank, and that
it would have been so entered if paid as stated. The ex-

planation is not satisfactory. There is a clear admission in the letter of the receipt of $300, and that the same was credited on the note. If there was but one note *prima facie* it would seem that that sum would have been credited on the note, and if so, there cannot be due the bank the sum recovered in this action. It devolves upon the bank to explain the letter referred to. The judgment, therefore, is contrary to the weight of evidence and is reversed, and the cause remanded.

REVERSED AND REMANDED.

THE other judges concur.

MCNAMARA & DUNCAN, PLAINTIFFS IN ERROR, V. ANTON CABON, DEFENDANT IN ERROR.

Judgment: FORM. A judgment in the following form is not void : "After hearing the proof it is the opinion of the court that the defendant, Anton Cabon, is indebted to the plaintiff in the sum of $100. It is therefore considered and adjudged by me that Anton Cabon pay to the plaintiff, McNamara & Duncan, the sum of $100.00 with interest from Dec. 20, 1883, and costs of this suit taxed at $3.15."

ERROR to the district court for Pierce county. Tried below before TIFFANY, J.

E. P. Weatherby, for plaintiffs in error.

H. C. Brome, for defendant in error.

MAXWELL, CH. J.

This action was commenced in the county court of Pierce county on the 20th day of December, 1883, and on

the 15th day of January, 1884, judgment by default was
entered against said defendant.

On the 22d of the following February a transcript of
said judgment was filed in the district court of said
county, and on the 29th day of January, 1885, an execution was issued out of said district court on said judgment
and levied on certain real estate in said county. On the
14th day of July, 1884, a motion was filed by the defendant in said district court asking that said execution be
quashed and that the transcript of judgment be stricken
from the files for the reason that there was no finding by
the court, and that there was no judgment entered on said
cause, and that said district court was without jurisdiction.

The finding and judgment of the court were in words
and figures as follows :

" After hearing the proof, it is the opinion of the court
that the defendant, Anton Cabon, is indebted to the plaintiff in the sum of $100.00. It is therefore considered
and adjudged by me that Anton Cabon pay to the plaintiff, McNamara & Duncan, the sum of $100.00 with in-
terest from Dec. 20, 1883, and costs of this suit taxed at
$3.15.

"JACOB B. SHAROT,
" Co. Judge."

The district court sustained the motion, to which the
plaintiff excepted, and now assigns the same for error.

The ruling of the court below seems to be based upon
the theory that the judgment in question was void.

Sec. 428 of the code of civil procedure defines a judgment to be "the final determination of the rights of the
parties in an action."

In *Lewis v. Watrus*, 7 Neb., 477, where the form was
"a judgment decreed in favor of plaintiff in the sum of
principal $174.70, interest 85 cents, judgment $175.55,"
and costs $9.30, it was held to be a final determination of
the rights of the parties to the action and a valid judg-

ment, although the language was untechnical. Citing *Taylor v. Runyan*, 3 Clarke (Ia.), 474; *Minkhart v. Hankler*, 19 Ill., 47; *Fish v. Emerson*, 44 N. Y., 376.

In *Ransdell v. Putnam*, 15 Neb., 642, it was held that the finding of facts by a court where a jury is waived need not be more specific than would be required of the verdict of a jury.

In decrees of foreclosure and sale the form for many years has been, after finding that the defendants executed the mortgage, that it was duly recorded, and the conditions of defeasance had been broken, to say: It is therefore considered that unless the defendants shall within —— days pay, etc. Such form is not appropriate in an action at law, yet we cannot hold that it is void. The judgment in the case at bar determines the amount 'due from the defendant to the plaintiff, and requires him to pay the same; and this, though informal, in a collateral proceeding, we must hold, under the definition of a judgment given by the code, to be a judgment. It follows that the judgment of the district court must be reversed and the cause remanded for further proceedings.

REVERSED AND REMANDED.

THE other judges concur.

J. C. GATZ, PLAINTIFF IN ERROR, V. ANTON CABON, DEFENDANT IN ERROR.

ERROR to the district court for Pierce county. Tried below before TIFFANY, J.

E. P. Weatherby, for plaintiff in error.

H. C. Brome, for defendant in error.

MAXWELL, CH. J.

The questions involved in this case are substantially the same as those which arose in *McNamara & Duncan v. Anton Cabon, ante* p. 589, and the same judgment will be entered as in that case. The judgment of the district court is reversed and the cause remanded for further proceedings.

REVERSED AND REMANDED.

OSWALD MULLER, PLAINTIFF IN ERROR, V. ANTON CABON, DEFENDANT IN ERROR.

ERROR to the district court for Pierce county. Tried below before TIFFANY, J.

E. P. Weatherby, for plaintiff in error.

H. C. Brome, for defendant in error.

MAXWELL, CH. J.

The same questions arise in this case as were determined in *McNamara & Duncan v. Anton Cabon, ante* p. 589, and the same judgment will be entered as in that case. The judgment of the district court is reversed and the cause remanded for further proceedings.

REVERSED AND REMANDED.

21
d54

VIRGIL ALLYN, PLAINTIFF IN ERROR, v. THE STATE
OF NEBRASKA, DEFENDANT IN ERROR.

1. **Criminal Law**: MISDEMEANOR: TRIAL WITHOUT PLEA.
   Where a defendant is put on trial for a misdemeanor without a
   plea to the indictment having been entered, it is a mere technical error or irregularity which does not affect any of his substantial rights and affords no ground for reversal of a judgment
   of conviction. *Vide State v. Hayes*, 24 N. W. Rep., 575.

2. ——: ACCESSORIES. The fact that a defendant was acting as
   the agent of another in the commission of an offense will afford
   no excuse or justification for the act in a prosecution therefor.

ERROR to the district court for Dawson county. Tried
below before TIFFANY, J.

G. W. McNamar, for plaintiff in error.

Wm. Leese, Attorney General, for defendant in error.

REESE, J.

Plaintiff in error was indicted for maintaining a nuisance. The trial resulted in a verdict of guilty, and a fine
of fifty dollars was imposed. From that judgment he
prosecutes error.

There are two principal questions presented for decision:

First. The record fails to show that plaintiff in error
was arraigned, or that he entered any plea to the indictment, or waived arraignment. It is claimed that the trial
in the absence of such plea or waiver was erroneous, and
that a new trial should be granted for that reason.

It must be conceded that at common law, both in England and in this country, it is almost universally held that
the trial of a party charged with a crime, without plea, is
erroneous. But under our system of criminal jurispru-
dence, as established by the code, the rule seems to be

38

pretty well settled that the omission to enter a plea to an indictment, especially in prosecutions for misdemeanor, is not necessarily fatal where the whole case was tried upon its merits, as upon a plea, and where the party has not been deprived of any of his substantial rights.

In *State v. Greene*, 23 N. W. Rep., 154, Reed, J., in writing the opinion of the court, says: "Treating the proceeding as a trial of defendant on the accusation contained in the indictment, the action of the court in putting him upon trial without a plea having been entered was a mere technical error or irregularity which in no manner affected any of his substantial rights. The fact that no plea had been entered was overlooked by the court and district attorney, through inadvertence, no doubt. The case was treated, however, at every stage of the proceeding, and by all of the parties, as though a plea had been entered. The allegations of the indictment were all regarded as denied by the defendant. The state was required to establish the charge in the indictment by the same character of evidence and with the same certainty which would have been required if the formal plea of not guilty had been entered." The conviction was sustained.

In Maxwell's Criminal Procedure, at page 541, the author says: "A party who personally and by his consent goes into court, practically on a plea of not guilty, should not, after verdict, be permitted to assign as a reason for setting aside the verdict that he was not asked to say whether he was guilty or not guilty before the trial. He has had the benefit of the plea of innocence in his favor and has been prejudiced in no right. Those cases that hold that this right cannot be waived, overlook the difference between the procedure under the code and at common law, where the accused was not allowed a copy of the indictment as a *right*, nor counsel to make his defense; where, in fact, all the machinery of the courts was brought to bear to secure, if possible, his conviction." See also, to the same effect, *State v. Hayes*, 24 N. W. Rep., 575. *State v. Cassady*, 12 Kas., 550. *Territory v. Shipley*, 2 Pac. Rep., 313.

While the proceeding was irregular, yet there was no prejudicial error, and the judgment cannot for that reason be reversed.

Second. It appears that the land upon which the nuisance was maintained was the property of the Brighton Ranch Company and it is contended that plaintiff was only their agent in the commission of the offense, and therefore the company should have been prosecuted if any one, and that this conviction cannot be sustained.

We do not care to discuss the question here, whether the corporation referred to was liable to indictment; nor whether or not a corporation may be indicted in this state, as these questions are not before us in this case. The law of principal and agent has no place in criminal procedure. If another person than a defendant procures him to commit the crime charged, such other person may be prosecuted under the provisions of section one of the criminal code, or as a principal; but we know of no rule of law which will allow the offender committing the criminal act to escape because he was acting as the agent of another. The ruling of the district court upon this part of the case was correct.

The judgment of the district court is affirmed.

JUDGMENT AFFIRMED.

THE other judges concur.

PATRICK HAGGERTY, PLAINTIFF IN ERROR, V. SAMUEL
A. WALKER, DEFENDANT IN ERROR.

1. **Default**: ANSWER. Unless a default is caused by the gross
laches of a defendant, or his authorized attorney, he should be
permitted to answer upon such terms as to the payment of costs
as may be prescribed by the court, at any time before judgment
is rendered; and where it is apparent that the answer presents a
meritorious defense, the court must permit the answer to be
filed.

2. **Practice in Supreme Court**: CORRECTING RECORD. The
affidavit of the clerk of the district court cannot be resorted to
for the purpose of correcting a transcript of the record certified to
by him. If a false or erroneous record is certified to by him it
should be corrected by a certified transcript of the record as it is.

3. **Answer** examined, and held to state a defense.

ERROR to the district court for Holt county. Tried
below before TIFFANY, J.

Thurston & Hall and *H. M. Uttley*, for plaintiff in error.

Thomas O'Day, for defendant in error.

REESE, J.

This action was instituted for the purpose of recovering
the amount alleged to be due upon a promissory note. An
order of attachment was issued and the property of plaintiff in error levied upon. It appears that on the 17th day
of February, 1886, a motion to discharge the attachment
was submitted to the district court, and on the 19th of
the same month the motion was sustained and the attachment dissolved. A motion for security for costs was filed
by plaintiff in error—but on what date we are not informed
—and on the 26th day of February the motion was heard,
but the necessary security having been given it was over-

ruled. On the same day, and in the absence of the attorney for plaintiff in error, a default was entered. On the 27th an answer was filed and with it a motion to set aside the default, and an affidavit of plaintiff in error showing his reliance on his attorney, his absence from court, and the *bona fides* of the defense pleaded in his answer. The motion to set aside the default was overruled and judgment rendered.

It further appears that subsequently a supplemental motion to set aside the judgment was made and was also overruled. A question arises as to whether an exception was taken to the ruling on this last motion. The record shows such to be the fact. An affidavit of the clerk is filed by which it is shown that no exception appears upon the court records.

Without stopping now to enquire whether or not an exception to this last order was essential to a review, we must hold that the certificate of the clerk to the transcript, which shows an exception, cannot be contradicted by the affidavit of the same officer. He is the custodian of the record; if an imperfect record is filed in the first instance the proper method of correcting it is by a perfect one, authenticated by the proper certificate. Sec. 408, Civil Code.

In *Blair v. West Point Manufacturing Company,* 7 Neb., 146, an application to set aside a default and permit a defendant to answer was overruled by the district court. In reviewing the case the court, by the present Chief Justice, says: "The court should have set the default aside and permitted the plaintiffs in error to answer. A party in default may be permitted to answer upon such terms as to the payment of costs as may be prescribed by the court, at any time before the judgment is rendered. And where it is apparent that the party in default has a meritorious defense to the action, the court must permit the answer to be filed. The court cannot deprive a suitor of a substantial right under the plea of the exercise of discretion." Citing *O'Dea v. Washington County*, 3 Neb., 122; *Mills v. Miller*, Id., 95.

In *Clutz v. Carter*, 12 Id., 113, a default had been entered for want of an answer, followed by a trial and judgment in the absence of the defendant. In a review of the order of the district court refusing to set aside the judgment, Judge COBB, in writing the opinion, says: "It is the spirit and policy of the law to give every party an opportunity to prosecute or defend his case in court, and courts will never deny such right except for the fault or gross laches of such party or his authorized attorney."

In the case at bar the default was entered on the same day the motion for security for costs was heard and decided. On the next day, and before judgment, the answer was filed and with it the affidavit of plaintiff in error and his motion to set aside the default. If the answer stated a defense the issues presented should have been tried. If any delay or expense was occasioned, the proper terms as to payment of costs should have been imposed in the discretion of the court.

The answer as shown by the abstract presented the defense that there was nothing due on the note upon which the suit was brought; that A. N. Shuster & Co., the payees, at the time the note was given, agreed with defendant that, if he would give the note for the amount expressed upon its face, they would forward him goods to the amount of $3,000, to make good certain overcharges and offsets claimed by him, growing out of previous transactions in the purchase of merchandise of them by him, but that they had failed so to do, to his damage, etc.; that plaintiff took the note without consideration, after maturity, and with full knowledge of all the facts connected with its execution and of his rights as against it. He demanded his set-off.

If Shuster & Co. actually owed plaintiff in error $3,000, as alleged, and procured his note for their claim, upon the promise that they would pay the $3,000 by a shipment of goods, and had failed to comply with their agreement—he not being at fault—he would have been entitled to his defense as against them. The fact, if true, that defendant in error received the note without consideration, after maturity, and with knowledge of plaintiff's rights, would not deprive him of this defense.

Under the rule stated in the cases above cited the default should have been set aside, and the issue presented should have been tried.

The judgment of the district court is reversed, the default set aside, and the cause remanded for further proceedings.

REVERSED AND REMANDED.

THE other judges concur.

THE STATE, EX REL. W. L. BERRY, v. H. A. BABCOCK, AUDITOR, AND G. L. LAWS, SECRETARY OF STATE.

1. **Construction of Statutes.** Statutes should be construed, if possible, so as to give effect to every clause, and one act should not be placed in antagonism with another prior act, unless such was clearly the intent of the legislature.

2. ———. All statutes *in pari materia* must be taken together and construed as if they were one law. *Hendrix v. Reiman*, 6 Neb., 516.

3. ———: REPEAL BY IMPLICATION. A statute will not be considered repealed by implication unless the repugnancy between the new provision and the former statute is plain and unavoidable. *Lawson v. Gibson*, 18 Id., 137.

4. **Precinct Bonds.** The provision of section 28 of chapter 18 of the Compiled Statutes of 1885, which requires the adoption of the amount of tax to be levied to meet the liability incurred by the issuance of bonds, is mandatory and must be complied with in the issuance of precinct bonds under the provisions of chapter 58 of the Session Laws of 1885, as well as in the issuance of county bonds.

ORIGINAL application for mandamus.

William V. Allen, for relator.

William Leese, Attorney General, and *Williams, Jenckes & Redlon*, for respondent.

REESE, J.

The county commissioners of Madison county submitted to the electors of Union Crcek precinct, in said county, a proposition to issue seven thousand dollars of precinct bonds to aid in the construction of a court house in the village of Madison, the county seat. The proposition, as submitted, was adopted, the bonds executed by the county officers and presented to the auditor and secretary of state for registration and certification. Those officers, for reasons which will hereafter appear, declined to register and certify the bonds, and this suit is brought for the purpose of compelling action by a peremptory writ of mandamus.

The cause is submitted upon a stipulation, which we here copy in full:

"It is hereby agreed by and between the parties hereto, that the annexed transcript marked exhibit 'A,' and which is incorporated into and made a part of this stipulation, is a true and accurate history and transcript of all things connected with and pertaining to the voting of $7,000 of precinct bonds, of Union Creek precinct, Madison county, Nebraska, on the 13th day of August, 1886. The relator having presented the bonds, duly executed and in proper form, to the defendant Babcock, auditor of state, for registration, and to the other defendant, as secretary of state, to be certified, they respectively refused to register and certify said bonds, solely on the ground that the commissioners of Madison county, in calling the election in the precinct to vote on the question of the issuance of said bonds, did not

embrace in the submission an additional proposition to
'adopt the amount of the tax to be levied to meet the liability incurred,' as provided in section 28, chapter 18,
Compiled Statutes of 1885—all other matters being adjudged and found by them to be strictly regular and
in conformity to the statute.   The parties submit this
question and no other to the consideration of the court.   In
submitting the question of the issuance of said precinct
bonds to the voters of Union Creek precinct, was it necessary to the validity of the election that there be embraced
in the submission an additional proposition 'adopting the
amount of the tax to be levied to meet the liability incurred,' by the voting of said bonds, as provided in section
28, chapter 18, Compiled Statutes of 1885?   If this shall
be answered in the negative, a writ of mandamus shall be
issued to the defendants, requiring them to respectively
register and certify said bonds.   If answered in the affirmative no writ shall be issued."

It will thus be seen that the question presented for decision is whether or not it was necessary to comply with
the provision of sections 27 and 28 of chapter 18, Compiled
Statutes of 1885, in submitting the question of the issuance
of the bonds to the voters of the precinct.   Our attention
is particularly directed to section 28, which is as follows:

"When the question submitted involves the borrowing
or expenditure of money, or issuance of bonds, the proposition of the question must be accompanied by a provision to levy a tax annually for the payment of interest, if
any, thereof, and no vote adopting the question proposed
shall be valid unless it likewise adopt the amount of tax to
be levied to meet the liability incurred."

It is believed by the auditor and secretary that the latter
clause of the foregoing section is in force, and that its provisions are mandatory; while it is contended on the part
of the relator that the provisions contained in subsequent
enactments have so far modified this section in its applica-

tion to the bonds in question as to render a compliance
with its terms unnecessary.

It is not our purpose to follow and discuss, in detail, the
very able and logical argument presented in the brief of
the attorney for relator, but must be content with a brief
statement of our conclusions and their application to the
case at bar.

It is a fundamental principle of law that in constructing
statutes all provisions on the same subject must be construed together, and if possible all should be harmonized
so that the whole should be consistent as if they were one
law. *Hendrix v. Reiman*, 6 Neb., 516. And, if possible, so
as to give effect to every clause; and one part should not
be placed in antagonism with another. *McCann v. Mc-
Lennan*, 2 Id., 286. It is also well settled that repeals of
statutes by implication are not favored, and a statute will
not be considered repealed by implication, unless the repugnancy between the new provision and the former statute is plain and unavoidable. *Lawson v. Gibson*, 18 Id.,
137.

The section (28) above quoted has been in force for a
number of years, and its provisions are mandatory, unless
modified by the act of March 6, 1885. Laws of 1885,
ch. 58. Comp. Stat., ch. 45. The section can receive but
one construction: "No vote adopting the question proposed
shall be valid unless it likewise adopt the amount of tax to
be levied to meet the liability incurred." Has this law
been changed? It is insisted that it has in so far as its
application to precinct bonds is concerned, and that this
change is affected by the act of 1885. This act gives authority to precincts, etc., to issue bonds to aid in the construction of court houses, and for other purposes therein
named, and that upon a petition being presented to that end
the county commissioners shall call an election for the purpose of voting upon the proposition of issuing the bonds.
"The notice, call, and election shall be governed by the

law regulating the election for voting bonds by a county."

Sections three and four are as follows:

"Sec. 3. The county commissioners or persons charged with levying the taxes for the county shall each year, until the bonds voted under the authority of this act be paid, levy upon the taxable property in the precinct, township, or village, a tax sufficient to pay the interest and five per cent of the principal of bonds issued under this act; and at the tax levy preceding the maturity of such bonds, levy an amount sufficient to pay the principal and interest due on said bonds.

"Sec. 4. All proceedings in relation to such election and the issuance of the bonds shall be in accordance with the provisions of this act."

It is insisted by the relator that "It being the duty of the commissioners to levy the tax to pay the bonds, it was not necessary for the people to vote on that question, and hence not necessary to include it in the submission;" that the duty to provide a fund to meet the payment of the bonds is vested solely in the county board, regardless of any vote upon that subject by the people.

We concede that the duty of providing the means of payment, by the levy of taxes, devolves upon the county board, and that no one else can discharge that duty. But the question to us is one of authority. Has the board the authority to levy the taxes without being directed so to do by the voters? It would have been entirely competent for the legislature to have incorporated the clause above quoted from section 28 into the body of the act of 1885, and the presence of such a provision would not have been in the least in conflict with any provision of the act. It would simply have been that, when the bonds were voted and the authority given to levy the taxes to meet the liability incurred, the county board should levy the necessary taxes each year until the bonds were paid. It seems to the mind of the writer that no one could consistently claim that a conflict would exist between such provisions. But as the provision already existed in section 28 it was unnecessary to re-enact it, and the whole ground was covered by the second provision of section one, which is: "Upon the reception of such petition the county commissioners shall give notice and call an election in the precinct, township, or village, as the case may be. Said notice, call, and election shall be governed by the law regulating the election for voting bonds by a county." Now by referring to section 28 of the prior act we find what the call (or proposition) shall be, and by that section the call or proposition in the case at bar must be measured.

This argument is not met by the provisions of section four above quoted. All proceedings in relation to the election and issuance of the bonds must be in accordance with the provisions of the act, so far as the provisions reach; but there is no provision regulating the notice to be given, the call to be issued, nor the manner of conducting the election. There is ample provision as to the presentation of the petition and the issuance of the bonds if the proposition be adopted. But as to other matters we are referred by the act itself to the law governing elections upon the subject of voting bonds by counties. This law says that "no vote adopting the question proposed shall be valid unless it likewise adopt the amount of tax to be levied to meet the liability incurred." The provision is mandatory and to it we must yield.

WRIT DENIED.

THE other judges concur.

WILLIAM E. SAVAGE, ADMINISTRATOR OF THE ESTATE
OF CHARLES A. SAVAGE, PLAINTIFF IN ERROR,
V. JONAS B. AIKEN, DEFENDANT IN ERROR.

1. **Money Had and Received:** EVIDENCE: FOREIGN JUDG-
MENT. On the 26th day of July, 1886, plaintiff instituted this
action against defendant upon a count for money had and received. Upon the trial, for the purpose of sustaining his case, he
introduced evidence tending to prove an account stated on the
12th of August, 1871. He also introduced a stipulation entered into between the parties, in a suit pending in the circuit
court of Adams county, Illinois, dated October 25th, 1877,
whereby defendant consented to a judgment in that action.
The stipulation was admitted over the objection of defendant;
Held, Error, as not tending to prove the allegations of the
petition.

2. **Pleadings:** REPLICATION. A plaintiff can recover only on the
cause of action stated in his petition. It is not the province of
a reply to introduce a new or different cause of action from that
stated in the petition.

3. **Account Stated:** INTEREST. Where an action is prosecuted
upon an account stated by a defendant, and in which he charges
himself with interest on money in his hands at the rate of ten
per cent per annum, this will imply a promise to pay interest
at that rate, if the proof shows the statement to have the effect
of an account stated.

4. **Money Had and Received:** EVIDENCE: PLEADINGS. If
in an action for money it is shown that payments have been
made or money collected upon the same account after the commencement of the suit, by judgment in a foreign court or otherwise, the recovery can only be for the balance remaining due.
But before a defense of that kind can be made, the issue must
be presented in the pleadings.

ERROR to the district court for Gage county. Tried below before BROADY, J.

Wm. H. Berry and *A. Hardy,* for plaintiff in error.

Hazlett & Bates and *L. W. Colby,* for defendant in error.

REESE, J.

This action was commenced in the district court of Gage county, on the 26th day of July, 1876. The allegation of the petition is "that on the first day of July, 1876, the defendant, Charles Savage, was indebted to the plaintiff in the sum of eleven thousand dollars for so much money by the defendant had and received for the use of the plaintiff, and which said sum of money was then due and payable, yet the defendant has not paid" the same, etc. An attachment was obtained on the ground of the non-residence of Savage, and his real estate was levied upon and sold.

It is developed by the evidence that C. A. Savage, the defendant in the action, now deceased, resided in Quincy, Illinois, the plaintiff therein in New Hampshire, and that considerable correspondence was had between them, each knowing the residence of the other, and that Savage had on two or three occasions sought to sell Aiken the lands in this state on his indebtedness to him. Apparently without noticing these offers, Aiken caused the attachment proceedings, without Savage's knowledge, and purchased the land at sheriff's sale. After the sale he sent the original claim to an attorney with instructions to bring suit for the whole amount, which was done, and on the 27th day of October, 1877, a written stipulation for judgment, signed by Savage, was filed and on which a judgment for seventeen thousand dollars was rendered. A few days afterward, but during the same term of court, defendant in error notified his attorneys that the Nebraska lands had been sold for "something over five thousand dollars," and directed that that amount should be deducted from the judgment. The attorney notified Savage of the fact, made the deduction and caused the judgment to be finally entered for $11,073.- 33. The deduction, however, was made prior to giving the information to Savage. This was the first that Savage knew of the proceedings in this state. There seems to have been nothing in Savage's conduct to warrant this duplicity on the part of defendant in error; but, as its consideration is not of vital importance, we need not notice it further at this time. It is proper, however, to remark that courts of justice are established for the purpose of protecting rights and enforcing remedies in a legitimate method, and not for the purpose of aiding designing men to take undue and dishonest advantages of others by reason of the liberal provisions of our laws.

Subsequent to this, Savage applied to the district court of Gage county to open the judgment under the provisions of section 82 of the civil code, and upon the opening of the judgment he filed his answer, in which he denies the indebtedness and alleged, in substance, that in the year 1863 plaintiff and defendant entered into a copartnership in the business of buying and selling lands in the state of Missouri; that by the terms of said copartnership plaintiff was to furnish the capital necessary to carry on the business, and defendant was to do all other things necessary in conducting it; that plaintiff furnished $11,400, which was invested in real estate; but that, contrary to the provisions of their contract, defendant was compelled, for the purpose of carrying on the business, to employ his own means in the payment of taxes and other expenses; that the last business transacted by said firm was in the year 1869; that subsequent to that year and prior to the first day of January, 1871, plaintiff had received from said firm $9,613.75; that no settlement of the business of said firm had ever been had, and that on a fair accounting but a trifling sum, if anything, would be found due plaintiff from defendant. The statute of limitations is also pleaded in the usual form.

On the 8th of March, 1884, the death of defendant was suggested, and on the 21st day of December, 1885, the final order of revivor was made and the cause revived in the name of plaintiff in error, as administrator of the estate of Charles A. Savage, deceased.

On the first day of June, 1886, defendant in error filed a reply by which he alleged, as answer to the first defense contained in the answer, that an accounting was had between plaintiff and Charles A. Savage, in his life-time, of the money furnished by defendant in error and property sold by Savage, and that the amount due and owing by Savage was agreed to, and that an account was stated between plaintiff and Savage, and on the 12th day of. August, 1871, a statement thereof was made by Savage to plaintiff. The defense of the statute of limitations was denied, and sundry payments and acknowledgments in writing alleged.

It is further alleged that after the commencement of this action and after the real estate owned by Savage, to the amount of $5,226.76, had been sold, plaintiff brought suit on the same cause of action set out in his petition in this case, in the circuit court of Adams county, in the state of Illinois; and that on the 3d day of October, 1877, Savage acknowledged in writing, the indebtedness sued upon in this action, and signed a stipulation therein which was filed and made part of the record in said cause, but by agreement in open court $5,226.67 was deducted from the amount agreed to be due from defendant to plaintiff in that action; and that by such action defendant is éstopped to defend further in this action. All other allegations of the answer are denied.

It seems that some objection was made to this reply, and on the 2d day of June, 1886, defendant in error took leave to file a supplemental petition, but for some reason it was never filed.

On the trial a witness was called who identified a paper, known as exhibit "A" in the record, as the writing and signature of the deceased. It consists of a statement of the account between him and defendant in error. By it it is shown that at that time, according to the accounts of deceased, there was $14,442.15 due defendant in error "on account of Missouri lands." This instrument was offered for the purpose of showing a closing up and settlement of their partnership matters, and proving an account stated. This was objected to as incompetent and barred by the statute of limitations. The objection was overruled. We think this ruling of the court was correct. The paper did have a tendency to prove the statement of the account between the parties, and if accepted as such and so treated by defendant in error, both parties would be bound by it in the absence of fraud or mistake. *McKinster v. Hitchcock,* 19 Neb., 100. The instrument was therefore competent to prove the act of Savage in stating the account, as well as to prove the terms of the statement. In case it was followed by proof of such conduct on the part of defendant in error as would bind him, the evidence would be sufficient to submit to the jury. The objection that it was barred by the statute of limitations could not be sustained, for the reason that, according to the issues, it was necessary to prove the indebtedness and follow up the proof with evidence of subsequent payment, acknowledgment, or promise sufficient to remove the bar. The question of limitation would then be one of fact for the jury upon the whole case.

Other instruments in writing, such as letters, statements, etc., from Savage to plaintiff in error, were introduced and received in evidence over the objection of plaintiff in error; but we do not deem it necessary to notice any of them, except the one referred to in the record as "plaintiff's exhibit I."

This is the stipulation referred to in the reply. It is as follows:

"Jonas B. Aiken,   }   In the circuit court
         v.   }   of
"Charles A. Savage. }   Adams county, Illinois.

"It is agreed that the amount due and owing from me to the plaintiff upon the account sued on in this case is seventeen thousand (17,000) dollars, and that judgment may be entered for that sum and costs of suit.   Dated October 25, 1877.   C. A. SAVAGE."

The stipulation was filed two days later and a judgment was entered for the amount named.   This evidence was offered and admitted over the objections of plaintiff in error in the evidence in chief offered by defendant in error in support of the allegations of the petition.

We are unable to see how this paper could have been admissible—especially at that stage of the trial.   It did not support any allegation of the petition, for it was not in existence for more than a year after the petition was filed, and hence could have been admitted only in support of a supplemental pleading, if at all.   Civil code, sec. 145. It is true that the fact was alleged in the reply, but "a plaintiff can recover only on the cause of action stated in his petition.   It is not the province of a reply to intro- duce new causes of action.   This can only be done by amendment of the petition."   *Hastings School District v. Caldwell, Hamilton & Co.*, 16 Neb., 68.   Maxwell's Pleading and Practice, 108.   *Durbin v. Fisk*, 16 O. S., 534.   Or by supplemental pleading.   Section 145, civil code.   The making of that stipulation was, in no sense, an acknowledgment of the cause of action stated in the petition in *this* suit, for it affirmatively appears that, at the time the suit was commenced in Illinois, the attorney for defendant in error did not have the statement of account here relied upon; and from the stipulation itself, it appears that that action was upon an account.   Again, it is difficult to see how a confession of an indebtedness of $17,000, if upon the same cause of action, could support an allegation of indebtedness made fifteen months before, of $11,000. Under the pleadings the stipulation should not have been admitted, and its admission was clearly error.

It is claimed that the judgment is excessive, and that no more than six per cent per annum could be allowed as in-

terest. If it be established to the satisfaction of the jury
that the statement rendered August 12, 1871, in connection with the conduct of defendant in error, amounted to an
account stated, then, as Savage charged himself with interest
at the rate of ten per cent, his estate would be bound by it
and that rate should be allowed.

On the trial the defense offered to prove the amount of
property obtained by defendant in error under the Illinois
judgment. This was excluded, and we think rightly.
There was no issue of that kind presented by the pleadings.
If money has been realized upon that judgment, it should be
deducted from the indebtedness and a judgment rendered
for what is due, if anything. But this can only be done by
presenting the issue by the proper answer.

The judgment of the district court is reversed and the
cause remanded for further proceedings, with leave to the
parties to file supplemental or amended pleadings if they
desire to do so, upon such terms as may be prescribed by
the district court.

REVERSED AND REMANDED.

THE other judges concur.

GEORGE ESTERLY & SON, PLAINTIFFS IN ERROR, V.
M. T. VAN SLYKE AND A. HUSTON, DEFENDANTS
IN ERROR.

Instructions to Jury. An instruction not warranted by the
pleadings nor evidence, will require the reversal of the judgment, if it have a tendency to mislead the jury.

ERROR to the district court for Fillmore county. Tried
below before MORRIS, J.

Ryan Bros., for plaintiffs in error.

John P. Maule, for defendants in error.

REESE, J.

This is an action upon two promissory notes, each for
$100, executed by defendants in error to plaintiffs in error
for the purchase price of an Esterly harvester and binder.
The cause has been tried three times. The first trial resulted in a verdict in favor of defendants; the second in a
verdict in favor of plaintiffs for $90. These verdicts were
set aside by the district court and new trials granted. The
third trial resulted in a verdict in favor of defendants,
which the court refused to molest, and proceedings in error
are now prosecuted by plaintiffs in this court.

The answer filed by defendants in the district court admitted the execution of the notes, but presented the defense,
substantially, that the harvester was taken on trial, but not
purchased; that it was taken upon the representation that
it was a good machine, properly constructed, and would do
good work; if it failed to comply with the representations
it was to be returned to the agent from whom it was received; that it was not as represented and failed to work,
notwithstanding, after notice from them to plaintiffs' agents,
they came to where it was and tried to adjust its parts so
that it would cut and bind grain according to the purpose
of its construction; that after the harvest was over,
plaintiffs agreed with defendants that they should retain it
until the next year, and that during the intervening time
plaintiffs would repair it and make it a good and perfect
machine, and one that would do good work; that relying
upon the promises so made by plaintiffs, the defendants,
on the 17th day of the following March, executed and delivered the notes upon which the action was brought. It
is further alleged that plaintiffs failed to comply with their

agreement to repair the machine, and that it was "entirely useless" to defendant as a harvester and binder, and they returned it to plaintiffs.

Plaintiffs, by their reply, deny the allegations of the answer and allege that the harvester was sold upon a written warranty alone.

This warranty is set out in the reply, but need not be here copied as it is in the usual form, requiring notice of failure, and time to be allowed to remedy the defects, if any, and upon failure to furnish a new machine or refund the purchase price. This warranty was dated July 18th, 1881, the day of the delivery of the harvester to defendants. The reason why we do not think the terms of the warranty are material here is, that the witnesses upon both sides agree in their testimony that plaintiff had notice of the fact that defendants claimed that the harvester failed to work, and their agents and employes went to where it was at various times and worked with it and replaced defective parts.

The evidence as to whether the machine was actually purchased, or whether it was taken and retained on trial, was conflicting, and the finding of the jury upon that question would not, of itself, warrant the setting aside of the verdict as not supported by proof.

It is undisputed that defendants received the harvester in 1881, that they made an effort to use it during the harvest of that year, and in the following March executed the notes upon which this action is founded. There is nothing in the pleadings which puts in issue the authority of Van Slyke to act for both himself and Huston in procuring the machine. Huston does not deny it, but in effect concedes it in his testimony.

The ninth instruction given the jury was as follows: "On the part of the defendant the court instructs you that if Huston did not sign the printed warranty and did not authorize Van Slyke to sign it, and did not afterwards ratify Van Slyke's act in signing it, he would not be bound by that written warranty if his acts afterwards did not ratify it.   That is to say, if he did not afterwards do something in connection with it, showing that he accepted of it,—you are to view all of this testimony together, and from a view of all of the facts and circumstances, come to the conclusion as to whether it was purchased at the first—when the order was made; whether the subsequent act of Mr. Huston ratified it or whether it was purchased at the second time when the notes were agreed to be given, and whether there was any warranty at that time or not. Now if there were a sale of the machine and the notes were given for the machine, any promise that might have been made by the general agent or any one authorized by the company, of what would be done in the future, would neither alter the contract nor be a defense to the note.   So I want the jury to distinctly understand if the contract was made at the time the notes were given, that was one thing; if they find that the contract was made at the time of the signing of this order, and these subsequent promises were made to induce these men to carry out their contract, it would not be a defense.   Whatever remedies he might have would be in some other action.   It is important to keep these things separate and by themselves, so as to let our best light settle these matters; as it is a matter for the enforcement of the law, whether justice is done by these parties as we see it, or whether they were entering on an ill-advised contract upon their side."

By this instruction the question of the authority of Van Slyke to make the original purchase or sign the instrument containing the warranty (or the subsequent ratification of what was done) is made a question of more or less importance to be decided by the jury.   As we have seen, it was not in the case and it should not have been submitted to the jury. *Newton Wagon Co. v. Diers*, 10 Neb., 284. *Turner v. O'Brien*, 11 Id., 108. *Steele v. Russell*, 5 Id., 211. *Smith v. Evans*, 13 Id., 314. We can not say that it was not prejudical, as it is clear that under it the jury might have entered into the inquiry and found against plaintiffs and in favor of Huston upon that point.

We do not deem it necessary to discuss all the propositions contained in this instruction; but we think that part by which the jury is instructed, in substance, that a change in the contract, after purchase, would afford no defense, is too strongly stated in plaintiff's favor. Suppose the harvester had been actually purchased in the first instance, upon the warranty contained in the order signed by Van Slyke. The notice, as we have seen, having been acted upon by plaintiff, was sufficient. Could it be maintained .that it would not be competent for the parties to make a new contract, especially after the failure of the harvester, if there was one, by which the old contract would be set aside or rescinded, and a new one made? We think not. But it is said by plaintiffs that the warranty given in the first instance "contained notice that no other warranty could be given by any agent." We do not so read it. The provision is, that "No agent has any authority to change above warranty." This certainly would not prevent an agent from making a new contract of conditional sale upon the same warranty, as to construction and capacity, rather than have a machine returned as worthless. It is true he could not change the ("above") warranty, but he and the general agent, Leffingwell, could rescind the old contract and make a new one on substantially the same terms as the old (as is claimed by defendants), and a failure to comply with it might constitute a defense. The terms of the warranty, if made as claimed by defendants, were not changed from the old or printed one in any material part, but that the machine should be made to comply with the original warranty of a good machine.

Again, as testified to by defendant Van Slyke, this agreement was made prior to the execution of the notes. Under it, it is claimed, they were given. They were accepted by plaintiffs, and they are now trying to enforce them by suit. It, of course, is charged with knowledge of the facts of their execution and delivery. *Chariton Plow Co. v. Davidson*, 16 Neb., 377. Having accepted the proceeds of the agreement, they ratified it, and are bound by its terms.

We do not see that the rule here stated is in any manner in conflict with that stated in *Wood, etc., Co. v. Crow*, 30 N. W. Rep., 609. In that case the only question was as to the authority of an agent to sell upon a different warranty from that which the purchaser knew was the only one he was authorized to give. In this case the notes were dated at a season of the year when such machines are not usually sold, and, as claimed by defendants, after the warranty given had failed and the conditions requiring notice and return had been waived.

The answer is quite voluminous, and in many respects is not clear or definite in its allegations. Matters of evidence are pleaded which might better have been omitted, and many questions were presented to the jury by the trial and instructions which, it seems to us, do not enter into the case, but which we do not think it necessary to discuss here. As we view the answer, there are but two defenses presented. One is, a failure of consideration for the notes; in other words, that the harvester was worthless when received. The other, that the sale was conditional, the machine taken on trial, and subject to the compliance on the part of plaintiff with the alleged agreement to make it a good machine. Either of these, if proven, would constitute a defense to the action. As to whether or not they are established is a question of fact for a trial jury to determine.

The judgment of the district court is reversed and the cause remanded for further proceedings.

REVERSED AND REMANDED.

THE other judges concur.

MILTON TOOTLE ET AL., PLAINTIFFS IN ERROR; V. LUTHER B. MABEN, DEFENDANT IN ERROR.

1. **Negotiable Instruments:** ACCOUNT.: PLEA OF PAYMENT. Where in an action on a promissory note and account the answer of the defendant was a plea of payment and over-payment, and there is a failure of proof to show payment of the account, a verdict for the defendant thereon cannot be sustained.

2. **Trial:** ISSUES. A cause should be submitted to the jury upon the issues made by the pleadings, and not upon incidental questions which may arise from the testimony.

ERROR to the district court for Holt county. Tried below before POST, J., sitting for TIFFANY, J.

Groff, Montgomery & Jeffrey and *Uttley & Small*, for plaintiffs in error.

M. P. Kinkaid, for defendant in error.

MAXWELL, CH. J.

This action was commenced in the county court of Holt county, where a judgment was rendered for the plaintiffs for the amount claimed, less $36.04. The defendant appealed to the district court, and in May, 1885, the plaintiffs filed their petition in said court, stating their cause of action to be:

That prior to August 14th, 1884, the plaintiffs sold and

delivered to Maben & McCormick goods, wares, and merchandise, for which said firm was indebted at that date to
the plaintiffs in the sum of $636.41; that on or about
said date the firm of Maben & McCormick was dissolved,
and its indebtedness to the plaintiffs was assumed by the
defendant, and he agreed with the plaintiffs to pay the
same; that pursuant to said agreement, on or about August 25, 1884, defendant did pay on said account the sum
of $130, and, in partial payment of the balance thereof,
gave his promissory note of which the following is a copy:

"$300.00.   DELOIT, NEB., Aug. 25, 1884.

"Thirty days after date, I promise to pay to the order
of Tootle, Maul & Co., at the bank of Neligh, three hundred dollars, value received, with interest at 10 per cent
per annum.   L. B. MABEN."

And that he promised to pay the balance within a short
time; that there was due from the defendant to the plaintiffs, upon said note and the balance of said account, a copy
of which was attached to the petition, marked 'Exhibit
A' and made a part thereof, including interest, the sum
of $517.71, for which, with interest and costs, the plaint-
iffs prayed judgment against the defendant. The following is a copy of the account, the principal of the note
being added thereto:

Tootle v. Maben.

MABEN & McCORMICK,
In Account with TOOTLE, MAUL & CO.,
S. W. Cor. Harney and Eleventh Sts.

1884.		DR.				CR.	
1	18	To Mdse......60	$ 27 07	6	3	By Cash	$ 75 00
		90	58 50	8	28		130 00
	21	60	17 16			Bills receivable	300 00
		90	31 77			Balance..........	206 41
2	14	60	26 04				
		90	10 00				
4	9	30	4 75				
		60	145 93				
		90	157 00				
6	3	60	140 48				
		90	79 48				
	4	90	7 65				
	7	90	2 00				
	30	90	3 58				
			$711 41				$711 41
		To Bal............	$206 41				
		" Int............	11 30				
		" Note..........	300 00	and	int.		
		Due.......	$517 71				

The defendant filed his answer as follows:

"First. He denies each and every material allegation contained in the petition not herein expressly admitted.

"Second. Admits the making of the promissory note, but alleges that it was given by him through mistake, he believing that he was indebted to the plaintiffs in the sum of said note at the time of making and delivering the same to plaintiffs, but he has since learned that he was not indebted to plaintiffs, but had overpaid them on a running account in the sum of about $100, as he is informed and believes, and said note was thus given without any consideration.

"Third. Alleges that plaintiffs are indebted to him for said $100 and seven per cent interest thereon from August 25, 1884, for which amount, with interest, he prays judgment against the plaintiffs."

The plaintiffs' reply is a general denial of all new matters contained in defendant's answer.

On the trial of the cause the jury returned a verdict in favor of the plaintiffs for the sum of $339.20.

A motion for a new trial having been made by the plaintiffs and overruled, judgment was entered on the verdict.

The principal errors relied upon are: First, That the court erred in giving the following instruction: "The giving and acceptance of a promissory note, as in this case, raises a presumption of settlement of all matters pertaining to the transactions at that time under consideration; therefore, to entitle plaintiffs to recover upon the account sued on, they must not only prove that the goods were not only in fact sold to defendant, or Maben & McCormick, but they must also prove by a preponderance of evidence that the said balance on said account was omitted from any settlement at the time of the execution of said note." Second, The verdict is contrary to the evidence.

It will be seen that the answer is a plea of confession and avoidance. It admits the account, but alleges that the defendant has paid it—in fact, paid more than was due thereon. The rule is well settled that under a plea of payment in the answer, the burden of proof is on the defendant to prove it. *N. P. R. R. Co. v. Adams,* 54 Penn. St., 94. *Gernon v. McCan,* 23 La. Ann., 89. *Knapp v. Runals,* 37 Wis., 135.

It does not require the citation of authorities, however, to sustain the proposition, as it is fundamental. No issue is made in the pleadings or proof that the note included the whole account. The note was not made upon a settlement of accounts between the parties, but upon the mere statement of an agent of the plaintiffs that so much was due. The defendant in his testimony claims that he was not bound by such note, and the plaintiffs were not if there was a mistake in the amount due from the defendant. The case was thus submitted to the jury upon a matter not at issue, and without proof that the defendant had paid the account the jury returned a verdict thereon in his favor. This they had no authority to do. The judgment of the district court is reversed and the cause remanded for further proceedings.

REVERSED AND REMANDED.

THE other judges concur.

THE PAXTON CATTLE COMPANY, PLAINTIFF IN ERROR, v. THE FIRST NATIONAL BANK OF ARAPAHOE, DEFENDANT IN ERROR.

1. **Corporations**: RECOVERY ON NOTE GIVEN BEFORE ORGANIZATION PERFECTED. Where after articles of incorporation were drawn up and signed by the promoters of a cattle company, but before they were recorded or filed for record in the office of the county clerk, and before the time fixed in such articles for the commencement of the business of such corporation, a president was selected for the corporation, by such promoters, and the president, in the presence and with the approval of all of such promoters, executed and delivered to one M. a note, in payment for, and in consideration of, the sale and delivery of certain horses, cattle, ranch, and other property to said corporation, which, after the perfecting of the said corporation and the time fixed for the commencement of the business thereof, came into its hands as its property, and continued to be used and enjoyed by it as such ; *Held,* That the endorsee of M. could recover on said note.

2. **Pleading**: REPLICATION. Where a defendant in an action alleges by way of answer any matter in bar of the plaintiff's action, the plaintiff may, by way of reply, allege any fact or facts not inconsistent with the facts alleged in his petition, by reason of which the defendant may be estopped to avail himself of such defense.

3. **Negotiable Instruments:** CONSIDERATION. The sale and relinquishment of an inchoate homestead, or other possessory right upon the public domain, together with the ranch and other improvements thereon; *Held,* To constitute a good and valid consideration for a promissory note.

ERROR to the district court for Red Willow county. Tried below before GASLIN, J.

John Dawson and *Calvin H. Frew,* for plaintiff in error.

W. S. Morlan, for defendant in error.

COBB, J.

Plaintiff commenced its action in the district court of Red Willow county by filing the following petition:

"1.   On the 12th day of July, 1884, the defendant was justly indebted to one J. B. Meserve, in the sum of five thousand five hundred dollars, balance due on the sale and delivery of certain horses, cattle, and a ranch, at that time sold and delivered to said defendant by J. B. Meserve, and said defendant then agreed to pay said J. B. Meserve said sum of $5,500 on the 1st day of April, 1885, with interest at eight per cent; and thereafter, in consideration of the foregoing, on the 14th day of July, 1884, the defendant, in accordance with the terms of said contract, and as at the time of said sale, mutually agreed, executed, and delivered to said J. B. Meserve its promise in writing, in words and figures following, to-wit:

'PAXTON, ILLINOIS, July 14, 1885.

In consideration of the sale and delivery of all the cattle, horses, and ranch by J. B. Meserve to the Paxton Cattle Company, of Ford county, Illinois, the said Paxton Cattle Company promises to pay J. B. Meserve $5,500 on April 1, 1885, with eight per cent interest, provided said company has then sold capital stock of said company so as to have the means to pay the same; and whenever any stock over $23,000 shall be sold then such sums shall be applied on this note of April 1, 1885.

> PAXTON CATTLE COMPANY,
> By GEORGE WRIGHT, Pres.'

"2. On the 1st day of April, 1885, defendant had sold capital stock of said company so as to have the means to pay said indebtedness to J. B. Meserve. Previous to the beginning of this suit, defendant had sold of the capital stock as follows, to-wit:

On the 14th day of July, 1884, $32,200.

On the 3d day of May, 1885, $1,000.

On the 20th day of July, 1885, $22,800.

"Total amount of capital stock sold, $56,000, from which the defendant realized the sum of $56,000.

"No part of said indebtedness has been paid except the sum of $490, on the 17th day of December, 1884.

"3. On the first day of March, 1886, the plaintiff loaned to the said J. B. Meserve the sum of $4,000, to be repaid on the 2d day of June, 1886, and in consideration of said loan the said J. B. Meserve executed and delivered to the plaintiff his promissory note in writing, in words and figures following, to-wit:

'$4,000.   ARAPAHOE, NEBRASKA, March 1st, 1886.

Ninety days after date, we or either of us promise to pay to the First National Bank of Arapahoe, Nebraska, or order, four thousand dollars, for value received, payable at the First National Bank of Arapahoe, Nebraska, with interest at the rate of ten per cent per annum from maturity until paid.

> J. B. MESERVE.'

"And to secure the payment of said promissory note, according to the tenor thereof, the said J. B. Meserve, on the 1st day of March, 1886, sold said claim against defendant, and delivered said instrument in writing of said Paxton

Cattle Company to this plaintiff, by writing endorsed thereon, as follows :

'ARAPAHOE, NEB., March 1st, 1886.

I hereby assign the within obligation to the First National
Bank of Arapahoe, as collateral security for the payment of
my note of this date, for the sum of $4,000, with the under-
standing that the said bank shall collect the amount due
thereon and apply the amount collected, first, to the payment
of my said note, and the surplus is to be paid to me.

[Signed]   J. B. MESERVE.'

"4. No part of said debt has been paid, and the plaintiff
is now the owner and holder of said obligation of Paxton
Cattle Co., by virtue of said sale and assignment, and
there is now due the plaintiff from the defendant thereon
the sum of $5,315.74, with interest at eight per cent from
April 1st, 1885, against said defendant."

On the first day of October, 1886, the defendant filed
its answer, setting up "that it is not now, nor was it ever,
incorporated; that no meeting for the election of officers
or the transaction of any other business was held in the
state of Nebraska by the pretended stockholders or directors of said company, the state in which the articles of incorporation were filed, which was on the 11th day of August,
1884, long after the instrument set forth in plaintiff's
petition was executed; that the said George Wright, who
executed said instrument, was never president of said company or association of persons, and had no authority to
sign the said instrument; that at the time of making said
instrument the Paxton Cattle Company consisted of the
following named persons: J. B. Meserve, the person mentioned in plaintiff's petition, George Wright, Calvin H.
Frew, O. D. Sackett; and the said J. B. Meserve had full
knowledge of all the facts connected with the attempt of
the above named persons to organize as a corporation.
Setting up further that the defendant, as a consideration
for said instrument and indebtedness, received from J. B.

Meserve cattle and ranch in Chase county, Nebraska, said ranch consisting of fourteen hundred and forty acres, the whole for an agreed sum of thirty-two thousand two hundred dollars, all of which has been paid except the sum mentioned in plaintiff's petition, that said ranch consisted of land held under the United States homestead and preemption laws, by persons who agreed with the said J. B. Meserve, for a consideration paid or to be paid, to convey said real estate to him or to the persons to be designated by him; and the said J. B. Meserve, as a part of said agreement, and as a consideration for said instrument mentioned in plaintiff's petition, agreed to obtain and perfect the title to said real estate and have it conveyed to said defendant; all of which was prior to the making proof and obtaining title to said real estate; that at the time of making said agreement said J. B. Meserve occupied and held, under the United States homestead laws, one hundred and sixty acres, as part of said fourteen hundred and forty acres, and agreed to convey said real estate upon the making of final proof and obtaining title to the same, the said company agreeing to furnish the necessary money to pay the expense of obtaining title to said real estate. All of the above agreements in regard to said real estate were fraudulently and corruptly made, for the purpose and with intent of violating the laws of the United States. Said J. B. Meserve has since made proof and has obtained title to said real estate, but has refused and still refuses to convey said one hundred and sixty acres to the defendant. Said one hundred and sixty is reasonably worth the sum of twelve hundred dollars; that defendant has not received title to any of said land except 320 acres; that the balance of said land which J. B. Meserve agreed to obtain the title and convey the same is reasonably worth the sum of seven thousand dollars."

On the 11th day of October, 1886, the plaintiff filed a reply to defendant's answer, to the 2d and 3d counts thereof.

40

"That on the 12th day of July, 1884, Calvin H. Frew, George Wright, J. B. Meserve, and O. D. Sackett agreed on articles of incorporation for said Paxton Cattle Company, and on the said 12th day of July all of said individuals subscribed said articles of incorporation and adopted for said Paxton Cattle Company the name of 'Paxton Cattle Company,' and afterwards, to-wit, on the 12th day of July, 1884, said individuals, for the purpose of completing said corporation and putting it into operation, assembled together and elected said Calvin H. Frew, secretary and treasurer, O. D. Sackett, vice president, and George Wright, president of said company ; and from said last mentioned date up to the present time said individuals, and others who have since the 12th day of July, 1884, associated themselves with said individuals and purchased capital stock of said company, have retained and assumed the name of 'Paxton Cattle Company,' and acted in a corporate capacity, with a full set of corporate officers, acting as such from said last mentioned date up to the present time.

"2d.   And on said 12th day of July, 1884, when said individuals were assembled as aforesaid, they elected the following board of directors, to-wit: George Wright, Calvin H. Frew, O. D. Sackett, and J. B. Meserve, and assumed full corporate powers, and at various times since have elected officers, bought, sold, and held property as a corporation, and each and every day from said 12th day of July, 1884, up to the present time, said individuals and this said association have represented themselves to be duly incorporated under the name of the 'Paxton Cattle Company,' and have assumed to be and acted as a corporation; and the same George Wright, from the time of his election as president of said company as aforesaid, up to the present time, has assumed to be and acted as president of said company, and is the only person who has acted as such officer or been recognized as president of said company.   After the election of said officers and directors, to-wit, on the

12th day of July, 1884, said individuals owning all the
capital stock of said company, and claiming to be duly incorporated under said name of 'Paxton Cattle Company,'
and acting in a corporate capacity, at a meeting when all
of said individuals and officers were present, for the benefit
of said corporation, agreed to buy the horses, cattle, and
ranch named in plaintiff's petition and defendant's answer,
and pay the said J. B. Meserve therefor the amount of
twenty-six thousand dollars; and it then and there paid
the said J. B. Meserve all of said $26,000, excepting the
sum of $5,000; and said George Wright, on the 14th day
of July, 1884, in the presence of all the officers and individuals of said company, and under their direction and
procurement, and with the consent of each and every officer
and individual of said company, signed the instrument in
writing set out in plaintiff's petition as president of said
company, as evidence of the debt due said J. B. Meserve
by said company. Said J. B. Meserve entered into said
contract with said company as a corporation duly incorporated, and accepted said instrument in writing subscribed by
said George Wright as president of said Paxton Cattle Company, as the promise in writing of said company, duly incorporated. At the time of the meeting of the individuals
aforesaid, on the 12th day of July, 1884, it was the agreement and understanding between all of them that said
Paxton Cattle Company would in all respects duly incorporate, and from said 12th day of July, 1884, up to the
present time, said company has assumed, exercised, and
practiced all the powers, privileges, and rights of a corporation duly incorporated under the laws of the state of Nebraska. And said instrument of writing, subscribed by
said George Wright as president, was assigned to said
plaintiff under the representation to this plaintiff that said
company was duly incorporated; and this plaintiff, relying
on said representations and the long and continued use on
the part of said defendant of said corporate powers and

privileges, accepted the assignment of said instrument and debt as collateral security for the note of J. B. Meserve set out in the petition.   The said J. B. Meserve has fully performed and complied with all the terms of the contract on his part entered into between him and said company, and said company, from the 14th day of July, 1884, up to the present time, has accepted the result of said contract with said J. B. Meserve, and kept and retained possession of all the horses, cattle, and ranch mentioned in said petition, and has enjoyed all the benefits, rights, privileges, and advantages of said contract from the 14th day of July, 1884, up to the present time, with no other authority, right, title, or consideration than that derived through said contract with said J. B. Meserve.   Since the filing of the articles of incorporation of said company in the office of the county clerk of Red Willow county, to-wit, on the 17th day of December, 1884, and at divers other times previous to filing the petition in this action, said defendant promised to pay the said J. B. Meserve the balance remaining due on said contract as set forth in said petition.

"2d. Plaintiff denies each and every allegation of 2d and 3d defenses in defendant's answer, not herein before specifically admitted."

There was a trial to the court with a finding and judgment for the plaintiff.   A motion for a new trial having been overruled, the defendant brings the cause to this court on error, and assigns the following errors:

"1st. The court erred in refusing to grant a new trial in this case.

"2d. The court erred in giving judgment for the plaintiff upon the note in question, because it was given before the articles of incorporation were filed, and before the day fixed in the charter for the company to commence doing business, and before $30,000 of the capital stock had been paid in as required by its charter.

"3d.   The court erred in permitting the defendant to

prove the new matter set up in the reply, because it stated a different cause of action from that stated in the petition.

"4th. The court erred in giving judgment for the defendant on the note before it was due.

"5th. The court erred in giving judgment for defendant, because the note was given for an illegal consideration.

"6th. The court erred in giving judgment for defendant when the petition did not state facts sufficient to constitute a cause of action."

Upon the trial there was introduced in evidence an agreed statement of facts, which is too lengthy to be inserted here, in full. Such parts of it only will be given as are deemed necessary to an understanding of the points relied upon. From such statement it appears that on the 12th day of July, 1884, Calvin H. Frew, O. D. Sackett, J. B. Meserve, and George Wright met at the office of Calvin H. Frew, in Paxton, Illinois, for the purpose of forming a corporation to be known as the "Paxton Cattle Company." And thereupon said parties agreed upon articles of incorporation as follows:

* * * *

"ART. 2. The principal place of transacting the business of this incorporation shall be at Paxton, Ill., with a branch office at McCook, Neb.

* * * *

"ART. 5. This incorporation shall commence its business on the 15th day of July, 1884, and shall terminate on the 15th day of July, 1904, unless sooner dissolved or renewed by a vote of two-thirds of the stock."

* * * *

These articles were signed by all of the above named persons, and were recorded in Red Willow county on the 11th day of August following.

On the said 12th day of July, 1884, the said incorporators, being all present, proceeded to elect the officers of said company, and elected George Wright, president; O. D.

Sackett, vice president; Calvin H. Frew, secretary and treasurer; and a board of directors as follows: George Wright, Calvin H. Frew, O. D. Sackett, and J. B. Meserve. That on said day said J. B. Meserve agreed to sell to the said Paxton Cattle Company, and did sell and convey to said company by bill of sale then and there executed and delivered, certain cattle, saddle ponies, mules, wagons, harness, "ranch equipments, cook stove, dishes, chains, tents, lumber, houses, sheds, fences, and everything else on said Meserve's ranch in Chase Co., Nebraska, on Frenchman river;" and it was then and there agreed that said Paxton Cattle Company should pay to said J. B. Meserve for the property that day agreed to be sold by said J. B. Meserve to said Company, the sum of twenty-six thousand dollars, and that the said J. B. Meserve should take in payment therefor the sum of ten thousand dollars in the capital stock of said company, at par, the remaining amount to be paid to him in money; and thereupon said J. B. Meserve executed and delivered to said Paxton Cattle Company the bill of sale above set forth; and thereupon the said J. B. Meserve, as manager for said Paxton Cattle Company, took possession of the ranch mentioned in said bill of sale, and all the horses, cattle, and personal property thereon, that had formerly belonged to J. B. Meserve; and the said Paxton Cattle Company, from the said 12th day of July, 1884, up to the present time, has kept possession of said ranch and property, and kept and retained possession of all the horses and cattle mentioned in said bill of sale, and has enjoyed all the benefits, privileges, and rights of said sale up to the present time, with no authority, title, or consideration other than that derived from said J. B. Meserve; that on the 14th day of July, 1884, at a meeting of all the officers and stockholders of said Paxton Cattle Company, the said company not having paid the amount still remaining unpaid to said J. B. Meserve, and there being still the sum of five thousand five hundred dollars unpaid, George Wright, its president, in the presence of and with the consent of all parties claiming to act as officers or stockholders of said company, executed and delivered to said J. B. Meserve the instrument in writing sued on in this action; that there was paid in of the stock of said company as follows: On the 14th day of July, 1884, there was sold and paid into the capital stock of said company twenty-six thousand dollars, and no more on that day; on the 30th day of May, 1885, one thousand dollars more of the capital stock of said company was sold and the amount paid in cash; on the 20th day of July, 1885, there was sold of the capital stock of said company $22,800 to various parties, as follows: To C. D. Fuller, $3,400; F. E. Cawley, $3,300; James K. Work, $5,100; to Dwight H. Loomis, $5,000, and $600 in addition to other parties. This stock was paid for by cattle delivered to and taken possession of by said company on the 20th day of July, 1885.

"That on the 1st day of March, 1886, the plaintiff in this action loaned to J. B. Meserve the sum of $4,000, to be paid on the 2d day of June, 1886, and in consideration of said loan said J. B. Meserve executed and delivered to said plaintiff his promissory note set out in his petition in this action; and to secure the payment of said promissory note, according to the tenor thereof, said J. B. Meserve on the said first day of March, 1886; sold said claim against defendants, and assigned and delivered the instrument in writing of said Paxton Cattle Company to the plaintiff, by writing endorsed thereon as set out in the petition; and afterwards, on the 31st day of August, 1886 said J. B. Meserve renewed the said note to the plaintiff, and there is still due on the renewal of said note of said J. B. Meserve to said plaintiff the sum of $4,000, and that said instrument in writing signed by George Wright, and set out in the petition, is held by the plaintiff as collateral security for said last mentioned note by said J. B. Meserve

to said plaintiff; and that there has nothing been paid on
the instrument purporting to be executed by said Paxton
Cattle Company and signed by George Wright, president,
except the sum of $490 on the 17th day of December, 1884;
that the meeting on the 12th day of July, 1884, when said
pretended articles of incorporation were acted upon and
signed, was held in the town of Paxton, Ford county, in
the state of Illinois, and that the pretended election of officers was held in the said town and state; and that there has
been no meeting of the pretended stockholders or directors
of said company ever held in the state of Nebraska or in
the town of McCook; that said articles of incorporation
were never filed in the office of the county clerk of Red
Willow county, Nebraska, until the 11th day of August,
1884, nor were said articles filed at any other place; that
said George Wright, who signed the instrument set out in
plaintiff's petition, pretended to act by the authority of an
election held in the town of Paxton, Illinois, on the 12th
day of July, 1884, and by no other official authority whatever; that at the time of the delivery of the bill of sale
above mentioned by J. B. Meserve, there was also delivered by said J. B. Meserve to the Paxton Cattle Company
an agreement in words and figures following:

"' Articles of agreement made this 12th day of July, 1884,
between J. B. Meserve, of McCook, in Red Willow county,
Neb., party of the first part, and Paxton Cattle Company,
of Paxton, Ford county, Illinois, party of the second part,
witnesseth: that the party of the first part has bargained,
sold, and will convey and deed, if so desired, with release
of homestead and release of dower by the wife of said first
party, unto second party, all his interest, right, title, or claim
of any nature or kind whatsoever, in and to the following
real estate, to-wit: W $\frac{1}{2}$ of nw $\frac{1}{4}$ of section 11, and sw $\frac{1}{4}$
of sw $\frac{1}{4}$ of section 2, and n $\frac{1}{2}$ of ne $\frac{1}{4}$ of section 10, and n $\frac{1}{2}$
of nw $\frac{1}{4}$ and sw $\frac{1}{4}$ of nw $\frac{1}{4}$ of section 10, and n $\frac{1}{2}$ of ne $\frac{1}{4}$ of
section 9, and south half of se $\frac{1}{4}$ of section 4, and the s $\frac{1}{2}$

of the s ½ of section 3, and sw ¼ of section 4, and se ¼ of section 5, and sw ¼ of section 5, and nw qr of ne qr of section 8, and n ½ of nw qr and sw qr of nw qr of section 8, and ne qr of section 7, and sw qr of section 6, each and all of said pieces being in town 5, range thirty-six west, in Chase county, Neb., lying along both sides of the French-man river; and second party is to be at all expense and outlay in perfecting the title to said land, and second party as the owner of said land, so far as first party's interest therein is concerned, has the sole control thereof; and first party covenants and agrees to do all he can to obtain and perfect the title to said land in and to the second party.

> "'J. B. MESERVE.
> "'PAXTON CATTLE COMPANY,
> "'By GEORGE WRIGHT, President.'

"That the legal title to the land mentioned in said contract was in the government of the United States at the time of the delivery of the same, and was held by various persons who had filed thereon under the homestead, pre-emption, and timber culture laws of the United States; that at the time of the execution and delivery of said contract, J. B. Meserve had a homestead entry on the south-west quarter of the south-west quarter of section 2, the north-west quarter of the north-west quarter of section 10, and the north half of the north-west quarter of section eleven, in township 5, range thirty-six west, in Chase county, being a portion of the land mentioned in said agreement; that since the delivery of said contract by said J. B. Meserve, the said J. B. Meserve has made proof upon said land described, and has received a receiver's final duplicate receipt from the receiver of the United States Land Office at Mc-Cook, Nebraska, but no patent has ever been issued to said J. B. Meserve therefor, and he has not conveyed nor attempted to convey since the making of said contract any title to said land to the Paxton Cattle Company; that the money necessary to prove up on said land was charged up to the Paxton Cattle Company; that the said J. B. Meserve, at the time of making the instrument set out in plaintiff's petition, sold to the Paxton Cattle Company, as shown by said agreement and bill of sale, in a lump, or as an entire consideration, for the sum of $26,000, the ranch, houses, horses, cattle, and other property mentioned in the bill of sale and agreement; that since the making of said agreement the Paxton Cattle Company has received the title to but 320 acres of said land mentioned in said agreement."

On the trial it was proved, on the part of the plaintiff, over objection by defendant's counsel, that the Paxton Cattle Company have ever since the 12th day of July, 1884, had persons who claimed to be officers of said company; that George Wright has claimed to be president of said Paxton Cattle Company.

Calvin H. Frew testified on the part of the defendant as follows:

"I have seen the agreement in regard to the land. I drew it. There was an agreement in addition to that put in writing in regard to the land mentioned in the agreement; he agreed to convey the land and perfect the title to the same to the Paxton Cattle Company. He was to get parties to take the timber claims; he was to work the lands and turn them over to the company the same as money. The company was to be at the expense. The company for Meserve was to procure the men to make those proofs. He objected to this going into the agreement. He said if that was written in the contract it might affect the title. He said it would leave the claims liable to contest. Meserve said at the time he made the contract the ranch was worth from $6,000 to $10,000. His own homestead was worth from twelve to fifteen hundred dollars. He (Meserve) said it was worth that much; that he could borrow $1,000 on it. The quarters the company got cost them $210 to $214 over and above what he paid the other parties.

"There were other persons claiming interests and rights to the property of the company besides Sackett, Wright, and J. B. Meserve. Other parties have purchased 10 shares, and they were purchased subsequent to the making of the instrument set out in the petition. The company has had no money at all; once or twice sold some cattle to pay up the debts. Only $1,000 of the capital stock was paid for in cash."

All of the above evidence was objected to by plaintiff as irrelevant, incompetent, and immaterial. Objection overruled and exceptions taken.

"Mr. Meserve has always met with us in Illinois, always except the last meeting or two. It is the same Meserve who acted as secretary and manager of the company. He still has interest in the company, and had at the commencement of this action.

"I estimated the value of the ranch lots of times. I don't think I estimated it at $6,000. We had one meeting on Saturday and then on Monday, in Illinois; had á meeting in November and December, 1884. I think perhaps we had another. We had a meeting to borrow some money in the year 1885. We had two or three meetings; then in 1886 we had just one meeting.

"We had to abandon our ranch. At the last meeting Mr. Meserve was elected secretary at Buckley, Illinois. I suppose he has had the custody of the papers. I suppose Meserve has kept the books at McCook. I think I know my own handwriting. I wrote the following letter. I have not the letter to which this is an answer. I could not tell whether I kept this letter. I don't pretend to keep all my letters. I keep some, and sometimes I keep them for awhile and then destroy them. I did not bring any letters with me in relation to the controversy."

Said letter was then introduced in evidence, which read as follows:

"PAXTON, ILL., Oct. 13th, 1885.

"*D. M. Tomlin, Esq., Cashier First National Bank, Arapahoe, Neb.:*

" DEAR SIR—Yours of 12th received. In reply I have
to say, 1st, it is not possible for the company to pay that
note now ; 2d, it is not due, notwithstanding it provides to
be paid April 1st, 1885.   If Hon. J. B. M. will sell shares
in the company which he agreed to do for the cash, the money
can be applied to pay that note.   He can do so if he tries.
It may be you are not informed about the merits of this
note, but Mr. M. has not even had the temerity to ask us
himself for it.   It can't by law be collected now.

"Very Respectfully,

"CALVIN H. FREW,

"*Secretary and Treas.*"

"At the time we made the contract with Meserve I did
not know how much money the company had in the treasury.   I was elected secretary and treasurer, and I suppose
I acted in that capacity.   I suppose I signed the paper as
secretary."

Q.   When did you, or any member of the company,
ever deny being an incorporation?

Objected to by defendant as immaterial, irrelevant, and
not proper cross-examination.   Objection overruled, and
defendant excepts.

A.   I don't know.

Q.   In whose name were the cattle held the last two
years ?

Objected to as not proper cross-examination.   Overruled,
and defendant excepted.

A.   I suppose the Paxton Cattle Company thought it
had some rights to it then.   Debts were created every day
in my name, in the name of George Wright, O. D. Sackett, J. B. Meserve, and John A. Koplins.

On re-direct examination defendant asked the following
question :

Q. · When was Mr. Frew secretary and treasurer?

Objected to as immaterial and irrelevant by plaintiff, and objections sustained, to which defendant excepted.

There was further evidence on the part of the plaintiff in rebuttal; but the foregoing is deemed sufficient for the purpose of a proper consideration of the grounds of error relied on.

As I understand the case, there is but one important point involved in it. It is not denied, nor can it be under the pleadings, admissions, and evidence, that long before the commencement of this action the plaintiff in error had been in existence both *defacto* and *dejure* as a corporation, under the laws of this state; but the contention is, that the action can not be maintained, for the reason that the instrument sued on was executed and delivered in point of time nearly one month before the filing and recording of the articles of incorporation of said company, and one day, in point of time, before that provided for in said articles for the commencement of the business of said incorporation. It is not denied that the consideration for which said instrument was given passed to the possession of said corporation and has been retained and enjoyed by it.

I have carefully examined the numerous cases cited by counsel for the plaintiff in error, to the proposition that " There could be no incorporation until the articles of incorporation were filed in the county clerk's office, as there should be a substantial compliance with the statute before the corporation could be considered *in esse*." This proposition is sustained by the cases of *Abbott v. Omaha Smelting Co.*, 4 Neb., 416; *Harris v. McGregor*, 29 Cal., 124; *Douthitt v. Stinson*, 63 Mo., 269, and *Stowe v. Flagg*, 72 Ill., 397; also *Bigelow v. Gregory*, 73 Id., 197. But these are all cases where parties were sued, either as natural persons or as partnerships, and sought to defend by pleading or proving corporate rights or powers. In all such cases I think it is held that the party alleging or relying upon such cor-

porate existence must prove at least a colorable compliance with all provisions of law upon which such
corporate existence is made to depend.   In the case at bar
the Paxton Cattle Company is sued as a corporation, and
sought to be held responsible for corporate acts antedating
its legal existence.   In other words, it is sought to make
it pay for property of which the corporation found itself
in possession upon coming into legal existence; and that at a
price and upon terms, in the agreeing upon and fixing
which, it had not, nor could have had, any legal voice.

There are well recognized principles of law under which
this may be done, supported by a line of well considered
cases, both American and English.   I will quote from two
of these cases, one of which is cited by counsel for plaintiff in error, in which it is held that the promoters of a
future incorporation, while the same exists only in prospect,
may contract obligations by which the corporation, when
legally organized, will be bound.

The case referred to is that of *Bell's Gap Railroad Company v. Christy*, 79 Pa. St., 54.   I quote from the syllabus: "Where a number of persons not incorporated, but
associated for a common object, intending to procure a
charter, authorize acts to be done in furtherance of their
object by one of their number, with the understanding that
he should be compensated, if such acts were necessary to
the organization and its objects and are accepted by the
corporation and the benefits enjoyed, they must be taken
cum onere and be compensated for."

In that case, while the court denied the claim of the
plaintiff for compensation · for his services in making a
pioneer survey of a route for a railroad, and procuring a
charter for the company, etc., it did so for the reason that
such services were procured and acquiesced in by less than
a majority of the active promoters of the scheme.   In the
opinion the court say: "We do not desire to controvert
the principles established in England, and to some extent

recognized in this country, that when the projectors of a company enter into contracts in behalf of a body not existing at the time, but to be called into existence afterwards, then, if the body for whom the projectors assumed to act does come into existence, it cannot take the benefit of the contract without performing that part of it which the projectors undertook that it should perform."

The case of *Low v. Railroad*, 45 N. H., 370, is quite in in point. The leading facts of the case may be shortly stated thus: The legislature of Vermont, in November, 1835, passed an act incorporating the Connecticut and Passumpsic Rivers Railroad Company, with power to construct a railroad from the south boundary of Vermont up the valleys of the Connecticut and Passumpsic to the north line of the state, the capital to be $2,000,000, and the act to be void unless $20,000 should be expended on the road within five years. Nothing having been done under the act, by an act of Oct. 31, 1843, the corporation was revived, subject to a similar condition, and Messrs. Fairbanks, Hall, and others were appointed commissioners to open books and receive subscriptions to the capital stock of the company. Near the close of the year 1844, for reasons stated in the case, there commenced a great revival of interest in the said line of railroad, and the plaintiff being largely concerned in business in Brantford, Vt., was engaged in the effort to awaken an interest in the enterprise of building the said railroad. Says the statement of the case: "The evidence tended to show that he collected maps, charts, and statistics showing the feasibility of the road and the probable amount of transportation upon it; that he was active in getting up meetings, public and private, of those interested at various places where the road was supposed likely to pass, at which meetings he was present and laid before the people assembled the material and data he had collected; and was successful in exciting a general interest and attention to the project. At some of these meetings Mr. Low sug-

gested to the persons present who took the principal lead
in the movement the necessity of some person being employed steadily in visiting and stirring up the people in
the different towns interested, in Vermont and New Hampshire, in visiting Boston and Canada, and inviting the attention of the capitalists to the advantages of the road, and
generally in forwarding the enterprise; that they all assented
to the suggestion and to the urgent need of such exertions,
and suggested to Mr. Low that he was the man, and the only
man, who could successfully accomplish the object. Mr.
Low stated his anxiety for the road and his willingness to do
what he could consistently, with due attention to his business; but that his business was large, requiring almost his
whole time, and that he could not afford to devote his time to
the railroad, as it was necessary that some one should do.
To which they replied that he must make it his business to
push forward the road, and assured him if he would do so
he should be abundantly compensated for his services and
expenses.   Mr. Low testified that he always expected to
be fully compensated and paid by the railroad company,
for his time and labor and neglect of his own business, and
that he devoted to this object almost all his time, from
Jan. 1, 1845, till the organization of the corporation on the
15th day of January, 1846.

"The gentlemen who gave these assurances to Mr. Low
were not corporators named in the charter, and no meeting
of the corporation had been held, or association formally
admitted; but they were active favorers of the enterprise,
intending to become stockholders, and actually taking
shares in it when the books were opened.

"The evidence tended to show that Mr. Low visited Boston and spent many weeks there, laboring to enlist the
co-operation of men of capital there; that he visited many
places in the vicinity of the route, and in Canada, to unite
their efforts and to encourage subscriptions." There was
evidence of other services rendered by Mr. Low of the

same general character; also, that to enlist the aid of one Harrison Gilmore, of Boston, he agreed to give him his best horse whenever the cars should run into Brantford, and that he accordingly did give him such a horse, which he testified was worth from $200 to $250.

After the organization of the company Mr. Low presented an account to the president, who was also disbursing agent for the company, for his expenses during the time for which his service was charged, which was allowed and paid; and at the same time he stated to the president that he had a claim for his services, and requested that it should be settled. This was not done, and the suit was finally brought for the value of such services and of the horse above referred to.

"The court charged the jury that by the charter all associates are corporators; that by the law of Vermont each corporator is charged with the duty of rendering all necessary service to carry out the provisions of the charter and to effect an organization; and that if any one performs necessary labor, and expends money in the discharge of such duty, and his action is assented to by the corporators, or, being known to them, is not objected to, and the corporation is organized and enjoys the benefit of such services, the law implies a promise to pay for them; that every person interested in the object for which an act of incorporation is granted, and who, with the knowledge and without the objection of the corporators, and with the assent and at the request of some of them, shall unite in assisting in the organization of the corporation, with a *bona fide* intention of becoming a member, by taking stock, and shall, as soon as books are opened, take stock, by subscribing for shares, is to be deemed an associate from the commencement of his labors, within the purview of the act of incorporation in this case, so far as the liability of the corporation for his services is concerned; that in this case, if some few of the corporators mentioned in the charter

41

requested the plaintiff to perform the services now in suit, or if the greater number of those who, like himself, became associates, and in the manner that he did—by subscribing for stock in the road and becoming members of the corporation, either requested the plaintiff to render such services, or knew of them and assented thereto, he will be deemed to have sufficient authority to render the services, and the law will raise a promise of the corporation to pay for said services, if necessary and reasonable."

To this instruction the defendant excepted.   .

"The defendant requested the court to instruct the jury that, prior to the organization no person, or persons, were competent to bind the corporation by contract, express or implied; that prior to the organization it would require the concurrence of a majority of the corporators named in the charter to bind the corporation by contract; that no subscription for stock could make the subscribers associates within the meaning of the charter before organization; that no intention to subscribe for stock, nor any acts done in furtherance of the objects of the enterprise could have that effect; that no one would become an associate within the meaning of the charter except after the organization, by being a subscriber for stock; that the corporation would be bound by no implied contract arising before organization; that the plaintiff is not entitled to recover anything on account of the horse delivered by him to Addison Gilmore, nor for the service performed at Montpelier in procuring a division of the charter, being of the kind called 'logrolling.'"   *   *   *   *   *   *

The court declined to give this instruction, to which the defendant excepted.

"But the court did instruct the jury that the corporation would be bound to pay for the horse delivered to Gilmore if they found upon consideration of all the evidence, and the nature of the employment, that Low was authorized to make such a contract in behalf of the corporation and

did so make it, and not otherwise.   *   *   *
The jury returned a verdict for the plaintiff which the defendants move may be set aside by reason of the preceding exceptions."

The court in the opinion say :

"The great question is, whether the plaintiff is entitled to recover of the incorporation, in any form, for services rendered by him antecedent to its organization, but which were necessary to enable it to complete that organization; and if so, whether the action of assumpsit can be maintained.

"In considering the first question it will be assumed for the present that the services were necessary, that they were rendered at the request of one or more of the original cor- porators or of those who were associated with them, and that the corporation accepted those services after its or- ganization, and enjoyed the benefits of them. Under such circumstances we are inclined to the opinion that it would become the duty of the corporation to pay for such services, and that in some form this duty could be enforced.

    *   *   *   *

"In such case it can avail nothing by way of defense, to show that in fact the party had no capacity to make such antecedent request, or to bind himself by a contract, as in the case of a corporation that was not organized at all, or imperfectly, any more than to show that in point of fact there was no such request or no contract made. But the promise is implied by law from the fact that the party, when it *had* capacity to contract, has taken its benefits, and, therefore, must be deemed to have taken its burthens at the same time; and he is estopped to controvert it either by showing a want of capacity to make a contract, or that none in fact was made. Upon the same principle a person entering into a contract with a corporation in their corpo- rate name is estopped to deny that it is duly constituted. *   *   *   The case of an infant is in point. He has not capacity to bind himself by a contract except for necessities, but if after he arrives at full age he apply the goods to his use he is bound to pay as he had promised. So, here, if the corporation, after its organization, has elected to receive the benefit of services rendered for it prior to such organization, the law may well imply a promise to make reasonable compensation for them."

I have quoted at great length from the above case because it seems to be very nearly or quite in point to the case at bar. When, under a general incorporation law, persons have drawn up and signed articles of incorporation, but have not yet filed them in the office of the county clerk, the status of the corporation is the same as where, under a different constitutional provision, a charter has been granted by special legislative enactment, but no organization has been effected under it.

From the agreed statement of facts above set out, it appears that after the articles of incorporation had been drawn up and signed by all of the promoters of the scheme and a full set of officers for the corporation had been elected, but before the said articles were filed in the county clerk's office, and before the time fixed for the commencement of the business of the corporation, the said officers and promoters entered into a contract with Meserve for the purchase on the part of the corporation of the cattle, horses, ranch, claims, and other property in Chase county, as stated in the agreed statement of facts, and in part payment therefor, by the president elected for said corporation, executed and delivered to him the note sued on. It is very clearly shown, both by the agreed statement of facts and other evidence, that the organization of the said Paxton Cattle Company was afterwards perfected by the filing of their articles of incorporation in the county clerk's office of Red Willow county, and that the company, through its officers and manager, has retained the possession of the property in Chase county, both real and personal, for which

the said note was given.   This, under the authority of the
foregoing cases, is the turning point in the case, and I think
the conclusion is inevitable, granting the entire want of
power on the part of the officers and promoters of the corporation to act as such at the date of the note, that the retaining possession of the consideration by the corporation
after its organization is a ratification of the contract with
all of its terms and obligations.

The plaintiff in error also makes the point that "The
court erred in allowing the defendant in error to prove the
new cause of action set up in the reply."   I do not understand the matters set up in the reply as constituting a new
cause of action, but only as stating facts in reply to the defense set up by the corporation defendant.

Bliss, in his work on Code Pleading, sec. 396, defines a
departure to consist "in leaving the case as made in the
complaint or petition in respect to some material matter,
and introducing new matter which is inconsistent with, or
which does not support it."   This, he says, "will not be
permitted."   It is true that it is alleged in the petition
that the note was executed and delivered by the corporation.   The answer alleges that at the time and date of the
execution of the note the corporation was without capacity
to contract, or even legal existence.   By the reply the
plaintiff alleges facts which under the law estops, or at
least denies, to the defendant the right to avail itself of that
defense.   This, I think, is one of the proper offices of a
reply.   It by no means abandons the cause of action as
originally pleaded, but fortifies it by the new facts rendered
necessary by the allegations of the answer.

The defendant also makes the point that " The contract
was void for illegality, as it was intended to violate a statute of the United States.   All of the ranch of 1,440 acres
was, at the time of making the contract, held under the
timber culture, homestead, and pre-emption laws of the
United States," etc.

It is provided by statute, section 1, chapter 38, Compiled
Stats., that " All contracts, promises, assumpsits, or undertakings, either written or verbal, which shall be made hereafter in good faith and without fraud, collusion, or circumvention, for sale, purchase, or payment of improvements
made on the lands owned by the government of the United
States, shall be deemed valid in law or equity, and may be
sued for and recovered as in other contracts." This section
was construed by this court in the case of *Mc Williams v.
Bridges*, 7 Neb., 419. I quote the statement of the facts
of the case from the opinion : "The evidence shows that
the consideration for giving the promissory note in question was the sale and surrender by Daniel A. Bishop of
his unperfected homestead claim upon the public lands, together with the improvements thereon consisting of a small
dwelling house, or shanty, about twenty-five acres of breaking, and a lot of forest trees." Also from the syllabus: "The
sale and surrender of a homestead claim upon the public
lands, together with the improvements made thereon, although conveying no interest in the land itself as against
the government, is a good consideration for a promissory
note; the improvements being subjects of legitimate bargain and sale."

This case clearly recognizes it to be the law, where a
note or other obligation is given, partly in consideration
of the release of an inchoate homestead or other claim on
the public lands, and in part for improvements or other
property on said lands, the instrument will be enforced.

This case is followed by that of *Simmons v. Yurann*, 11
Id., 516, and the more recent one of *Carkins v. Anderson*,
ante page 364.

The judgment of the district court is affirmed.

JUDGMENT AFFIRMED.

THE other judges concur.

IN RE LEWIS A. GROFF ET AL.

21 647
50 98
52 217

21 647
59 110

1. **Constitutional Law**: DISTRICT JUDGES. A bill to reapportion the state into judicial districts, and to provide judges therefor, passed the legislature in due form, but before being signed by the governor was changed, reducing the number of judges to one in the second district. *Held*, That the act being complete in itself as to the first, third, fourth, fifth, sixth, seventh, eighth, ninth, tenth, eleventh, and twelfth districts and capable of being executed, was not affected by the invalidity of that part of the act relating to the second district. *State v. McLelland*, 18 Neb., 243; *State v. Robinson*, 20 Id., 96, distinguished. That the provision in regard to the second district was null and void.

2. ——: ——. The act of 1885, providing for two judges in the second district, is valid, and the number of such judges cannot, under the constitution, be changed oftener than every four years.

3. ——: ——: APPROPRIATION. The appropriation made by the legislature of $95,000 for the payment of salaries of nineteen judges of the district court, is an appropriation in gross to be applied as far as necessary to the payment of the salaries of all judges of the district courts.

MAXWELL, CH. J.

This case is submitted to the court upon an agreed statement of facts, and, as the action is real and the facts agreed upon appear to bring the case within the provisions of section 567 of the code of civil procedure, it is our duty to consider it and render a decision upon the questions involved. The agreed statement is as follows:

"*To the Honorable, the Judges of the Supreme Court of the State of Nebraska:*

" Your petitioners, the undersigned, respectfully represent and show unto your honors that pursuant to the annexed act of the legislature of this state, your petitioners, Lewis A. Groff and M. R. Hopewell, have been by the governor of this state duly appointed each as one of the

judges of the district court for the third judicial district of
this state, and have duly qualified and entered upon the
discharge of their duties as such; and that in like manner
and pursuant to the same authority your petitioner, William Marshall, has been appointed and has qualified and
entered upon the discharge of his duties as one of the judges
of the district court for the fourth judicial district; and that
in like manner your petitioner, T. O. C. Harrison, has,
pursuant to the same authority, been appointed and has
qualified and entered upon the discharge of his duties as
one of the judges of the ninth judicial district; that your
petitioner, Stephen B. Pound, was duly elected judge of the
district court of the second judicial district at the general
election in October, 1875, and has since been twice elected
to said office upon the expiration of his term, so that he
has held said office continuously from the date of his said
first election down to the present time, and still does continue to occupy and enjoy the same; and that pursuant to
an act passed and approved March 10th, 1885, the Hon.
Samuel M. Chapman was, at the general election in November, 1886, duly elected to the office of additional judge
in said second judicial district, and has since duly qualified
and entered upon his duties as such, and still continues to
hold and enjoy. said office.

"And your petitioners further show unto your honors that
at the twentieth session of the legislature of this state, the
only appropriation made for the payment of salaries of
judges of the district court was as follows:

"'H. R. No. 446.

"'An act to provide for the payment of the .alaries of
the officers of the state government,

*   *   *   .

"' DISTRICT COURT.

Salary of nineteen judges at $2,500.......$47,500 $95,500
Salary of nineteen stenographers at......
    $1,500................................$28,500 $57,000.'

"And your petitioners further show that certain doubts
and controversies have arisen as to the validity and construction of the above mentioned acts of the legislature,
insomuch that the titles of your said petitioners and of said
Chapman to their respective offices have been drawn in
question, and as to the right of your petitioners to receive
and draw their respective salaries as incumbents of said
offices, and as to the duty and authority of your petitioner, H. A. Babcock, auditor of state, to draw and deliver his warrant upon the treasurer of the state for the
payment of same.

"And your petitioners further show that said doubts and
controversies have arisen from the following facts appearing upon the legislative records of this state, to-wit:

"First. That said act first herein mentioned was introduced into the senate at said twentieth session as a measure
entitled, 'Senate File No. 174. A bill for an act to apportion the state into judicial districts, and for the appointment and election of officers thereof.' That by the bill so
introduced the county of Lancaster, being a part of the
territory theretofore comprised in the second judicial district,
was constituted a district by itself, bearing that number,
and the counties of Cass and Otoe, being the remainder of
said territory, were constituted a district by themselves and
numbered the eleventh; and by a proviso it was declared
that in each of said districts there should be one judge, and
that in the first, fourth, ninth, and seventh districts each,
there should be two judges; that afterwards, by amendment, the clause creating said eleventh district was stricken
out and the counties of Cass and Otoe restored to the second district; that thereafter the bill was by the house so
amended as to strike the said first district from the clause
providing that in each of certain districts there should be
two judges; that thereafter the bill was so amended by the
house that the second district was inserted in the clause
of the bill providing that in each of certain districts there

should be two judges, and that thereafter a further amendment was made by the house by which the first district
was also inserted in said clause, and that as so amended the
bill was passed by the house and concurred in by the senate and ordered to be enrolled so as to incorporate both of
said amendments; but that, by some fault or oversight, the
amendment including the second district in said clause was
omitted by the person or persons entrusted with the enrollment thereof, so that the same was by inadvertence presented to the governor and signed by him without said
omission having been discovered.

"Second. That said first mentioned act does not in express terms repeal or refer to said act of March 10th, 1885.

" Your petitioners therefore respectfully pray that your
honors will take into due consideration and advise your
petitioners upon the following matters touching this present inquiry, and necessary for your petitioners to be informed upon in order that grave and important interests,
both of the public and of individuals, may not be put in
jeopardy.

" I. Is the said first named act valid for any purpose or
to any extent?

" II. Is said act, on account of said amendment being
omitted in enrollment, invalid as respects the second judicial
district alone?

" III. If said act is not invalidated, either as a whole
or as respects said second judicial district, on account of the
omission of said amendment, does the same amend, repeal, or supersede the provisions of the act of March 10th,
1885, creating an additional judge in the second judicial
district? *Smails v. White,* 4 Neb., 353.

" V. The object of this act being to increase the number of the district judges in the state, was it competent for
the legislature by that measure to ' vacate the office of any
judge?' Sec. 2, Art. VI. of the constitution.

"VI. The constitution having made appropriation to pay the salaries of all the judges whose offices were created by that instrument, should not the legislative appropriation be treated as in addition thereto and intended to provide for the payment of the salaries of judges whose offices are created by law? *State, ex rel. Roberts, v. Weston,* 4 Neb., 216.

"VII. The office of the district judge, being created by law, does not the constitution appropriate the salary therefor in the same manner as that for the six judges whose offices were created by the constitution?

"VIII. Should not the legislative appropriation for salaries of district judges and stenographers be treated as an appropriation in gross to be drawn upon without reference to apportionment to particular district?

"LEWIS A. GROFF.

"M. R. HOPEWELL.

"WILLIAM MARSHALL.

"T. O. C. HARRISON.

"S. B. POUND,
By JOHN H. AMES,
G. M. LAMBERTSON,
Attorneys.

"S. M. CHAPMAN,
By G. W. COVELL,
J. B. STRODE,
Attorneys.

"H. A. BABCOCK,
Auditor P. A."

The statute to apportion the state into judicial districts is as follows:

"S. F. 174.

"An act to apportion the state into judicial districts, and for the apportionment and election of officers thereof.

"*Be it enacted by the Legislature of the State of Nebraska:*

"Section 1. The state of Nebraska shall be divided into twelve judicial districts, as follows:

"First District — Richardson, Nemaha, Johnson, Pawnee, and Gage counties.

"Second District — Lancaster, Otoe, and Cass counties.

"Third District — Douglas, Sarpy, Washington, and Burt counties.

"Fourth District — Saunders, Butler, Colfax, Dodge, Platte, Merrick, and Nance counties.

"Fifth District — Saline, Jefferson, Fillmore, Thayer, Nuckolls, and Clay counties.

"Sixth District — Seward, York, Hamilton, and Polk counties.

"Seventh District — Cuming, Stanton, Wayne, Dixon, Dakota, Madison, Antelope, Pierce, Cedar, and Knox counties, Winnebago and Omaha reservations, and the unorganized territory north of Knox county.

"Eighth District — Adams, Webster, Kearney, Franklin, Harlan, and Phelps counties.

"Ninth District — Boone, Hall, Wheeler, Greeley, Garfield, Loup, Valley, Howard, and Blaine counties, and the unorganized territory west of Blaine county.

"Tenth District — Buffalo, Dawson, Custer, Lincoln, Logan, Sherman, Keith, and Cheyenne counties, and the unorganized territory west of Logan county.

"Eleventh District — Gosper, Furnas, Frontier, Red Willow, Hayes, Hitchcock, Chase, and Dundy counties.

"Twelfth District — Holt, Brown, Keya Paha, Cherry, Sheridan, Dawes, Sioux, and Box Butte counties, and the unorganized territory north of Holt and Keya Paha counties.

"*Provided*, That in the third district there shall be four judges of the district court; that in each of the following districts, to-wit: first, fourth, seventh, and ninth districts, there shall be two judges of the district court, and in each of the other of said districts there shall be one judge of the district court.   All judges shall be elected for the term of and hold their office for four years from and after the first day of January next succeeding their election.   The said judges shall be elected at the general election to be held in November, A.D. 1887, and every four years thereafter. Such judges shall have equal power, and shall each perform such duties as are now provided by law, or such as may hereafter be imposed upon them by law, and it shall be the duty of such judges to so divide and arrange the business of said court between them that the trial of causes may be speedy.   In each district having more than one judge of the district court, there shall be drawn in the manner now provided by law a panel of forty-eight jurors to serve as jurors in such court; *Provided*, That in any county in such districts where such number of jurors may not be required, the judges may, by appropriate rule, provide for the drawing of a less number; and *Provided, further*, When there shall be more than two judges of the district court in any one district, they may provide, by appropriate rule, for the drawing of a greater number of jurors.

"Sec. 2.   The judges now in office shall hold their position and perform the duties of their office in the districts hereby created in which they may reside, until the expiration of the term for which they were elected.

"Sec. 3.   The governor shall appoint judges to fill all vacancies created by this act, including the additional judges as provided in section 1 of this act, who shall hold their office until the next general election, when such vacancies shall be filled by election in same manner as such officer is elected in other districts.

"Sec. 4.   All acts or parts of acts in conflict with the provisions of this act are hereby repealed.

"Sec. 5.   Whereas, an emergency exists, this act shall take effect and be in force from and after its passage.

"H. H. Shedd,

"*President of the Senate.*

"Attest:

"Walt. M. Seely,

"*Secretary of the Senate.*

"N. V. Harlan,

"*Speaker of House of Representatives.*

"Attest:

"Brad. D. Slaughter,

"*Chief Clerk of House of Representatives.*

"Approved March 31, 1887.

"John M. Thayer,

"*Governor.*" .

The testimony before us shows that the provisions of the above act as here set out, so far as they relate to all the districts except the second, were properly passed by both houses of the legislature and signed by the governor; that as to the second district, the provision relating thereto as passed by both houses provided for two judges, but that the bill as signed by the governor contained a provision for only one judge.

Three questions necessarily arise out of the facts stated:

First.   Does the invalidity of the provision as to the second district affect the whole act and render it void?

In *State v. McLelland,* 18 Neb., 237, it was held that when a bill providing that, in each county containing not less than "15,000" inhabitants, a register of deeds should be elected, etc., had passed both houses of the legislature, but before being signed by the governor had been changed to read "1,500" and signed in that form, was of no force or effect; and the same ruling was had in *State v. Robinson,* 20 Neb., 96.   These cases were argued by able attorneys and were carefully considered, and the conclusion reached, in our view, is the correct one and it will be adhered to.

But do those decisions affect the entire bill in this case? In those cases it will be observed that there was but a single question involved, viz.: A register was to be elected in each county containing not less than 15,000 inhabitants. In the case at bar, however, there are twelve distinct, minor subjects, or propositions, embraced in the bill; each proposition prescribes the extent of territory comprising a judicial district and the number of judges to preside therein. In effect there are twelve bills all embraced in one title, dividing the state into judicial districts and providing for judges in such districts. It will be seen, therefore, that a defect in one proposition does not necessarily affect or defeat the others.

This question was before the supreme court of South Carolina in *State v. Platt*, 2 Richardson, 150. On the first of March, 1870, the legislature of that state passed an "act to revise, simplify, and abridge the rules, practice, pleadings, and forms of courts in that state." The nineteenth section of the enrolled act, to which the great seal of the state was affixed, and which was signed in the senate chamber by the president of the senate and the speaker of the house of representatives, and received the approval of the governor, provided that the courts for the county of Barnwell should be held at Barnwell; but it appeared by the journals of the two houses of the general assembly that the same section of the bill, as it finally passed both houses, provided that the courts for that county should be held at Blackville. By the law as it stood at the passage of the act the last named place was the county seat of Barnwell county. The court held that the nineteenth section of the act was void, and consequently that Blackville remained the county seat of Barnwell county. It is said (p. 155): "In order to determine whether an act has passed through all the requisite stages of legislative progress, its identity in each of these stages must be determined.   If the formalities of enrollment do not prevent us from looking into the journals in order to see that the bill had its proper reading, of what value will that be to us if we are estopped by the enrollment from inquiry as to what bill the journals have relation?   To give full force and effect to the constitution, if an issue of identity is raised, we must look into the bill or act at each step of its progress, to determine that that which has received part of the formalities requisite to its validity as a law is the same with that which has received the residue of such formalities.   Hitherto this question has been considered in the simplest form in which it is likely to arise, that is, upon the supposition that the act, regarded as a whole, is not the same, as appearing by the enrollment, with that which passed through the preceding stages of enactment.   In regard to this assumed case, we have no doubt but that we may look at the journals for the purpose of ascertaining the action of the houses, and into any evidence that may be appropriate to show the nature of the bill, the subject of such action.   A more difficult question here presents itself.   When, as in the present case, the act, as a whole, has unquestionably passed through all the requisite stages, but some part, either of a section or clause, or, as in the case at hand, a mere word, is found to constitute the difference between the act in its different stages of progress, it is necessary to look beyond the expressions of the constitution to its substantial meaning and extent.   As regards   . the general question, it is much simplified by the fact that the alleged error does not affect the general integrity or efficiency of the act, nor enter into any of the limitations and conditions by which the legislature sought to bound the scope and sphere of its provisions."   That portion of the act which had been passed properly was sustained.   To the same effect is *Jones v. Hutchinson*, 43 Ala., 725; *Peterman v. Huling*, 7 Casey, 436.

In *State v. Lancaster County*, 6 Neb., 474, it was held that if the constitutional portion of a statute was not dependent upon that which was unconstitutional, and was complete in itself and capable of being executed, it will be maintained. In that case the title of the bill was "An act to provide for township organization." Under that restrictive title the act provided for county officers, defined their duties, and provided for county organization and defined the corporate powers of a county.

The same rule was applied in *White v. The City of Lincoln*, 5 Neb., 515, where a portion of an act was sustained and a portion rejected as not conforming to the constitutional requirements; and so in *Holmburg v. Houck*, 16 Neb., 338; *State v. Lancaster County*, 17 Neb., 85; *State v. Hurds*, 19 Neb., 316, and *Ex parte Thomason*, 16 Neb., 239. We hold, therefore, that where a part of an act is not dependent upon that which is unconstitutional, and is complete in itself and capable of being executed, it will be maintained. So far as this act affects the eleven districts spoken of it fully complies with these conditions, and as to such districts must be sustained.

Second. Does the invalidity of the act in question, so far as it relates to the second district, affect either such district or the judges thereof?

Sec. 11, Art. VI. of the constitution, provides that, "The legislature, whenever two-thirds of the members elected to each house shall concur therein, may, in or after the year one thousand eight hundred and eighty, and not oftener than once in every four years, increase the number of judges of the district courts and the judicial districts of the state. Such districts shall be formed of compact territory and bounded by county lines, and such increase or any change in the boundaries of a district shall not vacate the office of any judge."

It will be seen that by the above section the legislature after the year 1880, and not oftener than once in every

42

four years, may increase the number of judges of the district courts and the judicial districts of the state, provided the change of boundary shall not vacate the office of any judge. During the session of the legislature in 1883, certain leading citizens of the third judicial district, together with members of the judiciary committee of each house, submitted to the judges of the supreme court—Judge Lake then being on the bench, the bill then pending before the legislature to increase the number of judges in the third district to two, it being alleged that that number was necessary to transact the business of that district. The section of the constitution above quoted was carefully considered, and it was the unanimous opinion of the judges that the constitution provided first, for an increase of judges in a district, and also for an increase in the number of judicial districts, in both cases under certain restrictions. The bill providing for two judges of the third district was thereupon passed and became a law, and Judge Wakeley was appointed the second judge in that district.

The question came before the supreme court in *State v. Stevenson*, 18 Neb., 416. During the session of the legislature in 1885 an act was passed for two judges in the second judicial district. This act was duly approved, and Judge Mitchell appointed judge. The case of *State v. Stevenson* was in fact a contest over the validity of the act providing for a second judge in the second district. It was ably argued and carefully considered, and the power of the legislature was sustained.

In the carefully prepared and able opinion of Judge COBB in that case, pp. 418–420, it is said: "Although the language of this section is that of a grant of power, yet it being found in an instrument which deals in prohibitions, restrictions, and reservations, and not in grants of power, it must be construed to be a restriction upon the general power of legislation inhering in the people as represented in the legislature.

"The power of legislation on the subject under consideration is, by the terms of the above section, restricted in more respects than one. It is not to be exercised at all until the lapse of four years after the general taking effect of the constitution, and then only by the concurrence of two-thirds of the members elect of each house of the legislature. To these restrictions it is claimed that the language of the section adds another, to-wit, that the power of legislating to effect the above objects becomes exhausted and lies dormant until the lapse of another term of four years. While it is not my present purpose to deny the above construction, I will say that if it is the true meaning of our constitution—if one legislature may pass an act which the next legislature may not amend or repeal, or if one legislature possesses a power which is denied to its successor, then I think it presents an anomaly in fundamental law-making, and is an exception to an otherwise universal rule. But in the view I take of the section of the constitution now under consideration, the power granted to the legislature, 'Whenever two-thirds of the members elected to each house shall concur therein,' to, 'in or after the year one thousand eight hundred and eighty, and not oftener than once in every four years, increase the number of judges of the district courts,' was not only not exhausted by the passage of the act of February 24, 1883, but is not exhausted by that of 1885.

"Section one of the article of the constitution under consideration provides that, 'The judicial power of this state shall be vested in a supreme court, district courts,' etc. Section nine provides that, 'The district courts shall have both chancery and common law jurisdiction, and such other jurisdiction as the legislature may provide,' etc. Section ten divides the state into six judicial districts, and provides that, 'In each of which shall be elected by the electors thereof one judge, who shall be judge of the district court therein,' etc. Then follows section eleven. That part of which is applicable to the question being examined is herein quoted.   It will thus be seen that the constitution provided for six district courts, and that until the year 1880, and until the legislature by a two-thirds vote of each house should otherwise provide, there should be but one judge to each of said courts.   But that after the year 1880, and by the legislative majority therein specified, the number of such judges might be increased.   The number of such judges had only been fixed by the language, 'The state shall be divided into six judicial districts, in each of which shall be elected by the electors thereof one judge.'   It is also true that, by the terms of the eleventh section, in and after the year 1880, the legislature, in the manner stated, may increase the number of judicial districts, and that would indirectly increase the number of judges, by force of the language of the tenth section, authorizing the electors of each of the original districts to elect one judge.   But the language of the section empowers the legislature to directly 'increase the number of judges of the district courts,' and surely when a power is granted to do a thing directly we need not justify the doing of it under another indirect and constructive grant of power.   There being then one judge provided for each of the six district courts, the legislature may, in or after 1880, increase this number.   May they increase it in one district, or in any or all of them? Obviously, not only from the language used but from the very nature of the subject-matter, in any or all the districts. But not in any oftener than once in four years. Under this power the legislature of 1883 increased the number of the judges of the district court of the third district.   But did such action exhaust the power of that legislature or any of its successors to increase the number of such judges in any or all of the other judicial districts not oftener than once in four years? I think not. If this construction and these conclusions are correct, then the act of 1885, under discussion, as well as the act of February 24, 1883, are fully warranted by the provisions of the constitution above quoted. The writer is of the opinion that there are other grounds upon which such legislation may be justified and defended against the charge of being inimical to the constitution of the state, but having, to my own satisfaction at least, found in the above considerations ample authority under the constitution for the legislation under consideration, the discussion of this branch of the case will not be further pursued."

It is apparent that the constitutional convention intended to provide adequate means to administer the law in all the counties in the state. It had already provided, in section 13, article I. of the constitution, that "All courts shall be open, and every person, for any injury done him in his lands, goods, person, or reputation, shall have remedy by due course of law, and justice administered without denial or delay." These provisions would be meaningless unless the legislature was clothed with power to furnish the necessary tribunals for the prompt disposition of cases pending in the courts. The convention, therefore, with the example of Cleveland, Cincinnati, and other cities, where there are a number of judges of courts of record of equal power holding separate and distinct courts at the same time, provided for such courts in this state, should the necessity arise; of which necessity the legislature—the representatives of the people—were to be the judges. The act of 1885, therefore, increasing the number of judges in the second district to two, is valid.

The second section of the act of 1887, above copied, provides that the judges now in office shall continue to hold their respective offices till the expiration of their terms, so that even if this act was valid as respects the second district, there could be no doubt as to the rights and duties of the judges in such district. But in addition to the prohibition against changing the number of judges oftener than once in four years, the provision reducing the number of judges to one, not having passed both houses of the legislature, is void.   It will be observed, too, that there is no attempt to repeal the act of 1885 providing for two judges in the second district, the language being, "All acts or parts of acts in conflict with the provisions of this act are hereby repealed."   The act of 1885 is not referred to, nor, so far as the bill shows, is it affected in any manner.   It is unnecessary, however, to decide this question as it does not arise in the case.

Third.   It is very evident that the appropriation to provide for the salaries of nineteen judges for two years, $95,-000, is an appropriation in gross; that is, so much money is appropriated for the payment of the judges of the district courts.   No one judge can claim his salary under such appropriation to the exclusion of another, but in case of a deficiency in the amount appropriated it must be divided *pro rata* among the different judges.   It is probable that, under section 25, article 16 of the constitution, even in the absence of an appropriation the auditor would be required to draw warrants for the salaries of the officers named in the constitution, but as in our view the sum appropriated for the payment of the district judges applies to all the judges alike, the question does not arise and therefore will not be decided.

The other questions which the court is requested to answer do not properly arise out of the facts stated, and an answer if given would be mere dicta; therefore they will not be decided.

ALL of the judges concurred.

JOHN ATKINSON, PLAINTIFF IN ERROR, V. DOMINICUS S. HASTY, DEFENDANT IN ERROR.

1. **County Court**: JURISDICTION. The county court of the county of which a deceased intestate was an inhabitant or resident has jurisdiction to appoint an administrator when these facts are shown and it is made to appear that an administrator is necessary. This jurisdiction is conferred by section 177 of chapter 23 of the Compiled Statutes.

2. ———: ———. During the first thirty days after the death of an intestate, the right of administration is conferred upon the next of kin (or widow, if there is one), or such person as they may select, if suitable and competent to discharge the trust. After the expiration of that time the right is conferred upon the principal creditors of the estate. If no such persons are competent or willing to accept the trust, it is the duty of the county judge to select such other person or persons as he may think proper (Sec. 178, Id.), and for this purpose the discretion is vested in the county judge, to be exercised for the best interest of the estate and those interested therein.

3. ———: PETITION FOR APPOINTMENT OF ADMINISTRATOR. After the expiration of the thirty days provided by section 178, chapter 23 of the Compiled Statutes, within which the widow or next of kin of an intestate may apply for administration of an estate, it is not necessary that a petition for the appointment of an administrator should allege that the person whose appointment is sought is the next of kin or selected by the next of kin to the intestate. Nor would it be necessary after the expiration of about two years after the decease to allege that there were no creditors competent or willing to accept the trust, in order to confer jurisdiction upon the county judge to appoint some other suitable person.

ERROR to the district court for Furnas county. Tried below before GASLIN, J.

John Dawson and *Ryan Bros.*, for plaintiff in error.

W. S. Morlan, for defendant in error.

REESE, J.

Defendant in error petitioned the county court of Furnas county for letters of administration on the estate of Elizabeth Atkinson, deceased. Upon final hearing plaintiff in error appeared by his attorneys and objected to the granting of administration to the petitioner, but the appointment was made, notwithstanding the objection. The cause was removed to the district court by proceedings in error, where the order of the county court was affirmed. Plaintiff in error brings the case to this court by similar proceedings.

The errors assigned relate to the ruling of the county court on the "objections" to the appointment of defendant in error, filed in that court. These objections were in writing and are as follows:

" *First.* The petition filed states said case in the county court, the county court having no jurisdiction.

" *Second.* The deceased, Elizabeth Atkinson, left no property of any nature whatever to administer.

" *Third.* The applicant, Dominicus S. Hasty, has no interest whatever in this case, and is not the proper party to administer said estate."

The first and second objections are not discussed in the brief of plaintiff in error, and will, therefore, not be noticed here. The whole case seems to be based upon the third; and even in this we must be limited to a very narrow compass, for the question as to whether defendant in error was or was not a proper person to receive the appointment (aside from strictly legal considerations) would depend upon the evidence adduced upon the hearing, none of which is before us.

It is said by plaintiff in his brief that the petition for the appointment " did not allege that defendant was next of kin or such a person as the next of kin requested to be appointed, nor that he was one of the principal creditors," nor that there were no such creditors competent nor willing to receive such appointment.

It is insisted that such allegations were necessary to confer jurisdiction on the county court. If it is true that a petition for the appointment of defendant in error was necessary, and if it is also true that such petition must contain the allegation mentioned in order to confer jurisdiction, then the position of plaintiff in error is correct, and the appointment of defendant in error was a nullity. But we cannot see that the theory of plaintiff in error is the correct one.

Section 178 of chapter 23 of the Compiled Statutes, which provides for the appointment of administrators, is as follows:

"Administration of the estate of a person dying intestate, shall be granted to some one or more of the persons hereinafter mentioned, and they shall be respectively entitled to the same, in the following order: *First.* The widow, or next of kin, or both, as the judge of probate may think proper, or such person as the widow or next of kin may request to have appointed, if suitable and competent to discharge the trust. *Second.* If the widow, or next of kin, or the person selected by them, shall be unsuitable or incompetent, or if the widow or next of kin shall neglect, for thirty days after the death of the intestate, to apply for administration, or to request that administration be granted to some other person, the same may be granted to one or more of the principal creditors, if any such are competent and willing to take it. *Third.* If there be no such creditor competent and willing to take administration, the same may be committed to such other person or persons as the judge of probate may think proper."

It appears by the record that the deceased died on the first day of March, 1883. The application for administration was made February 20th, 1885, nearly two years after

her death. The time within which any of the next of kin
had the exclusive right to the appointment, either for themselves or such suitable person as they might designate, had
expired.   More than a year and a half had expired within
which a creditor might have been appointed, but none
had applied for such appointment.   It then became the
duty of the county judge to commit the administration to
"such other person" as he might think proper.   The jurisdiction of the county court, by section 177, Id., is made to
depend upon the facts that the deceased had died intestate,
and was, at the time of his death, an inhabitant or resident
of the county in which the court is authorized to act. These
fully appeared by the petition and record before the court.
Therefore it had jurisdiction.   It was not necessary that
the petition should allege that defendant in error was next
of kin to the deceased, nor that the next of kin requested
his appointment, for the reason that the thirty days mentioned in the section had passed and the right of appointment no longer belonged exclusively to such persons. They
had waived their rights, as such, to the appointment.   The
fact of the death and residence being shown, the duty of
selecting an administrator devolved upon the court, under
the statute.   In the exercise of that duty, the court appointed defendant in error.   The record shows that on the
day on which the cause was heard, and presumably before
the final decision, a waiver of the right to administer and
request for the appointment of defendant in error was
filed by two daughters and a son of deceased, one of the
former being the wife of defendant in error.   Whether or
not they constituted all the heirs is not shown; but this is,
in our view, wholly immaterial, as no such waiver or request was necessary so long after the death of the intestate.
Neither could the fact that the petition and waiver were
filed, conflict in any degree with the legal right of the court
to appoint defendant in error, if he was thought to be a
proper person.   The matter was entirely within the discretion of the court.

In Maxwell's Practice in Justices' Courts, at page 315, the author, in discussing this question, says: "The discretion vested in the judge is to be exercised for the good of the estate, and should be so used as will be most conducive to the interests of those interested therein. Other things being equal, a person of good business capacity should be preferred; but in all cases, a person of integrity should be selected." There being nothing found in the record assailing either the capacity or integrity of defendant in error, we must presume he possesses the necessary qualifications and that his appointment was a proper one.

The decision of the district court is therefore affirmed.

JUDGMENT AFFIRMED.

THE other judges concur.

THE NEBRASKA LAND AND CATTLE COMPANY, PLAINTIFF IN ERROR, V. HENRY H. BOWIE, DEFENDANT IN ERROR.

Evidence examined, and *Held*, Not to sustain the finding of the district court.

ERROR to the district court for Buffalo county. Tried below before HAMER, J.

Calkins & Pratt, for plaintiff in error.

A. H. Connor and *Ira D. Marston*, for defendant in error.

REESE, J.

This was an action upon a promissory note, executed by plaintiff in error to its secretary, and by him transferred through mesne endorsements to defendant in error. The petition stated the facts in the usual form. The answer was a general denial. Judgment was rendered in favor of defendant in error for the amount named in the note, with interest.

Plaintiff in error prosecutes error to this court, and contends that there was no evidence to sustain the finding of the district court, there being no proof of the execution of the note or of the endorsements, which, in *Donovan v. Fowler*, 17 Neb., 247, was held to be necessary.

It is insisted by defendant in error that the proof sustains the allegations of the petition.

We here copy all the testimony introduced upon the trial:

Plaintiff, to maintain the issues on his part, called W. W. Pool, who, being sworn, in answer to questions by Gen. Connor, testified:

"My name is W. W. Pool. On the 31st day of March, 1883, I resided on a farm on the South Loup, and was secretary and superintendent of the Nebraska Land and Cattle Company."

Q. (Handing witness a paper.) Look at that paper and state if you have any recollection of signing a paper of which this is a copy, to Mr. Deen for $700?

A. I don't know about this being a copy of it. I have a recollection of a note of that amount to Deen.

Q. State, from any examination of that copy, if you have a recollection of signing such a note yourself that was endorsed to Deen?

A. I have no recollection of endorsing a particular note. If you had the original here, I could remember.

Q. Do you remember of buying horses from Deen?

A. Yes, sir.

Q. Remember the drawing of a note payable to yourself and endorsing it to him?

A. No, sir. But I remember of him giving a note for $700.

Q. Ever give him any other note for that amount?

A. Not that I know of.

Q. Ever pay that note?

A. No, sir.

By the court, to witness:

Q. Has that note ever been paid by the company, that you know of?

A. No, sir; not that I know of.

Plaintiff here offers said note in evidence.

Defense objects, on the ground that it is not shown to be properly executed, in that it is executed by an officer of the corporation to himself.

By the court:

Q. This note was given for horses purchased of Deen?

A. Yes, sir.

Q. To whom were the horses delivered?

A. To the Nebraska Land and Cattle Company.

Q. And they got the horses?

A. Yes, sir.

By Gen. Connor:

Q. And this note was made payable to you and endorsed by you to Deen?

A. I don't remember about the endorsement.

A. H. Connor, Esq., called and sworn, per se:

"Mr. Bowie, the plaintiff in this suit, brought that note to me for the purpose of collection. He stated to me—"

Defense objects as improper and incompetent. Sustained. Plaintiff excepts.

"I will say that Mr. Deen also told me—"

Defense objects, as irrelevant, improper, and hearsay. Sustained. Plaintiff excepts.

"I offer to prove that both these parties being present, Mr. Deen informed me, so did Mr. Bowie, that he had sold the note and the price for which he had sold it. I don't remember the amount he stated, and the note was in in Bowie's possession."

Defense excepts to above offer being made.

"I also offer to prove that I brought this action at the instance of Mr. Bowie, plaintiff here, and that he paid me an attorney's fee of $50."

Defense except.

The plaintiff, offering no further evidence, rested; whereupon the defendant, without producing any evidence, rested, and the case was submitted to the court upon the foregoing evidence.

The testimony of General Connor seems not to have been admitted, neither was the note before the court. A copy of the note was presented to the witness Pool, but he does not identify it as such. He has no recollection of the endorsement, and, to the mind of the writer, fails to connect the copy presented to him with the transaction in which a note was given, in any particular.

The allegation of the petition is, that plaintiff executed *the note* upon which the action was brought. This was denied by the answer, while there was proof that a note was given which had not been paid that the witness *knew of*, yet there was no proof that the note described in the petition had ever been executed or endorsed.

The judgment of the district court is reversed and the cause is remanded for further proceedings.

REVERSED AND REMANDED.

THE other judges concur.

B. F. FURROW ET AL. V. ELIZA ATHEY ET AL.

1. **Husband and Wife**: DEED TO WIFE. A deed of conveyance of real estate, executed by the husband directly to the
wife, in the absence of fraud, and when neither the rights of
creditors nor subsequent purchasers intervene, will convey to
her such real estate without the intervention of a third party as
trustee.

2. —— : HOMESTEAD. When the husband and wife occupy a
homestead, the title to which is in the name of the husband, a
deed of conveyance from the husband to the wife, signed and
acknowledged by him alone, is valid, although not signed and
acknowledged by the wife.

Appeal from the district court of Richardson county,
Tried below before BROADY, J.

A. Schoenheit, for appellants.

A. H. Babcock, E. W. Thomas, and *E. A. Tucker,* for
appellees.

REESE, J.

The first question presented in this case is, whether a
husband can convey his real estate to his wife without the
intervention of a third party as a trustee, in a case where
no fraud is shown, and the rights of creditors or other
third parties do not intervene.

As has been decided by this court, the deed from a husband to the wife was void by the common law. *Smith v.
Dean,* 15 Neb., 432. *Johnson v. Vandervort,* 16 Id., 144.
But in equity such deeds have been upheld when any
equitable reason therefor was shown. Id.

There is some evidence tending to prove a valuable consideration for the deed in question, growing out of money
received by the wife from her separate property, and given

to the husband. If this was true, it would raise an equity in favor of the wife which would support the deed.   There is sufficient evidence to sustain the finding of the court upon this point, and the decree could not therefore be molested.   But aside from this we can see no reason why the decree of the district court is not correct.

It appears that in 1868 Charles Furrow, the husband, now deceased, purchased the land in question from the United States. At that time he, with defendant, his wife, settled upon it, and they resided there together until his death, which occurred in 1880.   In 1879, while in poor health, he conveyed the premises to her.   It was their home.   They had a family of children, the plaintiffs, and the deed was evidently executed to her in order that she might be enabled to rear and educate the family in which she was as much interested as the husband, and which he fully understood at the time he made the conveyance.   If it had been made to a third party as a trustee, and by him conveyed to defendant, it perhaps would never have been questioned.   It is just as good without such intervention. *Huber v. Huber*, 10 Ohio, 373. *Garlick v. Strong*, 3 Paige, 452. *Coates v. Gerlach*, 44 Penn. St., 43. *Story v. Marshall*, 24 Tex., 305. *Barker v. Koneman*, 13 Cal., 9. *Deming v. Williams*, 26 Conn., 226. *Brookbank v. Kennard*, 41 Ind., 339. *Hunt v. Johnson*, 44 N. Y., 27. *Eddins v. Buck*, 23 Ark., 507.   *Wilder v. Brooks*, 10 Minn., 50.

It is next contended that the deed was void under the provisions of chapter 36 of the Compiled Statutes, and particularly under section 4 of said chapter, the property being the homestead at the time of the conveyance. Section 4 is as follows : "The homestead of a married person cannot be conveyed or encumbered unless the instrument by which it is conveyed or encumbered is executed and acknowledged by both husband and wife."

Statutes creating the homestead right were enacted for

the protection of the family of the husband or wife, if the head of the family were a debtor, and for the protection of the husband or wife against a conveyance or encumbrance by the other. Both can join in a conveyance, and by it the right of the children or other members of the family may be entirely destroyed; but where the title is held by the husband, he cannot sell without the consent of the wife expressed by signing and acknowledging the deed. The same rule applies to the wife where the title is held by her. In effect, an estate or interest in the land is created, of which the party not named in the deed cannot be divested by the sole act of the other. But in the case at bar no effort was made to divest the wife of her estate or right. That remained unimpaired. I can see no reason why she should be required to execute the deed to herself in order to its validity. Neither do I find any authority for such a holding. The reverse seems to be the rule. Thompson on Homesteads, 473. *Reihl v. Bingenheimer*, 28 Wis., 84.

The decree of the district court is affirmed.

DECREE AFFIRMED.

THE other judges concur.

THOMAS CLARK, PLAINTIFF IN ERROR, v. D. S. MORGAN & CO., DEFENDANTS IN ERROR.

1. **Practice in Supreme Court:** JURISDICTION. Where judgment was rendered November 5th, 1885, and a petition in error was filed in the supreme court December 24th, 1886, a motion to dismiss for want of jurisdiction was sustained, the petition in error being filed more than one year after the rendition of final judgment by the district court.

43

2. ———: ———: STIPULATION. Prior to the expiration of the time
within which a proceeding in error might be instituted in the
supreme court, the defendants in error stipulated with plaintiff
in error, waiving the issuance and service of summons in error,
and agreeing that the cause might be heard at a term then in
session. It was held that such waiver and stipulation did not
give authority to plaintiff in error to commence the action
after the expiration of the time fixed by statute, and after the
final adjournment of the term at which it was agreed the cause
should be submitted.

ERROR to the district court for Red Willow county.
Tried below before GASLIN, J.

J. Byron Jennings, for plaintiff in error.

John Dawson, for defendant in error.

REESE, J.

This cause is submitted upon a motion to dismiss. Subject to this, it is submitted generally. Our first inquiry
must, therefore, be directed to the questions presented by
the motion.

It appears from the record that final judgment was rendered in the district court on the 5th day of November,
1885. The petition in error and transcript were filed in
the supreme court on the 24th day of December, 1886.

Section 592 of the civil code, in so far as it is applicable
to this cause, is as follows:

"No proceedings for reversing, vacating, or modifying
judgments or final orders shall be commenced unless within
one year after the rendition of the judgment, or making of
the final order complained of."

As the petition in error and transcript were not filed
until after the expiration of the time fixed by law within
which the proceeding might be commenced, the objection is
well taken. *French v. English,* 7 Neb., 124.

A stipulation was entered into between the parties prior

to the commencement of the proceedings in error, by which the issuance and service of summons was waived by defendants in error, and it was agreed that the cause should be docketed and heard during the week assigned to the eighth judicial district in the January term, 1886; but as the cause was not filed until after the final adjournment of both that term and the next, the stipulation could only be held to be a waiver of the issuance and service of summons, and not as authority for the commencement of the action after the statutory bar had fully accrued.

The motion is sustained and the proceeding dismissed.

JUDGMENT ACCORDINGLY.

THE other judges concur.

EDWIN C. WEAVER, APPELLANT, v. MARK S. CRESS-MAN, JULIUS THIELE, AND THOMAS M. FRANSE, APPELLEES.

1. **Creditor's Bill.** Where an action in the nature of a creditor's bill is brought by a non-resident of the state against a non-resident, on a judgment rendered in another state, on which an execution had been returned unsatisfied, to reach funds belonging to the debtor in the hands of the clerk of a district court, the petition must show that there is no property of the debtor within the state subject to attachment or garnishment.

2. **Garnishment.** While the general rule is that funds in the hands of the clerk of a court are not subject to garnishment in an action at law, yet, in a proper case, a court of equity may subject such funds to the payment of the claims of a creditor.

3. **Foreign Judgment.** A judgment rendered in another state, when brought into this state is merely evidence, and to be available in this state a judgment must be recovered thereon in our courts.

4. ——: PARTIES. Where an action is brought in this state on a judgment recovered in another state, to subject certain property of the debtor alleged to have been assigned by him without consideration, the debtor is a necessary party to the suit.

APPEAL from the district court of Cuming county. Tried below before CRAWFORD, J.

H. C. Brome, for appellant.

J. Thiele, for appellees.

MAXWELL, CH. J.

In January, 1886, the plaintiff filed a petition in the district court of Cuming county, stating his cause of action as follows:

"That in October of the year 1878, one George W. Cressman, who then resided in the state of Pennsylvania, where this plaintiff then resided and now resides, was jointly indebted to this plaintiff in the sum of three hundred and seventy-five dollars; that in said month of October, 1878, plaintiff recovered a judgment against said George W. Cressman for three hundred and seventy-five dollars, or thereabouts, and costs upon said indebtedness, in the court of common pleas of Montgomery county, Pennsylvania, which was a court having jurisdiction of the subject matter and of the person of said George W. Cressman, defendant therein, which judgment was rendered in all respects according to law; that said judgment is still in full force and effect, and there is now due thereon about six hundred dollars; that thereafter an execution was duly issued upon said judgment to the proper officer and in the manner prescribed by the laws of Pennsylvania, and to the county therein where said George W. Cressman resides, which said execution was returned wholly unsatisfied, and still remains wholly unsatisfied and unpaid; and that plaintiff has heretofore exhausted his remedy at law upon said judgment and has utterly failed to collect the same; that about the year 1878 the said George W. Cressman had a certain interest in a mechanic's lien on certain property and real estate and fixtures in the village of West Point, in the county of Cuming, and state of Nebraska, which he assigned without consideration to one John C. Kloder, who, about the same time and as a part of the same transaction, assigned the same without consideration to Mark S. Cressman, one of the defendants herein; that said mechanic's lien was afterwards foreclosed in due form of law, and out of the proceeds of said foreclosure there are now twelve hundred dollars in the custody of the defendant, Julius Thiele, who is the clerk of the district court of Cuming county, Nebraska, as such clerk, which said twelve hundred dollars is a part in law and equity of the assets of said George W. Cressman, subject of right and in law and equity to the payment of his debts, but which is held by the defendant, Mark S. Cressman, as assignee of the said George W. Cressman, and to which said George W. Cressman now makes no claim whatever; that the defendant, Thomas M. Franse, makes some claim to said fund of twelve hundred dollars, or some portion thereof, the particulars of which claim are unknown to plaintiff herein, but which claim is adverse to plaintiff's claim herein; that plaintiff has used due diligence in the assertion and enforcement of his claim herein, and has been guilty of no laches or negligence in relation thereto; that the assignments above referred to were entirely voluntary and without consideration, and in fraud of the rights of plaintiff.

"The plaintiff therefore prays that said assignments be set aside in so far as they affect the rights of plaintiff; that this court adjudge and decree that so much of said fund of twelve hundred dollars as is necessary to pay plaintiff's claim, with costs, be applied to the payment and discharge thereof; that said defendant, Thiele, be ordered to pay the same, or so much thereof as may be necessary, to this plaintiff or his proper attorneys in discharge of said claim; that the rights and interest of defendant Frause, if any, in and to said fund, so far as the same may be adverse to those of this plaintiff, be determined and settled herein, and that if necessary a receiver of said fund be appointed to carry into effect the final judgment of this court herein, and for such other and further relief and equity as may be proper in the premises, and for costs of this action."

In March, 1886, default was entered against the defendant, Mark S. Cressman. The defendant, Thiele, demurred to the petition, upon the ground that the facts stated therein were not sufficient to constitute a cause of action. The demurrer was sustained and the action dismissed. The plaintiff appeals.

It will be observed that this is an equitable action, brought by a non-resident of the state against a non-resident, to reach funds alleged to be held by Thiele, the clerk of the district court of Cuming county. There is no allegation in the petition that the debtor, Geo. W. Cressman, has no property subject to attachment or garnishment within the state.

The general rule is, that a court of equity will not interpose until the creditor has exhausted his remedy at law; and a judgment recovered and execution issued thereon and returned unsatisfied are ordinarily required, and are considered the best evidence that the remedy at law does not exist. To this rule, however, there are a few exceptions; as where the debtor is a non-resident of the state, and has no attachable property in the state. In such cases no doubt a court of equity will grant relief. To do so, however, it must be made to appear that there is no attachable property of the debtor within the state, in order to justify the creditor in invoking the aid of a court of equity.

This action is neither a proceeding in aid of an execution, nor a garnishment under the statute, and if sustained it must be as a proceeding in the nature of a creditor's action in equity; and as such it wholly fails to show that the plaintiff has exhausted his legal remedies, and that a portion of the fund in question is the only property of the debtor available to apply on his claim. The petition, therefore, fails to state a cause of action.

2. While the general rule is, that money paid into the hands of the clerk of a court on a judgment, and money in his possession, held by virtue of his office, cannot be attached—*Ross v. Clarke*, 1 Dallas, 354; *Alston v. Clay*, 2 Haywood (N. C.), 171; *Hunt v. Stevens*, 3 Iredell, 365; *Drane v. McGavock*, 7 Humphreys, 132, *Farmers' Bank v. Beaston*, 7 Gill & Johnson, 421; *Murrell v. Johnson*, 3 Hill (S.C.), 12; *Bowden v. Schatzell*, Bailey Eq. R., 360—yet there are exceptions to this rule, as where money was in the hands of a clerk, arising from the sale of lands in partition, which money he had been ordered by the court to pay over to the parties entitled thereto. *Gaither v. Ballew*, 4 Jones, 488. And no doubt a court of equity in a proper case would subject funds in the hands of a clerk, belonging to a debtor, to the satisfaction of a creditor's claim.

3. Geo. W. Cressman is not made a party defendant. A judgment rendered in another state, when brought into this state, is merely evidence, and to be available in this state a judgment must be recovered thereon in our courts. The debtor in fact is the principal defendant, and before his property can be taken and applied to the satisfaction of an alleged claim of the plaintiff, he must have his day in court, and the court must find that there is still due and owing from the debtor to the creditor or his assigns a specific sum. Until the court has obtained jurisdiction of the debtor, how can it say that the plaintiff is a creditor and entitled to the relief sought? The judgment of the court below is clearly right and is affirmed.

JUDGMENT AFFIRMED.

THE other judges concur.

ELIZABETH S. PARKER, PLAINTIFF IN ERROR, V. WM.
  STARR, DEFENDANT IN ERROR.

1. **Summons**: SERVICE ON WIDOW AND MINOR CHILD. The
   return to a summons served on a widow and her minor children
   in the following form is sufficient:
   "This summons came to hand September 4th, 1871, at 2 o'clock
   P.M., and on this 5th day of September, 1871, I served this summons on Sarah Sanders in person, and Sarah E. Sanders and
   Charles Sanders by delivering to each of them a true and certified
   copy of this summons, with all the endorsements thereon. All
   of this done in Nemaha county, state of Nebraska.
                             "DAVIDSON PLASTERS, *Sheriff.*"

2. **Mortgage Foreclosure**: GUARDIAN FOR MINOR DEFEND-
   ANTS. In an action to foreclose a mortgage on real estate the
   failure of the court to appoint a guardian *ad litem* for minor defendants does not render the decree of foreclosure and sale void;
   at most, it is erroneous.

3. **Minors**. A female, on reaching the age of eighteen years, ceases
   to be a minor.

4. **Limitation of Actions**. One who has been in the open, notorious, exclusive, adverse possession of real estate for ten years
   becomes vested with a valid title to the same.

5. **Mortgage Foreclosure**: MISTAKE IN DESCRIPTION OF PREM-
   ISES. Where a mistake was made in the description of certain
   premises mortgaged, which mistake was carried through all the
   proceedings to foreclose the mortgage, sale of the premises, confirmation of sale, and deed to the purchaser, but it appeared
   that the premises intended to be mortgaged had actually been
   appraised and sold under such mortgage, and the purchaser had
   taken possession of the same; *Held*, No injury to the heirs of
   the mortgagor being shown, that the grantee of the purchaser
   was entitled to a decree correcting the mistake and quieting
   his title in said premises, but at his own cost and expense.

ERROR to the district court for Nemaha county. Tried
below before BROADY, J.

O. P. Mason, for plaintiff in error.

E. W. Thomas, for defendant in error.

MAXWELL, CH. J.

This is an action of ejectment brought by the plaintiff against the defendant to recover the possession of certain real estate in Nemaha county. The defendant claims title under the foreclosure of a mortgage executed by Daniel C. Saunders to one Hawley, November 1st, 1869, to secure the payment of three promissory notes of the same date, one of $650, due April 10th, 1870; one of $400, due November 1st, 1870, and one of $650, due May 1st, 1871.

The land mortgaged consisted of about one and one-half acres, and comprised a mill and water-power on the Little Nemaha river. In the mortgage the premises were described as being in the south-east quarter of section 16, township 6, range 13 E., in Nemaha county, whereas, in fact, the premises were located in the north-east quarter of said section.

Saunders died intestate December 16th, 1870, and the notes not being paid, Hawley commenced suit September 1st, 1871, to foreclose the mortgage, the widow and children of Saunders being defendants. A decree of foreclosure and sale was rendered, the premises sold to Hawley, the sale confirmed, and a deed made to him by the sheriff June 4th, 1872. Hawley took possession of the premises intended to be conveyed, and on November 1st, 1872, sold and transferred said premises to one John E. Walton, and in 1874 Walton and wife sold and conveyed to one Jonathan Higgins; in 1876 Higgins and wife conveyed to the defendant, who has retained possession from that time until the present, and made improvements thereon of an estimated value of $6,000. In all these proceedings and conveyances the property was described as in the south-east quarter of said section 16. Saunders left two children surviving him, viz., the plaintiff, who was born September 6th, 1855, and Charles Saunders, who was born in 1869. Charles Saunders died in 1876, and the widow of

Daniel C. Saunders, in April, 1884, conveyed her interest in the premises in question to the plaintiff.

The defendant has set up the facts in regard to the error in the description, and prays that the error may be corrected and the title quieted in him. Second, pleads the statute of limitations. Third, alleges that the plaintiff is estopped to claim the land, as the defendant and those under whom he claims have made valuable improvements on the land, and the plaintiff knew it, and that she has waited an unreasonable time before bringing suit.

On the trial of the cause a judgment was rendered in favor of the defendant.

The first ground of objection is, that the service of summons in the foreclosure proceedings was not sufficient to give the court jurisdiction. The return is as follows:

"This summons came to hand September 4th, 1871, at 2 o'clock P.M., and on this 5th day of September, 1871, I served this summons on Sarah Sanders in person, and Sarah E. Sanders and Charles Sanders, by delivering to each of them a true and certified copy of this summons with all the endorsements thereon. All of this done in Nemaha county, state of Nebraska."

                              "DAVIDSON PLASTERS,
                                        "Sheriff."

Section 76 of the code of civil procedure provides that, "When the defendant is a minor under the age of fourteen years, the service must be upon him and upon his guardian or father, or if neither of these can be found, then his mother, or the person having the care or control of the infant, or with whom he lives. If neither of these can be found, or if the minor be more than fourteen years of age, service on him alone shall be sufficient. The manner of service may be the same as in the case of adults."

It will be seen that the service was made upon the mother as well as upon the minors. They appear to have been living with their mother, and, so far as appears, she had the care and control of them.   The presumption is that the officer did his duty, and that the mother was properly served as guardian.   The service, therefore, was sufficient.

The failure of the court to appoint a guardian *ad litem* did not oust it of jurisdiction.   This question was before this court in *McCormick v. Paddock*, 20 Neb., 486, and *McAllister v. Lancaster Co. Bank*, 15 Neb., 295, and it was held that where a court by the service of its process acquires jurisdiction over the person of an insane defendant, the failure to appoint a guardian *ad litem* does not render the judgment void ; at most, it is only erroneous, to be corrected on error.   The same rule will apply to minor defendants.   *Simmons v. McKay*, 5 Bush, 25.   Freeman on Judgments, § 151.   *Walkenhorst v. Lewis*, 24 Kas., 420. *McMurray v. McMurray*, 66 N. Y., 175.

Second.   That the bar of the statute of limitations is complete in favor of the defendants.

Section 1, chapter 34, Compiled Statutes, provides that, "all male children under twenty-one and all females under eighteen years of age are declared to be minors ; but in case a female marries between the ages of sixteen and eighteen her minority ends."

The plaintiff reached the age of eighteen years on the 6th day of September, 1873, and then had the right to bring suit in her own name and transact business generally.   This action was begun in April, 1884.   The testimony clearly shows that the defendant and those under whom he claims have been in open, notorious, and exclusive possession for ten years next before this suit was brought after plaintiff attained her majority. ` Such possession vests a good and sufficient title in the defendant. *Gatling v. Lane*, 17 Neb., 79–83.   *Haywood v. Thomas*, 17 Neb., 240.   *Horbach v. Miller*, 4 Neb., 47.   *Pettit v. Black*, 13 Neb., 153.   *Trussel v. Lewis*, 13 Neb., 417. *Stettnische v. Lamb*, 18 Neb., 626.   The plaintiff's right to maintain the action, therefore, is barred.

Third. The right of the defendant to have the error in the description of the premises corrected in this proceeding. The testimony shows that the property intended to be mortgaged was the mill and water-power heretofore referred to, that that property was actually appraised and sold under the decree of foreclosure, and that the purchaser thereupon entered into possession, and that he and those claiming under him have retained possession until the present time. There is no claim that the failure in the proceedings to properly describe the property, affected in any manner the sale thereof, under the decree of foreclosure, or prevented any person from bidding at such sale. The plaintiff, therefore, has sustained no damages by reason of the misdescription, and the defendant is entitled to the relief sought; but at his own cost and expenses. In *Davenport v. Sovil*, 6 Ohio State, 460, the facts were somewhat similar to the case at bar, although in that case the land sold under the mortgage does not appear to have been that intended to be covered by the mortgage. The power of a court to correct a mistake of this kind is undoubted, and it is its duty in a proper case to grant the relief sought. *Blodgett v. Hobart*, 18 Vt., 414. *Cummings v. Freer*, 26 Mich., 128. *Quivey v. Baker*, 37 Cal., 465. *Donald v. Beals*, 57 Id., 399.

The judgment of the district court is clearly right, and as above modified as to costs, is affirmed.

JUDGMENT ACCORDINGLY.

THE other judges concur.

21
46
31
49

RANDALL S. BENTLEY, PLAINTIFF IN ERROR, V. CHARLES H. DAVIS, DEFENDANT IN ERROR.

1. **Arbitration:** AWARD. Where certain matters in difference between A. B. and C. D. were submitted to certain arbitrators, who made verbal award, which was ratified by the aforesaid parties by entering into a written agreement, signed by them and witnessed by said arbitrators; *Held*, That the parties had thereby accepted of said award, and no action could be brought upon the original items of account submitted to said arbitrators without showing some adequate cause for setting the award aside.

2. ———: ———. Matters not submitted to the arbitrators, or not considered by them in making the award, may be sued on as though no award had been made.

3. **Testimony,** *Held*, Insufficient to sustain the verdict.

ERROR to the district court for Franklin county. Tried below before GASLIN, J.

Ryan Bros. and *H. Whitmore*, for plaintiff in error.

Sheppard & Black, A. E. Fletcher, and *H. H. Wilson*, for defendant in error.

MAXWELL, CH. J.

In October, 1885, the plaintiff below (defendant in error) filed his petition in the district court of Franklin county, as follows:

"Plaintiff complains of defendant for the reason that defendant is owing to plaintiff, upon account, the sum of three hundred and twenty-five dollars thirty-two cents, ($325.32) and interest at seven per cent from August 1st, 1884." Then follows an itemized statement of the account.

"2d. Plaintiff further alleges that on or about October 17th, 1884, plaintiff delivered to defendant, at defendant's

request, the following promissory notes, the property of
plaintiff." A description of the notes is then set out; the
amount claimed under second count is $700.

In his answer the defendant alleges, "That on or about
May 15th, 1884, plaintiff and defendant entered into an
agreement in writing, whereby it was mutually agreed that
they would together deal in agricultural implements, and
other goods of various kinds, in the following manner, viz.:
The defendant was to procure goods on his own responsi-
bility for the carrying on of the business, and the plaintiff
agreed to sell said goods, and the net profits of the firm
were to be equally divided between the plaintiff and the
defendant, in full payment and satisfaction for the services
of each party to be rendered in and about the carrying on
of said business. The alleged claims of plaintiff in his
'Exhibit A,' attached to his petition, excepting the 'millet'
and 'insurance' and 'commission and real estate loans,' are
false claims and have entirely originated and grown out of
the business done under, and by virtue of, said agreement,
and that defendant never purchased, contracted for, or
received of plaintiff any of the property itemized in his said
account, nor authorized plaintiff to lay out or expend any
money or other property mentioned in said account, nor
ever sanctioned or agreed to pay said account, or any part
thereof, except as to the said millet seed and insurance items,
and that two items have been fully paid to plaintiff by
defendant.

" 3d. The defendant alleges that before this action was
brought, to-wit, on the 17th day of October, A.D. 1884, said
plaintiff and defendant had a full settlement of all claims
mentioned in plaintiff's petition, and plaintiff then and
there delivered to the defendant, who accepted the same, to-
wit, all the promissory notes mentioned in the second alleged
cause of action in plaintiff's petition, for the purpose of
enabling defendant to collect thereupon the sum of four
hundred thirty-seven dollars ninety cents ($437.90), and

apply the same in payment of the indebtedness then agreed by the parties hereto to be due from plaintiff to the defendant. Plaintiff then and there agreed with defendant that the plaintiff was then owing defendant on such settlement the sum of $437.90, and when that amount should be collected by the defendant out of said notes, the notes then remaining uncollected should be returned to plaintiff. Defendant alleges that he has not been able to collect on said notes the said sum of $437.90.

"Whereupon defendant asks that this suit be dismissed at plaintiff's cost."

The reply was a general denial of new matter.

On the trial of the cause the jury returned a verdict in favor of the defendant in error for the sum of $306.61, upon which judgment was rendered. The principal ground of error relied upon is, that the verdict is against the weight of evidence.

The testimony shows that about the 17th of October, 1884, the plaintiff and defendant submitted the matters in controversy to Martin Hollenbeck and George Rice; these two arbitrators chose a third, one Robert Stevenson. The three heard the parties and found there was due from Davis to Bentley the sum of $437.90. This award was verbal. Davis thereupon produced the notes in question, and left them in the possession of one of the arbitrators to be delivered to Bentley upon his signing the following agreement:

"FRANKLIN, Neb., October 17, 1884.

"This is to certify that all matters in difference between R. S. Bentley and Chas. H. Davis, in any way relating to, or growing out of, the agricultural implement business entered into by written contract between the undersigned bearing date May 15, 1884, and all matters in difference between same parties relating to, or in any way pertaining to, the loaning business done between May 15, 1884, and Oct. 15, 1884, is fully settled and satisfied. The said loan-

ing business refers only to the loans that were made by
said Davis as the agent of said Bentley to third parties."
  (Signed)   "R. S. BENTLEY,
                                         "CHARLES H. DAVIS.
"M. L. HOLLENBECK,
"GEO. B. RICE,
"ROBT. STEVENSON,
            Witnesses."

The testimony further shows that Bentley was to collect
out of these notes the sum of $437.90, and that thereupon
the balance of the notes were to be returned to Davis, and
that Bentley has not yet received, on said notes, said
amount due him thereon. Upon this state of facts, it is
evident that Davis was not entitled to a verdict. The
petition is framed upon the theory that there had been no
settlement, and all accounts which were submitted to the
arbitrators are set out as though no settlement had taken
place. This, in our view, is an incorrect mode of pleading.
The plaintiff and defendant by entering into an agreement
based upon the award thereby ratified the same, and if
mistakes had been made by the arbitrators, or the arbitrators considered matters which were not submitted or omitted to consider others which were submitted, those facts
should be set out as a reason for setting such award aside.
Hall v. Vanier, 6 Neb., 87.

As a general rule, courts will construe awards favorably
and make all reasonable presumptions and intendments in
favor of their validity. *Johnson v. Wilson*, Willes, 253.
Barnardiston v. Fowler, 10 Mod., 204. *Skillings v. Cool-
idge*, 14 Mass., 43. *Bogan v. Daughdrill*, 51 Ala., 312.
Fudickar v. Guardian Mut. Life Ins. Co., 62 N. Y. (17
Sick.), 392. *Locke v. Filley*, 14 Hun (N. Y.), 139.

At common law an award acts as a merger upon the
original claims upon which it is predicated whenever a new
duty is created thereby; but it does not bar an action upon
a demand not presented to the arbitrators or one not passed

upon by them. *Edwards v. Stevens*, 1 Allen, 315. *Pritchard v. Daly*, 73 Ill., 523. As all matters upon which this suit is predicated seem to have been submitted to the arbitrators named, and an award made by them, which the plaintiff, so far as appears, ratified and confirmed, this form of action cannot be maintained.

The verdict is against the clear weight of evidence and must be set aside.

The judgment of the district court is reversed and the cause remanded for further proceedings.

REVERSED AND REMANDED.

THE other judges concur.

THE NORWEGIAN PLOW COMPANY, PLAINTIFF IN ERROR, V. JOSEPH A. HAINES ET AL., DEFENDANTS IN ERROR.

Conversion: There being evidence of facts constituting a conversion of the property of the plaintiff by the defendants and the same having been fairly submitted to the jury by proper instructions, a verdict and judgment for the plaintiff upheld.

ERROR to the district court for Douglas county. Tried below before WAKELEY, J.

O. P. Mason, for plaintiff in error.

Groff, Montgomery & Jeffrey, for defendants in error.

COBB, J.

The plaintiff in error had recovered several judgments against one Fred Fischer, amounting in the aggregate to about $1,000, in justices' court, in Knox county. Execu-

44

tions were issued thereon, and placed in the hands of the sheriff. The sheriff, by his deputy, proceeded to levy said executions on the goods and chattels of said Fischer, who was engaged in the agricultural implement business at Creighton, in said county. It appears that Fischer had in his store, or shed adjoining thereto, a quantity of agricultural implements of his own, and also a quantity of the same general character of goods belonging to the defendants in error, which he held on commission. There is considerable conflict in the evidence as to what the deputy sheriff did by virtue of his said writs, in respect to that part of the said property which confessedly belonged to the defendants in error, but they claim that he levied upon the whole, and actually sold a part of it. This conflict in the evidence will be hereafter referred to.

The defendants in error brought this action in the district court of Douglas county, against the plaintiff in error, together with one Mower, their managing agent, and Reuben Bollman, sheriff of Knox county, for the conversion of that part of said property belonging to them, of the alleged value of $1;124. The answer consisted of a general denial.

There was a trial to a jury, with a verdict and judgment for the plaintiffs. The cause is brought to this court on error. Nine errors are assigned in the petition in error, all of which are not strictly followed up, nor insisted on, in the brief of counsel.

Adhering to a rule often laid down by this, as well as other courts, I will discuss those points only which are urged in the brief, remarking at the same time that there was no oral argument of the case.

The first point presented is, that "When the officer presented his executions and announced his intention to levy on said Fischer's goods, Fischer made no objection, or in any way manifested a desire to prevent the levy being placed on the Haines Bros.' goods," etc., with the conclusion that under such state of facts the plaintiffs below cannot recover.

This point presents a question of pleading, as well as one of law applicable to the evidence. As already stated, the petition charges the conversion of the goods by the defendants. The answer is a general denial. This put in issue two facts only; that of the ownership of the goods by the plaintiffs, and their conversion by the defendant. Had the defendant relied upon the conduct of the plaintiffs' agent, or bailee, as giving a license, or creating an estoppel, such conduct should have been set up in the answer as a special ground of defense. This view is fully sustained by the authority of the three Nebraska cases cited by counsel for defendants in error.

Second. That the trial court "allowed testimony to be introduced to show what was said by the officer when he came to levy the executions, but before the levy was made, as to what he intended to levy on."

Under this head I will quote from the abstract the evidence of the witnesses, as well on part of the plaintiffs as the defendant, so far as it bears directly upon what was said and done by the officer in making the levy.

First as to the evidence of Fred Fischer:

"Friday, Feb. 29, deputy sheriff came to my office; stated that he had in his possession five executions against me, in favor of the Norwegian Plow Company, and that he levied upon the building my office was in, all the contents in the building, and everything on the premises—he took possession of the premises and the contents of the safe. There were present, Mr. Fox, attorney for the company, and Mr. Mower, representative of plow company."

George L. Fischer testified: "I was present when deputy sheriff came to make levy. He said he had five executions in favor of Norwegian Plow Company, against Fred Fischer. That he attached that building, in which Fischer was doing business—everything in it, and everything on the premises."

On the contrary, witnesses for the defendants testified as follows :

E. B. Mower: "Am one of the defendants. Know plaintiffs. I was present when the levy was made on the goods of Fischer. I ·remember exactly what he said, which was, 'I take into my possession all the things belonging to Fred Fischer or that he has any title in.' After that I went to desk, and saw by the looks of things that some of the goods belonged to Haines Bros., and were held on commission ; told sheriff to get his men and separate the goods from the others so there would be no trouble about them. Knew we could not hold them ; had no idea of trying to. We didn't take a dollar's worth of Haines Bros.' goods that I know of. We found quite a number of plows, etc., lying out under an open shed and frozen into the mud. We had to get an axe to take them out. Every article that I knew of belonging to Haines Bros. was taken out and all put together in one place and kept separate. The goods we took were the goods Fischer had got from us, the Norwegian Plow Company. The shed was a flimsy affair, just a 'lean-to' against a building and open at the side and end. We separated the goods, putting those we took in one pile and Haines Bros.' in another. We moved these goods, some of them, about twenty-five feet, some only the length of them. As soon as goods were sorted and inventory made, I came down to Omaha and informed Haines Bros. Fischer never said anything to me about the goods; I heard him saying to Rothwell about the Haines goods, and I told Rothwell he had nothing to do with those goods at all, not to touch them, only to move them out of the way ; we only wanted the goods belonging to Fischer. Young Fischer came and demanded the Haines Bros.' goods from Rothwell. I told him 'We haven't got anything to do with those things, you can take them.' He said, ' You have got my building ; what am I going to do about it?' The building was

Fischer's. The sheriff told them that they couldn't take anything away until after the inventory; then they could have them all; that he had to sort them out to make the inventory, and he didn't want anything only what Fischer had an interest in. I told them we did not want the commission goods, and as soon as we sorted the others out, they could have the balance. The goods were handled in first-rate shape. Nothing scratched or injured; they were not injured five cents' worth. I was there helping all the time and saw."

W. L. Rothwell: "Was deputy sheriff of Knox county on February 29th, 1884; levied the executions against Fred Fischer; told him I levied on all property belonging to Fred Fischer, and any property he had any interest in. The property was under open sheds; all plows were frozen in the ground, balance covered with snow. Goods were all together when I went there. I didn't know one party's goods from another. Mr. Mower separated the commission goods from the other. He spoke particularly of Haines Bros.' goods, and said he didn't want to get hold of any of them. I told him we had better put the Haines Bros.' goods out by themselves, so when we come to sell we could take care of them. I had a watchman to take care of both piles. Some goods were outside when we went there. The only demand George Fischer ever made on me was as follows: I was going by his attorney's office one day and he came running down-stairs and shoved a paper into my face, saying, 'Release those goods.' I said, 'What goods?' He said, 'Those goods.' I said, 'I don't release any goods until after I have made a correct inventory.' He did not hand me the paper, but went back upstairs. I did not read paper; had no opportunity to do so. This occurred while I was taking inventory. I never removed these goods from the premises. They came to me several times and wanted me to take care of them. The goods I took appear in my return on the executions."

The conflict in the above evidence consists chiefly in the words used by the levying officer. Counsel say in the brief that under some circumstances these declarations might become a part of the *res gestæ*. According to the evidence of the witnesses of defendant in error, the words were a part of the act of the levy, hence a part of the *res gestæ*. This point runs almost imperceptibly into the

Fourth, which is, " That neither the officer nor the agent of the plaintiff in error had any intention of taking Haines Bros.' goods on the execution," etc.

As a general proposition I think that a conversion of property is not a question of intention, but of fact, and yet in the case at bar if it was the *bona fide* intention of the officer and of the agent of the plaintiff in error only to take sufficient control of Fischer's store to enable them to separate the goods belonging to Fischer from those belonging to others who had made him their commission merchant, in respect thereto, to the end that the officer might complete the levy of his execution upon the former, and such intention governed their conduct throughout the transaction, and could be shown and proven by their acts and other circumstances, it would have amounted to a defense. Such, as near as I can gather from the abstract, was the view of the trial court. But this presented a question, or questions, peculiarly proper for a jury, and, if presented to them by proper instructions, their verdict must be final.

Under the assignment which we are now considering the plaintiff in error complains of the giving of the 7th instruction. I incline to the opinion that this instruction, taken alone, is open to objection, but when considered in connection with those which immediately precede and follow it, it expresses the law as applicable to the evidence. I quote the 5th, 6th, 7th, and 8th instructions :

" 5. If you find that any of the plaintiffs' goods were actually sold at the execution sale, whether by design or through mistake, the plaintiffs' right to recover therefor is clear and undoubted.

"6. As to such as were not sold, you will inquire and determine whether or not the sheriff by his deputy levied upon them. If he did make a levy upon them within the definition and according to the test about to be given to you, then the plaintiffs are entitled to recover for such as were levied on, as well as for those, if any, which were sold.

"7. If you should find from the evidence that the goods in controversy, or a part of them, were within a building occupied by Fischer; and that the deputy sheriff declared that he levied upon all the property within the building; and that he thereupon took possession of plaintiffs' property and reduced it to his control and dominion, with the purpose and intent of perfecting his levy thereon and subjecting it to his execution, those acts would amount to a conversion of the goods, and entitle plaintiffs to recover, although the levy might have been abandoned thereafter.

"8. If, however, the plaintiffs' goods were intermingled with those belonging to Fischer in such a way that it was necessary for the deputy to take temporary possession of the whole for the purpose of separating them, and he took such possession and held it for that purpose for a sufficient time only to accomplish it, not doing or intending to do any acts for the purpose of levying on plaintiffs' goods, or subjecting them to his executions, this did not amount to a levy upon or conversion of any goods not actually sold or appropriated."

These instructions, I think, fairly presented to the jury the conflicting evidence of the Fischers on the one side, and of W. L. Rothwell, the deputy sheriff, and E. B. Mower, the agent of the plaintiff in error, on the other, as to the disputed facts in the case. As above stated, these facts presented a proper case for the consideration of the jury, and together with the undisputed fact that two plows and two harrows, the property of the defendants in error, were actually sold by the sheriff on the executions of plaintiff in error against Fischer, I think fully sustain the verdict and judgment.

The judgment of the district court is therefore affirmed.

JUDGMENT AFFIRMED.

THE other judges concur.

GRACE REED ET. AL., PLAINTIFFS IN ERROR, V. LUTHER B. MABEN, DEFENDANT IN ERROR.

1. **Attachment:** GENERAL RULE. Attachment, although an ancillary remedy, and applicable to a limited class of cases, yet within its limits rests upon its own facts, and not upon the facts of the action.

2. ———: CASE STATED. R. J. & Co. sued M. in the county court and obtained an order of attachment. On motion and hearing the attachment was dissolved. Upon the trial the defendant obtained judgment. Upon error in the district court the judgment dissolving the attachment was reversed, and upon appeal and re-trial of the action in the district court, at a subsequent term, the plaintiff obtained judgment. But the court made a special finding, that at the date of the commencement of the action the debt sued on was not due, and thereupon dissolved the attachment; *Held*, Error and reversed.

ERROR to the district court for Holt county. Tried below before TIFFANY, J.

Groff, Montgomery & Jeffrey and *Uttley & Small*, for plaintiffs in error.

M. P. Kinkaid, for defendant in error.

COBB, J.

This cause arises upon a petition and proceeding in error by the plaintiffs in error to the district court of Holt county, upon the alleged errors of said court in a certain attachment proceeding lately pending therein, in which they were plaintiffs and the defendant in error was defendant.

It appears from the record that the plaintiffs commenced an action against the defendant in the county court, for a certain bill of goods sold and delivered by them to him, and caused an order of attachment to be issued therein, and attached certain chattels of the defendant. The defendant answered to the merits, and also contested the attachment by motion. Upon the trial, judgment was rendered for the defendant, and upon the hearing of the motion the same was sustained and the attachment discharged. The judgment on the merits of the case was taken to the district court of said county by appeal, and the order discharging the attachment was also taken to that court by proceeding in error.

It appears from the manner in which the transcript is made up and presented to this court, that in the district court the matter of error was first heard. I here transcribe the journal entry, showing the action of the court thereon: "Now on this 19th day of May, 1885, this cause coming on for hearing, upon the motion of the defendant to strike the evidence from the files, for the reason that there was no bill of exceptions preserved as required by law, and the court after hearing the arguments of counsel and being fully advised in the premises, does overrule the motion. * * * Thereupon, on this day, this cause came on for hearing upon the petition in error and the evidence in the case, and the court, after hearing the arguments of counsel and being fully advised in the premises, does find as follows:

" 1. The court erred in discharging the attachment issued in said action upon the testimony in the record.

" It is therefore considered by the court that the judgment and order of the county court discharging the attachment ssued in said action from the property attached therein, be and the same is hereby reversed, and the attachment re-instated to all the property attached therein, and the costs taxed to the defendant in error," etc.

The case on appeal in the district court does not appear to have been disposed of at the same time or term with the above proceedings, as amended pleadings are shown to have been filed in the case as late as December 16th of the same year; and at some time not shown in the journal entries, the cause came on for trial on the amended petition and answer thereto, presumably to the court, "and" continues the journal entry, "the court being fully advised in the premises, finds that at the time of the commencement of this action the * * * cause of action in this case was not due, and that no cause of action existed in favor of plaintiffs against defendant at the time of the commencement of this action. And the court further finds that since the commencement of this action, and during the pendency thereof, the account described in the amended petition has matured, and there is now due to the plaintiffs on the cause of action in their amended petition this day filed, the sum of $270.78, and that plaintiffs should recover on said cause of action. Wherefore it is considered by the court that the plaintiffs, Reed, Jones & Co., have and recover of and from the defendant, L. B. Maben, the sum of $270.78, and that this judgment bear interest at the rate of 7 per cent per annum, and that defendant recover his costs herein expended, and that plaintiff recover no costs in this action."

It further appears that thereupon the plaintiffs moved the court for an order for the sale of the attached property, as upon execution to satisfy the judgment, which motion was by the court denied, * * * "and" continues the record, "the court further orders that the order of attachment in this case be discharged."

It appears that again on the 17th day of February, 1886, the plaintiffs moved the court "to correct the judgment heretofore rendered in this cause by striking out the judgment and order of the court made at the December, 1885, term, discharging the attachment issued in the case, and strike said order from the records, and allow the matter of attachment to stand upon the original order made in this case at the May, 1885, term," etc., which motion was denied. Thereupon the cause is brought to this court on error by the plaintiffs, who assign the following errors:

"1. The court erred in its judgment rendered herein on the 16th day of December, 1885, in overruling the plaintiffs' motion, for an order for the sale of the attached property.

"2. The court erred in its said judgment in ordering that the attachment in this cause be discharged.

"3. The court erred in its judgment rendered herein on the 17th day of February, 1886, in overruling the motion of the plaintiff to strike from the former judgment of the court the portion thereof discharging the attachment in the cause."

Before considering the points presented by this case, let us see what is not presented. In the first place, the judgment of the district court on the proceeding in error to the county court is not presented. That judgment was favorable to the plaintiffs and unfavorable to defendant. He took an exception to it in that court, but he does not bring it here for review. None of the papers upon which the attachment was attacked and dissolved in the county court, and upon which the judgment of that court was reviewed and reversed in the district court, are brought up in the record before us. The important and difficult question whether the order of the county court, dissolving the attachment, could properly be brought up on error to the district court simultaneously with the bringing of the whole case before that court by appeal, is not presented by the record before us. The order of the district court, allowing the plaintiffs to amend their petition, and, as claimed by counsel for defendant at the argument, allowing plaintiffs to present a different issue in the district court from that upon which the cause was tried in the county court, is not before us. And finally, the general judgment of the district court in favor of the plaintiffs is not presented to this court for review in this proceeding in error.

The only questions, then, now before us for review are those directly arising upon the refusal of the district court to order the sale of the attached property and its order dissolving the attachment.

Attachment is a proceeding ancillary to the main action, in which it is allowed. If the main action is attacked and overthrown the attachment goes with it. On the other hand, it often happens that while the cause of action is lawful and just, the ground of attachment is mistaken or false; hence judgment must be rendered for the plaintiff on the merits, but the attachment must be dissolved. As a matter of practice, however, if no ground of attachment exists, or the order has been issued without the proper affidavit or bond, as required by statute, the attention of the court must be called thereto, in some appropriate manner, and the question of sufficiency settled before the final judgment in the case. The sole object of an attachment is, that the property of the debtor may be taken into the custody of law and preserved, so that it may be applied to the payment of the judgment of the plaintiff when obtained. It therefore follows that, when this proceeding has answered its purpose, it would be idle to go back and inquire into its sufficiency.

Under the system of practice which formerly prevailed in some of the states, where actions were commenced by attachment, it has been held that, when upon the final trial it appeared from the pleadings or evidence in the case, it was one not proper to be commenced by attachment, the cause would be dismissed. See *Elliott v. Jackson*, 3 Wis., 649. But this rule is not applicable to our present system of practice, where, as above stated, the order of attachment is an ancillary proceeding. But even were it otherwise, in the case at bar the action was for goods, wares, and merchandise, sold and delivered, one in which the ancillary or collateral remedy by attachment is clearly admissible, upon the proper steps being taken. That such steps were taken must be presumed from the judgment of the district court upon the direct attack made upon the attachment in the county court, and brought into the former court by proceedings in error. Whether the price of such goods, wares, and merchandise was not due at the date of the commencement of the action, as found by the court, or what effect such fact or finding should have had upon the judgment of the court, are questions which, as before stated, are not before the court, and upon which I express no opinion; but certain it is, if the plaintiffs were entitled to prosecute their action to final and successful judgment, they were also entitled to whatever security they could derive through the ancillary remedy of attachment; dependent, of course, upon the existence of the facts upon which an attachment may issue under the provisions of the statute, and their pursuit of the statutory means for making such remedy available.

It seems evident that the action of the district court in refusing the order for the sale of the attached property, and in dissolving the attachment, was based upon its finding that the debt sued on was not due at the time of the commencement of the action, and not upon fact or deficiency applicable to the attachment proceedings, and accordingly, as we have seen, it cannot be upheld.

The judgment of the district court in denying the order for the sale of the attached property as upon execution, and in dissolving the attachment, is reversed, the attachment restored, and the attached property ordered to be sold as upon execution.

JUDGMENT ACCORDINGLY.

THE other judges concur.

GEO. W. EARLE, PLAINTIFF IN ERROR, V. B. BURCH
AND OTHERS, DEFENDANTS IN ERROR.

1. **Chattel Mortgage**: RIGHTS OF PURCHASER. Where the law declares a mortgage valid, as between the parties, but void as to creditors and subsequent purchasers in good faith, a creditor, in order to avail himself of the advantage of that character, must remain a creditor throughout the litigation. If he receive his pay in the mortgaged property, with knowledge of the mortgage, he will take it subject to the mortgage.

2. —— : ——. In such case, no one who has knowledge of such sale can become a subsequent purchaser of the property which is the subject thereof, in good faith, so as to avail himself of the advantage awarded to that class of purchasers.

3. **Parties in Action of Replevin.** The statutory rule that " all persons having an interest in the subject of the action, and in obtaining the relief demanded, may be joined as plaintiffs," etc., (code, § 40) is applicable, not only to actions formerly denominated equitable, but also to those formerly denominated legal, including actions of replevin.

4. **Replevin**: FINDING OF COURT. The defendants claiming only a special property in the goods replevied, and the court having found the value of said special property, which finding was within the value of the goods as proved at the trial; *Held*, Not necessary that the court should have found the general value of the property.

ERROR to the district court for Gage county. Tried below before BROADY, J.

A. H. Babcock and *T. D. Cobbey*, for plaintiff in error.

Burke & Prout and *Griggs & Rinaker*, for defendants in error.

COBB, J.

This was an action of replevin in the district court of Gage county. George W. Earle was plaintiff, and one George

Noll, a constable, was defendant; the property replevied, a stock of drugs, medicines, and fancy articles, such as are usually kept in a drug store. There are two lengthy abstracts in the case in this court; but I will state the facts of the case, as I understand them, after a careful examination of both, and frequent recurrences to the transcript, without specially following either.

One Dr. George W. Rightmire, of Wymore, was, as early as October 6, 1882, the owner and keeper of the drug store and stock of goods in question, on which day he executed the chattel mortgage thereof to B. Burch & Co., hereinafter referred to. On the 12th day of December, 1883, he executed the chattel mortgage of said stock of goods to Holland Norton, also hereinafter referred to. On the 14th day of January, 1884, he sold and delivered the said stock of goods to George W. Earle. Earle paid for the said goods by delivering to Rightmire certain overdue notes of the said Rightmire, amounting to about $4,000, which he held, and assuming an indebtedness of the said Rightmire, at his request, amounting to four or five hundred dollars. On the 25th day of February, 1884, Max Meyer & Co., having obtained a judgment against the said George W. Rightmire, and suing out an execution thereon, placed the same in the hands of Drew Ryan, constable, and caused him to levy upon and seize the said stock of goods to satisfy the same. On the 26th day of February, 1884, B. Burch & Co. and Holland Norton commenced a joint action of replevin against the said Drew Ryan, and replevied the said stock of goods from him, which said order of replevin was placed in the hands of George Noll, constable, for service, and by him served by seizing said goods, causing the same to be appraised, and upon the execution of a replevin bond by the plaintiff in said action, with security, he delivered the said goods to the said B. Burch & Co. and Holland Norton.

On the 13th day of March, 1884, this action was com-

menced.   The plaintiff (as is stated in the briefs of counsel
on either side), supposing that·said goods were still in the
possession of said George Noll, the said action of replevin
was brought against him, as defendant.   The goods replevied, however, in said last mentioned action were, as
appears from the statement of counsel in the brief, delivered to the said Earle, plaintiff, upon the giving of the
usual replevin bond.

Upon the application of B. Burch & Co., and Holland
Norton, and Max Meyer & Co., they were severally permitted by the court to be made defendants in the action,
and severally filed their answers, consisting of general denials, and on the part of said Max Meyer & Co. setting
up the obtaining of judgment by them against the said
George W. Rightmire, and the levy of an execution issued
upon said judgment upon said goods, and that, at the date
of said levy, the same were the property of, and in the
possession of, said Rightmire.   To which answer the plaintiff replied, denying each and every allegation thereof.

Upon the affidavit and motion of counsel the said Max
Meyer & Co. applied to the court for an order merging the
said action of B. Burch & Co. and Holland Norton against
Drew Ryan, and making it a part of this action.   While I
find no order of the court upon said motion in the record,
one was evidently regarded as made, allowing the motion.

The cause was tried to the court, a jury being waived.
I quote the findings and judgment of the court: "This
cause coming on to be heard, and having heretofore been
submitted on the pleadings and the evidence, on consideration whereof the court finds that at the commencement of the
original constituent action of *George W. Earle v. George
Noll*, constable, the defendants, B. Burch & Co. and Holland Norton, were entitled to the possession of the goods
replevied by virtue of a special property to the amount of
$430.08 to B. Burch & Co., and the amount of $1,252.89
to Holland Norton, and that the property replevied was

the property of plaintiff, subject to said aggregate lien of
$1,682.97 in favor of B. Burch & Co. and Holland Norton,
and that as between the parties to the other constituent
action of *Holland Norton and B. Burch & Co. v. Max
Meyer & Co.* (Drew Ryan), Max Meyer & Co. were entitled to the possession by virtue of a judgment lien to the
amount of 221\frac{38}{100}$; that by consent of Holland Nor-
ton and B. Burch & Co., Max Meyer & Co. are entitled
to said 221\frac{38}{100}$ out of the first money paid on the above
findings in favor of Holland Norton and B. Burch & Co.;
that the said right of possession of B. Burch & Co. and
Holland Norton is of the value of said aggregate sum
$1,682$\frac{97}{100}$, and I find their damages for detention one cent.
(After overruling the plaintiff's motion for a new trial.)
It is therefore considered, ordered, adjudged, and decreed by
the court that the defendants, B. Burch & Co. and Holland
Norton, have a return of the property, or in case a return
of said property can not be had, that the defendants, B.
Burch & Co. and Holland Norton, recover of said plaintiff
the said value, to-wit, the sum of one thousand six hundred
and eighty two and $\frac{97}{100}$ dollars, and one cent damages for
withholding the same, and costs of suit."

The cause is brought to this court by the plaintiff, on
error. He assigns the following errors, which are substantially the same as those assigned in his motion for a new
trial:

" 1. The court erred in finding that the defendants, B.
Burch & Co. and Holland Norton, were entitled to the
possession of the goods replevied at the commencement of
this action by reason of a special property amounting in
the aggregate to the sum of $1,682$\frac{97}{100}$ or any other amount.

" 2. The court erred in finding that the defendants, Max
Meyer & Co., were entitled to the possession of said goods
at the commencement of this action by virtue of a judgment
lien to the amount of 221\frac{38}{100}$, or any other amount.

" 3. The court erred in finding the right of possession of

45

said goods jointly in the defendants, B. Burch & Co. and Holland Norton, and finding their damages for detention, instead of separately finding the damages each had sustained.

"4. The court erred in admitting any evidence in support of the action of replevin of the stock of goods by B. Burch & Co. and Holland Norton, on the ground that their petition and affidavit in replevin showed on their face that they had no cause of action.

" 5. The court erred in not finding the value of the property in controversy.

"6. The court erred in rejecting evidence offered by plaintiff on the objection of the defendants.

"7. The court erred in admitting evidence offered by defendants over the objection of plaintiff.

".8. The court erred in admitting in evidence the chattel mortgage of George W. Rightmire to Holland Norton and to B. Burch & Co. over the objections of plaintiff.

"9. The findings of the court in favor of the defendants are against the weight of the evidence and are not sustained by sufficient evidence.

"10. The findings of the court in favor of the defendants are contrary to law.

"11. The findings are irregular and do not pass upon the issue involved in the action, and are not such findings as the law requires in an action of replevin, and no valid judgment can be rendered thereon." .

I will examine as many of the assignments as may be deemed necessary to a proper disposition of the case, but will not take them up in their order.

A good portion of the abstract, as presented by either party, is devoted to the evidence for and against the sale by Rightmire to Earle, and its *bona fides,* without reference to its *bona fide* character, as regards the mortgages to B. Burch & Co. and Holland Norton.   But the court having found in favor of Earle's title to the goods as against the general creditors of Rightmire, such evidence is immaterial to the questions before this court, and it will not be examined or considered, except in so far, if at all, as it may tend to throw light upon the question of his right to attack the said mortgages.

The mortgage from Rightmire to Holland Norton contains a clause of which the following is a copy:

"*Provided*, That the said George Rightmire shall have the right to sell and dispose of said property in the usual course of trade, and shall replenish said stock from time to time, as shall be required by the sale of said goods in the usual course of trade, and it is understood by and between the parties that all such goods as are purchased for the purpose of replenishing said stock shall be subject to, and be covered, by this mortgage, as though especially enumerated therein."

The mortgage from Rightmire to B. Burch & Co. was executed October 6th, 1882, nearly fifteen months before the sale of the goods by Rightmire to Earle. The firm of B. Burch & Co., so far as can be ascertained from the record, consisted of B. Burch, I. C. Burch, and M. H. Southwick. These parties were all sworn as witnesses at the trial, and each testified to the effect that they were frequently in the store of George W. Rightmire between the time of the execution and delivery of the said mortgage and the sale from Rightmire to Earle, and saw him selling and disposing of the mortgaged goods at retail, and that neither of them ever made any objections to his so doing.

I assume it to be the law that at the date of the sale from Rightmire to Earle these mortgages were good as between the parties thereto, respectively; but void as to the creditors of Rightmire and (subsequent) purchasers from him in good faith.

There was evidence tending to prove, and which I will assume does prove, that at the time of the sale from Rightmire to Earle the latter knew of the existence of the said mortgages. Indeed there is evidence to the effect that about the time of his purchase of the goods, Earle made a statement to one or more of the members of the firm of B. Burch & Co. that he was aware of their mortgage, and of the consideration for which it was given, and expressed the hope that it would soon be paid off. Under this state of facts, was he a purchaser in good faith? The words "in good faith," or their Latin equivalent, *bona fides,* have been often construed and their meaning defined when used as applicable to cases where the want of legality or the pursuit of strictly legal form consisted in a failure to comply with a recording or registration act, but I find no case, in the course of the examination which I have been able to make, where the want of good faith, or *bona fides,* has been imputed to a party acting with actual knowledge of a deed or mortgage of the character which the law declares fraudulent and void as to persons who stand in the relation toward the other parties which is occupied by him. And yet, upon principles fairly analogous to those governing many cases, and which must be upheld, it must be a sound rule of law that one cannot become a *bona fide* purchaser of property from another without the intention on his part to discharge all of the legal duties and obligations which such other person has incurred, in respect to such property, which is known to the purchaser at or before the time of the purchase. Now we have already seen that these mortgages were void as between the mortgagees and the creditors of the mortgagor, the class to which the plaintiff once belonged, and purchasers from him in good faith ; yet it cannot be denied that as between the parties to such mortgages they were legal and valid. Such being the case, could a third party with knowledge, by purchase, even paying a full consideration, acquire the rights of the mortgagor in respect to the property freed from the duty of applying it upon the mortgage? I think not. To state the proposition a little differently, if Rightmire had not, nor would have, any creditors, and had all the world notice of these mortgages, then they would be absolutely safe and legal. Of the two favored classes, creditors and purchasers in good faith, the first would be empty, and no one could enter the second without such knowledge, or notice, as would divest him of an essential element of his character—*bona fides.* But he had creditors, and the plaintiff belonged to that class. To him the mortgages were void, notwithstanding his knowledge, good faith, or ignorance not being necessary to his standing in that class. From that vantage ground he could have assailed the mortgages with the weapons of the law, and it may be presumed successfully. But when he descended to the arena of barter, and sought to become a purchaser, then it was necessary that he be clothed with the habiliments of good faith, good intentions, and must not know that by means of such transactions he is depriving a fellow purchaser of a purchase, conditional though it may be, yet as between the parties as honest and equally lawful as any which he may make.

It must be admitted that the plaintiff, neither in the character of creditor or purchaser, is chargeable with notice of the mortgages by reason of their having been recorded. The mortgages being void as to him, while he had no actual knowledge of their existence, the record was impotent to charge him therewith, and upon his acquiring actual knowledge there was no office for that by construction. It is evident that the trial court found as a matter of fact that at or before the purchase by the plaintiff he had actual knowledge of both mortgages, and there being evidence to sustain such finding, it cannot be disturbed.

The principal remaining question is, whether two parties having separate and distinct claims to the possession of the same property may unite such claims, and in their joint or combined names maintain an action of replevin therefor.

The following sections of the code are quoted as governing the consideration of this question :

"Sec. 40.   All persons having an interest in the subject
of the action, and in obtaining the relief demanded, may
join as plaintiffs, except as otherwise provided in this title;"
and

" Sec. 429.   Judgment may be given for or against
one or more of several plaintiffs, and for or against one or
more of several defendants ; it may determine the ultimate
rights of the parties on either side, as between themselves,
and it may grant to the defendant any affirmative relief to
which he may be entitled," etc.

" It shocks the prejudices of common-law pleaders to
speak of a union of plaintiffs, where there is not a joint
interest ; and such is the effect of legal education and long
habits of thinking, that what seems so natural in a proceeding to prevent a common injury, or to set aside a sale
for the benefit of creditors, or to subject to their respective
claims the assets of an estate, seems almost impossible in
case a sum of money is sought to be recovered in which
sundry persons have a several, and perhaps unequal,
interest.   But it has come to be generally conceded
that the rule is universal in its application, as it is in its
terms ; and if two or more are interested in the subject of
the action, and in the relief sought, they may unite as
plaintiffs for the recovery of money, or of specific real or
personal property."   Bliss on Code Pleading, § 74.

The case of Schiffer, Admr., and others v. The City of
EauClaire, 51 Wis., 385, was an action against the city
for damages for flooding a certain house and grounds owned
in severalty by several persons, all of whom joined as
plaintiffs.   The supreme court, sustaining the judgment of
the circuit court, overruling a demurrer to the petition,
say in the syllabus: "The statutory rule that 'all persons
having an interest in the subject of the action, and in obtaining the relief demanded, may be joined as plaintiffs,'
etc., is applicable not only to actions formerly denominated
equitable, but also those formerly denominated legal, in-

cluding those for the recovery of money only." Citing numerous cases from that and other courts. See also Dicey on Parties,* p. 380.

While it must be admitted that many of the cases cited by the court in the case last above mentioned, as well as by the author from whose work I have quoted, fall considerably short of establishing the construction of the code contended for, yet I believe it to be in the main correct, and that in sustaining the defense in this action wherein the separate and distinct claims of the several defendants, but upon the same property, are united in the one action and judgment, there was no error.

By the 5th assignment, plaintiff in error complains that the court failed to find the value of the property replevied.

Section 191 of the code provides as follows: "In all cases when the property has been delivered to the plaintiff, where the jury shall find upon issue joined, for the defendant, they shall also find whether the defendant had the right of property, or the right of possession only, at the commencement of the suit; and if they find either in his favor, they shall assess such damages as they think right and proper for the defendant; for which, with costs of suit, the court shall render judgment for the defendant."

Section 191a provides that, "The judgment in the cases mentioned in sections one hundred and ninety, and one hundred and ninety-one, and in section one thousand and forty-one, of said code, shall be for a return of the property, or the value thereof in case a return cannot be had, or the value of the possession of the same, and for damages for withholding said property and costs of suit."

In the case at bar, the defendants did not claim the value of the property, but of the possession thereof, as measured by their respective mortgages. The value of such possession was found by the court, and while, in order to make such finding, it must have believed the evidence to establish the value of the property itself, at a figure equal to or above that of his finding of the value of the defendants' possession thereof, the statute does not require that such belief be expressed in the finding. If the finding of the court of the value of the defendants' possession were, in the opinion of this court, unsustained by the evidence, either for want of sufficient value in the property itself, or in the mortgages of defendants, it would be reversed; but an examination of the bill of exceptions shows that it is not only fully sustained in respect to the general value of the property, but that it was the contention of the plaintiff throughout the trial, that such value, at some stage of the proceeding, was far greater than that of the possession, as found by the court.

The judgment of the district court is affirmed.

JUDGMENT AFFIRMED.

THE other judges concur.

HENRY G. WILEY AND H. FRED WILEY, PLAINTIFFS IN ERROR, V. PETER F. SHARS, DEFENDANT IN ERROR.

1. **Trial**: TRIAL COURT: FINDINGS OF FACT AND LAW. Where a jury is waived and questions of fact tried by the court, either party may request the court to state in writing the conclusions of fact found, separately from the conclusions of law; when such request is made, it is error for the court to refuse to make such findings, and the error is not cured by assigning findings on overruling a motion for a new trial.

2. **Chattel Mortgage**: DESCRIPTION OF PROPERTY. Where the description in a chattel mortgage was "twenty-three head of horses and mules, * * * * * all situated on their range on the South Loup river, * * * * * Above described chattels are now in their (the mortgagor's) possession and are owned by them," the testimony showed the range in question to be situated in Buffalo county, where the mortgage was filed for record, and that the horses and mules were all those possessed by the mortgagor; Held, A sufficient description.

ERROR to the district court for Buffalo county. Tried below before HAMER, J.

Calkins & Pratt, for plaintiff in error.

Ira D. Marston and *A. H. Connor*, for defendant in error.

MAXWELL, CH. J.

In February, 1884, the Nebraska' Land and Cattle Company of Buffalo county, to secure the sum of $4,500, executed a chattel mortgage to the Buffalo County Bank, of Kearney, upon personal property described in the mortgage as follows:

"Their entire herd of cattle, consisting of bulls, cows, calves, heifers, steers, etc., 500 head, more or less, said cattle being marked in part by ear labels in left ear, by cutting of the right ear, by being branded on the hip with the letter 'P,' and by various other marks and brands, and some with no marks or brands.   Also their entire flock of sheep, 2,000 head, more or less, twenty-three head of horses and mules, together with all their tools, farm machinery, etc., consisting of threshing machine, four self-binding harvesters, four mowing machines, five wagons, a lot of harness, plows, seeders, cultivators, etc.; also a lot of carpenter and blacksmith tools; also about 500 bushels of wheat, their entire herd of swine, 400 head, more or less, all situated on their range on the South Loup river, subject to a chattel mortgage dated February 7, 1884, to Fred O. Ellis, on cattle to secure payment of $5,000; also one to Wiley & Perry on Vermont Merino ewes, to secure payment of about $3,100.

"The above described chattels are now in their possession, are owned by them, and free from incumbrances in all respects except as stated."

The chattel mortgage was duly filed and indexed in the county clerk's office February 25, 1884.

On the 10th day of March, 1884, the defendant in error, who was then sheriff of Buffalo county, levied upon certain personal property belonging to said Nebraska Land and Cattle Company, in an action pending in the district court of that county, wherein Henry H. Bowie was plaintiff and the Nebraska Land and Cattle Company defendant, to-wit: "One bay mare, named Brownie; one white mare, named Babe; one brown mare, named Curlie; one bay horse, named Charlie; one brown horse, named Bean; one dark bay horse mule, named Nickel; one dark bay mare mule, named Jennie; one dark bay horse mule, named Sam Tilden; one sorrel mare, named Nellie, and one brown mare with four white feet, named Lucy."

And also on the same day, in an action pending in said court wherein R. R. Greer was plaintiff and the Nebraska Land and Cattle Company defendant, said defendant in error levied upon the following personal property of said company: "One sorrel horse, named Dick; one light brown horse mule, named Jack; one bay mare mule, named Dime; one lumber wagon, Jackson make; one double harness; one lumber wagon, Moline make; 200 bushels of wheat in bin No. 1; 150 bushels wheat in bin No. 2; 200 bushels in bin No. 3; 100 bushels wheat in bin No. 4; 50 bushels wheat in bin No. 5; 75 bushels wheat in bin No. 6; about 300 bushels of oats, and 60 bags of millet"

It is claimed that the Greer case has been settled, and as there is no proof except as to the horses taken under the Bowie attachment, the property levied upon under the Greer attachment need not be further considered. The property levied upon under the Bowie attachment had previously been included in the mortgage heretofore referred to, and re-taken on an order of replevin by the said Buffalo County Bank.

On the trial of the action of replevin a jury was

waived and the cause tried to the court, which found the issue in favor of the defendant below, and that the value of the property was $1,200, and that the defendant had a lien on said property in the sum of $815.65.

The plaintiff filed a request in writing that the court find the questions of law and fact separately, which the court neglected to do, to which exceptions were taken, and which neglect is now assigned for error.

Section 297 of the code provides that, "Upon the trial of questions of fact by the court, it shall not be necessary for the court to state its findings, except generally, for the plaintiff or defendant, unless one of the parties request it, with the view of excepting to the decision of the court upon the questions of law involved in the trial; in which case the court shall state in writing the conclusions of fact found separately from the conclusions of law."

The plaintiff clearly was entitled to a separate statement of the questions of law and fact. The court endeavored to remedy this defect in part, on overruling the motion for a new trial, by assigning as a reason for such ruling, "That the mortgage did not sufficiently describe the property in question, and further, that the plaintiffs were affected with notice, and were estopped as to defendants' attachment to claim under their mortgage." This, however, did not cure the error, as a court could thereby prevent a review of its own erroneous judgment. The time for filing a motion for a new trial is limited to three days, except in certain contingencies which need not be noticed, while there is no such limitation as to the time in which the court shall rule upon such motion.

It is evident that the principal objection is, that the mortgage does not sufficiently describe the property in question. The testimony clearly shows that the range on the South Loup river, where the property was located, was the company's farm in the county of Buffalo, and that the property described in the mortgage, the twenty-three head

of horses and mules, were all the horses and mules possessed by such company.

The description of property in a chattel mortgage should
be such as to enable third persons to identify the property,
aided by inquiries which the mortgage itself indicates and
directs. *Price v. McComas, ante* p. 195; S. C. 31 N. W.
R., 511. *Elder v. Miller*, 60 Me., 118. *Chapin v. Cram,*
40 Me., 561. *Bank v. Farrar*, 46 Me., 293.

In this case, as the number of horses and mules given
in the mortgage included all those possessed by the mortgagor, there was no uncertainty as to what animals were
mortgaged; and it was further stated in the mortgage that
"all (were) situated on their range on the South Loup
river," and "that the above described chattels are now in
their possession (and) are owned by them," etc. It will
thus be seen that the ownership, possession, and location of
the horses are all descriptive. The chattel mortgage, therefore, was constructive notice to all persons that the bank
had a lien upon twenty-three head of horses owned by the
mortgagor, and then in its possession on its farm in Buffalo
county.

In *Knapp v. Dietz*, 24 N. W. R., 471, it was held by
the supreme court of Wisconsin, that the description of
property in a chattel mortgage, as "41 Berkshire hogs and
65 grain sacks," was not so uncertain as to invalidate the
mortgage, the testimony showing that this included all the
hogs and grain sacks owned by the mortgagor; see also
cases cited in note.

In *Kenyon v. Framel*, 28 N. W. R., 37, it was held by
the supreme court of Iowa that a chattel mortgage in which
the property was described as "50 head of steers, about
twenty months old, now owned by me and in my possession in Independence township, Jasper county, Iowa,"
sufficiently described the property to enable an honest in-
quirer to identify it. See also *Yant v. Harvey*, 55 Iowa,
421. *Smith v. McLain*, 24 Id., 322.

This case differs from that of *Price v. McComas* in this:

In that case McComas possessed 98 head of steers, and the description in both mortgages applied to all of them. . No particular steers were identified in any manner; hence it was impossible to determine what particular steers were mortgaged. In this case, however, the description is sufficient to identify the property.

The maxim of the law is, "That is certain which may be rendered certain."

The question of estoppel has neither been pleaded nor proved, and is not before the court.

It follows that the judgment of the district court must be reversed, and the cause remanded for further proceedings.

REVERSED AND REMANDED.

THE other judges concur.

MEYER & RAAPKE, APPELLEES, V. JOSEPH D. STONE, APPELLANT.

1. **Evidence** examined, and *Held,* To bring the case within the rule stated in *Smith v. Sands,* 17 Neb., 498.

2. **Witnesses:** EXAMINATION. When a witness, in answer to an inquiry as to a former statement, answers that he does not remember having made such statement, it is not equivalent to a denial that he made the same, neither is an answer to such inquiry, "not in that language," or like words, equivalent to a denial.

APPEAL from the district court of Saline county.

Hastings & McGintie, for appellant.

Ryan Bros., for appellees.

MAXWELL, CH. J.

In December, 1883, the appellees filed in the district court of Saline county a petition against Joseph D. Stone, appellant, alleging that plaintiffs were a co-partnership, and creditors of one Francis M. Woodruff, and exhibit their petition for their own benefit, as well as such other creditors of said Woodruff as shall come in under their bill and contribute to the expenses of the suit. Appellees also allege that September 6th, 1882, Woodruff was, and still is, indebted to appellees for goods, wares, and merchandise in the sum of $435.80, and interest due on a certain judgment rendered by the county court of Saline county, and that the indebtedness existed long before July 6th, 1882, and that on the 25th day of September, 1882, execution was issued on the judgment and placed in a constable's hands for service, who afterwards returned the execution wholly unsatisfied, and that a transcript was filed in the district court of Saline county, May 11th, 1883; that long before July 6th, 1882, Woodruff was insolvent, and was threatened by his creditors, and made known these facts to Joseph D. Stone, appellant, and arranged with Stone that in case Woodruff's creditors attempted to compel payment of their claims, Woodruff should transfer his stock of goods, merchandise, etc., to Stone, to avoid payment of his debts, and to delay, hinder, and defraud his creditors; that Stone, as an inducement, promised Woodruff that he would take and hold and sell the goods, collect the accounts, and apply the proceeds to the payment of a small amount due to him (Stone), and account to Woodruff for the balance, and pay the same to Woodruff, or his creditors with whom settlement could be made for a small percentage of their claims; that he would hold the property, subject to Woodruff's directions, for above purposes; that on the 6th day of July, 1882, one of Woodruff's creditors threatened Woodruff with legal proceedings to compel payment of the debt due from him, and that thereupon, in pursuance of their previous bargain, Woodruff made a pretended sale of his goods, wares, and merchandise, fixtures, book accounts, etc., to Stone, for the sole purpose of hindering, delaying,

and defrauding Woodruff's creditors; that on the 6th day
of July, 1882, Woodruff was insolvent, which fact was
known to Stone; that Woodruff had no property aside from
the goods and property so transferred to Stone, which
were of the value of at least $4,500; that the debts of Wood-
ruff were equal to the same amount, and that Stone knew
of that fact.   Notwithstanding, Stone claims to have bought
the entire stock, etc., for $2,250, of which $340 he claims
was due to him and $250 were claims of creditors of Wood-
ruff held by Stone for collection, and these two amounts
were treated as payment *pro tanto* on said purchase price,
viz., $2,250; that there then remained $1,660 of the purchase price, for which appellant claims he gave four notes
to Woodruff in four equal payments at six, twelve, eighteen, and twenty-four months without interest; and appellees deny that Stone held claims in his own favor, or in
favor of any one else against Woodruff, and alleges that
the transfer was made on account of the inability of Woodruff to pay his debts, and to defraud his creditors and secure a
preference in favor of appellant and for the creditors whose
claims appellant held for collection; that neither appellant's
claim or either of those he held for collection were for
laborer's wages, and the purchase from Woodruff was not
in good faith, and was made by both parties to enable
Woodruff to avoid payment of his debts.

The petition also charges that Stone refuses to account
for the goods and accounts to the creditors, but claims he
absolutely purchased the same and again sold them to one
Jacob Starkey, about July 27th, 1882, for a full and adequate consideration, and that Starkey is selling and disposing of said property as his own, and that the sale by Stone
to Starkey was made prior to appellees' judgment; that
between July 6th and July 27th, 1882, Stone sold a large
amount of the goods and converted them to his own use,
and has been since July 6th, 1882, collecting the accounts,
and is acting in utter disregard of the rights of the creditors

of Woodruff, and in violation of the trust under which he
secured the property from Woodruff, by reason of which
appellees suffer irreparable injury; that on July 6th, 1882,
and for a long time prior, Woodruff was indebted to R. L.
McDonald & Co. in the sum of $124, and on the 17th day
of August, 1882, R. L. McDonald & Co. obtained a judgment against Woodruff for $125.50 and costs, $3.25, and
on September 18th, 1882, caused an execution to be issued
thereon which was duly returned October 16th, 1882, unsatisfied; that on the 1st day of February, 1883, R. L.
McDonald & Co. sold to appellees said judgment; that a
transcript thereof was filed in the district court of Saline
county, May 10th, 1883; no part of said judgment has ever
been paid; that on July 6th, 1882, and prior, Woodruff
was indebted to Silver Link Lodge No. 69, of the Independent Order of Odd Fellows, in the sum of $100, and
that Stone, in getting in possession of the property and
books of Woodruff, promised as a part consideration to pay
said debt out of the funds which should be collected from
said accounts; that he has collected of the accounts more
than sufficient to pay the debt, but has never paid it or
any part of it; that on the 9th day of April, 1883, said
lodge procured a judgment against Woodruff for the debt
and costs, taxed at $135, and on the same day procured to
be issued an execution on the judgment; that May 5th,
1883, the execution was returned wholly unsatisfied; that
on April 10th, 1883, said lodge sold said judgment to
appellees, who filed a transcript of the same in the district
court of Saline county on the 11th day of May, 1883; that
there is due appellees on the judgments aforesaid the sum of
$730, and seven per cent interest from December 1st, 1883,
and pray that Stone may be held liable and treated as a
trustee for the benefit of appellees, as creditors of Woodruff,
in respect to the property received from Woodruff; that an
accounting may be had of the value of the goods and
accounts, whether realized on or not by Stone, and that

Stone be required to pay to appellees on their judgments the value of the same; that the sale from Woodruff to Stone be declared to have been made in bad faith, and that Stone took the same only as trustee for the creditors of Woodruff, exclusive of Stone, and that the sale be declared null and void.

Stone, in his answer, denies the indebtedness of Woodruff and the several judgments and executions against him; denies the insolvency of Woodruff, his inability to pay his debts, and of all knowledge that Woodruff was threatened with judicial process to compel him to pay his debts; denies that he ever entered into an agreement with Woodruff to take his goods, hold, and sell them, in trust for Woodruff or for any creditor of Woodruff, and denies that he ever agreed in any way to assist Woodruff in effecting settlement with his creditors; denies he ever agreed to hold any property subject to Woodruff's directions, and alleges that on the 6th day of July, 1882, appellant bought of Woodruff a certain stock of goods, wares, and merchandise in the village of Friend, Saline county, Nebraska; that said stock was not worth more than the sum of $2,250, and defendant bought the same in good faith, gave its full value, viz., $2,250; that appellant had no knowledge whatever of any intention to hinder, defraud, or delay his creditors on the part of Woodruff, nor did said Stone buy said property with any intention to hinder, delay, or defraud any of Woodruff's creditors.

The reply is a general denial.

On the trial of the cause a jury was waived and the cause tried to the court, which rendered judgment as follows:

"This cause coming on to be heard before the court, and the court being fully advised in the premises, and after careful consideration the court finds for the plaintiffs, Meyer & Raapke, and against the defendant, J. D. Stone. The court finds that the sale of the goods and accounts

46

from Francis M. Woodruff to the defendant Stone, was fraudulent and void as against the creditors of the said Francis M. Woodruff. The court finds that at the time of said sale the accounts were worth $500, and the stock of goods was worth about $2,732, and that after defendant obtained the goods of the said Woodruff, he sold off the stock of goods at retail for about 20 days, and in the meantime putting in some new stock, and that at the end of that time he sold the stock of goods to a third party for $2,500. The court further finds that the said J. D. Stone had collected of the accounts $225, and that he has converted the property obtained of Woodruff to his own use, and that when he had some he held it in trust for the benefit of the creditors of said Woodruff; that he paid for the property to said Woodruff $2,000; all of which, except $70 evidenced by the last note, has been paid to the creditors of Woodruff, and that said Stone is entitled to a credit of $1,930 on his liability to the creditors of Woodruff; that there is due the plaintiffs, Meyer & Raapke, from Woodruff, of indebtedness contracted before the transfer of Woodruff to Stone, the sum of $882.14, in which sum said defendant Stone is liable to said plaintiffs, Meyer & Raapke. It is therefore considered, ordered, and adjudged that the plaintiff have and recover of and from the said defendant, J. D. Stone, the sum of $882.14, with interest from this date, and in default of payment of the same for 30 days, an execution issue therefor, and that plaintiff recover his costs herein expended, taxed at $————."

A reversal is sought, principally upon the grounds that the judgment is not sustained by the evidence. There is a large amount of testimony in the abstract tending to support the petition and also the answer. It would subserve no good purpose to set this testimony out at length. The conceded facts are that the goods and book accounts were worth considerably more than the amount paid for them by the appellant, the proof varying from $2,300 to $5,000

A considerable portion of the testimony against the appellant consists of admissions, said to have been made by him to various agents of other creditors. The appellant, when asked in regard to some of these admissions, answered as follows:

Q. At that time and place did you say to Van Slyck that he (Woodruff) came to your office one day and stated that they had drawn up a mortgage and wanted him to sign it, and that he either would have to sign it or they would get out an attachment right away; and I says to him, stay here a few minutes?

A. I have no recollection of any such transaction.

Q. At the same time and place did you further say in the same connection to Van Slyck: "And I went out the back door, the back way to Woodruff's store, and went down cellar and looked around and looked through the store, and asked the clerk how many dollars' worth of goods he thought there was in there, and he says $2,500, and I concluded there was fully that much, and I told him I would give him my note for $2,000, deducting out what he was owing me, payable in 6, 12, 18, and 24 months without interest?

A. I think I did not make any such a statement.

Q. At the same time did you say it happened Morton came along, and I called him in, drew up a bill of sale, and took possession of the goods and store?

A. No, sir.

Q. In the same conversation did you say to Van Slyck: I afterwards asked him if he had any debts of honor, and he said yes, that he owed the Odd Fellows about $100, and other small accounts amounting to $200; and I told him if he would turn over his notes and book accounts, I would collect them and pay these and turn the balance over to him or his creditors. And did you say I calculated it would take about $250 for this, for I would want about $50 for my trouble?

A.   I have no recollection of any such transaction.

Q.   At the same time did Van Slyck say to you how many notes and accounts were there, and you said between $1,100 and $1,200.

A.   Not in that language.

Q.   At the same time did Van Slyck ask you if you would turn a part out of them to Farrington & Co., and you said go and see Woodruff and see what he says about it. Whereupon Van Slyck went out, and after his return said Woodruff was willing and would be glad to have you do so; and did you say I don't propose to turn these accounts to anybody, but propose to collect these accounts and buy up his accounts on a shave and put the boy on his feet again?

A.   I did not use any such language.

Q.   In that conversation did you say to Van Slyck: "Do you know of anybody that wants to buy a stock of goods, etc., worth about $3,500 for the whole thing just as as it stands, and I think there is as many goods there as when I bought it, for I have bought a few groceries. There is a bargain in it at that money?"

A.   I think I did not say so.

Q.   At that time did you say to Van Slyck: "Do you know of anybody that wants to buy a stock of goods, worth about $3,500 for the whole thing just as it stands, and I think there is nearly as many goods there as when I bought it, for I have bought a few groceries. There is a bargain in it at that money?"

A.   Not in that language.

The statement of a witness, that he does not remember that he made certain statements to which his attention is called, is not equivalent to a denial of such statements, nor do equivocal allegations of "not in that language," and the like, have that effect. There is sufficient evidence to bring the case within the rule stated in *Smith v. Sands*, 17

Neb., 498, and to support the judgment rendered by the court below.

The judgment is therefore affirmed.

JUDGMENT AFFIRMED.

THE other judges concur.

THE STATE, EX REL. FRANK HOPKINS, v. SCHOOL DISTRICT NUMBER 7, IN SHERMAN COUNTY.

1. **School Bonds**: EVIDENCE OF VALIDITY. Official certificates of the calling of an election in a school district for the purpose of voting on a proposition to issue $3,500 in the bonds of said district for the purpose of borrowing money to build a school house, and purchase a site therefor, of the posting up of notices of such election, of the holding of such election, and the result thereof, and of the issuance of such bonds, signed by persons claiming to be the director, moderator, and treasurer of said district, and the judges and clerk of said election, which official certificates were received in evidence upon the agreement and stipulation of parties; *Held*, To be evidence of the corporate existence of such school district at the date of such proceedings.

2. ———: REGISTRATION CERTIFICATE: EVIDENCE. The certificate of the registration of a school district bond, endorsed on such bond, signed by the county clerk under his official seal, and dated April 9, 1874, introduced and received as evidence without objection; *Held* To be evidence of the corporate existence of the school district by which such bond purported to have been issued.

3. ———: EVIDENCE OF VALIDITY. The official certificate of · the director of a school district, that notice of a certain special school meeting held in said district was given by posting up notices of said meeting twenty days before the holding thereof, in three of the most public places in said district, which certificate was introduced and received in evidence under a stipulation of parties, in which it was recited that such "stipulation is for the purpose of using the same as testimony, instead of the

plaintiff or defendant being obliged to take depositions to prove
the same ;" *Held*, To be evidence of the due publication of the
notice of the calling of such special school meeting.

ORIGINAL application for mandamus.

Dawes, Foss & Stephens, for relator.

Aaron Wall, Nightingale Bros., and *Groff & Montgomery*,
for respondent.

COBB, J.

This was an original application to this court for an
alternative mandamus against school district No. 7, of
Sherman county, to compel the payment of certain bonds
issued by said district, for the purpose of borrowing
money to build and furnish a school house therein.   Due
service of the application and notice on the school district,
as well as upon the board of county commissioners, was
acknowledged by counsel in writing filed in the case.

Plaintiff, by his petition, alleged that on the 1st day of
April, 1874, and for more than five months prior thereto,
school district No. 7, in the county of Sherman, was a duly
and legally organized school district under the laws of this
state, and that, being so organized, the said school district
did, on the 1st day of April, 1874, at a special meeting
duly called and held according to law, and for the purpose
of building and furnishing a school house in said school
district, vote to borrow for the purpose aforesaid the sum
of $3,500, and to issue the bonds of said district as evi-
dence of said indebtedness.   And afterwards, to-wit, on
the 1st day of April, 1874, said school district board, being
duly and regularly in session and capable of transacting
business, and in pursuance of the vote theretofore had, executed the bonds of said school district, as follows, to-wit:
Seven bonds of five hundred dollars each, payable six

years from the date thereof, with interest at the rate of ten
per cent per annum, payable semi-annually, according to
the coupons thereto attached, at the banking house of
Saunders & Hardenburgh, New York City. Said bonds
were dated April 1, 1874, and were numbered 1, 2, 3, 4,
5, 6, and 7 respectively, and signed by W. D. Wilson,
director, John A. Hendricks, moderator, and H. Croston,
treasurer, of said district, and countersigned and attested
by the signature of E. S. Atkinson, county clerk of said
county, said county clerk certifying on said bonds that the
same had been registered in his office in accordance with
the provisions of an act to provide for the registration of
precinct, township, and school district bonds, approved
February 27, 1873, and that said law had been complied
with in all respects, so as to entitle the same to registration.
Said bonds were placed upon the market and sold by said
school district, and out of the proceeds thereof a school
house was erected and furnished in said school district,
which said school district has ever since continued to use
and occupy for said school district, and said school district
has never had any other or different district organization
than the one so as aforesaid formed.   That of said series of
bonds so as aforesaid issued, negotiated, and sold, the relator purchased three bonds for $500 each, designated as
numbers one, two, and three, for nearly the face of said
bonds, in the due course of business, before the said bonds
or any part thereof became due; that no part of the
principal or interest of said bonds has been paid, except
the interest coupons due prior to October 1, 1877; that
plaintiff is now the owner and holder of said bonds and
the unpaid interest coupons, and that there now remains
due thereon the sum of fifteen hundred dollars, with interest thereon from the first day of October, 1877, at the
rate of ten per cent per annum, together with said unpaid
coupons with interest thereon from maturity, as the same
severally became due, at the rate of ten per cent per

annum, amounting in all to the sum of three thousand
and ninety dollars, now due and unpaid; that the district
board of said school district has not at any time made a
report in writing to the county clerk of said county of the
amount of indebtedness of said school district, as required
by law, and requested said board to levy a tax to pay said
indebtedness, although by and on behalf of the relator
often requested so to do; that the relator has made demand of said school district to pay the interest and principal of said bonds as the same severally became due, but
that the said school district has ever neglected to pay the
same or any part thereof, and that, although the relator
has reported the said indebtedness of said school district to
the county clerk, and to the board of county commissioners
of said county, and to the treasurer of said county, and requested them to levy and collect a tax to pay the said indebtedness, yet they still refuse to do so, and upon technical grounds unknown to relator, said commissioners,
said clerk, and said treasurer affirm that they would not,
even though said indebtedness were reported to them by
said district board, levy and collect a tax for such purpose, and that relator is wholly remediless, etc.

There was an answer filed in the case for the school district, denying that on the 1st day of April, 1874, said
school district No. 7, of Sherman county, was duly and
legally organized as a school district under the laws of the
state; denying that it had a corporate existence, with power
to issue bonds; that it had any power whatever to issue
bonds; denying that on the 1st day of April, 1874, a special
meeting was held, duly called according to law, for the
purpose of building and furnishing a school house in said
district and to borrow money for such purpose, and to issue
bonds of said district as evidence of said indebtedness;
denying that John A. Hendricks, W. D. Wilson, and H.
Croston were, on the 1st day of April, 1874, authorized
or had power to issue bonds described in said plaintiff's

petition; denying that said pretended bonds were registered in accordance with the provisions of an act of the
legislature to provide for the registration of precinct, township, and school district bonds, approved February 27,
1873; denying that said law had been complied with in all
respects, so as to entitle said bonds to registration; denying
that said bonds were placed upon the market and sold by
said school district, and out of the proceeds thereof a school
house was erected and furnished in said district, but alleging the fact to be that said district received no value .
whatever for said bonds; denying that Frank Hopkins,
the relator, purchased a bond of $500, designated as No. 1
of said series, in the due course of business, before the same
became due; and denying that he is now the legal owner
and holder of said bond and said unpaid coupons, or ever
was the legal owner of said bond and said unpaid coupons,
or that he ever had any interest therein, or ever paid any
money therefor; alleging that said district did not borrow
any money from the relator or from any person or persons
as by law it might have done, or that said pretended officers
of said school district had any authority to issue any bonds
under an act to establish a system of public instruction
in the state of Nebraska, approved February 15, 1869, or
acts amendatory thereof, etc.

By stipulation of parties, signed by counsel for the relator on the one part, and for the school district on the
other part, there was presented by the relator, and received
in evidence, copies of the proclamation of the director
of said school district, calling an election in said school
district for the purpose of voting upon the proposition to
issue the bonds of said school district, in the sum of $3,-
500, payable in six years from the date thereof, in New
York City, with interest at 10 per cent, payable semi-annually, and to authorize the levy of a tax, each year, to pay
the interest as the same should become due, and to authorize the school board of said district to contract for the

building of a school house in said district, and for purchasing a site therefor.   Also of the certificate of John A. Hendricks and Thomas H. Crosten, judges, and William D.
Wilson, clerk of said election, certifying that upon said
proposition to issue $3,500 in bonds to build a school
house in said school district, there were cast at said
election six votes for said proposition and no votes against
it.   Also the certificate of W. D. Wilson, director of said
district, and John A. Hendricks and Thomas H. Crosten,
members of the school board of said district, certifying to
the holding of an election in said school district on the first
day of April, 1874, for the purpose of voting three thousand five hundred dollars in bonds, for the purpose of
building a school house and purchasing a site therefor, and
that "The majority of the votes cast, in said district, were
'unanimously' in favor of the bonds, being six votes polled
for the bonds, and none against the bonds."   Also, the
certificate of W. D. Wilson, director of said school district,
"that at a meeting of the qualified voters of said district,
held at the house of W. D. Wilson, on the 1st day of
April, 1874, which meeting was duly called, and notice thereof given as by law required, by posting up notices of said
meeting twenty days before the holding thereof, in three of
the most public places in said district, the question of issuing the bonds of said district for the purpose of raising
money to build and furnish a school house in said district
to the amount of thirty-five hundred dollars, in the sum of
$500 each, due in six years from date, bearing interest at
ten per cent, payable semi annually, was duly submitted to
the qualified voters, and carried, there being cast in favor
of said question six votes, and against it no votes.   * * *
That the existing debt of the said district is nothing; that
the population of said district is about fifty souls, and that
the said bonds are issued by the officers, thereunto authorized by law, and that their signatures are genuine."
    It is recited in the said stipulation that it is made for

the purpose of using the said copies "as testimony, instead of the plaintiff or defendant being obliged to take depositions to prove the same."

The relator also introduced his own deposition, in which he deposes that he is the owner of the school district bonds upon which this action is brought, describing the same; that he purchased the said bonds before they were due, to-wit, on or about the 1st day of April, 1878, of Arnold Gregory, of Barre, Orleans county, New York, in good faith and for a valuable consideration, to-wit, the sum of fifteen hundred dollars; that he is still the owner of the said bonds, and that the whole of the principal of the said three bonds, together with the interest, as represented by the coupons remaining attached to the said bonds, is still due and unpaid.

Upon an inspection of the three bonds and eighteen interest coupons, offered in evidence by the relator and received by the court, it appears that there was due thereon, on the first day of the present term of this court, for principal and interest of said bonds and coupons the sum of three thousand and ninety-two dollars and eighty-nine cents ($3,092.89).

An endorsement on each of said bonds signed by E. S. Atkinson, then county clerk of said county of Sherman, shows that said bonds were duly registered in the bond registry of said county on the 9th day of April, 1874.

It will scarcely fail to be observed that the petition contains several quite unnecessary allegations, the issue joined by the denial of which, by the respondent, will be treated as immaterial. But of the above class, probably, cannot be included the allegation of the corporate existence of the defendant school district, at the date of the vote upon and issuance of the bonds, as set out in the petition. The plaintiff having alleged in the petition that the defendant was a duly organized school district under the laws of the state at the date of the election and issuance of the bonds, and that allegation being denied by the defendant school district, or not being admitted, either directly or by failure to deny the same, it was necessary for the plaintiff to prove it. Under the law as it stood at the date of the proceedings involved in the case at bar, the best evidence of the corporate existence of the school district was, doubtless, the records of the county superintendent's office, together with the records of the district itself, in case it is one of those districts formed after the original division of the county into school districts. And being the best evidence, they were probably the only evidence of such fact admissible, except by agreement of parties. But in the case at bar copies of the several official certificates of the officers of the district having been presented and received by the court as evidence, upon the agreement and stipulation of the parties, and the school district appearing in the case as a corporation, without alleging or in any manner developing the date of the commencement of its corporate existence, subsequent to the date of the alleged corporate acts upon which its liability is claimed to arise, such evidence must be held to prove not only the facts therein certified to, but also the official character of the persons so certifying, and the existence of the corporation from which such official existence was necessarily derived.

In this connection it should be observed that the bonds introduced in evidence each contains on its back a certificate of the county clerk of its registration by him, under the provisions of the act of February 27, 1873. Gen. Stat., 883. This, in the absence of objection to its competency, is some evidence of the corporate existence of the school district purporting to have issued such bonds.

It must be conceded that the evidence of the due publication of the notice of the special meeting of the electors of said school district, at which the said bonds were voted, is not as formal as could be desired, but the certificate of the director of the district, that said notice was posted up in three of the most public places in the district twenty days before the day of such special meeting and election, comes before the court as evidence, by stipulation of the parties, and therefore must be accepted as evidence of this, the most important fact which it contains.

The said certificates of the director and other officers of said school district, received in evidence upon the stipulation of the parties as aforesaid, must be accepted as sufficient evidence of the fact of the holding of said election in said district, for the issuance of bonds, of the result of said election in favor of the issuance of the bonds, of the amount thereof, and of their actual execution by the officers of said district. The presentation of said bonds and coupons by the relator, together with his deposition of the fact of their purchase by him in good faith, and their present ownership by him, sufficiently proves the allegation of the petition that the said bonds had been placed on the market and sold by the said district, as well as their purchase and ownership by the plaintiff. There being no allegation of fraud or bad faith in the issuing of said bonds, in the answer, there is no necessity of proof of want of notice on the part of the plaintiff when he purchased them.

Neither in the original or amended petitions does the relator pray for a peremptory mandamus, but in each case prays for an alternative mandamus. Yet the school district having appeared and answered to the merits, and having stipulated for the reception of certain evidence going to the merits of the case, and having accepted service of notice upon which depositions have been taken, and the cause having been in court for more than two years, and finally submitted on the merits, it is deemed unnecessary to require a further answer on the part of the defendant.

The plaintiff, both in his original and amended petitions, alleges that he " has reported the said indebtedness of said school district to the county clerk, and to the board of county commissioners of said county, and to the county treasurer of said county, and requested them to levy and collect a tax to pay said indebtedness, yet they still refuse so to do; and upon technical grounds unknown to petitioner, the said commissioners and said clerk and treasurer affirm that they would not, even though said indebtedness were reported to them by said district board, levy and collect a tax for such purpose."

The county commissioners of Sherman county having by counsel accepted service of the petition, and waived copy and notice, and all irregularities and informalities, and W. A. Wilson, county treasurer, and John Wall, county clerk, having personally signed and joined in such acceptance and waiver, they may, by a liberal construction, be considered parties to this proceeding, although not named in the caption.

A peremptory mandamus will therefore issue to said school district, the said board of county commissioners, the county clerk, and treasurer of said county of Sherman, commanding the said school district and the school district board thereof, to make a report in writing to the county clerk and board of county commissioners of said county of the amount of indebtedness of said school district, upon the bonds and coupons of the relator, as hereinbefore ascertained and found, and of the amount of tax necessary to be levied to pay said indebtedness; commanding said board of county commissioners to levy a tax upon all taxable property of said school district No. 7 sufficient to pay said indebtedness, together with interest on two thousand eight hundred and eighty-nine and $\frac{17}{100}$ dollars thereof from the 4th day of January, 1887, at the rate of ten per cent per annum, and on two hundred and three and $\frac{72}{100}$ dollars thereof at the rate of seven per cent per annum, or, in the event that such tax should be so large as to be, in the opinion of said board of county commissioners, grievously burdensome, that they levy a tax sufficient to pay one-third of said indebtedness the first year, and continue to levy an equal amount annually thereafter until all of said indebtedness and interest thereon as aforesaid is paid in full; commanding said county treasurer to collect such tax and retain the same in a special fund, and so often as one hundred dollars are paid in, to pay the same to the clerk of this court in liquidation of said indebtedness of the relator as aforesaid, and commanding the said county clerk, as well as the said county treasurer and board of county commissioners, and each of them, that they and each of them severally and collectively do and perform each and every act necessary to be done and performed in order to levy and collect said tax, and pay said indebtedness of the relator as aforesaid.

JUDGMENT ACCORDINGLY.

THE other judges concur.

INDEX.

47

Execution.

Where stay of execution is taken, at the expiration thereof, joint execution may issue against judgment debtors and sureties in the stay bond. *State v. Fleming*...................... 321

Exemption.

1. The exemption of five hundred dollars in personal property in favor of a judgment debtor, provided by section 521 of the civil code, in lieu of a homestead, must depend upon the filing of the inventory as provided by section 522, and the selection of property claimed by the debtor to be exempt. *Mann v. Welton.*.. 541

2. Replevin cannot be maintained against an officer for property levied upon and claimed to be exempt under said section until after the inventory is filed and the appraisement and selection are made. *Mann v. Welton*................ 541

Extradition. See FUGITIVES FROM JUSTICE.

Fees.

Commission of one per cent on money collected on judgment without execution, is to be paid by judgment debtor. *State v. Bryant*.. 475

Final Order. See JUDGMENT.

Forcible Entry and Detention.

1. In absence of a stipulation to the contrary, where tenant fails and refuses to pay rent according to his lease, such refusal terminates lease, and tenant is liable to an action for forcible detention of the property ; in such case, no other notice than the three days' notice to quit is necessary. *Hendrickson v. Beeson & Sullivan*........................ 61

2. Complaint alleging that " plaintiff served notice on defendant, describing said premises to defendant," *Held*, A sufficient allegation that the notice was in writing. *Hitchcock v. McKinster*... 148

3. Objections to form of notice not considered, there being no bill of exceptions. *Id*.. 148

Forfeiture.

Of school lands where purchaser fails to pay interest. *State v. Graham*.. 329

Fraud.

1. Never presumed ; proof required. *Brown v. Herr*......... 113

2. Action for relief on ground of fraud may be commenced at any time within four years. *Parker v. Kuhn*.............. 413

3. Instructions asked in case stated examined, and *Held*, Properly refused. *Herold v. State*................................ 50

48

Liquors.

Non Compos Mentis. See DEED.

Notary Public.

Notice.

Officers.

Physicians. See MEDICINE.

Pleading.

Precinct.

Principal and Agent.

Principal and Sureties.

Probate Courts. See COURTS—COUNTY.

Protest.

Public Lands of the United States.

Purchaser. See Bona Fide Purchaser. Pendente Lite.

Railroads.

Real Estate.

Statutes Cited and Construed.

CIVIL CODE.

CRIMINAL CODE.

Stay of Execution. See EXECUTION.

Summons.

1. Party under indictment in county other than his residence not liable to civil action there. *Palmer v. Rowan*... 452

2. Service of summons upon defendant in the presence of

49

Trial.

Trusts.

2194 076

Lightning Source UK Ltd.
Milton Keynes UK
UKHW020209091118
331957UK00012B/1639/P